The Middle Ages · SIMPSON

The Sixteenth Century · GREENBLATT / LOGAN

The Early Seventeenth Century
MAUS

The Restoration and the Eighteenth Century
NOGGLE

The Romantic Period · LYNCH

The Victorian Age · ROBSON

The Twentieth and Twenty-First Centuries
RAMAZANI

THE NORTON ANTHOLOGY OF

ENGLISH
LITERATURE

TENTH EDITION

VOLUME A

THE MIDDLE AGES

THE NORTON ANTHOLOGY OF

ENGLISH LITERATURE

TENTH EDITION

Stephen Greenblatt, *General Editor*
COGAN UNIVERSITY PROFESSOR OF THE HUMANITIES
HARVARD UNIVERSITY

VOLUME A

THE MIDDLE AGES

James Simpson

W · W · NORTON & COMPANY
NEW YORK · LONDON

W. W. Norton & Company has been independent since its founding in 1923, when William Warder Norton and Mary D. Herter Norton first published lectures delivered at the People's Institute, the adult education division of New York City's Cooper Union. The firm soon expanded its program beyond the Institute, publishing books by celebrated academics from America and abroad. By midcentury, the two major pillars of Norton's publishing program— trade books and college texts—were firmly established. In the 1950s, the Norton family transferred control of the company to its employees, and today—with a staff of four hundred and a comparable number of trade, college, and professional titles published each year—W. W. Norton & Company stands as the largest and oldest publishing house owned wholly by its employees.

Editors: Julia Reidhead and Marian Johnson
Assistant Editor, Print: Rachel Taylor
Manuscript Editors: Michael Fleming, Katharine Ings, Candace Levy
Media Editor: Carly Fraser Doria
Assistant Editor, Media: Ava Bramson
Marketing Manager, Literature: Kimberly Bowers
Managing Editor, College Digital Media: Kim Yi
Production Manager: Sean Mintus
Text design: Jo Anne Metsch
Art director: Rubina Yeh
Photo Editor: Nelson Colon
Permissions Manager: Megan Jackson Schindel
Permissions Clearing: Nancy J. Rodwan
Cartographer: Adrian Kitzinger
Composition: Westchester Book Company
Manufacturing: LSC Crawfordsville

ISBN: 978-0-393-60302-6

W. W. Norton & Company, Inc., 500 Fifth Avenue, New York, NY 10110
wwnorton.com

W. W. Norton & Company Ltd., 15 Carlisle Street, London W1D 3BS

3 4 5 6 7 8 9 0

Contents*

The Middle Ages (to ca. 1485)

* Additional readings are available on the NAEL Archive (digital.wwnorton.com/englishlit10abc).

Preface to the Tenth Edition

For centuries the study of literature has occupied a central place in the Humanities curriculum. The power of great literature to reach across time and space, its exploration of the expressive potential of language, and its ability to capture the whole range of experiences from the most exalted to the everyday have made it an essential part of education. But there are significant challenges to any attempt to derive the full measure of enlightenment and pleasure from this precious resource. In a world in which distraction reigns, savoring works of literature requires quiet focus. In a society in which new media clamor for attention, attending to words on the page can prove difficult. And in a period obsessed with the present at its most instantaneous, it takes a certain effort to look at anything penned earlier than late last night.

The Norton Anthology of English Literature is designed to meet these challenges. It is deeply rewarding to enter the sensibility of a different place, to hear a new voice, to be touched by an unfamiliar era. It is critically important to escape the narrow boundaries of our immediate preoccupations and to respond with empathy to lives other than our own. It is moving, even astonishing, to feel that someone you never met is speaking directly to you. But for any of this to happen requires help. The overarching goal of the Norton Anthology—as it has been for over fifty-five years and ten editions—is to help instructors energize their classrooms, engage their students, and bring literature to life.* At a time when the Humanities are under great pressure, we are committed to facilitating the special joy that comes with encountering significant works of art.

The works anthologized in these six volumes generally form the core of courses designed to introduce students to English literature. The selections reach back to the earliest moments of literary creativity in English, when the language itself was still molten, and extend to some of the most recent experiments, when, once again, English seems remarkably fluid and open. That openness—a recurrent characteristic of a language that has never been officially regulated and that has constantly renewed itself—helps to account for the sense of freshness that characterizes the works brought together here.

One of the joys of literature in English is its spectacular abundance. Even within the geographical confines of England, Scotland, Wales, and

---

* For more on the help we offer and how to access it, see "Additional Resources for Instructors and Students," p. xx.

Ireland, where the majority of texts in this collection originated, one can find more than enough distinguished and exciting works to fill the pages of this anthology many times over. But English literature is not confined to the British Isles; it is a global phenomenon. This border-crossing is not a consequence of modernity alone. It is fitting that among the first works here is *Beowulf*, a powerful epic written in the Germanic language known as Old English about a singularly restless Scandinavian hero. *Beowulf's* remarkable translator in *The Norton Anthology of English Literature*, Seamus Heaney, was one of the great contemporary masters of English literature— he was awarded the Nobel Prize for Literature in 1995—but it would be potentially misleading to call him an "English poet" for he was born in Northern Ireland and was not in fact English. It would be still more misleading to call him a "British poet," as if the British Empire were the most salient fact about the language he spoke and wrote in or the culture by which he was shaped. What matters is that the language in which Heaney wrote is English, and this fact links him powerfully with the authors assembled in these volumes, a linguistic community that stubbornly refuses to fit comfortably within any firm geographical or ethnic or national boundaries. So too, to glance at other authors and writings in the anthology, in the twelfth century, the noblewoman Marie de France wrote her short stories in an Anglo-Norman dialect at home on both sides of the channel; in the sixteenth century William Tyndale, in exile in the Low Countries and inspired by German religious reformers, translated the New Testament from Greek and thereby changed the course of the English language; in the seventeenth century Aphra Behn touched readers with a story that moves from Africa, where its hero is born, to South America, where Behn herself may have witnessed some of the tragic events she describes; and early in the twentieth century Joseph Conrad, born in Ukraine of Polish parents, wrote in eloquent English a celebrated novella whose ironic vision of European empire gave way by the century's end to the voices of those over whom the empire, now in ruins, had once hoped to rule: the Caribbean-born Claude McKay, Louise Bennett, Derek Walcott, Kamau Brathwaite, V. S. Naipaul, and Grace Nichols; the African-born Chinua Achebe, J. M. Coetzee, Ngũgĩ Wa Thiong'o, and Chimamanda Ngozi Adichie; and the Indian-born A. K. Ramanujan and Salman Rushdie.

A vital literary culture is always on the move. This principle was the watchword of M. H. Abrams, the distinguished literary critic who first conceived *The Norton Anthology of English Literature*, brought together the original team of editors, and, with characteristic insight, diplomacy, and humor, oversaw seven editions. Abrams wisely understood that new scholarly discoveries and the shifting interests of readers constantly alter the landscape of literary history. To stay vital, the anthology, therefore, would need to undergo a process of periodic revision, guided by advice from teachers, as well as students, who view the anthology with a loyal but critical eye. As with past editions, we have benefited from detailed information on the works actually assigned and suggestions for improvements from 273 reviewers. Their participation has been crucial as the editors grapple with the task of strengthening the selection of more traditional texts while adding texts that reflect the expansion of the field of English studies.

With each edition, *The Norton Anthology of English Literature* has offered a broadened canon without sacrificing major writers and a selection of complete longer texts in which readers can immerse themselves. Perhaps the most emblematic of these great texts are the epics *Beowulf* and *Paradise Lost*. Among the many other complete longer works in the Tenth Edition are *Sir Gawain and the Green Knight* (in Simon Armitage's spectacular translation), Sir Thomas More's *Utopia*, Sir Philip Sidney's *Defense of Poesy*, William Shakespeare's *Twelfth Night* and *Othello*, Samuel Johnson's *Rasselas*, Aphra Behn's *Oroonoko*, Jonathan Swift's *Gulliver's Travels*, Laurence Sterne's *A Sentimental Journey through France and Italy*, Charles Dickens's *A Christmas Carol*, Robert Louis Stevenson's *The Strange Case of Dr. Jekyll and Mr. Hyde*, Rudyard Kipling's *The Man Who Would Be King*, Joseph Conrad's *Heart of Darkness*, Virginia Woolf's *Mrs. Dalloway*, James Joyce's *Portrait of the Artist as a Young Man*, Samuel Beckett's *Waiting for Godot*, Harold Pinter's *The Dumb Waiter*, and Tom Stoppard's *Arcadia*. To augment the number of complete longer works instructors can assign, and—a special concern—better to represent the achievements of novelists, the publisher is making available the full list of Norton Critical Editions, more than 240 titles, including such frequently assigned novels as Jane Austen's *Pride and Prejudice*, Mary Shelley's *Frankenstein*, Charles Dickens's *Hard Times*, and Chinua Achebe's *Things Fall Apart*. A Norton Critical Edition may be included with either package (volumes A, B, C and volumes D, E, F) or any individual volume at a discounted price (contact your Norton representative for details).

We have in this edition continued to expand the selection of writing by women in several historical periods. The sustained work of scholars in recent years has recovered dozens of significant authors who had been marginalized or neglected by a male-dominated literary tradition and has deepened our understanding of those women writers who had managed, against considerable odds, to claim a place in that tradition. The First Edition of the Norton Anthology included 6 women writers; this Tenth Edition includes 84, of whom 13 are newly added and 10 are reselected or expanded. Poets and dramatists whose names were scarcely mentioned even in the specialized literary histories of earlier generations—Aemilia Lanyer, Lady Mary Wroth, Margaret Cavendish, Mary Leapor, Anna Letitia Barbauld, Charlotte Smith, Letitia Elizabeth Landon, Mary Elizabeth Coleridge, Mina Loy, and many others—now appear in the company of their male contemporaries. There are in addition four complete long prose works by women— Aphra Behn's *Oroonoko*, Eliza Haywood's *Fantomina*, Jane Austen's *Love and Friendship*, and Virginia Woolf's *Mrs. Dalloway*—along with selections from such celebrated fiction writers as Maria Edgeworth, Jean Rhys, Katherine Mansfield, Doris Lessing, Margaret Atwood, Kiran Desai, Zadie Smith, and new authors Hilary Mantel and Chimamanda Ngozi Adichie.

Building on an innovation introduced in the First Edition, the editors have expanded the array of topical clusters that gather together short texts illuminating the cultural, historical, intellectual, and literary concerns of each of the periods. We have designed these clusters with three aims: to make them lively and accessible, to ensure that they can be taught effectively in a class meeting or two, and to make clear their relevance to the surrounding works of literature. Hence, for example, in the Sixteenth Century, a new cluster, "The Wider World," showcases the English fascination with narratives of adventure, exploration, trade, and reconnaissance. New in the Eighteenth Century, "Print Culture and the Rise of the Novel" offers statements on the emergence of what would become English literature's most popular form as well as excerpts from *Robinson Crusoe* and *Evelina*. And in the Romantic Period, a new cluster on "The Romantic Imagination and the 'Oriental Nations'" joins contemporary discussion of the literature of those nations with selections from William Beckford's *Vathek* and Byron's *The Giaour*, among other texts. Across the volumes the clusters provide an exciting way to broaden the field of the literary and to set masterpieces in a wider cultural, social, and historical framework

Now, as in the past, cultures define themselves by the songs they sing and the stories they tell. But the central importance of visual media in contemporary culture has heightened our awareness of the ways in which songs and stories have always been closely linked to the images that societies have fashioned and viewed. The Tenth Edition of *The Norton Anthology of English Literature* features fifty-six pages of color plates (in seven color inserts) and more than 120 black-and-white illustrations throughout the volumes, including six new maps. In selecting visual material—from the Sutton Hoo treasure of the seventh century to Yinka Shonibare's *Nelson's Ship in a Bottle* in the twenty-first century—the editors sought to provide images that conjure up, whether directly or indirectly, the individual writers in each section; that relate specifically to individual works in the anthology; and that shape and illuminate the culture of a particular literary period. We have tried to choose visually striking images that will interest students and provoke discussion, and our captions draw attention to important details and cross-reference related texts in the anthology.

Period-by-Period Revisions

The Middle Ages. Edited by James Simpson, this period, huge in its scope and immensely varied in its voices, continues to offer exciting surprises. The heart of the Anglo-Saxon portion is the great epic *Beowulf,* in the acclaimed translation by Seamus Heaney. Now accompanied by a map of England at the time, the Anglo-Saxon texts include the haunting poems "Wulf and Eadwacer" and "The Ruin" as well as an intriguing collection of Anglo-Saxon riddles. These new works join verse translations of the *Dream of the Rood,* the *Wanderer,* and *The Wife's Lament*. An Irish Literature selection features a tale from *The Tain* and a group of ninth-century lyrics. The Anglo-Norman section—a key bridge between the Anglo-Saxon period and the time of Chaucer—offers a new pairing of texts about the tragic story of Tristan and Ysolt; an illuminating cluster on the Romance, with three stories by Marie de France (in award-winning translations); and *Sir Orfeo,* a comic version of the Orpheus and Eurydice story. The Middle English section centers, as always, on Chaucer, with a generous selection of tales and poems glossed and annotated so as to heighten their accessibility. Simon Armitage's brilliant verse translation of *Sir Gawain and the Green Knight* appears once again, and we offer newly modernized versions both of Thomas Hoccleve's *My Complaint,* a startlingly personal account of the speaker's attempt to reenter society after a period of mental instability, and of the playfully ironic and spiritually moving *Second Shepherds' Play.* "Talking Animals," a delightful new cluster, presents texts by Marie de France, Chaucer, and Robert Henryson that show how medieval writers used animals in stories that reveal much about humankind.

The Sixteenth Century, edited by Stephen Greenblatt and George Logan, features eight extraordinary longer texts in their entirety: More's *Utopia* (with two letters from More to Peter Giles); Book 1 of Spenser's *Faerie Queene* and, new to this edition, the posthumously published *Mutabilitie Cantos,* which arguably offer some of Spenser's finest poetry; Marlowe's *Hero and Leander* and *Doctor Faustus,* Sidney's *Defense of Poesy*; and Shakespeare's *Twelfth Night* and *Othello,* which has been added to the Tenth Edition by instructor request. Two exciting new topical clusters join the section. "An Elizabethan Miscellany" is a full, richly teachable grouping of sixteenth-century poems in English, by writers from George Gascoigne to Michael Drayton to Thomas Campion, among others, and provides access the period's explosion of lyric genius. "The Wider World" showcases the English Renaissance fascination with narratives of adventure, exploration, trade, and reconnaissance. Ranging from Africa to the Muslim East to the New World, the texts are compelling reading in our contemporary global context and offer particularly suggestive insights into the world of Shakespeare's *Othello.*

The Early Seventeenth Century. At the heart of this period, edited by Katharine Eisaman Maus, is John Milton's *Paradise Lost,* presented in its entirety. New to the Tenth Edition are the Arguments to each book, which are especially helpful for students first reading this magnificent, compelling epic. Along with Milton's "Lycidas" and *Samson Agonistes,* which is new to this edition, other complete longer works include John Donne's *Satire 3* and *The Anatomy of the World: The First Anniversary*; Aemilia Lanyer's country-house poem "The Description of Cookham"; Ben Jonson's *Volpone* and the moving Cary-Morison ode; and John Webster's tragedy *The Duchess of Malfi.* Generous selections from Donne, Mary Wroth, George Herbert, Katherine Philips, Andrew Marvell, and others, as well as the clusters "Inquiry and Experience," "Gender Relations," and "Crisis of Authority," together make for an exciting and thorough representation of the period.

The Restoration and the Eighteenth Century. The impressive array of complete longer texts in this period, edited by James Noggle, includes Dryden's *Absalom and Achitophel* and *MacFlecknoe*; Aphra Behn's *Oroonoko* (now with its dedicatory epistle); Congreve's comedy *The Way of the World*; Swift's *Gulliver's Travels* (newly complete, with illustrations from the first edition); Pope's *Essay on Criticism, The Rape of the Lock,* and *Epistle to Dr. Arbuthnot*; Gay's *Beggar's Opera*; Eliza Haywood's novella of sexual role-playing, *Fantomina*; Hogarth's graphic satire "Marriage A-la-Mode"; Johnson's *Vanity of Human Wishes* and *Rasselas*; Laurence Sterne's *A Sentimental Journey through France and Italy* (new to this edition); Gray's "Elegy Written in a Country Churchyard"; and Goldsmith's "The Deserted Village." An exciting new topical cluster, "Print Culture and the Rise of the Novel," with selections by Daniel Defoe, Henry Fielding, Samuel Richardson, Frances Burney, Clara Reeve, and others, enables readers to explore the origins of English literature's most popular form.

The Romantic Period. Edited by Deidre Shauna Lynch, this period again offers many remarkable additions. Chief among them are two topical clusters: "Romantic Literature and Wartime," which, through texts by Godwin, Wordsworth, Coleridge, Barbauld, Byron, De Quincey, and others, explores the varied ways in which war's violence came home to English literature; and "The Romantic Imagination and the 'Oriental Nations,'" which shows how English writers of the late eighteenth and early nineteenth centuries looked eastward for new, often contradictory themes of cultural identity and difference and for "exotic" subjects that were novel and enticing to the English audience. Also new to this period are poems by Barbauld, Robinson, Charlotte Smith, Wordsworth, Shelley, Hemans, and Landon. We are excited to include an excerpt from *The History of Mary Prince, a West Indian Slave*—the first slave narrative by a woman. John Clare, the increasingly appreciated "natural poet," receives four new texts.

The Victorian Age, edited by Catherine Robson, offers an impressive array of complete longer works. New to the prose selections is Charles Dickens's *A Christmas Carol,* complete with its original illustrations. Dickens's celebrated tale, which entertains at the same time that it deals brilliantly with matters social, economic, and spiritual, joins Robert Louis Stevenson's *The Strange Case of Dr. Jekyll and Mr. Hyde,* Arthur Conan Doyle's *The Speckled Band,* Elizabeth Gaskell's *The Old Nurse's Story,* and Rudyard Kipling's *The Man Who Would Be King.* Authors with significant longer poems include Elizabeth Barrett Browning, Alfred, Lord Tennyson, Robert Browning, Dante Gabriel Rossetti, Christina Rossetti, Algernon Charles Swinburne, and Gerard Manley Hopkins. Plays include Oscar Wilde's *The Importance of Being Earnest* and George Bernard Shaw's controversial drama on prostitution, *Mrs Warren's Profession.* And, continuing the tradition of enabling readers to grapple with the period's most resonant and often fiercely contentious issues, the Tenth Edition offers an exciting new cluster, "Beacons of the Future? Education in Victorian Britain," which brings together powerful reflections by John Stuart Mill and others, government reports on the nature of education, and illuminating excerpts from *Hard Times, Alice's Adventures in Wonderland, Tom Brown's School Days,* and *Jude the Obscure.*

The Twentieth and Twenty-First Centuries. The editor, Jahan Ramazani, continues his careful revision of this, the most rapidly changing period in the anthology. Once again its core is three modernist masterpieces: Virginia Woolf's *Mrs. Dalloway,* James Joyce's *Portrait of the Artist as a Young Man,* and Samuel Beckett's *Waiting for Godot,* all complete. These works are surrounded by a dazzling array of other fiction and drama. New to the Tenth Edition are the recent recipient of the Nobel Prize for Literature, Kazuo Ishiguro, along with Hilary Mantel, Caryl Phillips, and Chimamanda Ngozi Adichie. Their works join Joseph Conrad's *Heart of Darkness,* Harold Pinter's *The Dumb Waiter,* Tom Stoppard's *Arcadia,* and stories by D. H. Lawrence, Katherine Mansfield, Jean Rhys, Doris Lessing, Nadine Gordimer, Kiran

Desai, and Zadie Smith. A generous representation of poetry centers on substantial selections from Thomas Hardy, William Butler Yeats, and T. S. Eliot, and extends out to a wide range of other poets, from A. E. Housman, Wilfred Owen, and W. H. Auden to Philip Larkin, Derek Walcott, and Seamus Heaney. Two new poets, frequently requested by our readers, join the anthology: Anne Carson and Simon Armitage; and there are new poems by Yeats, Heaney, Geoffrey Hill, and Carol Ann Duffy. Visual aids have proved very helpful in teaching this period, and new ones include facsimile manuscript pages of poems by Isaac Rosenberg and Wilfred Owen, plus five new maps, which illustrate, among other things, the dramatic changes in the British Empire from 1891 to the late twentieth century, the movement of peoples to and from England during this time, and the journeys around London of the central characters in Woolf's *Mrs. Dalloway*. Linton Kwesi Johnson, Bernardine Evaristo, Patience Agbabi, and Dajlit Nagra join Claude McKay, Louise Bennett, Kamau Brathwaite, Ngũgĩ Wa Thiong'o, M. NourbeSe Philip, Salman Rushdie, and Grace Nichols in the much-praised cluster "Nation, Race, and Language"—together they bear witness to the global diffusion of English, the urgency of issues of nation and identity, and the rich complexity of literary history.

Editorial Procedures and Format

The Tenth Edition adheres to the principles that have always characterized *The Norton Anthology of English Literature*. Period introductions, headnotes, and annotations are designed to enhance students' reading and, without imposing an interpretation, to give students the information they need to understand each text. The aim of these editorial materials is to make the anthology self-sufficient, so that it can be read anywhere—in a coffeeshop, on a bus, under a tree.

The *Norton Anthology of English Literature* prides itself on both the scholarly accuracy and the readability of its texts. To ease students' encounter with some works, we have normalized spelling and capitalization in texts up to and including the Romantic period—for the most part they now follow the conventions of modern English. We leave unaltered, however, texts in which such modernizing would change semantic or metrical qualities. From the Victorian period onward, we have used the original spelling and punctuation. We continue other editorial procedures that have proved useful in the past. After each work, we cite the date of first publication on the right; in some instances, this date is followed by the date of a revised edition for which the author was responsible. Dates of composition, when they differ from those of publication and when they are known, are provided on the left. We use square brackets to indicate titles supplied by the editors for the convenience of readers. Whenever a portion of a text is omitted, we indicate that omission with three asterisks. If the omitted portion is important for following the plot or argument, we provide a brief summary within the text or in a footnote. Finally, we have reconsidered annotations throughout and increased the number of marginal glosses for archaic, dialect, or unfamiliar words.

The Tenth Edition includes the useful "Literary Terminology" appendix, a quick-reference alphabetical glossary with examples from works in the anthology. We have also updated the General Bibliography that appears in the print volumes, as well as the period and author bibliographies, which appear online, where they can be easily searched and updated.

Additional Resources for Instructors and Students

The idea that a vital literary culture is always on the move applies not only to the print anthology but also to the resources that accompany it. For the Tenth Edition, we have added exciting new resources and improved and updated existing resources to make them more useful and easy to find.

We are pleased to launch the new NAEL Archive site, found at digital.wwnorton.com/englishlit10abc (for volumes A, B, C) and digital.wwnorton.com/englishlit10def (for volumes D, E, F). This searchable and sortable site contains thousands of resources for students and instructors in one centralized place at no additional cost. Following are some highlights:

- A series of twenty brand-new video modules designed to enhance classroom presentation of the literary works. These videos, conceived of and narrated by the anthology editors, bring various texts from the anthology to life by providing a closer look at a rarely seen manuscript, visiting a place of literary significance, or offering a conversation with a living writer.
- Over 1,000 additional readings from the Middle Ages to the turn of the twentieth century, edited, glossed, and annotated to the scholarly standards and with the sensitivity to classroom use for which the Norton Anthology is renowned. Teachers who wish to add to the selections in the print anthology will find numerous exciting works, including Wycherley's *The Country Wife*, Joanna Baillie's "A Mother to Her Waking Infant," and Edward Lear's "The Jumblies." In addition, there are many fascinating topical clusters—"The First Crusade: Sanctifying War," "Genius," and "The Satanic and Byronic Hero," to name only a few—all designed to draw readers into larger cultural contexts and to expose them to a wide spectrum of voices.
- Hundreds of images—maps, author portraits, literary places, and manuscripts—available for student browsing or instructor download for in-class presentation.
- Several hours of audio recordings.
- Annotated bibliographies for all periods and authors in the anthology.

The NAEL Archive also provides a wealth of teaching resources that are unlocked on instructor log-in:

- "Quick read" summaries, teaching notes, and discussion questions for every work in the anthology, from the much-praised *Teaching with* The Norton Anthology of English Literature: *A Guide for Instructors* by Naomi Howell (University of Exeter), Philip Schwyzer (University of Exeter), Judyta Frodyma (University of Northern British Columbia), and Sondra Archimedes (University of California–Santa Cruz).
- Downloadable PowerPoints featuring images and audio for in-class presentation

In addition to the resources in the NAEL Archive, Norton offers a downloadable coursepack that allows instructors to easily add high-quality Norton media to online, hybrid, or lecture courses—all at no cost. Norton Coursepacks work within existing learning management systems; there's no new system to learn, and access is free and easy. Content is customizable and includes over seventy-four reading-comprehension quizzes, short-answer questions with suggested answers, links to the video modules, and more.

The editors are grateful to the hundreds of teachers worldwide who have helped us improve *The Norton Anthology of English Literature*. A list of instructors who replied to a detailed questionnaire follows, under Acknowledgments. The editors would like to express appreciation for their help to Jessica Berman (University of Maryland Baltimore County), Lara Bovilsky (University of Oregon), Gordon Braden (University of Virginia), Bruce Bradley (Clongowes Wood College), Dympna Callaghan (Syracuse University), Ariel Churchill (Harvard University), Joseph Connors (Harvard University), Taylor Cowdery (University of North Carolina at Chapel Hill), Maria Devlin (Harvard University), Lars Engel (University of Tulsa), James Engell (Harvard University), Aubrey Everett (Harvard University), Anne Fernald (Fordham University), Kevis Goodman (University of California–Berkeley), Alexander Gourlay (RISD), John Hale (University of Otago), Stephen Hequembourg (University of Virginia), Seth Herbst (U.S. Military Academy, West Point), Rhema Hokama (Singapore University of Technology and Design), Jean Howard (Columbia University), Robert Irvine (University of Edinburgh), Thomas Keirstead (University of Toronto), Margaret Kelleher (University College Dublin), Cara Lewis (Indiana University Northwest), Mario Menendez (Harvard University), Tara Menon (New York University), John Miller (University of Virginia), Peter Miller (University of Virginia), A. J. Odasso (Wellesley College), Declan O'Keeffe (Clongowes Wood College), Juan Christian Pellicer (University of Oslo), Robert Pinsky (Boston University), Will Porter (Harvard University), Mark Rankin (James Madison University), Josephine Reece (Harvard University), Jessica Rosenberg (University of Miami), Suparna Roychoudhury (Mount Holyoke College), Peter Sacks (Harvard University), Ray Siemens (University of Victoria), Kim Simpson (University of Southampton), Bailey Sincox (Harvard University), Ramie Targoff (Brandeis University), Misha Teramura (Reed College), Gordon Teskey (Harvard University), Katie Trumpener (Yale University), Paul Westover (Brigham Young University), Katy Woodring (Harvard University), and Faye Zhang (Harvard University).

We also thank the people at Norton, an employee-owned publishing house with a commitment to excellence, who contributed to the Tenth Edition. In planning this edition, Julia Reidhead served, as she has in the past, as our wise and effective collaborator. In addition, we are now working with Marian Johnson, literature editor and managing editor for college books, a splendid new collaborator who has helped us bring the Tenth Edition to fruition. With admirable equanimity and skill, Carly Frasier Doria, electronic media editor and course guide editor, fashioned the new video modules and brought together the dazzling array of web resources and other pedagogical aids. We also thank Katharine Ings, Candace Levy, and Michael Fleming, manuscript editors; Sean Mintus, senior production manager; Kimberly Bowers, marketing manager for literature; Megan Jackson Schindel and Nancy Rodwan, permissions; Nelson Colon, photo editor; and Rachel Taylor and Ava Bramson, assistant editor and assistant media editor, respectively. All these friends provided us with indispensable help in meeting the challenge of representing the unparalleled range and variety of English literature.

STEPHEN GREENBLATT

Acknowledgments

The editors would like to express appreciation and thanks to the hundreds of teachers who provided reviews:

Michel Aaij (Auburn University at Montgomery), Jerry J. Alexander (Presbyterian College), Sarah Alexander (The University of Vermont), Marshall N. Armintor (University of North Texas), Marilyn Judith Atlas (Ohio University), Alison Baker (California State Polytechnic University, Pomona), Reid Barbour (University of North Carolina, Chapel Hill), Jessica Barnes-Pietruszynski (West Virginia State University), Jessica Barr (Eureka College), Chris Barrett (Louisiana State University), Craig Barrette (Brescia University), Carol Beran (St. Mary's College), Peter Berek (Amherst College), David Bergman (Towson University), Scott Black (University of Utah), William R. "Beau" Black III (Weatherford College), Justin Blessinger (Dakota State University), William E. Bolton (La Salle University), Wyatt Bonikowski (Suffolk University), Rebecca Bossie (University of Texas at El Paso), Bruce Brandt (South Dakota State University), Heather Braun (University of Akron), Mark Brown (University of Jamestown), Logan D. Browning (Rice University), Monica Brzezinski Potkay (College of William and Mary), Rebecca Bushnell (University of Pennsylvania), Claire Busse (La Salle University), Thomas Butler (Eastern Kentucky University), Jim Casey (Arcadia University), Susan P. Cerasano (Colgate University), Maria Chappell (University of Georgia), Brinda Charry (Keene State College), Susannah Chewning (Union County College), Lin Chih-hsin (National Chengchi University), Kathryn Chittick (Trent University), Rita Colanzi (Immaculata University), Nora Corrigan (Mississippi University for Women), David Cowart (University of South Carolina), Catherine Craft-Fairchild (University of St. Thomas), Susan Crisafulli (Franklin College), Jenny Crisp (Dalton State College), Ashley Cross (Manhattan College), James P. Crowley (Bridgewater State University), Susie Crowson (Del Mar College), Rebecca Crump (Louisiana State University), Cyrus Mulready (SUNY New Paltz), Lisa Darien (Hartwick College), Sean Dempsey (University of Arkansas), Anthony Ding (Grossmont Community College), Lorraine Eadie (Hillsdale College), Schuyler Eastin (San Diego Christian College), Gary Eddy (Winona State University), J. Craig Eller (Louisburg College), Robert Ellison (Marshall University), Nikolai Endres (Western Kentucky University), Robert Epstein (Fairfield University), Richard Erable (Franklin College), Simon C. Estok (Sungkyunkwan University), Michael Faitell (Mohawk Valley Community College), Jonathan Farina (Seton Hall University), Tyler Farrell (Marquette University),

Jennifer Feather (The University of North Carolina Greensboro), Annette Federico (James Madison University), Kerstin Feindert (Cosumnes River College), Maryanne Felter (Cayuga Community College), Benjamin Fischer (Northwest Nazarene University), Matthew Fisher (University of California, Los Angeles), Chris Fletcher (North Central University), Michael J. Flynn (The University of North Dakota), James E. Foley (Worcester State University), Walter C. Foreman (University of Kentucky), Ann Frank Wake (Elmhurst College), Michael D. Friedman (University of Scranton), Lee Garver (Butler University), Paul L. Gaston (Kent State University), Sara E. Gerend (Aurora University), Avilah Getzler (Grand View University), Edward Gieskes (University of South Carolina), Elaine Glanz (Immaculata University), Adam Golaski (Brown University), Rachel Goldberg (Northeastern CPS), Augusta Gooch (University of Alabama–Huntsville), Nathan Gorelick (Utah Valley University), Robert Gorsch (Saint Mary's College of California), Carey Goyette (Clinton Community College), Richard J. Grande (Pennsylvania State University, Abington), David A. Grant (Columbus State Community College), Sian Griffiths (Weber State University), Ann H. Guess (Alvin Community College), Audley Hall (NorthWest Arkansas Community College), Jenni Halpin (Savannah State University), Brian Harries (Concordia University Wisconsin), Samantha Harvey (Boise State University), Raychel Haugrud Reiff (University of Wisconsin–Superior), Erica Haugtvedt (The Ohio State University), Mary Hayes (University of Mississippi), Joshua R. Held (Indiana University, Bloomington), Roze Hentschell (Colorado State University), Erich Hertz (Siena College), Natalie Hewitt (Hope International University), Lisa Hinrichsen (University of Arkansas), Lorretta Holloway (Framingham State University), Catherine Howard (University of Houston), Chia-Yin Huang (Chinese Culture University), Sister Marie Hubert Kealy (Immaculata University), Elizabeth Hutcheon (Huntingdon College), Peter Hyland (Huron University College, Western University), Eileen Jankowski (Chapman University), Alan Johnson (Idaho State University), Brian Jukes (Yuba College), Kari Kalve (Earlham College), Parmita Kapadia (Northern Kentucky University), Deborah Kennedy (Saint Mary's University), Mark Kipperman (Northern Illinois University), Cindy Klestinec (Miami University–Ohio), Neal W. Kramer (Brigham Young University), Kathryn Laity (College of Saint Rose), Jameela Lares (University of Southern Mississippi), Caroline Levine (University of Wisconsin–Madison), Melinda Linscott (Idaho State University), Janet Madden (El Camino College), Gerald Margolis (Temple University), Elizabeth Mazzola (The City College of New York), Keely McCarthy (Chestnut Hill College), Cathryn McCarthy Donahue (College of Mount Saint Vincent), Mary H. McMurran (University of Western Ontario), Josephine A. McQuail (Tennessee Technological University), Brett Mertins (Metropolitan Community College), Christian Michener (Saint Mary's University), Brook Miller (University of Minnesota, Morris), Kristine Miller (Utah State University), Jacqueline T. Miller (Rutgers University), Richard J. Moll (University of Western Ontario), Lorne Mook (Taylor University), Rod Moore (Los Angeles Valley College), Rory Moore (University of California, Riverside), Grant Moss (Utah Valley University), Nicholas D. Nace (Hampden-Sydney College), Jonathan Naito (St. Olaf College), Mary Nelson (Dallas Baptist University), Mary Anne Nunn (Central Connecticut State University), John O'Brien (University of Virginia),

Onno Oerlemans (Hamilton College), Michael Oishi (Leeward Community College), Sylvia Pamboukian (Robert Morris University), Adam Parkes (University of Georgia), Michelle Parkinson (University of Wisconsin–River Falls), Geoffrey Payne (Macquarie University), Anna Peak (Temple University), Dan Pearce (Brigham Young University–Idaho), Christopher Penna (University of Delaware), Zina Petersen (Brigham Young University), Kaara L. Peterson (Miami University of Ohio), Keith Peterson (Brigham Young University–Hawaii), Professor Maggie Piccolo (Rowan University), Ann Pleiss Morris (Ripon College), Michael Pogach (Northampton Community College), Matthew Potolsky (The University of Utah), Miguel Powers (Fullerton College), Gregory Priebe (Harford Community College), Jonathan Purkiss (Pulaski Technical College), Kevin A. Quarmby (Oxford College of Emory University), Mark Rankin (James Madison University), Tawnya Ravy (The George Washington University), Joan Ray (University of Colorado, Colorado Springs), Helaine Razovsky (Northwestern State University of Louisiana), Vince Redder (Dakota Wesleyan University), Elizabeth Rich (Saginaw Valley State University), Patricia Rigg (Acadia University), Albert J. Rivero (Marquette University), Phillip Ronald Stormer (Culver-Stockton College), Kenneth Rooney (University College Cork, Ireland), David Ruiter (University of Texas at El Paso), Kathryn Rummell (California Polytechnic State University), Richard Ruppel (Chapman University), Jonathan Sachs (Concordia University), David A. Salomon (Russell Sage College), Abigail Scherer (Nicholls State University), Roger Schmidt (Idaho State University), William Sheldon (Hutchinson Community College), Christian Sheridan (Bridgewater College), Nicole Sidhu (East Carolina University), Lisa Siefker Bailey (Indiana University–Purdue University Columbus), Samuel Smith (Messiah College), Cindy Soldan (Lakehead University), Diana Solomon (Simon Fraser University), Vivasvan Soni (Northwestern University), Timothy Spurgin (Lawrence University), Felicia Jean Steele (The College of New Jersey), Carole Lynn Stewart (Brock University), Judy Suh (Duquesne University), Dean Swinford (Fayetteville State University), Allison Symonds (Cecil College), Brenda Tuberville (Rogers State University), Verne Underwood (Rogue Community College), Janine Utell (Widener University), Paul Varner (Abilene Christian University), Deborah Vause (York College of Pennsylvania), Nicholas Wallerstein (Black Hills State University), Rod Waterman (Central Connecticut State University), Eleanor Welsh (Chesapeake College), Paul Westover (Brigham Young University), Christopher Wheatley (The Catholic University of America), Miranda Wilcox (Brigham Young University), Brett D. Wilson (College of William & Mary), Lorraine Wood (Brigham Young University), Nicholas A. Wright (Marist College), Michael Wutz (Weber State University).

THE NORTON ANTHOLOGY OF

ENGLISH LITERATURE

TENTH EDITION

VOLUME A

THE MIDDLE AGES

The Middle Ages
to ca. 1485

The Middle Ages designates the time span roughly from the collapse of the Roman Empire to the Renaissance and Reformation. The adjective "medieval," coined from Latin *medium* (middle) and *aevum* (age), refers to whatever was made, written, or thought during the Middle Ages. The Renaissance was so named by nineteenth-century historians and critics because they associated it with an outburst of creativity attributed to a "rebirth" or revival of Latin and, especially, of Greek learning and literature. The word "Reformation" designates the powerful religious movement that began in the early sixteenth century and repudiated the supreme authority of the Roman Catholic Church. The Renaissance was seen as spreading from Italy in the fourteenth and fifteenth centuries to the rest of Europe, whereas the Reformation began in Germany and quickly affected all of Europe to a greater or lesser degree. The very idea of a Renaissance or rebirth, however, implies something dormant or lacking in the preceding era. More recently, there have been two nonexclusive tendencies in our understanding of the medieval period and what follows. Some scholars emphasize the continuities between

Pilgrims leaving Canterbury, ca. 1420. For more information about this image, see the color insert in this volume.

3

the Middle Ages and the later time now often called the Early Modern Period. Others emphasize the ways in which sixteenth-century writers in some sense "created" the Middle Ages, in order to highlight what they saw as the brilliance of their own time. Medieval authors, of course, did not think of themselves as living in the "middle"; they sometimes expressed the idea that the world was growing old and that theirs was a declining age, close to the end of time. Yet art, literature, and science flourished during the Middle Ages, rooted in both Christian and secular cultures that preserved, transmitted, and transformed classical tradition.

The works covered in this section of the anthology encompass a period of more than eight hundred years, from Cædmon's *Hymn* at the end of the seventh century to *Everyman* at the beginning of the sixteenth. The date 1485, the year of the accession of Henry VII and the beginning of the Tudor dynasty, is an arbitrary but convenient one to mark the "end" of the Middle Ages in England.

Although the Roman Catholic Church provided continuity from the seventh century on, the period was one of enormous historical, social, and linguistic change. To emphasize these changes and the events underlying them, we have divided the period into three primary sections: Anglo-Saxon Literature, Anglo-Norman Literature, and Middle English Literature in the Fourteenth and Fifteenth Centuries. The Anglo-Saxon invaders, who began their conquest of the southeastern part of Britain around 450, spoke an early form of the language we now call Old English. Old English displays its kinship with other Germanic languages (German or Dutch, for example) much more clearly than does contemporary British and American English, of which Old English is the ancestor. As late as the tenth century, part of an Old Saxon poem written on the Continent was transcribed and transliterated into the West Saxon dialect of Old English without presenting problems to its English readers. In form and content, Old English literature also has much in common with other Germanic literatures with which it shared a body of heroic as well as Christian stories. The major characters in *Beowulf* are pagan Danes and Geats, and the only connection to England is an obscure allusion to the ancestor of one of the kings of the Angles.

The changes already in progress in the language and culture of Anglo-Saxon England were greatly accelerated by the Norman Conquest of 1066. The ascendancy of a French-speaking ruling class had the effect of adding a vast number of French loan words to the English vocabulary. The conquest resulted in new forms of political organization and administration, architecture, and literary expression. In the twelfth century, through the interest of the Anglo-Normans in British history before the Anglo-Saxon Conquest, not only England but all of Western Europe became fascinated with a legendary hero named Arthur who makes his earliest appearances in Celtic literature. King Arthur and his knights became a staple subject of medieval French, English, and German literature. Selections from Latin, French, and Old Irish, as well as from Early Middle English, have been included here to give a sense of the cross-currents of languages and literatures in Anglo-Norman England and to provide background for later English literature in all periods.

Literature in English was both performed orally and written throughout the Middle Ages, but an awareness of and pride in a uniquely *English* literature did not actually exist before the late fourteenth century. In 1336 Edward III began a war to enforce his claims to the throne of France; the war continued intermittently for more than one hundred years until finally the English were driven from all their French territories, except for the port of Calais, in 1453. One result of the war and these losses was a keener sense on the part of England's nobility of their English heritage and identity. Toward the close of the fourteenth century, English finally began to displace French as the language for conducting business in Parliament and much official correspondence. Although the high nobility continued to speak French by preference, they were certainly bilingual, whereas some of the earlier Norman kings had known no English at all. It was becoming possible to obtain patronage for literary achievement in English. The decision of Chaucer (ca. 1340–1400) to emulate French and Italian poetry in his own vernacular is an indication of the change taking place in the status of English, and Chaucer's works were greatly to enhance the prestige of English as a vehicle for literature of high ambition. He was acclaimed by fifteenth-century poets as the embellisher of the English tongue; later writers called him the English Homer and the father of English poetry. His friend John Gower (ca. 1330–1408) wrote long poems in French and Latin before producing his last major work, the *Confessio Amantis* (The Lover's Confession), which in spite of its Latin title is composed in English.

The third and longest of the three primary sections, Middle English Literature in the Fourteenth and Fifteenth Centuries, is thus not only a chronological and linguistic division but implies a new sense of English as a literary medium that could compete with French and Latin in elegance and seriousness.

Book production throughout the medieval period was an expensive process. Until the invention of movable type in the mid-fifteenth century (introduced into England by Caxton in 1476), medieval books were reproduced by hand in manuscript (literally "written by hand"). While paper became increasingly common for less expensive manuscripts in the fifteenth century, manuscripts were until then written on carefully prepared animal (usually calf or sheep) skin, known as parchment or vellum. More expensive books could be illuminated both by colored and calligraphic lettering, and by visual images.

The institutions of book production developed across the period. In the Anglo-Saxon period, monasteries were the main centers of book production and storage. Until their dissolution in the 1530s, monastic and other religious houses continued to produce books, but from the early fourteenth century, particularly in London, commercial book-making enterprises came into being. These were loose organizations of various artisans such as parchmentmakers, scribes, flourishers, illuminators, and binders, who usually lived in the same neighborhoods in towns. A bookseller or dealer (usually a member of one of these trades) would coordinate the production of books to order for wealthy patrons, sometimes distributing the work of copying to different scribes, who would be responsible for different gatherings, or quires, of the same book. Such shops could call upon the services of professional scribes working in the bureaucracies of the royal court.

The market for books also changed across the period: while monasteries, other religious houses, and royal courts continued to fund the production of books, from the Anglo-Norman period books were also produced for (and sometimes by) noble and gentry households. From the fourteenth century the market was widened yet further, with wealthy urban patrons also ordering books. Some of these books were dedicated to single works, some largely to single genres; most were much more miscellaneous, containing texts of many kinds and (particularly in the Anglo-Norman period) written in different languages (especially Latin, French, and English). Only a small proportion of medieval books survive; large numbers were destroyed at the time of the dissolution of the monasteries in the 1530s.

Texts in Old English, Early Middle English, the more difficult texts in later Middle English (*Sir Gawain and the Green Knight, Piers Plowman*), and those in other languages are here given in translation. Chaucer and other Middle English works may be read in the original, even by the beginner, with the help of marginal glosses and notes. These texts have been spelled in a way that is intended to aid the reader. Analyses of the sounds and grammar of Middle English and of Old and Middle English prosody are presented on pages 20–26.

ANGLO-SAXON LITERATURE

From the first to the fifth century, England was a province of the Roman Empire and was named Britannia after its Celtic-speaking inhabitants, the Britons. The Britons adapted themselves to Roman civilization, of which the ruins survived to impress the poet of *The Wanderer*, who refers to them as "the ancient works of giants." The withdrawal of the Roman legions during the fifth century, in a vain attempt to protect Rome itself from the threat of Germanic conquest, left the island vulnerable to seafaring Germanic invaders. These belonged primarily to three related tribes: the Angles, the Saxons, and the Jutes. The name *English* derives from the Angles, and the names of the counties Essex, Sussex, and Wessex refer to the territories occupied by the East, South, and West Saxons.

The Anglo-Saxon occupation was no sudden conquest but extended over decades of fighting against the native Britons. The latter were, finally, largely confined to the mountainous region of Wales, where the modern form of their language is spoken alongside English to this day. The Britons had become Christians in the fourth century after the conversion of Emperor Constantine along with most of the rest of the Roman Empire, but for about 150 years after the beginning of the invasion, Christianity was maintained only in the remoter regions where the as yet pagan Anglo-Saxons failed to penetrate. In the year 597, however, a Benedictine monk (afterward St. Augustine of Canterbury) was sent by Pope Gregory as a missionary to King Ethelbert of Kent, the most southerly of the kingdoms into which England was then divided, and about the same time missionaries from Ireland began to preach Christianity in the north. Within 75 years the island was once more predominantly Christian. Before Christianity there had been no books. The impact of Christianity on literacy is evident from the fact that the first extended written specimen of the Old English (Anglo-Saxon) language is a code of laws promulgated by Ethelbert (ca. 560–616), the first English Christian king.

ANGLO-SAXON ENGLAND

In the centuries that followed the conversion, England produced many distinguished churchmen. One of the earliest of these was Bede, whose Latin *Ecclesiastical History of the English People*, which tells the story of the conversion and of the English church, was completed in 731; this remains one of our most important sources of knowledge about the period. In the next generation, Alcuin (735–804), a man of wide culture, became the friend and adviser of the Frankish emperor Charlemagne, whom he assisted in making the Frankish court a great center of learning; thus by the year 800 English culture had developed so richly that it overflowed its insular boundaries.

Lindisfarne Gospels. Opening of Gospel of St. Matthew, ca. 698. The veil of mysteries is drawn aside, and the author of the gospel text copies his book as if by divine dictation.

In the ninth century, the Christian Anglo-Saxons were themselves subjected to new Germanic invasions by the Danes who in their longboats repeatedly ravaged the coast, sacking Bede's monastery among others. Such a raid late in the tenth century inspired *The Battle of Maldon*, the last of the Old English heroic poems. The Danes also occupied the northern part of the island, threatening to overrun the rest. They were stopped by Alfred, king of the West Saxons from 871 to 899, who for a time united all the kingdoms of southern England. This most active king was also an enthusiastic patron of literature. He himself translated various works from Latin, the most important of which was Boethius's *Consolation of Philosophy*, a sixth-century Roman work also translated in the fourteenth century by Chaucer. Alfred probably also instigated a translation of Bede's *History* and the beginning of the *Anglo-Saxon Chronicle*: this year-by-year record in Old English of important events in England was maintained at one monastery until the middle of the twelfth century. Practically all of Old English poetry is preserved in copies made in the West Saxon dialect after the reign of Alfred.

Old English Poetry

The Anglo-Saxon invaders brought with them a tradition of oral poetry (see "Bede and Cædmon's *Hymn*," p. 30). Because nothing was written down before the conversion to Christianity, we have only circumstantial evidence of what that poetry must have been like. Aside from a few short inscriptions on small artifacts, the earliest records in the English language are in manuscripts produced at monasteries and other religious establishments, beginning in the seventh century. Literacy was mainly restricted to servants of the church, and so it is natural that the bulk of Old English literature deals with religious subjects and is mostly drawn from Latin sources. Under the expensive conditions of manuscript production, few texts were written down that did not pertain directly to the work of the church. Most of Old English poetry is contained in just four manuscripts.

Germanic heroic poetry continued to be performed orally in alliterative verse and was at times used to describe current events. *The Battle of Brunanburh,* which celebrates an English victory over the Danes in traditional alliterative verse, is preserved in the *Anglo-Saxon Chronicle. The Battle of Maldon* (in the NAEL Archive) commemorates a Viking victory in which the Christian English invoke the ancient code of honor that obliges a warrior to avenge his slain lord or to die beside him.

These poems show that the aristocratic, heroic, and kinship values of Germanic society continued to inspire both clergy and laity in the Christian era. As represented in the relatively small body of Anglo-Saxon heroic poetry that survives, this world shares many characteristics with the heroic world described by Homer. Nations are reckoned as groups of people related by kinship rather than by geographical areas, and kinship is the basis of the heroic code. The tribe is ruled by a chieftain who is called *king,* a word that has "kin" for its root. The *lord* (a word derived from Old English *hlaf,* "loaf," plus *weard,* "protector") surrounds himself with a band of retainers (many of them his blood kindred) who are members of his household. He leads his men in battle and rewards them with the spoils; royal generosity was one of the most important aspects of heroic behavior. In return, the retainers are obligated to fight to the death for their lord, and if he is slain, to avenge him or die in the attempt. Blood vengeance is regarded as a sacred duty, and in poetry, everlasting shame awaits those who fail to observe it.

Even though the heroic world of poetry could be invoked to rally resistance to the Viking invasions, it was already remote from the Christian world of Anglo-Saxon England. Nevertheless, Christian writers like the *Beowulf* poet were fascinated by the distant culture of their pagan ancestors and by the inherent conflict between the heroic code and a religion that teaches that we should "forgive those who trespass against us" and that "all they that take the sword shall perish with the sword." The *Beowulf* poet looks back on that ancient world with admiration for the courage of which it was capable and at the same time with elegiac sympathy for its inevitable doom.

For Anglo-Saxon poetry, it is difficult and probably futile to draw a line between "heroic" and "Christian," for the best poetry crosses that boundary. Much of the Christian poetry is also cast in the heroic mode: although the Anglo-Saxons adapted themselves readily to the ideals of Christianity, they did not do so without adapting Christianity to their own heroic ideal. Thus Moses and St. Andrew, Christ and God the Father are represented in the style of heroic verse. In *The Dream of the Rood,* the Cross speaks of Christ as "this young man, . . . strong and courageous." In Cædmon's *Hymn* the creation of heaven and earth is seen as a mighty deed, an "establishment of wonders." Anglo-Saxon heroines, too, are portrayed in the heroic manner. St. Helena, who leads an expedition to the Holy Land to discover the true Cross, is described as a "battle-queen." The biblical narrative related in the Anglo-Saxon poem *Judith* is recast in the terms of Germanic heroic poetry. Christian and heroic ideals are poignantly blended in *The Wanderer,* which laments the separation from one's lord and kinsmen and the transience of all earthly treasures. Love between man and woman, as described by the female speaker of *The Wife's Lament*, is disrupted by separation, exile, and the malice of kinfolk.

The world of Old English poetry is often elegiac. Men are said to be cheerful in the mead hall, but even there they think of war, of possible triumph but probable failure. Romantic love—one of the principal topics of later literature—appears hardly at all. Even so, at some of the bleakest moments, the poets powerfully recall the return of spring. The blade of the magic sword with which Beowulf has killed Grendel's mother in her sinister underwater lair begins to melt, "as ice melts / when the Father eases the fetters off the frost / and unravels the water ropes, He who wields power."

The poetic diction, formulaic phrases, and repetitions of parallel syntactic structures, which are determined by the versification, are difficult to reproduce in modern translation. A few features may be anticipated here and studied in the text of Cædmon's *Hymn*, printed below (pp. 31–32) with interlinear translation.

Poetic language is created out of a special vocabulary that contains a multiplicity of terms for *lord*, *warrior*, *spear*, *shield*, and so on. Synecdoche and metonymy are common figures of speech, as when "keel" is used for *ship* or "iron" for *sword*. A particularly striking effect is achieved by the kenning, a compound of two words in place of another as when *sea* becomes "whale-road" or *body* is called "life-house." The figurative use of language finds playful expression in poetic riddles, of which about one hundred survive. Common (and sometimes uncommon) creatures, objects, or phenomena are described in an enigmatic passage of alliterative verse, and the reader must guess their identity. Sometimes they are personified and ask, "What is my name?"

Because special vocabulary and compounds are among the chief poetic effects, the verse is constructed in such a way as to show off such terms by creating a series of them in apposition. In the second sentence of Cædmon's *Hymn*, for example, God is referred to five times appositively as "he," "holy Creator," "mankind's Guardian," "eternal Lord," and "Master Almighty." This use of parallel and appositive expressions, known as *variation*, gives the verse a highly structured and musical quality.

The overall effect of the language is to formalize and elevate speech. Instead of being straightforward, it moves at a slow and stately pace with steady indirection. A favorite mode of this indirection is irony. A grim irony pervades heroic poetry even at the level of diction where *fighting* is called "battle-play." A favorite device, known by the rhetorical term *litotes*, is ironic understatement. After the monster Grendel has slaughtered the Danes in the great hall Heorot, it stands deserted. The poet observes, "It was easy then to meet with a man / shifting himself to a safer distance."

More than a figure of thought, irony is also a mode of perception in Old English poetry. In a famous passage, the Wanderer articulates the theme of *Ubi sunt?* (where are they now?): "Where did the steed go? Where the young warrior? Where the treasure-giver? . . ." *Beowulf* is full of ironic balances and contrasts—between the aged Danish king and the youthful Beowulf, and between Beowulf, the high-spirited young warrior at the beginning, and Beowulf, the gray-haired king at the end, facing the dragon and death.

The formal and dignified speech of Old English poetry was always distant from the everyday language of the Anglo-Saxons, and this poetic idiom remained remarkably uniform throughout the roughly three hundred years that separate Cædmon's *Hymn* from *The Battle of Maldon.* This clinging to old forms—grammatical and orthographic as well as literary—by the Anglo-Saxon church and aristocracy conceals from us the enormous changes that were taking place in the English language and the diversity of its dialects. The dramatic changes between Old and Middle English did not happen overnight or over the course of a single century. The Normans displaced the English ruling class with their own barons and clerics, whose native language was a dialect of Old French that we call Anglo-Norman. Without a ruling literate class to preserve English traditions, the custom of transcribing vernacular texts in an earlier form of the West-Saxon dialect was abandoned, and both language and literature were allowed to develop unchecked in new directions.

For examples of Irish medieval literature, see "Cúchulainn's Boyhood Deeds," an excerpt from the Old Irish epic *Táin Bó Cuailnge* (The Cattle Raid of Cooley), and some delightful monastic lyrics (pp. 128–35).

ANGLO-NORMAN LITERATURE

The Normans, who took possession of England after the decisive Battle of Hastings (1066), were, like the Anglo-Saxons, descendants of Germanic adventurers, who at the beginning of the tenth century had seized a wide part of northern France. Their name is actually a contraction of "Norsemen." A highly adaptable people, they had adopted the French language of the land they had settled in and its Christian religion. Both in Normandy and in Britain they were great builders of castles, with which they enforced their political dominance, and magnificent churches. Norman bishops, who held land and castles like the barons, wielded both political and spiritual authority. The earlier Norman kings of England, however, were often absentee rulers, as much concerned with defending their Continental possessions as with ruling over their English holdings. The English Crown's French territories were enormously increased in 1154 when Henry II, the first of England's Plantagenet kings, ascended the throne. Through his marriage with Eleanor of Aquitaine, the divorced wife of Louis VII of France, Henry had acquired vast provinces in the southwest of France.

The presence of a French-speaking ruling class in England created exceptional opportunities for linguistic and cultural exchange. Four languages coexisted in the realm of Anglo-Norman England. Latin, as it had been for Bede, remained the international language of learning, used for theology, science, and history. It was not by any means a written language only but also a lingua franca by which different nationalities communicated in the church and the newly founded universities. The Norman aristocracy for the most part spoke French, but intermarriage with the native English nobility and the business of daily life between masters and servants encouraged bilingualism. Different dialects of English were spoken by Anglo-Saxons of all social levels. And different branches of the Celtic language group were spoken in Scotland, Ireland, Wales, Cornwall, and Brittany.

Inevitably, there was also literary intercourse among the different languages. The Latin Bible and Latin saints' lives provided subjects for a great

King Harold Fatally Struck in the Eye. Bayeux Tapestry, textile, ca. 1070–80. The decisive historical moment is captured as Harold falls victim to irrepressible horizontal attack. Note the dead being stripped of their armor, in the lower margin.

deal of Old English as well as Old French poetry and prose. The first medieval drama in the vernacular, *The Play of Adam*, with elaborate stage directions in Latin and realistic dialogue in the Anglo-Norman dialect of French, was probably produced in England during the twelfth century.

The Anglo-Norman aristocracy was especially attracted to Celtic legends and tales that had been circulating orally for centuries. The twelfth-century poets Thomas of England, Marie de France, and Chrétien de Troyes each claim to have obtained their narratives from Breton storytellers, who were probably bilingual performers of native tales for French audiences. *Sir Orfeo* may represent the kind of lay that served as a model for Marie. "Breton" may indicate that they came from Brittany, or it may have been a generic term for a Celtic bard. Marie speaks respectfully of the storytellers, while Thomas expresses caution about their tendency to vary narratives; Chrétien accuses them of marring their material, which, he boasts, he has retold with an elegant fusion of form and meaning. Marie wrote a series of short romances, which she refers to as "lays" originally told by Bretons. Her versions are the most original and sophisticated examples of the genre that came to be known as the Breton lay, represented here by Marie's *Milun, Lanval, Chevrefoil,* and *Bisclavret.* It is very likely that Henry II is the "noble king" to whom she dedicated her lays and that they were written for his court. Thomas composed a moving, almost operatic version of the adulterous passion of Tristran and Ysolt, very different from the powerful version of the same story by Beroul, also composed in the last half of the twelfth century. Chrétien is the principal creator of the romance of chivalry in which knightly adventures are a means of exploring psychological and ethical dilemmas that the knights must solve, in addition to displaying martial prowess in saving ladies from monsters, giants, and wicked knights. Chrétien, like Marie, is thought to have spent time in England at the court of Henry II.

Thomas, Marie, and Chrétien de Troyes were innovators of the genre that has become known as "romance." The word *roman* was initially applied in French to a work written in the French vernacular. Thus the twelfth-century *Roman de Troie* is a long poem in French about the Trojan War. While this work deals mainly with the siege of Troy, it also includes stories about the love of Troilus for Cressida and of Achilles for the Trojan princess Polyxena. Eventually, "romance" acquired the generic associations it has for us as a story about love and adventure.

Romance was the principal narrative genre for late medieval readers. Insofar as it was centrally concerned with love, it developed ways of representing psychological interiority with great subtlety. That subtlety itself provoked a subgenre of questions about love. Thus in the late twelfth century, Andreas Capellanus (Andrew the Chaplain) wrote a Latin treatise, the title of which may be translated *The Art of Loving Correctly* [*Honeste*]. In one part, Eleanor of Aquitaine, her daughter, the countess Marie de Champagne, and other noble women are cited as a supreme court rendering decisions on difficult questions of love—for example, whether there is greater passion between lovers or between married couples. Whether such "courts of love" were purely imaginary or whether they represent some actual court entertainment, they imply that the literary taste and judgment of women had a significant role in fostering the rise of romance in France and Anglo-Norman England.

In Marie's *Lanval* and in Chrétien's romances, the court of King Arthur had already acquired for French audiences a reputation as the most famous center of chivalry. That eminence is owing in large measure to a remarkable book in Latin, *The History of the Kings of Britain*, completed by Geoffrey of Monmouth, ca. 1136–38. Geoffrey claimed to have based his "history" on a book in the British tongue (i.e., Welsh), but no one has ever found such a book. He drew on a few earlier Latin chronicles, but the bulk of his history was probably fabricated from Celtic oral tradition, his familiarity with Roman history and literature, and his own fertile imagination. The climax of the book is the reign of King Arthur, who defeats the Roman armies but is forced to turn back to Britain to counter the treachery of his nephew Mordred. In 1155 Geoffrey's Latin was rendered into French rhyme by an Anglo-Norman poet called Wace, and fifty or so years later Wace's poem was turned by Layamon, an English priest, into a much longer poem that combines English alliterative verse with sporadic rhyme.

Layamon's work is one of many instances where English receives new material directly through French sources, which may in turn have been drawn from Celtic or Latin sources. There are two Middle English versions of Marie's *Lanval*, and the English romance called *Yvain and Gawain* is a cruder version of Chrétien's *Le Chevalier au Lion* (The Knight of the Lion). A marvelous English lay, *Sir Orfeo*, is a version of the Orpheus story in which Orpheus succeeds in rescuing his wife from the other world, for which a French original, if there was one, has never been found. Romance, stripped of its courtly, psychological, and ethical subtleties, had an immense popular appeal for English readers and listeners. Many of these romances are simplified adaptations of more aristocratic French poems and recount in a rollicking and rambling style the adventures of heroes like Guy of Warwick, a poor steward who must prove his knightly worth to win the love of Fair Phyllis. The ethos of many romances, aristocratic and popular alike, involves a knight proving his worthiness through nobility of character and brave deeds rather than through high birth. In this respect romances reflect the aspirations of a lower order of the nobility to rise in the world, as historically some of these nobles indeed did. William the Marshall, for example, the fourth son of a baron of middle rank, used his talents in war and in tournaments to become tutor to the oldest son of Henry II and Eleanor of Aquitaine. He married a great heiress and became one of the most powerful nobles in England and the subject of a verse biography in French, which often reads like a romance.

Of course, not all writing in Early Middle English depends on French sources or intermediaries. The *Anglo-Saxon Chronicle* continued to be written at the monastery of Peterborough. It is an invaluable witness for the changes taking place in the English language and allows us to see Norman rule from an English point of view. *The Owl and the Nightingale* (late twelfth century) is a witty and entertaining poem in which these two female birds engage in a fierce debate about the benefits their singing brings to humankind. The owl grimly reminds her rival of the sinfulness of the human condition, which her mournful song is intended to amend; the nightingale sings about the pleasures of life and love when lord and lady are in bed together. The poet, who was certainly a cleric, is well aware of the fashionable new romance literature; he specifically has the nightingale allude to Marie de France's lay *Laüstic*, the Breton word, she says, for "rossignol" in French and "nightingale" in English. The poet does not side with either bird; rather he has amusingly created the sort of dialectic between the discourses of religion and romance that is carried on throughout medieval literature.

There is also a body of Early Middle English religious prose aimed at women. Three saints' lives celebrate the heroic combats of virgin martyrs who suffer dismemberment and death; a tract entitled *Holy Maidenhead* paints the woes of marriage not from the point of view of the husband, as in standard medieval antifeminist writings, but from that of the wife. Related to these texts, named the Katherine Group after one of the virgin martyrs, is a religious work also written for women but in a very different spirit. The *Ancrene Wisse* (Guide for Anchoresses) is one of the finest works of English religious prose in any period. It is a manual of instruction written at the request of three sisters who have chosen to live as religious recluses. The author, who may have been their personal confessor, addresses them with affection, and, at times, with kindness and humor. He is also profoundly serious in his analyses of sin, penance, and love. In the selection included here from his chapter on penance, he imagines the enclosed life in richly metaphorical ways, mixing pleasure strangely with pain.

MIDDLE ENGLISH LITERATURE IN THE FOURTEENTH AND FIFTEENTH CENTURIES

The styles of *The Owl and the Nightingale* and *Ancrene Wisse* show that around the year 1200 both poetry and prose were being written for sophisticated and well-educated readers whose primary language was English. Throughout the thirteenth and early fourteenth centuries, there are many kinds of evidence that, although French continued to be the principal language of Parliament, law, business, and high culture, English was gaining ground. Several authors of religious and didactic works in English state that they are writing for the benefit of those who do not understand Latin or French. Anthologies were made of miscellaneous works adapted from French for English readers and original pieces in English. Most of the nobility were by now bilingual, and the author of an English romance written early in the fourteenth century declares that he has seen many nobles who cannot speak French. Children of the nobility and the merchant class were now learning French as a second language. By the 1360s the linguistic, political, and cultural climate had been prepared for the flowering of Middle English literature in the writings of Chaucer, Gower, Langland, and the *Gawain* poet.

The Fourteenth Century

War and disease were prevalent throughout the Middle Ages but never more devastatingly than during the fourteenth century. In the wars against France, the gains of two spectacular English victories, at Crécy in 1346 and Poitiers in 1356, were gradually frittered away in futile campaigns that ravaged the French countryside without obtaining any clear advantage for the English. In 1348 the first and most virulent epidemic of the bubonic plague—the Black Death—swept Europe, wiping out a quarter to a third of the population. The toll was higher in crowded urban centers. Giovanni Boccaccio's description of the plague in Florence, with which he introduces the *Decameron*, vividly portrays its ravages: "So many corpses would arrive in front of a church every day and at every hour that the amount of holy ground for burials was certainly insufficient for the ancient custom of giving each body its individual place; when all the graves were full, huge trenches were dug in all of the cemeteries of the churches and into them the new arrivals were dumped by the hundreds; and they were packed in there with dirt, one on top of another, like a ship's cargo, until the trench was filled." The resulting scarcity of labor and a sudden expansion of the possibilities for social mobility fostered popular discontent. In 1381 attempts to enforce wage controls and to collect oppressive new taxes provoked a rural uprising in Essex and Kent that dealt a profound shock to the English ruling class. The participants were for the most part tenant farmers, day laborers, apprentices, and rural workers not attached to the big manors. A few of the lower clergy sided with the rebels against their wealthy church superiors; the priest John Ball was among the leaders. The movement was quickly suppressed, but not before sympathizers in London had admitted the rebels through two city gates, which had been barred against them. The insurgents burned down the palace of the hated duke of Lancaster, and they summarily beheaded the archbishop of Canterbury and the treasurer of England, who had taken refuge in the Tower of London. The Church had become the target of popular resentment because it was among the greatest of the oppressive landowners and because of the wealth, worldliness, and venality of many of the higher clergy.

These calamities and upheavals nevertheless did not stem the growth of international trade and the influence of the merchant class. In the portrait of Chaucer's merchant, we see the budding of capitalism based on credit and interest. Cities like London ran their own affairs under politically powerful mayors and aldermen. Edward III, chronically in need of money to finance his wars, was obliged to negotiate for revenues with the Commons in the English Parliament, an institution that became a major political force during

The City. Ambrogio Lorenzetti, *Effects of Good Government in the City*, 1338–39. The extraordinary energies of urban culture are set in a dynamic relation of peace and competition: the external walls of the city protect against outside invasion, even as the skyscrapers compete for space and power within the city.

this period. A large part of the king's revenues depended on taxing the profitable export of English wool to the Continent. The Crown thus became involved in the country's economic affairs, and this involvement led to a need for capable administrators. These were no longer drawn mainly from the Church, as in the past, but from a newly educated laity that occupied a rank somewhere between that of the lesser nobility and the upper bourgeoisie. The career of Geoffrey Chaucer (ca. 1340–1400), who served Edward III and his successor Richard II in a number of civil posts, is typical of this class—with the exception that Chaucer was also a great poet.

In the fourteenth century, a few poets and intellectuals achieved the status and respect formerly accorded only to the ancients. Marie de France and Chrétien de Troyes had dedicated their works to noble patrons and, in their role as narrators, address themselves as entertainers and sometimes as instructors to court audiences. Dante (1265–1321) made himself the protagonist of *The Divine Comedy*, the sacred poem, as he called it, in which he revealed the secrets of the afterlife. After his death, manuscripts of the work were provided with lengthy commentaries as though it were Scripture, and public readings and lectures were devoted to it. Francis Petrarch (1304–1374) won an international reputation as a man of letters. He wrote primarily in Latin and contrived to have himself crowned "poet laureate" in emulation of the Roman poets whose works he imitated, but his most famous work is the sonnet sequence he wrote in Italian. Giovanni Boccaccio (1313–1375) was among Petrarch's most ardent admirers and carried on a literary correspondence with him.

Chaucer read these authors along with the ancient Roman poets and drew on them in his own works. Chaucer's *Clerk's Tale* is based on a Latin version Petrarch made from the last tale in Boccaccio's *Decameron*; in his prologue, the Clerk refers to Petrarch as "lauriat poete" whose sweet rhetoric illuminated all Italy with his poetry. Yet in his own time, the English poet Chaucer never attained the kind of laurels that he and others accorded to Petrarch. In his earlier works, Chaucer portrayed himself comically as a diligent reader of old books, as an aspiring apprentice writer, and as an eager spectator on the fringe of a fashionable world of courtiers and poets. In *The House of Fame*, he relates a dream of being snatched up by a huge golden eagle (the eagle and many other things in this work were inspired by Dante) that transports him to the palace of the goddess Fame. There he gets to see phantoms, like the shades in Dante's poem, of all the famous authors of antiquity. At the end of his romance *Troilus and Criseyde*, Chaucer asks his "litel book" to kiss the footsteps where the great ancient poets had passed before. Like Dante and Petrarch, Chaucer had an ideal of great poetry and, in his *Troilus* at least, strove to emulate it. But in *The House of Fame* and in his final work, *The Canterbury Tales*, he also views that ideal ironically and distances himself from it. The many surviving documents that record Geoffrey Chaucer's career as a civil servant do not contain a single word to show that he was also a poet. Only in the following centuries would he be canonized as the father of English poetry.

Chaucer is unlikely to have known his contemporary William Langland (ca. 1330–1388), who says in an autobiographical passage (see pp. 410–13), added to the third and last version of his great poem *Piers Plowman*, that he lived in London on Cornhill (a poor area of the city) among "lollers." "Loller" was a slang term for the unemployed and transients; it was later applied to followers of the religious and social reformer John Wycliffe, some of whom were burned at the stake for heresy in the next century. Langland assailed corruption in church and state, but he was certainly no radical. It is thought that he may have written the third version of *Piers Plowman*, which tones down his attacks on the church, after the rebels of 1381 invoked Piers as one of their own. Although Langland does not condone rebellion and his religion is not revolutionary, he nevertheless presents the most clear-sighted vision of social and religious issues in the England of his day. *Piers Plowman* is also a painfully honest search for the right way that leads to salvation. Though learned himself, Langland and the dreamer who represents him in the poem arrive at the insight that learning can be one of the chief obstacles on that way.

Langland came from the west of England, and his poem belongs to the "Alliterative Revival," a final flowering in the late fourteenth century of the verse form that goes all the way back to Anglo-Saxon England. Anglo-Saxon traditions held out longest in the west and north, away from London, where Chaucer and his audience were more open to literary fashions from the Continent.

John Gower (ca. 1330–1408) is a third major late-fourteenth-century English poet. While his first and second large works are written in French and Latin verse respectively, his *Confessio Amantis* (1390) is written in English four-stress couplets. Gower's first two works are severe satires; the *Confessio*, by contrast, broaches political and ethical issues from an oblique angle. Its primary narrative concerns the treatment of a suffering lover. His therapy consists of listening to, and understanding, many other narratives, many of which are drawn from classical sources. Like Chaucer, Gower anglicizes and absorbs classical Latin literature.

Admiration for the poetry of both Chaucer and Gower and the controversial nature of Langland's writing assured the survival of their work in many manuscripts. The work of a fourth major fourteenth-century English poet, who remains anonymous, is known only through a single manuscript, which contains four poems all thought to be by a single author: *Cleanness* and *Patience*, two biblical narratives in alliterative verse; *Pearl*, a moving dream vision in which a grief-stricken father is visited and consoled by his dead child, who has been transformed into a queen in the kingdom of heaven; and *Sir Gawain and the Green Knight*, the finest of all English romances. The plot of *Gawain* involves a folklore motif of a challenge by a supernatural visitor, first found in an Old Irish tale. The poet has made this motif a challenge to King Arthur's court and has framed the tale with allusions at the beginning and end to the legends that link Arthur's reign with the Trojan War and the founding of Rome and of Britain. The poet has a sophisticated awareness of romance as a literary genre and plays a game with both the hero's and the reader's expectations of what is supposed to happen in a romance. One could say that the broader subject of *Sir Gawain and the Green Knight* is "romance" itself, and in this respect the poem resembles Chaucer's *Canterbury Tales* in its author's interest in literary form.

Julian of Norwich (ca. 1342–ca. 1416) is a fifth major writer of this period. The first known woman writer in the English vernacular, the anchoress Julian participates in a Continental tradition of visionary writings, often by women. She spent a good deal of her life meditating and writing about a series of visions, which she called "showings," that she had received in 1373, when she was thirty years old. While very carefully negotiating the dangers of writing as a woman, and of writing sophisticated theology in the vernacular, Julian manages to produce visionary writing that is at once penetrating and serene.

The Fifteenth Century

In 1399 Henry Bolingbroke, the duke of Lancaster, deposed his cousin Richard II, who was murdered in prison. As Henry IV, he successfully defended his crown against several insurrections and passed it on to Henry V, who briefly united the country once more and achieved one last apparently decisive victory over the French at the Battle of Agincourt (1415). The premature death of Henry V in 1422, however, left England exposed to the civil wars known as the Wars of the Roses, the red rose being the emblem of the house of Lancaster; the white, of York. These wars did not end until 1485, when the Lancastrian Henry Tudor defeated the Yorkist Richard III at Bosworth Field and acceded to the throne as Henry VII.

The most prolific poet of the fifteenth century was the monk John Lydgate (ca. 1371–1449), who produced dream visions; a life of the Virgin; translations of French religious allegories; a *Troy Book*; *The Siege of Thebes*, which he framed as a "new" Canterbury tale; and a thirty-six-thousand-line poem called *The Fall of Princes*, a free translation of a French work, itself based on a Latin work by Boccaccio. The last illustrates the late medieval idea of tragedy, namely that emperors, kings, and other famous men enjoy power and fortune only to be cast down in misery. Lydgate shapes these tales as a "mirror" for princes—that is, as object lessons to the powerful men of his own day, several of whom were his patrons. A self-styled imitator of Chaucer, Lydgate had a reputation almost equal to Chaucer's in the fifteenth century. The other significant poet of the first half of the fifteenth century is Thomas Hoccleve (ca. 1367–1426). Like Lydgate, Hoccleve also wrote for powerful Lancastrian patrons, but his poetry is strikingly private, painfully concerned as it often is with his penury and mental instability. The searing poem *My Complaint* is an example of his work.

Religious works of all kinds continued to be produced in the fifteenth century, but under greater surveillance. The Lancastrian authorities responded to the reformist religious movement known as "Lollardy" in draconian ways. They introduced a statute for the burning of heretics (the first such statute) in 1401, and a series of measures designed to survey and censor theology in English in 1409. Despite this, many writers continued to produce religious works in the vernacular. Perhaps the most remarkable of these writers is Margery Kempe (ca. 1373–ca. 1438). Kempe made pilgrimages to the Holy Land, Rome, Santiago, and to shrines in Northern Europe; she also visited Julian of Norwich in about 1413. These journeys she records, in the context of her often fraught and painful personal life, in her *Book of Margery Kempe*. Both Julian of Norwich and Margery Kempe, in highly individual ways, allow us to see the medieval church and its doctrines from female points of view.

The Seasons. Limbourg Brothers, "February," *Les Très Riches Heures du Duc de Berry* (ca. 1411–16). The calm inevitability of cosmic, seasonal change is set above the uncertain yet inventive struggle of peasants, in the main frame, for heat and food. (See the color insert in this volume.)

Social, economic, and literary life continued as they had throughout all of the previously mentioned wars. The prosperity of the towns was shown by performances of the mystery plays—a sequence or "cycle" of plays based on the Bible and produced by the city guilds, the organizations representing the various trades and crafts. The cycles of several towns are lost, but those of York and Chester have been preserved, along with two other complete cycles, one possibly from Wakefield in Yorkshire, and the other titled the "N-Town" Cycle. Under the guise of dramatizing biblical history, playwrights such as the Wakefield Master manage to comment satirically on the social ills of the times. The century also saw the development of the morality play, in which personified vices and virtues struggle for the soul of "Mankind" or "Everyman." Performed by professional players, the morality plays were precursors of the professional theater that flourished in the reign of Elizabeth I.

The best of Chaucer's imitators was Robert Henryson (ca. 1425–ca. 1500), who, in the last quarter of the fifteenth century, wrote *The Testament of Cresseid*, a continuation of Chaucer's great poem *Troilus and Criseyde*. He also wrote the *Moral Fabilis of Esope*, among which *The Cock and the Fox*, is a remake of Chaucer's *Nun's Priest's Tale*.

The works of Sir Thomas Malory (ca. 1415–1471) gave the definitive form in English to the legend of King Arthur and his knights. Malory spent years in prison rendering into English a series of Arthurian romances that he translated and abridged chiefly from several enormously long thirteenth-century French prose romances. Malory was a passionate devotee of chivalry, which he personified in his hero Sir Lancelot. In the jealousies and rivalries that finally break up the round table and destroy Arthur's kingdom, Malory saw a distant image of the civil wars of his own time. A manuscript of Malory's works fell into the hands of William Caxton (ca. 1422–1492), who had introduced the new art of printing by movable type to England in 1476. Caxton divided Malory's tales into the chapters and books of a single long work, as though it were a chronicle history, and gave it the title *Morte Darthur*, which has stuck to it ever since. Caxton also printed *The Canterbury Tales*, some of Chaucer's earlier works, and Gower's *Confessio Amantis*. Caxton himself translated many of the works he printed for English readers: a history of Troy, a book on chivalry, Aesop's fables, *The History of Reynard the Fox*, and *The Game and Playe of Chesse*. The new technology extended literacy and made books more easily accessible to new classes of readers. Printing made the production of literature a business and made possible the bitter political and doctrinal disputes that, in the sixteenth century, were waged in print as well as on the field of battle.

MEDIEVAL ENGLISH

The medieval works in this anthology were composed in different states of the language. Old English, the language that took shape among the Germanic settlers of England, preserved its integrity until the Norman Conquest radically altered English civilization. Middle English, the first records of which date from the early twelfth century, was continually changing. Shortly after the introduction of printing at the end of the fifteenth century, it attained the form designated as Early Modern English. Old English is a very heavily inflected language. (That is, the words change form to indicate changes in function, such as person, number, tense, case, mood, and so on. Most languages have some inflection—for example, the personal pronouns in Modern English have different forms when used as objects—but a "heavily inflected" language, such as Greek or Latin, is one in which almost all classes of words undergo elaborate patterns of change.) The vocabulary of Old English is almost entirely Germanic. In Middle English, the inflectional system was weakened, and a large number of words were introduced into it from French, so that many of the older Anglo-Saxon words disappeared. Because of the difficulty of Old English, all selections from it in this book have been given in translation. So that the reader may see an example of the language, Cædmon's *Hymn* has been printed in the original, together with an interlinear translation. The present discussion, then, is concerned primarily with the relatively late form of Middle English used by Chaucer and the East Midland dialect in which he wrote.

The chief difficulty with Middle English for the modern reader is caused not by its inflections so much as by its spelling, which may be described as a rough-and-ready phonetic system, and by the fact that it is not a single standardized language, but consists of a number of regional dialects, each with its own peculiarities of sound and its own systems for representing sounds in writing. The East Midland dialect—the dialect of London and of Chaucer, which is the ancestor of our own standard speech—differs greatly from the dialect spoken in the west of England (the original dialect of *Piers Plowman*), from that of the northwest (*Sir Gawain and the Green Knight*), and from that of the north (*The Second Shepherds' Play*). In this book, the long texts composed in the more difficult dialects have been translated or modernized, and those that—like Chaucer, Gower, *Everyman*, and the lyrics—appear in the original, have been respelled in a way that is designed to aid the reader. The remarks that follow apply chiefly to Chaucer's East Midland English, although certain non-Midland dialectal variations are noted if they occur in some of the other selections.

I. The Sounds of Middle English: General Rules

The following general analysis of the sounds of Middle English will enable the reader who does not have time for detailed study to read Middle English aloud and preserve some of its most essential characteristics, without, however, worrying too much about details. The next section, "Detailed Analysis," is designed for the reader who wishes to go more deeply into the pronunciation of Middle English. The best way to absorb the sound of Middle English pronunciation is to listen to it; the NAEL Archive offers recordings of selections as an aid to this end.

Middle English differs from Modern English in three principal respects: (1) the pronunciation of the long vowels *a, e, i* (or *y*), *o,* and *u* (spelled *ou, ow*); (2) the fact that Middle English final *e* is often sounded; and (3) the fact that all Middle English consonants are sounded.

1. LONG VOWELS

Middle English vowels are long when they are doubled (*aa, ee, oo*) or when they are terminal (*he, to, holy*); *a, e,* and *o* are long when followed by a single consonant plus a vowel (*name, mete, note*). Middle English vowels are short when they are followed by two consonants.

Long *a* is sounded like the *a* in Modern English "father": *maken, madd.*

Long *e* may be sounded like the *a* in Modern English "name" (ignoring the distinction between the close and open vowel): *be, sweete.*

Long *i* (or *y*) is sounded like the *i* in Modern English "machine": *lif, whit; myn, holy.*

Long *o* may be sounded like the *o* in Modern English "note" (again ignoring the distinction between the close and open vowel): *do, soone.*

Long *u* (spelled *ou, ow*) is sounded like the *oo* in Modern English "goose": *hous, flowr.*

Note that in general Middle English long vowels are pronounced like long vowels in modern European languages other than English. Short vowels and diphthongs, however, may be pronounced as in Modern English.

2. FINAL E

In Middle English syllabic verse, final *e* is sounded, like the *a* in "sofa," to provide a needed unstressed syllable: *Another Nonnë with hire haddë she.* But (cf. *hire* in the example) final *e* is suppressed when not needed for the meter. It is commonly silent before words beginning with a vowel or *h.*

3. CONSONANTS

Middle English consonants are pronounced separately in all combinations—*gnat: g-nat; knave: k-nave; write: w-rite; folk: fol-k*. In a simplified system of pronunciation the combination *gh* as in *night* or *thought* may be treated as if it were silent.

II. The Sounds of Middle English: Detailed Analysis

1. SIMPLE VOWELS

Sound	Pronunciation	Example
long *a* (spelled *a, aa*)	*a* in "father"	*maken, maad*
short *a*	*o* in "hot"	*cappe*
long *e* close (spelled *e, ee*)	*a* in "name"	*be, sweete*
long *e* open (spelled *e, ee*)	*e* in "there"	*mete, heeth*
short *e*	*e* in "set"	*setten*
final *e*	*a* in "sofa"	*large*
long *i* (spelled *i, y*)	*i* in "machine"	*lif, myn*
short *i*	*i* in "wit"	*wit*
long *o* close (spelled *o, oo*)	*o* in "note"	*do, soone*
long *o* open (spelled *o, oo*)	*oa* in "broad"	*go, goon*
short *o*	*o* in "oft"	*pot*
long *u* when spelled *ou, ow*	*oo* in "goose"	*hous, flowr*
long *u* when spelled *u*	*u* in "pure"	*vertu*
short *u* (spelled *u, o*)	*u* in "full"	*ful, love*

Doubled vowels and terminal vowels are always long, whereas single vowels before two consonants other than *th* and *ch* are always short. The vowels *a*, *e*, and *o* are long before a single consonant followed by a vowel: *nāmë, sēkë* (sick), *hōly*. In general, words that have descended into Modern English reflect their original Middle English quantity: *līven* (to live), but *līf* (life).

The close and open sounds of long *e* and long *o* may often be identified by the Modern English spellings of the words in which they appear. Original long close *e* is generally represented in Modern English by *ee*: "sweet," "knee," "teeth," and "see" have close *e* in Middle English, but so does "be"; original long open *e* is generally represented in Modern English by *ea*: "meat," "heath," "sea," "great," and "breath" have open *e* in Middle English. Similarly, original long close *o* is now generally represented by *oo*: "soon," "food," "good," but also "do" and "to"; original long open *o* is represented either by *oa* or by *o*: "coat," "boat," and "moan," but also "go," "bone," "foe," and "home." Notice that original close *o* is now almost always pronounced like the *oo* in "goose," but that original open *o* is almost never so pronounced; thus it is often possible to identify the Middle English vowels through Modern English sounds.

The nonphonetic Middle English spelling of *o* for short *u* has been preserved in a number of Modern English words ("love," "son," and "come"), but in others *u* has been restored: "sun" (*sonne*), "run" (*ronne*).

For the treatment of final *e*, see "General Rules," "Final *e*."

2. DIPHTHONGS

Sound	Pronunciation	Example
ai, ay, ei, ay	between *ai* in "aisle" and *ay* in "day"	*saide, day, veine, preye*
au, aw	*ou* in "out"	*chaunge, bawdy*
eu, ew	*ew* in "few"	*newe*
oi, oy	*oy* in "joy"	*joye, point*
ou, ow	*ou* in "thought"	*thought, lowe*

Note that in words with *ou, ow* that in Modern English are sounded with the *ou* of "about," the combination indicates not the diphthong but the simple vowel long *u* (see "Simple Vowels").

3. CONSONANTS

In general, all consonants except *h* were always sounded in Middle English, including consonants that have become silent in Modern English, such as the *g* in *gnaw*, the *k* in *knight*, the *l* in *folk*, and the *w* in *write*. In noninitial *gn*, however, the *g* was silent as in Modern English "sign." Initial *h* was silent in short common English words and in words borrowed from French and may have been almost silent in all words. The combination *gh* as in *night* or *thought* was sounded like the *ch* of German *ich* or *nach*. Note that Middle English *gg* represents both the hard sound of "dagger" and the soft sound of "bridge."

III. Parts of Speech and Grammar

1. NOUNS

The plural and possessive of nouns end in *es*, formed by adding *s* or *es* to the singular: *knight, knightes*; *roote, rootes*. A final consonant is frequently doubled before *es*: *bed, beddes*. A common irregular plural is *yën*, from *yë*, "eye."

2. PRONOUNS

The chief comparisons with Modern English are as follows:

Modern English	East Midlands Middle English
I	*I, ich* (*ik* is a northern form)
you (singular)	*thou* (subjective); *thee* (objective)
her	*hir(e), her(e)*
its	*his*
you (plural)	*ye* (subjective); *you* (objective)
they	*they*
their	*hir* (*their* is a Northern form)
them	*hem* (*them* is a Northern form)

In formal speech, the second-person plural is often used for the singular. The possessive adjectives *my* and *thy* take *n* before a word beginning with a vowel or *h*: *thyn yë, myn host*.

3. ADJECTIVES

Adjectives ending in a consonant add final *e* when they stand before the noun they modify and after another modifying word such as *the, this, that,* or nouns or pronouns in the possessive: *a good hors*, but *the* (*this, my, the kinges*) *goode hors.* They also generally add *e* when standing before and modifying a plural noun, a noun in the vocative, or any proper noun: *goode men, oh goode man, faire Venus.*

Adjectives are compared by adding *er(e)* for the comparative, *est(e)* for the superlative. Sometimes the stem vowel is shortened or altered in the process: *sweete, swettere, swettest; long, lenger, lengest.*

4. ADVERBS

Adverbs are formed from adjectives by adding *e*, *ly*, or *liche*; the adjective *fair* thus yields *faire, fairly, fairliche.*

5. VERBS

Middle English verbs, like Modern English verbs, are either "weak" or "strong." Weak verbs form their preterites and past participles with a *t* or *d* suffix and preserve the same stem vowel throughout their systems, although it is sometimes shortened in the preterite and past participle: *love, loved; bend, bent; hear, heard; meet, met.* Strong verbs do not use the *t* or *d* suffix, but vary their stem vowel in the preterite and past participle: *take, took, taken; begin, began, begun; find, found, found.*

The inflectional endings are the same for Middle English strong verbs and weak verbs except in the preterite singular and the imperative singular. In the following paradigms, the weak verbs *loven* (to love) and *heeren* (to hear) and the strong verbs *taken* (to take) and *ginnen* (to begin) serve as models.

	Present Indicative	Preterite Indicative
I	*love, heere*	*loved(e), herde*
	take, ginne	*took, gan*
thou	*lovest, heerest*	*lovedest, herdest*
	takest, ginnest	*tooke, gonne*
he, she, it	*loveth, heereth*	*loved(e), herde*
	taketh, ginneth	*took, gan*
we, ye, they	*love(n) (th), heere(n) (th)*	*loved(e) (en), herde(n)*
	take(n) (th), ginne(n) (th)	*tooke(n), gonne(n)*

The present plural ending *eth* is southern, whereas the *e(n)* ending is Midland and characteristic of Chaucer. In the north, *s* may appear as the ending of all persons of the present. In the weak preterite, when the ending *e* gave a verb three or more syllables, it was frequently dropped. Note that in certain strong verbs like *ginnen* there are two distinct stem vowels in the preterite; even in Chaucer's time, however, one of these had begun to replace the other, and Chaucer occasionally writes *gan* for all persons of the preterite.

	Present Subjunctive	Preterite Subjunctive
Singular	*love, heere*	*lovede, herde*
	take, ginne	*tooke, gonne*
Plural	*love(n), heere(n)*	*lovede(n), herde(n)*
	take(n), ginne(n)	*tooke(n), gonne(n)*

In verbs like *ginnen*, which have two stem vowels in the indicative preterite, it is the vowel of the plural and of the second person singular that is used for the preterite subjunctive.

The imperative singular of most weak verbs is *e*: *(thou) love*, but of some weak verbs and all strong verbs, the imperative singular is without termination: *(thou) heer, taak, gin*. The imperative plural of all verbs is either *e* or *eth*: *(ye) love(th), heere(th), take(th), ginne(th)*.

The infinitive of verbs is *e* or *en*: *love(n), heere(n), take(n), ginne(n)*.

The past participle of weak verbs is the same as the preterite without inflectional ending: *loved, herd*. In strong verbs the ending is either *e* or *en*: *take(n), gonne(n)*. The prefix *y* often appears on past participles: *yloved, yherd, ytake(n)*.

OLD AND MIDDLE ENGLISH PROSODY

All the poetry of Old English is in the same verse form. The verse unit is the single line, because rhyme was not used to link one line to another, except very occasionally in late Old English. The organizing device of the line is alliteration, the beginning of several words with the same sound ("Foemen fled"). The Old English alliterative line contains, on the average, four principal stresses and is divided into two half-lines of two stresses each by a strong medial caesura, or pause. These two half-lines are linked to each other by alliteration; at least one of the two stressed words in the first half-line, and often both of them, begin with the same sound as the first stressed word of the second half-line (the second stressed word is generally nonalliterative). The fourth line of *Beowulf* is an example (*sc* has the value of modern *sh*; þ is a runic symbol with the value of modern *th*):

> Oft Scyld Scefing   sceaþena þreatum.

For further examples, see Cædmon's *Hymn*. It will be noticed that any vowel alliterates with any other vowel. In addition to the alliteration, the length of the unstressed syllables and their number and pattern is governed by a highly complex set of rules. When sung or intoned—as it was—to the rhythmic strumming of a harp, Old English poetry must have been wonderfully impressive in the dignified, highly formalized way that aptly fits both its subject matter and tone.

The majority of Middle English verse is either in alternately stressed rhyming verse, adapted from French after the conquest, or in alliterative verse that is descended from Old English. The latter preserves the caesura of Old English and in its purest form the same alliterative system, the two stressed words of the first half-line (or at least one of them) alliterating with the first stressed word in the second half-line. But most of the alliterative poets allowed themselves a number of deviations from the norm. All four stressed words may alliterate, as in the first line of *Piers Plowman*:

> In a summer season   when soft was the sun.

Or the line may contain five, six, or even more stressed words, of which all or only the basic minimum may alliterate:

> A fair field full of   folk found I there between.

There is no rule determining the number of unstressed syllables, and at times some poets seem to ignore alliteration entirely. As in Old English, any vowel may alliterate with any other vowel; furthermore, since initial *h* was silent or lightly pronounced in Middle English, words beginning with *h* are treated as though they began with the following vowel.

There are two general types of stressed verse with rhyme. In the more common, unstressed and stressed syllables alternate regularly as x X x X x X or with two unstressed syllables intervening as x x X x x X x x X or a combination of the two as x x X x X x x X (of the reverse patterns, only X x X x X x is common in English). There is also a line that can only be defined as containing a predetermined number of stressed syllables but an irregular number and pattern of unstressed syllables. Much Middle English verse has to be read without expectation of regularity; some of this was evidently composed in an irregular meter, but some was probably originally composed according to a strict metrical system that has been obliterated by scribes careless of fine points. One receives the impression that many of the lyrics—as well as the *Second Shepherds' Play*—were at least composed with regular syllabic alternation. In the play *Everyman*, only the number of stresses is generally predetermined but not the number or placement of unstressed syllables.

In pre-Chaucerian verse the number of stresses, whether regularly or irregularly alternated, was most often four, although sometimes the number was three and rose in some poems to seven. Rhyme in Middle English (as in Modern English) may be either between adjacent or alternate lines, or may occur in more complex patterns. Most of the *Canterbury Tales* are in rhymed couplets, the line containing five stresses with regular alternation—technically known as iambic pentameter, the standard English poetic line, perhaps introduced into English by Chaucer. In reading Chaucer and much pre-Chaucerian verse, one must remember that the final *e*, which is silent in Modern English, could be pronounced at any time to provide a needed unstressed syllable. Evidence seems to indicate that it was also pronounced at the end of the line, even though it thus produced a line with eleven syllables. Although he was a very regular metricist, Chaucer used various conventional devices that are apt to make the reader stumble until he or she understands them. Final *e* is often not pronounced before a word beginning with a vowel or *h*, and may be suppressed whenever metrically convenient. The same medial and terminal syllables that are slurred in Modern English are apt to be suppressed in Chaucer's English: *Canterb'ry* for *Canterbury*; *ev'r* (perhaps *e'er*) for *evere*. The plural in *es* may either be syllabic or reduced to *s* as in Modern English. Despite these seeming irregularities, Chaucer's verse is not difficult to read if one constantly bears in mind the basic pattern of the iambic pentameter line.

THE MIDDLE AGES

TEXTS	CONTEXTS
	43–ca. 420 Romans conquer Britons; Britania a province of the Roman Empire
	306–80 Reign of Constantine the Great (306–337) leads to adoption of Christianity as the official religion of the Roman Empire in 380
ca. 405 St. Jerome completes *Vulgate*, Latin translation of the Bible that becomes standard for the Roman Catholic Church	
	432 St. Patrick begins mission to convert Ireland
	ca. 450 Anglo-Saxon conquest of Britons begins
523 Boethius, *Consolation of Philosophy* (Latin)	
	597 St. Augustine of Canterbury's mission to Kent begins conversion of Anglo-Saxons to Christianity
	622–750 Spread of Islam throughout Middle East, North Africa, and Spain
ca. 658–80 Cædmon's *Hymn*, earliest poem recorded in English	
731 Bede completes *Ecclesiastical History of the English People*	
? ca. 750 *Beowulf* composed	
	ca. 787 First Viking raids on England
871–99 Texts written or commissioned by Alfred	**871–99** Reign of King Alfred
ca. 1000 Unique manuscript of *Beowulf* and *Judith*	
	1066 Norman Conquest by William I establishes French-speaking ruling class in England
	1095–1221 Crusades, including massacres of Jews in England, 1189–90
ca. 1135–38 Geoffrey of Monmouth's Latin *History of the Kings of Britain* gives pseudohistorical status to Arthurian and other legends	
	1152 Future Henry II marries Eleanor of Aquitaine, bringing vast French territories to the English crown
1154 End of *Peterborough Chronicle*, last branch of the *Anglo-Saxon Chronicle*	
? ca. 1165–80 Marie de France, *Lais* in Anglo-Norman French from Breton sources	

TEXTS	CONTEXTS
ca. 1170–91 Chrétien de Troyes, chivalric romances about knights of the Round Table	**1170** Archbishop Thomas Becket murdered in Canterbury Cathedral
? ca. 1200 Layamon's *Brut*	**1182** Birth of St. Francis of Assisi
? ca. 1215–25 *Ancrene Wisse*	**1215** Fourth Lateran Council requires annual confession. English barons force King John to seal Magna Carta (the Great Charter) guaranteeing baronial rights
ca. 1304–21 Dante Alighieri writing *Divine Comedy*	**1290** Expulsion of Jews from England
ca. 1340–1374 Giovanni Boccaccio active as writer in Naples and Florence	**ca. 1337–1453** Hundred Years' War
ca. 1340–1374 Francis Petrarch active as writer	**1348** Black Death ravages Europe
	1362 English first used in law courts and Parliament
1368 Chaucer, *Book of the Duchess*	
	1372 Chaucer's first journey to Italy
1373–93 Julian of Norwich, *Book of Showings*	
ca. 1375–1400 *Sir Gawain and the Green Knight*	
	1376 Earliest record of performance of cycle drama at York
1377–79 William Langland, *Piers Plowman* (B-Text)	
ca. 1380 Followers of John Wycliffe begin first complete translation of the Bible into English	
	1381 People's uprising briefly takes control of London before being suppressed
ca. 1385–87 Chaucer, *Troilus and Criseyde*	
ca. 1387–99 Chaucer working on *The Canterbury Tales*	
ca. 1390–92 John Gower, *Confessio Amantis*	
	1399 Richard II deposed by his cousin, who succeeds him as Henry IV
	1400 Richard II murdered
	1401 Execution of William Sawtre, first Lollard burned at the stake under new law against heresy
ca. 1410–49 John Lydgate active	
ca. 1420 Thomas Hoccleve, *My Complaint*	**1415** Henry V defeats French at Agincourt
ca. 1425 *York Play of the Crucifixion*	

TEXTS	CONTEXTS
	1431 English burn Joan of Arc at Rouen
ca. 1432–38 Margery Kempe, *The Book of Margery Kempe*	
ca. 1450–75 Wakefield mystery cycle, *Second Shepherds' Play*	
	1455–85 Wars of the Roses
ca. 1470 Sir Thomas Malory in prison working on *Morte Darthur*	
ca. 1475 Robert Henryson active	
	1476 William Caxton sets up first printing press in England
1485 Caxton publishes *Morte Darthur*, one of the first books in English to be printed	**1485** The earl of Richmond defeats the Yorkist king, Richard III, at Bosworth Field and succeeds him as Henry VII, founder of the Tudor dynasty
ca. 1510 *Everyman*	
	1575 Last performance of mystery plays at Chester

Anglo-Saxon Literature

BEDE (ca. 673–735) and CÆDMON'S *HYMN*

The Venerable Bede (the title by which he is known to posterity) became a novice at the age of seven and spent the rest of his life at the neighboring monasteries of Wearmouth and Jarrow. Although he may never have traveled beyond the boundaries of his native district of Northumbria, he achieved an international reputation as one of the greatest scholars of his age. Writing in Latin, the learned language of the era, Bede produced many theological works as well as books on science and rhetoric, but his most popular and enduring work is the *Ecclesiastical History of the English People* (completed 731). The *History* tells about the Anglo-Saxon conquest and the vicissitudes of the petty kingdoms that comprised Anglo-Saxon England; Bede's main theme, however, is the spread of Christianity and the growth of the English church. The latter were the great events leading up to Bede's own time, and he regarded them as the unfolding of God's providence. The *History* is, therefore, also a moral work and a hagiography—that is, it contains many stories of saints and miracles meant to testify to the grace and glory of God.

The story we reprint preserves what is probably the earliest extant Old English poem (composed sometime between 658 and 680) and the only biographical information, outside of what is said in the poems themselves, about any Old English poet. Bede tells how Cædmon, an illiterate cowherd employed by the monastery of Whitby, miraculously received the gift of song, entered the monastery, and became the founder of a school of Christian poetry. Cædmon was clearly an oral-formulaic poet, one who created his work by combining and varying formulas—units of verse developed in a tradition transmitted by one generation of singers to another. In this respect he resembles the singers of the Homeric poems and oral-formulaic poets recorded in the twentieth century, especially in the Balkan countries. Although Bede tells us that Cædmon had never learned the art of song, we may suspect that he concealed his skill from his fellow workmen and from the monks because he was ashamed of knowing "vain and idle" songs, the kind Bede says Cædmon never composed. Cædmon's inspiration and the true miracle, then, was to apply the meter and language of such songs, presumably including pagan heroic verse, to Christian themes.

Although most Old English poetry was written by lettered poets, they continued to use the oral-formulaic style. The *Hymn* is, therefore, a good short example of the way Old English verse, with its traditional poetic diction and interwoven formulaic expressions, is constructed. Eight of the poem's eighteen half-lines contain epithets describing various aspects of God: He is *Weard* (Guardian), *Meotod* (Measurer), *Wuldor-Fæder* (Glory-Father), *Drihten* (Lord), *Scyppend* (Creator), and *Frea* (Master). God is *heofonrices Weard* or *mancynnes Weard* (heaven's or mankind's Guardian), depending on the alliteration required. This formulaic style provides a richness of texture and meaning difficult to convey in translation. As Bede said about his own Latin paraphrase of the *Hymn*, no literal translation of poetry from one language to another is possible without sacrifice of some poetic quality.

Several manuscripts of Bede's *History* contain the Old English text in addition to Bede's Latin version. The poem is given here in a West Saxon form with a literal inter-linear translation. In Old English spelling, æ (as in Cædmon's name and line 3) is a vowel symbol that represents the vowel of Modern English *cat*; þ (line 2) and ð (line 7) both represented the sound *th*. The spelling *sc* (line 1) = *sh*; ġ (line 1) = *y* in *yard*; ċ (line 1)=*ch* in *chin*; c (line 2)=*k*. The space in the middle of the line indicates the caesura. The alliterating sounds that connect the half-lines are printed in bold italics.

From An Ecclesiastical History of the English People

[THE STORY OF CÆDMON]

Heavenly grace had especially singled out a certain one of the brothers in the monastery ruled by this abbess[1] for he used to compose devout and religious songs. Whatever he learned of holy Scripture with the aid of interpreters, he quickly turned into the sweetest and most moving poetry in his own language, that is to say English. It often happened that his songs kindled a contempt for this world and a longing for the life of Heaven in the hearts of many men. Indeed, after him others among the English people tried to compose religious poetry, but no one could equal him because he was not taught the art of song by men or by human agency but received this gift through heavenly grace. Therefore, he was never able to compose any vain and idle songs but only such as dealt with religion and were proper for his religious tongue to utter. As a matter of fact, he had lived in the secular estate until he was well advanced in age without learning any songs. Therefore, at feasts, when it was decided to have a good time by taking turns singing, whenever he would see the harp get-ting close to his place,[2] he got up in the middle of the meal and went home.

Once when he left the feast like this, he went to the cattle shed, which he had been assigned the duty of guarding that night. And after he had stretched himself out and gone to sleep, he dreamed that someone was standing at his side and greeted him, calling out his name. "Cædmon," he said, "sing me something."

And he replied, "I don't know how to sing; that is why I left the feast to come here—because I cannot sing."

"All the same," said the one who was speaking to him, "you have to sing for me."

"What must I sing?" he said.

And he said, "Sing about the Creation."

At this, Cædmon immediately began to sing verses in praise of God the Creator, which he had never heard before and of which the sense is this:

> Nu sculon *h*eriġean *h*eofonrices Weard
> Now we must praise heaven-kingdom's Guardian,

> *M*eotodes *m*eahte and his *m*odġeþanc
> the Measurer's might and his mind-plans,

---

1. Abbess Hilda (614–680), a grandniece of the first Christian king of Northumbria, founded Whitby, a double house for monks and nuns, in 657 and ruled over it for twenty-two years.

2. Oral poetry was performed to the accompani-ment of a harp; here the harp is being passed from one participant of the feast to another, each being expected to perform in turn.

weorc Wuldor-Fæder   swa he wundra ġehwæs
the work of the Glory-Father, when he of wonders of every one,

eċe Drihten   or onstealde
eternal Lord, the beginning established.[3]

He ærest sceop   ielda[4] bearnum
He first created for men's sons

heofon to hrofe   haliġ Scyppend
heaven as a roof, holy Creator;

ða middanġeard   moncynnes Weard
then middle-earth mankind's Guardian,

eċe Drihten   æfter teode
eternal Lord, afterwards made—

firum foldan   Frea ælmihtiġ
for men earth, Master almighty.

This is the general sense but not the exact order of the words that he sang in his sleep;[5] for it is impossible to make a literal translation, no matter how well-written, of poetry into another language without losing some of the beauty and dignity. When he woke up, he remembered everything that he had sung in his sleep, and to this he soon added, in the same poetic measure, more verses praising God.

The next morning he went to the reeve,[6] who was his foreman, and told him about the gift he had received. He was taken to the abbess and ordered to tell his dream and to recite his song to an audience of the most learned men so that they might judge what the nature of that vision was and where it came from. It was evident to all of them that he had been granted the heavenly grace of God. Then they expounded some bit of sacred story or teaching to him, and instructed him to turn it into poetry if he could. He agreed and went away. And when he came back the next morning, he gave back what had been commissioned to him in the finest verse.

Therefore, the abbess, who cherished the grace of God in this man, instructed him to give up secular life and to take monastic vows. And when she and all those subject to her had received him into the community of brothers, she gave orders that he be taught the whole sequence of sacred history. He remembered everything that he was able to learn by listening, and turning it over in his mind like a clean beast that chews the cud,[7] he converted it into sweetest song, which sounded so delightful that he made his teachers, in their

3. I.e., established the beginning of every one of the wonders.
4. The later manuscript copies read *eorpan*, "earth," for *ælda* (West Saxon *ielda*), "men's."
5. Bede is referring to his Latin translation, for which we have substituted the Old English text with interlinear translation.

6. Superintendent of the farms belonging to the monastery.
7. In Mosaic law "clean" animals, those that may be eaten, are those that both chew the cud and have a cloven hoof (cf. Leviticus 11.3 and Deuteronomy 14.6).

turn, his listeners. He sang about the creation of the world and the origin of the human race and all the history of Genesis; about the exodus of Israel out of Egypt and entrance into the promised land; and about many other stories of sacred Scripture, about the Lord's incarnation, and his passion,[8] resurrection, and ascension into Heaven; about the advent of the Holy Spirit and the teachings of the apostles. He also made many songs about the terror of the coming judgment and the horror of the punishments of hell and the sweetness of heavenly kingdom; and a great many others besides about divine grace and justice in all of which he sought to draw men away from the love of sin and to inspire them with delight in the practice of good works.[9] * * *

8. The suffering of Christ beginning on the night of the Last Supper and culminating with his death.
9. The great majority of extant Old English poems are on religious subjects like those listed here, but most are thought to be later than Cædmon.

THE DREAM OF THE ROOD

Ruthwell Cross, Ruthwell, Scotland, ca. 8th century. Not only is the cross sculpted with Christian images; it also has lines from *The Dream of the Rood* inscribed in runic letters. They may have been added at a later date.

The Dream of the Rood (i.e., of the Cross) is considered the finest of a large number of religious poems in Anglo-Saxon. Neither the author nor its date of composition is known. It appears in a late tenth-century manuscript located in Vercelli in northern Italy, a manuscript made up of Old English religious poems and sermons. The poem may antedate its manuscript, because some passages from the Rood's speech were carved, with some variations, in runes on a stone cross at some time after its construction early in the eighth century; this is the famous Ruthwell Cross, preserved near Dumfries in southern Scotland. The precise relation of the poem to this cross is, however, uncertain.

The experience of the Rood, often called "tree" in the poem—its humiliation at the hands of those who cut it down and made it into an instrument of punishment for criminals and its humility when the young hero Christ mounts it—has a suggestive relevance to the condition of the Dreamer. His isolation and melancholy is typical of exile figures in Anglo-Saxon poetry. For the Rood, however, glory has replaced torment, and at the end, the Dreamer's description

of Christ's entry into heaven with the souls he has liberated from Hell reflects the
Dreamer's response to the hope that has been brought to him. Christ and the Rood
both act in keeping with, and yet diametrically opposed to, a code of heroic action:
Christ is both heroic in mounting and passive in suffering on the Rood, while the
Rood is loyal to its lord, yet must participate in his death.

The Dream of the Rood[1]

Attend to what   I intend to tell you
a marvelous dream   that moved me at night
when human voices   are veiled in sleep.
In my dream I espied   the most splendid tree.
5   looming aloft   with light all around,
the most brilliant beam.   That bright tree was
covered with gold; gemstones gleamed
fairly fashioned down to its foot,   yet another five were standing[2]
high up on the crossbeam   —the Lord's angel beheld them—[3]
10   cast by eternal decree.   Clearly this was no criminal's gallows,[4]
but holy spirits   were beholding it there,
men on this earth,   all that mighty creation.
That tree was triumphant   and I tarnished by sin,
begrimed with evil.   I beheld Glory's trunk
15   garnished with grandeur,   gleaming in bliss,
all plated with gold;   precious gemstones
had gloriously graced   the Lord God's tree.
Yet I could see   signs of ancient strife:
beneath that gold   it had begun
20   bleeding on the right side.[5]   I was all bereft with sorrows;
that splendid sight made me afraid.   I beheld the sign rapidly
changing clothing and colors.   Now it was covered with moisture,
drenched with streaming blood,   now decked in treasure.
Yet I, lying there   for a long time,
25   sorrowfully beheld   the tree of our Savior
until I could hear it   call out to me,
the best of all wood   began speaking words:
    "That was years ago   —I yet remember—
that I was cut down   at the edge of the forest
30   torn up from my trunk.   There powerful enemies took me,
put me up to make a circus-play to lift   up and parade their criminals.
Soldiers bore me on their shoulders   till they set me up on a mountain;
more than enough foes made me stand fast.   I saw the lord of mankind
coming with great haste   so that he might climb up on me.

1. The translation by Alfred David is based on
Eight Old English Poems, 3rd ed., edited by John
C. Pope, revised by R. D. Fulk (2000).
2. This longer line and the two following, as well
as lines 20–23, 30–34, 39–43, 46–49, 59–70, 75–
76, and 133, contain additional stresses and are
designated as "hypermetric." Fewer than 500 such
lines survive in the corpus of Anglo-Saxon poetry.
3. The translation follows R. D. Fulk's emenda-
tion: "beheold on þam engel dryhtnes."
4. Constantine the Great, emperor from 306 to
337, erected a jeweled cross at the site of the crucifixion, transforming the Roman "felon's gallows" from a symbol of shame into a universal
icon of Christian art.
5. According to biblical tradition, following John
19.34, Christ was wounded by the centurion's
lance on the right side.

35   Then I did not dare   act against the Lord's word
           bow down or fall to pieces   when I felt the surface
           of the earth trembling.[6]   Although I might
           have destroyed the foes,   I stood in place.
      Then this young man stripped himself   —that was God Almighty—
40   strong and courageous;   he climbed up on the high gallows,
      brave in the sight of many,   as he set out to redeem mankind.
      I trembled when the man embraced me;   I dared not bow down to earth,
      stoop to the surface of the ground,   but I had to stand fast.
          I was reared a rood;   I raised up a mighty king,
45   the heavens' lord;   I dared not bow in homage.
      They drove dark nails into me;   the dints of those wounds can still be seen,
      open marks of malice;   but I did not dare maul any of them in return.
      They mocked both of us.   I was moistened all over with blood,
      shed from the man's side   after he had sent up his spirit.
50   On that mountain   I have endured many
           cruel happenings.   I saw the God of hosts
           direly stretched out.   Shades of darkness
           had clouded over   the corpse of the Lord,
           the shining radiance;   shadows went forth
55   dark under clouds.   All creation wept,
           mourning the king's fall: Christ was on the cross.
           "Yet from afar   fervent men came
           to that sovereign.   I saw all that.
      I was badly burdened with grief   yet bowed down to their hands,
60   submissive with most resolve.   There they took up almighty God,
      lifted him from that cruel torment.   Then the warriors left me there
      standing, blood all over me,   pierced everywhere with arrows.
      They laid him there, limb-wearied;   they stood at the head of his lifeless
           body.
65   There they beheld the lord of heaven,   and he rested there for a while,
      spent after that great struggle.   Then they set about to construct a sepulcher
      warriors in the slayer's[7] sight.   Out of bright stone they carved it;
      they laid the lord of victories into it.   They began singing a lay of sorrow,
      warriors sad as night was falling,   when they wished to journey back
70   wearily far from that famous lord;   he rested there with few followers.[8]
      We,[9] grieving there   for a good while,
           stood still in place;   the soldiers' voices
           faded away.   Finally men brought axes
           to fell us to earth.   That was a frightful destiny!
75   They buried us in a deep pit.   But thanes° of the Lord,   *retainers*
      friends learned about me[1] * * *
          * * * adorned me   with gold and silver.
          "Now, man so dear to me,   you may understand
          that I have gone through   grievous sufferings,
80   terrible sorrows.   Now the time has come

---

6. According to Matthew 27.51, the earth quaked at the crucifixion.

7. I.e., the Cross. See John 19.41–42.

8. An example of Anglo-Saxon litotes, ironically expressing something by its contrary. In fact, Christ's tomb is now deserted.

9. I.e., Christ's Cross and those on which the two thieves had been crucified.

1. The reference in this gap in the manuscript must be to the discovery of the Cross by St. Helena.

so that far and wide   men worship me
everywhere on earth,   and all creation,
pray to this sign.   On me the son of God
suffered a time;   therefore I now tower
85 in glory under heaven,   and I may heal
any one of those   in awe of me.
Long ago I became   the most cruel punishment,
most hated by men,   until I made open
the right way of life   to language-bearers.
90 So the lord of glory,   guardian of Heaven,
exalted me then   over all forest-trees,
as Almighty God   before all humankind
exalted over   all the race of women
His own mother,   Mary herself.
95   "Now I command you,   my man so dear,
to tell others   the events you have seen;
find words to tell   it was the tree of glory
Almighty God   suffered upon
for mankind's   so many sins
100 and for that ancient   offense of Adam.
There he tasted death;   yet the Redeemer arose
with his great might   to help mankind.
Then he rose to Heaven.   He will come again
to this middle-earth   to seek out mankind
105 on Judgment Day,   the Redeemer himself,
God Almighty   and his angels with him,
so that He will judge,   He who has power of the Judgment,
all humanity   as to the merits each
has brought about   in this brief life.
110 Nor may anyone   be unafraid
of the last question   the Lord will ask.
Before the multitude   he will demand
where a soul might be   who in the Savior's name
would suffer the death   He suffered on that tree.
115 But they shall fear   and few shall think
what to contrive   to say to Christ.
But no one there   need be afraid
who bears the best   sign on his breast.
And on this earth   each soul that longs
120 to exist with its savior   forevermore
must seek His kingdom   through that cross."
     Then compelled by joy,   I prayed to that tree
with ardent zeal,   where I was alone
with few followers.   Then my heart felt
125 an urge to set forth;   I have suffered
much longing since.   Now I live in hope,
venturing after   that victory-tree,
alone more often   than all other men,
to worship it well.   The will to do so
130 is much in my heart;   my protection
depends on the rood.   I possess but few
friends on this earth.   But forth from here

they have set out from worldly joys   to seek the King of Glory.
They dwell in Heaven now   with the High-father
135 living in glory,   and I look forward
constantly toward   that time the Lord's rood
which I beheld before   here on this earth
shall fetch me away   from this fleeting life
and bring me then   where bliss is eternal
140 to joy in Paradise   where the Lord's people
are joined at that feast   where joy lasts forever
and seat me there   where evermore
I shall dwell in glory,   together with the saints
share in their delights.   May the Lord be my friend,
145 who on earth long ago   on the gallows-tree
suffered agony   for the sins of men:
he redeemed us   and gave us life,
a home in Heaven.   Hope was made new
and blossomed with bliss   to those burning in fire.[2]
150 The Son was victorious   in venturing forth,
mighty and triumphant   when he returned with many,
a company of souls   to the Kingdom of God,
the Almighty Ruler,   to the joy of angels,
and all those holy ones   come to Heaven before.[3]
155 to live in glory,   when their Lord returned,
the Eternal King   to His own country.

2. This line and those following refer to the so-called Harrowing of Hell. After his death on the Cross, Christ descended into hell, from which he released the souls of certain patriarchs and prophets, conducting them into heaven (see *Piers Plowman*, Passus 18). The analogy is to the triumphal procession of a Roman emperor returning from war.
3. The line probably refers to a belief that God had sanctified a chosen few before the crucifixion.

BEOWULF

*B*eowulf, the oldest of the great long poems written in English, may have been composed more than twelve hundred years ago, in the first half of the eighth century, although some scholars would place it as late as the tenth century. As is the case with most Old English poems, the title has been assigned by modern editors, for the manuscripts do not normally give any indication of title or authorship. Linguistic evidence shows that the poem was originally composed in the dialect of what was then Mercia, the Midlands of England today. But in the unique late-tenth-century manuscript preserving the poem, it has been converted into the West-Saxon dialect of the southwest in which most of Old English literature survives. In 1731, before any modern transcript of the text had been made, the manuscript was seriously damaged in a fire that destroyed the building in London that housed the extraordinary collection of medieval English manuscripts made by Sir Robert Bruce Cotton (1571–1631). As a result of the fire and subsequent deterioration, a number of lines and words have been lost from the poem.

Beowulf. The opening page. Note the charred edges, caused by a fire in 1731.

It is possible that *Beowulf* may be the lone survivor of a genre of Old English long epics, but it must have been a remarkable and difficult work even in its own day. The poet was reviving the heroic language, style, and pagan world of ancient Germanic oral poetry, a world that was already remote to his contemporaries and that is stranger to the modern reader, in many respects, than the epic world of Homer and Virgil. With the help of *Beowulf* itself, a few shorter heroic poems in Old English, and later poetry and prose in Old Saxon, Old Icelandic, and Middle High German, we can only conjecture what Germanic oral epic must have been like when performed by the Germanic *scop*, or bard. The *Beowulf* poet himself imagines such oral performances by having King Hrothgar's court poet recite a heroic lay at a feast celebrating Beowulf's defeat of Grendel. Many of the words and formulaic expressions in *Beowulf* can be found in other Old English poems, but there are also an extraordinary number of what linguists call *hapax legomena*—that is, words recorded only once in a language. The poet may have found them elsewhere, but the high incidence of such words suggests that he was an original wordsmith in his own right.

Although the poem itself is English in language and origin, it deals not with native Englishmen but with their Germanic forebears, especially with two south Scandinavian tribes, the Danes and the Geats, who lived on the Danish island of Zealand and in southern Sweden. Thus the historical period the poem concerns—insofar as it may be said to refer to history at all—is some centuries before it was written—that is, a time after the initial invasion of England by Germanic tribes in the middle of the fifth century but before the Anglo-Saxon migration was completed. The one datable fact of history mentioned in the poem is a raid on the Franks in which Hygelac, the king of the Geats and Beowulf's lord, was killed, and this raid occurred in the year 520. Yet the poet's elliptical references to quasihistorical and legendary material show that his audience was still familiar with many old stories, the outlines of which we can only infer, sometimes with the help of later analogous tales in other Germanic languages. This knowledge was probably kept alive by other heroic poetry, of which little has been preserved in English, although much may once have existed.

It is now widely believed that *Beowulf* is the work of a single poet who was a Christian and that his poem reflects well-established Christian tradition. The conversion of the Germanic settlers in England had been largely completed during the seventh century. The Danish king Hrothgar's poet sings a song about the Creation (lines 87–98) reminiscent of Cædmon's *Hymn*. The monster Grendel is said to be a descendant of Cain. There are allusions to God's judgment and to fate (*wyrd*) but none to pagan deities. References to the New Testament are notably absent, but Hrothgar and Beowulf often speak of God as though their religion is monotheistic. With sadness the poet relates that, made desperate by Grendel's attacks, the Danes pray for help at heathen shrines—apparently backsliding just as the children of Israel had sometimes lapsed into idolatry.

Although Hrothgar and Beowulf are portrayed as morally upright and enlightened pagans, they fully espouse and frequently affirm the values of Germanic heroic poetry. In the poetry depicting this warrior society, the most important of human relationships was that which existed between the warrior—the thane—and his lord, a relationship based less on subordination of one man's will to another's than on mutual trust and respect. When a warrior vowed loyalty to his lord, he became not so much his servant as his voluntary companion, one who would take pride in defending him and fighting in his wars. In return, the lord was expected to take care of his thanes and to reward them richly for their valor; a good king, one like Hrothgar or Beowulf, is referred to by such poetic epithets as "ring-giver" and as the "helmet" and "shield" of his people.

Anglo-Saxon helmet, 6th to 7th centuries. Excavated at Sutton Hoo, Suffolk.

The relationship between kinsmen was also of deep significance to this society. If one of his kinsmen had been slain, a man had a moral obligation either to kill the slayer or to exact the payment of *wergild* (man-price) in compensation. Each rank of society was evaluated at a definite price, which had to be paid to the dead man's kin by the killer if he wished to avoid their vengeance—even if the killing had been an accident. In the absence of any legal code other than custom or any body of law enforcement, it was the duty of the family (often with the lord's support) to execute justice. The payment itself had less significance as wealth than as proof that the kinsmen had done what was right. The failure to take revenge or to exact compensation was considered shameful. Hrothgar's anguish over the murders committed by Grendel is not only for the loss of his men but also for the shame of his inability either to kill Grendel or to exact a "death-price" from the killer. "It is always better / to avenge dear ones than to indulge in mourning" (lines 1384–85), Beowulf says to Hrothgar, who has been thrown back into despair by the revenge-slaying of his old friend Aeschere by Grendel's mother.

Yet the young Beowulf's attempt to comfort the bereaved old king by invoking the code of vengeance may be one of several instances of the poet's ironic treatment of the tragic futility of never-ending blood feuds. The most graphic example in the poem of that irony is the Finnsburg episode, the lay sung by Hrothgar's hall-poet. The Danish princess Hildeburh, married to the Frisian king Finn—probably to put an end to a feud between those peoples—loses both her brother and her son when a bloody fight breaks out in the hall between a visiting party of Danes and her husband's men. The bodies are cremated together on a huge funeral pyre: "The glutton element flamed and consumed / the dead of both sides. Their great days were gone" (lines 1124–25).

Such feuds, the staple subject of Germanic epic and saga, have only a peripheral place in the poem. Instead, the poem turns on Beowulf's three great fights against preternatural evil, which inhabits the dangerous and demonic space surrounding human society. He undertakes the fight against Grendel to save the Danes from the monster and to exact vengeance for the men Grendel has slain. Another motive is to demonstrate his strength and courage and thereby to enhance his personal glory. Hrothgar's magnificent gifts become the material emblems of that glory. Revenge and glory also motivate Beowulf's slaying of Grendel's mother. He undertakes his last battle against the dragon, however, only because there is no other way to save his own people.

A somber and dignified elegiac mood pervades *Beowulf*. The poem opens and closes with the description of a funeral and is filled with laments for the dead. Our first view of Beowulf is of an ambitious young hero. At the end, he has become an old king, facing the dragon and death. His people mourn him and praise him, as does the poet, for his nobility, generosity, courage, and, what is less common in Germanic heroes, kindness to his people. The poet's elegiac tone may be informed by something more than the duty to "praise a prince whom he holds dear / and cherish his memory when that moment comes / when he has to be convoyed from his bodily home" (lines 3175–77). The entire poem could be viewed as the poet's lament for heroes like Beowulf who went into the darkness without the light of the poet's own Christian faith.

The verse translation here is by the Irish poet Seamus Heaney, who received the Nobel Prize for literature in 1995. Selections from Heaney's own poems appear in Volume F of this anthology.

TRIBES AND GENEALOGIES

1. The Danes (Bright-, Half-, Ring-, Spear-, North-, East-, South-, West-Danes; Shieldings, Honor-, Victor-, War-Shieldings; Ing's friends)

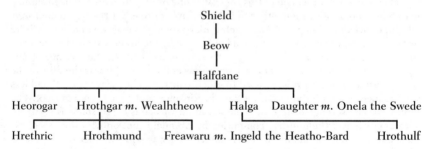

2. The Geats (Sea-, War-, Weather-Geats)

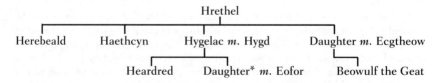

*The daughter of Hygelac who was given to Eofor may have been born to him by a former wife, older than Hygd.

3. The Swedes

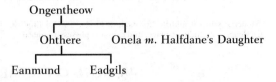

Ongentheow
Ohthere   Onela *m.* Halfdane's Daughter
Eanmund   Eadgils

4. Miscellaneous

A. The Half-Danes (also called Shieldings) involved in the fight at Finnsburg may represent a different tribe from the Danes described above. Their king Hoc had a son, Hnaef, who succeeded him, and a daughter Hildeburh, who married Finn, king of the Jutes.

B. The Jutes or Frisians are represented as enemies of the Danes in the fight at Finnsburg and as allies of the Franks or Hugas at the time Hygelac the Geat made the attack in which he lost his life and from which Beowulf swam home. Also allied with the Franks at this time were the Hetware.

C. The Heatho-Bards (i.e., "Battle-Bards") are represented as inveterate enemies of the Danes. Their king Froda had been killed in an attack on the Danes, and Hrothgar's attempt to make peace with them by marrying his daughter Freawaru to Froda's son Ingeld failed when the latter attacked Heorot. The attack was repulsed, although Heorot was burned.

The Poet's Song in Heorot

To give the reader a sample of the language, style, and texture of *Beowulf* in the original, we print the following passage, lines 90–98, in Old English with interlinear glosses. One may compare these lines with Cædmon's *Hymn* (p. 30) on the same theme. See the headnote there for the pronunciation of Old English characters.

> Sægde se þe cuþe
> Said   he who knew [how]

> *f*rumsceaft   *f*ira   *f*eorran   reccan,
> [the] origin [of] men   from far [time] [to] recount,

> cwæð þæt se Ælmightiga   *e*orðan worhte,
> said   that the Almighty   [the] earth wrought

> *w*lite-beorhtne *w*ang,   swa *w*æter bebugeð,
> beauty-bright   plain   as   water surrounds [it]

> gesette sige-hreþig   sunnan ond monan,
> set   triumph-glorious   sun   and moon

> *l*eoman   to *l*eohte   *l*andbuendum,
> beacons   as light   [for] land-dwellers

> ond ge*f*rætwade   *f*oldan   sceatas
> and adorned   [of] earth [the] grounds

> *l*eomum ond *l*eafum,   *l*if   eac gesceop
> [with] limbs and leaves,   life also [he] created

cynna   gehwylcum*   þara ðe   cwice hwyrfaþ.
[of] kinds [for] each   [of] those who living move about

*Modern syntax would be "for each of kinds." In Old English, the endings -a and -um indicate that
gewylcum is an indirect object and cynna, a possessive plural.

A NOTE ON NAMES

Old English, like Modern German, contained many compound words, most of
which have been lost in Modern English. Most of the names in *Beowulf* are compounds. Hrothgar is a combination of words meaning "glory" and "spear"; the name
of his older brother, Heorogar, comes from "army" and "spear"; Hrothgar's sons
Hrethric and Hrothmund contain the first elements of their father's name combined, respectively, with *ric* (kingdom, empire; Modern German *Reich*) and *mund*
(hand, protection). As in the case of the Danish dynasty, family names often alliterate. Masculine names of the warrior class have military associations. The importance of family and the demands of alliteration frequently lead to the designation of
characters by formulas identifying them in terms of relationships. Thus Beowulf is
referred to as "son of Ecgtheow" or "kinsman of Hygelac" (his uncle and lord).

The Old English spellings of names are mostly preserved in the translation. A few
rules of pronunciation are worth keeping in mind. Initial *H* before *r* was sounded,
and so Hrothgar's name alliterates with that of his brother Heorogar. The combination *cg* has the value of *dg* in words like "edge." The first element in the name of
Beowulf's father "Ecgtheow" is the same word as "edge," and, by the figure of speech
called synecdoche (a part of something stands for the whole), *ecg* stands for *sword* and
Ecgtheow means "sword-servant."

For more information about *Beowulf*, see "The Linguistic and Literary Contexts
of *Beowulf*," in the NAEL Archive.

Beowulf *

[PROLOGUE: THE RISE OF THE DANISH NATION]

So. The Spear-Danes[1] in days gone by
and the kings who ruled them had courage and greatness.
We have heard of those princes' heroic campaigns.
There was Shield Sheafson,[2] scourge of many tribes,
5   a wrecker of mead-benches, rampaging among foes.
This terror of the hall-troops had come far.
A foundling to start with, he would flourish later on
as his powers waxed and his worth was proved.
In the end each clan on the outlying coasts
10   beyond the whale-road had to yield to him
and begin to pay tribute. That was one good king.

*The translation is by Seamus Heaney.
1. There are different compound names for
tribes, often determined by alliteration in Old
English poetry. Line 1 reads, "*Hwæt, we Gar-
dena in gear-dagum,*" where alliteration falls on
Gar (spear) and *gear* (year). Old English hard and
soft *g* (spelled *y* in Modern English) alliterate.
The compound *geardagum* derives from "year,"
used in the special sense of "long ago," and "days"

and survives in the archaic expression "days of
yore."
2. Shield is the name of the founder of the Danish
royal line. Sheafson translates *Scefing*, i.e., *sheaf* +
the patronymic suffix *-ing*. Because Sheaf was a
"foundling" (line 7: *feasceaft funden*, i.e., found
destitute) who arrived by sea (lines 45–46), it is
likely that as a child Shield brought with him only
a sheaf, a symbol of fruitfulness.

Afterward a boy-child was born to Shield,
a cub in the yard, a comfort sent
by God to that nation. He knew what they had tholed,[3]
15   the long times and troubles they'd come through
without a leader; so the Lord of Life,
the glorious Almighty, made this man renowned.
Shield had fathered a famous son:
Beow's name was known through the north.
20   And a young prince must be prudent like that,
giving freely while his father lives
so that afterward in age when fighting starts
steadfast companions will stand by him
and hold the line. Behavior that's admired
25   is the path to power among people everywhere.
    Shield was still thriving when his time came
and he crossed over into the Lord's keeping.
His warrior band did what he bade them
when he laid down the law among the Danes:
30   they shouldered him out to the sea's flood,
the chief they revered who had long ruled them.
A ring-whorled prow rode in the harbor,
ice-clad, outbound, a craft for a prince.
They stretched their beloved lord in his boat,
35   laid out by the mast, amidships,
the great ring-giver. Far-fetched treasures
were piled upon him, and precious gear.
I never heard before of a ship so well furbished
with battle-tackle, bladed weapons
40   and coats of mail. The massed treasure
was loaded on top of him: it would travel far
on out into the ocean's sway.
They decked his body no less bountifully
with offerings than those first ones did
45   who cast him away when he was a child
and launched him alone out over the waves.[4]
And they set a gold standard up
high above his head and let him drift
to wind and tide, bewailing him
50   and mourning their loss. No man can tell,
no wise man in hall or weathered veteran
knows for certain who salvaged that load.
    Then it fell to Beow to keep the forts.
He was well regarded and ruled the Danes
55   for a long time after his father took leave
of his life on earth. And then his heir,
the great Halfdane,[5] held sway
for as long as he lived, their elder and warlord.
He was four times a father, this fighter prince:

3. Suffered, endured.
4. See n. 2, above. Since Shield was found destitute, "no less bountifully" is litotes or understatement; the ironic reminder that he came with

nothing (line 43) emphasizes the reversal of his
fortunes.
5. Probably named so because, according to one
source, his mother was a Swedish princess.

60   one by one they entered the world,
     Heorogar, Hrothgar, the good Halga,
     and a daughter, I have heard, who was Onela's queen,
     a balm in bed to the battle-scarred Swede.
       The fortunes of war favored Hrothgar.
65   Friends and kinsmen flocked to his ranks,
     young followers, a force that grew
     to be a mighty army. So his mind turned
     to hall-building: he handed down orders
     for men to work on a great mead-hall
70   meant to be a wonder of the world forever;
     it would be his throne-room and there he would dispense
     his God-given goods to young and old—
     but not the common land or people's lives.[6]
     Far and wide through the world, I have heard,
75   orders for work to adorn that wallstead
     were sent to many peoples. And soon it stood there
     finished and ready, in full view,
     the hall of halls. Heorot was the name[7]
     he had settled on it, whose utterance was law.
80   Nor did he renege, but doled out rings
     and torques at the table. The hall towered,
     its gables wide and high and awaiting
     a barbarous burning.[8] That doom abided,
     but in time it would come: the killer instinct
85   unleashed among in-laws, the blood-lust rampant.[9]

[HEOROT IS ATTACKED]

    Then a powerful demon,[1] a prowler through the dark,
     nursed a hard grievance. It harrowed him
     to hear the din of the loud banquet
     every day in the hall, the harp being struck
90   and the clear song of a skilled poet
     telling with mastery of man's beginnings,
     how the Almighty had made the earth
     a gleaming plain girdled with waters;
     in His splendor He set the sun and the moon
95   to be earth's lamplight, lanterns for men,
     and filled the broad lap of the world
     with branches and leaves; and quickened life
     in every other thing that moved.
      So times were pleasant for the people there
100 until finally one, a fiend out of hell,
     began to work his evil in the world.
     Grendel was the name of this grim demon

---

6. The king could not dispose of land used by all, such as a common pasture, or of slaves.
7. I.e., "Hart," from antlers fastened to the gables, or because the crossed gable-ends resembled a stag's antlers; the hart was also an icon of royalty.
8. An allusion to the future destruction of Heorot by fire, probably in a raid by the Heatho-Bards.

9. As told later (lines 2020–69), Hrothgar plans to marry a daughter to Ingeld, chief of the Heatho-Bards, in hopes of resolving a long-standing feud. See previous note.
1. The poet withholds the name for several lines. He does the same with the name of the hero as well as others.

haunting the marches, marauding round the heath
and the desolate fens; he had dwelt for a time
105 in misery among the banished monsters,
Cain's clan, whom the Creator had outlawed
and condemned as outcasts.[2] For the killing of Abel
the Eternal Lord had exacted a price:
Cain got no good from committing that murder
110 because the Almighty made him anathema
and out of the curse of his exile there sprang
ogres and elves and evil phantoms
and the giants too who strove with God
time and again until He gave them their reward.
115 　　So, after nightfall, Grendel set out
for the lofty house, to see how the Ring-Danes
were settling into it after their drink,
and there he came upon them, a company of the best
asleep from their feasting, insensible to pain
120 and human sorrow. Suddenly then
the God-cursed brute was creating havoc:
greedy and grim, he grabbed thirty men
from their resting places and rushed to his lair,
flushed up and inflamed from the raid,
125 blundering back with the butchered corpses.
　　Then as dawn brightened and the day broke,
Grendel's powers of destruction were plain:
their wassail was over, they wept to heaven
and mourned under morning. Their mighty prince,
130 the storied leader, sat stricken and helpless,
humiliated by the loss of his guard,
bewildered and stunned, staring aghast
at the demon's trail, in deep distress.
He was numb with grief, but got no respite
135 for one night later merciless Grendel
struck again with more gruesome murders.
Malignant by nature, he never showed remorse.
It was easy then to meet with a man
shifting himself to a safer distance
140 to bed in the bothies[3] for who could be blind
to the evidence of his eyes, the obviousness
of the hall-watcher's hate? Whoever escaped
kept a weather-eye open and moved away.
　　So Grendel ruled in defiance of right,
145 one against all, until the greatest house
in the world stood empty, a deserted wallstead.
For twelve winters, seasons of woe,
the lord of the Shieldings[4] suffered under
his load of sorrow; and so, before long,
150 the news was known over the whole world.

---

2. See Genesis 4.9–12.
3. Huts, outlying buildings. Evidently Grendel
wants only to dominate the hall.

4. The descendants of Shield, another name for
the Danes.

Sad lays were sung about the beset king,
the vicious raids and ravages of Grendel,
his long and unrelenting feud,
nothing but war; how he would never
155 parley or make peace with any Dane
nor stop his death-dealing nor pay the death-price.[5]
No counselor could ever expect
fair reparation from those rabid hands.
All were endangered; young and old
160 were hunted down by that dark death-shadow
who lurked and swooped in the long nights
on the misty moors; nobody knows
where these reavers from hell roam on their errands.
　　So Grendel waged his lonely war,
165 inflicting constant cruelties on the people,
atrocious hurt. He took over Heorot,
haunted the glittering hall after dark,
but the throne itself, the treasure-seat,
he was kept from approaching; he was the Lord's outcast.
170 　　These were hard times, heartbreaking
for the prince of the Shieldings; powerful counselors,
the highest in the land, would lend advice,
plotting how best the bold defenders
might resist and beat off sudden attacks.
175 Sometimes at pagan shrines they vowed
offerings to idols, swore oaths
that the killer of souls[6] might come to their aid
and save the people. That was their way,
their heathenish hope; deep in their hearts
180 they remembered hell. The Almighty Judge
of good deeds and bad, the Lord God,
Head of the Heavens and High King of the World,
was unknown to them. Oh, cursed is he
who in time of trouble has to thrust his soul
185 in the fire's embrace, forfeiting help;
he has nowhere to turn. But blessed is he
who after death can approach the Lord
and find friendship in the Father's embrace.

[THE HERO COMES TO HEOROT]

　　So that troubled time continued, woe
190 that never stopped, steady affliction
for Halfdane's son, too hard an ordeal.
There was panic after dark, people endured
raids in the night, riven by the terror.
　　When he heard about Grendel, Hygelac's thane
195 was on home ground, over in Geatland.
There was no one else like him alive.

---

5. I.e., *wergild* (man-price); monetary compensation for the life of the slain man is the only way, according to Germanic law, to settle a feud peacefully.

6. I.e., the devil. Heathen gods were thought to be devils.

In his day, he was the mightiest man on earth,
highborn and powerful. He ordered a boat
that would ply the waves. He announced his plan:
200   to sail the swan's road and seek out that king,
the famous prince who needed defenders.
Nobody tried to keep him from going,
no elder denied him, dear as he was to them.
Instead, they inspected omens and spurred
205   his ambition to go, whilst he moved about
like the leader he was, enlisting men,
the best he could find; with fourteen others
the warrior boarded the boat as captain,
a canny pilot along coast and currents.
210   Time went by, the boat was on water,
in close under the cliffs.
Men climbed eagerly up the gangplank,
sand churned in surf, warriors loaded
a cargo of weapons, shining war-gear
215   in the vessel's hold, then heaved out,
away with a will in their wood-wreathed ship.
Over the waves, with the wind behind her
and foam at her neck, she flew like a bird
until her curved prow had covered the distance,
220   and on the following day, at the due hour,
those seafarers sighted land,
sunlit cliffs, sheer crags
and looming headlands, the landfall they sought.
It was the end of their voyage and the Geats vaulted
225   over the side, out on to the sand,
and moored their ship. There was a clash of mail
and a thresh of gear. They thanked God
for that easy crossing on a calm sea.
       When the watchman on the wall, the Shieldings' lookout
230   whose job it was to guard the sea-cliffs,
saw shields glittering on the gangplank
and battle-equipment being unloaded
he had to find out who and what
the arrivals were. So he rode to the shore,
235   this horseman of Hrothgar's, and challenged them
in formal terms, flourishing his spear:
"What kind of men are you who arrive
rigged out for combat in your coats of mail,
sailing here over the sea-lanes
240   in your steep-hulled boat? I have been stationed
as lookout on this coast for a long time.
My job is to watch the waves for raiders,
any danger to the Danish shore.
Never before has a force under arms
245   disembarked so openly—not bothering to ask
if the sentries allowed them safe passage
or the clan had consented. Nor have I seen
a mightier man-at-arms on this earth

than the one standing here: unless I am mistaken,
250   he is truly noble. This is no mere
hanger-on in a hero's armor.
So now, before you fare inland
as interlopers, I have to be informed
about who you are and where you hail from.
255   Outsiders from across the water,
I say it again: the sooner you tell
where you come from and why, the better."
    The leader of the troop unlocked his word-hoard;
the distinguished one delivered this answer:
260   "We belong by birth to the Geat people
and owe allegiance to Lord Hygelac.
In his day, my father was a famous man,
a noble warrior-lord named Ecgtheow.
He outlasted many a long winter
265   and went on his way. All over the world
men wise in counsel continue to remember him.
We come in good faith to find your lord
and nation's shield, the son of Halfdane.
Give us the right advice and direction.
270   We have arrived here on a great errand
to the lord of the Danes, and I believe therefore
there should be nothing hidden or withheld between us.
So tell us if what we have heard is true
about this threat, whatever it is,
275   this danger abroad in the dark nights,
this corpse-maker mongering death
in the Shieldings' country. I come to proffer
my wholehearted help and counsel.
I can show the wise Hrothgar a way
280   to defeat his enemy and find respite—
if any respite is to reach him, ever.
I can calm the turmoil and terror in his mind.
Otherwise, he must endure woes
and live with grief for as long as his hall
285   stands at the horizon on its high ground."
    Undaunted, sitting astride his horse,
the coast-guard answered: "Anyone with gumption
and a sharp mind will take the measure
of two things: what's said and what's done.
290   I believe what you have told me, that you are a troop
loyal to our king. So come ahead
with your arms and your gear, and I will guide you.
What's more, I'll order my own comrades
on their word of honor to watch your boat
295   down there on the strand—keep her safe
in her fresh tar, until the time comes
for her curved prow to preen on the waves
and bear this hero back to Geatland.
May one so valiant and venturesome
300   come unharmed through the clash of battle."

So they went on their way. The ship rode the water,
broad-beamed, bound by its hawser
and anchored fast. Boar-shapes[7] flashed
above their cheek-guards, the brightly forged
305   work of goldsmiths, watching over
those stern-faced men. They marched in step,
hurrying on till the timbered hall
rose before them, radiant with gold.
Nobody on earth knew of another
310   building like it. Majesty lodged there,
its light shone over many lands.
So their gallant escort guided them
to that dazzling stronghold and indicated
the shortest way to it; then the noble warrior
315   wheeled on his horse and spoke these words:
"It is time for me to go. May the Almighty
Father keep you and in His kindness
watch over your exploits. I'm away to the sea,
back on alert against enemy raiders."
320   It was a paved track, a path that kept them
in marching order. Their mail-shirts glinted,
hard and hand-linked; the high-gloss iron
of their armor rang. So they duly arrived
in their grim war-graith[8] and gear at the hall,
325   and, weary from the sea, stacked wide shields
of the toughest hardwood against the wall,
then collapsed on the benches; battle-dress
and weapons clashed. They collected their spears
in a seafarers' stook, a stand of grayish
330   tapering ash. And the troops themselves
were as good as their weapons.
                       Then a proud warrior
questioned the men concerning their origins:
"Where do you come from, carrying these
decorated shields and shirts of mail,
335   these cheek-hinged helmets and javelins?
I am Hrothgar's herald and officer.
I have never seen so impressive or large
an assembly of strangers. Stoutness of heart,
bravery not banishment, must have brought you to Hrothgar."
340   The man whose name was known for courage,
the Geat leader, resolute in his helmet,
answered in return: "We are retainers
from Hygelac's band. Beowulf is my name.
If your lord and master, the most renowned
345   son of Halfdane, will hear me out
and graciously allow me to greet him in person,
I am ready and willing to report my errand."
      Wulfgar replied, a Wendel chief

---

7. Carved images of boars were placed on helmets,   8. "Graith": archaic for apparel.
probably as charms to protect the warriors.

renowned as a warrior, well known for his wisdom
350 and the temper of his mind: "I will take this message,
in accordance with your wish, to our noble king,
our dear lord, friend of the Danes,
the giver of rings. I will go and ask him
about your coming here, then hurry back
355 with whatever reply it pleases him to give."
　　With that he turned to where Hrothgar sat,
an old man among retainers;
the valiant follower stood foursquare
in front of his king: he knew the courtesies.
360 Wulfgar addressed his dear lord:
"People from Geatland have put ashore.
They have sailed far over the wide sea.
They call the chief in charge of their band
by the name of Beowulf. They beg, my lord,
365 an audience with you, exchange of words
and formal greeting. Most gracious Hrothgar,
do not refuse them, but grant them a reply.
From their arms and appointment, they appear well born
and worthy of respect, especially the one
370 who has led them this far: he is formidable indeed."
　　Hrothgar, protector of Shieldings, replied:
"I used to know him when he was a young boy.
His father before him was called Ecgtheow.
Hrethel the Geat⁹ gave Ecgtheow
375 his daughter in marriage. This man is their son,
here to follow up an old friendship.
A crew of seamen who sailed for me once
with a gift-cargo across to Geatland
returned with marvelous tales about him:
380 a thane, they declared, with the strength of thirty
in the grip of each hand. Now Holy God
has, in His goodness, guided him here
to the West-Danes, to defend us from Grendel.
This is my hope; and for his heroism
385 I will recompense him with a rich treasure.
Go immediately, bid him and the Geats
he has in attendance to assemble and enter.
Say, moreover, when you speak to them,
they are welcome to Denmark."
　　　　　　　　　　　　　　At the door of the hall,
390 Wulfgar duly delivered the message:
"My lord, the conquering king of the Danes,
bids me announce that he knows your ancestry;
also that he welcomes you here to Heorot
and salutes your arrival from across the sea.
395 You are free now to move forward
to meet Hrothgar in helmets and armor,
but shields must stay here and spears be stacked

---

9. Hygelac's father and Beowulf's grandfather.

until the outcome of the audience is clear."
　　　The hero arose, surrounded closely
400　by his powerful thanes. A party remained
under orders to keep watch on the arms;
the rest proceeded, led by their prince
under Heorot's roof. And standing on the hearth
in webbed links that the smith had woven,
405　the fine-forged mesh of his gleaming mail-shirt,
resolute in his helmet, Beowulf spoke:
"Greetings to Hrothgar. I am Hygelac's kinsman,
one of his hall-troop. When I was younger,
I had great triumphs. Then news of Grendel,
410　hard to ignore, reached me at home:
sailors brought stories of the plight you suffer
in this legendary hall, how it lies deserted,
empty and useless once the evening light
hides itself under heaven's dome.
415　So every elder and experienced councilman
among my people supported my resolve
to come here to you, King Hrothgar,
because all knew of my awesome strength.
They had seen me boltered[1] in the blood of enemies
420　when I battled and bound five beasts,
raided a troll-nest and in the night-sea
slaughtered sea-brutes. I have suffered extremes
and avenged the Geats (their enemies brought it
upon themselves; I devastated them).
425　Now I mean to be a match for Grendel,
settle the outcome in single combat.
And so, my request, O king of Bright-Danes,
dear prince of the Shieldings, friend of the people
and their ring of defense, my one request
430　is that you won't refuse me, who have come this far,
the privilege of purifying Heorot,
with my own men to help me, and nobody else.
I have heard moreover that the monster scorns
in his reckless way to use weapons;
435　therefore, to heighten Hygelac's fame
and gladden his heart, I hereby renounce
sword and the shelter of the broad shield,
the heavy war-board: hand-to-hand
is how it will be, a life-and-death
440　fight with the fiend. Whichever one death fells
must deem it a just judgment by God.
If Grendel wins, it will be a gruesome day;
he will glut himself on the Geats in the war-hall,
swoop without fear on that flower of manhood
445　as on others before. Then my face won't be there
to be covered in death: he will carry me away
as he goes to ground, gorged and bloodied;

---

1. Clotted, sticky.

he will run gloating with my raw corpse
and feed on it alone, in a cruel frenzy
450   fouling his moor-nest. No need then
to lament for long or lay out my body:[2]
if the battle takes me, send back
this breast-webbing that Weland[3] fashioned
and Hrethel gave me, to Lord Hygelac.
455   Fate goes ever as fate must."
    Hrothgar, the helmet of Shieldings, spoke:
"Beowulf, my friend, you have traveled here
to favor us with help and to fight for us.
There was a feud one time, begun by your father.
460   With his own hands he had killed Heatholaf
who was a Wulfing; so war was looming
and his people, in fear of it, forced him to leave.
He came away then over rolling waves
to the South-Danes here, the sons of honor.
465   I was then in the first flush of kingship,
establishing my sway over the rich strongholds
of this heroic land. Heorogar,
my older brother and the better man,
also a son of Halfdane's, had died.
470   Finally I healed the feud by paying:
I shipped a treasure-trove to the Wulfings,
and Ecgtheow acknowledged me with oaths of allegiance.
    "It bothers me to have to burden anyone
with all the grief that Grendel has caused
475   and the havoc he has wreaked upon us in Heorot,
our humiliations. My household guard
are on the wane, fate sweeps them away
into Grendel's clutches—but God can easily
halt these raids and harrowing attacks!
480   "Time and again, when the goblets passed
and seasoned fighters got flushed with beer
they would pledge themselves to protect Heorot
and wait for Grendel with their whetted swords.
But when dawn broke and day crept in
485   over each empty, blood-spattered bench,
the floor of the mead-hall where they had feasted
would be slick with slaughter. And so they died,
faithful retainers, and my following dwindled.
Now take your place at the table, relish
490   the triumph of heroes to your heart's content."

[FEAST AT HEOROT]

    Then a bench was cleared in that banquet hall
so the Geats could have room to be together
and the party sat, proud in their bearing,

---

2. I.e., for burial. Hrothgar will not need to give   3. Famed blacksmith in Germanic legend.
Beowulf an expensive funeral.

strong and stalwart. An attendant stood by
495   with a decorated pitcher, pouring bright
helpings of mead. And the minstrel sang,
filling Heorot with his head-clearing voice,
gladdening that great rally of Geats and Danes.
    From where he crouched at the king's feet,
500   Unferth, a son of Ecglaf's, spoke
contrary words. Beowulf's coming,
his sea-braving, made him sick with envy:
he could not brook or abide the fact
that anyone else alive under heaven
505   might enjoy greater regard than he did:
"Are you the Beowulf who took on Breca
in a swimming match on the open sea,
risking the water just to prove that you could win?
It was sheer vanity made you venture out
510   on the main deep. And no matter who tried,
friend or foe, to deflect the pair of you,
neither would back down: the sea-test obsessed you.
You waded in, embracing water,
taking its measure, mastering currents,
515   riding on the swell. The ocean swayed,
winter went wild in the waves, but you vied
for seven nights; and then he outswam you,
came ashore the stronger contender.
He was cast up safe and sound one morning
520   among the Heatho-Reams, then made his way
to where he belonged in Branding country,
home again, sure of his ground
in strongroom and bawn.[4] So Breca made good
his boast upon you and was proved right.
525   No matter, therefore, how you may have fared
in every bout and battle until now,
this time you'll be worsted; no one has ever
outlasted an entire night against Grendel."
    Beowulf, Ecgtheow's son, replied:
530   "Well, friend Unferth, you have had your say
about Breca and me. But it was mostly beer
that was doing the talking. The truth is this:
when the going was heavy in those high waves,
I was the strongest swimmer of all.
535   We'd been children together and we grew up
daring ourselves to outdo each other,
boasting and urging each other to risk
our lives on the sea. And so it turned out.
Each of us swam holding a sword,
540   a naked, hard-proofed blade for protection
against the whale-beasts. But Breca could never
move out farther or faster from me

---

4. Fortified outwork of a court or castle. The word was used by English planters in Ulster to describe fortified dwellings they erected on lands confiscated from the Irish [Translator's note].

than I could manage to move from him.
Shoulder to shoulder, we struggled on
545   for five nights, until the long flow
and pitch of the waves, the perishing cold,
night falling and winds from the north
drove us apart. The deep boiled up
and its wallowing sent the sea-brutes wild.
550   My armor helped me to hold out;
my hard-ringed chain-mail, hand-forged and linked,
a fine, close-fitting filigree of gold,
kept me safe when some ocean creature
pulled me to the bottom. Pinioned fast
555   and swathed in its grip, I was granted one
final chance: my sword plunged
and the ordeal was over. Through my own hands,
the fury of battle had finished off the sea-beast.
      "Time and again, foul things attacked me,
560   lurking and stalking, but I lashed out,
gave as good as I got with my sword.
My flesh was not for feasting on,
there would be no monsters gnawing and gloating
over their banquet at the bottom of the sea.
565   Instead, in the morning, mangled and sleeping
the sleep of the sword, they slopped and floated
like the ocean's leavings. From now on
sailors would be safe, the deep-sea raids
were over for good. Light came from the east,
570   bright guarantee of God, and the waves
went quiet; I could see headlands
and buffeted cliffs. Often, for undaunted courage,
fate spares the man it has not already marked.
However it occurred, my sword had killed
575   nine sea-monsters. Such night dangers
and hard ordeals I have never heard of
nor of a man more desolate in surging waves.
But worn out as I was, I survived,
came through with my life. The ocean lifted
580   and laid me ashore, I landed safe
on the coast of Finland.
                              Now I cannot recall
any fight you entered, Unferth,
that bears comparison. I don't boast when I say
that neither you nor Breca were ever much
585   celebrated for swordsmanship
or for facing danger on the field of battle.
You killed your own kith and kin,
so for all your cleverness and quick tongue,
you will suffer damnation in the depths of hell.
590   The fact is, Unferth, if you were truly
as keen or courageous as you claim to be
Grendel would never have got away with
such unchecked atrocity, attacks on your king,

havoc in Heorot and horrors everywhere.
595 But he knows he need never be in dread
of your blade making a mizzle of his blood
or of vengeance arriving ever from this quarter—
from the Victory-Shieldings, the shoulderers of the spear.
He knows he can trample down you Danes
600 to his heart's content, humiliate and murder
without fear of reprisal. But he will find me different.
I will show him how Geats shape to kill
in the heat of battle. Then whoever wants to
may go bravely to mead, when the morning light,
605 scarfed in sun-dazzle, shines forth from the south
and brings another daybreak to the world."
　　Then the gray-haired treasure-giver was glad;
far-famed in battle, the prince of Bright-Danes
and keeper of his people counted on Beowulf,
610 on the warrior's steadfastness and his word.
So the laughter started, the din got louder
and the crowd was happy. Wealhtheow came in,
Hrothgar's queen, observing the courtesies.
Adorned in her gold, she graciously saluted
615 the men in the hall, then handed the cup
first to Hrothgar, their homeland's guardian,
urging him to drink deep and enjoy it
because he was dear to them. And he drank it down
like the warlord he was, with festive cheer.
620 So the Helming woman went on her rounds,
queenly and dignified, decked out in rings,
offering the goblet to all ranks,
treating the household and the assembled troop,
until it was Beowulf's turn to take it from her hand.
625 With measured words she welcomed the Geat
and thanked God for granting her wish
that a deliverer she could believe in would arrive
to ease their afflictions. He accepted the cup,
a daunting man, dangerous in action
630 and eager for it always. He addressed Wealhtheow;
Beowulf, son of Ecgtheow, said:
"I had a fixed purpose when I put to sea.
As I sat in the boat with my band of men,
I meant to perform to the uttermost
635 what your people wanted or perish in the attempt,
in the fiend's clutches. And I shall fulfill that purpose,
prove myself with a proud deed
or meet my death here in the mead-hall."
This formal boast by Beowulf the Geat
640 pleased the lady well and she went to sit
by Hrothgar, regal and arrayed with gold.
　　Then it was like old times in the echoing hall,
proud talk and the people happy,
loud and excited; until soon enough
645 Halfdane's heir had to be away

to his night's rest. He realized
that the demon was going to descend on the hall,
that he had plotted all day, from dawn light
until darkness gathered again over the world
650   and stealthy night-shapes came stealing forth
under the cloud-murk. The company stood
as the two leaders took leave of each other:
Hrothgar wished Beowulf health and good luck,
named him hall-warden and announced as follows:
655   "Never, since my hand could hold a shield
have I entrusted or given control
of the Danes' hall to anyone but you.
Ward and guard it, for it is the greatest of houses.
Be on your mettle now, keep in mind your fame,
660   beware of the enemy. There's nothing you wish for
that won't be yours if you win through alive."

[THE FIGHT WITH GRENDEL]

    Hrothgar departed then with his house-guard.
The lord of the Shieldings, their shelter in war,
left the mead-hall to lie with Wealhtheow,
665   his queen and bedmate. The King of Glory
(as people learned) had posted a lookout
who was a match for Grendel, a guard against monsters,
special protection to the Danish prince.
And the Geat placed complete trust
670   in his strength of limb and the Lord's favor.
He began to remove his iron breast-mail,
took off the helmet and handed his attendant
the patterned sword, a smith's masterpiece,
ordering him to keep the equipment guarded.
675   And before he bedded down, Beowulf,
that prince of goodness, proudly asserted:
"When it comes to fighting, I count myself
as dangerous any day as Grendel.
So it won't be a cutting edge I'll wield
680   to mow him down, easily as I might.
He has no idea of the arts of war,
of shield or sword-play, although he does possess
a wild strength. No weapons, therefore,
for either this night: unarmed he shall face me
685   if face me he dares. And may the Divine Lord
in His wisdom grant the glory of victory
to whichever side He sees fit."
    Then down the brave man lay with his bolster
under his head and his whole company
690   of sea-rovers at rest beside him.
None of them expected he would ever see
his homeland again or get back
to his native place and the people who reared him.
They knew too well the way it was before,

695 how often the Danes had fallen prey
to death in the mead-hall. But the Lord was weaving
a victory on His war-loom for the Weather-Geats.
Through the strength of one they all prevailed;
they would crush their enemy and come through
700 in triumph and gladness. The truth is clear:
Almighty God rules over mankind
and always has.
                    Then out of the night
came the shadow-stalker, stealthy and swift.
The hall-guards were slack, asleep at their posts,
705 all except one; it was widely understood
that as long as God disallowed it,
the fiend could not bear them to his shadow-bourne.
One man, however, was in fighting mood,
awake and on edge, spoiling for action.
710   In off the moors, down through the mist-bands
God-cursed Grendel came greedily loping.
The bane of the race of men roamed forth,
hunting for a prey in the high hall.
Under the cloud-murk he moved toward it
715 until it shone above him, a sheer keep
of fortified gold. Nor was that the first time
he had scouted the grounds of Hrothgar's dwelling—
although never in his life, before or since,
did he find harder fortune or hall-defenders.
720 Spurned and joyless, he journeyed on ahead
and arrived at the bawn.[5] The iron-braced door
turned on its hinge when his hands touched it.
Then his rage boiled over, he ripped open
the mouth of the building, maddening for blood,
725 pacing the length of the patterned floor
with his loathsome tread, while a baleful light,
flame more than light, flared from his eyes.
He saw many men in the mansion, sleeping,
a ranked company of kinsmen and warriors
730 quartered together. And his glee was demonic,
picturing the mayhem: before morning
he would rip life from limb and devour them,
feed on their flesh; but his fate that night
was due to change, his days of ravening
735 had come to an end.
                    Mighty and canny,
Hygelac's kinsman was keenly watching
for the first move the monster would make.
Nor did the creature keep him waiting
but struck suddenly and started in;
740 he grabbed and mauled a man on his bench,
bit into his bone-lappings, bolted down his blood
and gorged on him in lumps, leaving the body

5. See p. 53, n. 4.

utterly lifeless, eaten up
hand and foot. Venturing closer,
745   his talon was raised to attack Beowulf
where he lay on the bed, he was bearing in
with open claw when the alert hero's
comeback and armlock forestalled him utterly.
The captain of evil discovered himself
750   in a handgrip harder than anything
he had ever encountered in any man
on the face of the earth. Every bone in his body
quailed and recoiled, but he could not escape.
He was desperate to flee to his den and hide
755   with the devil's litter, for in all his days
he had never been clamped or cornered like this.
Then Hygelac's trusty retainer recalled
his bedtime speech, sprang to his feet
and got a firm hold. Fingers were bursting,
760   the monster back-tracking, the man overpowering.
The dread of the land was desperate to escape,
to take a roundabout road and flee
to his lair in the fens. The latching power
in his fingers weakened; it was the worst trip
765   the terror-monger had taken to Heorot.
And now the timbers trembled and sang,
a hall-session[6] that harrowed every Dane
inside the stockade: stumbling in fury,
the two contenders crashed through the building.
770   The hall clattered and hammered, but somehow
survived the onslaught and kept standing:
it was handsomely structured, a sturdy frame
braced with the best of blacksmith's work
inside and out. The story goes
775   that as the pair struggled, mead-benches were smashed
and sprung off the floor, gold fittings and all.
Before then, no Shielding elder would believe
there was any power or person upon earth
capable of wrecking their horn-rigged hall
780   unless the burning embrace of a fire
engulf it in flame. Then an extraordinary
wail arose, and bewildering fear
came over the Danes. Everyone felt it
who heard that cry as it echoed off the wall,
785   a God-cursed scream and strain of catastrophe,
the howl of the loser, the lament of the hell-serf
keening his wound. He was overwhelmed,
manacled tight by the man who of all men
was foremost and strongest in the days of this life.
790   But the earl-troop's leader was not inclined
to allow his caller to depart alive:

---

6. In Hiberno-English the word "session" (*seissiún* in Irish) can mean a gathering where musicians and singers perform for their own enjoyment [Translator's note].

he did not consider that life of much account
to anyone anywhere. Time and again,
Beowulf's warriors worked to defend
795   their lord's life, laying about them
as best they could, with their ancestral blades.
Stalwart in action, they kept striking out
on every side, seeking to cut
straight to the soul. When they joined the struggle
800   there was something they could not have known at the time,
that no blade on earth, no blacksmith's art
could ever damage their demon opponent.
He had conjured the harm from the cutting edge
of every weapon.[7] But his going away
805   out of this world and the days of his life
would be agony to him, and his alien spirit
would travel far into fiends' keeping.
    Then he who had harrowed the hearts of men
with pain and affliction in former times
810   and had given offense also to God
found that his bodily powers failed him.
Hygelac's kinsman kept him helplessly
locked in a handgrip. As long as either lived,
he was hateful to the other. The monster's whole
815   body was in pain; a tremendous wound
appeared on his shoulder. Sinews split
and the bone-lappings burst. Beowulf was granted
the glory of winning; Grendel was driven
under the fen-banks, fatally hurt,
820   to his desolate lair. His days were numbered,
the end of his life was coming over him,
he knew it for certain; and one bloody clash
had fulfilled the dearest wishes of the Danes.
The man who had lately landed among them,
825   proud and sure, had purged the hall,
kept it from harm; he was happy with his nightwork
and the courage he had shown. The Geat captain
had boldly fulfilled his boast to the Danes:
he had healed and relieved a huge distress,
830   unremitting humiliations,
the hard fate they'd been forced to undergo,
no small affliction. Clear proof of this
could be seen in the hand the hero displayed
high up near the roof: the whole of Grendel's
835   shoulder and arm, his awesome grasp.

[CELEBRATION AT HEOROT]

    Then morning came and many a warrior
gathered, as I've heard, around the gift-hall,
clan-chiefs flocking from far and near
down wide-ranging roads, wondering greatly

---

7. Grendel is protected by a charm against metals.

840 at the monster's footprints. His fatal departure
was regretted by no one who witnessed his trail,
the ignominious marks of his flight
where he'd skulked away, exhausted in spirit
and beaten in battle, bloodying the path,
845 hauling his doom to the demons' mere.[8]
The bloodshot water wallowed and surged,
there were loathsome upthrows and overturnings
of waves and gore and wound-slurry.
With his death upon him, he had dived deep
850 into his marsh-den, drowned out his life
and his heathen soul: hell claimed him there.
      Then away they rode, the old retainers
with many a young man following after,
a troop on horseback, in high spirits
855 on their bay steeds. Beowulf's doings
were praised over and over again.
Nowhere, they said, north or south
between the two seas or under the tall sky
on the broad earth was there anyone better
860 to raise a shield or to rule a kingdom.
Yet there was no laying of blame on their lord,
the noble Hrothgar; he was a good king.
      At times the war-band broke into a gallop,
letting their chestnut horses race
865 wherever they found the going good
on those well-known tracks. Meanwhile, a thane
of the king's household, a carrier of tales,
a traditional singer deeply schooled
in the lore of the past, linked a new theme
870 to a strict meter.[9] The man started
to recite with skill, rehearsing Beowulf's
triumphs and feats in well-fashioned lines,
entwining his words.
                  He told what he'd heard
repeated in songs about Sigemund's exploits,[1]
875 all of those many feats and marvels,
the struggles and wanderings of Waels's son,[2]
things unknown to anyone
except to Fitela, feuds and foul doings
confided by uncle to nephew when he felt
880 the urge to speak of them: always they had been
partners in the fight, friends in need.
They killed giants, their conquering swords
had brought them down.
                  After his death
Sigemund's glory   grew and grew

---

8. A lake or pool, although we learn later that it
has an outlet to the sea. Grendel's habitat.
9. I.e., an extemporaneous heroic poem in alliterative verse about Beowulf's deeds.
1. Tales about Sigemund, his nephew Sinfjotli
(Fitela), and his son Sigurth are found in a 13th-

century Old Icelandic collection of legends
known as the *Volsung Saga*. Analogous stories
must have been known to the poet and his audience, though details differ.
2. Waels is the father of Sigemund.

885 *because of his courage when he killed the dragon,*
 the guardian of the hoard. Under gray stone
 he had dared to enter all by himself
 to face the worst without Fitela.
 But it came to pass that his sword plunged
890 *right through those radiant scales*
 and drove into the wall. The dragon died of it.
 His daring had given him total possession
 of the treasure-hoard, his to dispose of
 however he liked. He loaded a boat:
895 *Waels's son weighted her hold*
 with dazzling spoils. The hot dragon melted.
  Sigemund's name was known everywhere.
 He was utterly valiant and venturesome,
 a fence round his fighters and flourished therefore
900 *after King Heremod's[3] prowess declined*
 and his campaigns slowed down. The king was betrayed,
 ambushed in Jutland, overpowered
 and done away with. The waves of his grief
 had beaten him down, made him a burden,
905 *a source of anxiety to his own nobles:*
 that expedition was often condemned
 in those earlier times by experienced men,
 men who relied on his lordship for redress,
 who presumed that the part of a prince was to thrive
910 *on his father's throne and defend the nation,*
 the Shielding land where they lived and belonged,
 its holdings and strongholds. Such was Beowulf
 in the affection of his friends and of everyone alive.
 But evil entered into Heremod.
915 They kept racing each other, urging their mounts
 down sandy lanes. The light of day
 broke and kept brightening. Bands of retainers
 galloped in excitement to the gabled hall
 to see the marvel; and the king himself,
920 guardian of the ring-hoard, goodness in person,
 walked in majesty from the women's quarters
 with a numerous train, attended by his queen
 and her crowd of maidens, across to the mead-hall.
  When Hrothgar arrived at the hall, he spoke,
925 standing on the steps, under the steep eaves,
 gazing toward the roofwork and Grendel's talon:
 "First and foremost, let the Almighty Father
 be thanked for this sight. I suffered a long
 harrowing by Grendel. But the Heavenly Shepherd
930 can work His wonders always and everywhere.
 Not long since, it seemed I would never
 be granted the slightest solace or relief
 from any of my burdens: the best of houses

---

3. Heremod was a bad king, held up by the bard as the opposite of Beowulf, as Sigemund is held up as a heroic prototype of Beowulf.

glittered and reeked and ran with blood.
935 This one worry outweighed all others—
a constant distress to counselors entrusted
with defending the people's forts from assault
by monsters and demons. But now a man,
with the Lord's assistance, has accomplished something
940 none of us could manage before now
for all our efforts. Whoever she was
who brought forth this flower of manhood,
if she is still alive, that woman can say
that in her labor the Lord of Ages
945 bestowed a grace on her. So now, Beowulf,
I adopt you in my heart as a dear son.
Nourish and maintain this new connection,
you noblest of men; there'll be nothing you'll want for,
no worldly goods that won't be yours.
950 I have often honored smaller achievements,
recognized warriors not nearly as worthy,
lavished rewards on the less deserving.
But you have made yourself immortal
by your glorious action. May the God of Ages
955 continue to keep and requite you well."
  Beowulf, son of Ecgtheow, spoke:
"We have gone through with a glorious endeavor
and been much favored in this fight we dared
against the unknown. Nevertheless,
960 if you could have seen the monster himself
where he lay beaten, I would have been better pleased.
My plan was to pounce, pin him down
in a tight grip and grapple him to death—
have him panting for life, powerless and clasped
965 in my bare hands, his body in thrall.
But I couldn't stop him from slipping my hold.
The Lord allowed it, my lock on him
wasn't strong enough; he struggled fiercely
and broke and ran. Yet he bought his freedom
970 at a high price, for he left his hand
and arm and shoulder to show he had been here,
a cold comfort for having come among us.
And now he won't be long for this world.
He has done his worst but the wound will end him.
975 He is hasped and hooped and hirpling with pain,
limping and looped in it. Like a man outlawed
for wickedness, he must await
the mighty judgment of God in majesty."
  There was less tampering and big talk then
980 from Unferth the boaster, less of his blather
as the hall-thanes eyed the awful proof
of the hero's prowess, the splayed hand
up under the eaves. Every nail,
claw-scale and spur, every spike
985 and welt on the hand of that heathen brute

was like barbed steel. Everybody said
there was no honed iron hard enough
to pierce him through, no time-proofed blade
that could cut his brutal, blood-caked claw.
990   Then the order was given for all hands
to help to refurbish Heorot immediately:
men and women thronging the wine-hall,
getting it ready. Gold thread shone
in the wall-hangings, woven scenes
995 that attracted and held the eye's attention.
But iron-braced as the inside of it had been,
that bright room lay in ruins now.
The very doors had been dragged from their hinges.
Only the roof remained unscathed
1000 by the time the guilt-fouled fiend turned tail
in despair of his life. But death is not easily
escaped from by anyone:
all of us with souls, earth-dwellers
and children of men, must make our way
1005 to a destination already ordained
where the body, after the banqueting,
sleeps on its deathbed.
                Then the due time arrived
for Halfdane's son to proceed to the hall.
The king himself would sit down to feast.
1010 No group ever gathered in greater numbers
or better order around their ring-giver.
The benches filled with famous men
who fell to with relish; round upon round
of mead was passed; those powerful kinsmen,
1015 Hrothgar and Hrothulf, were in high spirits
in the raftered hall. Inside Heorot
there was nothing but friendship. The Shielding nation
was not yet familiar with feud and betrayal.[4]
    Then Halfdane's son presented Beowulf
1020 with a gold standard as a victory gift,
an embroidered banner; also breast-mail
and a helmet; and a sword carried high,
that was both precious object and token of honor.
So Beowulf drank his drink, at ease;
1025 it was hardly a shame to be showered with such gifts
in front of the hall-troops. There haven't been many
moments, I am sure, when men exchanged
four such treasures at so friendly a sitting.
An embossed ridge, a band lapped with wire
1030 arched over the helmet: head-protection
to keep the keen-ground cutting edge
from damaging it when danger threatened
and the man was battling behind his shield.

---

4. Probably an ironic allusion to the future usurpation of the throne from Hrothgar's sons by Hrothulf, although no such treachery is recorded of Hrothulf, who is the hero of other Germanic stories.

Next the king ordered eight horses
1035   with gold bridles to be brought through the yard
into the hall. The harness of one
included a saddle of sumptuous design,
the battle-seat where the son of Halfdane
rode when he wished to join the sword-play:
1040   wherever the killing and carnage were the worst,
he would be to the fore, fighting hard.
Then the Danish prince, descendant of Ing,
handed over both the arms and the horses,
urging Beowulf to use them well.
1045   And so their leader, the lord and guard
of coffer and strongroom, with customary grace
bestowed upon Beowulf both sets of gifts.
A fair witness can see how well each one behaved.
    The chieftain went on to reward the others:
1050   each man on the bench who had sailed with Beowulf
and risked the voyage received a bounty,
some treasured possession. And compensation,
a price in gold, was settled for the Geat
Grendel had cruelly killed earlier—
1055   as he would have killed more, had not mindful God
and one man's daring prevented that doom.
Past and present, God's will prevails.
Hence, understanding is always best
and a prudent mind. Whoever remains
1060   for long here in this earthly life
will enjoy and endure more than enough.
    They sang then and played to please the hero,
words and music for their warrior prince,
harp tunes and tales of adventure:
1065   there were high times on the hall benches,
and the king's poet performed his part
with the saga of Finn and his sons, unfolding
the tale of the fierce attack in Friesland
where Hnaef, king of the Danes, met death.[5]
1070   *Hildeburh*
              had little cause
to credit the Jutes:
              son and brother,
she lost them both
              on the battlefield.
She, bereft
              and blameless, they

---

5. The bard's lay is known as the Finnsburg Episode. Its allusive style makes the tale obscure in many details, although some can be filled in from a fragmentary Old English lay, which modern editors have entitled *The Fight at Finnsburg*. Hildeburh, the daughter of the former Danish king Hoc, was married to Finn, king of Friesland, presumably to help end a feud between their peoples. As the episode opens, the feud has already broken out again when a visiting party of Danes, led by Hildeburh's brother Hnaef, who has succeeded their father, is attacked by a tribe called the Jutes. The Jutes are subject to Finn but may be a clan distinct from the Frisians, and Finn does not seem to have instigated the attack. In the ensuing battle, both Hnaef and the son of Hildeburh and Finn are killed, and both sides suffer heavy losses.

foredoomed, cut down
                    and spear-gored. She,
1075   *the woman in shock,*
                    waylaid by grief,
Hoc's daughter—
                    how could she not
lament her fate
                    when morning came
and the light broke
                    on her murdered dears?
And so farewell
                    delight on earth,
1080   *war carried away*
                    Finn's troop of thanes
all but a few.
                    How then could Finn
hold the line
                    or fight on
to the end with Hengest,
                    how save
the rump of his force
                    from that enemy chief?
1085   *So a truce was offered*
                    as follows:[6] *first*
separate quarters
                    to be cleared for the Danes,
hall and throne
                    to be shared with the Frisians.
Then, second:
                    every day
at the dole-out of gifts
                    Finn, son of Focwald,
1090   *should honor the Danes,*
                    bestow with an even
hand to Hengest
                    and Hengest's men
the wrought-gold rings,
                    bounty to match
the measure he gave
                    his own Frisians—
to keep morale
                    in the beer-hall high.
1095   *Both sides then*
                    sealed their agreement.
With oaths to Hengest
                    Finn swore
openly, solemnly,
                    that the battle survivors
would be guaranteed
                    honor and status.

---

6. The truce was offered by Finn to Hengest, who succeeded Hnaef as leader of the Danes.

No infringement
                    by word or deed,
1100   *no provocation*
                    would be permitted.
Their own ring-giver
                    after all
was dead and gone,
                    they were leaderless,
in forced allegiance
                    to his murderer.
So if any Frisian
                    stirred up bad blood
1105   *with insinuations*
                    or taunts about this,
the blade of the sword
                    would arbitrate it.
A funeral pyre
                    was then prepared,
effulgent gold
                    brought out from the hoard.
The pride and prince
                    of the Shieldings lay
1110   *awaiting the flame.*
                    Everywhere
there were blood-plastered
                    coats of mail.
The pyre was heaped
                    with boar-shaped helmets
forged in gold,
                    with the gashed corpses
of wellborn Danes—
                    many had fallen.
1115   *Then Hildeburh*
                    ordered her own
son's body
                    be burnt with Hnaef's,
the flesh on his bones
                    to sputter and blaze
beside his uncle's.
                    The woman wailed
and sang keens,
                    the warrior went up.[7]
1120   *Carcass flame*
                    swirled and fumed,
they stood round the burial
                    mound and howled
as heads melted,
                    crusted gashes
spattered and ran
                    bloody matter.

---

7. The meaning may be that the warrior was placed up on the pyre, or went up in smoke. "Keens": lamentations or dirges for the dead.

The glutton element
                    flamed and consumed
1125   the dead of both sides.
                            Their great days were gone.
Warriors scattered
                to homes and forts
all over Friesland,
                    fewer now, feeling
loss of friends.
                Hengest stayed,
lived out that whole
                        resentful, blood-sullen
1130   winter with Finn,
                        homesick and helpless.
No ring-whorled prow
                            could up then
and away on the sea.
                        Wind and water
raged with storms,
                        wave and shingle
were shackled in ice
                        until another year
1135   appeared in the yard
                            as it does to this day,
the seasons constant,
                        the wonder of light
coming over us.
                    Then winter was gone,
earth's lap grew lovely,
                            longing woke
in the cooped-up exile
                        for a voyage home—
1140   but more for vengeance,
                            some way of bringing
things to a head:
                    his sword arm hankered
to greet the Jutes.
                    So he did not balk
once Hunlafing
                    placed on his lap
Dazzle-the-Duel,
                    the best sword of all,[8]
1145   whose edges Jutes
                    knew only too well.
Thus blood was spilled,
                        the gallant Finn
slain in his home
                    after Guthlaf and Oslaf[9]

8. Hunlafing may be the son of a Danish warrior called Hunlaf. The placing of the sword in Hengest's lap is a symbolic call for revenge.
9. It is not clear whether the Danes have traveled home and then returned to Friesland with reinforcements or whether the Danish survivors attack once the weather allows them to take ship.

back from their voyage
               made old accusation:
the brutal ambush,
             the fate they had suffered,
1150   all blamed on Finn.
               The wildness in them
had to brim over.
             The hall ran red
with blood of enemies.
               Finn was cut down,
the queen brought away
               and everything
the Shieldings could find
               inside Finn's walls—
1155   the Frisian king's
               gold collars and gemstones—
swept off to the ship.
               Over sea-lanes then
back to Daneland
             the warrior troop
bore that lady home.

               The poem was over,
the poet had performed, a pleasant murmur
1160   started on the benches, stewards did the rounds
with wine in splendid jugs, and Wealhtheow came to sit
in her gold crown between two good men,
uncle and nephew, each one of whom
still trusted the other;[1] and the forthright Unferth,
1165   admired by all for his mind and courage
although under a cloud for killing his brothers,
reclined near the king.
             The queen spoke:
"Enjoy this drink, my most generous lord;
raise up your goblet, entertain the Geats
1170   duly and gently, discourse with them,
be open-handed, happy and fond.
Relish their company, but recollect as well
all of the boons that have been bestowed on you.
The bright court of Heorot has been cleansed
1175   and now the word is that you want to adopt
this warrior as a son. So, while you may,
bask in your fortune, and then bequeath
kingdom and nation to your kith and kin,
before your decease. I am certain of Hrothulf.
1180   He is noble and will use the young ones well.
He will not let you down. Should you die before him,
he will treat our children truly and fairly.
He will honor, I am sure, our two sons,
repay them in kind, when he recollects

---

1. See p. 63, n. 4.

₁₁₈₅   all the good things we gave him once,
the favor and respect he found in his childhood."
She turned then to the bench where her boys sat,
Hrethric and Hrothmund, with other nobles' sons,
all the youth together; and that good man,
₁₁₉₀   Beowulf the Geat, sat between the brothers.

    The cup was carried to him, kind words
spoken in welcome and a wealth of wrought gold
graciously bestowed: two arm bangles,
a mail-shirt and rings, and the most resplendent
₁₁₉₅   torque of gold I ever heard tell of
anywhere on earth or under heaven.
There was no hoard like it since Hama snatched
the Brosings' neck-chain and bore it away
with its gems and settings to his shining fort,
₁₂₀₀   away from Eormenric's wiles and hatred,[2]
and thereby ensured his eternal reward.
Hygelac the Geat, grandson of Swerting,
wore this neck-ring on his last raid;[3]
at bay under his banner, he defended the booty,
₁₂₀₅   treasure he had won. Fate swept him away
because of his proud need to provoke
a feud with the Frisians. He fell beneath his shield,
in the same gem-crusted, kingly gear
he had worn when he crossed the frothing wave-vat.
₁₂₁₀   So the dead king fell into Frankish hands.
They took his breast-mail, also his neck-torque,
and punier warriors plundered the slain
when the carnage ended; Geat corpses
covered the field.
                  Applause filled the hall.
₁₂₁₅   Then Wealhtheow pronounced in the presence of the company:
"Take delight in this torque, dear Beowulf,
wear it for luck and wear also this mail
from our people's armory: may you prosper in them!
Be acclaimed for strength, for kindly guidance
₁₂₂₀   to these two boys, and your bounty will be sure.
You have won renown: you are known to all men
far and near, now and forever.
Your sway is wide as the wind's home,
as the sea around cliffs. And so, my prince,
₁₂₂₅   I wish you a lifetime's luck and blessings
to enjoy this treasure. Treat my sons
with tender care, be strong and kind.
Here each comrade is true to the other,
loyal to lord, loving in spirit.

2. The necklace presented to Beowulf is compared to one worn by the goddess Freya in Germanic mythology. In another story it was stolen by Hama from the Gothic king Eormenric, who is treated as a tyrant in Germanic legend, but how Eormenric came to possess it is not known.
3. Later we learn that Beowulf gave the necklace to Hygd, the queen of his lord Hygelac. Hygelac is here said to have been wearing it on his last expedition. This is the first of several allusions to Hygelac's death on a raid up the Rhine, the one incident in the poem that can be connected to a historical event documented elsewhere.

1230 The thanes have one purpose, the people are ready:
having drunk and pledged, the ranks do as I bid."
    She moved then to her place. Men were drinking wine
at that rare feast; how could they know fate,
the grim shape of things to come,
1235 the threat looming over many thanes
as night approached and King Hrothgar prepared
to retire to his quarters? Retainers in great numbers
were posted on guard as so often in the past.
Benches were pushed back, bedding gear and bolsters
1240 spread across the floor, and one man
lay down to his rest, already marked for death.
At their heads they placed their polished timber
battle-shields; and on the bench above them,
each man's kit was kept to hand:
1245 a towering war-helmet, webbed mail-shirt
and great-shafted spear. It was their habit
always and everywhere to be ready for action,
at home or in the camp, in whatever case
and at whatever time the need arose
1250 to rally round their lord. They were a right people.

[ANOTHER ATTACK]

    They went to sleep. And one paid dearly
for his night's ease, as had happened to them often,
ever since Grendel occupied the gold-hall,
committing evil until the end came,
1255 death after his crimes. Then it became clear,
obvious to everyone once the fight was over,
that an avenger lurked and was still alive,
grimly biding time. Grendel's mother,
monstrous hell-bride, brooded on her wrongs.
1260 She had been forced down into fearful waters,
the cold depths, after Cain had killed
his father's son, felled his own
brother with a sword. Branded an outlaw,
marked by having murdered, he moved into the wilds,
1265 shunned company and joy. And from Cain there sprang
misbegotten spirits, among them Grendel,
the banished and accursed, due to come to grips
with that watcher in Heorot waiting to do battle.
The monster wrenched and wrestled with him,
1270 but Beowulf was mindful of his mighty strength,
the wondrous gifts God had showered on him:
he relied for help on the Lord of All,
on His care and favor. So he overcame the foe,
brought down the hell-brute. Broken and bowed,
1275 outcast from all sweetness, the enemy of mankind
made for his death-den. But now his mother
had sallied forth on a savage journey,
grief-racked and ravenous, desperate for revenge.

She came to Heorot. There, inside the hall,
1280 Danes lay asleep, earls who would soon endure
a great reversal, once Grendel's mother
attacked and entered. Her onslaught was less
only by as much as an amazon warrior's
strength is less than an armed man's
1285 when the hefted sword, its hammered edge
and gleaming blade slathered in blood,
razes the sturdy boar-ridge off a helmet.
Then in the hall, hard-honed swords
were grabbed from the bench, many a broad shield
1290 lifted and braced; there was little thought of helmets
or woven mail when they woke in terror.
     The hell-dam was in panic, desperate to get out,
in mortal terror the moment she was found.
She had pounced and taken one of the retainers
1295 in a tight hold, then headed for the fen.
To Hrothgar, this man was the most beloved
of the friends he trusted between the two seas.
She had done away with a great warrior,
ambushed him at rest.
                              Beowulf was elsewhere.
1300 Earlier, after the award of the treasure,
the Geat had been given another lodging.
     There was uproar in Heorot. She had snatched their trophy,
Grendel's bloodied hand. It was a fresh blow
to the afflicted bawn. The bargain was hard,
1305 both parties having to pay
with the lives of friends. And the old lord,
the gray-haired warrior, was heartsore and weary
when he heard the news: his highest-placed adviser,
his dearest companion, was dead and gone.
1310 Beowulf was quickly brought to the chamber:
the winner of fights, the arch-warrior,
came first-footing in with his fellow troops
to where the king in his wisdom waited,
still wondering whether Almighty God
1315 would ever turn the tide of his misfortunes.
So Beowulf entered with his band in attendance
and the wooden floorboards banged and rang
as he advanced, hurrying to address
the prince of the Ingwins, asking if he'd rested
1320 since the urgent summons had come as a surprise.
     Then Hrothgar, the Shieldings' helmet, spoke:
"Rest? What is rest? Sorrow has returned.
Alas for the Danes! Aeschere is dead.
He was Yrmenlaf's elder brother
1325 and a soul-mate to me, a true mentor,
my right-hand man when the ranks clashed
and our boar-crests had to take a battering
in the line of action. Aeschere was everything
the world admires in a wise man and a friend.

1330 Then this roaming killer came in a fury
and slaughtered him in Heorot. Where she is hiding,
glutting on the corpse and glorying in her escape,
I cannot tell; she has taken up the feud
because of last night, when you killed Grendel,
1335 wrestled and racked him in ruinous combat
since for too long he had terrorized us
with his depredations. He died in battle,
paid with his life; and now this powerful
other one arrives, this force for evil
1340 driven to avenge her kinsman's death.
Or so it seems to thanes in their grief,
in the anguish every thane endures
at the loss of a ring-giver, now that the hand
that bestowed so richly has been stilled in death.
1345   "I have heard it said by my people in hall,
counselors who live in the upland country,
that they have seen two such creatures
prowling the moors, huge marauders
from some other world. One of these things,
1350 as far as anyone ever can discern,
looks like a woman; the other, warped
in the shape of a man, moves beyond the pale
bigger than any man, an unnatural birth
called Grendel by the country people
1355 in former days. They are fatherless creatures,
and their whole ancestry is hidden in a past
of demons and ghosts. They dwell apart
among wolves on the hills, on windswept crags
and treacherous keshes, where cold streams
1360 pour down the mountain and disappear
under mist and moorland.
                              A few miles from here
a frost-stiffened wood waits and keeps watch
above a mere; the overhanging bank
is a maze of tree-roots mirrored in its surface.
1365 At night there, something uncanny happens:
the water burns. And the mere bottom
has never been sounded by the sons of men.
On its bank, the heather-stepper halts:
the hart in flight from pursuing hounds
1370 will turn to face them with firm-set horns
and die in the wood rather than dive
beneath its surface. That is no good place.
When wind blows up and stormy weather
makes clouds scud and the skies weep,
1375 out of its depths a dirty surge
is pitched toward the heavens. Now help depends
again on you and on you alone.
The gap of danger where the demon waits
is still unknown to you. Seek it if you dare.
1380 I will compensate you for settling the feud

as I did the last time with lavish wealth,
coffers of coiled gold, if you come back."

[BEOWULF FIGHTS GRENDEL'S MOTHER]

Beowulf, son of Ecgtheow, spoke:
"Wise sir, do not grieve. It is always better
1385 to avenge dear ones than to indulge in mourning.
For every one of us, living in this world
means waiting for our end. Let whoever can
win glory before death. When a warrior is gone,
that will be his best and only bulwark.
1390 So arise, my lord, and let us immediately
set forth on the trail of this troll-dam.
I guarantee you: she will not get away,
not to dens under ground nor upland groves
nor the ocean floor. She'll have nowhere to flee to.
1395 Endure your troubles today. Bear up
and be the man I expect you to be."
    With that the old lord sprang to his feet
and praised God for Beowulf's pledge.
Then a bit and halter were brought for his horse
1400 with the plaited mane. The wise king mounted
the royal saddle and rode out in style
with a force of shield-bearers. The forest paths
were marked all over with the monster's tracks,
her trail on the ground wherever she had gone
1405 across the dark moors, dragging away
the body of that thane, Hrothgar's best
counselor and overseer of the country.
So the noble prince proceeded undismayed
up fells and screes, along narrow footpaths
1410 and ways where they were forced into single file,
ledges on cliffs above lairs of water-monsters.
He went in front with a few men,
good judges of the lie of the land,
and suddenly discovered the dismal wood,
1415 mountain trees growing out at an angle
above gray stones: the bloodshot water
surged underneath. It was a sore blow
to all of the Danes, friends of the Shieldings,
a hurt to each and every one
1420 of that noble company when they came upon
Aeschere's head at the foot of the cliff.
    Everybody gazed as the hot gore
kept wallowing up and an urgent war-horn
repeated its notes: the whole party
1425 sat down to watch. The water was infested
with all kinds of reptiles. There were writhing sea-dragons
and monsters slouching on slopes by the cliff,
serpents and wild things such as those that often
surface at dawn to roam the sail-road

1430 and doom the voyage. Down they plunged,
lashing in anger at the loud call
of the battle-bugle. An arrow from the bow
of the Geat chief got one of them
as he surged to the surface: the seasoned shaft
1435 stuck deep in his flank and his freedom in the water
got less and less. It was his last swim.
He was swiftly overwhelmed in the shallows,
prodded by barbed boar-spears,
cornered, beaten, pulled up on the bank,
1440 a strange lake-birth, a loathsome catch
men gazed at in awe.
                          Beowulf got ready,
donned his war-gear, indifferent to death;
his mighty, hand-forged, fine-webbed mail
would soon meet with the menace underwater.
1445 It would keep the bone-cage of his body safe:
no enemy's clasp could crush him in it,
no vicious armlock choke his life out.
To guard his head he had a glittering helmet
that was due to be muddied on the mere bottom
1450 and blurred in the upswirl. It was of beaten gold,
princely headgear hooped and hasped
by a weapon-smith who had worked wonders
in days gone by and adorned it with boar-shapes;
since then it had resisted every sword.
1455 And another item lent by Unferth
at that moment of need was of no small importance:
the brehon[4] handed him a hilted weapon,
a rare and ancient sword named Hrunting.
The iron blade with its ill-boding patterns
1460 had been tempered in blood. It had never failed
the hand of anyone who hefted it in battle,
anyone who had fought and faced the worst
in the gap of danger. This was not the first time
it had been called to perform heroic feats.
1465   When he lent that blade to the better swordsman,
Unferth, the strong-built son of Ecglaf,
could hardly have remembered the ranting speech
he had made in his cups. He was not man enough
to face the turmoil of a fight under water
1470 and the risk to his life. So there he lost
fame and repute. It was different for the other
rigged out in his gear, ready to do battle.
    Beowulf, son of Ecgtheow, spoke:
"Wisest of kings, now that I have come
1475 to the point of action, I ask you to recall
what we said earlier: that you, son of Halfdane
and gold-friend to retainers, that you, if I should fall

---

4. One of an ancient class of lawyers in Ireland [Translator's note]. The Old English word for Unferth's office, *thyle*, has been interpreted as "orator" and "spokesman."

and suffer death while serving your cause,
would act like a father to me afterward.
1480 If this combat kills me, take care
of my young company, my comrades in arms.
And be sure also, my beloved Hrothgar,
to send Hygelac the treasures I received.
Let the lord of the Geats gaze on that gold,
1485 let Hrethel's son take note of it and see
that I found a ring-giver of rare magnificence
and enjoyed the good of his generosity.
And Unferth is to have what I inherited:
to that far-famed man I bequeath my own
1490 sharp-honed, wave-sheened wonder-blade.
With Hrunting I shall gain glory or die."
　　After these words, the prince of the Weather-Geats
was impatient to be away and plunged suddenly:
without more ado, he dived into the heaving
1495 depths of the lake. It was the best part of a day
before he could see the solid bottom.
　　Quickly the one who haunted those waters,
who had scavenged and gone her gluttonous rounds
for a hundred seasons, sensed a human
1500 observing her outlandish lair from above.
So she lunged and clutched and managed to catch him
in her brutal grip; but his body, for all that,
remained unscathed: the mesh of the chain-mail
saved him on the outside. Her savage talons
1505 failed to rip the web of his war-shirt.
Then once she touched bottom, that wolfish swimmer
carried the ring-mailed prince to her court
so that for all his courage he could never use
the weapons he carried; and a bewildering horde
1510 came at him from the depths, droves of sea-beasts
who attacked with tusks and tore at his chain-mail
in a ghastly onslaught. The gallant man
could see he had entered some hellish turn-hole
and yet the water there did not work against him
1515 because the hall-roofing held off
the force of the current; then he saw firelight,
a gleam and flare-up, a glimmer of brightness.
　　The hero observed that swamp-thing from hell,
the tarn-hag in all her terrible strength,
1520 then heaved his war-sword and swung his arm:
the decorated blade came down ringing
and singing on her head. But he soon found
his battle-torch extinguished; the shining blade
refused to bite. It spared her and failed
1525 the man in his need. It had gone through many
hand-to-hand fights, had hewed the armor
and helmets of the doomed, but here at last
the fabulous powers of that heirloom failed.
　　Hygelac's kinsman kept thinking about

1530 his name and fame: he never lost heart.
Then, in a fury, he flung his sword away.
The keen, inlaid, worm-loop-patterned steel
was hurled to the ground: he would have to rely
on the might of his arm. So must a man do
1535 who intends to gain enduring glory
in a combat. Life doesn't cost him a thought.
Then the prince of War-Geats, warming to this fight
with Grendel's mother, gripped her shoulder
and laid about him in a battle frenzy:
1540 he pitched his killer opponent to the floor
but she rose quickly and retaliated,
grappled him tightly in her grim embrace.
The sure-footed fighter felt daunted,
the strongest of warriors stumbled and fell.
1545 So she pounced upon him and pulled out
a broad, whetted knife: now she would avenge
her only child. But the mesh of chain-mail
on Beowulf's shoulder shielded his life,
turned the edge and tip of the blade.
1550 The son of Ecgtheow would have surely perished
and the Geats lost their warrior under the wide earth
had the strong links and locks of his war-gear
not helped to save him: holy God
decided the victory. It was easy for the Lord,
1555 the Ruler of Heaven, to redress the balance
once Beowulf got back up on his feet.
    Then he saw a blade that boded well,
a sword in her armory, an ancient heirloom
from the days of the giants, an ideal weapon,
1560 one that any warrior would envy,
but so huge and heavy of itself
only Beowulf could wield it in a battle.
So the Shieldings' hero hard-pressed and enraged,
took a firm hold of the hilt and swung
1565 the blade in an arc, a resolute blow
that bit deep into her neck-bone
and severed it entirely, toppling the doomed
house of her flesh; she fell to the floor.
The sword dripped blood, the swordsman was elated.
1570   A light appeared and the place brightened
the way the sky does when heaven's candle
is shining clearly. He inspected the vault:
with sword held high, its hilt raised
to guard and threaten, Hygelac's thane
1575 scouted by the wall in Grendel's wake.
Now the weapon was to prove its worth.
The warrior determined to take revenge
for every gross act Grendel had committed—
and not only for that one occasion
1580 when he'd come to slaughter the sleeping troops,
fifteen of Hrothgar's house-guards

surprised on their benches and ruthlessly devoured,
and as many again carried away,
a brutal plunder. Beowulf in his fury
1585   now settled that score: he saw the monster
in his resting place, war-weary and wrecked,
a lifeless corpse, a casualty
of the battle in Heorot. The body gaped
at the stroke dealt to it after death:
1590   Beowulf cut the corpse's head off.
    Immediately the counselors keeping a lookout
with Hrothgar, watching the lake water,
saw a heave-up and surge of waves
and blood in the backwash. They bowed gray heads,
1595   spoke in their sage, experienced way
about the good warrior, how they never again
expected to see that prince returning
in triumph to their king. It was clear to many
that the wolf of the deep had destroyed him forever.
1600   The ninth hour of the day arrived.
The brave Shieldings abandoned the cliff-top
and the king went home; but sick at heart,
staring at the mere, the strangers held on.
They wished, without hope, to behold their lord,
Beowulf himself.
1605   Meanwhile, the sword
began to wilt into gory icicles
to slather and thaw. It was a wonderful thing,
the way it all melted as ice melts
when the Father eases the fetters off the frost
1610   and unravels the water-ropes, He who wields power
over time and tide: He is the true Lord.
    The Geat captain saw treasure in abundance
but carried no spoils from those quarters
except for the head and the inlaid hilt
1615   embossed with jewels; its blade had melted
and the scrollwork on it burned, so scalding was the blood
of the poisonous fiend who had perished there.
Then away he swam, the one who had survived
the fall of his enemies, flailing to the surface.
1620   The wide water, the waves and pools,
were no longer infested once the wandering fiend
let go of her life and this unreliable world.
    The seafarers' leader made for land,
resolutely swimming, delighted with his prize,
1625   the mighty load he was lugging to the surface.
His thanes advanced in a troop to meet him,
thanking God and taking great delight
in seeing their prince back safe and sound.
Quickly the hero's helmet and mail-shirt
1630   were loosed and unlaced. The lake settled,
clouds darkened above the bloodshot depths.
    With high hearts they headed away

along footpaths and trails through the fields,
roads that they knew, each of them wrestling
1635   with the head they were carrying from the lakeside cliff,
men kingly in their courage and capable
of difficult work. It was a task for four
to hoist Grendel's head on a spear
and bear it under strain to the bright hall.
1640   But soon enough they neared the place,
fourteen Geats in fine fettle,
striding across the outlying ground
in a delighted throng around their leader.
     In he came then, the thanes' commander,
1645   the arch-warrior, to address Hrothgar:
his courage was proven, his glory was secure.
Grendel's head was hauled by the hair,
dragged across the floor where the people were drinking,
a horror for both queen and company to behold.
1650   They stared in awe. It was an astonishing sight.

[ANOTHER CELEBRATION AT HEOROT]

     Beowulf, son of Ecgtheow, spoke:
"So, son of Halfdane, prince of the Shieldings,
we are glad to bring this booty from the lake.
It is a token of triumph and we tender it to you.
1655   I barely survived the battle under water.
It was hard-fought, a desperate affair
that could have gone badly; if God had not helped me,
the outcome would have been quick and fatal.
Although Hrunting is hard-edged,
1660   I could never bring it to bear in battle.
But the Lord of Men allowed me to behold—
for He often helps the unbefriended—
an ancient sword shining on the wall,
a weapon made for giants, there for the wielding.
1665   Then my moment came in the combat and I struck
the dwellers in that den. Next thing the damascened
sword blade melted; it bloated and it burned
in their rushing blood. I have wrested the hilt
from the enemy's hand, avenged the evil
1670   done to the Danes; it is what was due.
And this I pledge, O prince of the Shieldings:
you can sleep secure with your company of troops
in Heorot Hall. Never need you fear
for a single thane of your sept or nation,
1675   young warriors or old, that laying waste of life
that you and your people endured of yore."
     Then the gold hilt was handed over
to the old lord, a relic from long ago
for the venerable ruler. That rare smithwork
1680   was passed on to the prince of the Danes
when those devils perished; once death removed

that murdering, guilt-steeped, God-cursed fiend,
eliminating his unholy life
and his mother's as well, it was willed to that king
1685   who of all the lavish gift-lords of the north
was the best regarded between the two seas.
    Hrothgar spoke; he examined the hilt,
that relic of old times. It was engraved all over
and showed how war first came into the world
1690   and the flood destroyed the tribe of giants.
They suffered a terrible severance from the Lord;
the Almighty made the waters rise,
drowned them in the deluge for retribution.
In pure gold inlay on the sword-guards
1695   there were rune-markings correctly incised,
stating and recording for whom the sword
had been first made and ornamented
with its scrollworked hilt. Then everyone hushed
as the son of Halfdane spoke this wisdom:
1700   "A protector of his people, pledged to uphold
truth and justice and to respect tradition,
is entitled to affirm that this man
was born to distinction. Beowulf, my friend,
your fame has gone far and wide,
1705   you are known everywhere. In all things you are even-tempered,
prudent and resolute. So I stand firm by the promise of friendship
we exchanged before. Forever you will be
your people's mainstay and your own warriors'
helping hand.
                Heremod was different,
1710   the way he behaved to Ecgwela's sons.
His rise in the world brought little joy
to the Danish people, only death and destruction.
He vented his rage on men he caroused with,
killed his own comrades, a pariah king
1715   who cut himself off from his own kind,
even though Almighty God had made him
eminent and powerful and marked him from the start
for a happy life. But a change happened,
he grew bloodthirsty, gave no more rings
1720   to honor the Danes. He suffered in the end
for having plagued his people for so long:
his life lost happiness.
                So learn from this
and understand true values. I who tell you
have wintered into wisdom.
                It is a great wonder
1725   how Almighty God in His magnificence
favors our race with rank and scope
and the gift of wisdom; His sway is wide.
Sometimes He allows the mind of a man
of distinguished birth to follow its bent,
1730   grants him fulfillment and felicity on earth

and forts to command in his own country.
He permits him to lord it in many lands
until the man in his unthinkingness
forgets that it will ever end for him.
1735 He indulges his desires; illness and old age
mean nothing to him; his mind is untroubled
by envy or malice or the thought of enemies
with their hate-honed swords. The whole world
conforms to his will, he is kept from the worst
1740 until an element of overweening
enters him and takes hold
while the soul's guard, its sentry, drowses,
grown too distracted. A killer stalks him,
an archer who draws a deadly bow.
1745 And then the man is hit in the heart,
the arrow flies beneath his defenses,
the devious promptings of the demon start.
His old possessions seem paltry to him now.
He covets and resents; dishonors custom
1750 and bestows no gold; and because of good things
that the Heavenly Powers gave him in the past
he ignores the shape of things to come.
Then finally the end arrives
when the body he was lent collapses and falls
1755 prey to its death; ancestral possessions
and the goods he hoarded are inherited by another
who lets them go with a liberal hand.
    "O flower of warriors, beware of that trap.
Choose, dear Beowulf, the better part,
1760 eternal rewards. Do not give way to pride.
For a brief while your strength is in bloom
but it fades quickly; and soon there will follow
illness or the sword to lay you low,
or a sudden fire or surge of water
1765 or jabbing blade or javelin from the air
or repellent age. Your piercing eye
will dim and darken; and death will arrive,
dear warrior, to sweep you away.
    "Just so I ruled the Ring-Danes' country
1770 for fifty years, defended them in wartime
with spear and sword against constant assaults
by many tribes: I came to believe
my enemies had faded from the face of the earth.
Still, what happened was a hard reversal
1775 from bliss to grief. Grendel struck
after lying in wait. He laid waste to the land
and from that moment my mind was in dread
of his depredations. So I praise God
in His heavenly glory that I lived to behold
1780 this head dripping blood and that after such harrowing
I can look upon it in triumph at last.
Take your place, then, with pride and pleasure,

and move to the feast. Tomorrow morning
our treasure will be shared and showered upon you."
1785   The Geat was elated and gladly obeyed
the old man's bidding; he sat on the bench.
And soon all was restored, the same as before.
Happiness came back, the hall was thronged,
and a banquet set forth; black night fell
1790   and covered them in darkness.
                          Then the company rose
for the old campaigner: the gray-haired prince
was ready for bed. And a need for rest
came over the brave shield-bearing Geat.
He was a weary seafarer, far from home,
1795   so immediately a house-guard guided him out,
one whose office entailed looking after
whatever a thane on the road in those days
might need or require. It was noble courtesy.

[BEOWULF RETURNS HOME]

    That great heart rested. The hall towered,
1800   gold-shingled and gabled, and the guest slept in it
until the black raven with raucous glee
announced heaven's joy, and a hurry of brightness
overran the shadows. Warriors rose quickly,
impatient to be off: their own country
1805   was beckoning the nobles; and the bold voyager
longed to be aboard his distant boat.
Then that stalwart fighter ordered Hrunting
to be brought to Unferth, and bade Unferth
take the sword and thanked him for lending it.
1810   He said he had found it a friend in battle
and a powerful help; he put no blame
on the blade's cutting edge. He was a considerate man.
    And there the warriors stood in their war-gear,
eager to go, while their honored lord
1815   approached the platform where the other sat.
The undaunted hero addressed Hrothgar.
Beowulf, son of Ecgtheow, spoke:
"Now we who crossed the wide sea
have to inform you that we feel a desire
1820   to return to Hygelac. Here we have been welcomed
and thoroughly entertained. You have treated us well.
If there is any favor on earth I can perform
beyond deeds of arms I have done already,
anything that would merit your affections more,
1825   I shall act, my lord, with alacrity.
If ever I hear from across the ocean
that people on your borders are threatening battle
as attackers have done from time to time,
I shall land with a thousand thanes at my back
1830   to help your cause. Hygelac may be young

to rule a nation, but this much I know
about the king of the Geats: he will come to my aid
and want to support me by word and action
in your hour of need, when honor dictates
1835   that I raise a hedge of spears around you.
Then if Hrethric should think about traveling
as a king's son to the court of the Geats,
he will find many friends. Foreign places
yield more to one who is himself worth meeting."
1840   Hrothgar spoke and answered him:
"The Lord in his wisdom sent you those words
and they came from the heart. I have never heard
so young a man make truer observations.
You are strong in body and mature in mind,
1845   impressive in speech. If it should come to pass
that Hrethel's descendant dies beneath a spear,
if deadly battle or the sword blade or disease
fells the prince who guards your people
and you are still alive, then I firmly believe
1850   the seafaring Geats won't find a man
worthier of acclaim as their king and defender
than you, if only you would undertake
the lordship of your homeland. My liking for you
deepens with time, dear Beowulf.
1855   What you have done is to draw two peoples,
the Geat nation and us neighboring Danes,
into shared peace and a pact of friendship
in spite of hatreds we have harbored in the past.
For as long as I rule this far-flung land
1860   treasures will change hands and each side will treat
the other with gifts; across the gannet's bath,
over the broad sea, whorled prows will bring
presents and tokens. I know your people
are beyond reproach in every respect,
1865   steadfast in the old way with friend or foe."
    Then the earls' defender furnished the hero
with twelve treasures and told him to set out,
sail with those gifts safely home
to the people he loved, but to return promptly.
1870   And so the good and gray-haired Dane,
that highborn king, kissed Beowulf
and embraced his neck, then broke down
in sudden tears. Two forebodings
disturbed him in his wisdom, but one was stronger:
1875   nevermore would they meet each other
face to face. And such was his affection
that he could not help being overcome:
his fondness for the man was so deep-founded,
it warmed his heart and wound the heartstrings
1880   tight in his breast.
            The embrace ended
and Beowulf, glorious in his gold regalia,

stepped the green earth. Straining at anchor
and ready for boarding, his boat awaited him.
So they went on their journey, and Hrothgar's generosity
1885 was praised repeatedly. He was a peerless king
until old age sapped his strength and did him
mortal harm, as it has done so many.

Down to the waves then, dressed in the web
of their chain-mail and war-shirts the young men marched
1890 in high spirits. The coast-guard spied them,
thanes setting forth, the same as before.
His salute this time from the top of the cliff
was far from unmannerly; he galloped to meet them
and as they took ship in their shining gear,
1895 he said how welcome they would be in Geatland.
Then the broad hull was beached on the sand
to be cargoed with treasure, horses and war-gear.
The curved prow motioned; the mast stood high
above Hrothgar's riches in the loaded hold.
1900 The guard who had watched the boat was given
a sword with gold fittings, and in future days
that present would make him a respected man
at his place on the mead-bench.
Then the keel plunged
and shook in the sea; and they sailed from Denmark.
1905 Right away the mast was rigged with its sea-shawl;
sail-ropes were tightened, timbers drummed
and stiff winds kept the wave-crosser
skimming ahead; as she heaved forward,
her foamy neck was fleet and buoyant,
1910 a lapped prow loping over currents,
until finally the Geats caught sight of coastline
and familiar cliffs. The keel reared up,
wind lifted it home, it hit on the land.
The harbor guard came hurrying out
1915 to the rolling water: he had watched the offing
long and hard, on the lookout for those friends.
With the anchor cables, he moored their craft
right where it had beached, in case a backwash
might catch the hull and carry it away.
1920 Then he ordered the prince's treasure-trove
to be carried ashore. It was a short step
from there to where Hrethel's son and heir,
Hygelac the gold-giver, makes his home
on a secure cliff, in the company of retainers.
1925 The building was magnificent, the king majestic,
ensconced in his hall; and although Hygd, his queen,
was young, a few short years at court,
her mind was thoughtful and her manners sure.
Haereth's daughter behaved generously
1930 and stinted nothing when she distributed
bounty to the Geats.
Great Queen Modthryth

perpetrated terrible wrongs.[5]
If any retainer ever made bold
to look her in the face, if an eye not her lord's[6]
1935   stared at her directly during daylight,
the outcome was sealed: he was kept bound,
in hand-tightened shackles, racked, tortured
until doom was pronounced—death by the sword,
slash of blade, blood-gush, and death-qualms
1940   in an evil display. Even a queen
outstanding in beauty must not overstep like that.
A queen should weave peace, not punish the innocent
with loss of life for imagined insults.
But Hemming's kinsman[7] put a halt to her ways
1945   and drinkers round the table had another tale:
she was less of a bane to people's lives,
less cruel-minded, after she was married
to the brave Offa, a bride arrayed
in her gold finery, given away
1950   by a caring father, ferried to her young prince
over dim seas. In days to come
she would grace the throne and grow famous
for her good deeds and conduct of life,
her high devotion to the hero king
1955   who was the best king, it has been said,
between the two seas or anywhere else
on the face of the earth. Offa was honored
far and wide for his generous ways,
his fighting spirit and his farseeing
1960   defense of his homeland; from him there sprang Eomer,
Garmund's grandson, kinsman of Hemming,[8]
his warriors' mainstay and master of the field.
    Heroic Beowulf and his band of men
crossed the wide strand, striding along
1965   the sandy foreshore; the sun shone,
the world's candle warmed them from the south
as they hastened to where, as they had heard,
the young king, Ongentheow's killer
and his people's protector,[9] was dispensing rings
1970   inside his bawn. Beowulf's return
was reported to Hygelac as soon as possible,

---

5. The story of Queen Modthryth's vices is abruptly introduced as a foil to Queen Hygd's virtues. A transitional passage may have been lost, but the poet's device is similar to that of using the earlier reference to the wickedness of King Heremod to contrast with the good qualities of Sigemund and Beowulf.

6. This could refer to her husband or her father before her marriage. The story resembles folktales about a proud princess whose unsuccessful suitors are all put to death, although the unfortunate victims in this case seem to be guilty only of looking at her.

7. I.e., Offa I, a legendary king of the Angles. We know nothing about Hemming other than that

Offa was related to him. Offa II (757–96) was king of Mercia, and although the story is about the second Offa's ancestor on the Continent, this is the only English connection in the poem and has been taken as evidence to date its origins to 8th-century Mercia.

8. I.e., Eomer, Offa's son. See previous note. Garmund was presumably the name of Offa's father.

9. I.e., Hygelac. Ongentheow was king of the Swedish people called the Shylfings. This is the first of the references to wars between the Geats and the Swedes. One of Hygelac's war party named Eofer was the actual slayer of Ongentheow.

news that the captain was now in the enclosure,
his battle-brother back from the fray
alive and well, walking to the hall.
1975 Room was quickly made, on the king's orders,
and the troops filed across the cleared floor.
 After Hygelac had offered greetings
to his loyal thane in a lofty speech,
he and his kinsman, that hale survivor,
1980 sat face to face. Haereth's daughter
moved about with the mead-jug in her hand,
taking care of the company, filling the cups
that warriors held out. Then Hygelac began
to put courteous questions to his old comrade
1985 in the high hall. He hankered to know
every tale the Sea-Geats had to tell:
"How did you fare on your foreign voyage,
dear Beowulf, when you abruptly decided
to sail away across the salt water
1990 and fight at Heorot? Did you help Hrothgar
much in the end? Could you ease the prince
of his well-known troubles? Your undertaking
cast my spirits down, I dreaded the outcome
of your expedition and pleaded with you
1995 long and hard to leave the killer be,
let the South-Danes settle their own
blood-feud with Grendel. So God be thanked
I am granted this sight of you, safe and sound."
 Beowulf, son of Ecgtheow, spoke:
2000 "What happened, Lord Hygelac, is hardly a secret
any more among men in this world—
myself and Grendel coming to grips
on the very spot where he visited destruction
on the Victory-Shieldings and violated
2005 life and limb, losses I avenged
so no earthly offspring of Grendel's
need ever boast of that bout before dawn,
no matter how long the last of his evil
family survives.
 When I first landed
2010 I hastened to the ring-hall and saluted Hrothgar.
Once he discovered why I had come,
the son of Halfdane sent me immediately
to sit with his own sons on the bench.
It was a happy gathering. In my whole life
2015 I have never seen mead enjoyed more
in any hall on earth. Sometimes the queen
herself appeared, peace-pledge between nations,
to hearten the young ones and hand out
a torque to a warrior, then take her place.
2020 Sometimes Hrothgar's daughter distributed
ale to older ranks, in order on the benches:
I heard the company call her Freawaru

as she made her rounds, presenting men
with the gem-studded bowl, young bride-to-be
2025   to the gracious Ingeld,[1] in her gold-trimmed attire.
The friend of the Shieldings favors her betrothal:
the guardian of the kingdom sees good in it
and hopes this woman will heal old wounds
and grievous feuds.   But generally the spear
2030   is prompt to retaliate when a prince is killed,
no matter how admirable the bride may be.
     "Think how the Heatho-Bards are bound to feel,
their lord, Ingeld, and his loyal thanes,
when he walks in with that woman to the feast:
2035   Danes are at the table, being entertained,
honored guests in glittering regalia,
burnished ring-mail that was their hosts' birthright,
looted when the Heatho-Bards could no longer wield
their weapons in the shield-clash, when they went down
2040   with their beloved comrades and forfeited their lives.
Then an old spearman will speak while they are drinking,
having glimpsed some heirloom that brings alive
memories of the massacre; his mood will darken
and heart-stricken, in the stress of his emotion,
2045   he will begin to test a young man's temper
and stir up trouble, starting like this:
'Now, my friend, don't you recognize
your father's sword, his favorite weapon,
the one he wore when he went out in his war-mask
2050   to face the Danes on that final day?
After Withergeld[2] died and his men were doomed,
the Shieldings quickly claimed the field;
and now here's a son of one or other
of those same killers coming through our hall
2055   overbearing us, mouthing boasts,
and rigged in armor that by right is yours.'
And so he keeps on, recalling and accusing,
working things up with bitter words
until one of the lady's retainers lies
2060   spattered in blood, split open
on his father's account.[3] The killer knows
the lie of the land and escapes with his life.
Then on both sides the oath-bound lords
will break the peace, a passionate hate
2065   will build up in Ingeld, and love for his bride
will falter in him as the feud rankles.
I therefore suspect the good faith of the Heatho-Bards,
the truth of their friendship and the trustworthiness

---

1. King of the Heatho-Bards; his father, Froda, was killed by the Danes.
2. One of the Heatho-Bard leaders.
3. I.e., the young Danish attendant is killed because his father killed the father of the young Heatho-Bard who has been egged on by the old veteran of that campaign.

of their alliance with the Danes.

                            But now, my lord,

2070 I shall carry on with my account of Grendel,
the whole story of everything that happened
in the hand-to-hand fight.

                        After heaven's gem
had gone mildly to earth, that maddened spirit,
the terror of those twilights, came to attack us
2075 where we stood guard, still safe inside the hall.
There deadly violence came down on Hondscio
and he fell as fate ordained, the first to perish,
rigged out for the combat. A comrade from our ranks
had come to grief in Grendel's maw:
2080 he ate up the entire body.
There was blood on his teeth, he was bloated and furious,
all roused up, yet still unready
to leave the hall empty-handed;
renowned for his might, he matched himself against me,
2085 wildly reaching. He had this roomy pouch,
a strange accoutrement, intricately strung
and hung at the ready, a rare patchwork
of devilishly fitted dragon-skins.
I had done him no wrong, yet the raging demon
2090 wanted to cram me and many another
into this bag—but it was not to be
once I got to my feet in a blind fury.
It would take too long to tell how I repaid
the terror of the land for every life he took
2095 and so won credit for you, my king,
and for all your people. And although he got away
to enjoy life's sweetness for a while longer,
his right hand stayed behind him in Heorot,
evidence of his miserable overthrow
2100 as he dived into murk on the mere bottom.
    "I got lavish rewards from the lord of the Danes
for my part in the battle, beaten gold
and much else, once morning came
and we took our places at the banquet table.
2105 There was singing and excitement: an old reciter,
a carrier of stories, recalled the early days.
At times some hero made the timbered harp
tremble with sweetness, or related true
and tragic happenings; at times the king
2110 gave the proper turn to some fantastic tale;
or a battle-scarred veteran, bowed with age,
would begin to remember the martial deeds
of his youth and prime and be overcome
as the past welled up in his wintry heart.
2115   "We were happy there the whole day long
and enjoyed our time until another night
descended upon us. Then suddenly
the vehement mother avenged her son

and wreaked destruction. Death had robbed her,
2120 Geats had slain Grendel, so his ghastly dam
struck back and with bare-faced defiance
laid a man low. Thus life departed
from the sage Aeschere, an elder wise in counsel.
But afterward, on the morning following,
2125 the Danes could not burn the dead body
nor lay the remains of the man they loved
on his funeral pyre. She had fled with the corpse
and taken refuge beneath torrents on the mountain.
It was a hard blow for Hrothgar to bear,
2130 harder than any he had undergone before.
And so the heartsore king beseeched me
in your royal name to take my chances
underwater, to win glory
and prove my worth. He promised me rewards.
2135 Hence, as is well known, I went to my encounter
with the terror-monger at the bottom of the tarn.
For a while it was hand-to-hand between us,
then blood went curling along the currents
and I beheaded Grendel's mother in the hall
2140 with a mighty sword. I barely managed
to escape with my life; my time had not yet come.
But Halfdane's heir, the shelter of those earls,
again endowed me with gifts in abundance.
   "Thus the king acted with due custom.
2145 I was paid and recompensed completely,
given full measure and the freedom to choose
from Hrothgar's treasures by Hrothgar himself.
These, King Hygelac, I am happy to present
to you as gifts. It is still upon your grace
2150 that all favor depends. I have few kinsmen
who are close, my king, except for your kind self."
Then he ordered the boar-framed standard to be brought,
the battle-topping helmet, the mail-shirt gray as hoar-frost,
and the precious war-sword; and proceeded with his speech:
2155   "When Hrothgar presented this war-gear to me
he instructed me, my lord, to give you some account
of why it signifies his special favor.
He said it had belonged to his older brother,
King Heorogar, who had long kept it,
2160 but that Heorogar had never bequeathed it
to his son Heoroward, that worthy scion,
loyal as he was. Enjoy it well."
   I heard four horses were handed over next.
Beowulf bestowed four bay steeds
2165 to go with the armor, swift gallopers,
all alike. So ought a kinsman act,
instead of plotting and planning in secret
to bring people to grief, or conspiring to arrange
the death of comrades. The warrior king
2170 was uncle to Beowulf and honored by his nephew:

each was concerned for the other's good.
　　I heard he presented Hygd with a gorget,
the priceless torque that the prince's daughter,
Wealhtheow, had given him; and three horses,
2175　supple creatures brilliantly saddled.
The bright necklace would be luminous on Hygd's breast.
　　Thus Beowulf bore himself with valor;
he was formidable in battle yet behaved with honor
and took no advantage; never cut down
2180　a comrade who was drunk, kept his temper
and, warrior that he was, watched and controlled
his God-sent strength and his outstanding
natural powers. He had been poorly regarded
for a long time, was taken by the Geats
2185　for less than he was worth:[4] and their lord too
had never much esteemed him in the mead-hall.
They firmly believed that he lacked force,
that the prince was a weakling; but presently
every affront to his deserving was reversed.
2190　　The battle-famed king, bulwark of his earls,
ordered a gold-chased heirloom of Hrethel's[5]
to be brought in; it was the best example
of a gem-studded sword in the Geat treasury.
This he laid on Beowulf's lap
2195　and then rewarded him with land as well,
seven thousand hides; and a hall and a throne.
Both owned land by birth in that country,
ancestral grounds; but the greater right
and sway were inherited by the higher born.

[THE DRAGON WAKES]

2200　A lot was to happen in later days
in the fury of battle. Hygelac fell
and the shelter of Heardred's shield proved useless
against the fierce aggression of the Shylfings:[6]
ruthless swordsmen, seasoned campaigners,
2205　they came against him and his conquering nation,
and with cruel force cut him down

---

4. There is no other mention of Beowulf's unpromising youth. This motif of the "Cinderella hero" and others, such as Grendel's magic pouch, are examples of folklore material, probably circulating orally, that made its way into the poem.
5. Hygelac's father and Beowulf's grandfather.
6. There are several references, some of them lengthy, to the wars between the Geats and the Swedes. Because these are highly allusive and not in chronological order, they are difficult to follow and keep straight. This outline, along with the Genealogies (pp. 40–41), may serve as a guide. *Phase 1*: After the death of the Geat patriarch, King Hrethel (lines 2462–70), Ohthere and Onela, the sons of the Swedish king Ongentheow, invade Geat territory and inflict heavy casualties in a battle at Hreosnahill (lines 2472–78). *Phase 2*: The Geats invade Sweden under Haethcyn, King Hrethel's son who

has succeeded him. At the battle of Ravenswood, the Geats capture Ongentheow's queen, but Ongentheow counterattacks, rescues the queen, and kills Haethcyn. Hygelac, Haethcyn's younger brother, arrives with reinforcements; Ongentheow is killed in savage combat with two of Hygelac's men; and the Swedes are routed (lines 2479–89 and 2922–90). *Phase 3*: Eanmund and Eadgils, the sons of Ohthere (presumably dead), are driven into exile by their uncle Onela, who is now king of the Swedes. They are given refuge by Hygelac's son Heardred, who has succeeded his father. Onela invades Geatland and kills Heardred; his retainer Weohstan kills Eanmund; and after the Swedes withdraw, Beowulf becomes king (lines 2204–8, which follow, and 2379–90). *Phase 4*: Eadgils, supported by Beowulf, invades Sweden and kills Onela (lines 2391–96).

so that afterwards
                                    the wide kingdom
reverted to Beowulf. He ruled it well
for fifty winters, grew old and wise
2210   as warden of the land
                                    until one began
to dominate the dark, a dragon on the prowl
from the steep vaults of a stone-roofed barrow
where he guarded a hoard; there was a hidden passage,
unknown to men, but someone[7] managed
2215   to enter by it and interfere
with the heathen trove. He had handled and removed
a gem-studded goblet; it gained him nothing,
though with a thief's wiles he had outwitted
the sleeping dragon. That drove him into rage,
2220   as the people of that country would soon discover.
       The intruder who broached the dragon's treasure
and moved him to wrath had never meant to.
It was desperation on the part of a slave
fleeing the heavy hand of some master,
2225   guilt-ridden and on the run,
going to ground. But he soon began
to shake with terror;[8] . . . . . . in shock
the wretch . . . .
. . . . panicked and ran
2230   away with the precious . . . . . .
metalwork. There were many other
heirlooms heaped inside the earth-house,
because long ago, with deliberate care,
some forgotten person had deposited the whole
2235   rich inheritance of a highborn race
in this ancient cache. Death had come
and taken them all in times gone by
and the only one left to tell their tale,
the last of their line, could look forward to nothing
2240   but the same fate for himself: he foresaw that his joy
in the treasure would be brief.
                                    A newly constructed
barrow stood waiting, on a wide headland
close to the waves, its entryway secured.
Into it the keeper of the hoard had carried
2245   all the goods and golden ware
worth preserving. His words were few:
"Now, earth, hold what earls once held
and heroes can no more; it was mined from you first
by honorable men. My own people
2250   have been ruined in war; one by one
they went down to death, looked their last

---

7. The following section was damaged by fire. In
lines 2215–31 entire words and phrases are
missing or indicated by only a few letters. Editorial attempts to reconstruct the text are conjectural and often disagree.
8. Lines 2227–30 are so damaged that they defy
guesswork to reconstruct them.

on sweet life in the hall. I am left with nobody
to bear a sword or to burnish plated goblets,
put a sheen on the cup. The companies have departed.
2255 The hard helmet, hasped with gold,
will be stripped of its hoops; and the helmet-shiner
who should polish the metal of the war-mask sleeps;
the coat of mail that came through all fights,
through shield-collapse and cut of sword,
2260 decays with the warrior. Nor may webbed mail
range far and wide on the warlord's back
beside his mustered troops. No trembling harp,
no tuned timber, no tumbling hawk
swerving through the hall, no swift horse
2265 pawing the courtyard. Pillage and slaughter
have emptied the earth of entire peoples."
And so he mourned as he moved about the world,
deserted and alone, lamenting his unhappiness
day and night, until death's flood
2270 brimmed up in his heart.
                  Then an old harrower of the dark
happened to find the hoard open,
the burning one who hunts out barrows,
the slick-skinned dragon, threatening the night sky
with streamers of fire. People on the farms
2275 are in dread of him. He is driven to hunt out
hoards under ground, to guard heathen gold
through age-long vigils, though to little avail.
For three centuries, this scourge of the people
had stood guard on that stoutly protected
2280 underground treasury, until the intruder
unleashed its fury; he hurried to his lord
with the gold-plated cup and made his plea
to be reinstated. Then the vault was rifled,
the ring-hoard robbed, and the wretched man
2285 had his request granted. His master gazed
on that find from the past for the first time.
    When the dragon awoke, trouble flared again.
He rippled down the rock, writhing with anger
when he saw the footprints of the prowler who had stolen
2290 too close to his dreaming head.
So may a man not marked by fate
easily escape exile and woe
by the grace of God.
                The hoard-guardian
scorched the ground as he scoured and hunted
2295 for the trespasser who had troubled his sleep.
Hot and savage, he kept circling and circling
the outside of the mound. No man appeared
in that desert waste, but he worked himself up
by imagining battle; then back in he'd go
2300 in search of the cup, only to discover
signs that someone had stumbled upon

the golden treasures. So the guardian of the mound,
the hoard-watcher, waited for the gloaming
with fierce impatience; his pent-up fury
2305 at the loss of the vessel made him long to hit back
and lash out in flames. Then, to his delight,
the day waned and he could wait no longer
behind the wall, but hurtled forth
in a fiery blaze. The first to suffer
2310 were the people on the land, but before long
it was their treasure-giver who would come to grief.

    The dragon began to belch out flames
and burn bright homesteads; there was a hot glow
that scared everyone, for the vile sky-winger
2315 would leave nothing alive in his wake.
Everywhere the havoc he wrought was in evidence.
Far and near, the Geat nation
bore the brunt of his brutal assaults
and virulent hate. Then back to the hoard
2320 he would dart before daybreak, to hide in his den.
He had swinged the land, swathed it in flame,
in fire and burning, and now he felt secure
in the vaults of his barrow; but his trust was unavailing.

    Then Beowulf was given bad news,
2325 the hard truth: his own home,
the best of buildings, had been burned to a cinder,
the throne-room of the Geats. It threw the hero
into deep anguish and darkened his mood:
the wise man thought he must have thwarted
2330 ancient ordinance of the eternal Lord,
broken His commandment. His mind was in turmoil,
unaccustomed anxiety and gloom
confused his brain; the fire-dragon
had razed the coastal region and reduced
2335 forts and earthworks to dust and ashes,
so the war-king planned and plotted his revenge.
The warriors' protector, prince of the hall-troop,
ordered a marvelous all-iron shield
from his smithy works. He well knew
2340 that linden boards would let him down
and timber burn. After many trials,
he was destined to face the end of his days,
in this mortal world, as was the dragon,
for all his long leasehold on the treasure.

2345   Yet the prince of the rings was too proud
to line up with a large army
against the sky-plague. He had scant regard
for the dragon as a threat, no dread at all
of its courage or strength, for he had kept going
2350 often in the past, through perils and ordeals
of every sort, after he had purged
Hrothgar's hall, triumphed in Heorot
and beaten Grendel. He outgrappled the monster

and his evil kin.
                              One of his crudest
2355   hand-to-hand encounters had happened
       when Hygelac, king of the Geats, was killed
       in Friesland: the people's friend and lord,
       Hrethel's son, slaked a swordblade's
       thirst for blood. But Beowulf's prodigious
2360   gifts as a swimmer guaranteed his safety:
       he arrived at the shore, shouldering thirty
       battle-dresses, the booty he had won.
       There was little for the Hetware[9] to be happy about
       as they shielded their faces and fighting on the ground
2365   began in earnest. With Beowulf against them,
       few could hope to return home.
           Across the wide sea, desolate and alone,
       the son of Ecgtheow swam back to his people.
       There Hygd offered him throne and authority
2370   as lord of the ring-hoard: with Hygelac dead,
       she had no belief in her son's ability
       to defend their homeland against foreign invaders.
       Yet there was no way the weakened nation
       could get Beowulf to give in and agree
2375   to be elevated over Heardred as his lord
       or to undertake the office of kingship.
       But he did provide support for the prince,
       honored and minded him until he matured
       as the ruler of Geatland.
                                  Then over sea-roads
2380   exiles arrived, sons of Ohthere.[1]
       They had rebelled against the best of all
       the sea-kings in Sweden, the one who held sway
       in the Shylfing nation, their renowned prince,
       lord of the mead-hall. That marked the end
2385   for Hygelac's son: his hospitality
       was mortally rewarded with wounds from a sword.
       Heardred lay slaughtered and Onela returned
       to the land of Sweden, leaving Beowulf
       to ascend the throne, to sit in majesty
2390   and rule over the Geats. He was a good king.
           In days to come, he contrived to avenge
       the fall of his prince; he befriended Eadgils
       when Eadgils was friendless, aiding his cause
       with weapons and warriors over the wide sea,
2395   sending him men. The feud was settled
       on a comfortless campaign when he killed Onela.
           And so the son of Ecgtheow had survived
       every extreme, excelling himself
       in daring and in danger, until the day arrived
2400   when he had to come face to face with the dragon.
       The lord of the Geats took eleven comrades

9. A tribe of the Franks allied with the Frisians.   1. See p. 89, n. 6, Phases 3 and 4.

and went in a rage to reconnoiter.
By then he had discovered the cause of the affliction
being visited on the people. The precious cup
2405 had come to him from the hand of the finder,
the one who had started all this strife
and was now added as a thirteenth to their number.
They press-ganged and compelled this poor creature
to be their guide. Against his will
2410 he led them to the earth-vault he alone knew,
an underground barrow near the sea-billows
and heaving waves, heaped inside
with exquisite metalwork. The one who stood guard
was dangerous and watchful, warden of the trove
2415 buried under earth: no easy bargain
would be made in that place by any man.
    The veteran king sat down on the cliff-top.
He wished good luck to the Geats who had shared
his hearth and his gold. He was sad at heart,
2420 unsettled yet ready, sensing his death.
His fate hovered near, unknowable but certain:
it would soon claim his coffered soul,
part life from limb. Before long
the prince's spirit would spin free from his body.
2425   Beowulf, son of Ecgtheow, spoke:
"Many a skirmish I survived when I was young
and many times of war: I remember them well.
At seven, I was fostered out by my father,
left in the charge of my people's lord.
2430 King Hrethel kept me and took care of me,
was openhanded, behaved like a kinsman.
While I was his ward, he treated me no worse
as a wean[2] about the place than one of his own boys,
Herebeald and Haethcyn, or my own Hygelac.
2435 For the eldest, Herebeald, an unexpected
deathbed was laid out, through a brother's doing,
when Haethcyn bent his horn-tipped bow
and loosed the arrow that destroyed his life.
He shot wide and buried a shaft
2440 in the flesh and blood of his own brother.
That offense was beyond redress; a wrongfooting
of the heart's affections; for who could avenge
the prince's life or pay his death-price?
It was like the misery endured by an old man
2445 who has lived to see his son's body
swing on the gallows. He begins to keen
and weep for his boy, watching the raven
gloat where he hangs: he can be of no help.
The wisdom of age is worthless to him.
2450 Morning after morning, he wakes to remember
that his child is gone; he has no interest

2. A young child [Northern Ireland; Translator's note].

in living on until another heir
is born in the hall, now that his first-born
has entered death's dominion forever.
2455 He gazes sorrowfully at his son's dwelling,
the banquet hall bereft of all delight,
the windswept hearthstone; the horsemen are sleeping,
the warriors under ground; what was is no more.
No tunes from the harp, no cheer raised in the yard.
2460 Alone with his longing, he lies down on his bed
and sings a lament; everything seems too large,
the steadings and the fields.
                                    Such was the feeling
of loss endured by the lord of the Geats
after Herebeald's death. He was helplessly placed
2465 to set to rights the wrong committed,
could not punish the killer in accordance with the law
of the blood-feud, although he felt no love for him.
Heartsore, wearied, he turned away
from life's joys, chose God's light
2470 and departed, leaving buildings and lands
to his sons, as a man of substance will.
    "Then over the wide sea Swedes and Geats
battled and feuded and fought without quarter.
Hostilities broke out when Hrethel died.[3]
2475 Ongentheow's sons were unrelenting,
refusing to make peace, campaigning violently
from coast to coast, constantly setting up
terrible ambushes around Hreosnahill.
My own kith and kin avenged
2480 these evil events, as everybody knows,
but the price was high: one of them paid
with his life. Haethcyn, lord of the Geats,
met his fate there and fell in the battle.
Then, as I have heard, Hygelac's sword
2485 was raised in the morning against Ongentheow,
his brother's killer. When Eofor cleft
the old Swede's helmet, halved it open,
he fell, death-pale: his feud-calloused hand
could not stave off the fatal stroke.
2490   "The treasures that Hygelac lavished on me
I paid for when I fought, as fortune allowed me,
with my glittering sword. He gave me land
and the security land brings, so he had no call
to go looking for some lesser champion,
2495 some mercenary from among the Gifthas
or the Spear-Danes or the men of Sweden.
I marched ahead of him, always there
at the front of the line; and I shall fight like that
for as long as I live, as long as this sword
2500 shall last, which has stood me in good stead

3. See p. 89, n. 6, Phases 1 and 2.

late and soon, ever since I killed
Dayraven the Frank in front of the two armies.
He brought back no looted breastplate
to the Frisian king but fell in battle,
2505 their standard-bearer, highborn and brave.
No sword blade sent him to his death:
my bare hands stilled his heartbeats
and wrecked the bone-house. Now blade and hand,
sword and sword-stroke, will assay the hoard."

[BEOWULF ATTACKS THE DRAGON]

2510   Beowulf spoke, made a formal boast
for the last time: "I risked my life
often when I was young. Now I am old,
but as king of the people I shall pursue this fight
for the glory of winning, if the evil one will only
2515 abandon his earth-fort and face me in the open."
    Then he addressed each dear companion
one final time, those fighters in their helmets,
resolute and highborn: "I would rather not
use a weapon if I knew another way
2520 to grapple with the dragon and make good my boast
as I did against Grendel in days gone by.
But I shall be meeting molten venom
in the fire he breathes, so I go forth
in mail-shirt and shield. I won't shift a foot
2525 when I meet the cave-guard: what occurs on the wall
between the two of us will turn out as fate,
overseer of men, decides. I am resolved.
I scorn further words against this sky-borne foe.
    "Men-at-arms, remain here on the barrow,
2530 safe in your armor, to see which one of us
is better in the end at bearing wounds
in a deadly fray. This fight is not yours,
nor is it up to any man except me
to measure his strength against the monster
2535 or to prove his worth. I shall win the gold
by my courage, or else mortal combat,
doom of battle, will bear your lord away."
    Then he drew himself up beside his shield.
The fabled warrior in his war-shirt and helmet
2540 trusted in his own strength entirely
and went under the crag. No coward path.
    Hard by the rock-face that hale veteran,
a good man who had gone repeatedly
into combat and danger and come through,
2545 saw a stone arch and a gushing stream
that burst from the barrow, blazing and wafting
a deadly heat. It would be hard to survive
unscathed near the hoard, to hold firm
against the dragon in those flaming depths.

2550 Then he gave a shout. The lord of the Geats
unburdened his breast and broke out
in a storm of anger. Under gray stone
his voice challenged and resounded clearly.
Hate was ignited. The hoard-guard recognized
2555 a human voice, the time was over
for peace and parleying. Pouring forth
in a hot battle-fume, the breath of the monster
burst from the rock. There was a rumble under ground.
Down there in the barrow, Beowulf the warrior
2560 lifted his shield: the outlandish thing
writhed and convulsed and viciously
turned on the king, whose keen-edged sword,
an heirloom inherited by ancient right,
was already in his hand. Roused to a fury,
2565 each antagonist struck terror in the other.
Unyielding, the lord of his people loomed
by his tall shield, sure of his ground,
while the serpent looped and unleashed itself.
Swaddled in flames, it came gliding and flexing
2570 and racing toward its fate. Yet his shield defended
the renowned leader's life and limb
for a shorter time than he meant it to:
that final day was the first time
when Beowulf fought and fate denied him
2575 glory in battle. So the king of the Geats
raised his hand and struck hard
at the enameled scales, but scarcely cut through:
the blade flashed and slashed yet the blow
was far less powerful than the hard-pressed king
2580 had need of at that moment. The mound-keeper
went into a spasm and spouted deadly flames:
when he felt the stroke, battle-fire
billowed and spewed. Beowulf was foiled
of a glorious victory. The glittering sword,
2585 infallible before that day,
failed when he unsheathed it, as it never should have.
For the son of Ecgtheow, it was no easy thing
to have to give ground like that and go
unwillingly to inhabit another home
2590 in a place beyond; so every man must yield
the leasehold of his days.
                              Before long
the fierce contenders clashed again.
The hoard-guard took heart, inhaled and swelled up
and got a new wind; he who had once ruled
2595 was furled in fire and had to face the worst.
No help or backing was to be had then
from his highborn comrades; that hand-picked troop
broke ranks and ran for their lives
to the safety of the wood. But within one heart
2600 sorrow welled up: in a man of worth

the claims of kinship cannot be denied.
  His name was Wiglaf, a son of Weohstan's,
a well-regarded Shylfing warrior
related to Aelfhere.[4] When he saw his lord
2605 tormented by the heat of his scalding helmet,
he remembered the bountiful gifts bestowed on him,
how well he lived among the Waegmundings,
the freehold he inherited from his father[5] before him.
He could not hold back: one hand brandished
2610 the yellow-timbered shield, the other drew his sword—
an ancient blade that was said to have belonged
to Eanmund, the son of Ohthere, the one
Weohstan had slain when he was an exile without friends.
He carried the arms to the victim's kinfolk,
2615 the burnished helmet, the webbed chain-mail
and that relic of the giants. But Onela returned
the weapons to him, rewarded Weohstan
with Eanmund's war-gear. He ignored the blood-feud,
the fact that Eanmund was his brother's son.[6]
2620 Weohstan kept that war-gear for a lifetime,
the sword and the mail-shirt, until it was the son's turn
to follow his father and perform his part.
Then, in old age, at the end of his days
among the Weather-Geats, he bequeathed to Wiglaf
2625 innumerable weapons.
                    And now the youth
was to enter the line of battle with his lord,
his first time to be tested as a fighter.
His spirit did not break and the ancestral blade
would keep its edge, as the dragon discovered
2630 as soon as they came together in the combat.
  Sad at heart, addressing his companions,
Wiglaf spoke wise and fluent words:
"I remember that time when mead was flowing,
how we pledged loyalty to our lord in the hall,
2635 promised our ring-giver we would be worth our price,
make good the gift of the war-gear,
those swords and helmets, as and when
his need required it. He picked us out
from the army deliberately, honored us and judged us
2640 fit for this action, made me these lavish gifts—
and all because he considered us the best
of his arms-bearing thanes. And now, although
he wanted this challenge to be one he'd face
by himself alone—the shepherd of our land,

---

4. Although Wiglaf is here said to be a Shylfing (i.e.,
a Swede), in line 2607 we are told his family are
Waegmundings, a clan of the Geats, which is also
Beowulf's family. It was possible for a family to owe
allegiance to more than one nation and to shift sides
as a result of feuds. Nothing is known of Aelfhere.
5. I.e., Weohstan, who, as explained below, was
the slayer of Onela's nephew Eanmund. Possibly,

Weohstan joined the Geats under Beowulf after
Eanmund's brother, with Beowulf's help, avenged
Eanmund's death on Onela and became king of
the Shylfings. See p. 89, n. 6, Phase 2.
6. An ironic comment: since Onela wanted to
kill Eanmund, he rewarded Weohstan for killing
his nephew instead of exacting compensation or
revenge.

2645 a man unequaled in the quest for glory
and a name for daring—now the day has come
when this lord we serve needs sound men
to give him their support. Let us go to him,
help our leader through the hot flame
2650 and dread of the fire. As God is my witness,
I would rather my body were robed in the same
burning blaze as my gold-giver's body
than go back home bearing arms.
That is unthinkable, unless we have first
2655 slain the foe and defended the life
of the prince of the Weather-Geats. I well know
the things he has done for us deserve better.
Should he alone be left exposed
to fall in battle? We must bond together,
2660 shield and helmet, mail-shirt and sword."
Then he waded the dangerous reek and went
under arms to his lord, saying only:
"Go on, dear Beowulf, do everything
you said you would when you were still young
2665 and vowed you would never let your name and fame
be dimmed while you lived. Your deeds are famous,
so stay resolute, my lord, defend your life now
with the whole of your strength. I shall stand by you."
    After those words, a wildness rose
2670 in the dragon again and drove it to attack,
heaving up fire, hunting for enemies,
the humans it loathed. Flames lapped the shield,
charred it to the boss, and the body armor
on the young warrior was useless to him.
2675 But Wiglaf did well under the wide rim
Beowulf shared with him once his own had shattered
in sparks and ashes.
               Inspired again
by the thought of glory, the war-king threw
his whole strength behind a sword stroke
2680 and connected with the skull. And Naegling snapped.
Beowulf's ancient iron-gray sword
let him down in the fight. It was never his fortune
to be helped in combat by the cutting edge
of weapons made of iron. When he wielded a sword,
2685 no matter how blooded and hard-edged the blade,
his hand was too strong, the stroke he dealt
(I have heard) would ruin it. He could reap no advantage.
    Then the bane of that people, the fire-breathing dragon,
was mad to attack for a third time.
2690 When a chance came, he caught the hero
in a rush of flame and clamped sharp fangs
into his neck. Beowulf's body
ran wet with his life-blood: it came welling out.
    Next thing, they say, the noble son of Weohstan
2695 saw the king in danger at his side

and displayed his inborn bravery and strength.
He left the head alone,[7] but his fighting hand
was burned when he came to his kinsman's aid.
He lunged at the enemy lower down
2700 so that his decorated sword sank into its belly
and the flames grew weaker.
                  Once again the king
gathered his strength and drew a stabbing knife
he carried on his belt, sharpened for battle.
He stuck it deep in the dragon's flank.
2705 Beowulf dealt it a deadly wound.
They had killed the enemy, courage quelled his life;
that pair of kinsmen, partners in nobility,
had destroyed the foe. So every man should act,
be at hand when needed; but now, for the king,
2710 this would be the last of his many labors
and triumphs in the world.
                Then the wound
dealt by the ground-burner earlier began
to scald and swell; Beowulf discovered
deadly poison suppurating inside him,
2715 surges of nausea, and so, in his wisdom,
the prince realized his state and struggled
toward a seat on the rampart. He steadied his gaze
on those gigantic stones, saw how the earthwork
was braced with arches built over columns.
2720 And now that thane unequaled for goodness
with his own hands washed his lord's wounds,
swabbed the weary prince with water,
bathed him clean, unbuckled his helmet.
   Beowulf spoke: in spite of his wounds,
2725 mortal wounds, he still spoke
for he well knew his days in the world
had been lived out to the end—his allotted time
was drawing to a close, death was very near.
"Now is the time when I would have wanted
2730 to bestow this armor on my own son,
had it been my fortune to have fathered an heir
and live on in his flesh. For fifty years
I ruled this nation. No king
of any neighboring clan would dare
2735 face me with troops, none had the power
to intimidate me. I took what came,
cared for and stood by things in my keeping,
never fomented quarrels, never
swore to a lie. All this consoles me,
2740 doomed as I am and sickening for death;
because of my right ways, the Ruler of mankind
need never blame me when the breath leaves my body
for murder of kinsmen. Go now quickly,

---

7. I.e., he avoided the dragon's flame-breathing head.

dearest Wiglaf, under the gray stone
2745 where the dragon is laid out, lost to his treasure;
hurry to feast your eyes on the hoard.
Away you go: I want to examine
that ancient gold, gaze my fill
on those garnered jewels; my going will be easier
2750 for having seen the treasure, a less troubled letting-go
of the life and lordship I have long maintained."
　　And so, I have heard, the son of Weohstan
quickly obeyed the command of his languishing
war-weary lord; he went in his chain-mail
2755 under the rock-piled roof of the barrow,
exulting in his triumph, and saw beyond the seat
a treasure-trove of astonishing richness,
wall-hangings that were a wonder to behold,
glittering gold spread across the ground,
2760 the old dawn-scorching serpent's den
packed with goblets and vessels from the past,
tarnished and corroding. Rusty helmets
all eaten away. Armbands everywhere,
artfully wrought. How easily treasure
2765 buried in the ground, gold hidden
however skillfully, can escape from any man!
　　And he saw too a standard, entirely of gold,
hanging high over the hoard,
a masterpiece of filigree; it glowed with light
2770 so he could make out the ground at his feet
and inspect the valuables. Of the dragon there was no
remaining sign: the sword had dispatched him.
Then, the story goes, a certain man
plundered the hoard in that immemorial howe,
2775 filled his arms with flagons and plates,
anything he wanted; and took the standard also,
most brilliant of banners. 　　　　　Already the blade
of the old king's sharp killing-sword
had done its worst: the one who had for long
2780 minded the hoard, hovering over gold,
unleashing fire, surging forth
midnight after midnight, had been mown down.
　　Wiglaf went quickly, keen to get back,
excited by the treasure. Anxiety weighed
2785 on his brave heart—he was hoping he would find
the leader of the Geats alive where he had left him
helpless, earlier, on the open ground.
　　So he came to the place, carrying the treasure
and found his lord bleeding profusely,
2790 his life at an end; again he began
to swab his body. The beginnings of an utterance
broke out from the king's breast-cage.
The old lord gazed sadly at the gold.
　　"To the everlasting Lord of all,

2795 to the King of Glory, I give thanks
that I behold this treasure here in front of me,
that I have been allowed to leave my people
so well endowed on the day I die.
Now that I have bartered my last breath
2800 to own this fortune, it is up to you
to look after their needs. I can hold out no longer.
Order my troop to construct a barrow
on a headland on the coast, after my pyre has cooled.
It will loom on the horizon at Hronesness[8]
2805 and be a reminder among my people—
so that in coming times crews under sail
will call it Beowulf's Barrow, as they steer
ships across the wide and shrouded waters."
     Then the king in his great-heartedness unclasped
2810 the collar of gold from his neck and gave it
to the young thane, telling him to use
it and the war-shirt and gilded helmet well.
"You are the last of us, the only one left
of the Waegmundings. Fate swept us away,
2815 sent my whole brave highborn clan
to their final doom. Now I must follow them."
     That was the warrior's last word.
He had no more to confide. The furious heat
of the pyre would assail him. His soul fled from his breast
2820 to its destined place among the steadfast ones.

[BEOWULF'S FUNERAL]

     It was hard then on the young hero,
having to watch the one he held so dear
there on the ground, going through
his death agony. The dragon from underearth,
2825 his nightmarish destroyer, lay destroyed as well,
utterly without life. No longer would his snakefolds
ply themselves to safeguard hidden gold.
Hard-edged blades, hammered out
and keenly filed, had finished him
2830 so that the sky-roamer lay there rigid,
brought low beside the treasure-lodge.
     Never again would he glitter and glide
and show himself off in midnight air,
exulting in his riches: he fell to earth
2835 through the battle-strength in Beowulf's arm.
There were few, indeed, as far as I have heard,
big and brave as they may have been,
few who would have held out if they had had to face
the outpourings of that poison-breather
2840 or gone foraging on the ring-hall floor
and found the deep barrow-dweller

---

8. A headland by the sea. The name means "Whalesness."

on guard and awake.
                                    The treasure had been won,
bought and paid for by Beowulf's death.
Both had reached the end of the road
2845 through the life they had been lent.
                                    Before long
the battle-dodgers abandoned the wood,
the ones who had let down their lord earlier,
the tail-turners, ten of them together.
When he needed them most, they had made off.
2850 Now they were ashamed and came behind shields,
in their battle-outfits, to where the old man lay.
They watched Wiglaf, sitting worn out,
a comrade shoulder to shoulder with his lord,
trying in vain to bring him round with water.
2855 Much as he wanted to, there was no way
he could preserve his lord's life on earth
or alter in the least the Almighty's will.
What God judged right would rule what happened
to every man, as it does to this day.
2860   Then a stern rebuke was bound to come
from the young warrior to the ones who had been cowards.
Wiglaf, son of Weohstan, spoke
disdainfully and in disappointment:
"Anyone ready to admit the truth
2865 will surely realize that the lord of men
who showered you with gifts and gave you the armor
you are standing in—when he would distribute
helmets and mail-shirts to men on the mead-benches,
a prince treating his thanes in hall
2870 to the best he could find, far or near—
was throwing weapons uselessly away.
It would be a sad waste when the war broke out.
Beowulf had little cause to brag
about his armed guard; yet God who ordains
2875 who wins or loses allowed him to strike
with his own blade when bravery was needed.
There was little I could do to protect his life
in the heat of the fray, but I found new strength
welling up when I went to help him.
2880 Then my sword connected and the deadly assaults
of our foe grew weaker, the fire coursed
less strongly from his head. But when the worst happened
too few rallied around the prince.
     "So it is good-bye now to all you know and love
2885 on your home ground, the open-handedness,
the giving of war-swords. Every one of you
with freeholds of land, our whole nation,
will be dispossessed, once princes from beyond
get tidings of how you turned and fled
2890 and disgraced yourselves. A warrior will sooner
die than live a life of shame."

Then he ordered the outcome of the fight to be reported
to those camped on the ridge, that crowd of retainers
who had sat all morning, sad at heart,
2895   shield-bearers wondering about
the man they loved: would this day be his last
or would he return? He told the truth
and did not balk, the rider who bore
news to the cliff-top. He addressed them all:
2900   "Now the people's pride and love,
the lord of the Geats, is laid on his deathbed,
brought down by the dragon's attack.
Beside him lies the bane of his life,
dead from knife-wounds. There was no way
2905   Beowulf could manage to get the better
of the monster with his sword. Wiglaf sits
at Beowulf's side, the son of Weohstan,
the living warrior watching by the dead,
keeping weary vigil, holding a wake
2910   for the loved and the loathed.
                        Now war is looming
over our nation, soon it will be known
to Franks and Frisians, far and wide,
that the king is gone. Hostility has been great
among the Franks since Hygelac sailed forth
2915   at the head of a war-fleet into Friesland:
there the Hetware harried and attacked
and overwhelmed him with great odds.
The leader in his war-gear was laid low,
fell among followers: that lord did not favor
2920   his company with spoils. The Merovingian king
has been an enemy to us ever since.
     "Nor do I expect peace or pact-keeping
of any sort from the Swedes. Remember:
at Ravenswood,[9] Ongentheow
2925   slaughtered Haethcyn, Hrethel's son,
when the Geat people in their arrogance
first attacked the fierce Shylfings.
The return blow was quickly struck
by Ohthere's father.[1] Old and terrible,
2930   he felled the sea-king and saved his own
aged wife, the mother of Onela
and of Ohthere, bereft of her gold rings.
Then he kept hard on the heels of the foe
and drove them, leaderless, lucky to get away
2935   in a desperate rout into Ravenswood.
His army surrounded the weary remnant
where they nursed their wounds; all through the night
he howled threats at those huddled survivors,
promised to axe their bodies open

---

9. The messenger describes in greater detail the
Battle of Ravenswood. See the outline of the

Swedish wars on p. 89, n. 6.
1. I.e., Ongentheow.

2940 when dawn broke, dangle them from gallows
to feed the birds. But at first light
when their spirits were lowest, relief arrived.
They heard the sound of Hygelac's horn,
his trumpet calling as he came to find them,
2945 the hero in pursuit, at hand with troops.
    "The bloody swathe that Swedes and Geats
cut through each other was everywhere.
No one could miss their murderous feuding.
Then the old man made his move,
2950 pulled back, barred his people in:
Ongentheow withdrew to higher ground.
Hygelac's pride and prowess as a fighter
were known to the earl; he had no confidence
that he could hold out against that horde of seamen,
2955 defend his wife and the ones he loved
from the shock of the attack. He retreated for shelter
behind the earthwall. Then Hygelac swooped
on the Swedes at bay, his banners swarmed
into their refuge, his Geat forces
2960 drove forward to destroy the camp.
There in his gray hairs, Ongentheow
was cornered, ringed around with swords.
And it came to pass that the king's fate
was in Eofor's hands,[2] and in his alone.
2965 Wulf, son of Wonred, went for him in anger,
split him open so that blood came spurting
from under his hair. The old hero
still did not flinch, but parried fast,
hit back with a harder stroke:
2970 the king turned and took him on.
Then Wonred's son, the brave Wulf,
could land no blow against the aged lord.
Ongentheow divided his helmet
so that he buckled and bowed his bloodied head
2975 and dropped to the ground. But his doom held off.
Though he was cut deep, he recovered again.
    "With his brother down, the undaunted Eofor,
Hygelac's thane, hefted his sword
and smashed murderously at the massive helmet
2980 past the lifted shield. And the king collapsed,
the shepherd of people was sheared of life.
Many then hurried to help Wulf,
bandaged and lifted him, now that they were left
masters of the blood-soaked battle-ground.
2985 One warrior stripped the other,
looted Ongentheow's iron mail-coat,
his hard sword-hilt, his helmet too,
and carried the graith[3] to King Hygelac,

---

2. I.e., he was at Eofor's mercy. Eofor's slaying of Ongentheow was described in lines 2486–89, where no mention is made of his brother Wulf's part in the battle. They are the sons of Wonred. *Eofor* means boar; *Wulf* is the Old English spelling of wolf.
3. Possessions, apparel.

he accepted the prize, promised fairly
2990 that reward would come, and kept his word.
For their bravery in action, when they arrived home,
Eofor and Wulf were overloaded
by Hrethel's son, Hygelac the Geat,
with gifts of land and linked rings
2995 that were worth a fortune. They had won glory,
so there was no gainsaying his generosity.
And he gave Eofor his only daughter
to bide at home with him, an honor and a bond.
   "So this bad blood between us and the Swedes,
3000 this vicious feud, I am convinced,
is bound to revive; they will cross our borders
and attack in force when they find out
that Beowulf is dead. In days gone by
when our warriors fell and we were undefended,
3005 he kept our coffers and our kingdom safe.
He worked for the people, but as well as that
he behaved like a hero.
                        We must hurry now
to take a last look at the king
and launch him, lord and lavisher of rings,
3010 on the funeral road. His royal pyre
will melt no small amount of gold:
heaped there in a hoard, it was bought at heavy cost,
and that pile of rings he paid for at the end
with his own life will go up with the flame,
3015 be furled in fire: treasure no follower
will wear in his memory, nor lovely woman
link and attach as a torque around her neck—
but often, repeatedly, in the path of exile
they shall walk bereft, bowed under woe,
3020 now that their leader's laugh is silenced,
high spirits quenched. Many a spear
dawn-cold to the touch will be taken down
and waved on high; the swept harp
won't waken warriors, but the raven winging
3025 darkly over the doomed will have news,
tidings for the eagle of how he hoked and ate,
how the wolf and he made short work of the dead."[4]
   Such was the drift of the dire report
that gallant man delivered. He got little wrong
3030 in what he told and predicted.
                        The whole troop
rose in tears, then took their way
to the uncanny scene under Earnaness.[5]
There, on the sand, where his soul had left him,
they found him at rest, their ring-giver

---

4. The raven, eagle, and wolf—the scavengers who will feed on the slain—are "the beasts of battle," a common motif in Germanic war poetry. "Hoked": rooted about [Northern Ireland, Translator's note].
5. The site of Beowulf's fight with the dragon. The name means "Eaglesness."

3035 from days gone by. The great man
had breathed his last. Beowulf the king
had indeed met with a marvelous death.
    But what they saw first was far stranger:
the serpent on the ground, gruesome and vile,
3040 lying facing him. The fire-dragon
was scaresomely burned, scorched all colors.
From head to tail, his entire length
was fifty feet. He had shimmered forth
on the night air once, then winged back
3045 down to his den; but death owned him now,
he would never enter his earth-gallery again.
Beside him stood pitchers and piled-up dishes,
silent flagons, precious swords
eaten through with rust, ranged as they had been
3050 while they waited their thousand winters under ground.
That huge cache, gold inherited
from an ancient race, was under a spell—
which meant no one was ever permitted
to enter the ring-hall unless God Himself,
3055 mankind's Keeper, True King of Triumphs,
allowed some person pleasing to Him—
and in His eyes worthy—to open the hoard.
    What came about brought to nothing
the hopes of the one who had wrongly hidden
3060 riches under the rock-face. First the dragon slew
that man among men, who in turn made fierce amends
and settled the feud. Famous for his deeds
a warrior may be, but it remains a mystery
where his life will end, when he may no longer
3065 dwell in the mead-hall among his own.
So it was with Beowulf, when he faced the cruelty
and cunning of the mound-guard. He himself was ignorant
of how his departure from the world would happen.
The highborn chiefs who had buried the treasure
3070 declared it until doomsday so accursed
that whoever robbed it would be guilty of wrong
and grimly punished for their transgression,
hasped in hell-bonds in heathen shrines.
Yet Beowulf's gaze at the gold treasure
3075 when he first saw it had not been selfish.
    Wiglaf, son of Weohstan, spoke:
"Often when one man follows his own will
many are hurt. This happened to us.
Nothing we advised could ever convince
3080 the prince we loved, our land's guardian,
not to vex the custodian of the gold,
let him lie where he was long accustomed,
lurk there under earth until the end of the world.
He held to his high destiny. The hoard is laid bare,
3085 but at a grave cost; it was too cruel a fate
that forced the king to that encounter.

I have been inside and seen everything
amassed in the vault. I managed to enter
although no great welcome awaited me
3090 under the earthwall. I quickly gathered up
a huge pile of the priceless treasures
handpicked from the hoard and carried them here
where the king could see them. He was still himself,
alive, aware, and in spite of his weakness
3095 he had many requests. He wanted me to greet you
and order the building of a barrow that would crown
the site of his pyre, serve as his memorial,
in a commanding position, since of all men
to have lived and thrived and lorded it on earth
3100 his worth and due as a warrior were the greatest.
Now let us again go quickly
and feast our eyes on that amazing fortune
heaped under the wall. I will show the way
and take you close to those coffers packed with rings
3105 and bars of gold. Let a bier be made
and got ready quickly when we come out
and then let us bring the body of our lord,
the man we loved, to where he will lodge
for a long time in the care of the Almighty."
3110　　Then Weohstan's son, stalwart to the end,
had orders given to owners of dwellings,
many people of importance in the land,
to fetch wood from far and wide
for the good man's pyre:
　　　　　　　　　　　　　"Now shall flame consume
3115 our leader in battle, the blaze darken
round him who stood his ground in the steel-hail,
when the arrow-storm shot from bowstrings
pelted the shield-wall. The shaft hit home.
Feather-fledged, it finned the barb in flight."
3120　　Next the wise son of Weohstan
called from among the king's thanes
a group of seven: he selected the best
and entered with them, the eighth of their number,
under the God-cursed roof; one raised
3125 a lighted torch and led the way.
No lots were cast for who should loot the hoard
for it was obvious to them that every bit of it
lay unprotected within the vault,
there for the taking. It was no trouble
3130 to hurry to work and haul out
the priceless store. They pitched the dragon
over the cliff-top, let tide's flow
and backwash take the treasure-minder.
Then coiled gold was loaded on a cart
3135 in great abundance, and the gray-haired leader,
the prince on his bier, borne to Hronesness.
　　The Geat people built a pyre for Beowulf,

stacked and decked it until it stood foursquare,
hung with helmets, heavy war-shields
3140 and shining armor, just as he had ordered.
Then his warriors laid him in the middle of it,
mourning a lord far-famed and beloved.
On a height they kindled the hugest of all
funeral fires; fumes of woodsmoke
3145 billowed darkly up, the blaze roared
and drowned out their weeping, wind died down
and flames wrought havoc in the hot bone-house,
burning it to the core. They were disconsolate
and wailed aloud for their lord's decease.
3150 A Geat woman too sang out in grief;
with hair bound up, she unburdened herself
of her worst fears, a wild litany
of nightmare and lament: her nation invaded,
enemies on the rampage, bodies in piles,
3155 slavery and abasement. Heaven swallowed the smoke.
       Then the Geat people began to construct
a mound on a headland, high and imposing,
a marker that sailors could see from far away,
and in ten days they had done the work.
3160 It was their hero's memorial; what remained from the fire
they housed inside it, behind a wall
as worthy of him as their workmanship could make it.
And they buried torques in the barrow, and jewels
and a trove of such things as trespassing men
3165 had once dared to drag from the hoard.
They let the ground keep that ancestral treasure,
gold under gravel, gone to earth,
as useless to men now as it ever was.
Then twelve warriors rode around the tomb,
3170 chieftains' sons, champions in battle,
all of them distraught, chanting in dirges,
mourning his loss as a man and a king.
They extolled his heroic nature and exploits
and gave thanks for his greatness; which was the proper thing,
3175 for a man should praise a prince whom he holds dear
and cherish his memory when that moment comes
when he has to be convoyed from his bodily home.
So the Geat people, his hearth-companions,
sorrowed for the lord who had been laid low.
3180 They said that of all the kings upon earth
he was the man most gracious and fair-minded,
kindest to his people and keenest to win fame.

JUDITH

B iblical narrative inspired Anglo-Saxon poetry from its earliest recorded beginnings: the poet Cædmon (p. 30) is said, for example, to have composed poetry
on biblical subjects from Genesis to the Last Judgment. Although those texts do not
survive, up to one third of surviving Anglo-Saxon poetic texts are translations of
biblical material. Prose writers also produced ambitious biblical translations: at the
end of the tenth century Ælfric, Abbot of Eynsham (died ca. 1010), made partial
translations of many texts that he worked into sermon material; an Anglo-Saxon
version of the Pentateuch (the first five books of the Old Testament) was compiled
at about the same time. The prose translations are more or less faithful to the biblical text. The poetic translations, on the other hand, are much freer: they take liber-
ties with the narrative and style of the biblical sources, reshaping narratives and
placing the stories within a recognizably Germanic cultural setting.

One of the biblical books from which Ælfric drew material was the Book of Judith.
This book was regarded as apocryphal (i.e., not authentically a part of the Old Testament) by Protestant churches from the sixteenth century, but for all pre- and post-
Reformation Catholic readers it was an authentic part of the Hebrew Bible. The
narrative recounts the campaign of the Babylonian king Nebuchadnezzar to punish
many subject peoples who had refused to join him in his successful war against
Media (another ancient empire). Nebuchadnezzar's general Holofernes plunders and
razes many cities that resist his army, and others capitulate to him. He lays siege to
the strategic Israelite town of Bethulia, which blocks his route to Jerusalem (Bethulia
no longer exists, and its location in biblical times is uncertain). The leaders of the
suffering and thirsty population of Bethulia are almost ready to surrender, but the
pious, wealthy, and beautiful widow Judith rebukes them for their faintness of heart
and promises to liberate them if they will hold out a few days longer. After praying to
God in sackcloth and ashes, Judith dresses and adorns herself sumptuously. With
only one servant she enters the enemy camp, where all, and especially Holofernes
himself, are amazed at her beauty. She pretends to be fleeing a doomed people and
persuades Holofernes that she will lead him to victory over all the Israelite cities. The
Old English text begins four days after Judith's arrival, with Holofernes's invitation to
his principal warriors to a banquet, after which he plans to go to bed with the beautiful Israelite. Judith, however, has other plans.

The poet of *Judith* translated from the Latin text of the Bible (the so-called Vulgate
Bible, produced in the late fourth century). We do not know the date for this rendering
of the Book of Judith into Anglo-Saxon poetry, but it was probably composed sometime
in the tenth century (the one surviving text appears in the same late tenth-century
manuscript that contains *Beowulf*). Neither do we know the motives for this translation. Ælfric, writing in the late tenth century, made his translation of Judith to encourage the Anglo-Saxons in defense of their territory against the invading Vikings. The
text is, he says, "set down in our manner in English, as an example to you people that
you should defend your land with weapons against the invading army."*

The opening of the poem is lost (scholars estimate that some one hundred lines are
missing), but from the remainder we can see that the poet has freely reshaped the
biblical source and set the narrative within terms intelligible to an Anglo-Saxon audience. The poet has stripped the geographical, historical, and political complexity of

---

The Old English Heptateuch, ed. S. J. Crawford, Early English Text Society 160 (London, 1922), p. 48.

the story down to its bare essentials: the confrontation between Judith and Holofernes. Judith is the leader of an embattled people up against an exultant and terrifying enemy. Her only resources are her unfailing courage, her wits, and her faith in God. Within this concentrated narrative, the poet colors certain episodes by employing the traditional language and formulas of Anglo-Saxon poetry. Holofernes, for example, becomes riotous at the feast; "the beasts of battle" anticipate and enjoy *their* feast (cf. *Beowulf*, lines 3023–27); Judith is rewarded with Holofernes's battle gear, not with his household treasures as in the biblical narrative. Perhaps the most penetrating touch added by the Anglo-Saxon poet is the account of the net surrounding Holofernes's bed, from which he can see out but cannot be seen inside. This technology of tyrannical power undermines Holofernes's army in the end, since his men, waiting nervously around his bed because they are afraid to wake up their leader, lose precious time under attack from the Israelites.

Like the Abbess Hilda (see p. 31, n. 1), Judith is one of the women of power in Anglo-Saxon history and literature. Another is St. Helena, the mother of the emperor Constantine the Great: in the poem *Elene* she leads a Roman army to the Holy Land to discover the Cross on which Christ was crucified.

Judith[1]

        . . . She doubted
gifts in this wide earth; there she readily found
protection from the glorious Lord, when she had most need
of favour from the highest Judge, so that he, the Lord of creation,
5   defended her against the greatest terror. The glorious Father in the
       skies
granted her request, since she always possessed true faith
in the Almighty. I have heard then that Holofernes
eagerly issued invitations to a feast and provided all types of
magnificent wonders for the banquets; to it the lord of men
       summoned
10   the most experienced retainers. The warriors obeyed
with great haste; they came to the powerful lord and
proceeded to the leader of people. That was the fourth day
after Judith, prudent in mind,
this woman of elfin beauty first visited him.
15   They went into the feast to sit down,
proud men at the wine-drinking, bold mail-coated warriors,
all his companions in misfortune. There, along the benches,
deep bowls were carried frequently; full cups and pitchers
were also carried to the sitters in the hall. They received those,
       doomed to die,
20   brave warriors, though the powerful man did not expect it,
that terrible lord of heroes. Then Holofernes,
the gold-giving friend of his men, became joyous from the drinking.
He laughed and grew vociferous, roared and clamoured,
so that the children of men could hear from far away,
25   how the fierce one stormed and yelled;
arrogant and excited by mead, he frequently admonished

1. The translation is by Elaine Treharne, *Old and Middle English: An Anthology* (2000).

the guests that they enjoy themselves well.
So, for the entire day, the wicked one,
the stern dispenser of treasures,
30   drenched his retainers with wine until they lay unconscious,
the whole of his troop were as drunk as if they had been struck
        down in death,
drained of every ability. So, the men's lord commanded
the guests to be served, until the dark night approached
the children of men. Then corrupted by evil,
35   he commanded that the blessed maiden should be hastily fetched
to his bed, adorned with bracelets,
decorated with rings. The retainers quickly did
as their lord, the ruler of warriors,
commanded them. They stepped into the tumult
40   of the guest-hall where they found the wise Judith,
and then quickly
the warriors began to lead the
illustrious maiden to the lofty tent,
where the powerful man Holofernes, hateful to the Saviour,
45   rested himself during the night.
There was a beautiful
all-golden fly-net[2] that the commander
had hung around the bed, so that the wicked one,
the lord of warriors, could look through
50   on each of those sons of men who came in there,
but not one of the race of mankind could look
on him, unless, brave man, he commanded one
of his very iniquitous men to come
nearer to him for secret consultation. They quickly brought to bed
55   the prudent woman. Then the resolute heroes
went to inform their lord that the holy maiden
had been brought into his tent. Then the notorious one, that lord of
        cities,
became happy in his mind: he intended to violate
the bright woman with defilement and with sin. The Judge of glory,
60   the majestic Guardian, the Lord, Ruler of hosts, would not consent to
        that,
but he prevented him from that thing. Then the diabolical one,
the wanton and wicked man, departed
with a troop of his men to find his bed, where he would lose his life
forthwith within that one night. He had attained his violent end
65   on earth, just as he had previously deserved,
this severe lord of men, since he had dwelled under the roof
of clouds in this world. The mighty man then fell into the middle
of his bed, so drunk with wine that he possessed no sense
in his mind. The warriors stepped
70   out from that place with great haste,
men sated with wine, who led the traitor,
that hateful tyrant, to bed

---

2. Book of Judith 10.21: "A mosquito-net of purple interwoven with gold, emerald, and precious
stones." Here the "fly-net" is a kind of screen
enabling Holofernes to see outside his bed without being seen.

for the last time. Then the Saviour's
glorious handmaiden was very mindful
75 of how she could deprive the terrible one
of life most easily, before the impure and
foul one awoke. Then the Creator's maiden,
with her braided locks, took a sharp sword,
a hard weapon in the storms of battle, and drew it from the sheath
80 with her right hand. She began to call the Guardian of heaven
by name, the Saviour of all
the inhabitants of earth, and said these words:
   "God of creation, Spirit of comfort,
Son of the Almighty, I want to beseech you
85 for your mercy on me in my time of need,
glorious Trinity.[3] My heart is intensely
inflamed within me now, and my mind is troubled,
greatly afflicted with sorrows. Give me, Lord of heaven,
victory and true belief so I might cut down this bestower of torment
90 with this sword. Grant me my salvation,
mighty Lord of men: I have never had more need
of your mercy than now. Avenge now, mighty Lord,
eminent Bestower of glory, that which is so grievous in my mind,
so fervent in my heart." Then the highest Judge
95 inspired her immediately with great zeal, as he does to each
of the dwellers on earth who seek help from him
with reason and with true faith. Then she felt relief in her mind,
hope was renewed for the holy woman. She seized the heathen man
securely by his hair, pulled him shamefully towards her
100 with her hands, and skilfully placed
the wicked and loathsome man
so that she could most easily manage the miserable one
well. Then, the woman with braided locks struck
the enemy, that hostile one,
105 with the shining sword, so that she cut through half
of his neck, such that he lay unconscious,
drunk and wounded. He was not dead yet,
not entirely lifeless. The courageous woman
struck the heathen hound energetically
110 another time so that his head rolled
forwards on the floor. The foul body lay
behind, dead; the spirit departed elsewhere
under the deep earth and was oppressed there
and fettered in torment forever after,
115 wound round with serpents, bound with punishments,
cruelly imprisoned in hell-fire
after his departure. Enveloped in darkness,
he had no need at all to hope that he should get out from
that serpent-hall, but there he must remain
120 always and forever, henceforth without end,
in that dark home deprived of the joy of hope.

---

3. Anglo-Saxon *Drynesse*, "threeness." In lines 83–84, the heroine prays to the three persons of the Trinity. In the Apocrypha, she invokes the "Lord, God of Israel."

    Judith had won illustrious glory
in the battle as God, the Lord of heaven,
granted it so when he gave her her victory.
125   Then the prudent woman immediately placed
the warrior's head still bloody
into the sack in which her attendant,
a woman of pale complexion, an excellent handmaiden,
had brought food for them both; and then Judith
130   put it, all gory, into the hands of her
thoughtful servant to carry home.
Then both the courageous women
went from there straightaway,
until the triumphant women, elated,
135   got away out from that army
so that they could clearly see
the beautiful city walls of Bethulia
glitter. Then, ring-adorned,
they hurried forwards along the path
140   until, glad at heart, they had reached
the rampart gate. Warriors were sitting,
men watching, and keeping guard
in that stronghold, just as Judith the wise maiden
had asked, when she had previously
145   departed from the sorrowful people,
the courageous woman. The beloved woman had returned again
to the people, and the prudent woman
soon asked one of the men
from the spacious city to come towards her,
150   and hastily to let them in
through the gate of the city-wall; and she spoke these words
to the victorious people: "I am able to tell you
a memorable thing so that you need no longer
mourn in your minds. The Ruler, the Glory of kings,
155   is well disposed towards you. It had become revealed
throughout this wide world that glorious and triumphant success
is approaching and that honour has been granted by fate to you
because of the afflictions that you have long suffered."
    Then the city-dwellers were joyful
160   when they heard how the holy one spoke
over the high city-wall. The army was joyous
and people hurried to the fortress gate,
men and women, in multitudes and crowds,
groups and troops pressed forward and ran
165   towards the Lord's maiden in their thousands,
old and young. The mind of each one of the people
in that rejoicing city was gladdened
when they perceived that Judith had returned
to her native land; and then hastily
170   and reverently, they let her in.
    Then the prudent woman, adorned with gold, asked
her attentive handmaiden
to uncover the warrior's head

and to display it, bloodied, as proof
175 to the citizens of how she had been helped in battle.
Then the noble woman spoke to all the people:
"Victorious heroes, here you can gaze clearly
on the leader of the people, on this head
of the most hateful of heathen warriors,
180 of the unliving Holofernes,
who, among men, inflicted on us the worst torments,
grievous afflictions, and wished to add to these
even more; but God would not grant him
a longer life so that he could plague us
185 with wrongs. I deprived him of life
through God's help. Now I intend to ask
each of the men of these citizens,
each of the warriors, that you immediately
hasten to battle, as soon as the God of creation,
190 that glorious King, sends his radiant beam of light
from the east. Go forward carrying shields,
shields in front of your breasts and corslets,
gleaming helmets, into the troop of enemies;
fell the commanders, those leaders doomed to die
195 with shining swords. Your enemies
are condemned to death, and you will possess glory,
honour in conflict, just as mighty God has
given you that sign by my hand."
      Then a host of brave and keen men prepared quickly
200 for the battle. Noble warriors and retainers
stepped out; they carried triumphant banners;
heroes in helmets went forward to battle straightaway
from that holy city
at dawn of that same day. Shields clashed,
205 resounded loudly. The lean wolf rejoiced
in the forest, as did the dark raven,
a bloodthirsty bird: they both knew
that the warriors intended to provide them
with a feast from those doomed to die; but behind them flew
210 the eagle eager for food, dewy-winged
with dark plumage; the horn-beaked bird
sang a battle-song.[4] The warriors advanced,
men to battle, protected by shields,
hollow wooden shields, those who previously
215 had suffered the insolence of foreigners,
the insult of heathens. In the spear-play,
that was all grievously requited to
the Assyrians, when the Israelites
under their battle-banners had gone
220 to that camp. Then they boldly
let showers of arrows fly forwards,
battle arrows from horned bows,
firm arrows. Angry warriors

---

4. See *Beowulf*, lines 3024–27, n. 4 (p. 106).

roared loudly, sent spears
225   into the midst of the cruel ones. The native heroes
were angry against the hateful race,
resolute, they marched, determined,
they violently aroused their ancient enemies
who were drunk with mead. With their hands,
230   the retainers drew brightly adorned swords from their sheaths,
excellent sword-edges, zealously killed
the Assyrian warriors,
those evil schemers. They did not spare one
man's life from that army, neither the
235   lowly nor the powerful whom they could overcome.
   So, in the morning, the retainers
pursued the foreign people the entire time,
until the chief leaders of that army,
of those who were the enemies, perceived
240   that the Hebrew men had shown violent sword-brandishing
to them. They went to reveal
all that in words to the most
senior retainers, and they aroused the warriors
and announced fearfully to those drunk with mead
245   the dreadful news, the morning's terror,
the terrible battle. Then, I have heard, immediately
the warriors, doomed to perish, cast off sleep,
and the subdued men thronged in crowds
to the tent of the wicked man,
250   Holofernes. They intended to announce
the battle to their lord at once,
before the terrible force of the Israelites
came down on them. They all supposed
that the leader of the warriors and the bright maiden
255   were together in that beautiful tent:
Judith the noble one, and the licentious one,
terrible and fierce. There was not a single one of the men
who dared to wake the warrior
or inquire how the warrior
260   had got on with the holy maiden,
the Lord's woman. The armed force of the Israelites
approached; they fought vigorously
with hard swords, violently requited
their ancient grudges, that old conflict,
265   with shining swords. The Assyrian's
glory was destroyed in that day's work,
their pride humbled. Warriors stood
about their lord's tent very uneasy
and sombre in spirit. Then together they all
270   began to cough, to cry out loudly,
to gnash their teeth, suffering grief,
to no avail. Then their glory, success and brave deeds
were at an end. The men considered how to awaken
their lord; it did them no good.
275   It got later and later when one of the warriors

became bold in that he daringly risked going
into the tent, as need compelled him to.
He found on the bed his pale lord,
lying deprived of spirit,
280   devoid of life. Immediately, he fell
frozen to the floor, and began to tear at his hair
and clothing, wild in mind,
and he spoke these words to the warriors
who were outside, dejected:
285   "Here our own destruction is made clear,
the future signified, that the time of troubles
is pressing near when we shall now lose,
shall perish at the battle together. Here lies our protector
cut down and beheaded by the sword." Sorrowful, they
290   threw their weapons down then, and departed from him
      weary-spirited
to hasten in flight. The mighty people
fought them from behind, until the greatest part
of the army lay destroyed in battle
on that field of victory, cut down by swords
295   as a pleasure for the wolves and also as a joy
to bloodthirsty birds. Those who still lived fled
from the wooden weapons of their enemies. Behind them
came the army of the Hebrews, honoured with victory,
glorified with that judgement. The Lord God, the almighty Lord,
300   helped them generously with his aid.
Then quickly the valiant heroes
made a war-path through the hateful enemies
with their shining swords; cut down shields,
and penetrated the shield-wall. The Hebrew missile-throwers
305   were enraged in the battle,
the retainers at that time greatly desired
a battle of spears. There in the sand fell
the greatest part of the total number
of leaders of the Assyrians,
310   that hateful nation. Few returned
alive to their native land. The brave warriors
turned back to retreat among the carnage,
the reeking corpses. There was an opportunity for
the native inhabitants to seize from the most hateful
315   ancient enemies, the unliving ones,
bloody plunder, beautiful ornaments,
shield and broad sword, shining helmets,
precious treasures. The guardians of the country
had gloriously conquered their foes,
320   the ancient enemy, on that battlefield,
executed them with swords. Those who had been
the most hateful of living men while alive
rested in their tracks. Then the entire nation,
the greatest of tribes, the proud braided-haired ones,
325   for the space of one month carried and led
to the bright city of Bethulia

helmets and hip-swords, grey corslets,
men's armour decorated with gold,
more illustrious treasures than any man
330   among the wise could say.
All of that was earned by the warriors' glory,
bold under the banners and in battle
through the prudent counsel of Judith,
the daring maiden. The brave warriors
335   brought as her reward from that expedition
the sword of Holofernes and his gory helmet,
and likewise his ample mail-coat
adorned with red gold, and everything that the arrogant
lord of warriors owned by way of treasures or personal heirlooms,
340   rings and bright riches; they gave that to the bright
and ready-witted woman. For all of this Judith said
thanks to the Lord of hosts, who had given her honour
and glory in the kingdom of this earth, and also as her reward in
    heaven,
the reward of victory in heaven's glory, because she possessed true
    faith
345   in the Almighty. Indeed, at the end she did not doubt
in the reward which she had long yearned for. For that be glory
to the beloved Lord for ever and ever, who created wind and air,
the heavens and spacious earth, likewise the raging seas
and joys of heaven through his own individual grace.

THE WANDERER

The lament of *The Wanderer* is an excellent example of the elegiac mood so common in Anglo-Saxon poetry. Such poems look back to a time when oral poets performed heroic songs in the meter preserved, practiced, and recorded in original works by their Christian descendants. In celebration of Beowulf's victory over Grendel, Hrothgar's court poet performs a heroic lay about the Germanic hero Sigemund (lines 883–914). The elegiac tone common to *Beowulf* and these later poems, however, expresses the poets' profound feelings toward their ancestors who lived before St. Augustine brought the "good news" to Kent and initiated the conversion. Nowhere are those feelings expressed more poignantly than in *The Wanderer*.

As is true of most Anglo-Saxon elegiac laments, both the language and the structure of *The Wanderer* are difficult. At the beginning, the speaker (whom the poet identifies as an "earth-treader") voices hope of finding comfort after his many tribulations. After the poet's interruption, the Wanderer continues to speak—to himself—of his long search for a new home, describing how he must keep his thoughts locked within him while he makes that search. But these thoughts form the most vivid and moving part of his soliloquy—how, floating on the sea, dazed with sorrow and fatigue, he imagines that he sees his old companions, and how, as he wakens to reality, they vanish on the water like seabirds. The second part of the poem, beginning "Therefore

I don't know why," expands the theme from one man to all human beings in a world wasted by war and time. He derives such cold comfort as he can from asking the old question, "Where are they now, who were once so glad in the mead-hall?"

The Wanderer is preserved only in the Exeter Book, a manuscript dating to about 975 (although the poem may be much earlier), which contains the largest surviving collection of Anglo-Saxon poetry.

The Wanderer [1]

"Often the lone-dweller[2]   longs for relief,
the Almighty's mercy,   though melancholy,
his hands turning   time and again
the ocean's currents,   the ice-cold seas,
5   following paths of exile.   Fate is firmly set."
     So spoke the Wanderer,[3]   weary of hardships,
cruel combats,   the death of kinsmen.
     "Often alone,   always at daybreak
I must lament my cares;   not one remains alive
10 to whom I could utter   the thoughts in my heart,
tell him my sorrows.   In truth, I know that
for any eorl[4]   an excellent virtue
is to lock tight   the treasure chest
within one's heart,   howsoever he may think.
15 A downcast heart   won't defy destiny,
nor the sad spirit   give sustenance.
And therefore those   who thirst for fame
often bind fast   their breast chamber.
     "So I must hold in   the thoughts of my heart—
20 though often wretched,   bereft of my homeland,
far from kinfolk—   bind them with fetters,
since in days long past   with darkness of earth
I covered my gold-friend,[5]   and I fared from there
over the waves' bed,   winter-weary,
25 longing for a hall   and a lord of rings,
where near or far   I might find one
in the mead-hall   remembering me and my kin,
or else show favor   to a friendless man,
requite me with comfort.   One acquainted with pain
30 understands how cruel   a traveling companion
sorrow is for someone   with few friends at his side.
Exile attends him,   not twisted gold rings,
Heart-freezing frost,   not fruits of the earth.
He recalls tablemates   and treasure distributed,

---

1. The translation by Alfred David is based on *Eight Old English Poems*, 3rd ed., edited by John C. Pope, revised by R. D. Fulk. The translation is also indebted to comments by Professor Fulk.
2. Old English *an-haga*=one+hedge, enclosure— i.e., one who dwells alone in some sort of confinement.
3. Old English *eard-stapa*=earth+treader. The modern title—there is no title in the manuscript— derives from this compound noun.
4. *Eorl*=warrior. Only later did the Old English word come to designate a member of the British nobility.
5. Old English *gold-wine*=gold-friend, one of the many formulas applied to the lord, here in his role as dispenser of treasure to his retainers.

35 how from the first his friend and lord
 helped him to the feast. That happy time is no more.
  "This, indeed, anyone forced to forgo for long
 the beloved counsel of his lord knows well.
 Often when sorrow and sleep together
40 bind the poor lone-dweller in their embrace,
 he dreams he clasps and that he kisses
 his liege-lord again, lays head and hands
 on the lord's knees as he did long ago,
 enjoyed the gift-giving in days gone by.
45 Then the warrior, friendless, awakens again,
 sees before him the fallow waves,
 seabirds on the water spreading their wings,
 snow and hail falling and sleet as well.
 Then the heart's wounds grow heavier,
50 sadness for dear ones. Sorrow returns.
 Then through his mind pass memories of kinsmen—
 joyfully he greets them, eagerly gazes—
 his fellow warriors, the floating spirits,
 fade on their way. They fail to bring
55 much familiar talk —trouble is renewed—
 for any man who must often send
 his weary spirit over the waves' bed.
  "Therefore I don't know why my woeful heart
 should not wax dark in this wide world
60 when I look back on the life of eorls,
 how quickly they quit the mead-hall's floor,
 brave young men. So this middle-earth
 from day to day dwindles and fails;
 therefore no one is wise without his share of winters
65 in the world's kingdom. A wise man must be patient,
 not too hot of heart nor hasty of speech,
 not reluctant to fight nor too reckless,
 not too timid nor too glad, not too greedy,
 and never eager to commit until he can be sure.
70 A man should hold back his boast until
 that time has come when he truly knows
 to direct his heart on the right path.
  "A wise man must know the misery of that time
 when the world's wealth shall all stand waste,
75 just as in our own day all over middle-earth
 walls are standing wind-swept and wasted,
 downed by frost, and dwellings covered with snow.
 The mead-hall crumbles, its master lies dead,
 bereft of pleasures, all the warrior-band[6] perished,
80 boldly by the wall. Battle took some,
 bore them away; a bird carried one
 above the high waves; the gray wolf took another,
 divided him with death; dreary-spirited

---

6. Old English *duguth* = generally something that affords benefit or advantage, but here it specifically applies to a band of warriors.

an eorl buried another   in an earthen pit.
85 "Mankind's Creator   laid waste this middle-earth
till the clamor of city-dwellers   ceased to be heard
and ancient works of giants   stood empty.
He who wisely   contemplates this wall-stead,
and considers deeply   the darkness of this life,
90 mature in years,   remembers many
bloody battlegrounds   and so begins:
    'Where did the steed go? Where the young warrior?   Where the
        treasure-giver?
Where the seats of fellowship?   Where the hall's festivity?
Alas bright beaker!   Alas burnished warrior!
95 Alas pride of princes!   How the time has passed,
gone under night-helm   as if it never was!
A towering wall,   traced with serpent shapes,[7]
endures instead   of the dear warrior-band.
Strength of ash-spears   destroyed warriors,
100 slaughter-greedy weapons,   overwhelming fate,
and storms beat against   these stone-faced cliffs,
snow descending   seals up the ground,
drumming of winter   when darkness falls,
night shadows darken,   from the north send down
105 fierce hail-showers   in hatred of men.
All is wretchedness   in the realm of earth;
fate's work lays low   the world under heaven.
Here wealth is fleeting,   here friend is fleeting,
here family is fleeting,   here humankind is fleeting.
110 All this resting-place Earth   shall become empty.'"
    So said the wise man   as he sat in meditation.
A good man holds his words back,   tells his woes not too soon,
baring his inner heart   before knowing the best way,
an eorl who acts with courage.   All shall be well for him who seeks
        grace,
115 help from our Father in heaven   where a fortress stands for us all.

7. The reference is to a kind of serpentine ornamentation; examples from Roman times survive in Britain.

WULF AND EADWACER

The first three lines of this lyric poem consist of three grammatically coherent sentences, and yet they paint no coherent narrative situation. The reader is obliged to infer that situation from the juxtaposition of sentences: thus the gap of narrative sense between the first and second sentences begs the reader to supply a narrative. But what is that narrative? One might infer that the speaker's people and the male to whom the speaker refers are mutually hostile, and that if "he" comes to where the speaker is, he will be easily defeated. One might also assume that there is some special relation between that male and the speaker ("We are apart"). The fourth line might confirm the assumption that the special male is physically absent, and it appears to supply a proper name for him ("Wulf").

Each of these inferences is vulnerable, but the reader is impelled to make assumptions of this kind. The remaining twenty lines prompt many further conjectures. Faced with the vulnerability of those assumptions, we might respond variously. We might dismiss this poem as maddeningly incoherent, inviting us as it does to construct a narrative but refusing to supply the needed connectives. Or we might keep testing hypotheses, working from fundamental elements of narrative (e.g., he/I; here/there; now/then). Or we might step back from the enticing puzzles of the poem's texture to think about what kind of poem this is.

Wulf and Eadwacer (an editorial title) appears in the Exeter Book (ca. 975), along with (though not precisely grouped with) all the other so-called Old English elegies, such as *The Wanderer*. Many of these poems are narrated by a first-person narrator who suffers from temporal and physical dislocations. They are relatively short. They tend to suggest, without filling in, a narrative context. Sometimes the experience of worldly pain invites general reflection on the inevitable treacheries of earthly experience.

This poem, like only one other in this group, is voiced by a woman. We learn this for sure only in line 10 (through an adjectival ending). That fact also helps us to set the text in a larger tradition of usually feminine elegy, a genre exemplified especially by Ovid's *Heroides* (*Heroines*). Classical elegy gives voice to the victim of history—often a woman—whose suffering predominates when society demands her sacrifice, and whose suffering is so intense that it overrides any commitment to narrative. The fragmented, incoherently expressed *implied* narrative is part of the poem's point: it sharpens and concentrates the poignancy of the poem's painful expression. This is the voice of a vast tradition of European lyric love poetry, with both male and female narrators.

That understanding of genre accounts for the kind of puzzles we have already encountered. It also accounts for the way in which the pained voice in the present breaks forth over narration of the past ("Wulf, my Wulf"). But the puzzles remain: Is Wulf the narrator's husband or lover? Is the name "Wulf" (a possible proper name, but also a figure for the outlaw) conceptually symmetrical with "Eadwacer" (literally "property watcher"), thus designating the same male? Is the name "Eadwacer" used ironically with regard to the absent, outlawed "Wulf," given that the child of the couple's union is threatened by a literal wolf?

We can never know the answers to these questions, but neither, by the conventions of this genre, are we supposed to. What we do know for sure is that the shared song of this couple is joined painfully only through the longing caused by separation.

Wulf and Eadwacer[1]

It is as though my people have been given
A present. They wish to capture him
If he comes with a troop. We are apart.
Wulf is on one isle, I am on another.
5 Fast is that island set among the fens.
Murderous are the people who inhabit
That island. They will wish to capture him
If he comes with a troop. We are apart.
Grieved have I for my Wulf with distant longings.

---

1. The translation is by Richard Hamer, *A Choice of Anglo-Saxon Verse* (1970).

10 Then was it rainy weather, and I sad,
When the bold warrior laid his arms about me.
I took delight in that and also pain.
O Wulf, my Wulf, my longing for your coming
Has made me ill, the rareness of your visits,
15 My grieving spirit, not the lack of food.
Eadwacer, do you hear me? For a wolf
Shall carry to the woods our wretched whelp.
Men very easily may put asunder
That which was never joined, our song together.

THE WIFE'S LAMENT

In modern English translation, the speaker of this poem sounds much like the speaker in *The Wanderer*, lamenting his exile, isolation, and the loss of his lord. But in Old English the grammatical gender of the pronouns reveals that this speaker is a woman; the man she refers to as "my lord" must, therefore, be her husband. The story behind the lament remains obscure. All that can be made out for certain is that the speaker was married to a nobleman of another country; that her husband has left her (possibly forced into exile as a result of a feud); that his kinsmen are hostile to her; and that she is now living alone in a wilderness. Although the circumstances are shadowy, it is reasonable to conjecture that the wife may have been a "peace-weaver" (a woman married off to make peace between warring tribes), like Hildeburh and Freawaru, whose politically inspired marriages only result in further bloodshed (see *Beowulf*, pp. 64 and 85). The obscurity of the Old English text has led to diametrically opposed interpretations of the husband's feeling toward his wife. One interpretation holds that, for unexplained reasons, possibly because of his kinsmen's hostility to her, he has turned against her. The other, which is adopted in this translation, is that, in her mind at least, they share the suffering of his exile and their separation. Thus in the line here rendered "I must suffer the feud of my much-beloved," *fæhðu* (feud) is read by some as the technical term for a blood feud—the way it is used in *Beowulf* when Hrothgar says he settled a great feud started by Beowulf's father with *feo* (fee)—that is, monetary compensation (p. 52). Others take the word in a more general sense as referring to the man's enmity toward his wife. In either case, the woman's themes and language resemble those of male "wræccas" (outcasts or exiles; the Old English root survives in modern *wretch*, *wretched*, and *wrack*) in the Old English poems called "elegies" because of their elegiac content and mood.

The Wife's Lament[1]

Full of sorrow,   I shall make this song
about me, my own fate.   Surely I can tell

1. The translation by Alfred David is based on *Eight Old English Poems*, 3rd ed., edited by John C. Pope and revised by R. D. Fulk (2000).

what sufferings I endured   since I came of age,
both the new and old,   never more than now.
5   I must endure without end   the misery of exile.
    First my lord[2] departed   from his people
over tossing waves;   I worried when day came
in what land   my liege-lord could be.
Then I set out,   a friendless exile,
10   to seek a place   for my sore need.
My husband's kin   had hatched a plot,
conspiring secretly   to separate us,
so that we[3] widest apart   in the world's realms
lived in most misery,   and I languished.
15   My lord commanded me   to keep house here;
in this dwelling-place;   I had few dear ones,
devoted friends.   Therefore I feel downcast.
Then I learned my lord   was like myself—
down on his luck,   dreary-spirited,
20   secretly minding   murder in his heart.
A happy pair   we had promised each other,
that death alone   would ever divide us,
and nothing else.   All that is changed;
our nearness once   is now as though
25   it never had been.   Now, far or near, I must
bear the malice   of the man I loved.
    I was told to live   in a grove of trees,
under an oak   in an earthen cave.
That earth-hall is old;   yearning overcomes me.
30   These dales are dark   and the dunes high,
bitter bulwarks   overgrown with briers,
a joyless place.   Here my lord's departure
afflicts me cruelly.   Friends here on earth,
lovers lying together,   lounge in bed,
35   while at daybreak   I abandon
this earthen-pit   under the oak
to sit alone   the summer-long day.
There I may bewail   my many woes,
suffering of exile,   for I can never
40   obtain comfort   for all my cares
nor all the longing   this life brought me.
    If ever anyone   should feel anguish,
harsh pain at heart,   she[4] should put on
a happy appearance   while enduring
45   endless sorrows—   should she possess
all the world's bliss,   or be banished far away
from her homeland.   I believe my lord sits
by a stony   storm-beaten cliff,
that water-tossed   my weary friend

---

2. A woman would refer to her husband as her
"lord."
3. Old English *wit*, an example of the dual form,
used for two persons.
4. Old English *geong-man*. The identity of the
speaker has been debated, but most recent opinion holds it to be the wife herself, speaking
impersonally. The translation takes the liberty of
using "she" in reference to the speaker.

50 sits in a desolate home. He must suffer
much in his mind, remembering too often
a happier place. Woe unto him
who languishing waits for a loved one.

THE RUIN

The power of enduring yet decaying architecture is characteristic of post-imperial cultures. The imperialists may have left (as the Romans did when they quit Britain in 420), but their buildings remain for centuries, serving as figures for the fall of earthly kingdoms. Anglo-Saxon poets certainly admired things bound fast. Stable architecture is almost the last thing upon which the dying Beowulf looks: he beholds "those gigantic stones . . . how the earthwork / was braced with arches built over columns" (lines 2718–19). Some buildings constructed by Germanic kings are provisionally capable of resisting the ravages of time for a few generations (for example, Hrothgar's Heorot in *Beowulf*, lines 770–74), but only the Roman buildings inspire awe for their capacity to endure for centuries, to evoke memories of the glory of what has been almost entirely lost from mind, and for the fact that they, too, are finally subject to the destructive effects of what Anglo-Saxons called "wyrd," or fate (the ancestor of our word *weird*). *The Ruin*, though itself damaged in the Exeter Book (ca. 975), expresses awe, admiration, and grief as it surveys what seems almost certainly a Roman building for hot baths.

The Ruin[1]

Splendid this rampart is, though fate destroyed it,
The city buildings fell apart, the works
Of giants crumble. Tumbled are the towers,
Ruined the roofs, and broken the barred gate,
5 Frost in the plaster, all the ceilings gape,
Torn and collapsed and eaten up by age.
And grit holds in its grip, the hard embrace
Of earth, the dead departed master-builders,
Until a hundred generations now
10 Of people have passed by. Often this wall
Stained red and grey with lichen has stood by
Surviving storms while kingdoms rose and fell.
And now the high curved wall itself has fallen.
. . .[2]

20 The heart inspired, incited to swift action.
Resolute masons, skilled in rounded building

1. The translation is from Richard Hamer, *A Choice of Anglo-Saxon Verse* (1970).
2. Six lines are illegible here in the manuscript.

Wondrously linked the framework with iron bonds.
The public halls were bright, with lofty gables,
Bath-houses many; great the cheerful noise,
25 And many mead-halls filled with human pleasures.
Till mighty fate brought change upon it all.
Slaughter was widespread, pestilence was rife,
And death took all those valiant men away.
The martial halls became deserted places,
30 The city crumbled, its repairers fell,
Its armies to the earth. And so these halls
Are empty, and this red curved roof now sheds
Its tiles, decay has brought it to the ground,
Smashed it to piles of rubble, where long since
35 A host of heroes, glorious, gold-adorned,
Gleaming in splendor, proud and flushed with wine,
Shone in their armor, gazed on gems and treasure,
On silver, riches, wealth, and jewelry,
On this bright city with its wide domains.
40 Stone buildings stood, and the hot steam cast forth
Wide sprays of water, which a wall enclosed
In its bright compass, where convenient
Stood hot baths ready for them at the centre.
Hot streams poured forth over the clear grey stone,
45 To the round pool and down into the baths.

RIDDLES

"*S aga hwæt ic hatte*" ("Say what I am called") is a frequently repeated imperative in the corpus of Anglo-Saxon riddles. The Exeter Book (ca. 975) not only contains moving elegiac poems, such as *The Wanderer* (pp. 118–21), *The Wife's Lament* (pp. 123–25), and *Wulf and Eadwacer* (pp. 121–23), but also a striking collection of ninety or so riddles. Like the elegies, the riddles are conveyed by first-person narrators, and, also like the elegies, they refuse to disclose the full conditions of their utterance. Whereas that refusal produces an emotional charge in the elegies, in the riddles it produces an intriguing and cognitive challenge.

The Anglo-Saxon riddles are clearly related to a learned Latin tradition of enigmas (*aenigmata*). Even if their subject matter is derived from the empirical world of natural phenomena, of everyday objects and animals, they provoke subtle interpretive challenges that defamiliarize the everyday world. When a poem fails to supply the crucial term of recognition ("what I am") around which understanding rapidly organizes perception, then every feature of the familiar becomes suddenly fascinating. Outworn metaphors spring into rich conceptual life; that which is regarded as purely conceptual is returned to its material condition; the everyday event becomes a wonder; comedy leaps unexpectedly forth from a revitalized account of the humdrum. Things and creatures disclose their mysterious and layered life in the world.

The Riddles[1]

Riddle 1

My beak points downwards, and I travel low
And dig along the ground, move forward as
The wood's old foe propels me; and my lord
And guardian walks stooping at my tail,
5 Pushes and moves and drives me on the field,
Sows in my track. I sniff along the ground,
Brought from the forest, firmly bound, and borne
Upon the wagon; I have many wonders.
And as I move on one side there is green
10 And my clear track is dark upon the other.
A well-made point is driven through my back
And hangs beneath, and through my head another,
Firm, pointing forwards; what my teeth tear up
Falls down beside me, if he serves me well
15 Who, as my lord, controls me from behind.[2]

Riddle 2

Some enemy deprived me of my life
And took away my worldly strength, then wet me,
Dipped me in water, took me out again,
Set me in sunshine, where I quickly lost
5 The hairs I had. Later the knife's hard edge
Cut me with all impurities ground off.
Then fingers folded me; the bird's fine raiment
Traced often over me with useful drops
Across my brown domain, swallowed the tree-dye
10 Mixed up with water, stepped on me again
Leaving dark tracks. The hero clothed me then
With boards to guard me, stretched hide over me,
Decked me with gold; and thus the splendid work
Of smiths, with wire bound round, embellished me.
15 Now my red dye and all my decorations,
My gorgeous trappings far and wide proclaim
The Lord of Hosts, not grief for foolish sins.
If sons of men will make good use of me,
By that they shall be sounder, more victorious,
20 Their hearts more bold, their minds more full of joy,
Their spirits wiser; they shall have more friends,
Dear ones and kinsmen, truer and more good,
More kind and faithful, who will add more glory
And happiness by favors, who will lay
25 Upon them kindnesses and benefits,
And clasp them fast in the embrace of love.

1. Translations are from Richard Hamer, *A Choice of Anglo-Saxon Verse* (1970).   2. Solution: plow.

Say who I am, useful to men. My name
Is famous, good to men, and also sacred.[3]

Riddle 3

A moth ate words; a marvelous event
I thought it when I heard about that wonder,
A worm had swallowed some man's lay, a thief
In darkness had consumed the mighty saying
5   With its foundation firm. The thief was not
One whit the wiser when he ate those words.[4]

---

3. Solution: the Bible.   4. Solution: bookworm.

IRISH LITERATURE

The changes European literature underwent during the twelfth and thirteenth centuries were greatly indebted to Celtic influences. The legends about King Arthur and his knights, although they were assimilated to the feudal culture of the Anglo-Normans and transmitted by texts written in Latin, French, and English (see p. 13), were originally products of Celtic myth and legend. The folkloric otherworld elements and the major role played by women in those stories profoundly shaped and colored the literature we now think of as "romance." The French Tristran romances, the romances of Marie de France and Chrétien de Troyes, and even the legends of the Holy Grail could not have been imagined without their Celtic components.

The Celts overran central Europe, Spain, and the British Isles during the first millennium B.C.E. On the Continent and in Great Britain, south of the wall built by the emperor Hadrian (see the map inside the front cover), they were absorbed into the Roman Empire. However, the Celtic vernacular continued to be spoken as the native language, and Ireland never became a Roman province. The Anglo-Saxon invasions in the fifth and early sixth centuries, and the Danish invasions after the eighth, displaced the Celts in England, but Celtic language and culture continued to flourish in Wales (Welsh), in Cornwall (Cornish), in Scotland (Scottish Gaelic), across the English Channel in Brittany (Breton), and, of course, in Ireland (Gaelic). While still part of the Roman Empire, Britain and, in consequence, Ireland had been converted to Christianity. As portrayed in the Arthurian legend, the Christian Britons fought against barbaric Germanic invaders. Irish and Welsh missionaries, along with Roman ones, brought about the conversion of the Anglo-Saxons.

The earliest Celtic literature, like that of the Anglo-Saxons, was transmitted orally and little was copied down before the twelfth century. Nevertheless, the surviving monuments indicate its richness and its significance for the development of French and English medieval literature.

What follows are two examples of Irish literature, an excerpt from the Old Irish epic *Táin Bó Cuailnge* (The Cattle Raid of Cooley) and some delightful monastic lyrics written between the sixth and the ninth centuries.

CÚCHULAINN'S BOYHOOD DEEDS

Cúchulainn (koo-chúll-in), nephew of Ulster's king Conchobor, is the hero of the Old Irish epic *Táin Bó Cuailnge* (The Cattle Raid of Cooley), which tells of a great war between the kingdoms of Connacht and Ulster. The cause of the war that gives this epic work its title is the desire of Queen Medb of Connacht to obtain possession of the brown bull of Ulster to match one owned by her husband, King Ailill. The tales go back to ancient oral literature; the best surviving manuscript, pieced together in the twelfth century from different sources, although seriously defective, nevertheless tells powerful tales. This excerpt is part of the answer Medb and Ailill, leading the invading army, are given to the query "What sort of man . . . is this Hound of Ulster?"

Cúchulainn's Boyhood Deeds[1]

'There was another deed he did,' Fiacha Mac Fir Febe said. 'Cathbad the druid was staying with his son, Conchobor mac Nesa. He had one hundred studious men learning druid lore from him—this was always the number that Cathbad taught.

'One day a pupil asked him what that day would be lucky for. Cathbad said if a warrior took up arms for the first time that day his name would endure in Ireland as a word signifying mighty acts, and stories about him would last forever.

'Cúchulainn overheard this. He went to Conchobor and claimed his weapons. Conchobor said:

"By whose instruction?"

"My friend Cathbad's," Cúchulainn said.

"We have heard of him," Conchobor said, and gave him shield and spear. Cúchulainn brandished them in the middle of the house, and not one piece survived of the fifteen sets that Conchobor kept in store for new warriors or in case of breakage. He was given Conchobor's own weapons at last, and these survived. He made a flourish and saluted their owner the king and said:

"Long life to their seed and breed, who have for their king the man who owns these weapons."

'It was then that Cathbad came in and said:

"Do I see a young boy newly armed?"

"Yes," Conchobor said.

"Then woe to his mother's son," he said.

"What is this? Wasn't it by your own direction he came?" Conchobor said.

"Certainly not," Cathbad said.

"Little demon, why did you lie to me?" Conchobor said to Cúchulainn.

---

1. The translation is by Thomas Kinsella, *The Táin* (1969).

"It was no lie, king of warriors," Cúchulainn said. "I happened to hear him instructing his pupils this morning south of Emain, and I came to you then."

"Well," Cathbad said, "the day has this merit: he who arms for the first time today will achieve fame and greatness. But his life is short."

"That is a fair bargain," Cúchulainn said. "If I achieve fame I am content, though I had only one day on earth."

'Another day came and another druid asked what that day would be lucky for.

"Whoever mounts his first chariot today," Cathbad said, "his name will live forever in Ireland."

Cúchulainn overheard this also, and went to Conchobor and said:

"Friend Conchobor, my chariot!"

'A chariot was given to him. He clapped his hand to the chariot between the shafts, and the frame broke at his touch. In the same way he broke twelve chariots. At last they gave him Conchobor's chariot and that survived him.

'He mounted the chariot beside Conchobor's charioteer. This charioteer, Ibor by name, turned the chariot round where it stood.

"You can get out of the chariot now," the charioteer said.

"You think your horses are precious," Cúchulainn said, "but so am I, my friend. Drive round Emain now, and you won't lose by it."

'The charioteer set off.

'Cúchulainn urged him to take the road to the boy-troop, to greet them and get their blessing in return. After this he asked him to go further along the road. Cúchulainn said to the charioteer as they drove onward:

"Use your goad on the horses now."

"Which direction?" the charioteer said.

"As far as the road will take us!" Cúchulainn said.

'They came to Sliab Fuait. They met Conall Cernach there—for to Conall Cernach had fallen the care of the province boundary that day. Each of Ulster's heroic warriors had his day on Sliab Fuait, to take care of every man who came that way with poetry, and to fight any others. In this way everyone was challenged and no one slipped past to Emain unnoticed.

"May you prosper," Conall said. "I wish you victory and triumph."

"Conall, go back to the fort," Cúchulainn said, "and let me keep watch here a little."

"You would do for looking after men of poetry," Conall said. "But you are a little young still for dealing with men of war."

"It might never happen at all," Cúchulainn said. "Let us wander off, meanwhile," he said, "to view the shore of Loch Echtra. Warriors are often camped there."

"It is a pleasant thought," Conall said.

'They set off. Suddenly Cúchulainn let fly a stone from his sling and smashed the shaft of Conall Cernach's chariot.

"Why did you cast that stone, boy?" Conall said.

"To test my hand and the straightness of my aim," Cúchulainn said. "Now, since it is your Ulster custom not to continue a dangerous journey, go back to Emain, friend Conall, and leave me here on guard."

"If I must," Conall said.

'Conall Cernach wouldn't go beyond that point.

'Cúchulainn went on to Loch Echtra but found no one there. The charioteer said to Cúchulainn that they ought to go back to Emain, that they might
get there for the drinking.

"No," Cúchulainn said. "What is that peak there?"

"Sliab Mondairn," the charioteer said.

"Take me there," Cúchulainn said.

'They travelled on until they got there. On arriving at the mountain,
Cúchulainn asked:

"That white heap of stones on the mountain-top, what is it called?"

"The look-out place, Finncarn, the white cairn," the charioteer said.

"That plain there before us?" Cúchulainn said.

"Mag Breg, Breg Plain," the charioteer said.

'In this way he gave the name of every fort of any size between Temair
and Cenannos. And he recited to him also all fields and fords, all habita-
tions and places of note, and every fastness and fortress. He pointed out at
last the fort of the three sons of Nechta Scéne, who were called Foill (for
deceitfulness) and Fannall (the Swallow) and Tuachell (the Cunning). They
came from the mouth of the river Scéne. Fer Ulli, Lugaid's son, was their
father and Nechta Scéne their mother. Ulstermen had killed their father
and this is why they were at enmity with them.

"Is it these who say," Cúchulainn said, "that they have killed as many
Ulstermen as are now living?"

"They are the ones," the charioteer said.

"Take me to meet them," Cúchulainn said.

"That is looking for danger," the charioteer said.

"We're not going there to avoid it," Cúchulainn said.

'They travelled on, and turned their horses loose where bog and river
met, to the south and upstream of their enemies' stronghold. He took the
spancel-hoop of challenge from the pillar-stone at the ford and threw it as
far as he could out into the river and let the current take it—thus challenging the ban of the sons of Nechta Scéne.

'They took note of this and started out to find him.

'Cúchulainn, after sending the spancel-hoop downstream, lay down by
the pillar-stone to rest, and said to his charioteer:

"If only one man comes, or two, don't wake me, but wake me if they all
come."

'The charioteer waited meanwhile in terror. He yoked the chariot and
pulled off the skins and coverings that were over Cúchulainn, trying not to
wake him, since Cúchulainn had told him not to wake him for only one.

'Then the sons of Nechta Scéne came up.

"Who is that there?" said one.

"A little boy out in his chariot today for the first time," the charioteer
said.

"Then his luck has deserted him," the warrior said. "This is a bad beginning in arms for him. Get out of our land. Graze your horses here no
more."

"I have the reins in my hand," the charioteer said.

Then Ibor said to the warrior:

"Why should you earn enmity? Look, the boy is asleep."

"A boy with a difference!" cried Cúchulainn. "A boy who came here to look for fight!"

"It will be a pleasure," the warrior said.

"You may have that pleasure now, in the ford there," Cúchulainn said.

"You would be wise," the charioteer said, "to be careful of the man who is coming against you. Foill is his name," he said. "If you don't get him with your first thrust, you may thrust away all day."

"I swear the oath of my people that he won't play that trick on an Ulsterman again when my friend Conchobor's broad spear leaves my hand to find him. He'll feel it like the hand of an outlaw!"

'He flung the spear at him, and it pierced him and broke his back. He removed the trophies, and the head with them.

"Watch this other one," the charioteer said. "Fannall is his name, and he treads the water no heavier than swan or swallow."

"I swear he won't use that trick on an Ulsterman again," Cúchulainn said. "You have seen how I foot the pool in Emain."

'They met in the ford, and he killed the man and took away the trophies and the head.

"Watch this next one advancing against you," the charioteer said. "Tuachell is his name, and he wasn't named in vain. He has never fallen to any weapon."

"I have the *del chliss* for him, a wily weapon to churn him up and red-riddle him," Cúchulainn said.

'He threw the spear at him and tore him asunder where he stood. He went up and cut off his head. He gave the head and trophies to his charioteer.

'Then a scream rose up behind them from the mother, Nechta Scéne. Cúchulainn lifted the trophies off the ground and brought the three heads with him into the chariot, saying:

"I won't let go of these trophies until we reach Emain Macha."

'They set out for Emain Macha with all his spoils. Cúchulainn said to his charioteer:

"You promised us great driving. We'll need it now after our fight, with this chase after us."

'They travelled onward to Sliab Fuait. So fleet their haste across Breg Plain, as he hurried the charioteer, that the chariot-horses overtook the wind and the birds in flight, and Cúchulainn could catch the shot from his sling before it hit the earth.

'When they got to Sliab Fuait they found a herd of deer before them.

"What are those nimble beasts there?" Cúchulainn said.

"Wild deer," the charioteer said.

Cúchulainn said:

"Which would the men of Ulster like brought in, a dead one or a live one?"

"A live one would startle them more," the charioteer said. "It isn't everyone who could do it. Every man there has brought home a dead one. You can't catch them alive."

"I can," Cúchulainn said. "Use your goad on the horses, over the marsh."

'The charioteer did so until the horses bogged down. Cúchulainn got out and caught the deer nearest to him, the handsomest of all. He lashed the horses free of the bog and calmed the deer quickly. Then he tethered it between the rear shafts of the chariot.

'The next thing they saw before them was a flock of swans.

"Would the men of Ulster prefer to have these brought in alive or dead?" Cúchulainn said.

"The quickest and the most expert take them alive," the charioteer said.

'Cúchulainn immediately flung a little stone at the birds and brought down eight of them. Then he flung a bigger stone that brought down twelve more. He did this with his feat of the stunning-shot.

"Gather in our birds now," Cúchulainn said to his charioteer. "If I go out to them this wild stag will turn on you."

"But it's no easier if I go," the charioteer said. "The horses are so maddened that I can't get past them. I can't get over the two iron rims of the chariot wheels, they are so sharp. And I can't get past the stag; his antlers fill all the space between the chariot's shafts."

"Step out onto the antlers," Cúchulainn said. "I swear the oath of Ulster's people, I'll turn my head on him with such a stare, I'll fix him with such an eye, that he won't dare to stir or budge his head at you."

'He did this. Cúchulainn tied the reins and the charioteer gathered up the birds. Then Cúchulainn fastened the birds to the cords and thongs of the chariot. It was in this manner that they came back to Emain Macha: a wild stag behind the chariot, a swan-flock fluttering above, and the three heads of Nechta Scéne's sons inside the chariot.

'They came to Emain.

"A man in a chariot advancing upon us," cried the watcher in Emain Macha. "He'll spill the blood of the whole court unless you see to him and send naked women to meet him."

'Cúchulainn turned the left chariot-board toward Emain in insult, and he said:

"I swear by the oath of Ulster's people that if a man isn't found to fight me, I'll spill the blood of everyone in this court."

"Naked women to him!" Conchobor said.

'The women of Emain went forth, with Mugain the wife of Conchobor mac Nesa at their head, and they stripped their breasts at him.

"These are the warriors you must struggle with today," Mugain said.

'He hid his countenance. Immediately the warriors of Emain seized him and plunged him in a vat of cold water. The vat burst asunder about him. Then he was thrust in another vat and it boiled with bubbles the size of fists. He was placed at last in a third vat and warmed it till its heat and cold were equal. Then he got out and Mugain the queen gave him a blue cloak to go round him with a silver brooch in it, and a hooded tunic. And he sat on Conchobor's knee, and that was his seat ever after.

'What wonder,' Fiacha mac Fir Febe said, 'that the one who did this in his seventh year should triumph against odds and beat his match today, when he is fully seventeen years old?'

EARLY IRISH LYRICS

Monastic Irish scribes were also composers of beautiful lyrics, inspired by both the study and what could be seen from the study.

The Scholar and His Cat

I and white Pangur practice each of us his special art: his mind is set on hunting, my mind on my special craft.

I love (it is better than all fame) to be quiet beside my book, diligently pursuing knowledge. White Pangur does not envy me: he loves his childish craft.

When the two of us (this tale never wearies us) are alone together in our house, we have something to which we may apply our skill, an endless sport.

It is usual, at times, for a mouse to stick in his net, as a result of warlike battlings. For my part, into my net falls some difficult rule of hard meaning.

He directs his bright perfect eye against an enclosing wall. Though my clear eye is very weak I direct it against keenness of knowledge.

He is joyful with swift movement when a mouse sticks in his sharp paw. I too am joyful when I understand a dearly loved difficult problem.

Though we be thus at any time, neither of us hinders the other: each of us likes his craft, severally rejoicing in them.

He it is who is master for himself of the work which he does every day. I can perform my own work directed at understanding clearly what is difficult.

The Scribe in the Woods

A hedge of trees overlooks me; a blackbird's lay sings to me (an announcement which I shall not conceal); above my lined book the birds' chanting sings to me.

A clear-voiced cuckoo sings to me (goodly utterance) in a grey cloak from bush fortresses. The Lord is indeed good to me: well do I write beneath a forest of woodland.

The Lord of Creation

Let us adore the Lord, maker of wondrous works, great bright Heaven with its angels, the white-waved sea on earth.

My Hand Is Weary with Writing

My hand is weary with writing; my sharp great point is not thick; my slender-beaked pen juts forth a beetle-hued draft of bright blue ink.

A steady stream of wisdom springs from my well-colored neat fair hand; on the page it pours its draft of ink of the green-skinned holly.

I send my little dripping pen unceasingly over an assemblage of books of great beauty, to enrich the possessions of men of art—whence my hand is weary with writing.

Anglo-Norman Literature

THE MYTH OF ARTHUR'S RETURN

During the twelfth century, three authors, writing in Latin, Anglo-Norman French, and Middle English respectively, created a mostly legendary history of Britain for their Norman overlords (see p. 13). This "history" was set in the remote past, beginning with a foundation myth—a heroic account of national origins—modeled on Virgil's *Aeneid* and ending with the Anglo-Saxon conquest of the native islanders, the Britons, in the fifth and sixth centuries. The chief architect of the history is Geoffrey of Monmouth, who was writing his *History of the Kings of Britain* in Latin prose ca. 1136–38. His work was freely translated into French verse by Wace in 1155, and Wace in turn was translated into English alliterative poetry by Layamon in his *Brut* (ca. 1190).

Geoffrey of Monmouth and Wace wrote their histories of Britain primarily for an audience of noblemen and prelates who were descendants of the Norman conquerors of the Anglo-Saxons. Geoffrey wrote several dedications of his *History*, first to supporters of Matilda, the heiress presumptive of Henry I, and, when the Crown went instead to Stephen of Blois, to the new king's allies and to Stephen himself. Layamon tells us that Wace wrote his French version for Eleanor of Aquitaine, queen of Stephen's successor, Henry II. The prestige and power of ancient Rome still dominated the historical and political imagination of the feudal aristocracy, and the legendary history of the ancient kings of the Britons, especially of King Arthur, who had defeated Rome itself, served to flatter the self-image and ambitions of the Anglo-Norman barons. Perhaps the destruction of Arthur's Kingdom also provided a timely object lesson of the disastrous consequences of civil wars such as those over the English succession in which these lords were engaged.

Folklore and literature provide examples of a recurrent myth about a leader or hero who has not really died but is asleep somewhere or in some state of suspended life and will return to save his people. Evidently, the Bretons and Welsh developed this myth about Arthur in oral tradition long before it turns up in medieval chronicles. Geoffrey of Monmouth, Wace, and Layamon, and subsequent writers about Arthur, including Malory (see pp. 534–36), allude to it with varying degrees of skepticism.

The selections from Geoffrey of Monmouth and Wace are translated by Alfred David. The Layamon selection is translated by Rosamund Allen. For more information about Arthur, see the NAEL Archive.

GEOFFREY OF MONMOUTH: *From* The History of the Kings of Britain

But also the famous King Arthur himself was mortally wounded. When he was carried off to the island of Avalon to have his wounds treated, he bestowed the crown on his cousin Constantine, the son of Duke Cador in the year 542 after the Incarnation of our lord. May his soul rest in peace.

WACE: *From* Roman de Brut

Arthur, if the story is not false, was mortally wounded; he had himself carried to Avalon to be healed of his wounds. He is still there and the Britons expect him as they say and hope. He'll come from there if he is still alive. Master Wace, who made this book, won't say more about Arthur's end than the prophet Merlin rightly said once upon a time that one would not know whether or not he were dead. The prophet spoke truly: ever since men have asked and shall always ask, I believe, whether he is dead or alive. Truly he had himself taken to Avalon 542 years after the Incarnation. It was a pity that he had no offspring. He left his realm to Constantine, the son of Cador of Cornwall, and asked him to reign until his return.

LAYAMON: *From* Brut

Arthur was mortally wounded, grievously badly;
To him there came a young lad who was from his clan,
He was Cador the Earl of Cornwall's son;
The boy was called Constantine; the king loved him very much.
14270   Arthur gazed up at him, as he lay there on the ground,
And uttered these words with a sorrowing heart:
"Welcome, Constantine; you were Cador's son;
Here I bequeath to you all of my kingdom,
And guard well my Britons all the days of your life
14275   And retain for them all the laws which have been extant in my days
And all the good laws which there were in Uther's days.
And I shall voyage to Avalon, to the fairest of all maidens,
To the Queen Argante, a very radiant elf,
And she will make quite sound every one of my wounds,
14280   Will make me completely whole with her health-giving potions.
And then I shall come back to my own kingdom
And dwell among the Britons with surpassing delight."
After these words there came gliding from the sea
What seemed a short boat, moving, propelled along by the tide
14285   And in it were two women in remarkable attire,
Who took Arthur up at once and immediately carried him
And gently laid him down and began to move off.
And so it had happened, as Merlin said before:
That the grief would be incalculable at the passing of Arthur.
14290   The Britons even now believe that he is alive
And living in Avalon with the fairest of the elf-folk,
And the Britons are still always looking for when Arthur comes
     returning.
Yet once there was a prophet and his name was Merlin:
He spoke his predictions, and his sayings were the truth,
14295   Of how an Arthur once again would come to aid the English.

TRISTAN AND YSOLT

The story of Tristan (also known as "Tristran") and Ysolt remains ever fresh in the Western tradition for re-adaptation, from Wagner's opera (1857–59) to the 2006 movie. Two lovers, the brilliant and gifted Tristan and Ysolt, are "made for each other." The intensity of their mutual love is both expressed and sealed by the love potion they mistakenly drink as they travel by sea from Ireland to Cornwall, where Ysolt, bound by the inescapable needs of feudal power, is to marry King Mark of Cornwall, Tristan's uncle. This tragic story of love and its consequences was a runaway success in Europe from the mid-twelfth century forward: two twelfth-century Anglo-Norman versions, by Thomas of England (below) and Beroul (ca. 1160) survive, but the fame of Tristan and Ysolt was much more widely dispersed, as attested by other, shorter texts, such as *The Madness of Tristan* (below) and *Chevrefoil* (pp. 185–87), references in many other texts, and visual artifacts.

THOMAS OF ENGLAND

The tragic love story of Tristran and Ysolt, the wife of Tristran's maternal uncle King Mark, derives mainly from Breton, Welsh, and Irish sources, although it also incorporates motifs of Eastern tales that were probably transmitted to Europe from India via Arabic Spain. The romance of Tristran and Ysolt entered the mainstream of Western European literature through the Old French version in octosyllabic couplets by a twelfth-century author who identifies himself only as "Thomas" and of whom practically nothing else is known for certain. Only 3,143 lines (roughly a sixth) of the poem survive, in nine separate fragments. But we can reconstruct the story from the *Tristrams saga* (1226), a relatively faithful translation into Old Norse, and the Middle High German adaptation *Tristan und Isolde* (also early thirteenth century) by Gottfried von Strassburg, who names the author of his major source "Thomas of Britain."

Thomas's *Tristran* is written in a dialect of western France containing Anglo-Norman forms; he is likely to have composed the romance for the court of Henry II. Borrowings from Wace's *Brut* (see p. 137) prove that he wrote after 1155, probably some time before 1170. As Thomas himself tells his audience, "My lords, this tale is told in many ways." Comparisons with other early versions in French and German suggest that he was following a lost text from which he eliminated episodes he considered improbable or coarse, and to which he added new courtly and psychological dimensions. Thomas's work proved enormously influential not only by way of Gottfried's important poem (the source of Richard Wagner's opera *Tristan und Isolde*), but it may well have provided the inspiration and model for the love affair of Lancelot and Guinevere. That relationship first appears (already in progress) in Chrétien de Troye's romance *The Knight of the Cart* (see "King Arthur," in the NAEL Archive).

The romance of Tristran was drawn into the orbit of Arthurian romance, where Sir Tristran is the only knight who can match Sir Lancelot. After fighting a five-hour duel to a draw, they become fast friends. Tristran is thus a champion in war and tournaments, but in Thomas and in other Tristran romances he has other attributes as well: he is a master of the hunt, chess, and several languages; he is a gifted harp player; and he and Ysolt make an expert team in the art of deceiving a jealous husband.

Tristran starts life as an orphan. His own story is preceded by the romance of his parents: Rivalen and Blancheflor, the sister of King Mark. Rivalen is killed in battle before Tristran's birth; Blancheflor dies in childbirth. Tristran is fostered by his father's steward until he is kidnapped by merchants who lure the handsome youth aboard their ship to play chess and then set sail. A storm they blame on the kidnapping causes them to strand the youth on a deserted coast of his uncle's kingdom. Tristran's gifts and charm lead Mark to adopt him as a trusted servant, who is identified as his nephew when Tristran's foster-father arrives at the court in search of him. Mark contracts to marry the king of Ireland's daughter Ysolt and sends Tristran to escort the bride to England. On the return voyage, Tristran and Ysolt become lovers after they unwittingly drink a love potion her mother had prepared for Ysolt and Mark. On Ysolt's wedding night, her maid Brengvein takes her place in the marriage bed. Tristran and Ysolt scheme repeatedly to meet secretly and devise ways to allay Mark's suspicions and frustrate his attempts to surprise them. Finally, however, Tristran is exiled from Britain for good and pursues wars on the Continent. Eventually, fearing that Ysolt no longer loves him and hoping that he will get over his love for her, he marries a second Ysolt, "Ysolt of the White Hands," the sister of Tristran's young friend and admirer Caerdin. Tristran, however, cannot bring himself to consummate the marriage, and the second Ysolt remains an unwilling virgin. When Tristran is wounded by a poisoned spear, Caerdin sets sail for England to fetch the first Ysolt, who alone has it in her power to save Tristran's life.

Tristan and Isolde, French ivory, ca. 1350. The image depicts a night scene in which the reflection of the face of King Mark, hiding in the tree above, is spotted by the lovers in the pool below (note Ysolt's pointing finger).

Medieval people believed that given names sometimes foreshadowed one's destiny, and the French authors of Tristran's story interpreted *trist*, the Celtic root of the name, as French *triste* (sad). The sense of a tragic illicit love whose passion finds an ultimate fulfillment in death haunts the story of Tristran and Ysolt in Thomas and in the different versions that derive from it.

The geography of the Tristran romances varies from version to version. Tristran's homeland Lyonesse may originally have been Lothian in Scotland. In Marie de France's *Chevrefoil* (see pp. 185–87), it is in Wales. In Thomas it is Brittany, and the voyages across the English Channel and Irish Sea are episodes in which the sea itself plays a pivotal and symbolic role. The names Tristran and Ysolt vary according to the language of different versions. They are adopted here from the translation by A. T. Hatto (1960).

From Le Roman de Tristran

[THE DEATHS OF TRISTRAN AND YSOLT]

When Ysolt hears this message there is anguish in her heart, and pain, and sorrow, and grief—never yet has she known greater. Now she ponders deeply, and sighs and longs for Tristran, her lover. But she does not know how to come to him. She goes to speak with Brengvein. She tells her the whole story of the poisoned wound, the pain he is in and the misery, and how he lies there languishing, how and through whom he has sent for her—else his wound will never be healed. She has described all his torment and then asks advice what to do. And as they talk there begins a sighing, complaining, and weeping, and pain, sorrow, sadness, and grief, for the pity which they have on his account. Nevertheless they have discussed the matter and finally decide to set out on their journey and go away with Caerdin to treat Tristran's illness and succour him in his need.

They make ready towards evening and take what they will require. As soon as the others are all asleep, they leave very stealthily under cover of night by a lucky postern in the wall overlooking the Thames. The water has come up to it with the rising tide. The boat is all ready and the Queen has gone aboard it. They row, they sail with the ebb—quickly they fly before the wind. They make a mighty effort and keep on rowing till they are alongside the big ship. They hoist the yard and then they sail. They run before the waves as long as they have wind behind them. They coast along the foreign land past the port of Wissant, and then Boulogne, and Treport. The wind is strong and favourable and the ship that bears them is fleet. They sail past Normandy. They sail happily and joyfully, since they have the wind they want.

Tristran lies on his bed languishing of his wound. He can find no succour in anything. Medicine cannot avail him; nothing that he does affords him any aid. He longs for the coming of Ysolt, desiring nothing else. Without her he can have no ease—it is because of her that he lives so long. There, in his bed, he pines and he waits for her. He has high hopes that she will come and heal his malady, and believes that he will not live without her. Each day he sends to the shore to see if the ship is returning, with no other wish in his heart. And many is the time that he commands his bed to be made beside the sea and has himself carried out to it, to await and see the ship—what way she is making, and with what sail? He has no desire for anything, except for the coming of Ysolt: his whole mind, will, and desire are set on it. Whatever the world holds he rates of no account unless the Queen is coming to him. Then he has himself carried back again from the fear which he anticipates, for he dreads that she may not come, may not keep her faith with him, and he would much rather hear it from another than see the ship come without her. He longs to look out for the ship, but does not wish to know it, should she fail to come. There is anguish in his heart, and he is full of desire to see her. He often laments to his wife but does not tell her what he longs for, apart from Caerdin, who does not come. Seeing him delay so long Tristran greatly fears that Caerdin has failed in his mission.

Now listen to a pitiful disaster and a most sad mishap which must touch the hearts of all lovers! You never heard tell of greater sorrow arising from such love and such desire. Just there where Tristran is waiting and the lady is eager to arrive and has drawn close enough to see the land—gay they are on board and they sail lightheartedly—a wind springs up from the south and strikes them full in the middle of the yard, checking the whole ship in its course. The crew run to luff and turn the sail, they turn about whether they wish to or not. The wind gains in force and raises the swell, the deep begins to stir; the weather grows foul and the air thick, the waves rise, the sea grows black, it rains and sleets as the storm increases. Bowlines and shrouds snap. They lower the yard and drift along with the wind and waves. They had put out their boat on the sea, since they were close to their own country, but by ill luck they forgot it and a wave has smashed it to pieces. This at least they have now lost, and the tempest has grown so in violence that the best of sailors could never have kept his feet. All on board weep and lament and give vent to great grief, so afraid are they.

"Alas, poor me," cried Ysolt. "God does not wish me to live until I see my lover Tristran.—He wants me to be drowned in the sea! Tristran, if only I had spoken with you, I would not mind if I had then died. Dear love, when you hear that I am dead I know you will never again be consoled. You will be so afflicted by my death, following your long-drawn sufferings, that you will never be well again. My coming does not rest with me. God willing, I would come and take charge of your wound. For I have no other sorrow than that you are without aid; this is my sorrow and my grief. And I am very sad at heart, my friend, that you will have no support against death, when I die. My own death matters nothing to me—if God wills it, so be it. But when at last you learn of it, my love, I know that you will die of it. Such is our love, I can feel no grief unless you are in it. You cannot die without me, nor can I perish without you. If I am to be shipwrecked at sea, then you, too, must drown. But you cannot drown on dry land, so you have come to sea to seek me! I see your death before my eyes and know that I am soon to die. Dear friend, I fail in my desire, since I hoped to die in your arms and to be buried in one coffin with you. But now we have failed to achieve it. Yet it may still happen so: for if I am to drown here, and you, as I think, must also drown, a fish could swallow us, and so, my love, by good fortune we should share one sepulture, since it might be caught by someone who would recognize our bodies and do them the high honour befitting our love. But what I am saying cannot be.—Yet if God wills it, it must be!—But what would you be seeking on the sea? I do not know what you could be doing here. Nevertheless I am here, and here shall I die. I shall drown here, Tristran, without you. Yet it is a sweet comfort to me, my darling, that you will not know of my death. From henceforward it will never be known and I do not know who should tell it. You will live long after me and await my coming. If it please God you may be healed—that is what I most desire. I long for your recovery more than that I should come ashore. So truly do I love you, dear friend, that I must fear after my death, if you recover, lest you forget me during your lifetime or console yourself with another woman, Tristran, when I am dead. My love, I am indeed much afraid of Ysolt of the White Hands, at least. I do not know whether I ought to fear her; but, if you were to die before me, I would not long survive you. I do not know at all what to do, but you I do desire above all things. God grant we come together so that I may heal you, love, or that we two may die of one anguish!"

As long as the storm endures Ysolt gives vent to her sorrow and grief. The storm and foul weather last on the sea for five days and more; then the wind drops and it is fair. They have hoisted the white sail and are making good speed, when Caerdin espies the coast of Brittany. At this they are gay and light-hearted, they raise the sail right up so that it can be seen what sail it is, the white or the black. Caerdin wished to show its colour from afar, since it was the last day of the term that lord Tristran had assigned when they had set out for England.

While they are happily sailing, there is a spell of warm weather and the wind drops so that they can make no headway. The sea is very smooth and still, the ship moves neither one way nor the other save so far as the swell draws it. They are also without their boat. And now they are in great distress. They see the land close ahead of them, but have no wind with which to reach it. And so up and down they go drifting, now back, now forward. They cannot make any progress and are very badly impeded. Ysolt is much afflicted by it. She sees the land she has longed for and yet she cannot reach it: she all but dies of her longing. Those in the ship long for land, but the wind is too light for them. Time and again, Ysolt laments her fate. Those on the shore long for the ship, but they have not seen it yet. Thus Tristran is wretched and sorrowful, he often laments and sighs for Ysolt, whom he so much desires. The tears flow from his eyes, he writhes about, he all but dies of longing.

While Tristran endures such affliction, his wife Ysolt comes and stands before him. Meditating great guile she says: "Caerdin is coming, my love! I have seen his ship on the sea. I saw it making hardly any headway but nevertheless I could see it well enough to know that it is his. God grant it brings news that will comfort you at heart!"

Tristran starts up at this news. "Do you know for sure that it is his ship, my darling?" he asks. "Tell me now, what sort of sail is it?"

"I know it for a fact!" answered Ysolt. "Let me tell you, the sail is all black! They have hoisted it and raised it up high because they have no wind!"

At this Tristran feels such pain that he has never had greater nor ever will, and he turns his face to the wall and says: "God save Ysolt and me! Since you will not come to me I must die for your love. I can hold on to life no longer. I die for you, Ysolt, dear love! You have no pity for my sufferings, but you will have sorrow of my death. It is a great solace to me that you will have pity for my death."

Three times did he say "Dearest Ysolt." At the fourth he rendered up his spirit.

Thereupon throughout the house the knights and companions weep. Their cries are loud, their lament is great. Knights and serjeants rise to their feet and bear him from his bed, then lay him upon a cloth of samite and cover him with a striped pall.

And now the wind has risen on the sea. It strikes the middle of the sailyard and brings the ship to land. Ysolt has quickly disembarked, she hears the great laments in the street and the bells from the minsters and chapels. She asks people what news? and why they toll the bells so? and the reason for their weeping? Then an old man answers: "My lady, as God help me, we have greater sorrow than people ever had before. Gallant, noble Tristran, who was a source of strength to the whole realm, is dead! He was generous to the needy, a great succour to the wretched. He has died just now in his bed of a wound that his body received. Never did so great a misfortune befall this realm!"

As soon as Ysolt heard this news she was struck dumb with grief. So afflicted is she that she goes up the street to the palace in advance of the others, without her cloak. The Bretons have never seen a woman of her beauty; in the city they wonder whence she comes and who she may be. Ysolt goes to where she sees his body lying, and, turning towards the east, she prays for him piteously. "Tristran, my love, now that I see you dead, it is against reason for me to live longer. You died for my love, and I, love, die of grief, for I could not come in time to heal you and your wound. My love, my love, nothing shall ever console me for your death, neither joy nor pleasure nor any delight. May this storm be accursed that so delayed me on the sea, my sweetheart, so that I could not come! Had I arrived in time, I would have given you back your life and spoken gently to you of the love there was between us. I should have bewailed our fate, our joy, our rapture, and the great sorrow and pain that have been in our loving. I should have reminded you of this and kissed you and embraced you. If I had failed to cure you, then we could have died together. But since I could not come in time and did not hear what had happened and have come and found you dead, I shall console myself by drinking of the same cup. You have forfeited your life on my account, and I shall do as a true lover: I will die for you in return!"

She takes him in her arms and then, lying at full length, she kisses his face and lips and clasps him tightly to her. Then straining body to body, mouth to mouth, she at once renders up her spirit and of sorrow for her lover dies thus at his side.

Tristran died of his longing, Ysolt because she could not come in time. Tristran died for his love; fair Ysolt because of tender pity.

Here Thomas ends his book. Now he takes leave of all lovers, the sad and the amorous, the jealous and the desirous, the gay and the distraught, and all who will hear these lines. If I have not pleased all with my tale, I have told it to the best of my power and have narrated the whole truth, as I promised at the beginning. Here I have recounted the story in rhyme, and have done this to hold up an example, and to make this story more beautiful, so that it may please lovers, and that, here and there, they may find some things to take to heart. May they derive great comfort from it, in the face of fickleness and injury, in the face of hardship and grief, in the face of all the wiles of Love.

THE MADNESS OF TRISTAN

When a richly complex narrative is extremely familiar, later writers can adapt it allusively. Later twelfth-century Anglo-Norman writers adapted the story of Tristan and Ysolt in this way, in usually smaller versions that focus on a sequence, or even a single fragment, of the narrative (e.g., Marie de France's *Chevrefoil*, pp. 185–87). In the Anglo-Norman text presented here, known as the *Oxford Madness of Tristan*, the author shapes his or her own new narrative as a fragment within, and by frequent reference to, the broader, well-known narrative of Thomas. A further example of the "Madness of Tristan" narrative survives, in the *Berne Madness of*

Tristan (the manuscripts of these two texts are held in Oxford and Berne, respectively).

That the narrative of Tristan and Ysolt should collapse into fragments is itself peculiarly apt, given that this story of illicit, intensely private love can have no ultimate coherence, and given that the lovers must retreat into tiny, private moments of isolated joy. The intensity of that joy is heightened by contrast with the self-destructive, self-mutilating disguises that Tristan must adopt in order to see his lover. These disguises are extreme: Tristan disfigures himself to appear as a court jester (or *fole*) to such an extent that he borders on madness (*folie*). Even as he uses the truth to disguise himself (the fool declares his love for Queen Ysolt in the presence of the king and the court), so too does the possibility of that love's fulfilment recede (the courtiers all laugh at the jester's declaration of love). The struggle to maintain one's identity becomes so demanding as to fragment identity, and to merge extreme pain and joy. Tristan must hide his true self from everyone around him—from his friend, and from the king and his court. The compulsion to hide becomes so engrained, indeed, that Tristan, to our surprise and shock, finally disguises himself (unnecessarily) from Ysolt when he uses a false voice even in the intimacy of her chamber. It is no accident that Tristan should say that he will live with Ysolt in a wholly transparent, crystal palace, suspended in the air: a narrative marked by ever-thickening opacity and dissembling, in which even the most intimate relationships need to be disguised, produces a dream of pure transparency. Tokens of recognition and identity, so crucial to romance narratives, serve here almost endlessly to block and defer recognition, producing a seeming romance in reverse, and far from producing private, life-giving understanding, the precious signs of intimacy here become instruments of emotional cruelty.

Deferral of joy seems to be painfully indefinite, until Husdent the dog joyfully recognizes his master (note the distant echoes of the dog of Ulysses as he returns to Ithaca), and until Tristan changes his voice. Tristan, we realize, has been disguising himself deliberately from Ysolt—and from us.

From The Madness of Tristan[1]

Miserable, dejected, sad, and downcast, Tristan dwelt in his land.[2] He meditated on what he could do, for he lacked all solace: a cure would solace him, or, if there were none, better to die. Better to die once and for all, than for ever to be so distraught, and better to die once and for all, than forever languish in pain. To live in anguish is death itself; anxiety defeats and destroys man. Just so did pain, grief, anxiety, and distress defeat Tristan. He saw there was no cure for him: without solace he would have to die. Death, then, was certain, since he had lost his love, his joy, since he had lost Ysolt the queen. He wished to die, he desired to die, but only so long as she knew he was dying for love of her, for if she knew it, he would at least die more easily. He suspected everyone and hid his mind from them, fearing betrayal. Above all he hid his mind from Caerdin, his friend, for he feared that if he told him his plan, he would prevent him. For he wished and intended to go straight to England, not with a horse but entirely on foot, so as not to be recognized in

---

1. The translation and select notes are derived from Judith Weiss, *The Birth of Romance: An Anthology* (1992).

2. Tristan's "land" is Brittany, home of Caerdin and his sister, Ysolt of the White Hands, whom Tristan marries.

that land. Because he was well known there, he would be soon spotted. But no one notices a poor man on foot; no one at court takes heed of a poor, bare messenger. He intended to disguise himself and so change his appearance that no one would ever know he was Tristan, however hard they looked. Neither family, neighbors, fellows, nor friends would discover his identity. He kept his thoughts so quiet that he said nothing to anyone; he was wise, for disclosing secrets beforehand often brings great harm. No misfortune, I believe, will ever befall the man who thus hides, and will not reveal, his thoughts. Telling and disclosing secrets is often the cause of many disasters. People suffer from their own thoughtlessness.

Tristan prudently held his counsel and thought hard. He did not long delay: in bed at night he took his decision, and early in the morning he set out on his road. He did not stop till he reached the sea. He came to the sea and found the ship ready and all that he needed. The ship was large, fine and strong, a good merchants' boat. Its cargo came from many lands, and it was bound for England.

The sailors hauled up the sail and weighed anchor. They were eager to be on the high seas: there was a good wind for sailing. Then Tristan the brave appeared and said to them: "My lords, God save you all! Where are you going, God willing?" "To England, with luck!" they replied. Tristan said to the sailors: "I wish you a good voyage! My lords, take me with you: we both want to go to Britain." They said to him: "Agreed: come along then, embark." Tristan approached and went on board. The wind swelled the topsail and they went speedily through the waves, cutting through the deep sea. They had their will and plenty of good wind. They ran straight for England, spending two nights and a day on the voyage, and on the second day, if the record is true, they came to the port, at Tintagel.

King Mark dwelt there, as did Queen Ysolt, and a great court was gathered there, following the custom of the king. Tintagel was a very fine, strong castle, impervious to attack or siege-engine. . . . [3] It stood by the sea, in Cornwall, its tower large and strong: it was built by giants long ago. All its stones were of marble, superbly laid and joined. The wall was checkered with red and blue blocks. There was a gate to the castle, handsome, large, and strong; the entry and exit were well guarded by two valiant men.

There dwelt King Mark, with Britons and with Cornish-men, because of the castle, which he loved, and so did Queen Ysolt. Round about were many meadows, many woods for game, fresh water, fish-ponds and fine fields. Ships sailing by on the sea would arrive at the castle's port. People from other lands, both friends and strangers, looking for the king would there come to him from over the sea, and that is why he loved it so. The spot was lovely and delightful, the land good and fruitful, and thus once upon a time Tintagel was called the enchanted castle. It was rightly called so, because twice a year, once in winter and once in summer, truly no one can see it, neither a local man nor anyone else, however hard they try—so say the people in the neighborhood. Tristan's ship arrived and carefully dropped anchor in the port.

---

3. Here there is a gap in the text of a line and a half.

Tristan jumped up and left ship, and sat down on the shore. He sought and asked for news of King Mark and his whereabouts. They told him he was in town and held a great court. "And where is Queen Ysolt and Brenguain, her lovely handmaid?" "Indeed, they are here: it's not long since I saw them. But Queen Ysolt, as usual, certainly looks very sad." When Tristan heard Ysolt's name, he fetched a sigh from his heart. He decided on a trick to help him see his mistress.

He knew well there was no device to be found to enable him to talk to her. Prowess, knowledge, intelligence, skill—all were of no avail, for King Mark, he well knew, hated him above all things, and if he could catch him alive, he was convinced he would kill him. Then he thought of his mistress and said: "What does it matter if he kills me? I ought to die for love of her. Alas! I already die every day. Ysolt, for you I suffer so much. Ysolt, for you I so much wish to die. Ysolt, if you knew I was here, I'm not sure you would talk to me. I've gone mad for your love, yet I'm here and you don't know it. I don't know how I can talk to you, hence my anguish.

"Now I want to try something else, to see if I succeed: I'll pretend I'm a fool, behave as if mad. Isn't that clever and a stroke of cunning? That's shrewd: since neither time nor place are on my side, nothing wiser can be done. Whoever holds me silly, I'll be wiser than he, and whoever holds me a fool will have stupider men at home."

Tristan kept to this decision. He saw a fisherman coming towards him. He wore a tunic of coarse wool, with open sides, and a hood. Tristan saw him and beckoned to him and led him off with him in secret. "My friend," he said, "let's change clothes. You shall have mine, which are good. I will have your tunic, which pleases me greatly, for I often dress in such clothes." The fisherman saw the clothes were good, took them, and gave him his, and when he had them he was delighted and went off like a shot.

Tristan had some scissors, which he would carry about with him. He treasured them: Ysolt had given him them. With the scissors he shaved his hair on the top of his head: he certainly looked idiotic and crazy. Then he cut a cross-shaped tonsure. He knew how to transform his voice completely. He stained his face with an herb he had brought from his own land: he smeared it with its juice and then it changed color and went dark. No man alive, seeing and hearing him, would have recognized him or claimed him as Tristan. He took a stake from a hedge and held it on his shoulder. He went straight towards the castle; everyone who saw him was afraid.

When the porter saw him, he summed him up as a mad fool. He said to him: "Come here! Where have you been so long?"

The fool replied: "I was at the wedding of the Abbot of St. Michael's Mount, my old friend. He married an abbess, a fat nun. There was not a priest, abbot, monk, or clerk in orders, of whatever kind, from Besançon to the Mount, who was not invited to the wedding, and they all brought staves and crosses. There, in the pastures below Bel Encumbre,[4] they jump and play in the shade. I left them, because today I've got to serve the king at table."

---

4. Bel Encumbre is in Normandy; St. Michael's Mount probably refers to the Cornish monastery of that name. Besançon is in eastern France. Here it simply means "from far off."

The porter replied: "Come in, Urgan the Hairy's son. You are large and hairy, to be sure, and thus very like him."[5] The fool entered by the wicket gate. The young men ran up to him, shouting at him as men do to a wolf: "Look at the fool! Hu! hu! hu! hu!" The young men and the squires were intent on attacking him with branches of boxwood. They accompanied him across the courtyard, following the mad boy. He turned on them many times, playing the fool at will. If one attacked him on the right, he turned and struck towards the left. He came to the door of the hall and entered, stake over his shoulder. At once the king, from his seat on the royal dais, noticed him. He said: "There's a good servant. Make him come forward." Many jumped up and went to meet him, greeting him in accordance with his looks. Then they brought the fool, stake over his shoulder, before the king. Mark said: "Welcome, friend. Where are you from? What do you seek here?"

The fool said: "Indeed I'll tell you whence I am and what I seek. My mother was a whale and dwelt in the sea like a siren,[6] but I've no idea where I was born. But I will know who brought me up: a great tigress suckled me, in the rocks where she found me. She found me under a block of stone, thought I was her cub, and fed me from her breast. But I have a most beautiful sister: I will give her to you, if you like, in exchange for Ysolt, whom you love so much." The king laughed and then replied: "What would the wonder of the world say to that?" "King, I'll give you my sister for Ysolt, whom I love dearly. Let's make a bargain, let's make an exchange: it's good to try out something new. You're quite tired of Ysolt: get to know someone else. Give her to me, I'll take her. I'll be of service to you, king, out of love."

The king listened to him and laughed, and said to the fool: "God help you, tell me what you would do with the queen, or where you would put her, if I gave her into your power, to take away?" "King," said the fool, "Up there in the air I have a hall where I live. It's large and splendid, made of glass, and the sun comes streaming in. It's in the air, hanging from the clouds; the wind neither rocks nor shakes it. Beside the hall is a paneled room made of crystal. At daybreak, the sun floods it with light."

The king and the rest laughed at this. They spoke among themselves, saying: "This is a good fool, he talks well. He can speak on anything." "King," said the fool, "I adore Ysolt: my heart suffers and aches for her. I am Trantris, who loved her so, and will as long as I live."

Ysolt heard him, sighed deeply, and was angry and furious with the fool. She said: "Who let you in here? Fool, you aren't Trantris, you lie." The fool listened more carefully to Ysolt than to the others; he was well aware she was angry from the changed color in her face.

Then he said: "Queen Ysolt, I am Trantris who used to love you. You must remember when I was wounded—there were many who knew it well—in fighting the Morholt, who wanted to claim tribute from you.[7] In fighting, I

---

5. Urgan appears in other Tristan narratives as a giant defeated and killed by Tristan.
6. The whale mother appears in the *Berne Madness of Tristan*, but the siren comparison occurs only here.
7. Many Tristan narratives depict Mark's kingdom as having to pay tribute to Ireland, first in money, then in beautiful children. Morholt, the maternal uncle of Ysolt, is a huge warrior who comes to Cornwall to enforce the tribute and is slain by Tristan in single combat. A piece of Tristan's sword is left embedded in the Morholt's skull and is kept by Ysolt and her mother. Tristan himself is apparently mortally wounded and seeks cure in Ireland, disguised as Trantris (an anagram of Tristran). Ysolt, an expert with curative plants, cures him completely.

had the luck to kill him, I don't deny it. I was badly wounded, for the sword was poisoned. It damaged my hip bone and the virulent poison fomented, clinging to the bone and turning it black; there was then such pain there that no doctor could cure it and I thought I would die of it. I put out to sea, to die there, so badly did the suffering torment me. The wind got up and a great storm drove my boat to Ireland. I had to land in the country I most had reason to fear, for I had killed the Morholt, your uncle, Queen Ysolt; hence I was afraid of the land. But I was wounded and wretched. I tried taking pleasure in my harp, but it gave me no comfort, despite my love for it. Very soon people heard tell of my skill at harping. At once I was summoned to court just as I was, in my wounded state. Thanks to the queen, there I was cured of my wound. I taught you fine lays to the harp, Breton lays from our land.[8] You must remember, my lady Queen, how the medicine cured me. There I named myself Trantris: am I not him? What do you think?"

Ysolt replied: "No indeed! For he was a fine and noble man, and you, who call yourself Trantris, are coarse, ugly, and horrible. Now be off, stop shouting at me. I don't care for your jokes or for you." The fool turned about at these words and began playing the madman to perfection. He struck those he found in his way, escorting them from the dais to the door. Then he shouted at them: "Madmen, be off, out of here! Let me confer with Ysolt: I've come here to court her." The king laughed, for he enjoyed this very much. Ysolt flushed and kept silence.

And the king was well aware of it. He said to the fool: "Rascal, come here. Isn't Queen Ysolt your mistress?" "Yes indeed! I won't deny it."

Ysolt answered: "You're a liar! Throw the fool out!" The fool laughed in reply, and spoke as he wished to Ysolt: "Don't you remember, Queen Ysolt, what the king did when he wanted to send me on a mission? He sent me to get you, whom he's now married. I went there as a merchant, seeking my fortune. I was much hated in the land because I had killed the Morholt: that's why I went as a merchant and that was very shrewd. I was to seek you for the king's use, your lord, whom I see here, who was hardly loved in that land, while I was bitterly hated. I was a splendid knight, enterprising and brave, afraid of no one, from Scotland to Rome."

Ysolt replied: "That's a good story. You're a disgrace to knights, for you're a congenital idiot. A pity you're still alive! Get out, for God's sake!" The fool heard her and laughed.

Then he continued, like this: "My lady Queen, you must remember the dragon I killed, when I arrived in your land. I struck its head from its body,[9] cut its tongue and removed it, thrusting it in my hose. And from the poison I got such a fever, I was sure I would die; I lay fainting by the road. Your mother and you saw me and saved me from death. With skill and powerful medicine you cured me of the poison.[1]

"Do you remember the bath I sat in? You nearly killed me there. You were about to perform that amazing feat once you had unsheathed my sword.

---

8. Tristan's skill at the harp is one of his most famous characteristics, depicted in art as well as literature.

9. Tristan returns to Ireland a second time, to arrange the marriage of Ysolt and Mark. He confronts and kills a dragon. This narrative from Thomas's *Tristran* is preserved in the Norse trans-lation of Thomas.

1. This is the second time Ysolt and her mother cure Tristan in Ireland. The first cure is after Tristan's fight with Morholt. Tristan's illness from fighting the dragon is contracted in his second voyage to Ireland, this time to arrange the marriage of Ysolt and Tristan's uncle Mark.

When you drew it out and found the notch in it, then you thought, rightly, the Morholt had perished by it. You quickly thought of a clever idea: you opened your casket and found inside the piece you had taken out of his head. You matched the piece to the sword: it fitted at once. You were very bold, at once to try and kill me in the bath with my own sword.[2] How full of fury woman is! And at your cry, the queen came, for she had heard you. You know how I made my peace, for I kept begging for mercy; and besides, I had to defend you against the man intent on taking you.[3] You would not have him at any price for you found him odious. Ysolt, I defended you from him. Isn't what I say true?"

"It's not true, it's a lie; it's your own fantasies you relate. You went drunk to bed last night, and drunkenness made you dream." "True: I am drunk, from such a drink that I'll never be sober.

"Don't you remember when your father and mother gave you to me? They put us to sea, on the ship; I was to bring you here to the king. When we were on the open sea, I'll tell you what we did. The day was fine and hot, we were on the high seas and you were thirsty from the heat. Don't you remember, king's daughter? We both drank from the same cup: you drank it, I drank it. I've been drunk on it ever after,[4] but that intoxication costs me dear."

When Ysolt heard this, she wrapped her mantle around her and stood up, wishing to go. The king seized her and made her sit down; he seized her by her ermine cloak and sat her down again beside him. "Patience, Ysolt my love; let's hear this folly through to the end. Fool," said the king, "now I'd like to hear the ways you can be of service."

The fool answered Mark: "I have served kings and counts." "Do you know about dogs? And horses?" "Yes," he said, "I've had some fine ones!" The fool told him: "King, when I want to hunt in woods or forest, with my greyhounds I take the cranes flying up there in the skies; with my leash-hounds I take swans and white and grey geese, one after another. When I go out with my hunting-dogs I take many coots and bitterns." Mark laughed heartily at the fool and so did everyone, great and small. Then he said to the fool: "My friend, my dear brother, what can you catch in the marshes?"

The fool began to laugh and replied: "King, whatever I find, I take, for with my goshawks I take the forest wolves and the great bears. I catch the boars with my gerfalcons, neither hills or valleys protect them. I'll take roebuck and fallow-deer with my little high-flying falcons and with my sparrowhawk, the fox, with his fine tail. With my merlin I'll take the hare, with my falcon, the wild-cat and beaver. When I come back home, then I'm a good fencer with my stake: no one escapes a blow of mine, no matter how well he covers. I know how to share out the logs between the squires and the grooms. I know how to tune both harp and rote,[5] and then sing to the melody. I know how to love a noble queen and no lover under heaven is my equal. I know how to cut wood-chips with my knife, and throw them into

---

2. In curing Tristan, Ysolt discovers the notch in Tristan's sword that exactly matches the fragment extracted from her uncle Morholt's head, and thereby understands that Tristan had killed her uncle. She threatens to kill Tristan in his bath with the sword, but is dissuaded from doing so.
3. An Irish court officer had falsely claimed to have killed the dragon, and he demanded the hand of Ysolt in recompense.
4. In some Tristan texts, the effects of the love potion wear off after three or four years, while in others they endure for life.
5. The rote was a triangular zither.

streams.[6] Am I not a good servant? Today I've served you with my stake." Then he struck those around him with the stake. "Leave the king's presence!" he said. "All go back to your lodgings! Have you not eaten? Why do you stay?"

The king laughed at every word, delighted with the fool. Then he summoned a squire to bring him his horse, saying he wished to go out and amuse himself, as was his custom. His knights went with him, and so did the squires, to relieve boredom.

"By your leave, my lord," said Ysolt, "I'm ill, my head aches. I will go and rest in my chamber. I cannot listen to this din." Then the king let her go. She jumped up and left, entering her chamber in deep thought. She called herself miserable and wretched. She came to her bed and sat down; the lamentation she made was very great.

"Alas!" she said, "why was I born? My heart is heavy and sad. Brenguain, my fair sister," she said, "really, I'm almost dead. If I were dead, I'd be better off, since my life is so bitter and hard. I meet hostility wherever I look. Indeed, Brenguain, I don't know what to do, for a fool has arrived over there, his hair in a cross-shaped tonsure. He arrived in an evil hour, for he has caused me much pain. Really, this fool, this mad scoundrel, must be a soothsayer or magician, for he knows my life and my situation from top to bottom, my dear friend. Indeed, Brenguain, I wonder who revealed my secrets to him, since no one except you, I and Tristan, was privy to them. But this beggar, I think, knows them all by magic. Never did any man speak more truly, for he never got a single word wrong."

Brenguain replied: "It's Tristan himself, I'm sure I'm right." "No, Brenguain, for he's ugly and hideous and deformed, and Tristan is so shapely, a handsome man, well made, well educated. You could not find in any land a knight of greater renown. So I'll never believe it's my lover Tristan. But curses on this fool! Cursed be his life and cursed be the ship that brought him here! Pity he didn't drown in the waves, out there in the deep sea!"

"Be quiet, my lady," Brenguain said. "Now you are offensive. Where did you learn such talents? You're well acquainted with cursing!" "Brenguain, he put me out of my wits. Never did I hear a man talk so." "By St. John, my lady, I believe he's Tristan's messenger." "Indeed, I'm not sure, I don't know him. But go to him, my dear friend, speak with him, if you can, and discover if you know him."

Brenguain, who was courteous, jumped up, and went straight to the hall, but there she found neither freeman nor serf, only the fool, sitting on a bench. Everyone else had gone to their lodgings in the city. Brenguain saw him and stopped, at a distance, and Tristan recognized her very well. Then he threw down his stake and said: "Welcome, Brenguain. Noble Brenguain, I beg you, for God's sake, to have pity on me."

Brenguain replied: "And why do you want me to pity you?" "Oh come! I am Tristan, living in pain and grief. I am Tristan, in misery for the love of Queen Ysolt." Brenguain said: "No, it's my belief you're not." "Indeed, Brenguain, I really am. Tristan was my name when I came here and I truly am he. Brenguain, don't you remember, when we left Ireland together, how I had you in

6. See *Chevrefoil* (pp. 185–87) for a depiction of Tristan's skill as carver of secret messages to Ysolt.

my care, you and Ysolt, who now won't recognize me? When the queen came towards me, holding you by the right hand, she gave the charge of you into my hands. You must remember, beautiful Brenguain. She charged me with Ysolt and you; she required me, she begged me, to receive you into my care and guard you as best I could. Then she gave you a flask, by no means large but small, telling you to guard it well if you desired her friendship.[7] When we were on the open sea, the weather grew warm. I wore a tunic, I was hot and sweating, I was thirsty, and asked for drink: you know if I'm telling the truth. A lad sitting at my feet got up, and took the flask. He poured into a silver goblet the drink that he found there, then placed the goblet in my hand and, needing it, I drank. I offered half to Ysolt, who was thirsty and wanted to drink. Beautiful Brenguain, would that I had never drunk that drink, or known you. Beautiful Brenguain, don't you remember?" Brenguain replied: "No, indeed."

"Brenguain, since I first loved Ysolt, she would tell it to no other: you knew and heard of it and you allowed the affair. Nobody in the world knew of it, nobody except we three." Brenguain heard what he told her; she went off quickly towards the chamber. He jumped up and followed her, begging for mercy. Brenguain came to Ysolt and smiled at her, according to their custom.[8] Ysolt's face changed color and paled, and at once she feigned illness. The chamber was immediately emptied because the queen was unwell.

And Brenguain went for Tristan and led him straight to the chamber. When he entered and saw Ysolt, he approached her, wishing to kiss her. But she retreated, much mortified; she stood, sweating, not knowing what to do. Tristan saw that she shunned him. He was crestfallen and ashamed. He stepped back a little to the wall, near the door.

Then he gave vent to some of his desires: "Indeed, I would never have thought that of you, Ysolt, noble Queen, nor Brenguain, your maidservant. Alas! to have lived long enough to see you treating me with such scorn and repugnance! In whom can I trust, when Ysolt won't deign to love me, when Ysolt considers me so base that she now has no memory of me? Ah! Ysolt, ah! my dear, the loving heart is slow to forget. We prize the leaping fountain, whose fine stream runs freely; but the moment it dries, and the water neither rushes nor springs, it is worth praise no longer. Nor is love, when it's disloyal."

Ysolt answered: "My brother, I can't tell. I look at you and I'm dismayed, for I see nothing in you to say you're Tristan the Lover." Tristan replied: "Queen Ysolt, I am Tristan, who used to love you. Don't you remember the seneschal who embroiled us with the king? We were both young then and shared a lodging. One night, when I went out, he got up and followed me. It had snowed and he traced my footsteps. He came to the palisade and crossed it, spied on us in your chamber, and the next day accused us. I believe he was the first to denounce us to the king.[9]

"Again, you must remember the dwarf, whom you so used to fear. He did not care about my pleasure: he was about us day and night. He was put

---

7. This is the love potion prepared for Ysolt and King Mark.
8. This seems to be an agreed signal between Ysolt and Brenguain.

9. A court officer notices that the footprints of Tristan in the snow lead to Ysolt's chamber; he eventually tells the king.

there to spy on us, and carried out this service in a crazy fashion. On one occasion we had been bled; like any lovers in distress, who plan all kinds of cunning, ingenious and artful tricks in order to achieve meetings, pleasure and delight, we did the same. We had been bled in your room, where we were lying. But that crazy dwarf, son of a bitch, sprinkled flour between our beds, thus thinking to discover whether there really was love between us.[1] But I noticed it: feet together, I jumped into your bed. The wound in my arm spurted from the jump and bloodied your bed; I jumped back the same way and made my own bed bloody.

"Then King Mark arrived and found your bloodstained bed; at once he came to mine and found my bloody sheets. Queen, for love of you, I was then banished from court. Don't you remember, my darling, a little love-token I once sent you, a little dog I got for you? That was Petit Cru,[2] whom you dearly loved. And there is one thing, Ysolt my love, which you must remember.

"When the Irishman came to court, the king showed him honour and affection. He was a harper, he knew how to harp; you knew him well. The king gave you to the harper: he gaily carried you off and was about to enter his ship. I was in the forest and heard about it. I took a rote[3] and followed on horseback at a gallop. He won you through his harp, and I won you through my rote.[4]

"Queen, you must remember when the king banished me and I longed to speak with you, my love. I thought of a ruse, I came to the orchard where we had often been happy. I sat under a pine in the shade and cut woodchips with my knife, which served as signs between us when I wanted to come to you. A spring rose in that place, which ran by the chamber. I threw the chips in the water and the stream carried them along. When you saw the chips, you would know for sure that I would come that night, to delight in taking my pleasure.

"At once the dwarf took notice: he ran to tell King Mark. That night the king entered the garden and climbed into the pine. I came later, knowing nothing, but when I had been there a while, I noticed the shadow of the king sitting in the pine above me. You approached from the other direction. Then I was indeed terrified, but you must know I feared lest your haste were too great. But thank God, He didn't permit it. You saw the shadow, as I had, you stepped back, and I begged you to reconcile me with the king, if you could, or else ask him to pay my wages and let me leave the kingdom. This saved us, and I was reconciled with King Mark.[5]

"Beautiful Ysolt, do you remember the oath you went through for me? When you left the boat, I held you gently in my arms. I had disguised myself thoroughly, as you told me to; I kept my head well down. I well remember what you then told me—to fall, holding you. Ysolt, my love, isn't that true? You fell gently to the ground, opening your thighs and letting me fall between them, and everyone saw it. As I see it, that's how you were saved,

1. The dwarf does not appear in the Thomas fragments except in the orchard scene. His flour trick appears in other Tristan texts.
2. Petit Cru is a magical dog that appears in other Tristan texts.
3. A triangular zither, with strings on both sides of the soundbox.
4. This is the episode known as "the harp and the rote," which appears in other Tristan texts. The Irish harper, having asked for, and been

granted, an unspecified reward for his music, demands Ysolt. Mark is bound by his promise to hand her over.
5. This episode appears in many Tristan texts (see also the ivory carving reproduced on p. 139). In Beroul's version, Tristan and Ysolt, both conscious of the shadow of the king in the tree above them, immediately conduct a dialogue that suggests their innocence to the unwitting Mark as he listens to them.

Ysolt, at the trial from the oath that you made in the king's court."[6] The queen listened to him, carefully noting every word. She examined him and sighed deeply; she did not know what on earth to say, for he did not look like Tristan in face, appearance, or clothes. But from what he said, she understood very well he told the truth, without a word of a lie. This filled her heart with anguish and she had no idea what to do. It would be mad and deceitful to recognize him as Tristan, when she saw, thought, and believed he was not Tristan but another. And Tristan could see very well that she quite failed to know him.

Then he said: "My lady Queen, how well you showed your nobility when you loved me without disdain. Now I can truly complain of your treachery. Now I see you distant and false, now I've convicted you of deceit. But I've seen the day, my love, when you truly loved me. When Mark banished us and drove us from the court, we took each other by the hand and left the hall. Then we went to the forest and found a most beautiful place there, a grotto in a rock. In front, the entry was narrow; inside, it was vaulted and well shaped, as beautiful as a picture, the stone finely and richly carved. In that vault we lived as long as we stayed in the forest. There I trained Husdent, my dearly loved dog, not to bark.[7] With my dog and with my hawk, I kept us fed every day.

"My lady Queen, you're well aware how we were then found. The king himself found us, and the dwarf he took with him. But God was shielding us, when he found us lying apart and the sword between us. The king took the glove from his hand and put it over your face, gently and without a word, for he saw a sunbeam which had burnt and reddened it. Then the king went away and left us sleeping there; after that, he had no suspicion of anything wrong between us. He dismissed the anger he had toward us and soon sent for us.[8]

"Ysolt, you must remember: it was then I gave you Husdent, my dog. What have you done with him? Show him to me." Ysolt replied: "I have him, upon my word! I have the dog you speak of: indeed, you shall see him at once. Brenguain, go and get the dog; bring him, along with his lead." She rose and jumped to her feet, she came to Husdent, who frisked for joy. She untied him, letting him go. He bounded off.

Tristan said to him: "Come here, Husdent! Once you were mine, now I'm taking you back." Husdent saw him, at once knew him, and greeted him, rightly, with joy. I have never heard tell of a dog making a greater fuss of his master than Husdent did, so much love did he show him. He rushed at him, head high, rubbing him with his muzzle, patting him with his paws. Never did an animal show such joy: it was pitiful to see.

Ysolt was amazed. She was ashamed and blushed to see him giving him such a welcome as soon as he heard his voice, for he was vicious and badly bred, and would bite and harm all those who played with him and all those who handled him. No one could get to know him or handle him except the queen and Brenguain, so obnoxious had he been since losing his master, who had nurtured and trained him.

6. Ysolt undertakes to clear herself of the charge of adultery by undergoing trial, either by oath or by the ordeal of the red-hot iron. On the day, she has arranged that as she lands from a boat, the disguised Tristan should offer to help carry her to shore and stumble in the process. She can then truly and safely swear that nobody, except the king and this "feeble pilgrim," has ever been between her thighs.
7. Husdent appears in many Tristan texts.
8. This central episode occurs in all versions of the story. The separation of the lovers by the sword is taken by Mark to indicate their chaste love.

Tristan held Husdent and stroked him. He said to Ysolt: "He remembers me, who nurtured and trained him, better than you do, whom I loved so much. There's such great nobility in a dog, such great deceit in woman." Ysolt heard him and changed color; she shuddered and sweated with anguish. Tristan said to her: "My lady Queen, how loyal you once were!

"Don't you remember how we were lying in the orchard when the king appeared, discovered us, and quickly withdrew? He planned a wicked deed: out of spite he would kill you. But thank God, He wouldn't have it, for I realized in time. I had to leave you, my love, for the king wished to disgrace us. Then you gave me your beautiful ring, richly made of pure gold, and I received it and left, commending you to the one true God."[9]

Ysolt said: "Tokens will convince me. Have you the ring? Show it to me." He drew out the ring and gave it to her. Ysolt took it and looked at it; then she burst out weeping, she wrung her hands, she was distraught. "Alas for the day I was born!" she said, "I've finally lost my love, for I know well that no other man would have this ring if he were alive. Alas, I will never be comforted!" But when Tristan saw her weep, he was seized with pity, and rightly so.

Then he said: "My lady queen, now you are beautiful and true. Now I will no longer hide, but make myself heard and known." He altered his tone and spoke in his true voice.

Ysolt realized at once. She threw her arms around his neck and kissed his face and eyes.

Then Tristan said to Brenguain, who was overcome with delight: "Give me some water, my beauty: I'll wash my dirty face."

At once Brenguain brought the water and he soon cleansed his face: he washed off all the stain from the herb and its juice, along with the sweat. He resumed his own looks, and he held Ysolt in his arms. Such was the joy she had from her lover, whom she held by her side, that it knew no bounds. She would not let him leave that night, and promised him good lodging and a fine, well-made bed. Tristan desired only queen Ysolt, nothing but her. He was joyful and happy; he realized now he was well lodged.

9. This episode appears in the first of the fragments of Thomas's poem.

ANCRENE WISSE
(GUIDE FOR ANCHORESSES)

In the twelfth and thirteenth centuries, there was a movement toward a more solitary religious life and a more personal encounter with God. In the early days of Christianity, monasticism had originated with the desert fathers, men who withdrew to the wilderness in order to lead a life of prayer and meditation. The fifth and sixth centuries saw the growth and spread of religious orders, men and women living in religious communities, especially the Benedictine order of monks, founded in Italy by St. Benedict. New orders founded in the eleventh and twelfth centuries—

the Cistercians, for example—emphasized a more actively engaged and individual spirituality. The Dominican and Franciscan orders of friars were not confined to their houses but were preaching and teaching orders who staffed the newly founded universities.

Along with the new orders, a number of both men and women chose to become anchorites or hermits, living alone or in small groups. In his *Rule*, St. Benedict had described such solitaries with a military metaphor: "They have built up their strength and go from the battle line in the ranks of their brothers to the single combat of the desert. Self-reliant now, without the support of another, they are ready with God's help to grapple single-handed with the vices of body and mind." Benedict's battle imagery anticipates the affinities between this solitary kind of spirituality and the literary form of romance, both of which were developing in the twelfth and thirteenth centuries. The individual soul confined in its enclosure fights temptation, as Sir Gawain rides out alone in the wilderness to seek the Green Chapel and encounters temptation along the way. The wilderness in romance often contains hermits, who may be genuinely holy men, or they may be enchanters like Archimago, disguised as a holy hermit, in the *Faerie Queene*. The influence of romance on religion and of religion on romance is also strikingly seen in portrayals of Christ as a knight who jousts for the love and salvation of human souls, which is a motif common to *Ancrene Wisse*, William Herebert's poem "What is he, this lordling, that cometh from the fight" (p. 427), and *Piers Plowman* (see p. 415).

Anchoress (the feminine form of *anchorite*, from the Greek *anachoretes*, "one who retires") refers to a religious recluse who, unlike a hermit, lives in an enclosure, attached to a church, from which she never emerges. Anchoresses and anchorites might live singly, like Julian of Norwich (see pp. 430–31), or in small groups. *Ancrene Wisse* (ca. 1215) was originally written for three young sisters, who, the author says in an aside in one manuscript, come from a noble family with ample means to support them. The author of *Ancrene Wisse* addresses the sisters in a colloquial, urbane, and personal prose style that distinguishes the guide both as a book of religious instruction and as a literary achievement of Early Middle English. Note in particular the richly metaphorical transformations of pleasure and pain.

The excerpt comes from Part 6, to which the author gave the title "Penitence."[1]

From Ancrene Wisse (Guide for Anchoresses)

[THE SWEETNESS AND PAINS OF ENCLOSURE]

Now perhaps someone complains that she cannot feel any sweetness from God or sweetness within herself. Let her not wonder in the least if she is not Mary, for she must buy sweetness with exterior bitterness; but not with bitterness of any kind at all, for some lead away from God, for example every worldly grief that does not make for health in the soul. Thus it is written in the Gospel, of the three Marys, *that coming, they might anoint Jesus,*[2] *not going.* These Marys, it says, these bitternesses, were coming to anoint Our Lord. The bitter things which we suffer for His love come to anoint Our Lord, who reaches out toward us like one who has been anointed, and makes himself soft and sweet to touch. And was not He Himself a recluse in Mary's womb? These two things belong properly to an anchoress: narrowness of

---

1. The translation is from *The Ancrene Riwle*, translated by M. B. Salu (Exeter: University of

Exeter Press, 1990; first published 1955).
2. Mark 16.1.

room, and bitterness; for the womb, where Our Lord was a recluse, is a narrow dwelling, and this word "Mary", as I have often said, means "bitterness". If you then suffer bitter things in a narrow place you are His fellow-recluses, since He was a recluse in Mary's womb. Are you confined within four great walls? He was confined in a narrow cradle, confined when He was nailed to the cross, and fast enclosed in a sepulchre of stone. Mary's womb and this sepulchre were His anchor-houses. In neither was He a Man mingling with the world, but as it were apart from the world, to show anchoresses that with the world they should have nothing in common. "Yes," you will answer me, "but He went out of both." Yes, then go you out of both your anchor-houses too, as He did, without breaking them, and leave them both whole. That is what will happen when the spirit goes out at the end, without any breaking, without making any scar on its two houses. One is the body, the other is its outer house which is like the outer wall about the castle.

All that I have said about mortification of the flesh is not intended for you, my dear sisters, who sometimes suffer more than I would have you, but for some who are quite likely to read this and who treat themselves too gently. Nonetheless, young trees are encircled about with thorns for fear animals will feed on them while they are tender. You are young trees planted in God's orchard. The hardships which I have spoken of are the thorns, and it is necessary for you to be encircled with them, so that the beast of hell, when he sneaks towards you, intending to bite you, may be hurt by their sharpness and turn back frightened by all those hardships. Be glad and be well content if there is not much talk about you, and if you are of little account, for a thorn is sharp and unnoticeable. Be encircled, then, by these two things. You ought not, however, to allow any evil reports about yourselves. Giving scandal is a mortal sin, that is, saying or doing something in such a way that a bad interpretation may easily be put upon it, resulting in sins of evil thought or evil speech on the part of those who misinterpret, and on the part of others, and sins also of deed. You should be content that there be no talk of you at all, any more than there is of the dead, and if you incur disdain from Slurry, the cook's boy, who washes and dries the dishes in the kitchen, you should be happy in your hearts. Then you will be mountains lifted up towards heaven, for see what is said by the lady in the sweet Book of Love, *My beloved cometh, leaping upon the mountains, skipping over the hills.*[3] "My love comes leaping," she says, "upon the mountains, that is, he treads them underfoot, making them vile, allows them to be trodden on, to be outrageously chastised, and shows on them his own footmarks, so that by them people might follow him, and discover how he was trodden upon, as his traces show." These are the high mountains, like Montjoy and the mountains of Armenia. The hills, which are lower, and which the lady herself says He skips over, He had no confidence in, because of their weakness; they might not be able to bear such a tread and He skips over them, leaves them alone and avoids them until they grow higher, out of hills into mountains. Only His shadow passes over them and covers them as He skips over them; that is, He lays over them some likeness of His earthly life, His shadow as it were; but the mountains receive the impression of His own feet and in their lives they show what His life was like, how and where He went, in what lowliness and in what sorrow He led

3. Song of Solomon 2.8.

His earthly life. The good Paul spoke of such mountains and said with humility: *We are cast down: but we perish not. Bearing about in our body the mortification of Jesus, that the life also of Jesus may be made manifest in our bodies.*[4] "We suffer," he said, "all tribulation and all shame, but that is our happiness, to bear upon our body the mortification of Jesus Christ, so that in us there may be made plain the kind of life that was His on earth." God knows, they who do this prove to us their love of Our Lord. "Lovest thou me?" Then show it, for love does show itself in exterior actions. St. Gregory says, *The proof of love is the manifestation of its effect.*[5] However hard a thing may be, true love lightens it and makes it easy and sweet. *Love makes all things easy.* What do men and women suffer for false love and for unclean love? And how much more they would still be willing to suffer! And what is more strange than that true, real love, sweet beyond all other, cannot drive us forward as the love of sin does? And yet, I know one man who wears at the same time a heavy coat of mail and a hair-shirt fastened painfully about his waist, thighs, and arms with broad, thick bands of iron; to bear the sweat which this causes is agony; he fasts, watches, and performs great labours, and yet, Christ knows, laments that this gives him no pain at all, and he often asks me to teach him some means of mortifying his body. All that is bitter he finds sweet in the love of Our Lord. God knows, he still weeps to me and says that God has forgotten him because He has not sent him any great illness. These, God knows, are the effects of love, for as he often says to me, no evil thing that God might do to him, even though He should cast him into hell with those who are lost, could ever, he believes, make him love Him any the less. Anyone who imagines that it could, is more confounded than a thief taken with his theft. I know a woman too, who suffers not much less than this. We can only thank God for the strength which He gives them and humbly acknowledge our own weakness. Let us love what is good in them and thus it comes to belong to us, for, as St. Gregory says, love is of such great power that it makes others' good our own, without any effort on our part, as has been said before.[6] We have arrived now, I think, at the seventh part, which is entirely concerned with love, which makes the heart pure.

---

4. 2 Corinthians 4.9–10.
5. Gregory the Great, *Homilies* 30.1 (*Patrologia Latina* 76.1220).

6. See Gregory, *Moralia in Job* 6.10 (*Patrologia Latina* 76.461).

ROMANCE

Romances satisfy our deepest imaginative desires. If we most fear loss of identity in separation from what we hold dearest and from what makes us what we are, romances allay that fear. As they imagine narratives of separation, errancy, and loss, they therapeutically deliver endings of reintegration, recovery, and return. That which was lost is found.

The word *romans* was originally a simple linguistic designation, meaning "French," since French was derived from Latin, the language of Rome. In the twelfth century, however, the word narrowed in meaning, coming to designate narrative (forms of *roman* still mean "novel" in French, Italian, and German). The word then became particularly associated with a genre of narrative. It came to designate stories of separation and return, disintegration and reintegration.

Certainly classical Greek literature has examples of "romance" narrative, stories that involve separation, testing, and travel, all the prelude to, and premise of, a final homecoming and recognition. Homer's *Odyssey* is fundamentally a romance; five later Greek narratives of this kind also survive (first through fourth centuries C.E.). The broader modal commitment of romance to "comedy" (a story with a happy ending) also has classical roots. Romances are "comic" stories not because they make us laugh but, rather, like Shakespeare's comedies, they make us feel good through happy endings.

The dynamic French-speaking court cultures of twelfth-century France and England gave the genre its most powerful, undying impetus. Chrétien de Troyes (fl. 1160–90) is its greatest exponent in his Arthurian romances, but the rich set of Tristan materials and the lays of Marie de France are also of exceptional importance. The genre, once deeply planted in the twelfth century in French, flourishes anew in all European vernacular languages and in each historical period of European and American culture. It remains energetically immune to the literary plant killers of moralistic objection, high literary disdain for escapist entertainment, and satire.

The fundamental characteristic of romances is structural, not stylistic. They can be short or long, oral or literary, but to be romances they must have, or adapt, a particular story structure. Romances classically have a tripartite structure: integration (or implied integration); disintegration; and reintegration. They begin in, or at least imply, a protected, civilized state of some integrated social unit (e.g., family). That state is disrupted, expelling a member of the unit (the hero or heroine of the story, who is usually young) into a wild place. Undergoing the tests of that wild place is the premise of return to the integrated, civilized state of familial and/or social unity. Successfully undergoing tests in the wild often results in marriage,

The Dance of Mirth. *The Romance of the Rose,* ca. 1500. The scene illustrates a moment in the thirteenth-century French poem. Note the splendor and circularity of this aristocratic performance of amorous ritual.

in which case return to home and family is also return to an enlarged home and family.

This story pattern is characteristic of many fairy stories, medieval romances, Shakespearean comedies, novels, and popular movies. It not only represents desire but activates desire in its readers: the pleasure we take in such stories derives from our desire for the reintegration of lives in a coherent and constructive narrative. The desired pattern can also, of course, be adapted in many variations. In particular, it can be activated in order to be frustrated: some protagonists, particularly adulterous ones like Tristan and Ysolt, never reach home, forever needing to defer that unreachable happy ending of recognition.

Romances, then, are symbolic stories, replaying and allaying the fears of the young as they face the apparently insuperable challenges of the adult world. Their deepest wisdom is this: civilization is not a unitary concept. To enter and remain in the world of civilized order, we must, say romances, have commerce with all that threatens it. To regain Rome at the center, we must first be tested in the marginal wilds of romance. To be recognized and found, we must first be lost.

The romances offered here exemplify different possibilities derived from this story structure. *Sir Orfeo* is the only classic example, true in almost every respect to the model sketched above. *Sir Gawain and the Green Knight* and Chaucer's *Wife of Bath's Tale*, following this cluster, play fascinating games with classic romance structure. *Milun* and *Lanval* suggest different possibilities for romance within the tight and suffocating context of the medieval court. *Chevrefoil* expresses the way the aspiration to achieve a happy ending is all the more painfully intense because impossible. The earlier sample from Thomas's *Tristran* (pp. 140–43) underlines the inevitable end of such an impossible passion.

MARIE DE FRANCE

M uch of twelfth-century French literature was composed in England in the Anglo-Norman dialect (see p. 11). Prominent among the earliest poets writing in the French vernacular, who shaped the genres, themes, and styles of later medieval European poetry, is the author who, in an epilogue to her *Fables*, calls herself Marie de France. That signature tells us only that her given name was Marie and that she was born in France, but circumstantial evidence from her writings shows that she spent much of her life in England. A reference to her in a French poem written in England around 1180 speaks of "dame Marie" who wrote "lais" much loved and praised, read, and heard by counts, barons, and knights and indicates that her poems also appealed to ladies who listened to them gladly and joyfully.

Three works can be safely attributed to Marie, probably written in the following order: the *Lais* [English "lay" refers to a short narrative poem in verse], the *Fables*, and *St. Patrick's Purgatory*. Marie's twelve lays are short romances (they range from 118 to 1,184 lines), each of which deals with a single event or crisis in the affairs of noble lovers. In her prologue, Marie tells us that she had heard these *performed*, and in several of the lays she refers to the Breton language and Breton storytellers—that is, professional minstrels from the French province of Brittany or the Celtic parts of Great Britain. Marie's lays provide the basis of the genre that came to be known as the "Breton lay." In the prologue Marie dedicates the work to a "noble king," who is most likely to have been Henry II of England, who reigned from 1154 to 1189.

The portrait of the author that emerges from the combination of these works is of a highly educated noblewoman, proficient in Latin and English as well as her native French, with ideas of her own and a strong commitment to writing. Scholars have proposed several Maries of the period who fit this description to identify the author. A likely candidate is Marie, abbess of Shaftesbury, an illegitimate daughter of Geoffrey of Anjou and thus half-sister of Henry II. Correct or not, such an identification points to the milieu in which Marie moved and to the kind of audience she was addressing.

Many of Marie's lays contain elements of magic and mystery. Medieval readers would recognize that *Lanval* is about a mortal lover and a fairy bride, although the word "fairy" is not used in the tale. In the Middle Ages fairies were not thought of as the small creatures they became in Elizabethan and later literature. Fairies are supernatural, sometimes dangerous, beings who possess magical powers and inhabit another world. Their realm in some respects resembles the human (fairies have kings and queens), and fairies generally keep to themselves and disappear when humans notice them. But the tales are often about crossovers between the human and fairy worlds. *Sir Orfeo* and Chaucer's *Wife of Bath's Tale* are such stories.

Marie's narrative *Milun* has a tight family unit at its core, but that unit is divided in time and space by an oppressive marital system. Testing consists of long deferral; ability to recognize signs; and intergenerational violence, between father and son, that turns out to be constructive.

Chevrefoil, the shortest of Marie's lays, tells of a brief encounter between Tristran (here Tristram) and Ysolt (the Queen). The lay exemplifies the pain of their separation as well as the stratagems by which the lovers are forced to communicate and meet. The title refers to an image from the natural world that serves as a symbol of the inextricable and fatal character of the love that binds them to one another.

Marie wrote in eight-syllable couplets, which was the standard form of French narrative verse, employed also by Wace and Chrétien de Troyes. Here is what the beginning of Marie's prologue to the *Lais* says about her view of a writer's duty and, implicitly, of her own talent:

Ki Deu ad duné escïence	He to whom God has given knowledge
E de parler bon' eloquence	And the gift of speaking eloquently,
Ne s'en deit taisir ne celer,	Must not keep silent nor conceal the gift.
Ainz se deit volunters mustrer.	But he must willingly display it.

All translations of Marie's lays are by Dorothy Gilbert. All notes are by the translator.

Milun

    Who wishes various tales to tell
must vary forms to do it well,
speak a propos, with reason, sense,
for this will please the audience.
5 Just now I shall begin "Milun,"
revealing, by a brief sermon
just how it happened, how and why
this tale was formed and named, this *lai*.

    In South Wales he was born, Milun.
10 From the day he was dubbed, no one
he found, no single chevalier,
could knock him off his destrier.[1]

---

1. Steed (French).

He excelled among chevaliers,
noble and valiant, proud and fierce;
15 well known he was in Ireland,
in Norway, also in Gotland,
in Logres and in Albany[2]
many watched Milun enviously.
Loved for his prowess, though, Milun;
20 and many princes honored him.
    In his same country lived a lord;
I do not know what name he had.
He had a daughter, beautiful,
and a most courtly demoiselle.[3]
25 Much she heard mention of Milun
and she began to love the man.
She sent a messenger; she'd be
if it should please him, his *amie*.[4]
This news filled Milun with delight;
30 he thanked the demoiselle for it,
willingly said he'd be her lover—
be true, and never quit her, never!
Quite courtly his response to her.
Rich gifts he gave the messenger,
35 and great affection promised him.
    "Now, friend, see to it," said Milun,
"that I may speak with my *amie*,
that we meet with due secrecy.
Carry to her my golden ring;
40 on my behalf this message bring,
that when it pleases her, then she
send thee here; I'll return with thee."
    The servant took his leave, to tell
this message to the demoiselle,
45 gave her the ring, and said he'd well
performed the task, and done her will.
The girl was overjoyed to hear
that love had thus been granted her.

    So in a garden, set nearby
50 her chamber, in great jollity
of spirit, she kept rendez-vous;
Oh, frequently they met, these two!
He came so much,[5] he loved so well,
that she conceived, this demoiselle.
55 When she perceived she was *enceinte*,[6]
she summoned Milun, made her plaint,
and told him what had come to pass;
honor and good name lost, alas,
since she'd engaged in this affair.

2. Logres is England; Albany is an old name for
Scotland.
3. Young lady; damsel (French).
4. Friend, lover.
5. The double entendre of English "came"—"he
came so much"—does not occur in Marie's original or, as far as I know, in Marie's language; I
have not found it in the many ribald tales of the
period. I have retained it in this translation,
thinking the pun consistent with Marie's wit and
worldly spirit.
6. Pregnant (French).

60 Judgment on her would be severe:
   torture by sword, or she might be
   sold into foreign slavery.
   The ancients had such customs then,
   and in that time such things were done.
65 Milun responded that he would
   do what her counsel said he should.
       "Take this child," said she, "at its birth;
   my married sister lives up north,
   up in Northumberland's her home.
70 She's a rich, wise, and worthy dame.
   If in writing you display it,
   if in words you speak and say it,
   this is your sister's child you bring,
   a cause of her great suffering,
75 it will be nurtured well, she'll see,
   boy, girl, whichever one it be.
   And hang around its neck your ring,
   also a letter you must bring,
   written within, its father's name
80 and the hard story of its dame.
   When the child's big, and fully grown,
   and to sufficient age has come
   so it can reason understand,
   letter and ring into its hand
85 she should give, so it may discover
   while it cares for these things, its father."

       They kept her counsel thoroughly
   through the term of her pregnancy
   until the damsel's time to bear.
90 Then an old woman cared for her,
   with whom she trusted all she did.
   This dame concealed all, all she hid,
   never gave hint of the affair
   by word, by manner, or by air.
95   Beautiful was the damsel's son.
   Around its neck the ring she hung,
   also a pouch of silk; within
   the letter, which no one had seen.
   She laid all in a cradle; over
100 these treasures tucked a linen cover.
   She placed beneath the infant's head
   a useful pillow, fine and good;
   a coverlet placed over him
   hemmed all about with marten skin.
105 All, the old woman gave Milun
   who, in the garden, took his son.
   He bade his serving-folk that they
   transport the infant loyally.
   Through all the towns upon their way
110 they seven times stopped on each day

to rest, let the child suck, and then
bathe him, put him to bed again.
They took the straightest route, and there
found the dame, gave the child to her.
115 And she received the child with joy—
letter and seal and little boy.
When she discovered who he was
her loving care was marvelous!
Those who had brought the baby boy
120 to their own country went their way.

Out of his country went Milun,
a warrior, hired, to win renown.
Meanwhile his sweetheart was at home.
Her sire bestowed her on a man,
125 a baron of that region, rich
and powerful, his fame worth much.
And when she learned this was her fate
past reason she was desolate.
Much she regretted her affair
130 with Milun, for her deeds felt fear.
She'd borne a child, a serious fault,
straightway her lord would know of it.
"Alas," she said, "what shall I do?
Me, take a lord? Not possible!
135 No longer virgin, no more maid,
I'll all my days be serving maid.
I little knew how things would be;
I thought to marry my *ami*.[7]
We'd have concealed the liaison,
140 never heard talk by anyone.
Why live? To die is best for me.
But I am not the least bit free,
all around me are guardians,
young ones and old, my chamberlains,
145 who loathe love, with great enmity,
always, and who love misery.
I am compelled to suffer thus—
if only I could die! Alas!"
The time came; she was given away;
150 led to her lord upon the day.[8]

Back to his country came Milun,
a pensive and a grieving man.
Great pain he showed, great sorrow felt,
but he took comfort from the thought
155 that nearby lay the country which
was home to her he loved so much.
Milun considered how he could

---

7. Friend, lover (masculine form of *amie*).
8. The line in the original seems ambiguous. In
sis sires l'en ad amenee, *sires* could refer either to
the father, so keen to marry his daughter off to
the baron and lead her to him, or to the baron
himself, now her lord.

alert his love, or send her word
that he was, once again, at home
160 without the message being known.
A letter he composed, Milun,
and sealed. He had a much-loved swan;
he placed the letter round its throat
and in its feathers hid the note.
165 He called one of his squires to come,
And with this speech instructed him:
    "Change thy clothes; quickly go," said he,
"to the *chastel*[9] of my *amie*.
My swan thou shalt transport with thee;
170 take care that, for a surety,
that maid, manservant, either one
present my sweetheart with the swan!"
    He did as he was bid, this man;
at that he left and took the swan.
175 The route he knew, the straightest road,
and came there, quickly as he could,
on his way passing through the town;
now to the main gate he has come.
The porter saw him, called to him:
180   "Hear me, friend," called out Milun's man.
"My occupation, you must know,
is catching birds; that's what I do.
In a field under Caerleon,
with my snare, I have caught a swan.
185 I wish protection, strong and sure;
thus I present the swan to her
so that I not be hindered here,
charged and accused, as now I fear."
    To him replied the officer:
190   "Friend, for sure no one speaks with her.
Nevertheless I will find out
if I could locate near, some spot
where I could take you, lead you there.
Then I would let you speak with her."
195   The porter went into the hall.
He saw two knights there, that was all,
at a large table; seated thus,
they much amused themselves at chess.
The porter came back hastily,
200 and led the man in such a way
that no one saw him in the hall,
noticed or hindered them at all.
Now at the chamber, at his call
the door was opened; a *pucelle*[1]
205 went to her lady, took the swan;
thus was the presentation done.

---

9. Castle (Anglo-Norman French).
1. A "maid," in most of the English senses. Here, it means a maidservant. In line 135 it obviously

means a virgin; in line 136, a maidservant. It can also mean a "maiden, young girl" in a more general sense.

The lady called her valet, then,
And gave instructions to the man;
    "See that my swan here is well fed,
210 cared for, and has sufficient food."
    "Dame," said the man who'd brought the swan,
"this is a gift for you alone,
splendid, and fit for royalty!
How beautiful, how fine, just see!"
215 He put it in her hands, and she
received the present graciously.
    Her fingers felt the head, the throat;
under the feathers felt the note.
She trembled; her blood froze; the swan,
220 the note, she knew, was from Milun.
Some recompense she gave his man;
then he could go, his task was done.
    She was alone now in the room;
she called a servant girl to come;
225 unlaced the letter from the swan;
broke the seal, saw the name "Milun"
right at the top. Oh, certainly
she knew the name of her *ami*!
A hundred times she kissed the note,
230 weeping before speech passed her throat.
There at the top, the text she read,
all he confided, all he said,
the great distress and agony
that Milun suffered, night and day:
235   "Now it was at her pleasure whether
to kill him, or see him recover
If some device she could discover
whereby they two could speak together
she should write back to him in turn
240 and send the letter with the swan.
First the bird must have care and rest,
then she must starve him, let him fast,
three days; and then around his throat
she must attach her answering note,
245 and let him go; then he would come
flying once more to his first home."
    When she had read all that he wrote,
and understood all in the note,
she kept the swan; he sojourned there.
250 Fine food and drink he had from her!
A month, in her chamber, had good care.

    But now hear more of this affair!
How she found, by her stratagem,
parchment and ink, made use of them,
255 wrote such a letter as he sought,
and with a ring sealed up her note.
The swan she then allowed to fast,

and then into the air it cast
with the note, and the famished bird
260   craving and longing for its food
flew hastily, until it came
to its first shelter, its first home.
To the town, to the house, the swan
flew; to the feet, then, of Milun.
265   When he sees it, how joyful he!
He held its wings delightedly,
summoned a steward, so he could
give the pet swan its well-earned food.
From the swan's neck he took the note,
270   from end to end read all she wrote;
tokens and greetings in the feathers
gave him delights well known to lovers:
    "Without him I can know no good,
no joy; his sentiments he should
275   return, as she'd done, by the swan."
Hastily he'll comply, Milun.

     Twenty years these two lived this way,
The knight Milun and his *amie*,
always the swan their emissary,
280   no other intermediary.
Thus they would cause the bird to fast,
then let him fly off with his trust.
Then the one who received the bird
knew very well to give him food.
285   Sometimes they met, she and Milun.
No lover's so afflicted, none
so much constrained or so beset
they cannot find a way to meet.

     The lady who had nursed their son
290   devoted such attention
he grew of age under her care;
and then she dubbed him chevalier.
He was a fine young handsome man!
Letter and ring she gave him then,
295   explained to him who was his mother,
and told the fortunes of his father:
the best, she said, of chevaliers,
how worthy, and how bold and fierce,
no better knight upon this earth
300   for reputation, valor, worth.
And when she had revealed this truth
and he had listened well enough,
his father's prowess and this word
made him rejoice at all he heard.
305   Then to himself he thought and spoke:
    "He'll be considered small by folk,
if he was sired by such a man,

a chevalier of such renown,
who does not seek a greater fame,
310 leaving the land from which he came."
    Convinced of this necessity,
only one night more would he stay,
and took his leave the following day.
The lady then had much to say
315 of admonitions; those bestowed,
she gave him money for the road.
    At Southampton he passed straight through,
since over sea he meant to go.
To Barfluet[2] he went straightway,
320 and so he came to Brittany.
    He tourneyed there; gave largesse; sought
wealthy men's friendship. When he fought,
and raised his lance in any joust,
invariably he came off best.
325 He loved the poor knights; when he won
riches and prizes, the young man
took the poor in his service; he
shared the won wealth most lavishly.
In one land he'd no wish to stay,
330 but in all countries over sea
he bore with him his fame, his valor,
so courtly that he knew much honor.
His prowess, largess, his great fame
at length to his own country came,
335 that there was from that land a youth
who crossed the sea to prove his worth,
whose prowess, generosity,
largesse, were all so great that he,
this famous, nameless chevalier,
340 was called by all the knights "Sans Peer."[3]
    Praise of this fine knight reached Milun,
this man who'd such distinction won,
much Milun suffered, much complained
to himself of this knight, so famed.
345 While he himself set forth on journeys,
bore arms, engaged himself in tourneys,
none, in the country of his birth,
must prized, or praised, be, for his worth!
A plan he then resolved upon:
350 he'd cross the sea, make haste, be gone,
and with this chevalier he'd joust,
injure him, harm him, do his worst.
Rage spurred him to pursue this course;
if he could knock the man off horse
355 he'd finally be disgraced; that done,
Milun would then seek out his son,
who from the country was long gone,

2. Modern Barfleur.   3. I.e., "Without Equal."

his whereabouts and fate unknown.
To his *amie* he made this known;
360   he wished her blessing on this plan.
All his heart's feelings to reveal,
he sent the letter with its seal,
to my best knowledge, by the swan.
Her desire she must tell in turn.
365   When she had heard thus from her lover,
she thanked him greatly for the favor,
since, if their son he could discover,
he must leave home, the seas cross over,
find out the fortunes of the boy;
370   never would she stand in his way.
This message of hers reached Milun;
appareled splendidly, he soon
sailed to, then passed through, Normandy;
and traveled on to Brittany.
375   He cultivated folk, and went
seeking out any tournament,
rich lodgings he took frequently,
rewarding service courteously.
    All that one winter, I believe,
380   In that land Milun chose to live;
many good knights chose to retain.
Then, after Easter, once again
it was the time for tournaments,
also of wars and violence.[4]
385   They gathered at Mount Saint Michel,
Normans and Bretons and, as well,
Flemings and French assembled there,
but Englishmen were rather rare.
Milun, one of the earliest
390   came, bold and fierce, upon his quest.
Now the fine chevalier he sought;
for certain, people could point out
the region that the knight was from,
his arms, his shield, and so quite soon
395   they'd shown the warrior to Milun,
who now most closely studied him.
Tourniers gathered now; each knight
who wished to joust, soon found a fight;
who wished to search the ranks, could choose
400   soon enough, chance to win or lose,
encounter with an adversary.
    But, let me tell you Milun's story.
He was most valiant in the fray,
and he received much praise that day,
405   but the youth I have told of, he
over all, got *le dernier cri*.[5]

---

4. Tournaments and warfare were banned by the Church at certain times of the year, including Lent, in keeping with the principle of "the truce of God." The ban was sometimes ignored.
5. That is, the youth got the loudest, greatest cry of acclaim from observers and participants.

No one could match him, of the rest
in tourneying or in a joust.
How he behaved, Milun took note,
410 how well he spurred, how well he smote,
for all his envy of the knight
his skill filled Milun with delight.
He sought the ranks; he met the youth;
there they engaged and jousted, both.
415 Milun struck so ferociously
his foe's lance shattered, truth to say,
but he was not unhorsed; in turn
so hardily he struck Milun
that from his charger he fell down.
420 At that, the young man could discern
under the visor, the white hair,
white beard; his grief was hard to bear!
Milun's horse by the reins he led
to him; bestowed it on him; said,
425   "Sire, mount up, do! I am distraught,
I'm greatly troubled in my thought
that to a fine man of your age
I've dealt such insult, such outrage!"
   Milun leaped on his horse, much pleased;
430 on the youth's finger recognized
the ring, as he returned the horse,
and to the young man he spoke thus:
   "Friend, listen! Say, by God above,
by the Omnipotent's sweet love,
435 what name is that borne by thy father?
What is thy name? Who is thy mother?
I wish to know the truth. I've been,
much, a great traveler; much I've seen,
much sought in countries where I went,
440 battle and war and tournament;
never, by strike of chevalier
did I fall from my destrier.
Thou hast, though, jousting, unhorsed me;
wonderfully could I love thee!"
445   The other said, "I'll speak to you
about my father—what I know.
In Wales, I think, the man was born,
and given there the name Milun.
He loved a rich man's daughter; he
450 in secrecy engendered me.
Sent to Northumbria, there placed,
I was well nourished, taught, and raised!
An aunt of mine there nurtured me,
long kept me in her company,
455 gave me arms and a destrier,
and it was she who sent me here.
I've long lived here. But now I want
to leave; my longing, my intent
is to make voyage over sea

460 to my own country, hastily,
know the condition of my father
and his behavior toward my mother.
I will show him my golden ring
and certain tokens I will bring;
465 that he'll disown me, I've no fear;
but he will love me, hold me dear."
　　When he spoke thus, Milun, for sure
could not sit still and listen more;
quickly he leaped up, seized the skirt
470 of the youth's hauberk, his mailed shirt;
　　"My God", he said, "healed is Milun!
by my faith, friend, you are my son!
I've searched for thee, I've sought for thee,
this year, my country left for thee."
475 　　The youth heard; from his horse leaped down
and tenderly he kissed Milun.
Such joyous mein had son and father,
such happy speech made to each other
that other folk who watched nearby
480 wept both for pity and for joy.

　　The tournament broke up. Milun
left, all impatience; with his son
he greatly longed to speak at leisure,
impart to him his plans and pleasure.
485 They at a hostel spent the night,
in joyousness and in delight,
a goodly crowd of knights was there.
Milun could tell his son, and share
how he had come to love his mother,
490 how she was given, by her father,
to a lord of that region; he,
Milun, still loved her, faithfully,
and she him, most devotedly.
And how the swan then came to be
495 bearer of letters, go-between;
they dared not trust a human being.
　　The son said, "By my faith, dear father,
I shall bring you and her together!
This lord of hers I will dispatch,
500 and see you married! Made a match!"
　　They spoke no more of this affair.
Next day their task was to prepare
to leave; bid their friends farewell; and then
to their own land at last return.
505 Hastily they passed over seas,
fair winds they had, auspicious breeze.
They met, as they went on their way,
riding toward them, a servant boy.
He was sent by Milun's *amie*,
510 and meant to go to Brittany;

she sent this lad, and a report—
but now his journey was cut short!
A letter, sealed, he gave Milun;
in speech, he urged the man to come
515 quickly to her, he must not tarry!
Her lord was dead! Milun must hurry!
When he had heard this news, Milun
thought it seemed marvelous to him,
and he explained all to his son.
520 Delay or hindrance there was none;
they traveled on until they'd come
to the dame's castle, to her home.
In her son she took much delight—
a worthy, valiant, noble knight!
525 No word they sought from relative;
no counsel took, of none asked leave,
but the son brought the two together
and gave his mother to his father.
In happiness and sweetest joy
530 they lived from then on, night and day.

    Of their good fortune and their love
the ancients made the *lai* above,
and I, who wrote the story down,
delighted much to tell this one.

Lanval

    The story of another *lai*,
just as it happened, I will say.
It's of a young, most noble man;
he was called Lanval in Breton.
5   At Carlisle there was sojourning
Arthur, the valiant, courtly King;
Scottish and Pictish peoples laid
waste all that land, in war and raid.
Down into Logres[1] they would come
10 and often they did cruel harm.
The King was there at Pentecost,
lodging there for that summer feast,
Gifts to his barons and his counts
he gave, in great munificence.
15 And to those of the Table Round
—no greater band on earth!—good land,
and wives to wed, he gave them all,
save for one man, who'd served him well,
Lanval. The King forgot this man;
20 none put in a good word for him.

---

1. An ancient name for England.

For his great valor, his largesse,
his manly beauty, his prowess,
he was much envied by most men;
they made a show of loving him.
25 But if he'd met with some mischance,
No day would that be for laments!
A king's son, of high lineage,
he was far from his heritage!
Though of King Arthur's house, he had
30 spent all his money and his good,
for Arthur gave him not a thing,
and he asked nothing of the King.
Lanval was much disturbed by now,
pensive, he was, and sorrowful.
35 Be not dismayed, lords, at the thought
that such a man would be distraught,
foreigner in a foreign place—
where to find help, protection, grace?
This chevalier of whom I tell,
40 who'd served King Arthur long and well,
mounted one day his destrier[2]
for pleasure, and relief from care.
He mounted, and rode out of town,
came to a meadow all alone,
45 by a swift stream got down, to see
his horse was trembling terribly.
Unsaddling it, he let it go
roll in the field, as horses do.
Folding his cloak beneath his head
50 he lay down, made the field his bed
still pensive, deep in his malaise.
Nothing, it seemed, could bring him ease.
He lay there thus, heartsick, heartsore,
and down along the river's shore
55 he saw two girls approaching; never
had he seen fairer women, ever!
Splendidly, richly, they were dressed,
in garments closely, tightly laced,
bliauts[3] of dark silk with the laces,
60 and oh, how beautiful their faces!
Two golden bowls the elder bore,
of splendid workmanship, and pure;
it's true; pure gold each lovely bowl;
the younger woman bore a towel.
65 They were advancing straightaway
just up to where the young knight lay.
Now courteous Lanval rose to greet

2. A charger, or warhorse. It was a powerful and
very expensive mount, ordinarily used for combat
rather than pleasure riding.
3. Long, close-fitting tunics, with long, full sleeves.
Under the *bliaut*, in Marie's period, were ordinarily
worn two other garments. The *chemise* was worn
next to the skin; it had a long, full, pleated skirt.
Over the chemise was worn a *chainse*, a garment
made of linen or hemp with long tight sleeves and
a skirt so long it might trail on the ground. The
chainse might show just a bit above the *bliaut* at
the neck and below the hem.

the women, got up to his feet.
First they saluted the young man;
70 and then their message gave to him.
"Sir Lanval, our own demoiselle,[4]
so worthy, wise and beautiful,
has sent us here to find you thus;
she bids you come to her with us.
75 We shall conduct you safely there,
for the pavilion is quite near."
With the girls went the chevalier,[5]
but of his horse he took no care,
he left it grazing while he went.
80 The damsels led him to a tent,
splendidly set, magnificent.
Not Semiramis,[6] opulent
and at the zenith of her power,
her wealth, her wisdom in full flower,
85 nor that Octavian, great Rome's lord,[7]
could that door—its right flap!—afford.
On top, a golden eagle sat.
I do not know the worth of it,
nor of the tent ropes or the poles
90 that gave support to all the walls.
No king exists beneath the sky
who could afford all, possibly.
In the tent lay the demoiselle;
the lily, the new rose as well,
95 that in the summertime appear—
Oh, she was so much lovelier!
She lay upon a gorgeous bed;
—worth a great castle was the spread—
and her chemise[8] was all she wore.
100 Her body so well formed, so fair!
A costly cloak, of ermine fur,
and Alexandrine silk, she wore;
from the heat it protected her.
Her side, though, was revealed and bare.[9]
105 Face, neck and breast bare too, and white
as hawthorn bloom, as delicate.
Into the tent then, Lanval came;

4. A young lady, an unmarried woman of gentle birth (English "damsel").
5. Horseman, knight (French).
6. A mythical Assyrian queen, wife of Ninus, founder of Nineveh, whom she succeeded as ruler. Famed for her beauty, wisdom, and voluptuousness, she was said to have built Babylon and its hanging gardens, founded certain other ancient cities, conquered Egypt, and unsuccessfully attacked India.
7. Caesar Augustus (63 B.C.E.–C.E. 14), the first Roman emperor.
8. See note to line 59. An undergarment with a long, full, pleated skirt, it was ordinarily worn under a chainse, a long dress with very tight sleeves. Over that was worn the tunic or bliaut,

with long, full sleeves.
9. Some readers have seen a contradiction or at least a confusion in this description in which the pucelle lies only in her chemise (line 99) but a few lines down is described having an ermine fur cloak pulled over her to shield her from the heat (lines 101–3). As Marie says, ... En sa chemise senglement. / Mut ot le cors bien fait e gent / Un chier mantel de blanc hermine, / Couvert de purpre alexandrine, / Ot pur le chaut sur li geté; / Tut ot descovert le costé, / Le vis, le col, e la peitrine ... The fur cloak protects her, presumably covers her, but perhaps not completely? Or one can see her bare side and her bare face, neck and breast, presumably from the side or perhaps through her supernatural abilities.

the lovely girl called out to him.
He sat down, just beside the bed.
110   "Lanval, fair friend," the damsel said,
"I've come for you. I've come from far,
I've left my land, to seek you here.
If you are courtly, wise and brave,
joy beyond measure you shall have,
115 greater than emperors or kings—
for I love you above all things."
    He saw her beauty; felt within
the spark ignite, the glow begin
to set his heart alight, to spread,
120 and with due courtesy, he said:
    "Fair one: if you should wish to give
to me such joy, to give your love,
I know of nothing you might ask
I would not honor as my task
125 if it lay in my power at all—
though good, or evil, might befall.
I will do all that you require;
forsake all those I might desire,
and never seek to part from you—
130 this, above all, I wish to do!"
    When the girl heard him thus declare
so forcefully his love for her,
her love, her body, she gave, both.
Lanval was now on the right path!
135   After, she had a boon to give:
anything he might wish to have
was his to hold and to possess;
should he bestow great gifts, largesse,
she would find a sufficiency.
140 This was a pleasant place to be;
the more he lavished, more he gave,
more gold and silver would he have!
    "Friend," she said, "I admonish you—
command! beseech! In all you do,
145 tell our sweet secret to no one.
Here is my warning, all and sum.
Betray us, and you lose your lover;
I shall be lost to you for ever.
Lost to your sight; lost, our amours;
150 my body never pleasure yours."
    He would obey her, Lanval said,
her command he well understood.
    He lay beside her on the bed;
here was a lodging sweet and good!
155 He lay by her all afternoon,
nearly till evening came on,
and would have lingered if he could
and if she had more stay allowed.
    She said, "You must get up, sweet friend.

160　Even this time must have an end.
　　Go away, now! Here I shall stay,
　　but listen: I have this to say:
　　when you may wish for us to speak,
　　there's no place you may know or seek
165　where one may meet with one's *amie*[1]
　　without reproach or calumny
　　that I shall not seek out as well,
　　to be with you, to do your will.
　　We shall be seen there by no other,
170　none hear the words we speak together."
　　　　Full of deep joy at what she said,
　　he kissed her, then got out of bed.
　　Those who had led him to the tent
　　now gave him clothes most elegant.
175　Thus dressed anew, beneath the sky
　　No man was handsomer than he!
　　　　Lanval was neither boor nor fool;
　　they brought him water and a towel;
　　he washed and dried his hands. That done,
180　they brought a supper to the man.
　　His love and he took this repast—
　　who could refuse so fine a feast!
　　Served it was with great courtesy,
　　which he accepted happily.
185　Many and fine the dishes were,
　　all pleasing to the chevalier,
　　for often his *amie* he kissed,
　　and he embraced and held her fast.
　　When they had finished every course,
190　the damsels led him to his horse,
　　saddled up expeditiously:
　　there too, he found great courtesy!
　　　　He took his leave, got on his mount;
　　off to the city then he went.
195　Often he looked back; for our knight
　　Lanval felt great dismay and fright.
　　Shaken by all these strange events,
　　disturbed, depressed in heart and sense,
　　amazed, he could not trust his thought.
200　Had it all truly been, or not?

　　　　Home again, at his hostelry,
　　he saw his men—dressed splendidly!
　　That night he was a lavish host:
　　where his wealth came from, no one guessed.
205　If in that town a chevalier
　　needed a lodging, he came there;
　　Lanval would see to it; he'd come,
　　and splendidly be waited on.

1. Friend, lover (French).

Lanval gave gifts to chevaliers;
210 and Lanval ransomed prisoners;
jongleurs² he dressed in fineries;
and many were his honorees!
Foreigner, intimate, they all
had gifts from generous Lanval.
215 Great was his joy and his delight;
at times by day, at times by night,
often she came, his sweet *amie*,
to do his will most happily.

That year, I understand, quite soon
220 after the feast of good Saint John,³
a group, perhaps, of thirty knights,
met for amusement and delights
within a garden, very near
a tower where stayed Queen Guinevere.
225 Among these chevaliers, Gawain;⁴
his cousin, handsome Sir Yvain.⁵
Gawain, that noble, valiant man,
who was so loved by everyone,
spoke out: "God, *seigneurs*!⁶ We do wrong
230 to Lanval, our companion,
so courtly and so generous;
his sire is rich, illustrious,
a king! We should have brought Lanval!"
At that the knights turned, and they all
235 went off to Lanval's lodging; there
begged and convinced the chevalier.
At a carved window chanced to lean,
looking about and down, the queen;
three ladies were attending her.
240 She noticed the King's household there;
She knew and recognized Lanval.
She made occasion then to call
one of her ladies to go find
the fairest damsels, most refined,
245 they'd join her in the garden there,
and frolic where the knights all were.
More than thirty she brought with her
descending with her down the stair.
The knights, delighted with the meeting,
250 gave all the women joyful greeting,
taking them by the hands; their speech
lacked no refinement, each to each.
Lanval, though, stood alone, apart,
impatient, tumult in his heart,

2. Jugglers, jesters (French).
3. The Feast of St. John is Midsummer Day, June 24.
4. Gawain, the son of King Lot, is Arthur's nephew. In many Arthurian tales he is the finest of Arthur's knights and a model of perfect chivalry and *courtoisie*.
5. There are three Arthurian knights known as Yvain (there is some evidence that they may actually be the same person), but this man is undoubtedly Yvain the Valiant (*li preuz*).
6. Lords (French).

255   he longed for his *amie* so much—
       to kiss her, hold her, know her, know her touch—
       how poor, how small, all other joy
       with his own pleasure not nearby!
          But the queen saw the lone young lover,
260   and lost no time, but hurried over
       sat down beside him, spoke his name,
       unburdened all her heart to him.
          "Dear Lanval," said Queen Guinevere,[7]
       you are much honored and held dear—
       you may possess my love entire!
265   Speak to me! Tell me your desire!
       Freely I give you *druerie*;[8]
       you must rejoice in taking me!"
          "Lady," said Lanval, "let me be!"
270   I care not for your *druerie*.
       I've served my king well, kept my faith—
       I'll never compromise my oath!
       No to your love, dame, no's the word—
       I will not wrong my sovereign lord!"
275   At that the queen was furious,
       and she spoke slander, spoke it thus:
          "Lanval," she said, "I know, I sense
       you do not care for dalliance;
       but it is often rumored, sire,
280   for women you have no desire!
       But youths and squires, well-trained young men
       You seek out; you disport with them.
       Oh, coward! Boor! Unnatural,
       your service to my lord, Lanval!
285   He has lost God—I fear it—since
       he's known your vicious influence!"[9]
          Lanval heard—and with grief intense—
       but was not slow in his defense.
       In fury, though, he spoke such words
290   he much repented afterwards.
          "This calling that you claim I have,
       Lady, I have no knowledge of;
       but I love, and possess the love
       of one who should be prized above
295   all other women whom I've seen;
       I say this truth to you, my queen,
       and you had better understand—
       some servant girl she has at hand,
       the poorest in her retinue,
300   is, Lady Queen, worth more than you

---

7. Guinevere is not named in Marie's original text; she is always referred to as *la reïne* (i.e., "the queen"). . . . Since this queen is undoubtedly the figure known in Arthurian literature (e.g., the romances of Chrétien de Troyes, who was probably Marie's near contemporary) as Guinevere, I have taken the liberty of supplying her name.

8. Love, or courtly love; or a love affair. In other medieval works, it can mean a love token.

9. In other words, Arthur has lost his salvation, is damned, through Lanval's supposed influence.

in beauty—body and in face—
in breeding, virtue, goodness, grace!"
    At that the queen abandoned him,
    and she went weeping to her room.
305 Great was her grief, rage, wounded pride,
    she was so shamed and vilified.
    Wretched at heart, she went to bed,
    never would she get up, she said,
    until the king had got redress
310 for that which caused her such distress.
    The king came riding from the wood,
    joyful; the sport that day was good!
    He went straight to the queen's abode.
    She saw him and complained aloud;
315 "Mercy!" she cried; at his feet fell;
    she'd been dishonored by Lanval!
    Love he'd demanded, *druerie*,
    She had refused him, loyally;
    he had humiliated her,
320 boasting of an *amie* so fair,
    noble, refined and elegant,
    even her poorest maidservant,
    the lowliest one serving her,
    was finer than Queen Guinevere.
325   Terrible was King Arthur's wrath;
    in his great rage he swore an oath,
    if in the court this was proved truth,
    Lanval must hang, or burn to death.
    The king stormed out. He left the room,
330 he called on barons, three of them,
    to summon Lanval; sent them off.
    Lanval was sorrowful enough;
    back to his lodging he had gone.
    He knew full well what he had done;
335 utterly lost was his *amie*—
    he had revealed their *druerie*!
    Alone now in his room, Lanval
    was pensive, deeply miserable.
    His love he summoned, over and over—
340 there was no answer from his lover.
    He sighed, lamented, made complaint;
    at times he fell down in a faint;
    a hundred times he tried to call,
    Mercy! Speak to your love Lanval!
345 He cursed his heart, he cursed his mouth,
    a wonder, did not seek his death.
    Neither his wailings, shouts and cries,
    self-lacerations, agonies,
    could make his love have mercy, hear,
350 and to the wretched man appear.
    Alas, poor Lanval! What to do?
        The men of Arthur's retinue

arrived now, with their grave import:
without delay, he must to court.
355 The summons of the king they bore;
he was accused by Guinevere.
He went with them, in misery,
wishing they would just make him die.
    Before the king Lanval has come:
360 he stands there pensive, mute, struck dumb,
his bearing shows his great distress.
The king speaks, his rage manifest.
    "Vassal, you've done great wrong to me![1]
Disgusting act! Your villainy
365 traduces, shames me! Vile, obscene,
you slander and abuse the queen!
You boast, then, madly, recklessly,
that you've so noble an *amie*
her serving maid is lovelier
370 and finer than Queen Guinevere!"
    Lanval denied he'd said one thing
shaming, dishonoring his king.
Word for word he denied the scene—
he'd made not trial of the queen.
375 But then that claim he'd spoken of,
he said, was true; he had a love
of whom he'd made, in fact, that boast,
and so she'd gone; his love was lost.
Desolate, he said he'd submit
380 to the decision of the court.
    The king was in a tearing rage;
he called all knights in his ménage[2]
to counsel him on protocol;
he wished no adverse thoughts at all!
385 They came at his commandment, whether
they wanted to or not; together
they were assembled. There they weighed
judicially, decreed and said
that Lanval needs must have his day
390 in court, but must pledge faithfully
that he'd attend; give solemn word;
present himself before his lord.
The court would be its full size then;
now it was just the household men.
395 These barons went back to the king,
there to announce their reasoning;
the pledges he required, at that.
    Lanval stood, lone and desolate.

---

1. The word *vassal* had several meanings. It could commonly be a form of address appropriate to a young man of noble rank, either a comrade or someone to whom one must extend the courtesies of rank. It could also refer to any noble, worthy young man or to a noble or knight who had sworn fealty to a lord. Here, Arthur uses it in the latter sense, especially to emphasize his belief that Lanval has betrayed and traduced the bond between the two of them.
2. Household (French).

With him there were no friends or kin—
400 but bail was offered by Gawain;
his confreres followed, one by one.
The king said, "I'll release this man,
but all each man here holds from me—
lands, fiefs—you'll pledge in surety."
405 They pledged. No more was to be done.
Lanval was to his lodging gone,
escorted, for the others came,
with much chastisement and much blame.
His grief they made reproaches of,
410 cursing his ludicrous, mad love.
Each day the barons came to call;
they wanted to be sure Lanval
ate and drank, did so properly.
They feared he might go mad, or die.

415 Then on the designated day
the knights all gathered faithfully.
The king and queen were there as well.
The pledge was honored by Lanval.
Many there felt concern and grief;
420 a hundred men, it's my belief,
would have done all within their might
to liberate from trial this knight.
He'd been accused most wrongfully!
Now for the verdict. What would be
425 the finding, and the king's demands?
Now all was in the barons' hands.
All of them were assembled there;
many perplexed and saddened for
this foreigner, this noble knight—
430 with them, he had so hard a plight!
Some wished him harm though, following
the wishes of their lord and king.
Cornwall's Count then addressed the court;
"We have a task; we'll not fall short,
435 whoever weeps, whoever sings,
right must prevail above all things.
The king has charged, before us all,
a vassal I have heard you call
Lanval; charged him with felony,
440 gross misdeed, gross activity,
boasting, it seems, of an *amie*,
infuriating my lady.
The king alone desires to sue.
Now by the faith I owe to you,
445 there should, to speak the truth, not be
for response, a necessity,
save that for one's *seigneur*, one's king,
honor is due in everything.
We, with an oath, can bind Lanval,

450 and the king will excuse us all.
If Lanval can make warranty,
and she comes forward, this *amie*,
and it is true—proof can be seen—
this statement that enraged the queen,
455 then pardon will be his by right,
since he did not speak out from spite.
And if he cannot prove his claim,
then we must go and say to him
his service to the king is lost;
460 he must be banished for his boast."

They sent a message to the knight;
they said, announced, that now, by right
he must send for his love to come
defend, protect, and succor him.
465 He said this was not possible:
no chance that she would help Lanval!
They returned to the judges' place;
no help from Lanval in his case!
King Arthur pressed them to make haste
470 for the queen's sake. No time to waste!
The verdict was about to come.

They saw two damsels riding on
two lovely palfreys ambling near;
the girls were wonderfully fair!
475 Rich purple taffeta they wore
next to their skin, and nothing more.
The knights looked on delightedly!
Gawain, and with him riders three,
went to Lanval, gave him the news,
480 and pointed out the demoiselles.
Full of joy, Gawain begged Lanval—
is one of them your *amie*? Speak! Tell!
But these girls Lanval did not know,
where they came from or meant to go.
485 Still they approached, and still they rode
their palfreys; still in graceful mode
dismounted just before the dais
that was King Arthur's honored space.
Their beauty was astonishing.
490 One said politely to the king:
"Royal sire, make available
a chamber, and adorn it well
with silken curtains; for my dame
wishes for lodging in your home."
495 Arthur obliged; he did this deed,
summoned two chevaliers, to lead
the ladies to an upper floor.
For the time being, they said no more.
The king then asked the knights, meanwhile,

500 for judgment, finding, in the trial.
He was incensed, he said to them,
so dilatory they had been.
     "Sire," they said, "we debate. We're keen.
Thanks to the ladies you have seen
505 we have not reached a verdict yet.
Now let us all get on with it."
     Pensive and anxious, they all met,
noisy and brawling and upset.

While their fear hung on them this way
510 two girls in beautiful array—
Phrygian silk stuff was what they wore,[3]
and Spanish mules these damsels bore—
were observed riding by the way.
This gave the vassals all great joy!
515 Each to each said that these would save
Lanval, the worthy and the brave.
Up to him now there came Yvain
leading companions after him.
     "Sire," he said, "now you must rejoice!
520 For God's love, speak! Give us your voice!
Two demoiselles are coming here,
splendidly dressed and passing fair,
one of them surely your *amie*!"
But Lanval replied hastily
525 neither he knew; all Yvain got:
     "I know them not; I love them not."
     They arrived now, these demoiselles;
before the king, got off their mules.
Many admired them in that place
530 for form, complexion, and for face
and said, more worthy than the queen
they were, more than she'd ever been.

The elder, with great courtesy,
spoke wisely, with propriety.
535   "King, sire, have a chamber ready
that can accommodate my lady.
She's on her way to speak to you."
He gave commands to lead the two
where the two others were led before.
540 But of the mules they took no care.
     The damsels once provided for
the king gave his commands once more.
The judgment! Now, without delay!
Too much was squandered of the day,
545 and the queen's fury had increased;
she had not broken yet her fast.

---

3. Phrygia was an ancient state located in what is now central Turkey.

They were about to answer, when
they could see coming from the town,
upon her horse, a girl. On earth
550 none had such beauty, none such worth!
A pure white palfrey was her mount;
gentle it was and elegant.
Form—neck and head—so beautiful
on earth was no such animal.
555 Splendid adornments bore this mount;
under sweet heaven no king nor count
could ever buy them, have and hold
unless his lands were pledged or sold.
Dressed was this damsel in this wise:
560 In a white *chainse* and a chemise[4]
in two parts laced together, so
all down her sides the flesh could show.
Her form was fine, her hips were low,
her neck white as a branch in snow,
565 brilliant her eyes, her face was white,
lovely her mouth, nose set just right,
brown her eyebrows, her forehead fair,
her head of curly, quite blonde hair;
gold thread could not give off such light
570 as did her hair in sunbeams bright.
A mantle of dark silk she wore
with the skirts gathered close to her,
sparrowhawk on her fist she bore,
following her, a levrier.[5]
575 In the town no one, small or great,
in childhood or in aged state
there was, who did not rush to be
where she rode, where they too could see.
Her beauty caused no gab, no jokes,
580 but slowly she approached these folks.
The judges who observed her thus,
thought her a wonder, marvelous;
not one of them who looked her way
but felt a kindling warmth of joy.

585 Barons who loved the knight Lanval
went to him speedily to tell
how there was come a demoiselle
who, if God pleased, could save him still.
"Sire—dear companion—here rides one
590 who's neither tawny, nor dull brown.[6]
In all the world, she's loveliest
of all the women who exist!"

That Lanval heard, and raised his head;
He knew her well from what they said,

4. See n. 3, p. 172; n. 8, p. 173.
5. A greyhound.

6. Dark complexions were considered unattractive
in the Middle Ages.

595   he gasped, and blood rose to his face.
     He answered them, and with some haste.
        "Faith!" he said, "that is my *amie*!
     I do not care who slaughters me
     if she shows me no mercy, for
600   all my cure is in seeing her."

       Into the palace rode the lady;
     none there had ever seen such beauty.
     Before the king she stepped down, then
     she was well seen by everyone.
605   Dismounted, she let fall her cloak
     for better view by all the folk.
     The king, so courtly and well bred,
     rose up to greet her where she stood;
     the others honored her as well,
610   and wished to serve the demoiselle.
     When they'd seen all there was to see
     and praised her beauty fittingly,
     she spoke to Arthur in this way,
     for she was not inclined to stay.
615   "King, I have loved thy vassal. See,
     there he stands; Lanval, it is he!
     Here in thy court he stands accused;
     Lanval must not be here abused
     for what he spoke; thou, King, must know
620   the queen was wrong; it was not so,
     he never sought her love at all!
     As for the boast made by Lanval,
     if his acquittal come through me,
     let thy good barons set him free!"
625   King Arthur granted that it must
     be as the Court found right and just;
     of all the judges, one and all
     determined to acquit Lanval,
     and by their finding he was free.

630   The lady left, for such as she
     not even Arthur could retain,
     with his fine servants; she was gone.
       Before the hall there had been set
     a block of stone, dark marble. That
635   the heavier men could use to mount
     when to King Arthur's court they went.
     Lanval jumped up upon this stone;
     when his love out the door had come,
     riding her palfrey, up behind
640   leaped Lanval, in a single bound!
     With her he went to Avalon[7]

---

7. A mystical island that figures in a number of Arthurian legends; King Arthur's sword, Excalibur, was said to have been forged there.

—or so they say, those called Breton—
to an isle, a most lovely one,
she carried off this fine young man!
645 More of Lanval no one has heard;
I cannot tell another word.

Chevrefoil[1]

Much pleased am I to tell the tale,
the *lai* that folk call *Chevrefoil*.
I shall recount the truth, the sum,
why it was made, and how: for whom.

5 Folk have told me it, several,
and I've found written tales as well,
of Tristram and the Queen's affairs,
what an exalted love was theirs,
from which much sorrow came their way:
10 how they both perished in one day.
King Mark was raging, furious,
his nephew, Tristram, gave him cause.
Tristram was banished, for he'd been
the secret lover of the Queen.
15 To his own country he had gone,
to Southern Wales, where he was born.
For a full year was his sojourn,
in exile; he could not return,
But then he chose, most recklessly,
20 to risk death and calamity.
That choice should not astonish you,
for loyal lovers, steadfast, true,
are troubled, full of doleful thought,
when their great longings are not met.
25 So Tristram, pensive, doleful, found
he must go, leave his home and land.
Straightway he sought Cornwall again,
for it was there he'd find the Queen.
In the forest he hid, alone,
30 for he wished notice by no one.
Only in evening he stole out,
needing a lodging for the night.
He met some poor folk, peasantry;
glad of their hospitality
35 he asked, what news? The King, what quest
did he pursue, what business?
The King had summoned, so they heard,

1. In English, "honeysuckle." Literally it means "Goat-leaf." See note to line 115. In Anglo-Norman of this period the vowel sound in "foil" would be *ay*, and the rhyme with English "tale" would be closer than in modern French.

all of the barons, every lord.
To Tintagel they must repair;
40 Mark desired court to be held there.
At Pentecost they'd gather, all,
to meet in joyous festival,
the Queen among the company.
Tristram heard, full of joy and glee,
45 for if she took that road, for sure
Tristram must catch a sight of her.
    The day the King moved house, Tristram
was hidden in the woods again.
And on the route that he well knew,
50 the route the party must pass through,
a hazel branch he cut and split,
squared it, and made a staff from it.
When he had pared and smoothed the staff,
he carved his name there with his knife.
55 The Queen would likely see it there;
she would be watching, well aware,
for it had happened once before
such a stick was perceived by her—
her lover's stick she'd recognize
60 when it appeared before her eyes.
He wrote just this, and nothing more;
he had made known to her before
that in that place he lay in wait,
long tarrying, in a hopeful state,
65 to catch a glimpse of her and know
how meeting her was possible;
live he could not, if not with her.
The two of them were similar
to honeysuckle, which must find
70 a hazel, and around it bind;
when it enlaces it all round,
both in each other are all wound.
Together they will surely thrive,
but split asunder, they'll not live.
75 Quick is the hazel tree's demise;
quickly the honeysuckle dies.
"So with us never, *belle amie*,[2]
me without you, you without me."
    The Queen came riding. As she rode
80 she watched the upward-sloping road.
She saw the staff; perceived it well,
could certainly those letters spell.
Attending chevaliers who led her
as they rode on their way together
85 she told to stop; she gave command;
she wished to rest and would descend.
    Her men obeyed; did not say nay!

---

2. In English, "fair sweetheart," "fair friend," "beautiful lover."

and from her knights she went some way,
calling to her her maid Brenguein,
90   so greatly trusted by the Queen.
A distance, small, along the road,
she went; found him within the wood,
who loved her most of any being;
great joy they had, he and the Queen.
95   He spoke, at leisure; time allowed;
she spoke, at pleasure, all she would;
and then she told him how he could
win from his uncle an accord.
Much grieved the King was when he sent
100   Sir Tristram into banishment;
accused he had been, by some other.[3]
They parted then; she left her lover,
but as they separated, both
wept much, each of them was so loath.
105   Back home to Wales Sir Tristram went
until his uncle for him sent.

For all the joy that he had known
when Tristram had his lover seen,
and for the words he then wrote down
110   at the fond urging of the Queen—
to keep those words in memory
Tristram, who well knew minstrelsy,
made, for remembrance, a new *lai*;
briefly I name it; let me say,
115   *Gotelef*[4] the English call this tale;
and the French call it *Chevrefoil*.
Now I've recounted all that's true
about this *lai* I've told to you.

3. In the various versions of the Tristan story, various people reveal the affair between the knight and the queen. In the mid-twelfth-century Old French work by Beroul, three wicked barons observe Tristan and Yseut the Fair in a "compromising situation" and plot to discredit the knight; in Thomas of Britain's *Tristran*, much of which is lost, Brangein turns against her mistress and tells the king that she is unfaithful not with Tristran but with another man.
4. I.e., "Goat-leaf." The word is not attested in Middle English.

SIR ORFEO
ca. 1300

*S*ir Orfeo is a reworking of the tragic classical myth of Orpheus and his wife, Eurydice. When Eurydice died of a snake bite, Orpheus followed her to the underworld. Having so pleased Pluto and Proserpina with his music, Orpheus was granted Eurydice's release, on condition he not look back to his wife as she followed him from Hades. Orpheus did look back, and so lost his wife. The medieval narrative evokes this tragedy to replace it with the comedy of reunification, not only of husband and wife but also of king and subjects. Orfeo's abdication, his entry into the forest and the underworld, his charming of the fairy kingdom with his music: all permit the rescue of his paralyzed, lacerated wife, Eurydice, and their joyful return home.

The poem was probably translated from a French romance of the kind called a Breton lay. The English translation was likely made before 1300, but it has survived in only three manuscripts of later date. Some scholars believe that the best of these, the Auchinleck manuscript, might once have been read by Chaucer, whose *Franklin's Tale* is also a Breton lay.

The text presented here is flexibly based on the Auchinleck manuscript. The metrical form is the four-stress couplet, the standard English form used to translate French octosyllabic couplets.

Sir Orfeo

We reden ofte and finden ywrite—
As thise clerkes doon° us wite°—   *cause / to learn*
The layes that been of harping[1]
Been yfounde° of freely° thing.   *composed / pleasant*
5 Some been of werre° and some of wo,   *war*
And some of joye and mirthe also,
And some of trecherye and of gile;
And some of happes° that fellen° while,°   *events / occurred / once*
And some of bourdes° and ribaudye,°   *jokes / ribaldry*
10 And manye been of faïrye.[2]
Of alle thing that men may see,
Most of love forsoothe they be.
In Britain° thise layes been wrought,   *Brittany*
First yfounde° and forth ybrought.   *composed*
15 Of aventures that felle° by dayes[3]   *occurred*
The Britons° therof maden layes: *Bretons*
Whan they mighte owher° yheere°   *anywhere / hear*
Of any merveiles that ther were,
They tooken hem hir harpes with game,°   *pleasure*
20 Maden layes and yaf° hem name.   *gave*
    Of aventures that han bifalle
I can some telle, but nought alle.
Herkneth, lordinges° that been trewe,   *gentlemen*
I wol you telle of Sir Orfewe.
25   Orfeo was a riche° king,   *noble*
In Engelond an heigh lording,
A stalworth° man and hardy bo,°   *valiant / both*
Large° and curteis° he was also,   *generous / courteous*
His fader was come of King Pluto,
30 And his moder of King Juno,
That somtime were as goddes yholde°   *considered*

---

1. I.e., composed to be sung to the harp.
2. Fairyland and, more commonly, the otherworld and its supernatural inhabitants.
3. Once.

For aventures that they dide and tolde.
    This king sojourned in Traciens°   *Thrace*
That is a citee of noble defens°   *fortification*
35 (For Winchester was cleped° tho°   *called / then*
Traciens withouten no°).   *denial*
Orfeo most of any thing
Loved the glee° of harping: *music*
Siker° was every good harpour   *certain*
40 Of him to have muche honour.
Himself he lerned for to harpe,
And laide° theron his wittes sharpe;°   *applied / keenly*
He lerned so ther nothing was
A bettre harpour in no plas.°   *place*
45 In al the world was no man bore°   *born*
That ones° Orfeo sat bifore,   *once*
And° he mighte of his harping heere,   *if*
But he sholde thinke that he were
In oon of the joyes of Paradis,
50 Swich melodye in his harping is.
    Orfeo hadde a queene of pris°   *excellence*
That was ycleped° Dame Heurodis,   *named*
The fairest lady for the° nones°   *that / matter*
That mighte goon° on body and bones,   *walk*
55 Ful of love and of goodnesse—
But no man may telle hir fairnesse.
    Bifel so, the comsing° of May,   *beginning*
When merye and hot is the day,
And away been winter showres,
60 And every feeld is ful of flowres,
And blosme breme° on every bough   *glorious*
Overal° wexeth° merye ynough,   *everywhere / grows*
This eeche° queene Dame Heurodis   *same*
Took with hire two maides of pris°   *excellence*
65 And wente in the undertide°   *forenoon*
To playe in an orchard-side,
To see the flowres sprede° and springe   *open*
And to heere the fowles singe.
    They setten hem down alle three
70 Faire° under an impe-tree;° *fairly / grafted fruit tree*
And wel soone this faire queene
Fel on sleepe upon the greene.
The maidens durste hire not awake,
But lete hire lie and reste take.
75 So she slepte til afternoon
That undertide was al ydoon.°   *passed*
But as soone as she gan wake
She cried and loothly bere° gan make: *outcry*
She frotte° hir hondes and hir feet   *tore at*
80 And cracched° hir visage—it bledde weet;° *scratched / wet*
Hir riche robe she al torit,°   *tore apart*
And was ravised° out of her wit.   *ravished*
The two maidenes hire biside

Ne durste with hire no leng° abide,   *longer*
85 But runne to the palais right
And tolde bothe squier and knight
That hir queene awede° wolde,   *go mad*
And bad hem go and hire atholde.°   *restrain*
Knightes runne and ladies also,
90 Damiseles sixty and mo,°   *more*
In th' orchard to the queene they come,
And hire up in armes nome,°   *took*
And broughte hire to bed at laste,
And heelde hire there fine° faste.   *very*
95 But evere she heeld° in oo° cry,   *continued / one*
And wolde uppe° and awy.°   *get up / go away*
    Whan the king herde that tiding
Nevere him nas worse for no thing:
Orfeo cam with knightes tene°   *ten*
100 To chambre right bifore the queene,
And looked and saide with greet° pitee,   *great*
"O leve° lif, what aileth thee?—   *dear*
That evere yit hast been so stille,
And now thou gredest° wonder shille.°   *cry out / shrilly*
105 Thy body that was so whit ycore°   *excellent*
With thine nailes is all totore.°   *torn*
Allas, thy rode° that was so reed°   *complexion / red*
Is as wan as thou were deed.°   *dead*
And also thy fingres smale
110 Been al bloody and al pale.
Allas, thy lovesome yën° two   *eyes*
Looketh so° man dooth on his fo.   *as*
A, dame, ich° biseeche mercy—   *I*
Lete been al this reweful° cry,   *pitiful*
115 And tel me what° thee is and how,   *what the matter with*
And what thing may thee helpe now."
    Tho° lay she stille at the laste,   *then*
And gan to weepe swithe° faste,°   *very / hard*
And saide thus the king unto:
120 "Allas, my lord Sir Orfeo,
Sitthen° we first togider were   *since*
Ones wrothe° nevere we nere,   *angry*
But evere ich have yloved thee
As my lif, and so thou me.
125 But now we mote° deele° atwo—   *must / separate*
Do thy best, for I moot° go."   *must*
    "Allas," quath he, "forlorn ich am!
Whider wilt thou go and to wham?°   *whom*
Whider thou goost ich wil with thee,
130 And whider I go thou shalt with me."
"Nay, nay, sire, that nought nis.[4]
Ich wil thee telle al how it is:
As ich lay this undertide°   *forenoon*

---

4. I.e., that's no use.

And slepte under oure orchard-side,
135 Ther come to me two faire knightes,
Wel y-armed al to rightes,
And bad me comen on hying°   *in haste*
And speke with hir lord the king;
And ich answerede at° wordes bolde   *in*
140 That I ne durste nought ne I nolde.°   *would not*
They prikked again as they mighte drive.[5]
Tho° cam hir king also blive°   *then / straightway*
With an hundred knightes and mo,
And damiseles an hundred also,
145 Alle on snow-white steedes;
As white as milk were hir weedes:°   *clothes*
I ne seigh° nevere yit bifore   *saw*
So faire creatures ycore.°   *splendid*
The king hadde a crown on his heed:°   *head*
150 It nas of silver n'of gold reed,°   *red*
But it was of a precious stoon;
As brighte as the sonne it shoon.
And as soone as he to me cam,
Wolde ich, nolde ich, he me nam°   *took*
155 And made me with him to ride
Upon a palfrey him biside,
And broughte me to his palais
Wel attired° in eech a ways,°   *equipped / way*
And shewed me castels and towrs,
160 Riveres, forestes, frith° with flowres,   *meadow*
And his riche steedes eechcon,
And sithen° broughte me again hoom   *afterward*
Into oure owene orche-yard,°   *orchard*
And saide to me thus afterward,
165 'Looke tomorwe that thou be
Right here under this impe-tree,
And thanne thou shalt with us go,
And live with us everemo.°   *evermore*
And if thou makest us ylet,°   *resistance*
170 Where° thou be, thou worst° yfet.°   *wherever / shall be / fetched*
And al totore° thy limes al   *torn apart*
That no thing thee helpe shal.
And though thou beest so totorn,
Yit thou worst° with us yborn.'"°   *shall be / carried off*
175   When king Orfeo herde this cas,°   *circumstance*
"O, weel,"° quath he, "allas, allas!   *woe*
Lever me were to lete° my lif   *leave*
Than thus to lese° the queene my wif."   *lose*
He asked conseil at° eech a man,   *from*
180 But no man him helpe can.
    Amorwe° the undertide is come,   *next day*
And Orfeo hath his armes ynome,°   *taken*
And wel ten hundred knightes with him,

---

5. I,e., they rode as fast as they could.

Eech y-armed, stout and grim.
185 And with the queene wenten he°   *they*
Right unto that impe-tree.
They made sheltrom° in eech a side,   *military formation*
And saide they wolde ther abide
And die there everichoon,
190 Er the queene sholde from hem goon.
And yit amiddes hem full right
The queene was away ytwight,°   *snatched*
With° faïrye forth ynome:°   *by / taken*
Men wiste nevere wher she was bicome.[6]
195   Tho° was ther crying, weep and wo;   *then*
The king into his chambre is go
And ofte swooned upon the stoon,°   *floor*
And made swich dool and swich moon[7]
That nye° his lif was yspent°—   *nearly / finished*
200 Ther was noon amendement.°   *remedy*
   He clepte° togider his barouns,   *called*
Eerles, lordes of renouns,°   *great names*
And whan they alle ycomen were,
"Lordinges," he saide, "bifor you here
205 Ich ordaine myn heigh steward
To wite° my kingdom afterward;   *keep*
In my stede been he shal
To keepe my londes overal.°   *everywhere*
For now I have my queene ylore,°   *lost*
210 The faireste lady that evere was bore,°   *born*
Nevere eft° I nil° no womman see;   *again / will not*
In wildernesse now wil ich tee°   *go*
And live ther for everemore,
With wilde beestes in holtes° hore.°   *woods / gray*
215 And whan ye wite° that I be spent,°   *learn / dead*
Make you than a parlement
And chese° you° a newe king: *choose / for yourselves*
Now dooth youre best with al my thing."
   Tho° was ther weeping in the halle,   *then*
220 And greet° cry among hem alle;   *great*
Unnethe° mighte olde or yong   *scarcely*
For weeping speke a word with tonge.
They kneeled alle adown in fere°   *together*
And prayede him if his wille were,
225 That he ne sholde from hem go.
"Do way," quath he, "it shal be so."
   Al his kingdom he forsook;
But° a sclavin° on him he took: *only / pilgrim's cloak*
He hadde no kirtel° ne noon hood,   *short coat*
230 Shert ne yit noon other good.
But his harp he took algate,°   *at any rate*
And dide him barefoot out at yate:°   *gate*

---

6. No one knew what had become of her.   7. And made such lamentation and such complaint.

	No man moste° with him go.	must
	O way,° what° ther was weep and wo,	alas / how
235	Whan he that hadde been king with crown	
	Wente so poorelich out of town.	
	Thrugh the wode° and over heeth	wood
	Into the wildernesse he geeth.°	goes
	Nothing he fint° that him is aise,°	finds / easy
240	But evere he liveth in greet malaise.	
	He that hadde wered° the fowe and gris,[8]	worn
	And on bed the purper° bis,°	purple / linen
	Now on harde heeth he lith,°	lies
	With leves and grasse he him writh.°	covers
245	He that hadde had castels and towres,	
	Rivere foreest, frith° with flowres,	meadow
	Now though it ginne snowe and freese,	
	This king moot° make his bed in meese.°	must / moss
	He that hadde had knightes of pris,°	renown
250	Bifore him kneeling and ladis,	
	Now seeth he nothing that him liketh,°	pleases
	But wilde wormes° by him striketh.°	snakes / glide
	He that hadde yhad plentee	
	Of mete and drinke, of eech daintee,	
255	Now may he alday° digge and wrote°	constantly / scrounge
	Er he finde his fille of roote.	
	In somer he liveth by wilde fruit	
	And berien° but goode lite,[9]	berries
	In winter may he nothing finde	
260	But roote, grasses, and the rinde.°	bark
	Al his body away was dwined°	wasted
	For misaise, and al tochined.°	scarred
	Lord, who may telle of the sore	
	This king suffered ten yeer and more?	
265	His heer of his beerd, blak and rowe,°	rugged
	To his girdel-stede° was growe.	waist
	His harp wheron was al his glee	
	He hidde in an holwe tree,	
	And whan the weder was cleer and bright,	
270	He took his harp to him wel right,	
	And harped at his owene wille:°	pleasure
	In al the woode the soun gan shille,°	resound
	That wilde beestes that ther beeth	
	For joy abouten him they teeth;°	draw
275	And alle the fowles that ther were	
	Come and sete on eech a brere°	briar
	To here his harping afine,°	to the end
	So muche melodye was therine.	
	When he his harping lete° wolde,	leave off
280	No beest by him abide nolde.	
	Ofte he mighte see him bisides	
	In the hote undertides°	mornings

8. White and gray fur; i.e., royal ermine.   9. Little good.

The king of fairy with his route°   *company*
Come to hunte him al aboute
285 With dinne, cry, and with blowing,
And houndes also with him berking.
But no beeste they ne nome°   *took*
Ne nevere he niste wher they bicome.[1]
And otherwhile he mighte see,
290 As a greet oost° by him tee,°   *host / passed*
Wel atourned° ten hundred knightes,   *equipped*
Eech y-armed to his rightes,°   *fittingly*
Of countenance stout and fiers,°   *fierce*
With manye displayed° baners,   *unfurled*
295 And eech his swerd ydrawe holde,
But nevere he niste° wher they wolde,   *knew not*
And somwhile he seigh° other thing: *saw*
Knightes and ladies come dauncing,
In quainte° atir, degisely,°   *elegant / wonderfully*
300 Quainte pas° and softely.   *step*
Tabours° and trumpes yede° him by, *drums / went*
And al manere mïnstracy.°   *minstrelsy*
  And on a day he seigh° biside   *saw*
Sixty ladies on horse ride,
305 Gentil and jolif° as brid° on ris°— *pretty / bird / bough*
Nought oo man amonges hem nis.
And eech a faucon on hond beer,°   *bore*
And riden on hawking by river.
Of game they founde wel good haunt,°   *plenty*
310 Maulardes,° hairoun,° and cormeraunt. *mallards / herons*
The fowles of° the water ariseth;   *from*
The faucons hem wel deviseth:°   *descry*
Eech faucon his preye slough.°   *slew*
That seigh° Orfeo and lough:°   *saw / laughed*
315 "Parfay!"° quath he, "ther is fair game! *by faith*
Thider ich wil,° by Goddes name.   *will go*
Ich was ywon° swich° werk to see." *accustomed / such*
He aroos and thider gan tee.°   *draw*
To a lady he was ycome,
320 Biheeld, and hath wel undernome,°   *understood*
And seeth by al thing that it is
His owene queene Dame Heurodis,
Yerne° biheeld hire and she him eke,° *eagerly / also*
But neither to other a word ne speke.
325 For misaise that she on him seigh°   *saw*
That hadde been so riche and heigh,
The teres felle out of hir ye.
The othere ladies this ysye°   *saw*
And maked hire away to ride:
330 She moste° with him no lenger° abide. *must / longer*
  "Allas," quath he, "now me is wo.
Why nil° deeth now me nought slo?° *will not / slay*

---

1. Nor did he ever learn what happened to them.

Allas, wrecche,° that I ne mighte   *wretched one*
Die now after this sighte.
335 Allas, too longe last° my lif   *lasts*
Whan I ne dar nought to my wif—
Ne she to me—oo word ne speke.
Allas, why nil myn herte breke?
Parfay,"° quath he, "tide what bitide,   *by faith*
340 Whider so thise ladies ride
The selve° waye ich wil strecche:°   *same / go*
Of lif ne deeth me nothing recche."°   *care*
    His sclavin° he dide on also spak°   *cloak / at once*
And heeng° his harp upon his bak,   *hung*
345 And hadde wel good wil to goon:
He ne spared neither stub ne stoon.[2]
In at a roche° the ladies rideth   *rock, cave*
And he after and nought abideth.
    Whan he was in the roche ago
350 Wel three mile other° mo,   *or*
He cam into a fair countrey,
As bright so° sonne on somers day,   *as*
Smoothe and plain° and alle greener: *flat*
Hil ne dale nas ther noon seene.
355 Amidde the lond a castel he seigh,°   *saw*
Riche and real° and wonder heigh.   *royal*
Al the utemoste° wal   *outmost*
Was cleer° and shined as crystal.   *bright*
An hundred towres ther were aboute,
360 Degiseliche,° and batailed[3] stoute.   *wonderful*
The butres° cam out of the diche   *buttress*
Of reed gold y-arched riche.[4]
The vousour° was anourned° al   *vaulting / adorned*
Of eech manere divers aumal.°   *enamel*
365 Within ther were wide wones,°   *halls*
And alle were fulle of precious stones.
The worste pilar on to biholde
Al it was of burnist golde.
Al that land was evere light,
370 For when it sholde be therk° and night   *dark*
The riche stones lighte gonne[5]
As brighte as dooth at noon the sonne.
No man may telle ne thinke in thought
The riche werk that ther was wrought.
375 By alle thing him thinkth it is
The proude court of Paradis.
    In this castel the ladies alighte:
He wolde in after, if he mighte.
Orfeo knokketh at the yate:°   *gate*
380 The porter was redy therate
And asked what he wolde have ydo.°   *done*

2. I.e., neither stump nor stone prevented him.
3. I.e., furnished with battlements.
4. I.e., made of red gold that arched splendidly: gold was commonly described as red in Middle English.
5. Did light it.

"Parfay,° ich am a minstrel, lo,   *by faith*
To solace° thy lord with my glee   *delight*
If[6] his sweete wille be."
385   The porter undide the gate anoon
And lete him into the castel goon.
    Than he gan looke aboute al
And seigh,° lying within the wal,   *saw*
Of folk that ther were thider ybrought,
390   And thoughte° dede,° and nere nought:[7]   *seemed / dead*
Some stoode withouten hade,°   *head*
And some none armes hade,
And some thurgh the body hadde wounde,
And some laye woode° ybounde;   *mad*
395   And some armed on horse sete,
And some astrangled as they ete,
And some were in watre adreint,°   *drowned*
And some with fire al forshreint,°   *shriveled*
Wives ther laye on child-bedde,
400   Some dede and some awedde.°   *driven mad*
And wonder fele° ther laye bisides   *many*
Right as they slepte hir undertides°   *forenoons*
Each was thus in this world ynome,°   *taken*
With° faïrye thider ycome.   *by force of*
405   Ther he seigh his owene wif,
Dame Heurodis, his leve° lif,   *dear*
Sleepe under an impe-tree:
By hir clothes he knew it was she.
    Whan he hadde seen thise mervailes alle
410   He wente into the kinges halle.
Than seigh he ther a seemly sighte:
A tabernacle[8] wel ydight°—   *arrayed*
Hir maister king therinne sete,
And hir queene fair and sweete.
415   Hir crownes, hir clothes shoon so brighte
That unnethe° he biholde hem mighte.   *with difficulty*
    Whan he hadde seen al this thing,
He kneeled adoun bifor the king:
"O lord," he saide, "if thy wil were,
420   My minstracye thou sholdest yheere."°   *hear*
The king answerede, "What man art thou
That art hider ycomen now?
Ich, ne noon that is with me,
Ne sente never after thee.
425   Sith° that ich here regne° gan   *since / reign*
I ne foond° nevere so hardy man   *found*
That hider to us durste wende
But° that ich him wolde ofsende."°   *unless / send for*
"Lord," quath he, "ye trowe° wel   *may believe*
430   I nam but a poore minstrel,

---

6. If it.
7. Were not.
8. I.e., an alcove.

And, sire, it is the maner of us
To seeche many a lordes hous.
And theigh° we not welcome be,   *though*
Yit we mote° profere forth oure glee."°   *must / music*
435   Bifor the king he sat adown
And took his harp so merye of soun,
And tempreth° it as he wel can.   *tunes*
And blisful notes he ther gan
That alle that in the palais were
440   Come to him for to heere,
And lieth adown to his feete,
Hem thinkth his melodye so sweete.
The king herkneth and sit° ful stille: *sits*
To heere his glee he hath good wille.
445   Good bourde° he hadde of his glee: *entertainment*
The riche queene also hadde she.
        Whan he hadde stint° of his harping,   *ceased*
Then saide to him the riche king,
"Minstrel, me liketh wel thy glee.
450   Now aske of me what it may be—
Largeliche° ich wil thee paye   *generously*
Now speke and thou might it assaye."
"Sire," he saide, "ich praye thee
That thou woldest yive me
455   The eeche° lady, bright on blee,°   *very / of hue*
That sleepeth under the impe-tree."
"Nay," quath the king, "that nought nere:⁹
A sory couple of you it were;
For thou art lene,° rowe,° and blak,   *lean / rough*
460   And she is lovesom, withoute lak.°   *blemish*
A loothly thing it were forthy°   *therefore*
To seen hire in thy compaigny."
        "O sire," he saide, "gentil king,
Yit were it a wel fouler thing
465   To heere a lesing° of thy mouthe.   *lie*
So, sire, as ye saide nouthe°   *now*
What ich wolde aske, have I wolde,
A kinges word moot° needes be holde."   *must*
"Thou sayest sooth," the king saide than,
470   "And sith° I am a trewe man,   *since*
I wol wel that it be so:
Taak hire by the hond and go.
Of hire ich wol that thou be blithe."
        He kneeled adown and thanked him swithe;°   *quickly*
475   His wif he took by the hond
And dide him swithe out of that lond,
And wente° him out of that thede:°   *turned / country*
Right as he cam the way he yede.°   *went*
        So longe he hath the way ynome°   *taken*
480   To Winchester he is ycome,

9. I.e., that wouldn't do.

That somtime was his owene citee,
But no man knew that it was he.
No forther than the townes ende
For knoweleche¹ he durste wende.
485 But in a beggeres bild° ful narwe°   house / small
Ther he hath take his herbarwe°   lodging
(To him and to his owene wife),
As a minstrel of poore lif,
And asked tidinges of that lond,
490 And who the kingdom heeld in hond.
The poore begger in his cote°   hovel
Tolde him everich° a grote°—   every / bit
How hir queene was stole awy,°   away
Ten yeer goon, with° faïry.   by
495 And now hir king in exile yede°   went
But no man wiste° in which thede;°   knew / country
And how the steward the lond gan holde,
And othere many thinges him tolde.
    Amorwe ayain the noon-tide²
500 He maked his wif ther abide,
And beggeres clothes he borwed anoon,°   straightaway
And heeng° his harp his rigge° upon,   hung / back
And wente him into that citee,
That men mighte him biholde and see.
505 Bothe eerles and barouns bolde,
Burgeis° and ladies him gan biholde: burgesses
"Lord," they saide, "swich° a man!   such
How longe the heer° him hangeth upon!   hair
Lo, how his beerd hangeth to his knee!
510 He is yclungen° also° a tree!"   withered / as
    And as he yede° in the streete,   walked
With his steward he gan meete.
And loude he sette him on a cry,
"Sir steward," he saide, "grant mercy!
515 Ich am an harpour of hethenesse:°   heathen country
Help me now in this distresse."
The steward saide, "Com with me, com:
Of that I have thou shalt have som.
Eech harpour is welcome me to
520 For my lordes love, Sir Orfeo."
    Anoon they wente into the halle,
The steward and the lordes alle.
The steward wessh° and wente to mete,   washed
And manye lordes by him sete.
525 Ther were trumpours° and tabourers,°   trumpeters / drummers
Harpours fele,° and crouders:°   many / fiddlers
Muche melodye they maked alle.
And Orfeo sat stille in halle.
And herkneth; whan they been al stille,
530 He took his harp and tempered° shille°—   played / loudly

1. I.e., for fear of being recognized.   2. In the morning toward noontime.

The blisfullest notes he harped there
That evere man yherde with ere.
Eech man liked wel his glee.
   The steward looked and gan ysee,
535 And the harp knew also blive.°   *right away*
"Minstrel," he saide, "so mote° thou thrive,   *may*
Where haddest thou this harp and how?
I praye that thou me telle now."
"Lord," quath he, "in uncouthe° thede,°   *strange / country*
540 Thurgh a foreest as I yede,°   *walked*
I foond° lying in a dale   *found*
A man with° lions totorn° smale,   *by / torn to bits*
And wolves him frette° with teeth so sharp.   *bit*
By him I foond this eeche° harp   *very*
545 Wel ten yeer it is ago."
"O," quath the steward, "now me is wo!
That was my lord Sir Orfeo.
Allas, wrecche, what shal I do
That have swich° a lord ylore?°   *such / lost*
550 A, way,° that evere ich was ybore°   *woe / born*
That him was so harde grace y-yarked,°   *ordained*
And so vile deeth ymarked."°   *appointed*
Adown he fel aswoone to grounde.
His barouns him tooke up that stounde°   *time*
555 And telleth him how that it geeth:°   *goes*
It is no boote° of mannes deeth.   *remedy*
   King Orfeo knew wel by than°   *that*
His steward was a trewe man
And loved him as him oughte to do,
560 And stondeth up and saith thus, "Lo,
Steward, herkne now this thing:
If ich were Orfeo the king
And hadde ysuffered ful yore°   *long*
In wildernesse muche sore,
565 And hadde ywonne my queene awy°   *away*
Out of the lond of faïry,
And hadde ybrought the lady hende°   *gracious*
Right here to the townes ende,
And with a begger hir in° ynome,°   *lodging / taken*
570 And were myselve hider ycome
Poorelich to thee thus stille,°   *secretly*
For to assaye° thy goode wille,   *test*
And° ich founde thee thus trewe,   *if*
Thou ne sholdest it nevere rewe:°   *regret*
575 Sikerliche,° for love or ay,°   *surely / dread*
Thou sholdest be king after my day.
If thou of my deeth haddest been blithe,
Thou sholdest have voided° also swithe." *been dismissed*
   Tho° alle tho° that therinne sete   *then / those*
580 That it was Orfeo underyete,°   *understood*
And the steward wel him knew:
Over and over the boord° he threw   *table*

And fel adown to his feete.
So dide eech lord that ther sete,
585 And alle they saide at oo° crying,   *one*
"Ye beeth oure lord, sire, and oure king."
Glade they were of his live:
To chambre they ladde him as blive,°   *at once*
And bathed him and shaved his beard,
590 And tired° him as a king apert.°   *dressed / openly*
And sith° with greet processioun   *after*
They broughte the queene into the town,
With alle manere minstracye.
Lord, ther was greet melodye:
595 For joye they wepte with hir yë
That hem so sound° ycomen sye.°   *healthy / saw*
   Now Orfeo newe corouned° is,   *crowned*
And his queene Dame Heurodis,
And lived longe afterward,
600 And sitthen° king was the steward.   *afterward*
   Harpours in Britain after than°   *that*
Herde how this merveile bigan
And made a lay of good liking,°   *well-pleasing*
And nempned° it after the king.   *named*
605 That lay is "Orfeo" yhote:°   *called*
Good is the lay, sweete is the note.
   Thus cam Sir Orfeo out of his care:
God grante us alle wel to fare.

Middle English Literature in the Fourteenth and Fifteenth Centuries

SIR GAWAIN AND THE GREEN KNIGHT
ca. 1375–1400

etween the *Ancrene Wisse* and the later fourteenth century, writers deployed English for many genres, especially saints' lives and romances. The finest Arthurian romance in English survives in only one manuscript, which also contains three religious poems—*Pearl, Patience,* and *Purity*—generally believed to be by the same poet. Nothing is known about the author except what can be inferred from the works. The dialect of the poems locates them in a remote corner of the northwest midlands between Cheshire and Staffordshire, and details of Sir Gawain's journey north show that the author was familiar with the geography of that region. But if author and audience were provincials, *Sir Gawain* and the other poems in the manuscript reveal them to have been highly sophisticated and well acquainted both with the international culture of the high Middle Ages and with ancient insular traditions.

Sir Gawain belongs to the so-called Alliterative Revival. After the Norman Conquest, alliterative verse doubtless continued to be recited by oral poets. At the beginning, the *Gawain* poet pretends that this romance is an oral poem and asks the audience to "listen" to a story, which he has "heard." Alliterative verse also continued to appear in Early Middle English texts. Layamon's *Brut* (see p. 137) is the outstanding example. During the late fourteenth century there was a renewed flowering of alliterative poetry, especially in the north and west of Britain, which includes *Piers Plowman* and a splendid poem known as *The Alliterative Morte Darthur*.

The *Gawain* poet's audience evidently valued the kind of alliterative verse that Chaucer's Parson caricatures as "Rum-Ram-Ruf by lettre" (see p. 359, line 43). They would also have understood archaic poetic diction surviving from Old English poetry such as *athel* (noble) and words of Scandinavian origin such as *skete* (quickly) and *skifted* (alternated). They were well acquainted with French Arthurian romances and the latest fashions in clothing, armor, and castle building. In making Sir Gawain, Arthur's sister's son, the preeminent knight of the Round Table, the poet was faithful to an older tradition. The thirteenth-century French romances, which in the next century became the main sources of Sir Thomas Malory, had made Sir Lancelot the best of Arthur's knights and Lancelot's adultery with Queen Guinevere the central event on which the fate of Arthur's kingdom turns. In *Sir Gawain* Lancelot is only one name in a list of Arthur's knights. Arthur is still a youth, and the court is in its springtime. Sir Gawain epitomizes this first blooming of Arthurian chivalry, and the reputation of the court rests upon his shoulders.

Ostensibly, Gawain's head is what is at stake. The main plot belongs to a type that folklorists classify as the "Beheading Game," in which a supernatural challenger offers to let his head be cut off in exchange for a return blow. The earliest written occurrence

Baronial Feasting. Limbourg Brothers, "January," from *Les Très Riches Heures du Duc de Berry,* ca. 1411–16. This wall hanging depicts the Trojan War as if it were invading the protected space of the duke's feast.

of this motif is in the Middle Irish tale of *Bricriu's Feast.* The *Gawain* poet could have encountered it in several French romances as well as in oral tradition. But the outcome of the game here does not turn only on the champion's courage as it does in *Bricriu's Feast.* The *Gawain* poet has devised another series of tests for the hero that link the beheading with his truth, the emblem of which is the pentangle—a five-pointed star—displayed on Gawain's coat of arms and shield. The word *truth* in Middle English as in Chaucer's ballade of that name (see pp. 362–63), and in Passus 1 of *Piers Plowman* (see p. 394), means not only what it still means now—a fact, belief, or idea held to be "true"—but what is conveyed by the old-fashioned variant from the same root: *troth*—that is, faith pledged by one's word and owed to a lord, a spouse, or anyone who puts someone else under an obligation. In this respect, Sir Gawain is being measured against a moral and Christian ideal of chivalry. Whether or not he succeeds in that contest is a question carefully left unresolved—perhaps as a challenge for the reader.

The poet has framed Gawain's adventure with references in the first and last stanzas to what are called the "Brutus books," the foundation stories that trace the origins of Rome and Britain back to the destruction of Troy. See, for example, the selection from Geoffrey of Monmouth's *History of the Kings of Britain* (p. 136). A cyclical sense of history as well as of the cycles of the seasons of the year, the generations of humankind, and of individual lives runs through *Sir Gawain and the Green Knight.*

The poem is written in stanzas that contain a group of alliterative lines (the number of lines in a stanza varies). The line is longer and does not contain a fixed number or pattern of stresses like the classical alliterative measure of Old English poetry. Each stanza closes with five short lines rhyming *a b a b a.* The first of these rhyming lines contains just one stress and is called the "bob"; the four three-stress lines that follow are called the "wheel." For details on alliterative verse, see "Old and Middle English Prosody" (pp. 25–26). The opening stanza is printed below in Middle English with an interlinear translation. The stressed alliterating sounds have been italicized.

> **S**ithen the *s*ege and the *a*ssaut was *s*esed at Troye,
> After the siege and the assault was ceased at Troy,
>
> The *b*orgh *b*rittened and *b*rent to *b*rondes and askes,
> The city destroyed and burned to brands and ashes,

The *t*ulk that the *t*rammes of *t*resoun ther wroght
The man who the plots of treason there wrought

Was *t*ried for his *t*richerie, the *t*rewest on erthe.
Was tried for his treachery, the truest on earth.

Hit was *E*nnias the *a*thel and his *h*ighe kynde,
It was Aeneas the noble and his high race,

That sithen de*p*reced *p*rovinces, and *p*atrounes bicome
Who after subjugated provinces, and lords became

*W*elneghe of al the *w*ele in the *w*est iles.
Wellnigh of all the wealth in the west isles.

Fro *r*iche *R*omulus to *R*ome *r*icchis hym swythe,
Then noble Romulus to Rome proceeds quickly,

With gret *b*obbaunce that *b*urghe he *b*iges upon fyrst
With great pride that city he builds at first

And *n*evenes hit his aune *n*ome, as hit *n*ow hat;
And names it his own name, as it now is called;

*T*icius to *T*uskan and *t*eldes bigynnes,
Ticius (goes) to Tuscany and houses begins,

*L*angaberde in *L*umbardie *l*yftes up homes,
Longbeard in Lombardy raises up homes,

And *f*er over the French *f*lod, *F*elix Brutus
And far over the English Channel, Felix Brutus

On mony *b*onkkes ful *b*rode Bretayn he settes
On many banks very broad Britain he sets

Wyth *w*ynne,
With joy,

*W*here *w*erre and *w*rake and *w*onder
Where war and strife and wondrous happenings

Bi sythes has wont therinne,
On occasions have dwelled therein

And oft *b*othe *b*lysse and *b*lunder
And often both joy and strife

Ful *sk*ete has *sk*yfted synne.
Very swiftly have alternated since.

Sir Gawain and the Green Knight*

FITT[1] i

Once the siege and assault of Troy had ceased,
with the city a smoke-heap of cinders and ash,
the traitor who contrived such betrayal there
was tried for his treachery, the truest on earth;[2]
5   Aeneas, it was, with his noble warriors
who went conquering abroad, laying claim to the crowns
of the wealthiest kingdoms in the western world.
Mighty Romulus[3] quickly careered towards Rome
and conceived a city in magnificent style
10 which from then until now has been known by his name.
Ticius constructed townships in Tuscany
and Langobard[4] did likewise building homes in Lombardy.
And further afield, over the Sea of France,
Felix Brutus[5] founds Britain on broad banks
15   most grand.
          And wonder, dread and war
          have lingered in that land
          where loss and love in turn
          have held the upper hand.

20 After Britain was built by this founding father
a bold race bred there, battle-happy men
causing trouble and torment in turbulent times,
and through history more strangeness has happened here
than anywhere else I know of on Earth.
25 But most regal of rulers in the royal line
was Arthur, who I heard is honored above all,
and the inspiring story I intend to spin
has moved the hearts and minds of many—
an awesome episode in the legends of Arthur.
30 So listen a little while to my tale if you will
and I'll tell it as it's told in the town where it trips from
          the tongue;
          and as it has been inked
          in stories bold and strong,
35   where loyal letters linked
          have lasted loud and long.

It was Christmas at Camelot—King Arthur's court,
where the great and the good of the land had gathered,
the right noble lords of the ranks of the Round Table

---

* The translation is by Simon Armitage.
1. "Fitt" is a technical term used by the *Gawain* poet, and other late-medieval English alliterative poets, to designate the longer divisions of a poem.
2. The treacherous knight is Aeneas, who was a traitor to his city, Troy, according to medieval tradition, but Aeneas was actually tried by the Greeks for his refusal to hand his sister Polyxena over to them.
3. Like Aeneas, the legendary founder of Rome is here given Trojan ancestry.
4. The reputed founder of Lombardy. Ticius is not otherwise known.
5. Great-grandson of Aeneas and legendary founder of Britain, not elsewhere given the name *Felix* (Latin, "happy").

40   all roundly carousing and reveling in pleasure.
Time after time, in tournaments of joust,
they had lunged at each other with leveled lances
then returned to the castle to carry on their caroling,
for the feasting lasted a full fortnight and one day,
45   with more food and drink than a fellow could dream of.
The hubbub of their humor was heavenly to hear:
pleasant dialogue by day and dancing after dusk,
so house and hall were lit with happiness
and lords and ladies were luminous with joy.
50   With all the wonder in the world they gathered there as one:
the most chivalrous and courteous knights known to Christendom;
the most wonderful women to have walked in this world;
the handsomest king to be crowned at court.
All these fair folk in their first age, together in
55   that hall:
         most fortunate under heaven,
         with Arthur, that man of high will;
         no bolder band could ever
         be found on field or hill.

60   With New Year so young it still yawned and stretched
helpings were doubled on the dais that day.
And as king and company were coming to the hall
the choir in the chapel fell suddenly quiet,
then a chorus erupted from the courtiers and clerks:
65   "Noel," they cheered, then "Noel, Noel,"
"New Year Gifts!" the knights cried next
as they pressed forwards to offer their presents,
teasing with frivolous favors and forfeits,
till those ladies who lost couldn't help but laugh,
70   and the undefeated were far from forlorn.[6]
Their merrymaking rolled on in this manner until mealtime,
when, worthily washed, they went to the table,
and were seated in order of honor, as was apt,
with Guinevere in their gathering, gloriously framed
75   at her place on the platform, pricelessly curtained
by silk to each side, and canopied across
with tasteful tapestries of Toulouse and Tharsia,
studded with stones and stunning gems
beyond pocket or purse, beyond what pennies
80   could buy.
         But not one stone outshone
         the quartz of the queen's eyes;
         with hand on heart, no one
         could argue otherwise.

85   But Arthur would not eat until all were served.
He brimmed with ebullience, being almost boyish
in his love of life, and what he liked the least
was to sit still watching the seasons slip by.

6. The forfeit that made the ladies who lost laugh was in all likelihood a kiss.

His blood was busy and he buzzed with thoughts,
90 and the matter which played on his mind at that moment
was his pledge to take no portion from his plate
on such a special day until a story was told:
some far-fetched yarn or outrageous fable,
the tallest of tales, yet one ringing with truth,
95 like the action-packed epics of men-at-arms.
Or till some chancer had challenged his chosen knight,
dared him, with a lance, to lay life on the line,
to stare death face-to-face and accept defeat
should fortune or fate smile more favorably on his foe.
100 Within Camelot's castle this was the custom,
and at feasts and festivals when the fellowship
would meet.
With features proud and fine
he stood there tall and straight,
105 a king at Christmastime
amid great merriment.

And still he stands there just being himself,
chatting away charmingly, exchanging views.
Good Sir Gawain is seated by Guinevere,
110 and on his other side Agravain the Hard Hand sits,
both nephews of the king and notable knights.
At the head of the board sat Bishop Baldwin,
with Ywain, son of Urien, to eat beside him.
First those sitting on the dais[7] were splendidly served,
115 then those stalwarts seated on the benches to the sides.
The first course comes in to the fanfare and clamor
of blasting trumpets hung with trembling banners,
then pounding double-drums and dinning pipes,
weird sounds and wails of such warbled wildness
120 that to hear and feel them made the heart float free.
Flavorsome delicacies of flesh were fetched in
and the freshest of foods, so many in fact
there was scarcely space to present the stews
or to set the soups in the silver bowls on
125 the cloth.
Each guest received his share
of bread or meat or broth;
a dozen plates per pair—
plus beer or wine, or both.

130 Now, on the subject of supper I'll say no more
as it's obvious to everyone that no one went without.
Because another sound, a new sound, suddenly drew near,
which might signal the king to sample his supper,
for barely had the horns finished blowing their breath
135 and with starters just spooned to the seated guests,

---

7. A raised platform. Although the Round Table is referred to (line 39), the king and queen, along with the most prominent members of the court, are seated above the rest.

a fearful form appeared, framed in the door:
a mountain of a man, immeasurably high,
a hulk of a human from head to hips,
so long and thick in his loins and his limbs
140   I should genuinely judge him to be a half giant,
or a most massive man, the mightiest of mortals.
But handsome, too, like any horseman worth his horse,
for despite the bulk and brawn of his body
his stomach and waist were slender and sleek.
145   In fact in all features he was finely formed
                it seemed.
                Amazement seized their minds,
                no soul had ever seen
                a knight of such a kind—
150   entirely emerald green.

And his gear and garments were green as well:
a tight fitting tunic, tailored to his torso,
and a cloak to cover him, the cloth fully lined
with smoothly shorn fur clearly showing, and faced
155   with all-white ermine, as was the hood,
worn shawled on his shoulders, shucked from his head.
On his lower limbs his leggings were also green,
wrapped closely round his calves, and his sparkling spurs
were green-gold, strapped with stripy silk,
160   and were set on his stockings, for this stranger was shoeless.
In all vestments he revealed himself veritably verdant!
From his belt hooks and buckle to the baubles and gems
arrayed so richly around his costume
and adorning the saddle, stitched onto silk.
165   All the details of his dress are difficult to describe,
embroidered as it was with butterflies and birds,
green beads emblazoned on a background of gold.
All the horse's tack—harness strap, hind strap,
the eye of the bit, each alloy and enamel
170   and the stirrups he stood in were similarly tinted,
and the same with the cantle and the skirts of the saddle,
all glimmering and glinting with the greenest jewels.
And the horse: every hair was green, from hoof
                to mane.
175   A steed of pure green stock.
                Each snort and shudder strained
                the hand-stitched bridle, but
                his rider had him reined.

The fellow in green was in fine fettle.
180   The hair of his head was as green as his horse,
fine flowing locks which fanned across his back,
plus a bushy green beard growing down to his breast,
which hung with the splendid hair from his head
and was lopped in a line at elbow length
185   so half his arms were gowned in green growth,

crimped at the collar, like a king's cape.
The mane of his mount was groomed to match,
combed and knotted into curlicues
then tinseled with gold, tied and twisted
190 green over gold, green over gold.
The fetlocks were finished in the same fashion
with bright green ribbon braided with beads,
as was the tail—to its tippety-tip!
And a long, tied thong lacing it tight
195 where bright and burnished gold bells chimed clearly.
No waking man had witnessed such a warrior
or weird warhorse—otherworldly, yet flesh
        and bone.
       His look was lightning bright
200   said those who glimpsed its glow.
       It seemed no man there might
       survive his violent blow.

Yet he wore no helmet and no hauberk either,
no armored apparel or plate was apparent,
205 and he swung no sword nor sported any shield,
but held in one hand a sprig of holly—
of all the evergreens the greenest ever—
and in the other hand held the mother of all axes,
a cruel piece of kit I kid you not:
210 the head was an ell in length at least
and forged in green steel with a gilt finish;
its broad-edged blade brightly burnished,
it could shear a man's scalp and shave him to boot.
The handle which fitted that fiend's great fist
215 was inlaid with iron, end to end,
with green pigment picking out impressive designs.
From stock to neck, where it stopped with a knot,
a lace was looped the length of the haft,
trimmed with tassels and tails of string
220 fastened firmly in place by forest-green buttons.
And he kicks on, canters through that crowded hall
towards the top table, not the least bit timid,
cocksure of himself, sitting high in the saddle.
"And who," he bellows, without breaking breath,
225 "is governor of this gaggle? I'll be glad to know.
It's with him and no one else that I'll hold
        a pact."
       He held them with his eyes,
       and looked from right to left,
230   not knowing, of those knights,
       which person to respect.

The guests looked on. They gaped and they gawked
and were mute with amazement: what did it mean
that human and horse could develop this hue,
235 should grow to be grass-green or greener still,

like green enamel emboldened by bright gold?
Some stood and stared then stepped a little closer,
drawn near to the knight to know his next move;
they'd seen some sights, but this was something special,
240 a miracle or magic, or so they imagined.
Yet several of the lords were like statues in their seats,
left speechless and rigid, not risking a response.
The hall fell hushed, as if all who were present
had slipped into sleep or some trancelike state.
245   No doubt
          not all were stunned and stilled
          by dread, but duty bound
          to hold their tongues until
          their sovereign could respond.

250 Then the king acknowledged this curious occurrence,
cordially addressed him, keeping his cool.
"A warm welcome, sir, this winter's night.
My name is Arthur, I am head of this house.
Won't you slide from that saddle and stay awhile,
255 and the business which brings you we shall learn of later."
"No," said the knight, "by Him in highest heaven,
I'm not here to idle in your hall this evening.
But because your acclaim is so loudly chorused,
and your castle and brotherhood are called the best,
260 the strongest men to ever mount the saddle,
the worthiest knights ever known to the world,
both in competition and true combat,
and since courtesy, so it's said, is championed here,
I'm intrigued, and attracted to your door at this time.
265 Be assured by this holly stem here in my hand
that I mean no menace. So expect no malice,
for if I'd slogged here tonight to slay and slaughter
my helmet and hauberk wouldn't be at home
and my sword and spear would be here at my side,
270 and more weapons of war, as I'm sure you're aware;
I'm clothed for peace, not kitted out for conflict.
But if you're half as honorable as I've heard folk say
you'll gracefully grant me this game which I ask for
          by right."
275   Then Arthur answered, "Knight
          most courteous, if you claim
          a fair, unarmored fight,
          we'll see you have the same."

"I'm spoiling for no scrap, I swear. Besides,
280 the bodies on these benches are just bum-fluffed bairns.
If I'd ridden to your castle rigged out for a ruck
these lightweight men wouldn't last a minute.
But it's Yuletide—a time of youthfulness, yes?
So at Christmas in this court I lay down a challenge:
285 if a person here present, within these premises,

is big or bold or red-blooded enough
to strike me one stroke and be struck in return,
I shall give him as a gift this gigantic cleaver
and the axe shall be his to handle how he likes.
290   I'll kneel, bare my neck and take the first knock.
So who has the gall? The gumption? The guts?
Who'll spring from his seat and snatch this weapon?
I offer the axe—who'll have it as his own?
I'll afford one free hit from which I won't flinch,
295   and promise that twelve months will pass in peace,
                then claim
             the duty I deserve
             in one year and one day.
             Does no one have the nerve
300   to wager in this way?"

If flustered at first, now totally foxed
were the household and the lords, both the highborn and
        the low.
Still stirruped, the knight swiveled round in his saddle
looking left and right, his red eyes rolling
305   beneath the bristles of his bushy green brows,
his beard swishing from side to side.
When the court kept its counsel he cleared his throat
and stiffened his spine. Then he spoke his mind:
"So here is the House of Arthur," he scoffed,
310   "whose virtues reverberate across vast realms.
Where's the fortitude and fearlessness you're so famous for?
And the breathtaking bravery and the big-mouth bragging?
The towering reputation of the Round Table,
skittled and scuppered by a stranger—what a scandal!
315   You flap and you flinch and I've not raised a finger!"
Then he laughed so loud that their leader saw red.
Blood flowed to his fine-featured face and he raged
                inside.
             His men were also hurt—
320   those words had pricked their pride.
             But born so brave at heart
             the king stepped up one stride.

"Your request," he countered, "is quite insane,
and folly finds the man who flirts with the fool.
325   No warrior worth his salt would be worried by your words,
so in heaven's good name hand over the axe
and I'll happily fulfill the favor you ask."
He strides to him swiftly and seizes his arm;
the man dismounts in one mighty leap.
330   Then Arthur grips the axe, grabs it by its haft
and takes it above him, intending to attack.
Yet the stranger before him stands up straight,
highest in the house by at least a head,
but stands there sternly, stroking his beard,

335 drawing down his coat, countenance undaunted,
     about to be bludgeoned, but no more bothered
     than a guest at the table being given a goblet
                    of wine.
               By Guinevere, Gawain
340   now to his king inclines
               and says, "I stake my claim.
               May this melee be mine."

     "Should you call me, courteous lord," said Gawain to
          his king,
     "to rise from my seat and stand at your side,
345 politely take leave of my place at the table
     and quit without causing offence to my queen,
     then I would come to your counsel before this great court.
     For I find it unfitting, as my fellow knights would,
     when a deed of such daring is dangled before us
350 that you take on this trial—tempted as you are—
     when brave, bold men are seated on these benches,
     men never matched in the mettle of their minds,
     never beaten or bettered in the field of battle.
     I am weakest of your warriors and feeblest of wit;
355 loss of my life would be least lamented.
     Were I not your nephew my life would mean nothing;
     to be born of your blood is my body's only claim.
     Such a foolish affair is unfitting for a king,
     so; being first to come forward, it should fall to me.
360 And if my proposal is improper, let no other person
                    stand blame."
               The knighthood then unites
               and each knight says the same:
               their king can stand aside
365   and give Gawain the game.

     So the sovereign instructed his knight to stand.
     Getting to his feet he moved graciously forward
     and knelt before Arthur, taking hold of the axe.
     Letting go of it, Arthur then held up his hand
370 to give young Gawain the blessing of God
     and hope he finds firmness in heart and fist.
     "Take care, young cousin, to catch him cleanly,
     use full-blooded force then you needn't fear
     the blow which he threatens to trade in return."
375 Gawain, with the weapon, walked towards the warrior,
     and they stood face-to-face, not one man afraid.
     Then the green knight spoke, growled at Gawain:
     "Before we compete, repeat what we've promised.
     And start by saying your name to me, sir,
380 and tell me the truth so I can take it on trust."
     "In good faith," said the knight, "Gawain is my name.
     I heave this axe, and whatever happens after,
     in twelvemonth's time I'll be struck in return

with any weapon you wish, and by you and you
385   alone."
           The green man speaks again:
           "I swear on all I know,
           I'm glad it's you, Gawain,
           who'll drive the axe-head home."

390 "Gawain," said the green knight, "by God, I'm glad
the favor I've called for will fall from your fist.
You've perfectly repeated the promise we made
and the terms of the contest are crystal clear.
Except for one thing: you must solemnly swear
395 that you'll seek me yourself; that you'll search me out
to the ends of the earth to earn the same blow
as you'll dole out today in this decorous hall."
"But where will you be? Where's your abode?
You're a man of mystery, as God is my maker.
400 Which court do you come from and what are you called?
There is knowledge I need, including your name,
then I shall use all my wit to work out the way,
and keep to our contract, so cross my heart."
"But enough at New Year. It needs nothing more,"
405 said the warrior in green to worthy Gawain.
"I could tell you the truth once you've taken the blow;
if you smite me smartly I could spell out the facts
of my house and home and my name, if it helps,
then you'll pay me a visit and vouch for our pact.
410 Or if I keep quiet you might cope all the better,
loafing and lounging here, looking no further. But
           we stall!
           Now grasp that gruesome axe
           and show your striking style."
415   He answered, "Since you ask,"
           and touched the tempered steel.

The green knight took his stance, prepared to be struck,
bent forward, revealing a flash of green flesh
as he heaped his hair to the crown of his head,
420 the nape of his neck now naked and ready.
Gawain grips the axe and heaves it heavenwards,
plants his left foot firmly on the floor in front,
then swings it swiftly towards the bare skin.
The cleanness of the strike cleaved the spinal cord
425 and parted the fat and the flesh so far
that the bright steel blade took a bite from the floor.
The handsome head tumbles onto the earth
and the king's men kick it as it clatters past.
Blood gutters brightly against his green gown,
430 yet the man doesn't shudder or stagger or sink
but trudges towards them on those tree-trunk legs
and rummages around, reaches at their feet
and cops hold of his head and hoists it high,

and strides to his steed, snatches the bridle,
435 steps into the stirrup and swings into the saddle
still gripping his head by a handful of hair.
Then he settles himself in his seat with the ease
of a man unmarked, never mind being minus
            his head!
440   He wheeled his bulk about,
            that body which still bled.
            They cowered in the court
            before his speech was said.

For that scalp and skull now swung from his fist;
445 to the noblest at the table he turned the face
and it opened its eyelids, stared straight ahead
and spoke this speech, which you'll hear for yourselves:
"Sir Gawain, be wise enough to keep your word
and faithfully follow me until you find me,
450 as you vowed in this hall within hearing of these horsemen.
You're charged with getting to the Green Chapel,
to reap what you've sown. You'll rightfully receive
that what is due to be dealt to you as New Year dawns.
Men know my name as the Green Chapel knight,
455 and even a fool couldn't fail to find me.
So come, or be called a coward forever."
With a tug of the reins he twisted around
and, head still in hand, galloped out of the hall,
so the hooves brought fire from the flame in the flint.
460 Which kingdom he came from they hadn't a clue,
no more than they knew where he made for next.
            And then?
            Well, with the green man gone
            they laughed and grinned again.
465   And yet such goings-on
            were magic to those men.

And although King Arthur was awestruck at heart
no sign of it showed. Instead he spoke
to his exquisite queen with courteous words:
470 "Dear lady, don't be daunted by this deed today,
it's in keeping that such strangeness should occur at Christmas
between sessions of banter and seasonal song,
amid the lively pastimes of ladies and lords.
And at least I'm allowed to eat at last,
475 having witnessed such wonder, wouldn't you say?"
Then he glanced at Gawain and spoke gracefully:
"Now hang up your axe[8]—one hack is enough."
So it dangled from the drape behind the dais
so that men who saw it would be mesmerized and amazed,
480 and give voice, on its evidence, to that stunning event.
Then the two of them turned and walked to the table,

8. A colloquial expression equivalent to "bury the hatchet," but here with an ironic literal sense.

the monarch and his knight, and men served the meal—
double dishes apiece, rare delicacies,
all manner of food—and the music of minstrels.
485 And they danced and sang till the sun went down
                that day.
            But mind your mood, Gawain,
            lest dread make you delay,
            or lose this lethal game
490   you've promised you will play.

FITT ii

This happening was a gift—just as Arthur had asked for
and had yearned to hear of while the year was young.
And if guests had no subject as they strolled to their seats,
now this serious concern sustained their chatter.
495 And Gawain had been glad to begin the game,
but don't be so shocked should the plot turn pear-shaped:
for men might be merry when addled with mead
but each year, short lived, is unlike the last
and rarely resolves in the style it arrived.
500 So the festival finishes and a new year follows
in eternal sequence, season by season.
After lavish Christmas come the lean days of Lent
when the flesh is tested with fish and simple food.
Then the world's weather wages war on winter:
505 cold shrinks earthwards and the clouds climb;
sun-warmed, shimmering rain comes showering
onto meadows and fields where flowers unfurl;
woods and grounds wear a wardrobe of green;
birds burble with life and build busily
510 as summer spreads, settling on slopes as
                it should.
            Now every hedgerow brims
            with blossom and with bud,
            and lively songbirds sing
515   from lovely, leafy woods.

So summer comes in season with its subtle airs,
when the west wind sighs among shoots and seeds,
and those plants which flower and flourish are a pleasure
as their leaves let drip their drink of dew
520 and they sparkle and glitter when glanced by sunlight.
Then autumn arrives to harden the harvest
and with it comes a warning to ripen before winter.
The drying airs arrive, driving up dust
from the face of the earth to the heights of heaven,
525 and wild sky wrestles the sun with its winds,
and the leaves of the lime lie littered on the ground,
and grass that was green turns withered and gray.
Then all which had risen over-ripens and rots
and yesterday on yesterday the year dies away,

530 and winter returns, as is the way of the world
                    through time.
                At Michaelmas[9] the moon
                stands like that season's sign,
                a warning to Gawain
535   to rouse himself and ride.

Yet he stayed until All Saints' Day[1] by his sovereign's side,
and they feasted in the name of their noble knight
with the revels and riches of the Round Table.
The lords of that hall and their loving ladies
540 were sad and concerned for the sake of their knight,
but nevertheless they made light of his load.
Those joyless at his plight made jokes and rejoiced.
Then sorrowfully, after supper, he spoke with his uncle,
and openly talked of the trip he must take:
545 "Now, lord of my life, I must ask for your leave.
You were witness to my wager. I have no wish
to retell you the terms—they're nothing but a trifle.
I must set out tomorrow to receive that stroke
from the knight in green, and let God be my guide."
550 Then the cream of Camelot crowded around:
Ywain and Eric and others of that ilk,
Sir Dodinal the Dreaded, the Duke of Clarence,
Lancelot, Lionel, Lucan the Good,
and Sir Bors and Sir Bedevere—both big names,
555 and powerful men such as Mador de la Port.
This courtly committee approaches the king
to offer up heartfelt advice to our hero.
And sounds of sadness and sorrow were heard
that one as worthy and well liked as Gawain
560 should suffer that strike but offer no stroke in
                    reply.
                Yet keeping calm the knight
                just quipped, "Why should I shy
                away. If fate is kind
565   or cruel, man still must try."

He remained all that day and in the morning he dressed,
asked early for his arms and all were produced.
First a rug of rare cloth was unrolled on the floor,
heaped with gear which glimmered and gleamed,
570 and the stout knight steps onto it and handles the steel.
He tries on his tunic of extravagant silk,
then the neatly cut cloak, closed at the neck,
its lining finished with a layer of white fur.
Then they settled his feet into steel shoes
575 and clad his calves, clamped them with greaves,
then hinged and highly polished plates
were knotted with gold thread to the knight's knees.

9. September 29.   1. November 1.

Then leg guards were fitted, lagging the flesh,
attached with thongs to his thick-set thighs.
580 Then comes the suit of shimmering steel rings
encasing his body and his costly clothes:
well burnished braces to both of his arms,
good elbow guards and glinting metal gloves,
all the trimmings and trappings of a knight tricked out
585   to ride:
            a metal suit that shone;
            gold spurs which gleam with pride;
            a keen sword swinging from
            the silk belt to his side.

590 Fastened in his armor he seemed fabulous, famous,
every link looking golden to the very last loop.
Yet for all that metal he still made it to mass,
honored the Almighty before the high altar.
After which he comes to the king and his consorts
595 and asks to take leave of the ladies and lords;
they escort and kiss him and commended him to Christ.
Now Gringolet is rigged out and ready to ride
with a saddle which flickered with fine gold fringes
and was set with new studs for the special occasion.
600 The bridle was bound with stripes of bright gold,
the apparel of the panels was matched in appearance
to the color of the saddlebows and cropper and cover,
and nails of red gold were arrayed all around,
shining splendidly like splintered sunlight.
605 Then he holds up his helmet and hastily kisses it;
it was strongly stapled and its lining was stuffed,
and sat high on his head, fastened behind
with a colorful cloth to cover his neck
embroidered and bejeweled with brilliant gems
610 on the broad silk border, and with birds on the seams
such as painted parrots perched among periwinkles
and turtle doves and true lover's knots, tightly entwined
as if women had worked at it seven winters
                at least.
615   The diamond diadem
            was greater still. It gleamed
            with flawless, flashing gems
            both clear and smoked, it seemed.

Then they showed him the shining scarlet shield
620 with its pentangle painted in pure gold.[2]
He seized it by its strap and slung it round his neck;
he looked well in what he wore, and was worthy of it.
And why the pentangle was appropriate to that prince
I intend to say, though it will stall our story.

---

2. A five-pointed star, formed by five lines drawn without lifting the pencil from the paper; as Solomon's sign (line 625), a mystical significance was attributed to it.

625 It is a symbol that Solomon once set in place
and is taken to this day as a token of fidelity,
for the form of the figure is a five-pointed star
and each line overlaps and links with the last
so is ever eternal, and when spoken of in England
630 is known by the name of the endless knot.
So it suits this soldier in his spotless armor,
fully faithful in five ways five times over.
For Gawain was as good as the purest gold—
devoid of vices but virtuous, loyal
635   and kind,
   so bore that badge on both
   his shawl and shield alike.
   A prince who talked the truth:
   known as the noblest knight.

640 First he was deemed flawless in his five senses;
and secondly his five fingers were never at fault;
and thirdly his faith was founded in the five wounds
Christ received on the cross, as the creed recalls.
And fourthly, if that soldier struggled in skirmish
645 one thought pulled him through above all other things:
the fortitude he found in the five joys
which Mary had conceived in her son, our Savior.[3]
For precisely that reason the princely rider
had the shape of her image inside his shield,
650 so by catching her eye his courage would not crack.
The fifth set of five which I heard the knight followed
included friendship and fraternity with fellow men,
purity and politeness that impressed at all times,
and pity, which surpassed all pointedness. Five things
655 which meant more to Gawain than to most other men.
So these five sets of five were fixed in this knight,
each linked to the last through the endless line,
a five-pointed form which never failed,
never stronger to one side or slack at the other,
660 but unbroken in its being from beginning to end
however its trail is tracked and traced.
So the star on the spangling shield he sported
shone royally, in gold, on a ruby red background,

3. The Annunciation, Nativity, Resurrection, Ascension, and Assumption. These overlap but are not similar to the Five Joyful Mysteries of the Rosary, which were not formally established until the 16th century.

the pure pentangle as people have called it
665   for years.
           Then, lance in hand, held high,
           and got up in his gear
           he bids them all good-bye
           one final time, he fears.

670 Spiked with the spurs the steed sped away
     with such force that the fire-stones sparked underfoot.
     All sighed at the sight, and with sinking hearts
     they whispered their worries to one another,
     concerned for their comrade. "A pity, by Christ,
675 if a lord so noble should lose his life.
     To find his equal on earth would be far from easy.
     Cleverer to have acted with caution and care,
     deemed him a duke—a title he was due—
     a leader of men, lord of many lands;
680 better that than being battered into oblivion,
     beheaded by an ogre, through headstrong pride.
     Whoever knew any king to take counsel of a knight
     in the grip of an engrossing Christmas game?"
     Warm tears welled up in their weepy eyes
685 as gallant Sir Gawain galloped from court
                 that day.
           He sped from home and hearth
           and went his winding way
           on steep and snaking paths,
690   just as the story says.

     Now through England's realm he rides and rides,
     Sir Gawain, God's servant, on his grim quest,
     passing long dark nights unloved and alone,
     foraging to feed, finding little to call food,
695 with no friend but his horse through forests and hills
     and only our Lord in heaven to hear him.
     He wanders near to the north of Wales
     with the Isles of Anglesey off to the left.
     He keeps to the coast, fording each course,
700 crossing at Holy Head and coming ashore
     in the wilds of the Wirral, whose wayward people
     both God and good men have quite given up on.[4]
     And he constantly enquires of those he encounters
     if they know, or not, in this neck of the woods,
705 of a great green man or a Green Chapel.
     No, they say, never. Never in their lives.
     They know of neither a chap nor a chapel
                 so strange.
           He trails through bleak terrain.
710   His mood and manner change

---

4. Gawain travels from Camelot north to the northern coast of Wales, opposite the islands of Anglesey, where he turns east across the Dee to the forest of Wirral in Cheshire.

at every twist and turn
towards that chosen church.

In a strange region he scales steep slopes;
far from his friends he cuts a lonely figure.
715 Where he bridges a brook or wades through a waterway
it's no surprise to find that he faces a foe
so foul or fierce he is bound to use force.
So momentous are his travels among the mountains
to tell just a tenth would be a tall order.
720 Here he scraps with serpents and snarling wolves,
here he tangles with wodwos⁵ causing trouble in the crags,
or with bulls and bears and the odd wild boar.
Hard on his heels through the highlands come giants.
Only diligence and faith in the face of death
725 will keep him from becoming a corpse or carrion.
And the wars were one thing, but winter was worse:
clouds shed their cargo of crystallized rain
which froze as it fell to the frost-glazed earth.
Nearly slain by sleet he slept in his armor,
730 bivouacked in the blackness amongst bare rocks
where meltwater streamed from the snow-capped summits
and high overhead hung chandeliers of ice.
So in peril and pain Sir Gawain made progress,
crisscrossing the countryside until Christmas
735   Eve. Then
at that time of tiding,
he prayed to highest heaven.
Let Mother Mary guide him
towards some house or haven.

740 That morning he moves on, skirts the mountainside,
descends a deep forest, densely overgrown,
with vaulting hills to each half of the valley
and ancient oaks in huddles of hundreds.
Hazel and hawthorn are interwoven,
745 decked and draped in damp, shaggy moss,
and bedraggled birds on bare, black branches
pipe pitifully into the piercing cold.
Under cover of the canopy he girded Gringolet
through mud and marshland, a man all alone,
750 concerned and afraid in case he should fail
in the worship of our Deity, who, on that date
was born the Virgin's son to save our souls.
He prayed with heavy heart. "Father, hear me,
and Lady Mary, our mother most mild,
755 let me happen on some house where mass might be heard,
and matins in the morning; meekly I ask,
and here I utter my pater, ave

---

5. Wild men of the woods.

and creed."
He rides the path and prays,
760   dismayed by his misdeeds,
and signs Christ's cross and says,
"Be near me in my need."

No sooner had he signed himself three times
than he became aware, in those woods, of high walls
765   in a moat, on a mound, bordered by the boughs
of thick-trunked timber which trimmed the water.
The most commanding castle a knight ever kept,
positioned in a site of sweeping parkland
with a palisade of pikes pitched in the earth
770   in the midst of tall trees for two miles or more.
He stopped and stared at one side of that stronghold
as it sparkled and shone within shimmering oaks,
and with helmet in hand he offered up thanks
to Jesus and Saint Julian,[6] both gentle and good,
775   who had courteously heard him and heeded his cry.
"A lodging at last. So allow it, my Lord."
Then he girded Gringolet with his gilded spurs,
and purely by chance chose the principal approach
to the building, which brought him to the end of the bridge
780   with haste.
The drawbridge stood withdrawn,
the front gates were shut fast.
Such well-constructed walls
would blunt the storm wind's blast.

785   In the saddle of his steed he halts on the slope
of the delving moat with its double ditch.
Out of water of wondrous depth, the walls
then loomed overhead to a huge height,
course after course of crafted stone,
790   then battlements embellished in the boldest style
and turrets arranged around the ramparts
with lockable loopholes set into the lookouts.
The knight had not seen a more stunning structure.
Further in, his eye was drawn to a hall
795   attended, architecturally, by many tall towers
with a series of spires spiking the air
all crowned by carvings exquisitely cut.
Uncountable chimneys the color of chalk
sprutted from the roof and sparkled in the sun.
800   So perfect was that vision of painted pinnacles
clustered within the castle's enclosure
it appeared that the place was cut from paper.[7]
Then a notion occurred to that noble knight:
to seek a visit, get invited inside,
805   to be hosted and housed, and all the holy days

6. Patron saint of hospitality.
7. Paper castles were a common table decoration at feasts.

remain.
Responding to his call
a pleasant porter came,
a watchman on the wall,
810   who welcomed Sir Gawain.

"Good morning," said Gawain, "will you go with a message
to the lord of this house to let me have lodging?"
"By Saint Peter," said the porter, "it'll be my pleasure,
and I'll warrant you'll be welcome for as long as you wish."
815 Then he went on his way, but came back at once
with a group who had gathered to greet the stranger;
the drawbridge came down and they crossed the ditch
and knelt in the frost in front of the knight
to welcome this man in a way deemed worthy.
820 Then they yielded to their guest, yanked open the gate,
and bidding them to rise he rode across the bridge.
He was assisted from the saddle by several men
and the strongest amongst them stabled his steed.
Then knights, and the squires of knights, drew near,
825 to escort him, with courtesy, into the castle.
As he took off his helmet, many hasty hands
stretched to receive it and to serve this noble knight,
and his sword and his shield were taken aside.
Then he made himself known to nobles and knights
830 and proud fellows pressed forwards to confer their respects.
Still heavy with armor he was led to the hall
where a fire burned bright with the fiercest flames.
Then the master of the manor emerged from his chamber,
to greet him in the hall with all due honor,
835 saying, "Behave in my house as your heart pleases.
To whatever you want you are welcome, do what
        you will."
    "My thanks," Gawain exclaimed,
    "May Christ reward you well."
840   Then firmly, like good friends,
    arm into arm they fell.

Gawain gazed at the lord who greeted him so gracefully,
the great one who governed that grand estate,
powerful and large, in the prime of his life,
845 with a bushy beard as red as a beaver's,
steady in his stance, solid of build,
with a fiery face and fine conversation:
and it suited him well, so it seemed to Gawain,
to keep such a castle and captain his knights.
850 Escorted to his quarters the lord quickly orders
that a servant be assigned to assist Gawain,
and many were willing to wait on his word.
They brought him to a bedroom, beautifully furnished
with fine silken fabrics finished in gold
855 and curious coverlets lavishly quilted

in bright ermine and embroidered to each border.
Curtains ran on cords through red-gold rings,
tapestries from Toulouse and Turkistan
were fixed against walls and fitted underfoot.
860 With humorous banter Gawain was helped out
of his chain-mail coat and costly clothes,
then they rushed to bring him an array of robes
of the choicest cloth. He chose, and changed,
and as soon as he stood in that stunning gown
865 with its flowing skirts which suited his shape
it almost appeared to the persons present
that spring, with its spectrum of colors, had sprung;
so alive and lean were that young man's limbs
a nobler creature Christ had never created, they declared.
870   This knight,
             whose country was unclear,
             now seemed to them by sight
             a prince without a peer
             in fields where fierce men fight.

875 In front of a flaming fireside a chair
was pulled into place for Gawain, and padded
with covers and quilts all cleverly stitched,
then a cape was cast across the knight
of rich brown cloth with embroidered borders,
880 finished inside with the finest furs,
ermine, to be exact, and a hood which echoed it.
Resplendently dressed he settled in his seat;
as his limbs thawed, so his thoughts lightened.
Soon a table was set on sturdy trestles
885 covered entirely with a clean white cloth
and cruets of salt and silver spoons.
In a while he washed and went to his meal.
Staff came quickly and served him in style
with several soups all seasoned to taste,
890 double helpings as was fitting, and a feast of fish,
some baked in bread, some browned over flames,
some boiled or steamed, some stewed in spices
and subtle sauces which the knight savored.
Four or five times he called it a feast,
895 and the courteous company happily cheered him
                    along:
             "On penance plates you dine—[8]
             there's better board to come."
             The warming, heady wine
900   then freed his mind for fun.

Now through tactful talk and tentative enquiry
polite questions are put to this prince;
he responds respectfully, and speaks of his journey

8. "Penance" because, although sumptuous, the meal consists of fish dishes appropriate to a fasting day.

from the Court of Arthur, King of Camelot,
905   the royal ruler of the Round Table,
and he says they now sit with Gawain himself,
who has come here at Christmastime quite by chance.
Once the lord has gathered that his guest is Gawain
he likes it so well that he laughs out loud.
910   All the men of that manor were of the same mind,
being happy to appear promptly in his presence,
this person famed for prowess and purity,
whose noble skills were sung to the skies,
whose life was the stuff of legend and lore.
915   Then knight spoke softly to knight, saying
"Watch now, we'll witness his graceful ways,
hear the faultless phrasing of flawless speech;
if we listen we will learn the merits of language
since we have in our hall a man of high ˌonor.
920   Ours is a graceful and giving God
to grant that we welcome Gawain ⸝ɔ ɔur guest
as we sing of His birth who was ˡɔɾn to save us.
         We few
      shall learn a lesson ʰere
925   in tact and manⁿers true,
      and hopefullʸ we'll hear
      love's tender language, too."

Once dinner was done Gawain drew to his feet
and darkness neared as day became dusk.
930   Chaplains went off to the castle's chapels
to sound the bells hard, to signal the hour
of evensong, summoning each and every soul.
The lord goes alone, then his lady arrives,
concealing herself in a private pew.
935   Gawain attends, too; tugged by his sleeve
he is steered to a seat, led by the lord
who greets Gawain by name as his guest.
No man in the world is more welcome, are his words.
For that he is thanked. And they hug there and then,
940   and sit as a pair through the service in prayer.
Then she who desired to see this stranger
came from her closet with her sisterly crew.
She was fairest amongst them—her face, her flesh,
her complexion, her quality, her bearing, her body,
945   more glorious than Guinevere, or so Gawain thought,
and in the chancel of the church they exchanged courtesies.
She was hand in hand with a lady to her left,
someone altered by age, an ancient dame,
well respected, it seemed, by the servants at her side.
950   Those ladies were not the least bit alike:
one woman was young, one withered by years.
The body of the beauty seemed to bloom with blood,
the cheeks of the crone were wattled and slack.
One was clothed in a kerchief clustered with pearls

955 which shone like snow—snow on the slopes
of her upper breast and bright bare throat.
The other was noosed and knotted at the neck,
her chin enveloped in chalk-white veils,
her forehead fully enfolded in silk
960 with detailed designs at the edges and hems;
nothing bare, except for the black of her brows
and the eyes and nose and naked lips
which were chapped and bleared and a sorrowful sight.
A grand old mother, a matriarch she might
965   be hailed.
        Her trunk was square and squat,
        her buttocks bulged and swelled.
        Most men would sooner squint
        at her whose hand she held.

970 Then Gawain glanced at the gracious-looking woman,
and by leave of the lord he approached those ladies
saluting the elder with a long, low bow,
holding the other for a moment in his arms,
kissing her respectfully and speaking with courtesy.
975 They request his acquaintance, and quickly he offers
to serve them unswervingly should they say the word.
They take him between them and talk as they walk
to a hearth full of heat, and hurriedly ask
for specially spiced cakes, which are speedily fetched,
980 and wine filled each goblet again and again.
Frequently the lord would leap to his feet
insisting that mirth and merriment be made:
hauling off his hood he hoisted it on a spear—
a prize, he promised, to the person providing
985 most comfort and cheer at Christmastime.
"And my fellows and friends shall help in my fight
to see that it hangs from no head but my own."
So the laughter of that lord lights up the room,
and Gawain and the gathering are gladdened by games
990   till late.
        So late, his lordship said,
        that lamps should burn with light.
        Then, blissful, bound for bed,
        Sir Gawain waved good night.

995 So the morning dawns when man remembers
the day our Redeemer was born to die,
and every house on earth is joyful for Lord Jesus.
Their day was no different, being a diary of delights:
banquets and buffets were beautifully cooked
1000 and dutifully served to diners at the dais.
The ancient elder sat highest at the table
with the lord, I believe, in the chair to her left;
the sweeter one and Gawain took seats in the center
and were first at the feast to dine; then food

1005 was carried around as custom decrees
and served to each man as his status deserved.
There was feasting, there was fun, and such feelings of joy
as could not be conveyed by quick description,
yet to tell it in detail would take too much time.
1010 But I'm aware that Gawain and the beautiful woman
found such comfort and closeness in each other's company
through warm exchanges of whispered words
and refined conversation free from foulness
that their pleasure surpassed all princely sports
1015   by far.
      Beneath the din of drums
      men followed their affairs,
      and trumpets thrilled and thrummed
      as those two tended theirs.

1020 They drank and danced all day and the next
and danced and drank the day after that,
then Saint John's Day[9] passed with a gentler joy
as the Christmas feasting came to a close.
Guests were to go in the grayness of dawn,
1025 so they laughed and dined as the dusk darkened,
swaying and swirling to music and song.
Then at last, in the lateness, they upped and left
toward distant parts along different paths.
Gawain offered his good-byes, but was ushered by his host
1030 to his host's own chamber and the heat of its chimney,
waylaid by the lord so the lord might thank him
profoundly and profusely for the favor he had shown
in honoring his house at that hallowed season
and lighting every corner of the castle with his character.
1035 "For as long as I live my life shall be better
that Gawain was my guest at God's own feast."
"By God," said Gawain, "but the gratitude goes to you.
May the High King of Heaven repay your honor.
Your requests are now this knight's commands.
1040 I am bound by your bidding, no boon is too high
      to say."
      At length his lordship tried
      to get his guest to stay.
      But proud Gawain replied
1045   he must now make his way.

Then the lord of the castle inquired courteously
of what desperate deed in the depth of winter
should coax him from Camelot, so quickly and alone,
before Christmas was over in his king's court.
1050 "What you ask," said the knight, "you shall now know.
A most pressing matter prized me from that place:
I myself am summoned to seek out a site

9. December 27.

and I have not the faintest idea where to find it.
But find it I must by the first of the year, and not fail
1055 for all the acres in England, so the Lord help me.
Consequently this inquiry I come to ask of you:
that you tell me, in truth, if you have heard the tale
of a green chapel and the ground where it stands,
or the guardian of those grounds who is colored green.
1060 For I am bound by a bond agreed by us both
to link up with him there, should I live that long.
As dawn on New Year's Day draws near,
if God sees fit, I shall face that freak
more happily than I would the most wondrous wealth!
1065 With your blessing, therefore, I must follow my feet.
In three short days my destiny is due,
and I would rather drop dead than default from duty."
Then laughing the lord of the house said, "Stay longer.
I'll direct you to your rendezvous when the time is right,
1070 you'll get to the green chapel, so give up your grieving.
You can bask in your bed, bide your time,
save your fond farewells till the first of the year
and still meet him by midmorning to do as you might.
       So stay.
1075   A guide will get you there
      at dawn on New Year's Day.
      The place you need is near,
      two miles at most away."

Then Gawain was giddy with gladness, and declared,
1080 "For this more than anything I thank you thoroughly,
and shall work to do well at whatever you wish,
until that time, attending every task."
The lord squeezed Gawain's arm and seated him at his side,
and called for the ladies to keep them company.
1085 There was pleasure aplenty in their private talk,
the lord delighting in such lively language,
like man who might well be losing his mind.
Then speaking to Gawain, he suddenly shouted:
"You have sworn to serve me, whatever I instruct.
1090 Will you hold to that oath right here and now?"
"You may trust my tongue," said Gawain, in truth,
"for within these walls I am servant to your will."
The lord said warmly, "You were weary and worn,
hollow with hunger, harrowed by tiredness,
1095 yet joined in my reveling right royally every night.
You relax as you like, lie in your bed
until mass tomorrow, then go to your meal
where my wife will be waiting; she will sit at your side
to accompany and comfort you in my absence from court.
1100   So lounge:
      at dawn I'll rise and ride
      to hunt with horse and hound."

The gracious knight agreed
and, bending low, he bowed.

1105   "Furthermore," said the master, "let's make a pact.
Here's a wager: what I win in the woods will be yours,
and what you gain while I'm gone you will give to me.
Young sir, let's swap, and strike a bond,
let a bargain be a bargain, for better or worse."
1110   "By God," said Gawain, "I agree to the terms,
and I find it pleasing that you favor such fun."
"Let drink be served and we'll seal the deal,"
the lord cried loudly, and everyone laughed.
So they reveled and caroused uproariously,
1115   those lords and ladies, for as long as they liked;
then with immaculate exchanges of manners and remarks
they slowed and they stood and they spoke softly.
And with parting kisses the party dispersed,
footmen going forward with flaring torches,
1120   and everybody was brought to their bed at long last,
                to dream.
            Before they part the pair
            repeat their pact again.
            That lord was well aware
1125   of how to host a game.

FITT iii

Well before sunrise the servants were stirring;
the guests who were going had called for their grooms,
and they scurried to the stables to strap on the saddles,
trussing and tying all the trammel and tack.
1130   The high-ranking nobles got ready to ride,
jumped stylishly to their saddles and seized the reins,
then cantered away on their chosen courses.
The lord of that land was by no means last
to be rigged out for riding with the rest of his men.
1135   After mass he wolfed down a meal, then made
for the hills in a hurry with his hunting horn.
So as morning was lifting its lamp to the land
his lordship and his huntsmen were high on horseback,
and the canny kennel men had coupled the hounds
1140   and opened the cages and called them out.
On the bugles they blew three long, bare notes
to a din of baying and barking, and any dogs
which wandered at will were whipped back into line
by a hundred hunters, or so I heard tell,
1145   at least.
            The handlers hold their hounds,
            the huntsmen's hounds run free.
            Each bugle blast rebounds
            between the trunks of trees.

1150 As the cry went up the wild creatures quaked.
The deer in the dale, quivering with dread
hurtled to high ground, but were headed off
by the ring of beaters who bellowed boisterously.
The stags of the herd with their high-branched heads
1155 and the broad-horned bucks were allowed to pass by,
for the lord of the land had laid down a law
that man should not maim the male in close season.
But the hinds were halted with hollers and whoops
and the din drove the does to sprint for the dells.
1160 Then the eye can see that the air is all arrows:
all across the forest they flashed and flickered,
biting through hides with their broad heads.
What! They bleat as they bleed and they die on the banks,
and always the hounds are hard on their heels,
1165 and the hunters on horseback come hammering behind
with stone-splitting cries, as if cliffs had collapsed.
And those animals which escaped the aim of the archers
were steered from the slopes down to rivers and streams
and set upon and seized at the stations below.
1170 So perfect and practiced were the men at their posts
and so great were the greyhounds which grappled with the deer
that prey was pounced on and dispatched with speed
                    and force.
           The lord's heart leaps with life.
1175   Now on, now off his horse
           all day he hacks and drives.
           And dusk comes in due course.

So through a lime-leaf border the lord led the hunt,
while good Gawain lay slumbering in his sheets,
1180 dozing as the daylight dappled the walls,
under a splendid cover, enclosed by curtains.
And while snoozing he heard a slyly made sound,
the sigh of a door swinging slowly aside.
From below the bedding he brings up his head
1185 and lifts the corner of the curtain a little
wondering warily what it might be.
It was she, the lady, looking her loveliest,
most quietly and craftily closing the door,
nearing the bed. The knight felt nervous;
1190 lying back he assumed the shape of sleep
as she stole towards him with silent steps,
then cast up the curtain and crept inside,
then sat down softly at the side of his bed.
And awaited his wakening for a good long while.
1195 Gawain lay still, in his state of false sleep,
turning over in his mind what this matter might mean,
and where the lady's unlikely visit might lead.
Yet he said to himself, "Instead of this stealth
I should openly ask what her actions imply."
1200 So he stirred and stretched, turned on his side,

The Temptation of Sir Gawain by Bertilak's Wife. Gawain may think he is protected, but bedrooms are dangerous places.

lifted his eyelids and, looking alarmed,
crossed himself hurriedly with his hand, as if saving
       his life.
      Her chin is pale, her cheeks
1205   are ruddy red with health;
      her smile is sweet, she speaks
      with lips that love to laugh:

"Good morning, Sir Gawain," said the graceful lady,
"You sleep so soundly one might sidle in here.
1210 You're tricked and trapped! But let's make a truce,
or I'll bind you in your bed, and you'd better believe me."
The lady laughed, making light of his quandary.
"Good morning, madam," Gawain said merrily.
"I'll contentedly attend whatever task you set,
1215 and in serving your desires I shall seek your mercy,
which seems my best plan, in the circumstances!"
And he loaded his light-hearted words with laughter.
"But my gracious lady, if you grant me leave,
will you pardon this prisoner and prompt him to rise,
1220 then I'll quit these covers and pull on my clothes,
and our words will flow more freely back and forth."
"Not so, beautiful sir," the sweet lady said.
"Bide in your bed—my own plan is better.
I'll tuck in your covers corner to corner,
1225 then playfully parley with the man I have pinned.
Because I know your name—the knight Sir Gawain,
famed through all realms whichever road he rides,
whose princely honor is highly praised
amongst lords and ladies and everyone alive.
1230 And right here you lie. And we are left all alone,

with my husband and his huntsmen away in the hills
and the servants snoring and my maids asleep
and the door to this bedroom barred with a bolt.
I have in my house an honored guest
1235 so I'll make the most of my time and stay talking
                    a while.
            You're free to have my all,
            do with me what you will.
            I'll come just as you call
1240   and swear to serve you well."

"In good faith," said Gawain, "such gracious flattery,
though I am not him of whom you speak.
I don't dare to receive the respect you describe
and in no way warrant such worthy words.
1245 By God, I would be glad, if you agreed it fitting,
to devote myself through speech or deed
to the prize of your praise—my joy in it would be pure."
Said the gracious lady, "Sir Gawain, in good faith,
how improper on my part if I were to imply
1250 any slur or slight on your status as a knight.
But what lady in this land wouldn't latch the door,
wouldn't rather hold you as I do here—
in the company of your clever conversation,
forgetting all grief and engaging in joy—
1255 than hang on to half the gold that she owns?
I praise the Lord who upholds the high heavens,
for I have what I hoped for above all else by
                    His grace."
            That lovely-looking maid,
1260   she charmed him and she chased.
            But every move she made
            he countered, case by case.

"Madam," said our man, "may Mary reward you,
in good faith, I have found your fairness noble.
1265 Some fellows are praised for the feats they perform;
I hardly deserve to receive such respect.
It is you who is genuinely joyful and generous."
"By Mary," she declared, "it's quite the contrary.
Were I the wealthiest woman in the world
1270 with priceless pearls in the palm of my hand
to bargain with and buy the best of all men,
then for all the signs you have shown me, sir,
of kindness, courtesy and exquisite looks—
a picture of perfection now proved to be true—
1275 no person on this planet would be picked before you."
"In fairness," said Gawain, "you found far better.
But I'm proud of the price you would pay from your purse,
and will swear to serve you as my sovereign lady.
Let Gawain be your servant and Christ your Savior."
1280 Then they muse on many things through morning and midday,
and the lady stares with a loving look,

but Gawain acts graciously and remains on guard,
and although no woman could be warmer or more winning,
he is cool in his conduct, on account of the scene he
1285   foresees:
            the strike he must receive,
            as cruel fate decrees.
            The lady begs her leave—
            at once Gawain agrees.

1290 She glanced at him, laughed and gave her good-bye,
then stood, and stunned him with astounding words:
"May the Lord repay you for your prize performance.
But I know that Gawain could never be your name."
"But why not?" the knight asked nervously,
1295 afraid that some fault in his manners had failed him.
The beautiful woman blessed him, then rebuked him:
"A good man like Gawain, so greatly regarded,
the embodiment of courtliness to the bones of his being,
could never have lingered so long with a lady
1300 without craving a kiss, as politeness requires,
or coaxing a kiss with his closing words."
"Very well," said Gawain, "Let it be as you wish.
I shall kiss at your command, as becomes a knight,
and further, should it please you, so press me no more."
1305 The lady comes close, cradles him in her arms,
leans nearer and nearer, then kisses the knight.
Then they courteously commend one another to Christ,
and without one more word the woman is away.
Rapidly he rises and makes himself ready,
1310 calls for his chamberlain, chooses his clothes,
makes himself ready, then marches off to mass.
Then he went to a meal which was made and waiting,
and was merry and amused till the moon had silvered
                the view.
1315   No man felt more at home
            tucked in between those two,
            the cute one and the crone.
            Their gladness grew and grew.

And the lord of the land still led the hunt,
1320 driving hinds to their death through holts and heaths,
and by the setting of the sun had slaughtered so many
of the does and other deer that it beggared belief.
Then finally the folk came flocking to one spot
and quickly they collected and counted the kill.
1325 Then the leading lords and their loyal men
chose the finest deer—those fullest with fat—
and ordered them cut open by those skilled in the art.
They assessed and sized every slain creature
and even on the feeblest found two fingers worth of fat.
1330 Through the sliced-open throat they seized the stomach
and the butchered innards were bound in a bundle.
Next they lopped off the legs and peeled back the pelt

and hooked out the bowels through the broken belly,
but carefully, being cautious not to cleave the knot.
1335 Then they clasped the throat, and clinically they cut
the gullet from the windpipe, then garbaged the guts.
Then the shoulder blades were severed with sharp knives
and slotted through a slit so the hide stayed whole.
Then the beasts were prized apart at the breast,
1340 and they went to work on the gralloching again,
riving open the front as far as the hind fork,
fetching out the offal, then with further purpose
filleting the ribs in the recognized fashion.
And the spine was subject to a similar process,
1345 being pared to the haunch so it held as one piece
then hoisting it high and hacking it off.
And its name is the numbles, as far as I know, and
                    just that.
              Its hind legs pulled apart
1350   they slit the fleshy flaps,
              then cleave and quickly start
              to break it down its back.

Then the heads and necks of hinds were hewn off,
and the choice meat of the flanks chopped away from the chine,
1355 and a fee for the crows was cast into the copse.
Then each side was skewered, stabbed through the ribs
and heaved up high, hung by its hocks,
and every person was paid with appropriate portions.
Using pelts for plates, the dogs pogged out
1360 on liver and lights and stomach linings
and a blended sop of blood and bread.
The kill horn was blown and the bloodhounds bayed.
Then hauling their meat they headed for home,
sounding howling wails on their hunting horns,
1365 and as daylight died they had covered the distance
and had come to the castle where the knight was ensconced,
                    adjourned
              in peace, with fires aflame.
              The huntsman has returned,
1370   and when he greets Gawain
              warm feelings are confirmed.

Then the whole of the household was ordered to the hall,
and the women as well with their maids in waiting.
And once assembled he instructs the servants
1375 that the venison be revealed in full view,
and in excellent humor he asked that Gawain
should see for himself the size of the kill,
and showed him the side slabs sliced from the ribs.
"Are you pleased with this pile? Have I won your praise?
1380 Does my skill at this sport deserve your esteem?"
"Yes indeed," said the other. "It's the hugest haul
I have seen this seven years in the winter season."

"And I give it all to you, Gawain," said the master,
"for according to our contract it is yours to claim."
1385 "Just so," said Gawain, "and I'll say the same,
for whatever I've won within these walls
such gains will be graciously given to you."
So he held out his arms and hugged the lord
and kissed him in the comeliest way he could.
1390 "You're welcome to my winnings—to my one profit,
though I'd gladly have given you any greater prize."
"I'm grateful," said the lord, "and Gawain, this gift
would carry more worth if you cared to confess
by what wit you won it. And when. And where."
1395 "That wasn't our pact," he replied. "So don't pry.
You'll be given nothing greater, the agreement we have
            holds good!"
        They laugh aloud and trade
        wise words which match their mood.
1400   When supper's meal is made
        they dine on dainty food.

Later, they lounged by the lord's fire,
and were served unstintingly with subtle wines
and agreed to the game again next morning
1405 and to play by the rules already in place:
any takings to be traded between the two men
at night when they met, no matter what the merchandise.
They concurred on this contract in front of the court,
and drank on the deal, and went on drinking
1410 till late, when they took their leave at last,
and every person present departed to bed.
By the third cackle of the crowing cock
the lord and his liegemen are leaping from their beds,
so that mass and the morning meal are taken,
1415 and riders are rigged out ready to run as
                day dawns.
        They leave the levels, loud
        with howling hunting horns.
        The huntsmen loose the hounds
1420   through thickets and through thorns.

Soon they picked up a scent at the side of a swamp,
and the hounds which first found it were urged ahead
by wild words and shrill shouting.
The pack responded with vigor and pace,
1425 alert to the trail, forty lurchers at least.
Then such a raucous din rose up all around them
it ricocheted and rang through the rocky slopes.
The hounds were mushed with hollers and the horn,
then suddenly they swerved and swarmed together
1430 in a wood, between a pool and a precipice.
On a mound, near a cliff, on the margins of a marsh
where toppled stones lay scattered and strewn,

they coursed towards their quarry with huntsmen at heel.
Then a crew of them ringed the hillock and the cliff,
1435   until they were certain that inside their circle
was the beast whose being three bloodhounds had sensed.
Then they riled the creature with their rowdy ruckus,
and suddenly he breaks the barrier of beaters,
—the biggest of wild boars has bolted from his cover—
1440   ancient in years and estranged from the herd,
savage and strong, a most massive swine,
truly grim when he grunted. And the group were aggrieved,
for three were thrown down by the first of his thrusts;
then he fled away fast without further damage.
1445   The other huntsmen bawled "hi" and "hay, hay,"
blasted on their bugles, blew to regroup,
so the dogs and the men made a merry din,
tracking him nosily, testing him time and time
               again.
1450   The boar would stand at bay
        and aim to maul and maim
        the thronging dogs, and they
        would yelp and yowl in pain.

Then the archers advanced with their bows and took aim,
1455   shooting arrows at him which were often on target,
but their points could not pierce his impenetrable shoulders
and bounced away from his bristly brow.
The smooth, slender shafts splintered into pieces,
and the heads glanced away from wherever they hit.
1460   Battered and baited by such bombardment,
in frenzied fury he flies at the men,
hurts them horribly as he hurtles past
so that many grew timid and retreated a tad.
But the master of the manor gave chase on his mount,
1465   the boldest of beast hunters, his bugle blaring,
trumpeting the tally-ho and tearing through thickets
till the setting sun slipped from the western sky.
So the day was spent in pursuits of this style,
while our lovable young lord had not left his bed,
1470   and, cosseted in costly quilted covers, there he
              remained.
        The lady, at first light,
        did not neglect Gawain,
        but went to wake the knight
1475   and meant to change his mind.

She approaches the curtains, parts them and peeps in,
at which Sir Gawain makes her welcome at once,
and with prompt speech she replies to the prince,
settling by his side and laughing sweetly,
1480   looking at him lovingly before launching her words.
"Sir, if you truly are Gawain it seems wondrous to me
that a man so dedicated to doing his duty

cannot heed the first rule of honorable behavior,
which has entered through one ear and exited the other;
1485 you have already lost what yesterday you learned
in the truest lesson my tongue could teach."
"What lesson?" asked the knight. "I know of none,
though if discourtesy has occurred then blame me, of course."
"I encouraged you to kiss," the lady said kindly,
1490 "and to claim one quickly when one is required,
an act which ennobles any knight worth the name."
"Dear lady," said the other, "don't think such a thing,
I dare not kiss in case I am turned down.
If refused, I'd be at fault for offering in the first place."
1495 "In truth," she told him, "you cannot be turned down.
If someone were so snooty as to snub your advance,
a man like you has the means of his muscles."
"Yes, by God," said Gawain, "what you say holds good.
But such heavy-handedness is frowned on in my homeland,
1500 and so is any gift not given with grace.
What kiss you command I will courteously supply,
have what you want or hold off, whichever
           the case."
       So bending from above
1505   the fair one kissed his face.
       The two then talk of love:
       its grief; also its grace.

"I would like to learn," said the noble lady,
"and please find no offence, but how can it follow
1510 that a lord so lively and young in years,
a champion in chivalry across the country—
and in chivalry, the chiefmost aspect to choose,
as all knights acknowledge, is loyalty in love,
for when tales of truthful knights are told
1515 in both title and text the topic they describe
is how lords have laid down their lives for love,
endured for many days love's dreadful ordeal,
then vented their feelings with avenging valor
by bringing great bliss to a lady's bedroom—
1520 and you the most notable knight who is known,
whose fame goes before him . . . yes, how can it follow
that twice I have taken this seat at your side
yet you have not spoken the smallest syllable
which belongs to love or anything like it.
1525 A knight so courteous and considerate in his service
really ought to be eager to offer this pupil
some lessons in love, and to lead by example.
Why, are you, whom all men honor, actually ignorant,
or do you deem me too dull to hear of dalliances?
1530   I come
       to learn of love and more,
       a lady all alone.
       Perform for me before

my husband heads for home."

1535   "In faith," said Gawain, "may God grant you fortune.
It gives me great gladness and seems a good game
that a woman so worthy should want to come here
and take pains to play with your poor knight,
unfit for her favors—I am flattered indeed.
1540   But to take on the task of explaining true love
or touch on the topics those love tales tell of,
with yourself, who I sense has more insight and skill
in the art than I have, or even a hundred
of the likes of me, on earth where I live,
1545   would be somewhat presumptuous, I have to say.
But to the best of my ability I'll do your bidding,
bound as I am to honor you forever
and to serve you, so let our Savior preserve me!"
So the lady tempted and teased him, trying
1550   to entice him to wherever her intentions might lie.
But fairly and without fault he defended himself,
no sin on either side transpiring, only happiness
             that day.
           At length, when they had laughed,
1555   the woman kissed Gawain.
           Politely then she left
           and went her own sweet way.

Roused and risen he was ready for mass,
and then men sumptuously served the morning meal.
1560   Then he loitered with the ladies the length of the day
while the lord of the land ranged left and right
in pursuit of that pig which stampeded through the uplands,
breaking his best hounds with its back-snapping bite
when it stood embattled . . . then bowmen would strike,
1565   goading it to gallop into open ground
where the air was alive with the huntsman's arrows.
That boar made the best men flinch and bolt,
till at last his legs were like lead beneath him,
and he hobbled away to hunker in a hole
1570   by a stony rise at the side of a stream.
With the bank at his back he scrapes and burrows,
frothing and foaming foully at the mouth,
whetting his white tusks. The hunters waited,
irked by the effort of aiming from afar
1575   but daunted by the danger of daring to venture
            too near.
           So many men before
           had fallen prey. They feared
           that fierce and frenzied boar
1580   whose tusks could slash and tear.

Till his lordship hacks up, urging on his horse,
spots the swine at standstill encircled by men,

then handsomely dismounts and unhands his horse,
brandishes a bright sword and goes bounding onwards,
1585 wades through the water to where the beast waits.
Aware that the man was wafting a weapon
the hog's hairs stood on end, and its howling grunt
made the fellows there fear for their master's fate.
Then the boar burst forward, bounded at the lord,
1590 so that beast and hunter both went bundling
into white water, and the swine came off worst,
because the moment they clashed the man found his mark,
knifing the boar's neck, nailing his prey,
hammering it to the hilt, bursting the hog's heart.
1595 Screaming, it was swept downstream, almost slipping
      beneath.
      At least a hundred hounds
      latch on with tearing teeth.
      Then, dragged to drier ground,
1600   the dogs complete its death.

The kill was blown on many blaring bugle
and the unhurt hunters hollered and whooped.
The chief amongst them, in charge of the chase,
commanded the bloodhounds to bay at the boar,
1605 then one who was wise in woodland ways
began carefully to cut and carve up the carcass.
First he hacks off its head and hoists it aloft,
then roughly rives it right along the spine;
he gouges out the guts and grills them over coals,
1610 and blended with bread they are tidbits for the bloodhounds.
Next he fetches out the fillets of glimmering flesh
and retrieves the intestines in time-honored style,
then the two sides are stitched together intact
and proudly displayed on a strong pole.
1615 So with the swine swinging they swagger home,
the head of the boar being borne before the lord
who had fought so fiercely in the ford till the beast
      was slain.
      The day then dragged, it seemed,
1620   before he found Gawain,
      who comes when called, most keen
      to countenance the claim.

Now the lord is loud with words and laughter
and speaks excitedly when he sees Sir Gawain;
1625 he calls for the ladies and the company of the court
and he shows off the meat slabs and shares the story
of the boar's hulking hugeness, and the full horror
of the fight to the finish as it fled through the forest.
And Gawain is quick to compliment the conquest,
1630 praising it as proof of the lord's prowess,
for such prime pieces of perfect pork
and such sides of swine were a sight to be seen.

Then admiringly he handles the boar's huge head,
feigning fear to flatter the master's feelings.
1635 "Now Gawain," said the lord, "I give you this game,
as our wager warranted, as well you remember."
"Certainly," said Sir Gawain. "It shall be so.
And graciously I shall give you my gains in exchange."
He catches him by the neck and courteously kisses him,
1640 then a second time kisses him in a similar style.
"Now we're even," said Gawain, "at this eventide;
the clauses of our contract have been kept and you have what
          I owe."
          "By Saint Giles," the just lord says,
1645   "You're now the best I know.
          By wagering this way
          your gains will grow and grow."

Then the trestle tables were swiftly assembled
and cast with fine cloths. A clear, living light
1650 from the waxen torches awakened the walls.
Places were set and supper was served,
and a din arose as they reveled in a ring
around the fire on the floor, and the feasting party
made much pleasant music at the meal and after,
1655 singing seasonal songs and carol dancing
with as much amusement as a mouth could mention.
The young woman and Gawain sat together all the while.
And so loving was that lady towards the young lord,
with stolen glances and secret smiles
1660 that the man himself was maddened and amazed,
but his breeding forbade him rebuking a lady,
and though tongues might wag he returned her attention
          all night.
          Before his friends retire
1665   his lordship leads the knight,
          heads for his hearth and fire
          to linger by its light.

They supped and swapped stories, and spoke again
of the night to come next, which was New Year's Eve.
1670 Gawain pleaded politely to depart by morning,
so in two days' time he might honor his treaty.
But the lord was unswerving, insisting that he stayed:
"As an honest soul I swear on my heart,
you shall find the Green Chapel to finish your affairs
1675 long before dawn on New Year's Day.
So lie in your room and laze at your leisure
while I ride my estate, and, as our terms dictate,
we'll trade our trophies when the hunt returns.
I have tested you twice and found you truthful.
1680 But think tomorrow *third time throw best*.
Now, a lord can feel low whenever he likes,
so let's chase cheerfulness while we have the chance."

So those gentlemen agreed that Gawain would stay,
and they took more drink, then by torchlight retired to
1685   their beds.
    Our man then sleeps, a most
    reposed and peaceful rest.
    As hunters must, his host
    is up at dawn and dressed.

1690 After mass the master grabs a meal with his men
and asks for his mount on that marvelous morning.
All those grooms engaged to go with their lord
were high on their horses before the hall gates.
The fields were dazzling, fixed with frost,
1695 and the crown of sunrise rose scarlet and crimson,
scalding and scattering cloud from the sky.
At the fringe of the forest the dogs were set free
and the rumpus of the horns went ringing through the rocks.
They fall on the scent of a fox, and follow,
1700 turning and twisting as they sniff out the trail.
A young harrier yowls and a huntsman yells,
then the pack come panting to pick up the scent,
running as a rabble along the right track.
The fox scurries ahead, they scamper behind,
1705 and pursue him at speed when he comes within sight,
haranguing him with horrific ranting howls.
Now and then he doubles back through thorny thickets,
or halts and harkens in the hem of a hedge,
until finally, by a hollow, he hurdles a fence,
1710 and carefully he creeps by the edge of a copse,
convinced that his cunning has conned those canines!
But unawares he wanders where they lie in wait,
where greyhounds are gathered together, a group
     of three.
1715   He springs back with a start,
    then twists and turns and flees.
    With heavy, heaving heart
    he tracks towards the trees.

It was one of life's delights to listen to those hounds
1720 as they massed to meet him, marauding together.
They bayed bloodily at the sight of his being,
as if clustering cliffs had crashed to the ground.
Here he was ambushed by bushwhacking huntsmen
waiting with a welcome of wounding words;
1725 there he was threatened and branded a thief,
and the team on his tail gave him no time to tarry.
Often, in the open, the pack tried to pounce,
then that crafty Reynard[1] would creep into cover.
So his lordship and his lords were merrily led

---

1. The Old French word for "fox" (*goupil*) gave way to "Reynard" as a result of the immense success of stories about the cunning fox Reynard, anti-hero of the *Roman de Reynard*.

1730 in this manner through the mountains until midafternoon,
while our handsome hero snoozed contentedly at home,
kept from the cold of the morning by curtains.
But love would not let her ladyship sleep
nor suppress the purpose which suppressed her heart.
1735 She rose from her rest and rushed to his room
in a flowing robe that reached to the floor
and was finished inside with fine-trimmed furs.
Her head went unhooded, but heavenly gems
were entwined in her tresses in clusters of twenty.
1740 She wore nothing on her face; her neck was naked,
and her shoulders were bare to both back and breast.
She comes into his quarters and closes the door,
throws the window wide open and wakes Gawain,
right away rouses him with ringing words for
1745   his ear.
    "Oh, sir, how can you sleep
    when morning comes so clear?"
    And though his dreams are deep
    he cannot help but hear.

1750 Yes he dozes in a daze, dreams and mutters
like a mournful man with his mind on dark matters—
how destiny might deal him a death blow on the day
when he grapples with the guardian of the Green Chapel;
of how the strike of the axe must be suffered without struggle.
1755 But sensing her presence there he surfaces from sleep,
comes quickly from the depths of his dreams to address her.
Laughing warmly she walks towards him
and finds his face with the friendliest kiss.
In a worthy style he welcomes the woman
1760 and seeing her so lovely and alluringly dressed,
every feature so faultless, her complexion so fine,
a passionate heat takes hold in his heart.
They traded smiles and speech tripped from their tongues,
and a bond of friendship was forged there, all blissful
1765   and bright.
    They talk with tenderness
    and pride, and yet their plight
    is perilous unless
    sweet Mary minds her knight.

1770 For that noble princess pushed him and pressed him,
nudged him ever nearer to a limit where he needed
to allow her love or impolitely reject it.
He was careful to be courteous and avoid uncouthness,
and more so for the sake of his soul should he sin
1775 and be counted a betrayer by the keeper of the castle.
"I shall not succumb," he swore to himself.
With affectionate laughter he fenced and deflected
all the loving phrases which leapt from her lips.
"You shall bear the blame," said the beautiful one,

1780 "if you feel no love for the lady you lie with,
and wound her, more than anyone on earth, to the heart.
Unless, of course, there is a lady in your life
to whom you are tied and so tightly attached
that the bond will not break, as I must now believe.
1785 So in honesty and trust now tell me the truth;
for all the love alive, do not lessen the truth
        with guile."
       "You judge wrong, by Saint John,"
       he said to her, and smiled.
1790   "There is no other one
       nor will be for this while!"

"Those words," said the woman, "are the worst of all.
But I asked, and you answered, and now I ache.
Kiss me as I wish and I shall walk away
1795 in mourning like a lady who loved too much."
Stooping and sighing she kisses him sweetly,
then withdraws from his side, saying as she stands,
"But before we part will you find me some small favor?
Give me some gift—a glove at least,
1800 that might leaven my loss when we meet in my memory."
"Well it were," said Gawain. "I wish I had here
my most precious possession as a present for your love,
for over and over you deserve and are owed
the highest prize I could hope to offer.
1805 But I would not wish on you a worthless token,
and it strikes me as unseemly that you should receive
nothing greater than a glove as a keepsake from Gawain.
I am here on an errand in an unknown land
without men bearing bags of beautiful things,
1810 which my regard for you, lady, makes me regret;
but man must live by his means, and neither mope
        nor moan."
       The pretty one replies:
       "Nay, knight, since you decline
1815   to pass to me a prize,
       you must have one of mine."

She offers him a ring of rich, red gold,
and the stunning stone set upon it stood proud,
beaming and burning with the brightness of the sun;
1820 what wealth it was worth you can well imagine.
But he would not accept it, and said straight away,
"By God, no tokens will I take at this time;
I have nothing to give, so nothing will I gain."
She insists he receive it but still he resists,
1825 and swears, on his name as a knight, not to swerve.
Snubbed by his decision, she said to him then,
"You refuse my ring because you find it too fine,
and don't care to be deeply indebted to me;
so I give you my girdle, a lesser thing to gain."

1830 From around her body she unbuckled the belt
which fastened the frock beneath her fair mantle,
a green silk girdle trimmed with gold,
exquisitely edged and hemmed by hand.
And she sweetly beseeched Sir Gawain to receive it,
1835 in spite of its slightness, and hoped he would accept.
But still he maintained he intended to take
neither gold nor girdle, until by God's grace
the challenge he had chosen was finally achieved.
"With apologies I pray you be not displeased,
1840 but end all your offers, for always against them
        I am.
            For all your grace I owe
            a thousand thank-you's, ma'am.
            I shall through sun and snow
1845   remain your loyal man."

"And now he spurns my silk," the lady responded,
"so simple in itself, or so it appears,
so little and unlikely, worth nothing, or less.
But the knight who knew of the power knitted in it
1850 would pay a high price to possess it, perhaps.
For the body which is bound within this green belt,
as long as it is buckled robustly about him,
will be safe against anyone who seeks to strike him,
and all the slyness on earth wouldn't see him slain."
1855 The man mulled it over, and it entered his mind
it might just be the jewel for the jeopardy he faced
and save him from the strike in his challenge at the chapel.
With luck, it might let him escape with his life.
So relenting at last he let her speak,
1860 and promptly she pressed him to take the present,
and he granted her wish, and she gave with good grace,
though went on to beg him not to whisper a word
of this gift to her husband, and Gawain agreed;
those words of theirs within those walls
1865   should stay.
            His thanks are heartfelt, then.
            No sooner can he say
            how much it matters, when
            the third kiss comes his way.

1870 Then the lady departed, leaving him alone,
for no more merriment could be had from that man.
And once she has quit he clothes himself quickly,
rises and dresses in the richest of robes,
stowing the love-lace safely aside,
1875 hiding it away from all hands and eyes.
Then he went at once to the chapel of worship,
privately approached the priest and implored him
to allow his confession, and to lead him in life

so his soul might be saved when he goes to his grave.
1880 Then fully and frankly he spoke of his sins,
no matter how small, always seeking mercy,
beseeching the counselor that he receive absolution.
The priest declares him so clean and so pure
that the Day of Doom could dawn in the morning.
1885 Then in merrier mood he mingled with the ladies,
caroling and carousing and carrying on
as never before, until nightfall. Folk feel
          and hear
       and see his boundless bliss
1890   and say, "Such charm and cheer;
       he's at his happiest
       since his arrival here."

And long let him loiter there, looked after by love.
Now the lord of the land was still leading his men,
1895 finishing off the fox he had followed for so long.
He vaults a fence to flush out the victim,
hearing that the hounds are harrying hard.
Then Reynard scoots from a section of scrub
and the rabble of the pack rush right at his heels.
1900 Aware of its presence the wary lord waits,
then bares his bright sword and swishes at the beast,
which shirks from its sharpness, and would have shot away
but a hound flew forward before it could flee
and under the hooves of the horses they have him,
1905 worrying the wily one with wrathful baying.
The lord hurtles from his horse and heaves the fox up,
wrestles it from the reach of those ravenous mouths,
holds it high over head and hurrahs manfully
while the bloodthirsty bloodhounds bay and howl.
1910 And the other huntsmen hurried with their horns
to catch sight of the slaughter and celebrate the kill.
And when the courtly company had come together
the buglers blew with one mighty blast,
and the others hallooed with open throats.
1915 It was the merriest music ever heard by men,
that rapturous roar which for Reynard's soul
         was raised.
       The dogs, due their reward,
       are patted, stroked and praised.
1920   Then red fur rips—Reynard
       out of his pelt is prised.

Then with night drawing near they headed homewards,
blaring their bugles with the fullness of their breath.
And at last the lord lands at his lovely home,
1925 to find, by the heat of the fireside, his friend
the good Sir Gawain, in glad spirits
on account of the company he had kept with the ladies.

His blue robe flowed as far as the floor,
his soft-furred surcoat suited him well,
1930 and the hood which echoed it hung from his shoulders.
Both hood and coat were edged in ermine.
He meets the master in the middle of the room,
greets him graciously, with Gawain saying:
"I shall first fulfill our formal agreement
1935 which we fixed in words when the drink flowed freely."
He clasps him tight and kisses him three times
with as much emotion as a man could muster.
"By the Almighty," said the master, "you must have had luck
to profit such a prize—if the price was right."
1940 "Oh fiddlesticks to the fee," said the other fellow.
"As long as I have given the goods which I gained."
"By Mary," said the master, "mine's a miserable match.
I've hunted for hours with nothing to my name
but this foul-stinking fox—fling its fur to the devil—
1945 so poor in comparison with such priceless things,
these presents you impart, three kisses perfect
                    and true."
            "Enough!" the knight entreats,
            "I thank you through and through."
1950   The standing lord then speaks
            of how the fox fur flew!

And with meals and mirth and minstrelsy
they made as much amusement as any mortal could,
and among those merry men and laughing ladies
1955 Gawain and his host got giddy together;
only lunatics and drunkards could have looked more delirious.
Every person present performed party pieces
till the hour arrived when revelers must rest,
and the company in that court heard the call of their beds.
1960 And lastly, in the hall, humbly to his host,
our knight says good night and renews his gratitude.
"Your uncountable courtesies have kept me here
this Christmas—be honored by the High King's kindness.
If it suits, I submit myself as your servant.
1965 But tomorrow morning I must make a move;
if you will, as you promised, please appoint some person
to guide me, God willing, towards the Green Chapel,
where my destiny will dawn on New Year's Day."
"On my honor," he replied. "With hand on heart,
1970 every promise I made shall be put into practice."
He assigns him a servant to steer his course,
to lead him through the land without losing time,
to ride the fastest route between forest
                    and fell.
1975   Gawain will warmly thank
            his host in terms that tell;
            towards the womenfolk
            the knight then waves farewell.

It's with a heavy heart that guests in the hall
1980 are kissed and thanked for their care and kindness,
and they respond with speeches of the same sort,
commending him to our Savior with sorrowful sighs.
Then politely he leaves the lord and his household,
and to each person he passes he imparts his thanks
1985 for taking such trouble in their service and assistance
and such attention to detail in attendance of duty.
And every guest is grieved at the prospect of his going,
as if honorable Gawain were one of their own.
By tapering torchlight he was taken to his room
1990 and brought to his bed to be at his rest.
But if our knight sleeps soundly I couldn't say,
for the matter in the morning might be muddying
       his thoughts.
     So let him lie and think,
1995   in sight of what he sought.
     In time I'll tell if tricks
     work out the way they ought.

FITT iv

Now night passes and New Year draws near,
drawing off darkness as our Deity decrees.
2000 But wild-looking weather was about in the world:
clouds decanted their cold rain earthwards;
the nithering north needled man's very nature;
creatures were scattered by the stinging sleet.
Then a whip-cracking wind comes whistling between hills
2005 driving snow into deepening drifts in the dales.
Alert and listening, Gawain lies in his bed;
his lids are lowered but he sleeps very little
as each crow of the cock brings his destiny closer.
Before day had dawned he was up and dressed
2010 for the room was livened by the light of a lamp.
To suit him in his metal and to saddle his mount
he called for a servant, who came quickly,
bounded from his bedsheets bringing his garments.
He swathes Sir Gawain in glorious style,
2015 first fastening clothes to fend off the frost,
then his armor, looked after all the while by the household:
the buffed and burnished stomach and breastplates,
and the rings of chain mail, raked free of rust,
all gleaming good as new, for which he is grateful
2020   indeed.
     With every polished piece
     no man shone more, it seemed
     from here to ancient Greece.
     He sent then for his steed.

2025 He clothes himself in the costliest costume:
his coat with the brightly emblazoned badge

mounted on velvet; magical minerals
inside and set about it; embroidered seams;
a lining finished with fabulous furs.
2030 And he did not leave off the lady's lace girdle;
for his own good, Gawain won't forget that gift.
Then with his sword sheathed at his shapely hips
he bound himself twice about with the belt,
touchingly wrapped it around his waist.
2035 That green silk girdle truly suited Sir Gawain
and went well with the rich red weaves that he wore.
But our man bore the belt not merely for its beauty,
or the appeal of its pennants, polished though they were,
or the gleam of its edges which glimmered with gold,
2040 but to save his skin when presenting himself,
without shield or sword, to the fatal swing of
the axe.
Now in his gear and gown
he turns towards those ranks
2045 who served with such renown
and offers thorough thanks.

Then his great horse Gringolet was got up ready.
The steed had been stabled in comfort and safety
and snorted and stamped in readiness for the ride.
2050 Gawain comes closer to examine his coat,
saying soberly to himself, swearing on his word:
"There are folk in this castle who keep courtesy to the forefront;
their master maintains them—happiness to them all.
And let his lordship's lady be loved all her life.
2055 If they choose, out of charity, to cherish a guest,
showing kindness and care, then may heaven's King
who reigns over all reward them handsomely.
For as long as I live in the lands of this world
I shall practice every means in my power to repay him."
2060 Then he steps in the stirrup and vaults to the saddle
and his servant lifts his shield which he slings on his shoulder,
then he girds on Gringolet with his golden spurs
who clatters from the courtyard, not stalling to snort
or prance.
2065 His man was mounted, too,
who lugged the spear and lance.
"Christ keep this castle true,"
he chanted. "Grant good chance."

The drawbridge was dropped, and the double-fronted gates
2070 were unbarred and each half was heaved wide open.
As he clears the planking he crosses himself quickly,
and praises the porter, who kneels before the prince
and prays that God be good to Gawain.
Then he went on his way with the one whose task
2075 was to point out the road to that perilous place
where the knight would receive the sorry stroke.

They scrambled up bankings where branches were bare,
clambered up cliff faces where the cold clings.
The clouds which had climbed now cooled and dropped
2080 so the moors and the mountains were muzzy with mist
and every hill wore a hat of mizzle on its head.
The streams on the slopes seemed to fume and foam,
whitening the wayside with spume and spray.
They wandered onwards through the wildest woods
2085 till the sun, at that season, came skyward, showing
its hand.
On hilly heights they ride,
snow littering the land.
The servant at his side
2090 then has them slow and stand.

"I have accompanied you across this countryside, my lord,
and now you are near the site you have named
and have steered and searched for with such singleness of mind.
But there's something I should like to share with you, sir,
2095 because upon my life, you're a lord that I love,
so if you value your health you'll hear my advice:
the place you proceed to is held to be perilous.
In that wilderness lives a wildman, the worst in the world,
he is brooding and brutal and loves bludgeoning people.
2100 He's more powerful than any person alive on this earth
and four times the figure of any fighting knight
in Arthur's house, or Hector or any other hero.
He chooses the green chapel for his grim goings-on,
and to pass through that place unscathed is impossible,
2105 for he deals out death blows by dint of his hands,
a man without measure who shows no mercy.
Be it chaplain or churl who rides by the chapel,
monk or priest, whatever man or person,
he loves murdering more than he loves his own life.
2110 So I say, just as sure as you sit in your saddle,
if you come there you'll be killed, of that there's no question.
Trust me, he could trample you twenty times over
or more.
He's lurked about too long
2115 engaged in grief and gore.
His hits are swift and strong—
he'll fell you to the floor."

"Therefore, good Sir Gawain, let the man go,
and for God's sake travel an alternate track,
2120 ride another road, and be rescued by Christ.
I'll head off home, and with hand on heart
I shall swear by God and all his good saints,
and on all earthly holiness, and other such oaths,
that your secret is safe, and not a soul will know
2125 that you fled in fear from the fellow I described."
"Many thanks," said Gawain, in a terse tone of voice,

"and for having my interests at heart, be lucky.
I'm certain such a secret would be silent in your keep.
But as faithful as you are, if I failed to find him
2130 and were to flee in fear in the fashion you urge,
I'd be christened a coward, and could not be excused.
So I'll trek to the chapel and take my chances,
say my piece to that person, speak with him plainly,
whether fairness or foulness follows, however fate
2135   behaves.
          He may be stout and stern
          and standing armed with stave,
          but those who strive to serve
          our Lord, our Lord will save."

2140 "By Mary," said the servant, "you seem to be saying
you're hell-bent on heaping harm on yourself
and losing your life, so I'll delay you no longer.
Set your helmet on your head and your lance in your hand
and ride a route through that rocky ravine
2145 till you're brought to the bottom of that foreboding valley,
then look towards a glade a little to the left
and you'll see in the clearing the site itself,
and the hulking person who inhabits the place.
Now God bless and good-bye, brave Sir Gawain;
2150 for all the wealth in the world I wouldn't walk with you
or go further in this forest by a single footstep."
With a wrench on the reins he reeled around
and heel-kicked the horse as hard as he could,
and was gone from Gawain, galloping hard
2155   for home.
          "By Christ, I will not cry,"
          announced the knight, "or groan,
          but find my fortune by
          the grace of God alone."

2160 Then he presses ahead, picks up a path,
enters a steep-sided grove on his steed
then goes by and by to the bottom of a gorge
where he wonders and watches—it looks a wild place:
no sign of a settlement anywhere to be seen
2165 but heady heights to both halves of the valley
and set with saber-toothed stones of such sharpness
no cloud in the sky could escape unscratched.
He stalls and halts, holds the horse still,
glances side to side to glimpse the green chapel
2170 but sees no such thing, which he thinks is strange,
except at mid-distance what might be a mound,
a sort of bald knoll on the bank of a brook
where fell water surged with frenzied force,
bursting with bubbles as if it had boiled.
2175 He heels the horse, heads for that mound,
grounds himself gracefully and tethers Gringolet,

looping the reins to the limb of a lime.
Then he strides forwards and circles the feature,
baffled as to what that bizarre hill could be:
2180   it had a hole at one end and at either side,
and its walls, matted with weeds and moss,
enclosed a cavity, like a kind of old cave
or crevice in the crag—it was all too unclear to
        declare.
2185   "Green Church?" chunters the knight.
        "More like the devil's lair
        where at the nub of night
        he dabbles in dark prayers."

"For certain," he says, "this is a soulless spot,
2190   a ghostly cathedral overgrown with grass,
the kind of kirk where that camouflaged man
might deal in devotions on the devil's behalf.
My five senses inform me that Satan himself
has tricked me in this tryst, intending to destroy me.
2195   This is a haunted house—may it go to hell.
I never came across a church so cursed."
With head helmeted and lance in hand
he scrambled towards skylight in that strange abyss.
Then he heard on the hillside, from behind a hard rock
2200   and beyond the brook, a blood-chilling noise.
What! It cannoned though the cliffs as if they might crack,
like the scream of a scythe being ground on a stone.
What! It whined and wailed, like a waterwheel.
What! It rasped and rang, raw on the ear.
2205   "My God," cried Gawain, "that grinding is a greeting.
My arrival is honored with the honing of an axe
           up there.
        Then let the Lord decide.
        'Oh well,' won't help me here.
2210   I might well lose my life
        but freak sounds hold no fear."

Then Gawain called as loudly as his lungs would allow,
"Who has power in this place to honor his pact?
Because good Gawain now walks on this ground.
2215   If anyone wants anything then hurry and appear
to do what he needs—it's now or it's never."
"Abide," came a voice from above the bank.
"You'll cop for what's coming to you quickly enough."
Yet he went at his work, whetting the blade,
2220   not showing until it was sharpened and stropped.
Then out of the crags he comes, through the cave mouth,
whirling into view with a wondrous weapon,
a Danish-style axe for dealing the dint,
with a brute of a blade curving back to the haft
2225   filed on a stone, a four footer at least
by the look of the length of its shining lace.

And again he was green, as a year ago,
with green flesh, hair and beard, and a fully green face,
and firmly on green feet he came stomping forwards,
2230 the handle of that axe like a staff in his hand.
At the edge of the water, he will not wade
but vaults the stream with the shaft, and strides
with an ominous face onto earth covered over
             with snow.
2235   Our brave knight bowed, his head
         hung low—but not too low!
         "Sweet Sir," the green man said,
         "Your visit keeps your vow."

The green knight spoke again, "God guard you, Gawain.
2240 Welcome to my world after all your wandering.
You have timed your arrival like a true traveler,
honoring the terms that entwine us together.
Twelvemonths ago at this time you took what was yours,
and with New Year come you are called to account.
2245 We're very much alone, beyond view in this valley,
no person to part us—we can do as we please.
Pull your helmet from your head and take what you're owed.
Show no more struggle than I showed myself
when you severed my head with a single smite."
2250 "No," said good Gawain, "by my life-giving God,
I won't gripe or begrudge the grimness to come,
so keep to one stroke and I'll stand stock-still,
won't whisper a word of unwillingness, or one
             complaint."
2255   He bowed to take the blade
         and bared his neck and nape,
         but, loath to look afraid,
         he feigned a fearless state.

Suddenly the green knight summons up his strength,
2260 hoists the axe high over Gawain's head,
lifts it aloft with every fiber of his life
and begins to bring home a bone-splitting blow.
Had he seen it through as thoroughly as threatened
the knight, being brave, would have died from the blow.
2265 But glimpsing the axe at the edge of his eye
bringing death earthwards as it arced through the air,
and sensing its sharpness, Gawain shrank at the shoulders.
The swinging axman swerved from his stroke,
and reproached the young prince with some proud words:
2270 "You are not Gawain," he goaded, "with his good name,
who faced down every foe in the field of battle
but now flinches with fear at the foretaste of harm.
Never could I hear of such cowardice from that knight.
Did I budge or even blink when you aimed the axe,
2275 or carp or quibble in King Arthur's castle,
or flap when my head went flying to my feet?

But entirely untouched, you are terror struck.
I'll be found the better fellow, since you were so feeble
        and frail."
2280   Gawain confessed, "I flinched
         at first, but will not fail.
         Though once my head's unhitched
         it's off once and for all!"

"So be brisk with the blow, bring on the blade.
2285 Deal me my destiny and do it out of hand,
and I'll stand the stroke without shiver or shudder
and be wasted by your weapon. You have my word."
"Take this then," said the other, throwing up the axe,
with a menacing glare like the gaze of a maniac.
2290 Then he launches his swing but leaves him unscathed,
withholds his arm before harm could be done.
And Gawain was motionless, never moved a muscle,
but stood stone-still, or as still as a tree stump
anchored in the earth by a hundred roots.
2295 Then the warrior in green mocked Gawain again:
"Now you've plucked up your courage I'll dispatch you properly.
May the honorable knighthood heaped on you by Arthur—
if it proves to be powerful—protect your neck."
That insulting slur drew a spirited response:
2300 "Thrash away then, thug, your threats are hollow.
Such huffing and fussing—you'll frighten your own heart."
"By God," said the green man, "since you speak so grandly
there'll be no more shilly-shallying, I shall shatter you,
        I vow."
2305   He stands to strike, a sneer
         comes over lip and brow.
         Gawain is gripped by fear,
         no hope of rescue now.

Hoisted and aimed, the axe hurtled downwards,
2310 the blade bearing down on the knight's bare neck,
a ferocious blow, but far from being fatal
it skewed to one side, just skimming the skin
and finely snicking the fat of the flesh
so that bright red blood shot from body to earth.
2315 Seeing it shining on the snowy ground
Gawain leapt forward a spear's length at least,
grabbed hold of his helmet and rammed it on his head,
brought his shield to his side with a shimmy of his shoulder,
then brandished his sword before blurting out brave words,
2320 because never since birth, as his mother's babe,
was he half as happy as here and now.
"Enough swiping, sir, you've swung your swing.
I've borne one blow without backing out,
go for me again and you'll get some by return,
2325 with interest! Hit out, and be hit in an instant,
        and hard.

One axe attack—that's all.
Now keep the covenant
agreed in Arthur's hall
2330 and hold the axe in hand."

The warrior steps away and leans on his weapon,
props the handle in the earth and slouches on the head
and studies how Gawain is standing his ground,
bold in his bearing, brave in his actions,
2335 armed and ready. In his heart he admires him.
Then remarking merrily, but in a mighty voice,
with reaching words he rounded on the knight:
"Be a mite less feisty, fearless young fellow,
you've suffered no insulting or heinous incident
2340 beyond the game we agreed on in the court of your king.
One strike was promised—consider yourself well paid!
From any lingering loyalties you are hereby released.
Had I mustered all my muscles into one mighty blow
I would have hit more harshly and done you great harm.
2345 But my first strike fooled you—a feint, no less—
not fracturing your flesh, which was only fair
in keeping with the contract we declared that first night,
for with truthful behavior you honored my trust
and gave up your gains as a good man should.
2350 Then I missed you once more, and this for the morning
when you kissed my pretty wife then kindly kissed me.
So twice you were truthful, therefore twice I left
   no scar.
  The person who repays
2355 will live to feel no fear.
  The third time, though, you strayed,
  and felt my blade therefore."

"Because the belt you are bound with belongs to me;
it was woven by my wife so I know it very well.
2360 And I know of your courtesies, and conduct, and kisses,
and the wooing of my wife—for it was all my work!
I sent her to test you—and in truth it turns out
you're by the far the most faultless fellow on earth.
As a pearl is more prized than a pea which is white,
2365 in good faith, so is Gawain, amongst gallant knights.
But a little thing more—it was loyalty that you lacked:
not because you're wicked, or a womanizer, or worse,
but you loved your own life; so I blame you less."
Gawain stood speechless for what seemed a great while,
2370 so shocked and ashamed that he shuddered inside.
The fire of his blood brought flames to his face
and he shrank out of shame at what the other had said.
Then he tried to talk, and finding his tongue, said:
"A curse upon cowardice and covetousness.
2375 They breed villainy and vice, and destroy all virtue."
Then he grabbed the girdle and ungathered its knot
and flung it in fury at the man before him.
"My downfall and undoing; let the devil take it.

Dread of the death blow and cowardly doubts
2380 meant I gave in to greed, and in doing so forgot
the freedom and fidelity every knight knows to follow.
And now I am found to be flawed and false,
through treachery and untruth I have totally failed," said
Gawain.
2385 "Such terrible mistakes,
and I shall bear the blame.
But tell me what it takes
to clear my clouded name."

The green lord laughed, and leniently replied:
2390 "The harm which you caused me is wholly healed.
By confessing your failings you are free from fault
and have openly paid penance at the point of my axe.
I declare you purged, as polished and as pure
as the day you were born, without blemish or blame.
2395 And this gold-hemmed girdle I present as a gift,
which is green like my gown. It's yours, Sir Gawain,
a reminder of our meeting when you mix and mingle
with princes and kings. And this keepsake will be proof
to all chivalrous knights of your challenge in this chapel.
2400 But follow me home. New Year's far from finished—
we'll resume our reveling with supper and song.
What's more
my wife is waiting there
who flummoxed you before.
2405 This time you'll have in her
a friend and not a foe."

"Thank you," said the other, taking helmet from head,
holding it in hand as he offered his thanks.
"But I've loitered long enough. The Lord bless your life
2410 and bestow on you such honor as you surely deserve.
And mind you commend me to your fair wife,
both to her and the other, those honorable ladies
who kidded me so cleverly with their cunning tricks.
But no wonder if a fool finds his way into folly
2415 and be wiped of his wits by womanly guile—
it's the way of the world. Adam fell because of a woman,
and Solomon because of several, and as for Samson,
Delilah was his downfall, and afterwards David
was bamboozled by Bathsheba and bore the grief.[2]
2420 All wrecked and ruined by their wrongs; if only
we could love our ladies without believing their lies.
And those were foremost of all whom fortune favored,
excellent beyond all others existing under heaven,"
he cried.
2425 "Yet all were charmed and changed
by wily womankind.

---

2. Lines 2146–49 single out well-known male figures from the Hebrew Scriptures whom Gawain reads
as having fallen on account of female deception. The relevant references are as follows: for Adam,
Genesis 3:6; Solomon, 1 Kings 11:3; Samson, Judges 16:4–18; and David, 2 Samuel 11:1–15.

I suffered just the same,
but clear me of my crime."

"But the girdle," he went on, "God bless you for this gift.
2430 And I shall wear it with good will, but not for its gold,
nor its silks and streamers, and not for the sake
of its wonderful workmanship or even its worth,
but as a sign of my sin—I'll see it as such
when I swagger in the saddle—a sad reminder
2435 that the frailty of his flesh is man's biggest fault,
how the touch of filth taints his tender frame.
So when praise for my prowess in arms swells my pride,
one look at this love-lace will lessen my ardor.
But I will ask one thing, if it won't offend:
2440 since I stayed so long in your lordship's land
and was hosted in your house—let Him reward you
who upholds the heavens and sits upon high—
will you make known your name? And I'll ask nothing else."
"Then I'll treat you to the truth," the other told him,
2445 "Here in my homelands they call me Bertilak de Hautdesert.
And in my manor lives the mighty Morgan le Fay,
so adept and adroit in the dark arts,
who learned magic from Merlin—the master of mystery—
for in earlier times she was intimately entwined
2450 with that knowledgeable man, as all you knights know
        back home.
            Yes, 'Morgan the Goddess'—
            I will announce her name.
            There is no nobleness
2455   she cannot take and tame."

"She guided me in this guise to your great hall
to put pride on trial, and to test with this trick
what distinction and trust the Round Table deserves.
She imagined this mischief would muddle your minds
2460 and that grieving Guinevere would go to her grave
at the sight of a specter making ghostly speeches
with his head in his hands before the high table.
So that ancient woman who inhabits my home
is also your aunt—Arthur's half sister,
2465 the daughter of the duchess of Tintagel; the duchess
who through Uther, was mother to Arthur, your king.
So I ask you again, come and greet your aunt
and make merry in my house; you're much loved there,
and, by my faith, I am as fond of you my friend
2470 as any man under God, for your great truth."
But Gawain would not. No way would he go.
So they clasped and kissed and made kind commendations
to the Prince of Paradise, and then parted in the cold,
        that pair.
2475   Our man, back on his mount
            now hurtles home from there.

The green knight leaves his ground
to wander who-knows-where.

So he winds through the wilds of the world once more,
2480   Gawain on Gringolet, by the grace of God,
under a roof sometimes and sometimes roughing it,
and in valleys and vales had adventures and victories
but time is too tight to tell how they went.
The nick to his neck was healed by now;
2485   thereabouts he had bound the belt like a baldric—
slantwise, as a sash, from shoulder to side,
laced in a knot looped below his left arm,
as a sign that his honor was stained by sin.
So safe and sound he sets foot in court,
2490   and great joy came to the king in his castle
when tidings of Gawain's return had been told.
The king kissed his knight and so did the queen,
and Gawain was embraced by his band of brothers,
who made eager enquiries, and he answered them all
2495   with the tale of his trial and tribulations,
and the challenge at the chapel, and the great green chap,
and the love of the lady, which led to the belt.
And he showed them the scar at the side of his neck,
confirming his breach of faith, like a badge
2500   of blame.
    He grimaced with disgrace,
    he writhed in rage and pain.
    Blood flowed towards his face
    and showed his smarting shame.

2505   "Regard," said Gawain, as he held up the girdle,
"the symbol of sin, for which my neck bears the scar;
a sign of my fault and offence and failure,
of the cowardice and covetousness I came to commit.
I was tainted by untruth. This, its token,
2510   I will drape across my chest till the day I die.
For man's crimes can be covered but never made clean;
once sin is entwined it is attached for all time."
The king gave comfort, then the whole of the court
allow, as they laugh in lovely accord,
2515   that the lords and ladies who belong to the Table,
every knight in the brotherhood, should bear such a belt,
a bright green belt worn obliquely to the body,
crosswise, like a sash, for the sake of this man.
So that slanting green stripe was adopted as their sign,
2520   and each knight who held it was honored ever after,
as all the best books on romance remind us:
an adventure which happened in Arthur's era,
as the chronicles of this country have stated clearly.
Since fearless Brutus first set foot
2525   on these shores, once the siege land assault at Troy
           had ceased,

our coffers have been crammed
with stories such as these.
Now let our Lord, thorn-crowned,
2530   bring us to perfect peace. AMEN.

HONY SOYT QUI MAL PENCE[3]

3. "Shame be to the man who has evil in his mind" (Anglo-Norman French). This is practically identical to the motto of the Order of the Garter ("Honi soit qui mal y pense"). The order was founded ca. 1350; apparently a copyist of the poem associated this order with the one founded to honor Gawain.

GEOFFREY CHAUCER
ca. 1340–1400

Medieval social theory held that society was made up of three "estates": the nobility, composed of a small hereditary aristocracy, whose mission on earth was to rule over and defend the body politic; the church, whose duty was to look after the spiritual welfare of that body; and everyone else, the large mass of commoners who were supposed to do the work that provided for its physical needs. By the late fourteenth century, however, these basic categories were layered into complex, interrelated, and unstable social strata among which birth, wealth, profession, and personal ability all played a part in determining one's status in a world that was rapidly changing—economically, politically, and socially. Chaucer's life and his works, especially *The Canterbury Tales*, were profoundly influenced by these forces. A growing and prosperous middle class was beginning to play increasingly important roles in church and state, blurring the traditional class boundaries, and it was into this middle class that Geoffrey Chaucer was born.

Chaucer was the son of a prosperous wine merchant and probably spent his boyhood in the mercantile atmosphere of London's Vintry, where ships docked with wines from France and Spain. Here he would have mixed daily with people of all sorts, heard several languages spoken, become fluent in French, and received schooling in Latin. Instead of apprenticing Chaucer to the family business, however, his father was apparently able to place him, in his early teens, as a page in one of the great aristocratic households of England, that of the countess of Ulster, who was married to Prince Lionel, the second son of Edward III. There Chaucer would have acquired the manners and skills required for a career in the service of the ruling class, not only in the role of personal attendant in royal households but in a series of administrative posts. (For Chaucer's portrait, see the color insert in this volume.)

We can trace Chaucer's official and personal life in a considerable number of surviving historical documents, beginning with a reference, in Elizabeth of Ulster's household accounts, to an outfit he received as a page (1357). He was captured by the French and ransomed in one of Edward III's campaigns during the Hundred Years War (1359). He was a member of King Edward's personal household (1367) and took part in several diplomatic missions to Spain (1366), France (1368), and Italy (1372). As controller of customs on wool, sheepskins, and leather for the port of London (1374–85), Chaucer audited and kept books on the export taxes, which were one of the Crown's main sources of revenue. During this period he was living in a rent-free apartment over one of the gates in the city wall, probably as a perquisite of the customs job. He served as a justice of the peace and knight of the shire (the title given to members of Parliament) for the county of Kent (1385–86) where he moved after giving up the controllership. As clerk of the king's works (1389–91), Chaucer was responsible for the maintenance of numerous royal residences, parks, and other holdings; his duties included supervision of the construction of the nave of Westminster Abbey and of stands and lists for a celebrated tournament staged by Richard II. While the records show Chaucer receiving many grants and annuities in addition to his salary for these services, they also show that at times he was being pressed by creditors and obliged to borrow money.

These activities brought Chaucer into association with the ruling nobility of the kingdom, with Prince Lionel and his younger brother John of Gaunt, duke of Lancaster, England's most powerful baron during much of Chaucer's lifetime; with

Middle-class Prosperity. Jan van Eyck, *The Arnolfini Portrait*, 1434. Note the way the religious elements of the scene are secondary to the fine, rich qualities of fabric represented here.

their father, King Edward; and with Edward's grandson, who succeeded to the throne as Richard II. Near the end of his life, Chaucer addressed a comic *Complaint to His Purse* to Henry IV—John of Gaunt's son, who had usurped the crown from his cousin Richard—as a reminder that the treasury owed Chaucer his annuity. Chaucer's wife, Philippa, served in the households of Edward's queen and of John of Gaunt's second wife, Constance, daughter of the king of Castile. A Thomas Chaucer, who was probably Chaucer's son, was an eminent man in the next generation, and Thomas's daughter Alice was married successively to the earl of Salisbury and the duke of Suffolk. The gap between the commoners and the aristocracy would thus have been bridged by Chaucer's family in the course of three generations.

None of these documents contains any hint that this hardworking civil servant wrote poetry, although poetry would certainly have been among the diversions cultivated at English courts in Chaucer's youth. That poetry, however, would have been in French, which still remained the fashionable language and literature of the English aristocracy, whose culture in many ways had more in common with that of the French nobles with whom they warred than with that of their English subjects. Chaucer's earliest models, works by Guillaume de Machaut (1300?–1377) and Jean Froissart (1333?–1400?), the leading French poets of the day, were lyrics and narratives about courtly love, often cast in the form of a dream in which the poet acted as a protagonist or participant in some aristocratic love affair. The poetry of Machaut and Froissart derives from the thirteenth-century *Romance of the Rose*, a long dream allegory in which the dreamer suffers many agonies and trials for the love of a symbolic rosebud. Chaucer's apprentice work may well have been a partial translation of the twenty-one-thousand-line *Romance*. His first important original poem is *The Book of the Duchess*, an elegy in the form of a dream vision commemorating John of Gaunt's first wife, the young duchess of Lancaster, who died in 1368.

The diplomatic mission that sent Chaucer to Italy in 1372 was in all likelihood a milestone in his literary development. Although he may have acquired some knowledge of the language and literature from Italian merchants and bankers posted in London, this visit and a subsequent one to Florence (1378) brought him into direct contact with the Italian Renaissance. He likely acquired manuscripts of works by Dante, Petrarch, and Boccaccio—the last two still alive at the time of Chaucer's visit, although he probably did not meet them. These writers provided him with models of new verse forms, new subject matter, and new modes of representation. *The House of Fame*, still a dream vision, takes the poet on a journey in the talons of a gigantic eagle to the celestial palace of the goddess Fame, a trip that at many points affectionately parodies Dante's journey in the *Divine Comedy*. In his dream vision *The Parliament of Fowls* (pp. 504–22), all the birds meet on St. Valentine's Day to choose their mates; their "parliament" humorously depicts the ways in which different classes in human society think and talk about love. Boccaccio provided sources for two of Chaucer's finest poems—although Chaucer never mentions his name. *The Knight's Tale*, the first of *The Canterbury Tales*, is based on Boccaccio's romance *Il Teseida* (The Story of Theseus). His longest completed poem, *Troilus and Criseyde* (ca. 1385), which tells the story of how Trojan Prince Troilus loved and finally lost Criseyde to the Greek warrior Diomede, is an adaptation of Boccaccio's *Il Filostrato* (The Love-Stricken). Chaucer reworked the latter into one of the greatest love poems in any language. Even if he had never written *The Canterbury Tales*, *Troilus* would have secured Chaucer a place among the major English poets.

A final dream vision provides the frame for Chaucer's first experiment with a series of tales, the unfinished *Legend of Good Women*. In the dream, Chaucer is accused of heresy and antifeminism by Cupid, the god of love himself, and ordered to do penance by writing a series of "legends"—that is, saints' lives, of Cupid's martyrs, women who were betrayed by false men and died for love. Perhaps a noble patron, possibly Queen Anne, asked the poet to write something to make up for telling about Criseyde's betrayal of Troilus.

Throughout his life Chaucer also wrote moral and religious works, chiefly translations. Besides French, which was a second language for him, and Italian, Chaucer also read Latin. He made a prose translation of the Latin *Consolation of Philosophy*, written by the sixth-century Roman statesman Boethius while in prison awaiting execution for crimes for which he had been unjustly condemned. The *Consolation* became a favorite book for the Middle Ages, providing inspiration and comfort through its lesson that worldly fortune is deceitful and ephemeral and through the platonic doctrine that the body itself is only a prison house for the soul that aspires to eternal things. The influence of Boethius is deeply ingrained in both *The Knight's Tale* and *Troilus*. The ballade *Truth* compresses the Boethian and Christian teaching into three stanzas of homely moral advice.

Thus long before Chaucer conceived of *The Canterbury Tales*, his writings were many-faceted: they embrace prose and poetry; human and divine love; French, Italian, and Latin sources; secular and religious influences; comedy and philosophy. Moreover, different elements are likely to mix in the same work, often making it difficult to extract from Chaucer simple, direct, and certain meanings.

This Chaucerian complexity owes much to the wide range of Chaucer's learning and his exposure to new literary currents on the Continent but perhaps also to the special social position he occupied as a member of a new class of civil servants. Born into the urban middle class, Chaucer, through his association with the court and service of the Crown, had attained the rank of "esquire," roughly equivalent to what would later be termed a "gentleman." His career brought him into contact with overlapping bourgeois and aristocratic social worlds, without his being securely anchored in either. Although he was born a commoner and continued to associate with commoners in his official life, he did not live as a commoner; and although his training and service at court, his wife's connections, and probably his poetry brought him into contact with the nobility, he must always have been conscious of the fact that he did not really belong to that society of which birth alone could make one a true member. Situated at the intersection of these social worlds, Chaucer had the gift of being able to view with both sympathy and humor the behaviors, beliefs, and pretensions of the diverse people who comprised the levels of society. Chaucer's art of being at once involved in and detached from a given situation is peculiarly his own, but that art would have been appreciated by a small group of friends close to Chaucer's social position—men like Sir Philip de la Vache, to whom Chaucer addressed the humorous envoy to *Truth*. Chaucer belongs to an age when poetry was read aloud. A beautiful frontispiece to a manuscript of *Troilus* pictures the poet's public performance before a magnificently dressed royal audience, and he may well have been invited at times to read his poems at court. But besides addressing a listening audience, to whose allegedly superior taste and sensibility the poet often ironically defers (for example, *The General Prologue*, lines 745–48), Chaucer has in mind discriminating readers whom he might expect to share his sense of humor and his complex attitudes toward the company of "sondry folk" who make the pilgrimage to Canterbury.

The text given here is from E. T. Donaldson's *Chaucer's Poetry: An Anthology for the Modern Reader* (1958, 1975) with some modifications. For *The Canterbury Tales* the Hengwrt Manuscript has provided the textual basis. The spelling has been altered to improve consistency and has been modernized in so far as is possible without distorting the phonological values of the Middle English. A discussion of Middle English pronunciation, grammar, and prosody is included in the introduction to "The Middle Ages" (pp. 20–26).

The Canterbury Tales

Chaucer's original plan for *The Canterbury Tales*— if we assume it to be the same as that which the fictional Host proposes at the end of *The General Prologue*—projected about one hundred twenty stories, two for each pilgrim to tell on the way to Canterbury and two more on the way back. Chaucer actually completed only twenty-two and the beginnings of two others. He did write an ending, for the Host says to the Parson, who tells the last tale, that everyone except him has told "his tale." Indeed, the pilgrims never even get to Canterbury. The work was probably first conceived in 1386, when Chaucer was living in Greenwich, some miles east of London. From his house he might have been able to see the pilgrim road that led toward the shrine of the famous English saint, Thomas à Becket, the archbishop of Canterbury who was murdered in his cathedral in 1170. Medieval pilgrims were notorious tale tellers, and the sight and sound of the bands riding toward Canterbury may well have suggested to Chaucer the idea of using a fictitious pilgrimage as a framing device for a number of stories. Collections of stories linked by such a device were common in the later Middle Ages. Chaucer's contemporary John Gower had used one in his *Lover's Confession* (see p. 366). The most famous medieval framing tale besides Chaucer's is Boccaccio's *Decameron*, in which ten different narrators each tell a tale a day for ten days. Chaucer could have known the *Decameron*, which contains tales with plots analogous to plots found also in *The Canterbury Tales*, but these stories were widespread, and there is no proof that Chaucer got them from Boccaccio.

Chaucer's artistic exploitation of the device is, in any case, altogether his own. Whereas in Gower a single speaker relates all the stories, and in Boccaccio the ten speakers—three young gentlemen and seven young ladies—all belong to the same sophisticated social elite, Chaucer's pilgrim narrators represent a wide spectrum of ranks and occupations. This device, however, should not be mistaken for "realism." It is highly unlikely that a group like Chaucer's pilgrims would ever have joined together and communicated on such seemingly equal terms. That is part of the fiction, as is the tacit assumption that a group so large could have ridden along listening to one another tell tales in verse. The variety of tellers is matched by the diversity of their tales: tales are assigned to appropriate narrators and juxtaposed to bring out contrasts in genre, style, tone, and values. Thus the Knight's courtly romance about the rivalry of two noble lovers for a lady is followed by the Miller's fabliau of the seduction of an old carpenter's young wife by a student. In several of *The Canterbury Tales* there is a fascinating accord between the narrators and their stories, so that the story takes on rich overtones from what we have learned of its teller in *The General Prologue* and elsewhere, and the teller's character itself grows and is revealed by the story. Chaucer conducts two fictions simultaneously—that of the individual tale and that of the pilgrim to whom he has assigned it. He develops the second fiction not only through *The General Prologue* but also through the "links," the interchanges among pilgrims connecting the stories. These interchanges sometimes lead to quarrels. Thus *The Miller's Tale* offends the Reeve, who takes the figure of the Miller's foolish, cuckolded carpenter as directed personally at himself, and he retaliates with a story satirizing an arrogant miller very much like the pilgrim Miller. The antagonism of the two tellers provides comedy in the links and enhances the comedy of their tales. The links also offer interesting literary commentary on the tales by members of the pilgrim audience, especially the Host, whom the pilgrims have declared "governour" and "juge" of the storytelling. Further dramatic interest is created by the fact that several tales respond to topics taken up by previous tellers. The Wife of Bath's thesis that women should have sovereignty over men in marriage gets a reply from the Clerk, which in turn elicits responses from the Merchant and the Franklin. The tales have their own logic and interest quite apart from the framing fiction; no other medieval framing fiction, however, has such varied and lively interaction between the frame and the individual stories.

The composition of none of the tales can be accurately dated; most of them were written during the last fourteen years of Chaucer's life, although a few were probably written earlier and inserted into *The Canterbury Tales*. The popularity of the poem in late medieval England is attested by the number of surviving manuscripts: more than eighty, none from Chaucer's lifetime. It was also twice printed by William Caxton, who introduced printing to England in 1476, and often reprinted by Caxton's early successors. The manuscripts reflect the unfinished state of the poem—the fact that when he died Chaucer had not made up his mind about a number of details and hence left many inconsistencies. The poem appears in the manuscripts as nine or ten "fragments" or blocks of tales; the order of the poems within each fragment is generally the same, but the order of the fragments themselves varies widely. The fragment containing *The General Prologue*; the Knight's, Miller's, and Reeve's tales; and the Cook's unfinished tale, always comes first; and the fragment consisting of *The Parson's Tale* and *The Retraction* always comes last. But the others, such as that containing the Wife of Bath's, the Friar's, and the Summoner's tales or that consisting of the Physician's and Pardoner's tales or the longest fragment, consisting of six tales concluding with the Nun's Priest's tale, are by no means stable in relation to one another. The order followed here, that of the Ellesmere manuscript, has been adopted as the most nearly satisfactory.

THE GENERAL PROLOGUE

Chaucer did not need to make a pilgrimage himself to meet the types of people that his fictitious pilgrimage includes, because most of them had long inhabited literature as well as life: the ideal Knight, who had taken part in all the major expeditions and battles of the crusades during the last half-century; his fashionably dressed son, the Squire, a typical young lover; the lady Prioress, the hunting Monk, and the flattering Friar, who practice the little vanities and larger vices for which such ecclesiastics were conventionally attacked; the prosperous Franklin; the fraudulent Doctor; the lusty and domineering Wife of Bath; the austere Parson; and so on down through the lower orders to that spellbinding preacher and mercenary, the Pardoner, peddling his paper indulgences and phony relics. One meets all these types throughout medieval literature, but particularly in a genre called estates satire, which sets out to expose and pillory typical examples of corruption at all levels of society. (For more information on estates satire, see "Medieval Estates and Orders" in the NAEL Archive.) A remarkable number of details in *The General Prologue* could have been taken straight out of books as well as drawn from life. Although it has been argued that some of the pilgrims are portraits of actual people, the impression that they are drawn from life is more likely to be a function of Chaucer's art, which is able to endow types with a reality we generally associate only with people we know. The salient features of each pilgrim leap out randomly at the reader, as they might to an observer concerned only with what meets the eye. This imitation of the way our minds actually perceive reality may make us fail to notice the care with which Chaucer has selected his details to give an integrated sketch of the person being described. Most of these details give something more than mere verisimilitude to the description. The pilgrims' facial features, the clothes they wear, the foods they like to eat, the things they say, and the work they do are all clues not only to their social rank but to their moral and spiritual condition and, through the accumulation of detail, to the condition of late-medieval society, of which, collectively, they are representative. What uniquely distinguishes Chaucer's prologue from more conventional estates satire, such as the *Prologue* to *Piers Plowman*, is the suppression in all but a few flagrant instances of overt moral judgment. The narrator, in fact, seems to be expressing chiefly admiration and praise at the superlative skills and accomplishments of this particular group, even such dubious ones as the Friar's begging techniques or the Manciple's success in cheating the learned lawyers who employ him. The reader is left free to draw out the ironic implications of details presented with such seeming artlessness, even while falling in with the easygoing mood of "felaweship" that pervades Chaucer's prologue to the pilgrimage.

FROM THE CANTERBURY TALES

The General Prologue

Whan that April with his° showres soote°		*its / fresh*
The droughte of March hath perced to the roote,		
And bathed every veine[1] in swich° licour,°		*such / liquid*
Of which vertu[2] engendred is the flowr;		
5 Whan Zephyrus eek° with his sweete breeth		*also*
Inspired[3] hath in every holt° and heeth°		*grove / field*
The tendre croppes,° and the yonge sonne[4]		*shoots*
Hath in the Ram his halve cours yronne,		
And smale fowles° maken melodye		*birds*
10 That sleepen al the night with open yë°—		*eye*
So priketh hem° Nature in hir corages[5]—		*them*
Thanne longen folk to goon° on pilgrimages,		*go*
And palmeres for to seeken straunge strondes		
To ferne halwes,[6] couthe° in sondry° londes;		*known / various*

---

1. I.e., in plants.
2. By the power of which.
3. Breathed into. "Zephyrus": the west wind.
4. The sun is young because it has run only half-way through its course in Aries, the Ram—the first sign of the zodiac in the solar year.

5. Their hearts.
6. Far-off shrines. "Palmeres": palmers, wide-ranging pilgrims—especially those who sought out the "straunge strondes" (foreign shores) of the Holy Land.

15 And specially from every shires ende
    Of Engelond to Canterbury they wende,
    The holy blisful martyr⁷ for to seeke
    That hem hath holpen° whan that they were seke.°   *helped / sick*
        Bifel° that in that seson on a day,   *It happened*
20 In Southwerk⁸ at the Tabard as I lay,
    Redy to wenden on my pilgrimage
    To Canterbury with ful° devout corage,   *very*
    At night was come into that hostelrye
    Wel nine and twenty in a compaignye
25 Of sondry folk, by aventure° yfalle   *chance*
    In felaweshipe, and pilgrimes were they alle
    That toward Canterbury wolden° ride.   *would*
    The chambres and the stables weren wide,
    And wel we weren esed° at the beste.⁹   *accommodated*
30 And shortly,° whan the sonne was to reste,¹   *in brief*
    So hadde I spoken with hem everichoon°   *every one*
    That I was of hir felaweshipe anoon,°   *at once*
    And made forward² erly for to rise,
    To take oure way ther as³ I you devise.°   *describe*
35   But nathelees,° whil I have time and space,⁴   *nevertheless*
    Er° that I ferther in this tale pace,°   *before / proceed*
    Me thinketh it accordant to resoun⁵
    To telle you al the condicioun
    Of eech of hem, so as it seemed me,
40 And whiche they were, and of what degree,°   *social rank*
    And eek° in what array that they were inne: *also*
    And at a knight thanne° wol I first biginne.   *then*
        A Knight ther was, and that a worthy man,
    That fro the time that he first bigan
45 To riden out, he loved chivalrye,
    Trouthe and honour, freedom and curteisye.⁶
    Ful worthy was he in his lordes werre,°   *war*
    And therto hadde he riden, no man ferre,°   *farther*
    As wel in Cristendom as hethenesse,⁷
50 And⁸ evere honoured for his worthinesse.
        At Alisandre⁹ he was whan it was wonne;

7. St. Thomas à Becket, murdered in Canterbury Cathedral in 1170.
8. Southwark, site of the Tabard Inn, was then a suburb of London, south of the Thames River.
9. In the best possible way.
1. Had set.
2. I.e., (we) made an agreement.
3. Where.
4. I.e., opportunity.
5. It seems to me according to reason.
6. Courtesy. "Trouthe": integrity. "Freedom": generosity of spirit.
7. Heathen lands. "Cristendom" here designates specifically only crusades waged by the nations of Roman Catholic Western Europe in lands under other dispensations, primarily Arabic, Turkish, and Moorish Islam but also, as indicated in the list of the Knight's campaigns given below, the Christian Eastern Orthodox Church. Conspicu-

ous by absence is any reference to major battles in the Hundred Years War, fought between French and English Catholics. For excerpts from Christian, Jewish, and Arabic texts on the First Crusade, see the NAEL Archive.
8. I.e., and he was.
9. The capture of Alexandria in Egypt (1365) was considered a famous victory, although the Crusaders abandoned the city after a week of looting. Below: "Pruce" (Prussia), "Lettow" (Lithuania), and "Ruce" (Russia) refer to campaigns by the Teutonic Order of Knights on the shores of the Baltic Sea in northern Europe against the Eastern Orthodox Church, "Algezir" (Algeciras), and "Belmarye" (Belmarin), to southern Spain and Morocco; "Lyeis" (Ayash), seaport near Antioch, modern Syria), "Satalye," "Palatye" (Antalya and Balat, modern Turkey), "Tramissene" (Tlemcen, modern Algeria).

Ful ofte time he hadde the boord bigonne[1]
Aboven alle nacions in Pruce;
In Lettou had he reised,° and in Ruce,   *campaigned*
55 No Cristen man so ofte of his degree;
In Gernade° at the sege eek hadde he be   *Granada*
Of Algezir, and riden in Belmarye;
At Lyeis was he, and at Satalye,
Whan they were wonne; and in the Grete See°   *Mediterranean*
60 At many a noble arivee° hadde he be.   *military landing*
    At mortal batailes[2] hadde he been fifteene,
And foughten for oure faith at Tramissene
In listes[3] thries,° and ay° slain his fo.   *thrice / always*
    This ilke° worthy Knight hadde been also   *same*
65 Sometime with the lord of Palatye[4]
Again° another hethen in Turkye;   *against*
And everemore he hadde a soverein pris.°   *reputation*
And though that he were worthy, he was wis,[5]
And of his port° as meeke as is a maide.   *demeanor*
70 He nevere yit no vilainye° ne saide   *rudeness*
In al his lif unto no manere wight:[6]
He was a verray,° parfit,° gentil° knight.   *true / perfect / noble*
But for to tellen you of his array,
His hors° were goode, but he was nat gay.[7]   *horses*
75 Of fustian° he wered° a gipoun[8]   *thick cloth / wore*
Al bismotered with his haubergeoun,[9]
For he was late° come from his viage,°   *lately / expedition*
And wente for to doon his pilgrimage.
    With him ther was his sone, a yong Squier,[1]
80 A lovere and a lusty bacheler,
With lokkes crulle° as° they were laid in presse.   *curly / as if*
Of twenty yeer of age he was, I gesse.
Of his stature he was of evene° lengthe,   *moderate*
And wonderly delivere,° and of greet° strengthe.   *agile / great*
85 And he hadde been som time in chivachye[2]
In Flandres, in Artois, and Picardye,
And born him wel as of so litel space,[3]
In hope to stonden in his lady° grace.   *lady's*
    Embrouded° was he as it were a mede,[4]   *embroidered*
90 Al ful of fresshe flowres, white and rede;°   *red*
Singing he was, or floiting,° al the day: *whistling*
He was as fressh as is the month of May.
Short was his gowne, with sleeves longe and wide.
Wel coude he sitte on hors, and faire ride;

1. Sat in the seat of honor at military feasts.
2. Tournaments fought to the death.
3. Lists, tournament grounds.
4. A Muslim: alliances of convenience were often made during the Crusades between Christians and Muslims.
5. I.e., he was wise as well as bold.
6. Any sort of person. In Middle English, negatives are multiplied for emphasis, as in these two lines: "nevere," "no," "ne," "no."
7. I.e., gaily dressed.

8. Tunic worn underneath the coat of mail.
9. All rust-stained from his hauberk (coat of mail).
1. The vague term "Squier" (Squire) here seems to be the equivalent of "bacheler" (line 80), a young knight still in the service of an older one.
2. On cavalry expeditions. The places in the next line are sites of skirmishes in the constant warfare between the English and the French.
3. I.e., considering the little time he had been in service.
4. Mead, meadow.

95   He coude songes make, and wel endite,°   *compose verse*
      Juste[5] and eek° daunce, and wel portraye° and write.   *also / sketch*
      So hote° he loved that by nightertale[6]   *hotly*
      He slepte namore than dooth a nightingale.
      Curteis he was, lowely,° and servisable,   *humble*
100   And carf biforn his fader at the table.[7]
          A Yeman hadde he[8] and servants namo°   *no more*
      At that time, for him liste[9] ride so;
      And he[1] was clad in cote and hood of greene.
      A sheef of pecok arwes,° bright and keene,   *arrows*
105   Under his belt he bar° ful thriftily;°   *bore / properly*
      Wel coude he dresse° his takel° yemanly:[2]   *tend to / gear*
      His arwes drouped nought with fetheres lowe.
      And in his hand he bar a mighty bowe.
      A not-heed° hadde he with a brown visage.   *close-cut head*
110   Of wodecraft wel coude° he al the usage.   *knew*
      Upon his arm he bar a gay bracer,[3]
      And by his side a swerd° and a bokeler,[4]   *sword*
      And on that other side a gay daggere,
      Harneised° wel and sharp as point of spere;   *mounted*
115   A Cristophre[5] on his brest of silver sheene;°   *bright*
      An horn he bar, the baudrik[6] was of greene.
      A forster° was he soothly,° as I gesse.   *forester / truly*
          Ther was also a Nonne, a Prioresse,
      That of hir smiling was ful simple and coy.[7]
120   Hir gretteste ooth was but by sainte Loy!°   *Eloi*
      And she was cleped° Madame Eglantine.   *named*
      Ful wel she soong° the service divine,   *sang*
      Entuned° in hir nose ful semely;[8]   *chanted*
      And Frenssh she spak ful faire and fetisly,°   *elegantly*
125   After the scole° of Stratford at the Bowe[9]—   *school*
      For Frenssh of Paris was to hire unknowe.
      At mete° wel ytaught was she withalle:°   *meals / besides*
      She leet° no morsel from hir lippes falle,   *let*
      Ne wette hir fingres in hir sauce deepe;
130   Wel coude she carye a morsel, and wel keepe°   *take care*
      That no drope ne fille° upon hir brest.   *should fall*
      In curteisye was set ful muchel hir lest.[1]
      Hir over-lippe° wiped she so clene   *upper lip*
      That in hir coppe° ther was no ferthing° seene   *cup / bit*
135   Of grece,° whan she dronken hadde hir draughte;   *grease*
      Ful semely after hir mete she raughte.°   *reached*
      And sikerly° she was of greet disport,[2]   *certainly*

---

5. Joust, fight in a tournament.
6. At night.
7. It was a squire's duty to carve his lord's meat.
8. I.e., the Knight. The "Yeman" (Yeoman) is an independent commoner who acts as the Knight's military servant.
9. It pleased him to.
1. I.e., the Yeoman.
2. In a workmanlike way.
3. Wrist guard for archers.
4. Buckler (a small shield).

5. St. Christopher medal.
6. Baldric (a supporting strap).
7. Sincere and shy. The Prioress is the mother superior of her nunnery.
8. In a seemly, proper manner.
9. The French she learned in a convent school in Stratford-at-the-Bow, a suburb of London, was evidently not up to the Parisian standard.
1. I.e., her chief delight lay in good manners.
2. Of great good cheer.

And ful plesant, and amiable of port,°   *mien*
And pained hire to countrefete cheere[3]
140 Of court, and to been statlich° of manere,   *dignified*
And to been holden digne[4] of reverence.
But, for to speken of hir conscience,
She was so charitable and so pitous°   *merciful*
She wolde weepe if that she saw a mous
145 Caught in a trappe, if it were deed° or bledde.   *dead*
Of[5] smale houndes hadde she that she fedde
With rosted flessh, or milk and wastelbreed;°   *fine white bread*
But sore wepte she if oon of hem were deed,
Or if men smoot it with a yerde smerte;[6]
150 And al was conscience and tendre herte.
Ful semely hir wimpel° pinched° was,   *headdress / pleated*
Hir nose tretis,° hir yën° greye as glas,   *well-formed / eyes*
Hir mouth ful smal, and therto° softe and reed,° *moreover / red*
But sikerly° she hadde a fair forheed: *certainly*
155 It was almost a spanne brood,[7] I trowe,°   *believe*
For hardily,° she was nat undergrowe.   *assuredly*
Ful fetis° was hir cloke, as I was war;°   *becoming / aware*
Of smal° coral aboute hir arm she bar   *dainty*
A paire of bedes, gauded all with greene,[8]
160 And theron heeng° a brooch of gold ful sheene,° *hung / bright*
On which ther was first writen a crowned A,[9]
And after, *Amor vincit omnia.*[1]
   Another Nonne with hire hadde she
That was hir chapelaine,° and preestes three.[2]   *secretary*
165   A Monk ther was, a fair for the maistrye,[3]
An outridere[4] that loved venerye,°   *hunting*
A manly man, to been an abbot able.°   *worthy*
Ful many a daintee° hors hadde he in stable,   *fine*
And whan he rood,° men mighte his bridel heere *rode*
170 Ginglen° in a whistling wind as clere   *jingle*
And eek° as loude as dooth the chapel belle   *also*
Ther as this lord was kepere of the celle.[5]
The rule of Saint Maure or of Saint Beneit,
By cause that it was old and somdeel strait[6]—
175 This ilke° Monk leet olde thinges pace,°   *same / pass away*
And heeld° after the newe world the space.°   *held / course*
He yaf° nought of that text a pulled hen[7]   *gave*
That saith that hunteres been° nought holy men,   *are*
Ne that a monk, whan he is recchelees,[8]
180 Is likned til° a fissh that is waterlees—   *to*
This is to sayn, a monk out of his cloistre;

---

3. And took pains to imitate the behavior.
4. And to be considered worthy.
5. I.e., some.
6. If someone struck it with a rod sharply.
7. A handsbreadth wide.
8. Provided with green beads to mark certain prayers. "A paire": string (i.e., a rosary).
9. An A with an ornamental crown on it.
1. "Love conquers all" (Latin).
2. The three get reduced to just one nun's priest.

3. I.e., a superlatively fine one.
4. A monk charged with supervising property distant from the monastery. Monasteries obtained income from large landholdings.
5. Prior of an outlying cell (branch) of the monastery.
6. Somewhat strict. St. Maurus and St. Benedict were authors of monastic rules.
7. He didn't give a plucked hen for that text.
8. Reckless, careless of rule.

But thilke° text heeld he nat worth an oystre.　　　　*that same*
And I saide his opinion was good:
What° sholde he studye and make himselven wood°　　*why / crazy*
185　Upon a book in cloistre alway to poure,°　　　　*pore*
Or swinke° with his handes and laboure,　　　　*work*
As Austin bit?[9] How shal the world be served?
Lat Austin have his swink to him reserved!
Therefore he was a prikasour° aright.　　　　*hard rider*
190　Grehoundes he hadde as swift as fowl in flight.
Of priking° and of hunting for the hare　　　　*riding*
Was al his lust,° for no cost wolde he spare.　　　　*pleasure*
I sawgh his sleeves purfiled° at the hand　　　　*fur lined*
With gris,° and that the fineste of a land;　　　　*gray fur*
195　And for to festne his hood under his chin
He hadde of gold wrought a ful curious[1] pin:
A love-knotte in the grettere° ende ther was.　　　　*greater*
His heed was balled,° that shoon as any glas,　　　　*bald*
And eek his face, as he hadde been anoint:
200　He was a lord ful fat and in good point;[2]
His yën steepe,° and rolling in his heed,　　　　*protruding*
That stemed as a furnais of a leed,[3]
His bootes souple,° his hors in greet estat°　　*supple / condition*
Now certainly he was a fair prelat.[4]
205　He was nat pale as a forpined° gost:　　　　*wasted away*
A fat swan loved he best of any rost.
His palfrey° was as brown as is a berye.　　　　*saddle horse*
　　A Frere ther was, a wantoune° and a merye,　　　*jovial*
A limitour,[5] a ful solempne° man.　　　　*ceremonious*
210　In alle the ordres foure is noon that can°　　　*knows*
So muche of daliaunce° and fair langage:　　　*sociability*
He hadde maad ful many a mariage
Of yonge wommen at his owene cost;
Unto his ordre he was a noble post.[6]
215　Ful wel biloved and familier was he
With frankelains over al[7] in his contree,
And with worthy wommen of the town—
For he hadde power of confessioun,
As saide himself, more than a curat,°　　　　*parish priest*
220　For of° his ordre he was licenciat.[8]　　　　*by*
Ful swetely herde he confessioun,
And plesant was his absolucioun.
He was an esy man to yive penaunce
Ther as he wiste to have[9] a good pitaunce;°　　　*donation*
225　For unto a poore ordre for to yive

9. I.e., as St. Augustine bids. St. Augustine had written that monks should perform manual labor.
1. Of careful workmanship.
2. In good shape, plump.
3. That glowed like a furnace with a pot in it.
4. Prelate (an important churchman).
5. The "Frere" (Friar) is a member of one of the four religious orders whose members live by begging; as a "limitour" he has been granted by his order exclusive begging rights within a certain limited area.
6. I.e., pillar, a staunch supporter.
7. I.e., with franklins everywhere. Franklins were well-to-do country men.
8. I.e., licensed to hear confessions.
9. Where he knew he would have.

Is signe that a man is wel yshrive,[1]
For if he yaf, he dorste make avaunt°   *boast*
He wiste° that a man was repentaunt;   *knew*
For many a man so hard is of his herte
230 He may nat weepe though him sore smerte:[2]
Therfore, in stede of weeping and prayeres,
Men mote° yive silver to the poore freres.[3]   *may*
   His tipet° was ay farsed° ful of knives   *hood / stuffed*
And pinnes, for to yiven faire wives;
235 And certainly he hadde a merye note;
Wel coude he singe and playen on a rote;°   *fiddle*
Of yeddinges he bar outrely the pris.[4]
His nekke whit was as the flowr-de-lis;°   *lily*
Therto he strong was as a champioun.
240 He knew the tavernes wel in every town,
And every hostiler° and tappestere,°   *innkeeper / barmaid*
Bet° than a lazar or a beggestere.[5]   *better*
For unto swich a worthy man as he
Accorded nat, as by his facultee,[6]
245 To have with sike° lazars aquaintaunce: *sick*
It is nat honeste,° it may nought avaunce,°   *dignified / profit*
For to delen with no swich poraile,[7]
But al with riche, and selleres of vitaile;°   *foodstuffs*
And over al ther as[8] profit sholde arise,
250 Curteis he was, and lowely of servise.
Ther was no man nowher so vertuous:°   *effective*
He was the beste beggere in his hous.°   *friary*
And yaf a certain ferme for the graunt;[9]
Noon of his bretheren cam ther in his haunt.[1]
255 For though a widwe° hadde nought a sho,°   *widow / shoe*
So plesant was his *In principio*[2]
Yit wolde he have a ferthing° er he wente;   *small coin*
His purchas was wel bettre than his rente.[3]
And rage he coude as it were right a whelpe;[4]
260 In love-dayes[5] ther coude he muchel° helpe,   *much*
For ther he was nat lik a cloisterer,
With a thredbare cope, as is a poore scoler,
But he was lik a maister[6] or a pope.
Of double worstede was his semicope,°   *short robe*
265 And rounded as a belle out of the presse.°   *bell mold*
Somwhat he lipsed° for his wantounesse°   *lisped / affectation*

---

1. Shriven, absolved.
2. Although he is sorely grieved.
3. Before granting absolution, the confessor must be sure the sinner is contrite; moreover, the absolution is contingent on the sinner's performance of an act of satisfaction. In the case of Chaucer's Friar, a liberal contribution served both as proof of contrition and as satisfaction.
4. He absolutely took the prize for ballads.
5. "Beggestere": female beggar. "Lazar": leper.
6. It was not suitable because of his position.
7. I.e., poor trash. The oldest order of friars had been founded by St. Francis to administer to the spiritual needs of precisely those classes the Friar avoids.
8. Everywhere.
9. And he paid a certain rent for the privilege of begging.
1. Assigned territory.
2. A friar's usual salutation: Latin for "In the beginning [was the Word]" (John 1.1).
3. I.e., the money he got through such activity was more than his proper income.
4. And he could flirt wantonly, as if he were a puppy.
5. Days appointed for the settlement of lawsuits out of court.
6. A man of recognized learning.

To make his Englissh sweete upon his tonge;
And in his harping, whan he hadde songe,°   *sung*
His yën twinkled in his heed aright
270   As doon the sterres° in the frosty night.   *stars*
This worthy limitour was cleped Huberd.
    A Marchant was ther with a forked beerd,
In motelee,[7] and hye on hors he sat,
Upon his heed a Flandrissh° bevere hat,   *Flemish*
275   His bootes clasped faire and fetisly.°   *elegantly*
His resons° he spak ful solempnely,   *opinions*
Souning° alway th' encrees of his winning.°   *implying / profit*
He wolde the see were kept for any thing[8]
Bitwixen Middelburgh and Orewelle.
280   Wel coude he in eschaunge sheeldes[9] selle.
This worthy man ful wel his wit bisette:°   *employed*
Ther wiste° no wight° that he was in dette,   *knew / person*
So statly° was he of his governaunce,[1]   *dignified*
With his bargaines,° and with his chevissaunce.°   *bargainings / borrowing*
285   Forsoothe° he was a worthy man withalle;   *in truth*
But, sooth to sayn, I noot° how men him calle.   *don't know*
    A Clerk[2] ther was of Oxenforde also
That unto logik hadde longe ygo.[3]
As lene was his hors as is a rake,
290   And he was nought right fat, I undertake,
But looked holwe,° and therto sobrely.   *hollow*
Ful thredbare was his overeste courtepy,
For he hadde geten him yit no benefice,[4]
Ne was so worldly for to have office.°   *secular employment*
295   For him was levere[5] have at his beddes heed
Twenty bookes, clad in blak or reed,
Of Aristotle and his philosophye,
Than robes riche, or fithele,° or gay sautrye.[6]   *fiddle*
But al be that he was a philosophre[7]
300   Yit hadde he but litel gold in cofre;°   *coffer*
But al that he mighte of his freendes hente,°   *take*
On bookes and on lerning he it spente,
And bisily gan for the soules praye
Of hem that yaf him wherwith to scoleye.°   *study*
305   Of studye took he most cure° and most heede.   *care*
Nought oo° word spak he more than was neede,   *one*
And that was said in forme[8] and reverence,
And short and quik,° and ful of heigh sentence:[9]   *lively*

---

7. Motley, a cloth of mixed color.
8. I.e., he wished the sea to be guarded at all costs. The sea route between Middelburgh (in the Netherlands) and Orwell (in Suffolk) was vital to the Merchant's export and import of wool—the basis of England's chief trade at the time.
9. Shields were units of transfer in international credit, which he exchanged at a profit.
1. The management of his affairs.
2. The Clerk is a student at Oxford; to become a student, he would have had to signify his intention of becoming a cleric, but he was not bound

to proceed to a position of responsibility in the church.
3. Who had long since matriculated in philosophy.
4. Ecclesiastical living, such as the income a parish priest receives. "Courtepy": outer cloak.
5. He would rather.
6. Psaltery (a kind of harp).
7. The word may also mean alchemist, someone who tries to turn base metals into gold. The Clerk's "philosophy" does not pay either way.
8. With decorum.
9. Elevated thought.

310	Souning° in moral vertu was his speeche,	*resounding*
	And gladly wolde he lerne, and gladly teche.	
	A Sergeant of the Lawe, war and wis,[1]	
	That often hadde been at the Parvis[2]	
	Ther was also, ful riche of excellence.	
	Discreet he was, and of greet reverence—	
315	He seemed swich, his wordes weren so wise.	
	Justice he was ful often in assise°	*circuit courts*
	By patente[3] and by plein° commissioun.	*full*
	For his science° and for his heigh renown	*knowledge*
	Of fees and robes hadde he many oon.	
320	So greet a purchasour° was nowher noon;	*speculator in land*
	Al was fee simple[4] to him in effect—	
	His purchasing mighte nat been infect.[5]	
	Nowher so bisy a man as he ther nas;°	*was not*
	And yit he seemed bisier than he was.	
325	In termes hadde he caas and doomes[6] alle	
	That from the time of King William[7] were falle.	
	Therto he coude endite and make a thing,[8]	
	Ther coude no wight pinchen° at his writing;	*make trivial objection*
	And every statut coude° he plein° by rote.[9]	*knew / entire*
330	He rood but hoomly° in a medlee cote,[1]	*unpretentiously*
	Girt with a ceint° of silk, with barres[2] smale.	*belt*
	Of his array telle I no lenger tale.	
	A Frankelain[3] was in his compaignye:	
	Whit was his beerd as is the dayesye;°	*daisy*
335	Of his complexion he was sanguin.[4]	
	Wel loved he by the morwe a sop in win.[5]	
	To liven in delit° was evere his wone,°	*sensual delight / wont*
	For he was Epicurus[6] owene sone,	
	That heeld opinion that plein° delit	*full*
340	Was verray° felicitee parfit.°	*true / perfect*
	An housholdere and that a greet was he:	
	Saint Julian[7] he was in his contree.	
	His breed, his ale, was always after oon;[8]	
	A bettre envined° man was nevere noon.	*wine-stocked*
345	Withouten bake mete was nevere his hous,	
	Of fissh and flessh, and that so plentevous°	*plenteous*
	It snewed° in his hous of mete° and drinke,	*snowed / food*
	Of alle daintees that men coude thinke.	

1. Wary and wise. The Sergeant is not only a practicing lawyer but one of the high justices of the nation.
2. The Paradise, the porch of St. Paul's Cathedral, a meeting place for lawyers and their clients.
3. Royal warrant.
4. Owned outright without legal impediments.
5. Invalidated on a legal technicality.
6. Law cases and decisions. "By termes": i.e., by heart.
7. I.e., the Conqueror (reigned 1066–87).
8. Compose and draw up a deed.
9. By heart.
1. A coat of mixed color.
2. Transverse stripes.

3. The "Frankelain" (Franklin) is a prosperous country man, whose lower-class ancestry is no impediment to the importance he has attained in his county.
4. A reference to the fact that the Franklin's temperament ("humor") is dominated by blood as well as to his red face (see p. 271, n. 8).
5. I.e., in the morning he was very fond of a piece of bread soaked in wine.
6. The Greek philosopher whose teaching is popularly believed to make pleasure the chief goal of life.
7. The patron saint of hospitality.
8. Always of the same high quality.

After° the sondry sesons of the yeer   *according to*
350 So chaunged he his mete° and his soper.°   *dinner / supper*
    Ful many a fat partrich hadde he in mewe,°   *cage*
    And many a breem,° and many a luce° in stewe[9]   *carp / pike*
    Wo was his cook but if his sauce were
    Poinant° and sharp, and redy all his gere.   *spicy*
355 His table dormant in his halle alway
    Stood redy covered all the longe day.[1]
    At sessions ther was he lord and sire.
    Ful ofte time he was Knight of the Shire.[2]
    An anlaas° and a gipser° al of silk   *dagger / purse*
360 Heeng at his girdel,[3] whit as morne° milk.   *morning*
    A shirreve° hadde he been, and countour.[4]   *sheriff*
    Was nowhere swich a worthy vavasour.[5]
      An Haberdasshere and a Carpenter,
    A Webbe,° a Dyere, and a Tapicer°—   *weaver / tapestry maker*
365 And they were clothed alle in oo liveree[6]
    Of a solempne and greet fraternitee.
    Ful fresshe and newe hir gere apiked° was;   *trimmed*
    Hir knives were chaped° nought with bras,   *mounted*
    But al with silver; wrought ful clene and weel
370 Hir girdles and hir pouches everydeel.°   *altogether*
    Wel seemed eech of hem a fair burgeis°   *burgher*
    To sitten in a yeldehalle° on a dais.   *guildhall*
    Everich, for the wisdom that he can,[7]
    Was shaply° for to been an alderman.   *suitable*
375 For catel° hadde they ynough and rente,°   *property / income*
    And eek hir wives wolde it wel assente—
    And elles certain were they to blame:
    It is ful fair to been ycleped° "Madame,"   *called*
    And goon to vigilies all bifore,[8]
380 And have a mantel royalliche ybore.[9]
      A Cook they hadde with hem for the nones,[1]
    To boile the chiknes with the marybones,°   *marrowbones*
    And powdre-marchant tart and galingale.[2]
    Wel coude he knowe° a draughte of London ale.   *recognize*
385 He coude roste, and seethe,° and broile, and frye,   *boil*
    Maken mortreux,° and wel bake a pie.   *stews*
    But greet harm was it, as it thoughte° me,   *seemed to*
    That on his shine a mormal° hadde he,   *ulcer*
    For blankmanger,[3] that made he with the beste.
390   A Shipman was ther, woning° fer by weste°—   *dwelling / in the west*
    For ought I woot,° he was of Dertemouthe.[4]   *know*

---

9. Fishpond.
1. Tables were usually dismounted when not in use, but the Franklin kept his mounted and set ("covered"), hence "dormant."
2. County representative in Parliament. "Sessions": i.e., sessions of the justices of the peace.
3. Hung at his belt.
4. Auditor of county finances.
5. Feudal landholder of lowest rank; a provincial gentleman.
6. In one livery, i.e., the uniform of their "frater-nitee" or guild, a partly religious, partly social organization.
7. Was capable of.
8. I.e., at the head of the procession. "Vigilies": feasts held on the eve of saints' days.
9. Royally carried.
1. For the occasion.
2. "Powdre-marchant" and "galingale" are flavoring materials.
3. A white stew or mousse.
4. Dartmouth, a port in the southwest of England.

He rood upon a rouncy° as he couthe,[5]	*large nag*
In a gowne of falding° to the knee.	*heavy wool*
A daggere hanging on a laas° hadde he	*strap*
395 Aboute his nekke, under his arm adown.	
The hote somer hadde maad his hewe° al brown;	*color*
And certainly he was a good felawe.	
Ful many a draughte of win hadde he drawe[6]	
Fro Burdeuxward, whil that the chapman sleep:[7]	
400 Of nice° conscience took he no keep;°	*fastidious / heed*
If that he faught and hadde the hyer° hand,	*upper*
By water he sente hem hoom to every land.[8]	
But of his craft, to rekene wel his tides,	
His stremes° and his daungers° him bisides,[9]	*currents / hazards*
405 His herberwe° and his moone, his lodemenage,[1]	*anchorage*
There was noon swich from Hulle to Cartage.[2]	
Hardy he was and wis to undertake;[3]	
With many a tempest hadde his beerd been shake;	
He knew alle the havenes° as they were	*harbors*
410 Fro Gotlond to the Cape of Finistere,[4]	
And every crike° in Britaine° and in Spaine.	*inlet / Brittany*
His barge ycleped was the Maudelaine.°	*Magdalene*
With us ther was a Doctour of Physik:°	*medicine*
In al this world ne was ther noon him lik	
415 To speken of physik and of surgerye.	
For° he was grounded in astronomye,°	*because / astrology*
He kepte° his pacient a ful greet deel[5]	*tended to*
In houres by his magik naturel.[6]	
Wel coude he fortunen the ascendent	
420 Of his images[7] for his pacient.	
He knew the cause of every maladye,	
Were it of hoot or cold or moiste or drye,	
And where engendred and of what humour:[8]	
He was a verray parfit praktisour.[9]	
425 The cause yknowe,° and of his° harm the roote,	*known / its*
Anoon he yaf the sike man his boote.°	*remedy*
Ful redy hadde he his apothecaries	
To senden him drogges° and his letuaries,°	*drugs / medicines*
For eech of hem made other for to winne:	
430 Hir frendshipe was nought newe to biginne.	

5. As best he could.
6. Drawn, i.e., stolen.
7. Merchant slept. "Fro Burdeuxward": from Bordeaux; i.e., while carrying wine from Bordeaux (the wine center of France).
8. He drowned his prisoners.
9. Around him.
1. Pilotage, the art of navigation.
2. From Hull (in northern England) to Cartagena (in Spain).
3. Shrewd in his undertakings.
4. From Gotland (an island in the Baltic) to Finisterre (the westernmost point in Spain).
5. Closely.
6. Natural—as opposed to black—magic. "In houres": i.e., the astrologically important hours (when conjunctions of the planets might help his

recovery).
7. Assign the propitious time, according to the position of stars, for using talismanic images. Such images, representing either the patient himself or points in the zodiac, were thought to be influential on the course of the disease.
8. Diseases were thought to be caused by a disturbance of one or another of the four bodily "humors," each of which, like the four elements, was a compound of two of the elementary qualities mentioned in line 422: the melancholy humor, seated in the black bile, was cold and dry (like earth); the sanguine, seated in the blood, hot and moist (like air); the choleric, seated in the yellow bile, hot and dry (like fire); the phlegmatic, seated in the phlegm, cold and moist (like water).
9. True perfect practitioner.

Wel knew he the olde Esculapius.[1]
And Deiscorides and eek Rufus,
Olde Ipocras, Hali, and Galien,
Serapion, Razis, and Avicen,
435 Averrois, Damascien, and Constantin,
Bernard, and Gatesden, and Gilbertin.
Of his diete mesurable° was he,   *moderate*
For it was of no superfluitee,
But of greet norissing° and digestible.   *nourishment*
440 His studye was but litel on the Bible.
In sanguin° and in pers° he clad was al,   *blood red / blue*
Lined with taffata and with sendal;°   *silk*
And yit he was but esy of dispence;°   *expenditure*
He kepte that he wan in pestilence.[2]
445 For° gold in physik is a cordial,[3]   *because*
Therfore he loved gold in special.
    A good Wif was ther of biside Bathe,
But she was somdeel deef,° and that was scathe.°   *a bit deaf / a pity*
Of cloth-making she hadde swich an haunt,°   *skill*
450 She passed° hem of Ypres and of Gaunt.[4]   *surpassed*
In al the parissh wif ne was ther noon
That to the offring[5] bifore hire sholde goon,
And if ther dide, certain so wroth° was she   *angry*
That she was out of alle charitee.
455 Hir coverchiefs° ful fine were of ground°—   *headcovers / texture*
I dorste° swere they weyeden° ten pound   *dare / weighed*
That on a Sonday weren° upon hir heed.   *were*
Hir hosen° weren of fin scarlet reed,°   *leggings / red*
Ful straite yteyd,[6] and shoes ful moiste° and newe.   *supple*
460 Bold was hir face and fair and reed of hewe.
She was a worthy womman al hir live:
Housbondes at chirche dore[7] she hadde five,
Withouten° other compaignye in youthe—   *not counting*
But therof needeth nought to speke as nouthe.°   *now*
465 And thries hadde she been at Jerusalem;
She hadde passed many a straunge° streem;   *foreign*
At Rome she hadde been, and at Boloigne,
In Galice at Saint Jame, and at Coloigne:[8]
She coude° muchel of wandring by the waye: *knew*
470 Gat-toothed[9] was she, soothly for to saye.

---

1. The Doctor is familiar with the treatises that the Middle Ages attributed to the "great names" of medical history, whom Chaucer names: the purely legendary Greek demigod Aesculapius; the Greeks Dioscorides, Rufus, Hippocrates, Galen, and Serapion; the Persians Hali and Rhazes; the Arabians Avicenna and Averroës; the early Christians John (?) of Damascus and Constantine Afer; the Scotsman Bernard Gordon; the Englishmen John of Gatesden and Gilbert, the former an early contemporary of Chaucer.
2. He saved the money he made during the plague time.
3. A stimulant. Gold was thought to have some

medicinal properties.
4. Ypres and Ghent ("Gaunt") were Flemish clothmaking centers.
5. The offering in church, when the congregation brought its gifts forward.
6. Tightly laced.
7. In medieval times, weddings were performed at the church door.
8. Rome, Boulogne (in France), St. James (of Compostella) in Galicia (Spain), and Cologne (in Germany) were all sites of shrines much visited by pilgrims.
9. Gap-toothed, thought to be a sign of amorousness.

Upon an amblere[1] esily she sat,
Ywimpled° wel, and on hir heed an hat   *veiled*
As brood as is a bokeler or a targe,[2]
A foot-mantel° aboute hir hipes large,   *riding skirt*
475   And on hir feet a paire of spores° sharpe.   *spurs*
In felaweshipe wel coude she laughe and carpe:°   *talk*
Of remedies of love she knew parchaunce,°   *as it happened*
For she coude of that art the olde daunce.[3]
      A good man was ther of religioun,
480   And was a poore Person° of a town,   *parson*
But riche he was of holy thought and werk.
He was also a lerned man, a clerk,
That Cristes gospel trewely° wolde preche;   *faithfully*
His parisshens° devoutly wolde he teche.   *parishioners*
485   Benigne he was, and wonder° diligent,   *wonderfully*
And in adversitee ful pacient,
And swich he was preved° ofte sithes.°   *proved / times*
Ful loth were him to cursen for his tithes,[4]
But rather wolde he yiven, out of doute,[5]
490   Unto his poore parisshens aboute
Of his offring[6] and eek of his substaunce:°   *property*
He coude in litel thing have suffisaunce.°   *sufficiency*
Wid was his parissh, and houses fer asonder,
But he ne lafte° nought for rain ne thonder,   *neglected*
495   In siknesse nor in meschief,° to visite   *misfortune*
The ferreste° in his parissh, muche and lite,[7]   *farthest*
Upon his feet, and in his hand a staf.
This noble ensample° to his sheep he yaf   *example*
That first he wroughte,[8] and afterward he taughte.
500   Out of the Gospel he tho° wordes caughte,°   *those / took*
And this figure° he added eek therto: *metaphor*
That if gold ruste, what shal iren do?
For if a preest be foul, on whom we truste,
No wonder is a lewed° man to ruste.   *uneducated*
505   And shame it is, if a preest take keep,°   *heed*
A shiten° shepherde and a clene sheep.   *befouled*
Wel oughte a preest ensample for to yive
By his clennesse how that his sheep sholde live.
He sette nought his benefice[9] to hire
510   And leet° his sheep encombred in the mire   *left*
And ran to London, unto Sainte Poules,[1]
To seeken him a chaunterye[2] for soules,
Or with a bretherhede to been withholde,[3]

---

1. Horse with an easy gait.
2. "Bokeler" and "targe": small shields.
3. I.e., she knew all the tricks of that trade.
4. He would be most reluctant to invoke excommunication in order to collect his tithes.
5. Without doubt.
6. The offering made by the congregation of his church was at the Parson's disposal.
7. Great and small.
8. I.e., he practiced what he preached.

9. I.e., his parish. A priest might rent his parish to another and take a more profitable position.
1. St. Paul's Cathedral.
2. Chantry, i.e., a foundation that employed priests for the sole duty of saying masses for the souls of wealthy deceased persons. St. Paul's had many of them.
3. Or to be employed by a brotherhood; i.e., to take a lucrative and fairly easy position as chaplain with a parish guild (see this page, n. 6).

But dwelte at hoom and kepte wel his folde,
515 So that the wolf ne made it nought miscarye:[4]
He was a shepherde and nought a mercenarye.
And though he holy were and vertuous,
He was to sinful men nought despitous,°   scornful
Ne of his speeche daungerous° ne digne,°   disdainful / haughty
520 But in his teching discreet and benigne,
To drawen folk to hevene by fairnesse
By good ensample—this was his bisinesse.
But it° were any persone obstinat,   if there
What so he were, of heigh or lowe estat,
525 Him wolde he snibben° sharply for the nones:[5]   scold
A bettre preest I trowe° ther nowher noon is.   believe
He waited after[6] no pompe and reverence,
Ne maked him a spiced conscience,[7]
But Cristes lore° and his Apostles twelve   teaching
530 He taughte, but first he folwed it himselve.
      With him ther was a Plowman, was his brother,
That hadde ylad° of dong° ful many a fother[8]   carried / dung
A trewe swinkere° and a good was he,   worker
Living in pees° and parfit charitee.   peace
535 God loved he best with al his hoole° herte   whole
At alle times, though him gamed or smerte,[9]
And thanne his neighebor right as himselve.[1]
He wolde thresshe, and therto dike° and delve,°   work hard / dig
For Cristes sake, for every poore wight,
540 Withouten hire, if it laye in his might.
His tithes payed he ful faire and wel,
Bothe of his propre swink[2] and his catel.°   property
In a tabard° he rood upon a mere.°   workman's smock / mare
      Ther was also a Reeve° and a Millere,   estate manager
545 A Somnour, and a Pardoner[3] also,
A Manciple,° and myself—ther were namo.   steward
      The Millere was a stout carl° for the nones.   fellow
Ful big he was of brawn° and eek of bones—   muscle
That preved[4] wel, for overal ther he cam
550 At wrastling he wolde have alway the ram.[5]
He was short-shuldred, brood,° a thikke knarre.[6]   broad
Ther was no dore that he nolde heve of harre,[7]
Or breke it at a renning° with his heed.°   running / head
His beerd as any sowe or fox was reed,°   red
555 And therto brood, as though it were a spade;
Upon the cop right[8] of his nose he hade
A werte,° and theron stood a tuft of heres,   wart

4. See John 10.11–13.
5. On the spot, promptly.
6. I.e., awaited, expected.
7. Nor did he assume an overfastidious conscience, a holier-than-thou attitude.
8. Load.
9. Whether he was pleased or grieved.
1. Matthew 22.36–40.
2. His own work.

3. "Somnour" (Summoner): server of summonses to the ecclesiastical court. "Pardoner": dispenser of papal pardons (see p. 277, 2nd n. 7).
4. Proved, i.e., was evident.
5. A ram was frequently offered as the prize in wrestling, a village sport.
6. Sturdy fellow.
7. He would not heave off (its) hinge.
8. Right on the tip.

Rede as the bristles of a sowes eres;°   *ears*
His nosethirles° blake were and wide.   *nostrils*
560 A swerd and a bokeler° bar° he by his side.   *shield / bore*
His mouth as greet was as a greet furnais.°   *furnace*
He was a janglere° and a Goliardais,[9]   *chatterer*
And that was most of sinne and harlotries.°   *obscenities*
Wel coude he stelen corn and tollen thries[1]—
565 And yit he hadde a thombe[2] of gold, pardee.° *by heaven*
A whit cote and a blew hood wered° he.   *wore*
A baggepipe wel coude he blowe and soune,°   *sound*
And therwithal° he broughte us out of towne. *therewith*
  A gentil Manciple[3] was ther of a temple,
570 Of which achatours° mighte take exemple *buyers of food*
For to been wise in bying of vitaile;°   *victuals*
For wheither that he paide or took by taile,[4]
Algate he waited so in his achat[5]
That he was ay biforn and in good stat.[6]
575 Now is nat that of God a ful fair grace
That swich a lewed° mannes wit shal pace° *uneducated / surpass*
The wisdom of an heep of lerned men?
Of maistres° hadde he mo than thries ten   *masters*
That weren of lawe expert and curious,°   *cunning*
580 Of whiche ther were a dozeine in that hous
Worthy to been stiwardes of rente° and lond *income*
Of any lord that is in Engelond,
To make him live by his propre good[7]
In honour dettelees but if he were wood,[8]
585 Or live as scarsly° as him list° desire, *economically / it pleases*
And able for to helpen al a shire
In any caas° that mighte falle° or happe, *event / befall*
And yit this Manciple sette hir aller cappe![9]
  The Reeve was a sclendre° colerik[1] man; *slender*
590 His beerd was shave as neigh° as evere he can; *close*
His heer was by his eres ful round yshorn;
His top was dokked[2] lik a preest biforn;° *in front*
Ful longe were his legges and ful lene,
Ylik a staf, ther was no calf yseene.°   *visible*
595 Wel coude he keepe° a gerner° and a binne— *guard / granary*
Ther was noon auditour coude on him winne.[3]
Wel wiste° he by the droughte and by the rain *knew*
The yeelding of his seed and of his grain.
His lordes sheep, his neet,° his dayerye,° *cattle / dairy herd*
600 His swin, his hors, his stoor,° and his pultrye *stock*

9. Goliard, teller of ribald stories.
1. Take toll thrice—i.e., deduct from the grain far more than the lawful percentage.
2. Thumb. Ironic allusion to a proverb: "An honest miller has a golden thumb."
3. The Manciple is the business agent of a community of lawyers in London (a "temple").
4. By tally, i.e., on credit.
5. Always he was on the watch in his purchasing.
6. Financial condition. "Ay biforn": i.e., ahead of the game.

7. His own money.
8. Out of debt unless he were crazy.
9. This Manciple made fools of them all.
1. Choleric describes a person whose dominant humor is yellow bile (choler)—i.e., a hot-tempered person. The Reeve is the superintendent of a large farming estate.
2. Cut short; the clergy wore the head partially shaved.
3. I.e., find him in default.

wholly

Was hoolly° in this Reeves governinge,
And by his covenant yaf[4] the rekeninge,
Sin° that his lord was twenty-yeer of age. *since*
There coude no man bringe him in arrerage.[5]
605 Ther nas baillif, hierde, nor other hine,
That he ne knew his sleighte and his covine[6]
They were adrad° of him as of the deeth.° *afraid / plague*
His woning° was ful faire upon an heeth;° *dwelling / meadow*
With greene trees shadwed was his place.
610 He coude bettre than his lord purchase.° *acquire goods*
Ful riche he was astored° prively.° *stocked / secretly*
His lord wel coude he plesen subtilly,
To yive and lene° him of his owene good,° *lend / property*
And have a thank, and yit a cote and hood.
615 In youthe he hadde lerned a good mister:° *occupation*
He was a wel good wrighte, a carpenter.
This Reeve sat upon a ful good stot° *stallion*
That was a pomely° grey and highte° Scot. *dapple / was named*
A long surcote° of pers° upon he hade,[7] *overcoat / blue*
620 And by his side he bar° a rusty blade. *bore*
Of Northfolk was this Reeve of which I telle,
Biside a town men clepen Baldeswelle.° *Bawdswell*
Tukked[8] he was as is a frere aboute,
And evere he rood the hindreste of oure route.[9]
625 A Somnour[1] was ther with us in that place
That hadde a fir-reed° cherubinnes[2] face, *fire-red*
For saucefleem° he was, with yën narwe, *pimply*
And hoot° he was, and lecherous as a sparwe,° *hot / sparrow*
With scaled° browes blake and piled[3] beerd: *scabby*
630 Of his visage children were aferd.° *afraid*
Ther nas quiksilver, litarge, ne brimstoon,
Boras, ceruce, ne oile of tartre noon,[4]
Ne oinement that wolde dense and bite,
That him mighte helpen of his whelkes° white, *pimples*
635 Nor of the knobbes° sitting on his cheekes. *lumps*
Wel loved he garlek, oinons, and eek leekes,
And for to drinke strong win reed as blood.
Thanne wolde he speke and crye as he were wood;° *mad*
And whan that he wel dronken hadde the win,
640 Thanne wolde he speke no word but Latin:
A fewe termes hadde he, two or three,
That he hadde lerned out of som decree;
No wonder is—he herde it al the day,
And eek ye knowe wel how that a jay° *parrot*

4. And according to his contract he gave.
5. Convict him of being in arrears financially.
6. There was no bailiff (i.e., foreman), shepherd, or other farm laborer whose craftiness and plots he didn't know.
7. He had on.
8. With clothing tucked up like a friar.
9. Hindmost of our group.
1. The "Somnour" (Summoner) is an employee of the ecclesiastical court, whose duty is to bring to court persons whom the archdeacon—the justice of the court—suspects of offenses against canon law. By this time, however, summoners had generally transformed themselves into corrupt detectives who spied out offenders and blackmailed them by threats of summonses.
2. Cherubs, often depicted in art with red faces.
3. Uneven, partly hairless.
4. These are all ointments for diseases affecting the skin, probably diseases of venereal origin.

645 Can clepen "Watte"[5] as wel as can the Pope—
But whoso coude in other thing him grope,°   *examine*
Thanne hadde he spent all his philosophye;[6]
Ay *Questio quid juris*[7] wolde he crye.
He was a gentil harlot° and a kinde;   *rascal*
650 A bettre felawe sholde men nought finde:
He wolde suffre,° for a quart of win,   *permit*
A good felawe to have his concubin
A twelfmonth, and excusen him at the fulle;[8]
Ful prively° a finch eek coude he pulle.[9]   *secretly*
655 And if he foond° owher° a good felawe   *found / anywhere*
He wolde techen him to have noon awe
In swich caas of the Ercedekenes curs,[1]
But if[2] a mannes soule were in his purs,
For in his purs he sholde ypunisshed be.
660 "Purs is the Ercedekenes helle," saide he.
But wel I woot he lied right in deede:
Of cursing° oughte eech gilty man him drede,   *excommunication*
For curs wol slee° right as assoiling° savith—   *slay / absolution*
And also war him of a *significavit*.[3]
665 In daunger[4] hadde he at his owene gise°   *disposal*
The yonge girles of the diocise,
And knew hir conseil,° and was al hir reed.[5]   *secrets*
A gerland hadde he set upon his heed
As greet as it were for an ale-stake,[6]
670 A bokeler hadde he maad him of a cake.
With him ther rood a gentil Pardoner[7]
Of Rouncival, his freend and his compeer,°   *comrade*
That straight was comen fro the Court of Rome.[8]
Ful loude he soong,° "Com hider, love, to me."   *sang*
675 This Somnour bar to him a stif burdoun:[9]
Was nevere trompe° of half so greet a soun.   *trumpet*
This Pardoner hadde heer as yelow as wex,
But smoothe it heeng° as dooth a strike° of flex;°   *hung / hank / flax*
By ounces[1] heenge his lokkes that he hadde,
680 And therwith he his shuldres overspradde,°   *overspread*
But thinne it lay, by colpons,° oon by oon;   *strands*
But hood for jolitee° wered° he noon,   *nonchalance / wore*
For it was trussed up in his walet:°   *pack*

---

5. Call out: "Walter"—like modern parrots' "Polly."
6. I.e., learning.
7. "What point of law does this investigation involve?" A Latin phrase frequently used in ecclesiastical courts.
8. Fully. Ecclesiastical courts had jurisdiction over many offenses that today would come under civil law, including sexual offenses.
9. "To pull a finch" (pluck a bird) is to have sexual relations with a woman.
1. Archdeacon's sentence of excommunication.
2. Unless.
3. And also one should be careful of a *significavit* (Latin for the writ that transferred the guilty offender from the ecclesiastical to the civil arm

for punishment).
4. Under his domination.
5. Was their chief source of advice.
6. A tavern was signalized by a pole ("ale-stake"), rather like a modern flagpole, projecting from its front wall; on this hung a garland, or "bush."
7. A Pardoner dispensed papal pardon for sins to those who contributed to the charitable institution that he was licensed to represent; this Pardoner purported to be collecting for the hospital of Roncesvalles ("Rouncival") in Spain, which had a London branch.
8. The papal court.
9. I.e., provided him with a strong bass accompaniment.
1. I.e., thin strands.

	Him thoughte he rood al of the newe jet.°	*fashion*
685	Dischevelee° save his cappe he rood al bare.	*with hair down*
	Swiche glaring yën hadde he as an hare.	
	A vernicle² hadde he sowed upon his cappe,	
	His walet biforn him in his lappe,	
	Bretful° of pardon, come from Rome al hoot.°	*brimful / hot*
690	A vois he hadde as smal° as hath a goot;°	*high-pitched / goat*
	No beerd hadde he, ne nevere sholde have;	
	As smoothe it was as it were late yshave:	
	I trowe° he were a gelding³ or a mare.	*believe*
	But of his craft, fro Berwik into Ware,⁴	
695	Ne was ther swich another pardoner;	
	For in his male° he hadde a pilwe-beer°	*bag / pillowcase*
	Which that he saide was Oure Lady veil;	
	He saide he hadde a gobet° of the sail	*piece*
	That Sainte Peter hadde whan that he wente	
700	Upon the see, til Jesu Crist him hente.°	*seized*
	He hadde a crois° of laton,° ful of stones,	*cross / brassy metal*
	And in a glas he hadde pigges bones,	
	But with thise relikes⁵ whan that he foond°	*found*
	A poore person° dwelling upon lond,⁶	*parson*
705	Upon° a day he gat° him more moneye	*in / got*
	Than that the person gat in monthes twaye;	
	And thus with feined° flaterye and japes°	*false / tricks*
	He made the person and the peple his apes.°	*dupes*
	But trewely to tellen at the laste,	
710	He was in chirche a noble ecclesiaste;	
	Wel coude he rede a lesson and a storye,°	*liturgical narrative*
	But alderbest° he soong an offertorye,⁷	*best of all*
	For wel he wiste° whan that song was songe,	*knew*
	He moste° preche and wel affile° his tonge	*must / sharpen*
715	To winne silver, as he ful wel coude—	
	Therefore he soong the merierly° and loude.	*more merrily*
	Now have I told you soothly in a clause⁸	
	Th'estaat, th'array, the nombre, and eek the cause	
	Why that assembled was this compaignye	
720	In Southwerk at this gentil hostelrye	
	That highte the Tabard, faste° by the Belle;⁹	*close*
	But now is time to you for to telle	
	How that we baren us¹ that ilke° night	*same*
	Whan we were in that hostelrye alight;	
725	And after wol I telle of oure viage,°	*trip*
	And al the remenant of oure pilgrimage.	
	But first I praye you of youre curteisye	
	That ye n'arette it nought my vilainye²	

2. Portrait of Christ's face as was said to have been impressed on St. Veronica's handkerchief, i.e., a souvenir reproduction of a famous relic in Rome.
3. A neutered stallion, i.e., a eunuch.
4. I.e., from one end of England to the other.
5. Relics, i.e., the pigs' bones that the Pardoner represented as saints' bones.

6. Upcountry.
7. Part of the mass sung before the offering of alms.
8. I.e., in a short space.
9. Another tavern in Southwark.
1. Bore ourselves.
2. That you do not attribute it to my boorishness.

Though that I plainly speke in this matere
730 To telle you hir wordes and hir cheere,°   *behavior*
Ne though I speke hir wordes proprely;°   *accurately*
For this ye knowen also wel as I:
Who so shal telle a tale after a man
He moot° reherce,° as neigh as evere he can,   *must / repeat*
735 Everich a word, if it be in his charge,°   *responsibility*
Al speke he³ nevere so rudeliche and large,°   *broadly*
Or elles he moot telle his tale untrewe,
Or feine° thing, or finde° wordes newe;   *make up / devise*
He may nought spare⁴ although he were his brother:
740 He moot as wel saye oo word as another.
Crist spak himself ful brode° in Holy Writ,   *broadly*
And wel ye woot no vilainye° is it;   *rudeness*
Eek Plato saith, who so can him rede,
The wordes mote be cosin to the deede.
745   Also I praye you to foryive it me
Al° have I nat set folk in hir degree   *although*
Here in this tale as that they sholde stonde:
My wit is short, ye may wel understonde.
   Greet cheere made oure Host⁵ us everichoon,
750 And to the soper sette he us anoon.°   *at once*
He served us with vitaile° at the beste.   *food*
Strong was the win, and wel to drinke us leste.°   *it pleased*
A semely man oure Hoste was withalle
For to been a marchal⁶ in an halle;
755 A large man he was, with yën steepe,°   *prominent*
A fairer burgeis° was ther noon in Chepe⁷—   *burgher*
Bold of his speeche, and wis, and wel ytaught,
And of manhood him lakkede right naught.
Eek therto he was right a merye man,
760 And after soper playen he bigan,
And spak of mirthe amonges othere thinges—
Whan that we hadde maad oure rekeninges⁸—
And saide thus, "Now, lordinges, trewely,
Ye been to me right welcome, hertely.°   *heartily*
765 For by my trouthe, if that I shal nat lie,
I sawgh nat this yeer so merye a compaignye
At ones in this herberwe° as is now.   *inn*
Fain° wolde I doon you mirthe, wiste I⁹ how.   *gladly*
And of a mirthe I am right now bithought,
770 To doon you ese, and it shal coste nought.
   "Ye goon to Canterbury—God you speede;
The blisful martyr quite you youre meede.¹
And wel I woot as ye goon by the waye
Ye shapen you² to talen° and to playe,   *converse*
775 For trewely, confort ne mirthe is noon

3. Although he speak.
4. I.e., spare anyone.
5. The landlord of the Tabard Inn.
6. Marshal, one who was in charge of feasts.
7. Cheapside, business center of London.
8. Had paid our bills.
9. If I knew.
1. Pay you your reward.
2. Intend.

To ride by the waye domb as stoon;°   stone
And therefore wol I maken you disport
As I saide erst,° and doon you som confort;   before
And if you liketh alle, by oon assent,
780 For to stonden at³ my juggement,
And for to werken as I shall you saye,
Tomorwe whan ye riden by the waye—
Now by my fader° soule that is deed,   father's
But° ye be merye I wol yive you myn heed!°   unless / head
785 Holde up youre handes withouten more speeche."
　　Oure counseil was nat longe for to seeche;°   seek
Us thought it was not worth to make it wis,⁴
And graunted him withouten more avis,°   deliberation
And bade him saye his voirdit° as him leste.⁵   verdict
790 "Lordinges," quod he, "now herkneth for the beste;
But taketh it nought, I praye you, in desdain.
This is the point, to speken short and plain,
That eech of you, to shorte° with oure waye   shorten
In this viage, shal tellen tales twaye°—   two
795 To Canterburyward, I mene it so,
And hoomward he shal tellen othere two,
Of aventures that whilom° have bifalle;   once upon a time
And which of you that bereth him best of alle—
That is to sayn, that telleth in this cas
800 Tales of best sentence° and most solas°—   meaning / delight
Shal have a soper at oure aller cost,⁶
Here in this place, sitting by this post,
Whan that we come again fro Canterbury.
And for to make you the more mury°   merry
805 I wol myself goodly° with you ride—   kindly
Right at myn owene cost—and be youre gide.
And who so wol my juggement withsaye°   contradict
Shal paye al that we spende by the waye.
And if ye vouche sauf that it be so,
810 Telle me anoon, withouten wordes mo,°   more
And I wol erly shape me⁷ therefore."
　　This thing was graunted and oure othes swore
With ful glad herte, and prayden him⁸ also
That he wolde vouche sauf for to do so,
815 And that he wolde been oure governour,
And of oure tales juge and reportour,°   accountant
And sette a soper at a certain pris,°   price
And we wol ruled been at his devis,°   disposal
In heigh and lowe; and thus by oon assent
820 We been accorded to his juggement.
And therupon the win was fet° anoon;   fetched
We dronken and to reste wente eechoon°   each one
Withouten any lenger° taryinge.   longer

3. Abide by.　　　　　　　　　　　6. At the cost of us all.
4. We didn't think it worthwhile to make an　7. Prepare myself.
issue of it.　　　　　　　　　　　　8. I.e., we begged him.
5. It pleased.

Amorwe° whan that day bigan to springe   *in the morning*
825 Up roos oure Host and was oure aller cok,[9]
And gadred us togidres in a flok,
And forth we riden, a litel more than pas,°   *walking pace*
Unto the watering of Saint Thomas;[1]
And ther oure Host bigan his hors arreste,°   *halt*
830 And saide, "Lordes, herkneth if you leste:°   *it please*
Ye woot youre forward° and it you recorde:[2]   *agreement*
If evensong and morwesong° accorde,°   *morning song / agree*
Lat see now who shal telle the firste tale.
As evere mote° I drinken win or ale,   *may*
835 Who so be rebel to my juggement
Shal paye for al that by the way is spent.
Now draweth cut er that we ferrer twinne:[3]
He which that hath the shorteste shal biginne.
"Sire Knight," quod he, "my maister and my lord,
840 Now draweth cut, for that is myn accord.°   *will*
Cometh neer," quod he, "my lady Prioresse,
And ye, sire Clerk, lat be youre shamefastnesse°—   *modesty*
Ne studieth nought. Lay hand to, every man!"
Anoon to drawen every wight bigan,
845 And shortly for to tellen as it was
Were it by aventure, or sort, or cas,[4]
The soothe° is this, the cut fil° to the Knight;   *truth / fell*
Of which ful blithe and glad was every wight,
And telle he moste° his tale, as was resoun,   *must*
850 By forward and by composicioun,[5]
As ye han herd. What needeth wordes mo?
And whan this goode man sawgh that it was so,
As he that wis was and obedient
To keepe his forward by his free assent,
855 He saide, "Sin° I shal biginne the game,   *since*
What, welcome be the cut, in Goddes name!
Now lat us ride, and herkneth what I saye."
And with that word we riden forth oure waye,
And he bigan with right a merye cheere°   *countenance*
860 His tale anoon, and saide as ye may heere.

9. Was rooster for us all.
1. A watering place near Southwark.
2. You recall it.

3. Go farther. "Draweth cut": i.e., draw straws.
4. Whether it was luck, fate, or chance.
5. By agreement and compact.

[*The Knight's Tale* is a romance of 2,350 lines, which Chaucer had written before beginning *The Canterbury Tales*—one of several works assumed to be earlier that he inserted into the collection. It is probably the same story, with only minor revisions, that Chaucer referred to in *The Legend of Good Women* as "al the love of Palamon and Arcite." These are the names of the two heroes of *The Knight's Tale*, kinsmen and best friends who are taken prisoner at the siege and destruction of ancient Thebes by Theseus, the ruler of Athens. Gazing out from their prison cell in a tower, they fall in love at first sight and almost at the same moment with Theseus's sister-in-law, Emily, who is taking an early-morning walk in a garden below their window. After a bitter rivalry, they are at last reconciled through a tournament in which Emily is the prize. Arcite wins the tournament, but, as he lies dying after being thrown by his horse, he makes a noble speech encouraging Palamon and Emily to marry. The tale is an ambitious combination of classical setting and mythology, romance plot, and themes of fortune and destiny.]

The Miller's Prologue and Tale

The Miller's Tale belongs to a genre known as the "fabliau": a short story in verse that deals satirically, often grossly and fantastically as well as hilariously, with intrigues and deceptions about sex or money (and often both these elements in the same story). These are the tales Chaucer is anticipating in *The General Prologue* when he warns his presumably genteel audience that they must expect some rude speaking (see lines 727–44). An even more pointed apology follows at the end of *The Miller's Prologue*. Fabliau tales exist everywhere in oral literature; as a literary form they flourished in France, especially in the thirteenth century. By having Robin the Miller tell a fabliau to "quite" (to requite or pay back) the Knight's aristocratic romance, Chaucer sets up a dialectic between classes, genres, and styles that he exploits throughout *The Canterbury Tales*.

The Prologue

Whan that the Knight hadde thus his tale ytold,	
In al the route° nas° ther yong ne old	*group / was not*
That he ne saide it was a noble storye,	
And worthy for to drawen° to memorye,	*recall*
5 And namely° the gentils everichoon.	*especially*
Oure Hoste lough° and swoor, "So mote I goon,[1]	*laughed*
This gooth aright: unbokeled is the male.°	*pouch*
Lat see now who shal telle another tale.	
For trewely the game is wel bigonne.	
10 Now telleth ye, sire Monk, if that ye conne,°	*can*
Somwhat to quite° with the Knightes tale."	*repay*
The Millere, that for dronken[2] was al pale,	
So that unnethe° upon his hors he sat,	*with difficulty*
He nolde° avalen° neither hood ne hat,	*would not / take off*
15 Ne abiden no man for his curteisye,	
But in Pilates vois[3] he gan to crye,	
And swoor, "By armes[4] and by blood and bones,	
I can° a noble tale for the nones,	*know*
With which I wol now quite the Knightes tale."	
20 Oure Hoste sawgh that he was dronke of ale,	
And saide, "Abide, Robin, leve° brother,	*dear*
Som bettre man shal telle us first another.	
Abide, and lat us werken thriftily."°	*with propriety*
"By Goddes soule," quod he, "that wol nat I,	
25 For I wol speke or elles go my way."	

---

1. So might I walk—an oath.
2. I.e., drunkenness.
3. The harsh voice usually associated with the

character of Pontius Pilate in the mystery plays.
4. I.e., by God's arms, a blasphemous oath.

Oure Host answerde, "Tel on, a devele way!⁵
Thou art a fool; thy wit is overcome."
"Now herkneth," quod the Millere, "alle and some.⁶
But first I make a protestacioun°   *public affirmation*
30   That I am dronke: I knowe it by my soun.°   *tone of voice*
And therfore if that I misspeke° or saye,   *speak or say wrongly*
Wite it⁷ the ale of Southwerk, I you praye;
For I wol telle a legende° and a lif   *saint's life*
Bothe of a carpenter and of his wif,
35   How that a clerk hath set the wrightes cappe."⁸
     The Reeve answerde and saide, "Stint thy clappe!⁹
Lat be thy lewed° dronken harlotrye.°   *ignorant / obscenity*
It is a sinne and eek° a greet folye   *also*
To apairen° any man or him defame,   *injure*
40   And eek to bringen wives in swich fame.°   *reputation*
Thou maist ynough of othere thinges sayn."
     This dronken Millere spak ful soone again,
And saide, "Leve° brother Osewold,   *dear*
Who hath no wif, he is no cokewold.°   *cuckold*
45   But I saye nat therfore that thou art oon.
Ther ben ful goode wives many oon,°   *a one*
And evere a thousand goode ayains oon badde.
That knowestou wel thyself but if thou madde.°   *rave*
Why artou angry with my tale now?
50   I have a wif, pardee,° as wel as thou,   *by God*
Yit nolde° I, for the oxen in my plough,   *would not*
Take upon me more than ynough°   *enough*
As deemen of myself that I were oon:¹
I wol bileve wel that I am noon.
55   An housbonde shal nought been inquisitif
Of Goddes privetee,° nor of his wif.   *secrets*
So² he may finde Goddes foison° there,   *plenty*
Of the remenant° needeth nought enquere."°   *rest / inquire*
     What sholde I more sayn but this Millere
60   He nolde his wordes for no man forbere,
But tolde his cherles tale in his manere.
M'athinketh° that I shal reherce° it here,   *I regret / repeat*
And therefore every gentil wight I praye,
Deemeth nought, for Goddes love, that I saye
65   Of yvel entente, but for° I moot reherse   *because*
Hir tales alle, be they bet° or werse,   *better*
Or elles falsen° som of my matere.   *falsify*
And therfore, whoso list it nought yheere°   *hear*
Turne over the leef,° and chese° another tale,   *page / choose*
70   For he shal finde ynowe,° grete and smale,   *enough*
Of storial³ thing that toucheth gentilesse,°   *gentility*
And eek moralitee and holinesse:
Blameth nought me if that ye chese amis.

---

5. I.e., in the devil's name.   9. Stop your chatter.
6. Each and every one.   1. To think that I were one (a cuckold).
7. Blame it on.   2. Provided that.
8. I.e., how a clerk made a fool of a carpenter.   3. Historical, i.e., true.

The Millere is a cherl, ye knowe wel this,
75 So was the Reeve eek, and othere mo,
And harlotrye° they tolden bothe two.   *ribaldry*
Aviseth you,[4] and putte me out of blame:
And eek men shal nought maken ernest of game.

The Tale

Whilom° ther was dwelling at Oxenforde   *once upon a time*
80 A riche gnof° that gestes heeld to boorde,[5]   *churl*
And of his craft he was a carpenter.
With him ther was dwelling a poore scoler,
Hadde lerned art[6] but al his fantasye°   *desire*
Was turned for to lere° astrologye,   *learn*
85 And coude a certain of conclusiouns,
To deemen by interrogaciouns,[7]
If that men axed° him in certain houres   *asked*
Whan that men sholde have droughte or elles showres,
Or if men axed him what shal bifalle
90 Of every thing—I may nat rekene hem alle.
This clerk was cleped° hende[8] Nicholas.   *called*
Of derne love he coude, and of solas,[9]
And therto he was sly and ful privee,°   *secretive*
And lik a maide meeke for to see.
95 A chambre hadde he in that hostelrye
Allone, withouten any compaignye,
Ful fetisly ydight[1] with herbes swoote,°   *sweet*
And he himself as sweete as is the roote
Of licoris or any setewale.[2]
100 His *Almageste*[3] and bookes grete and smale,
His astrelabye, longing for[4] his art,
His augrim stones,[5] layen faire apart
On shelves couched° at his beddes heed;   *set*
His presse° ycovered with a falding reed;[6]   *storage chest*
105 And al above ther lay a gay sautrye,°   *psaltery (harp)*
On which he made a-nightes melodye
So swetely that al the chambre roong,°   *rang*
And *Angelus ad Virginem*[7] he soong,
And after that he soong the *Kinges Note*.[8]
110 Ful often blessed was his merye throte.
And thus this sweete clerk his time spente
After his freendes finding and his rente.[9]

4. Take heed.
5. I.e., took in boarders.
6. Who had completed the first stage of university education (the trivium).
7. I.e., and he knew a number of propositions on which to base astrological analyses (which would reveal the matters in the next three lines).
8. Courteous, handy, attractive.
9. I.e., he knew about secret love and pleasurable practices.
1. Elegantly furnished.
2. Setwall, a spice.

3. The 2nd-century treatise by Ptolemy, still the standard astronomy textbook in the 14th century.
4. Belonging to. "Astrelabye": astrolabe, an astronomical instrument.
5. Counters used in arithmetic.
6. Red coarse woolen cloth.
7. "The Angel to the Virgin" (Latin), an Annunciation hymn.
8. Probably a popular song of the time.
9. In accordance with his friends' provision and his own income.

This carpenter hadde wedded newe° a wif   *lately*
Which that he loved more than his lif.
115 Of eighteteene yeer she was of age;
Jalous he was, and heeld hire narwe in cage,
For she was wilde and yong, and he was old,
And deemed himself been lik a cokewold[1]
He knew nat Caton,[2] for his wit was rude,
120 That bad men sholde wedde his similitude:[3]
Men sholde wedden after hir estat,[4]
For youthe and elde° is often at debat.   *age*
But sith that he was fallen in the snare,
He moste endure, as other folk, his care.
125   Fair was this yonge wif, and therwithal
As any wesele° hir body gent and smal.[5]   *weasel*
A ceint she wered, barred[6] al of silk;
A barmcloth° as whit as morne° milk   *apron / morning*
Upon hir lendes,° ful of many a gore;°   *loins / flounce*
130 Whit was hir smok,° and broiden° al bifore   *undergarment / embroidered*
And eek bihinde, on hir coler° aboute,   *collar*
Of° col-blak silk, withinne and eek withoute;   *with*
The tapes° of hir white voluper°   *ribbons / cap*
Were of the same suite of[7] hir coler;
135 Hir filet° brood° of silk ana set ful hye;   *headband / broad*
And sikerly° she hadde a likerous° yë;   *certainly / wanton*
Ful smale ypulled[8] were hir browes two,
And tho were bent,° and blake as any slo.°   *arching / sloeberry*
She was ful more blisful on to see
140 Than is the newe perejonette° tree,   *pear*
And softer than the wolle° is of a wether;°   *wool / ram*
And by hir girdel° heeng° a purs of lether,   *belt / hung*
Tasseled with silk and perled with latoun.[9]
In al this world, to seeken up and down,
145 Ther nis no man so wis that coude thenche°   *imagine*
So gay a popelote° or swich° a wenche.   *doll / such*
Ful brighter was the shining of hir hewe
Than in the Towr[1] the noble° yforged newe.   *gold coin*
But of hir song, it was as loud and yerne°   *lively*
150 As any swalwe° sitting on a berne.°   *swallow / barn*
Therto she coude skippe and make game°   *play*
As any kide or calf folwing his dame.°   *mother*
Hir mouth was sweete as bragot or the meeth,[2]
Or hoord of apples laid in hay or heeth.°   *heather*
155 Winsing° she was as is a joly° colt,   *skittish / high-spirited*
Long as a mast, and upright° as a bolt.°   *straight / arrow*
A brooch she bar upon hir lowe coler
As brood as is the boos° of a bokeler;°   *boss / shield*

---

1. I.e., suspected of himself that he was like a cuckold.
2. Dionysius Cato, the supposed author of a book of maxims used in elementary education.
3. Commanded that one should wed his equal.
4. Men should marry according to their condition.
5. Slender and delicate.

6. A belt she wore, with transverse stripes.
7. The same kind as, i.e., black.
8. Delicately plucked.
9. I.e., with brassy spangles on it.
1. The Tower of London, the Mint.
2. "Bragot" and "meeth" (mead) are honey drinks.

Hir shoes were laced on hir legges hye.
160 She was a primerole,° a piggesnye,³   *primrose*
For any lord to leggen° in his bedde,   *lay*
Or yit for any good yeman to wedde.
      Now sire, and eft° sire, so bifel the cas   *again*
That on a day this hende Nicholas
165 Fil° with this yonge wif to rage° and playe,   *happened / flirt*
Whil that hir housbonde was at Oseneye⁴
(As clerkes been ful subtil and ful quainte),°   *clever*
And prively he caughte hire by the queinte,⁵
And saide, "Ywis,° but° if ich° have my wille,   *truly / unless / I*
170 For derne° love of thee, lemman, I spille,"°   *secret / die*
And heeld hire harde by the haunche-bones,°   *thighs*
And saide, "Lemman,° love me al atones,⁶   *sweetheart*
Or I wol dien, also° God me save."   *so*
And she sproong° as a colt dooth in a trave,⁷   *sprang*
175 And with hir heed she wried° faste away;   *twisted*
She saide, "I wol nat kisse thee, by my fay.°   *faith*
Why, lat be," quod she, "lat be, Nicholas!
Or I wol crye 'Out, harrow,° and allas!'   *help*
Do way youre handes, for your curteisye!"
180   This Nicholas gan mercy for to crye,
And spak so faire, and profred him so faste,⁸
That she hir love him graunted atte laste,
And swoor hir ooth by Saint Thomas of Kent⁹
That she wolde been at his comandement,
185 Whan that she may hir leiser¹ wel espye.
"Myn housbonde is so ful of jalousye
That but ye waite° wel and been privee   *be on guard*
I woot right wel I nam but deed,"² quod she.
"Ye moste been ful derne° as in this cas."   *secret*
190   "Nay, therof care thee nought," quod Nicholas.
"A clerk hadde litherly biset his while,³
But if he coude a carpenter bigile."
And thus they been accorded and ysworn
To waite° a time, as I have told biforn.   *watch for*
195 Whan Nicholas hadde doon this everydeel,°   *every bit*
And thakked° hire upon the lendes° weel,   *patted / loins*
He kiste hire sweete, and taketh his sautrye,
And playeth faste, and maketh melodye.
      Thanne fil° it thus, that to the parissh chirche,   *befell*
200 Cristes owene werkes for to wirche,°   *perform*
This goode wif wente on an haliday:°   *holy day*
Hir forheed shoon as bright as any day,
So was it wasshen whan she leet° hir werk.   *left*
Now was ther of that chirche a parissh clerk,⁴

---

3. A pig's eye, a name for a common flower.
4. A town near Oxford.
5. Elegant (thing); a euphemism for the female genitals.
6. Right now.
7. Frame for holding a horse to be shod.
8. I.e., made such vigorous advances.

9. Thomas à Becket.
1. I.e., opportunity.
2. I am no more than dead, I am done for.
3. Poorly employed his time.
4. Assistant to the parish priest, not a cleric or student.

205	The which that was ycleped° Absolon:	*called*
	Crul° was his heer, and as the gold it shoon,	*curly*
	And strouted° as a fanne⁵ large and brode;	*spread out*
	Ful straight and evene lay his joly shode.⁶	
	His rode° was reed, his yën greye as goos.°	*complexion / goose*
210	With Poules window corven⁷ on his shoos,	
	In hoses° rede he wente fetisly.°	*stockings / elegantly*
	Yclad he was ful smale° and proprely,	*finely*
	Al in a kirtel° of a light waget°—	*tunic / blue*
	Ful faire and thikke been the pointes⁸ set—	
215	And therupon he hadde a gay surplis,°	*surplice*
	As whit as is the blosme upon the ris.°	*bough*
	A merye child° he was, so God me save.	*young man*
	Wel coude he laten blood, and clippe,⁹ and shave,	
	And maken a chartre of land, or acquitaunce;¹	
220	In twenty manere° coude he trippe and daunce	*ways*
	After the scole of Oxenforde tho,°	*then*
	And with his legges casten° to and fro,	*prance*
	And playen songes on a smal rubible;°	*fiddle*
	Therto he soong somtime a loud quinible,²	
225	And as wel coude he playe on a giterne:°	*guitar*
	In al the town nas brewhous ne taverne	
	That he ne visited with his solas,°	*entertainment*
	Ther any gailard tappestere³ was.	
	But sooth to sayn, he was somdeel squaimous°	*a bit squeamish*
230	Of° farting, and of speeche daungerous.⁴	*about*
	This Absolon, that joly° was and gay,	*pretty, amorous*
	Gooth with a cencer° on the haliday,	*incense burner*
	Cencing the wives of the parissh faste,	
	And many a lovely look on hem he caste,	
235	And namely° on this carpenteres wif:	*especially*
	To looke on hire him thoughte a merye lif.	
	She was so propre° and sweete and likerous,⁵	*neat*
	I dar wel sayn, if she hadde been a mous,	
	And he a cat, he wolde hire hente° anoon.	*pounce on*
240	This parissh clerk, this joly Absolon,	
	Hath in his herte swich a love-longinge°	*lovesickness*
	That of no wif ne took he noon offringe—	
	For curteisye he saide he wolde noon.	
	The moone, whan it was night, ful brighte shoon,°	*shone*
245	And Absolon his giterne° hath ytake—	*guitar*
	For paramours° he thoughte for to wake—	*love*
	And forth he gooth, jolif° and amorous,	*pretty*
	Til he cam to the carpenteres hous,	
	A litel after cokkes hadde ycrowe,	

5. Wide-mouthed basket for separating grain from chaff.
6. Parting of the hair.
7. Carved with intricate designs, like the tracery in the windows of St. Paul's.
8. Laces for fastening the tunic and holding up the hose.

9. Let blood and give haircuts. Bleeding was a medical treatment performed by barbers.
1. Legal release. "Chartre": deed.
2. Part requiring a very high voice.
3. Gay (merry) barmaid.
4. Prudish about (vulgar) talk.
5. Wanton, appetizing.

250 And dressed him up by a shot-windowe[6]
    That was upon the carpenteres wal.
    He singeth in his vois gentil and smal,°   *dainty*
    "Now dere lady, if thy wille be,
    I praye you that ye wol rewe° on me,"   *have pity*
255 Ful wel accordant to his giterninge.[7]
    This carpenter awook and herde him singe,
    And spak unto his wif, and saide anoon,
    "What, Alison, heerestou nought Absolon
    That chaunteth thus under oure bowres° wal?"   *bedroom's*
260 And she answerde hir housbonde therwithal,
    "Yis, God woot, John, I heere it everydeel."°   *every bit*
      This passeth forth. What wol ye bet than weel?[8]
    Fro day to day this joly Absolon
    So woweth° hire that him is wo-bigoon: *woos*
265 He waketh° al the night and al the day;   *stays awake*
    He kembed° his lokkes brode[9] and made him gay;   *combed*
    He woweth hire by menes and brocage,[1]
    And swoor he wolde been hir owene page°   *personal servant*
    He singeth, brokking° as a nightingale;   *trilling*
270 He sente hire piment,° meeth,° and spiced ale,   *spiced wine / mead*
    And wafres° piping hoot out of the gleede;°   *pastries / coals*
    And for she was of towne,[2] he profred meede°—   *money*
    For som folk wol be wonnen for richesse,
    And som for strokes,° and som for gentilesse.   *blows (force)*
275 Somtime to shewe his lightnesse and maistrye,[3]
    He playeth Herodes[4] upon a scaffold° hye.   *platform, stage*
    But what availeth him as in this cas?
    She loveth so this hende Nicholas
    That Absolon may blowe the bukkes horn;[5]
280 He ne hadde for his labour but a scorn.
    And thus she maketh Absolon hir ape,[6]
    And al his ernest turneth til° a jape.°   *to / joke*
    Ful sooth is this proverbe, it is no lie;
    Men saith right thus: "Alway the nye slye
285 Maketh the ferre leve to be loth."[7]
    For though that Absolon be wood° or wroth,   *furious*
    By cause that he fer was from hir sighte,
    This nye° Nicholas stood in his lighte.   *nearby*
      Now beer° thee wel, thou hende Nicholas,   *bear*
290 For Absolon may waile and singe allas.
      And so bifel it on a Saterday
    This carpenter was goon til Oseney,
    And hende Nicholas and Alisoun
    Accorded been to this conclusioun,
295 That Nicholas shal shapen° hem a wile°   *arrange / trick*

---

6. Took his position by a hinged window.
7. In harmony with his guitar playing.
8. Better than well.
9. I.e., wide-spreading.
1. By go-betweens and agents.
2. Because she was a town woman.
3. Facility and virtuosity.

4. Herod, a role traditionally played as a bully in the mystery plays.
5. Blow the buck's horn, i.e., go whistle, waste his time.
6. I.e., thus she makes a monkey out of Absolon.
7. Always the sly man at hand makes the distant dear one hated.

This sely[8] jalous housbonde to bigile,
And if so be this game wente aright,
She sholden sleepen in his arm al night—
For this was his desir and hire° also.   *hers*
300 And right anoon, withouten wordes mo,
This Nicholas no lenger wolde tarye,
But dooth ful softe unto his chambre carye
Bothe mete and drinke for a day or twaye,
And to hir housbonde bad hire for to saye,
305 If that he axed after Nicholas,
She sholde saye she niste° wher he was—   *didn't know*
Of al that day she sawgh him nought with yë:
She trowed° that he was in maladye,   *believed*
For for no cry hir maide coude him calle,
310 He nolde answere for no thing that mighte falle.°   *happen*
    This passeth forth al thilke° Saterday   *this*
That Nicholas stille in his chambre lay,
And eet,° and sleep,° or dide what him leste,[9]   *ate / slept*
Til Sonday that the sonne gooth to reste.
315   This sely carpenter hath greet mervaile
Of Nicholas, or what thing mighte him aile,
And saide, "I am adrad,° by Saint Thomas,   *afraid*
It stondeth nat aright with Nicholas.
God shilde° that he deide sodeinly!   *forbid*
320 This world is now ful tikel,° sikerly: *precarious*
I sawgh today a corps yborn to chirche
That now a° Monday last I sawgh him wirche.°   *on / work*
Go up," quod he unto his knave° anoon,   *manservant*
"Clepe° at his dore or knokke with a stoon.°   *call / stone*
325 Looke how it is and tel me boldely."
    This knave gooth him up ful sturdily,
And at the chambre dore whil that he stood
He cride and knokked as that he were wood,°   *mad*
"What? How? What do ye, maister Nicholay?
330 How may ye sleepen al the longe day?"
But al for nought: he herde nat a word.
An hole he foond ful lowe upon a boord,
Ther as the cat was wont in for to creepe,
And at that hole he looked in ful deepe,
335 And atte laste he hadde of him a sighte.
    This Nicholas sat evere caping° uprighte   *gaping*
As he hadde kiked° on the newe moone.   *gazed*
Adown he gooth and tolde his maister soone
In what array° he saw this ilke° man.   *condition / same*
340   This carpenter to blessen him[1] bigan,
And saide, "Help us, Sainte Frideswide![2]
A man woot litel what him shal bitide.
This man is falle, with his astromye,°   *astronomy*
In som woodnesse° or in som agonye.   *madness*

8. Poor innocent.
9. He wanted.

1. Cross himself.
2. Patron saint of Oxford.

345 I thoughte ay° wel how that it sholde be: *always*
Men sholde nought knowe of Goddes privetee.° *secrets*
Ye, blessed be alway a lewed° man *ignorant*
That nought but only his bileve° can.° *creed / knows*
So ferde° another clerk with astromye: *fared*
350 He walked in the feeldes for to prye° *gaze*
Upon the sterres,° what ther sholde bifalle, *stars*
Til he was in a marle-pit³ yfalle—
He saw nat that. But yit, by Saint Thomas,
Me reweth sore⁴ for hende Nicholas.
355 He shal be rated of⁵ his studying,
If that I may, by Jesus, hevene king!
Get me a staf that I may underspore,° *pry up*
Whil that thou, Robin, hevest° up the dore. *heave*
He shal⁶ out of his studying, as I gesse."
360 And to the chambre dore he gan him dresse.⁷
His knave was a strong carl° for the nones,° *fellow / purpose*
And by the haspe he haaf° it up atones: *heaved*
Into° the floor the dore fil° anoon. *on / fell*
This Nicholas sat ay as stille as stoon,
365 And evere caped up into the air.
This carpenter wende° he were in despair, *thought*
And hente° him by the shuldres mightily, *seized*
And shook him harde, and cride spitously,° *vehemently*
"What, Nicholay, what, how! What! Looke adown!
370 Awaak and thenk on Cristes passioun!⁸
I crouche⁹ thee from elves and fro wightes."° *wicked creatures*
Therwith the nightspel saide he anoonrightes¹
On foure halves° of the hous aboute, *sides*
And on the thresshfold° on the dore withoute: *threshold*
375 "Jesu Crist and Sainte Benedight,° *Benedict*
Blesse this hous from every wikked wight!
For nightes nerye the White Pater Noster.²
Where wentestou,° thou Sainte Petres soster?° *did you go / sister*
And at the laste this hende Nicholas
380 Gan for to sike° sore, and saide, "Allas, *sigh*
Shal al the world be lost eftsoones° now?" *again*
    This carpenter answerde, "What saistou?
What, thenk on God as we doon, men that swinke."° *work*
    This Nicholas answerde, "Fecche me drinke,
385 And after wol I speke in privetee
Of certain thing that toucheth me and thee.
I wol telle it noon other man, certain."
    This carpenter gooth down and comth again,

3. Pit from which a fertilizing clay is dug.
4. I sorely pity.
5. Scolded for.
6. I.e., shall come.
7. Took his stand.
8. I.e., Christ's suffering and crucifixion.
9. Make the sign of the cross on.
1. The night-charm he said right away (to ward off evil spirits).

2. Pater Noster is Latin for "Our Father," the beginning of the Lord's Prayer. The line is obscure, but a conjectural reading would be, "May the White 'Our Father' (or 'Our White Father') [either a prayer or the personification of a protecting power] defend [*nerye*] (us) against nights." The "nightspel" is a jumble of Christian references and pagan superstition.

And broughte of mighty° ale a large quart, ° strong
390 And when that eech of hem hadde dronke his part,
This Nicholas his dore faste shette,° shut
And down the carpenter by him he sette,
And saide, "John, myn hoste lief° and dere, beloved
Thou shalt upon thy trouthe° swere me here word of honor
395 That to no wight thou shalt this conseil° wraye;° secret / disclose
For it is Cristes conseil that I saye,
And if thou telle it man,[3] thou art forlore,° lost
For this vengeance thou shalt have therfore,
That if thou wraye me, thou shalt be wood."[4]
400 "Nay, Crist forbede it, for his holy blood,"
Quod tho this sely° man. "I nam no labbe,° innocent / tell-tale
And though I saye, I nam nat lief to gabbe.[5]
Say what thou wilt, I shal it nevere telle
To child ne wif, by him that harwed helle."[6]
405 "Now John," quod Nicholas, "I wol nought lie.
I have yfounde in myn astrologye,
As I have looked in the moone bright,
That now a Monday next, at quarter night,[7]
Shal falle a rain, and that so wilde and wood,° furious
410 That half so greet was nevere Noees° flood. Noah's
This world," he saide, "in lasse° than an hour less
Shal al be dreint,° so hidous is the showr. drowned
Thus shal mankinde drenche° and lese° hir lif." drown / lose
This carpenter answerde, "Allas, my wif!
415 And shal she drenche? Allas, myn Alisoun!"
For sorwe of this he fil almost[8] adown,
And saide, "Is there no remedye in this cas?"
"Why yis, for[9] Gode," quod hende Nicholas,
"If thou wolt werken after lore and reed[1]—
420 Thou maist nought werken after thyn owene heed;° head
For thus saith Salomon that was ful trewe,
'Werk al by conseil and thou shalt nought rewe.'° be sorry
And if thou werken wolt by good conseil,
I undertake, withouten mast or sail,
425 Yit shal I save hire and thee and me.
Hastou nat herd how saved was Noee
Whan that oure Lord hadde warned him biforn
That al the world with water sholde be lorn?"° lost
"Yis," quod this carpenter, "ful yore° ago." long
430 "Hastou nat herd," quod Nicholas, "also
The sorwe of Noee with his felaweshipe?
Er° that he mighte gete his wif to shipe, before
Him hadde levere,[2] I dar wel undertake,
At thilke time than alle his wetheres[3] blake

---

3. To anyone.
4. Go mad.
5. And though I say it myself, I don't like to gossip.
6. By Him that harrowed (despoiled) hell—i.e.,
Christ.
7. I.e., shortly before dawn.

8. Almost fell.
9. I.e., by.
1. Act according to learning and advice.
2. He had rather.
3. Rams. I.e., he'd have given all the black rams
he had.

435 That she hadde had a ship hirself allone.[4]
And therfore woostou° what is best to doone? *do you know*
This axeth° haste, and of an hastif° thing *requires / urgent*
Men may nought preche or maken tarying.
Anoon go gete us faste into this in° *lodging*
440 A kneeding trough or elles a kimelin° *brewing tub*
For eech of us, but looke that they be large,° *wide*
In whiche we mowen swimme as in a barge,[5]
And han therinne vitaile suffisaunt[6]
But for a day—fy° on the remenaunt! *fie*
445 The water shal aslake° and goon away *diminish*
Aboute prime[7] upon the nexte day.
But Robin may nat wite° of this, thy knave, *know*
Ne eek thy maide Gille I may nat save.
Axe nought why, for though thou axe me,
450 I wol nought tellen Goddes privetee.° *secrets*
Suffiseth thee, but if thy wittes madde,° *go mad*
To han° as greet a grace as Noee hadde. *have*
Thy wif shal I wel saven, out of doute.
Go now thy way, and speed thee heraboute.
455 But whan thou hast for hire° and thee and me *her*
Ygeten us thise kneeding-tubbes three,
Thanne shaltou hangen hem in the roof ful hye,
That no man of oure purveyance° espye. *preparations*
And whan thou thus hast doon as I have said,
460 And hast oure vitaile faire in hem ylaid,
And eek an ax to smite the corde atwo,
Whan that the water comth that we may go,
And broke an hole an heigh[8] upon the gable
Unto the gardinward,[9] over the stable,
465 That we may freely passen forth oure way,
Whan that the grete showr is goon away,
Thanne shaltou swimme as merye, I undertake,
As dooth the white doke° after hir drake. *duck*
Thanne wol I clepe,° 'How, Alison? How, John? *call*
470 Be merye, for the flood wol passe anoon.'
And thou wolt sayn, 'Hail, maister Nicholay!
Good morwe, I see thee wel, for it is day!'
And thanne shal we be lordes al oure lif
Of al the world, as Noee and his wif.
475 But of oo thing I warne thee ful right:
Be wel avised° on that ilke night *warned*
That we been entred into shippes boord
That noon of us ne speke nought a word,
Ne clepe, ne crye, but been in his prayere,
480 For it is Goddes owene heeste dere[1]
Thy wif and thou mote hange fer atwinne,[2]

---

4. The reluctance of Noah's wife to board the ark
is a traditional comic theme in the mystery plays.
5. In which we can float as in a vessel.
6. Sufficient food.
7. 9:00 a.m.

8. On high.
9. Toward the garden.
1. Precious commandment.
2. Far apart.

For that bitwixe you shal be no sinne—
Namore in looking than ther shal in deede.
This ordinance is said: go, God thee speede.
485 Tomorwe at night whan men been alle asleepe,
Into oure kneeding-tubbes wol we creepe,
And sitten there, abiding Goddes grace.
Go now thy way, I have no lenger space°   *time*
To make of this no lenger sermoning.
490 Men sayn thus: 'Send the wise and say no thing.'
Thou art so wis it needeth thee nat teche:
Go save oure lif, and that I thee biseeche."
    This sely carpenter gooth forth his way:
Ful ofte he saide allas and wailaway,
495 And to his wif he tolde his privetee,
And she was war,° and knew it bet° than he,   *aware / better*
What al this quainte cast was for to saye.[3]
But nathelees she ferde° as she wolde deye,   *acted*
And saide, "Allas, go forth thy way anoon.
500 Help us to scape,° or we been dede eechoon.   *escape*
I am thy trewe verray wedded wif:
Go, dere spouse, and help to save oure lif."
    Lo, which a greet thing is affeccioun!°   *emotion*
Men may dien of imaginacioun,
505 So deepe° may impression be take.   *deeply*
This sely carpenter biginneth quake;
Him thinketh verrailiche° that he may see   *truly*
Noees flood come walwing° as the see   *rolling*
To drenchen° Alison, his hony dere.   *drown*
510 He weepeth, waileth, maketh sory cheere;
He siketh° with ful many a sory swough,°   *sighs / groan*
And gooth and geteth him a kneeding-trough,
And after a tubbe and a kimelin,
And prively he sente hem to his in,°   *dwelling*
515 And heeng° hem in the roof in privetee;   *hung*
His° owene hand he made laddres three,   *with his*
To climben by the ronges° and the stalkes°   *rungs / uprights*
Unto the tubbes hanging in the balkes,°   *rafters*
And hem vitailed,° bothe trough and tubbe,   *victualed*
520 With breed and cheese and good ale in a jubbe,°   *jug*
Suffising right ynough as for a day.
But er° that he hadde maad al this array,   *before*
He sente his knave, and eek his wenche also,
Upon his neede[4] to London for to go.
525 And on the Monday whan it drow to[5] nighte,
He shette° his dore withouten candel-lighte,   *shut*
And dressed° alle thing as it sholde be,   *arranged*
And shortly up they clomben° alle three.   *climbed*
They seten° stille wel a furlong way[6]   *sat*

---

3. What all this clever plan meant.   6. The time it takes to go a furlong (one-eighth
4. On an errand for him.   of a mile).
5. Drew toward.

530   "Now, Pater Noster, clum,"[7] saide Nicholay,
    And "Clum" quod John, and "Clum" saide Alisoun.
    This carpenter saide his devocioun,
    And stille he sit° and biddeth° his prayere,   *sits / prays*
    Awaiting on the rain, if he it heere.°   *might hear*
535   The dede sleep, for wery bisinesse,
    Fil° on this carpenter right as I gesse   *fell*
    Aboute corfew time,[8] or litel more.
    For travailing of his gost[9] he groneth sore,
    And eft° he routeth,° for his heed mislay.[1]   *then / snores*
540   Down of the laddre stalketh Nicholay,
    And Alison ful softe adown she spedde:
    Withouten wordes mo they goon to bedde
    Ther as the carpenter is wont to lie.
    Ther was the revel and the melodye,
545   And thus lith° Alison and Nicholas   *lies*
    In bisinesse of mirthe and of solas,°   *pleasure*
    Til that the belle of Laudes[2] gan to ringe,
    And freres° in the chauncel° gonne singe.   *friars / chancel*
    This parissh clerk, this amorous Absolon,
550   That is for love alway so wo-bigoon,
    Upon the Monday was at Oseneye,
    With compaignye him to disporte and playe,
    And axed upon caas a cloisterer[3]
    Ful prively after John the carpenter;
555   And he drow him apart out of the chirche,
    And saide, "I noot:[4] I sawgh him here nought wirche°   *work*
    Sith Saterday. I trowe that he be went
    For timber ther oure abbot hath him sent.
    For he is wont for timber for to go,
560   And dwellen atte grange[5] a day or two.
    Or elles he is at his hous, certain.
    Where that he be I can nought soothly sayn."
    This Absolon ful jolif was and light,[6]
    And thoughte, "Now is time to wake al night,
565   For sikerly,° I sawgh him nought stiringe   *certainly*
    Aboute his dore sin day bigan to springe.
    So mote° I thrive, I shal at cokkes crowe   *may*
    Ful prively knokken at his windowe
    That stant° ful lowe upon his bowres° wal.   *stands / bedroom's*
570   To Alison now wol I tellen al
    My love-longing,° for yet I shal nat misse   *lovesickness*
    That at the leeste way[7] I shal hire kisse.
    Som manere confort shal I have, parfay.°   *in faith*
    My mouth hath icched al this longe day:
575   That is a signe of kissing at the leeste.

---

7. Hush (?). "Pater Noster": Our Father.
8. Probably about 8:00 p.m.
9. Affliction of his spirit.
1. Lay in the wrong position.
2. The first church service of the day, before daybreak.

3. Here a member of the religious order of Osney Abbey. "Upon caas": by chance.
4. Don't know.
5. The outlying farm belonging to the abbey.
6. Was very amorous and cheerful.
7. I.e., at least.

Al night me mette[8] eek I was at a feeste.
Therfore I wol go sleepe an hour or twaye,
And al the night thanne wol I wake and playe."
     Whan that the firste cok hath crowe, anoon
580 Up rist° this joly lovere Absolon,   rises
And him arrayeth gay at point devis.[9]
But first he cheweth grain[1] and licoris,
To smellen sweete, er he hadde kembd° his heer.   combed
Under his tonge a trewe-love[2] he beer,°   bore
585 For therby wende° he to be gracious.°   supposed / pleasing
He rometh° to the carpenteres hous,   strolls
And stille he stant° under the shot-windowe—   stands
Unto his brest it raughte,° it was so lowe—   reached
And ofte he cougheth with a semisoun.°   small sound
590 "What do ye, hony-comb, sweete Alisoun,
My faire brid,[3] my sweete cinamome?°   cinnamon
Awaketh, lemman° myn, and speketh to me.   sweetheart
Wel litel thinken ye upon my wo
That for your love I swete° ther I go.   sweat
595 No wonder is though that I swelte° and swete: melt
I moorne as doth a lamb after the tete.°   teat
Ywis, lemman, I have swich love-longinge,
That lik a turtle° trewe is my moorninge: dove
I may nat ete namore than a maide."
600   "Go fro the windowe, Jakke fool," she saide.
"As help me God, it wol nat be com-pa-me.°   come-kiss-me
I love another, and elles I were to blame,
Wel bet° than thee, by Jesu, Absolon.   better
Go forth thy way or I wol caste a stoon,
605 And lat me sleepe, a twenty devele way."[4]
     "Allas," quod Absolon, "and wailaway,
That trewe love was evere so yvele biset.[5]
Thanne kis me, sin that it may be no bet,
For Jesus love and for the love of me."
610   "Woltou thanne go thy way therwith?" quod she.
"Ye, certes, lemman," quod this Absolon.
"Thanne maak thee redy," quod she. "I come anoon."
And unto Nicholas she saide stille,°   quietly
"Now hust,° and thou shalt laughen al thy fille."   hush
615 This Absolon down sette him on his knees,
And said, "I am a lord at alle degrees,[6]
For after this I hope ther cometh more.
Lemman, thy grace, and sweete brid, thyn ore!"°   mercy
     The windowe she undooth, and that in haste.
620 "Have do," quod she, "come of and speed thee faste,
Lest that oure neighebores thee espye."
     This Absolon gan wipe his mouth ful drye:
Derk was the night as pich or as the cole,

8. I dreamed.
9. To perfection.
1. Grain of paradise; a spice.
2. Sprig of a cloverlike plant.

3. Bird or bride.
4. In the name of twenty devils.
5. Ill-used.
6. In every way.

And at the windowe out she putte hir hole,
625 And Absolon, him fil no bet ne wers,[7]
But with his mouth he kiste hir naked ers,
Ful savourly,° er he were war of this.   with relish
Abak he sterte,° and thoughte it was amis,   started
For wel he wiste a womman hath no beerd.°   beard
630 He felte a thing al rough and longe yherd,°   haired
And saide, "Fy, allas, what have I do?"
   "Teehee," quod she, and clapte the windowe to.
And Absolon gooth forth a sory pas.[8]
   "A beerd, a beerd!"[9] quod hende Nicholas,
635 "By Goddes corpus,° this gooth faire and weel."   body
  This sely Absolon herde everydeel,°   every bit
And on his lippe he gan for anger bite,
And to himself he saide, "I shal thee quite."°   repay
  Who rubbeth now, who froteth° now his lippes   wipes
640 With dust, with sond,° with straw, with cloth, with chippes,   sand
But Absolon, that saith ful ofte allas?
"My soule bitake° I unto Satanas,°   commit / Satan
But me were levere[1] than all this town," quod he,
"Of this despit° awroken° for to be.   insult / avenged
645 Allas," quod he, "allas I ne hadde ybleint!"°   turned aside
His hote love was cold and al yqueint,°   quenched
For fro that time that he hadde kist hir ers
Of paramours he sette nought a kers,[2]
For he was heled° of his maladye.   cured
650 Ful ofte paramours he gan defye,°   renounce
And weep° as dooth a child that is ybete.   wept
A softe paas[3] he wente over the streete
Until° a smith men clepen daun Gervais,[4]   to
That in his forge smithed plough harneis:°   equipment
655 He sharpeth shaar and cultour[5] bisily.
This Absolon knokketh al esily,°   quietly
And saide, "Undo, Gervais, and that anoon."°   at once
  "What, who artou?" "It am I, Absolon."
"What, Absolon? What, Cristes sweete tree!°   cross
660 Why rise ye so rathe?° Ey, benedicite,°   early / bless me
What aileth you? Som gay girl, God it woot,
Hath brought you thus upon the viritoot.[6]
By Sainte Note, ye woot wel what I mene."
  This Absolon ne roughte nat a bene[7]
665 Of al his play. No word again he yaf:
He hadde more tow on his distaf[8]
Than Gervais knew, and saide, "Freend so dere,
This hote cultour in the chimenee° here,   fireplace
As lene[9] it me: I have therwith to doone.

---

7. It befell him neither better nor worse.
8. I.e., walking sadly.
9. A trick (slang), but with a play on line 629.
1. I had rather.
2. He didn't care a piece of cress for woman's love.
3. I.e., quiet walk.
4. Master Gervais.

5. He sharpens plowshare and coulter (the turf cutter on a plow).
6. I.e., on the prowl.
7. Didn't care a bean.
8. I.e., more on his mind.
9. I.e., please lend.

The Middle Ages (to ca. 1485)

Scepter, from the Sutton Hoo Treasure, ca. 625 C.E.

Discovered in 1939, among other items (jewelry, pottery, fragments of a helmet and shield), in a funeral ship buried in a mound near the coast of East Anglia, the scepter—probably a symbol of royal authority—consists of a massive ceremonial whetstone carved with faces and attached to a ring of twisted bronze wires mounted by an intricately carved stag. The treasure suggests the one laden on Scyld's funeral ship in *Beowulf* (lines 26–52; p. 43) and the material world imagined throughout the poem; the scepter evokes the "gold standard . . . / high above [the king's] head."

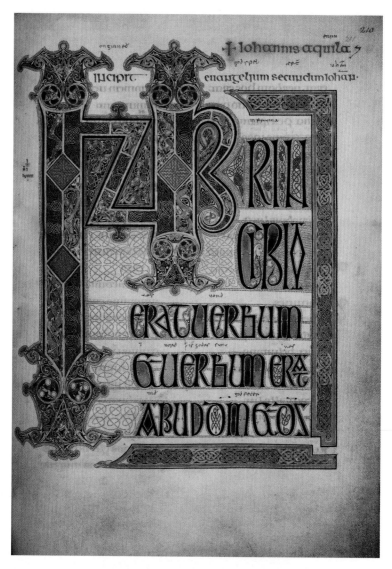

Lindisfarne Gospels, opening page of the Gospel of St. John

This gospel book was produced in the early eighth century in the monastery at Lindisfarne, an island off the coast of Northumbria in northeastern England. The book was written on vellum (animal skin). This magnificent page expresses the dynamic cultural encounter of different traditions. The large, easily legible letters form the beginning of the Gospel of St. John in Latin ("*In Principio erat verbum et verbum erat apud Deum, et Deus . . .*" ["In the beginning was the word, and the Word was with God, and God . . ."]); within the letters of that learned language, which voice a Christian theology influenced by Greek philosophical ideas, the illuminator mixes Germanic pre-Christian visual and vernacular elements: the complex, abstract, interlaced patterns, with animal and human forms (see the snake tucked into the stem of the capital "P" and the human face that emerges from the "c" of "cipio"), fill and/or surround the letters; and a later, tenth-century monk has provided an interlinear translation of the Latin (beginning "onginneth godspel"), written above the Latin heading "*incipit evangelium*" ("[Here] begins the gospel . . .").

Noah urging his wife to board the ark, ca. 1290

Noah's trouble getting his wife to board the ark was a popular subject in medieval drama and art (See Chaucer, *The Miller's Tale*, lines 430–35; pp. 291–92). In this illustration from a Psalter, Noah admonishes his wife with his left hand and grabs her wrist with the right, urging her to come aboard. Concealed, riding piggyback on the wife, a winged devil comes along as a stowaway. Below, he exits through the hull among drowned bodies on the seafloor. Other manuscripts show the serpent plugging the hole with his tail.

Plowing, the Luttrell Psalter, ca. 1330

The Psalter made for Sir Geoffrey Luttrell is sumptuously illustrated with idealized depictions of family, servants, workers, animals, and their activities (plowing, sowing, harvesting, feasting, playing) on the lord's estate; it is also elaborately decorated with foliage and grotesques. The Plowman here is a symbolic figure of order like Chaucer's Plowman (p. 274) and Langland's Piers Plowman (p. 391). The image echoes line 6 of the Psalm above: "Si dicebam motus est pes meus, misericordia tua, domine, adiuvabat me" (If I said: My foot is moved: thy mercy, Lord, helped me); "pes" (foot) anticipates the plow foot that moves the soil.

The Wilton Diptych,
Flemish school,
1395–96

Richard II commissioned this double-panel painting, both pious and political, not long before his deposition. In it he is portrayed as a boy, perhaps ten years old, the age at which he became king. Two English kings, St. Edmund and St. Edward "the Confessor," and John the Baptist, Richard's patron saint, present the young king to the Virgin and Child, who are surrounded by angels. The Christ Child blesses the red-cross standard of St. George (the patron saint of England), about to be given into the kneeling king's open hands. Richard's robe and the angels' sleeves display his personal emblem, a white hart (punning on *riche-hart*).

The Crucifixion, Lapworth Missal, 1398

This late medieval manuscript illumination typically portrays the humanity of
Christ: frail, eyes closed, head inclining on his shoulder. At the sides stand the
Virgin mother, who swoons in the arms of Mary Magdalene, and St. John the
Evangelist. The skull signifies Golgotha (place of skulls), the site of the
Crucifixion. According to medieval legend, the tree of knowledge had stood on
the same site and Adam was buried there: thus the skull is that of Adam,
whose original sin is being redeemed by the blood that the angels are collecting. The sun and moon symbolize the New and Old Testaments: as the sun
illuminates the moon, the light of the New Testament reveals the hidden
truths of the Old. Symbols of the four evangelists appear in the corners of the
intricately decorated frame.

Portrait of Chaucer, ca. 1411

In his poem *The Regiment of Princes*, Hoccleve, a younger disciple of Chaucer, memorializes "My maistir Chaucer, flour of eloquence, / Mirour of fructuous entendement, / O universel fadir in science!" One manuscript preserves a small portrait of Chaucer that Hoccleve placed in the margin so "That they that han of him lost thought and mynde / By this peynture may ageyn him fynde." Chaucer holds a rosary in his left hand; attached to his gown, a penknife (formerly used for making and mending quill pens) or pen case functions as a symbol of authorship.

Manuscript illumination of pilgrims leaving Canterbury, ca. 1420

Chaucer's pilgrims never get to Canterbury, but they do in the prologue to John Lydgate's *The Siege of Thebes*. In the prologue, Lydgate, a monk of Bury St. Edmund's and an enthusiastic follower of Chaucer, tells how on his own pilgrimage to Canterbury he encounters Chaucer's pilgrims. The Host invites the monk to join the company on their return journey and calls on him to tell the first tale. Lydgate is the middle figure in a monk's cowl, costumed more soberly than Chaucer's Monk (pp. 265–66). The cathedral and walls of Canterbury appear in the background.

Limbourg Brothers, *Tres Riches Heures* of John, duke of Berry, February scene, folio 2v

This page forms part of the splendid book of hours (a prayer book of daily and occasional prayers) commissioned by John, duke of Berry (d. 1416), third son of John II of France. The illuminated manuscript, produced in 1412–16, begins with a page devoted to the activities of each month. This page is for the month of February. Like the opening of Chaucer's *Canterbury Tales,* written just twenty or so years earlier, the scene is divided between the natural, cyclical movement of the cosmos above and the human world below. The semicircle at top represents the sun in its chariot moving as it always does (according to Ptolemaic astronomy) between the zodiacal signs of Aquarius and Pisces (the Fish). The rectangle below represents peasants working to survive in winter conditions: taking stock to market, chopping firewood, warming themselves by the fire. The semi-circle is divided by the necessity of numbers; the rectangle, by contrast, reveals that the human, constructed world is subject to accident: note, for example, the birds eating the accidentally spilled seeds.

The Money Lender and His Wife, Quentin Metsys, 1514

Metsys (d. 1530) worked in Antwerp (modern Belgium), one of the major trading centers of northwestern Europe in the later Middle Ages. Here we see the material world depicted in all its mesmeric attraction (note the gaze of both husband and wife, fixed on the coins as they are weighed); we also see how the material world pulls the gaze away from the spiritual world: the wife's eyes have drifted from her prayer book to the coins. The turn of both gazes seems oblivious to the possible spiritual consequences of obsessively material focus: neither husband nor wife seems to take in

the fact that the scales that weigh the money might remind them of the weighing of souls at the Last Judgment. Neither does the couple take in the spiritual resonances of the objects on the shelves behind them (for example, apple and extinguished candle). The entire painting, indeed, is an essay in observation and attention (note, for example, the convex mirror in the foreground, which reveals a figure in the room absorbed in a book).

670 I wol bringe it thee again ful soone."
　　Gervais answerde, "Certes, were it gold,
Or in a poke nobles alle untold,[1]
Thou sholdest have, as I am trewe smith.
Ey, Cristes fo,[2] what wol ye do therwith?"
675 "Therof," quod Absolon, "be as be may.
I shal wel telle it thee another day."
And caughte the cultour by the colde stele.°   *handle*
Ful softe out at the dore he gan to stele,
And wente unto the carpenteres wal:
680 He cougheth first and knokketh therwithal
Upon the windowe, right as he dide er.°   *before*
　　This Alison answerde, "Who is ther
That knokketh so? I warante[3] it a thief."
"Why, nay," quod he, "God woot, my sweete lief,°   *dear*
685 I am thyn Absolon, my dereling.°   *darling*
Of gold," quod he, "I have thee brought a ring—
My moder yaf it me, so God me save;
Ful fin it is and therto wel ygrave:°   *engraved*
This wol I yiven thee if thou me kisse."
690 　　This Nicholas was risen for to pisse,
And thoughte he wolde amenden[4] al the jape:°   *joke*
He sholde kisse his ers er that he scape.
And up the windowe dide he hastily,
And out his ers he putteth prively,
695 Over the buttok to the haunche-boon.
　　And therwith spak this clerk, this Absolon,
"Speek, sweete brid, I noot nought wher thou art."
This Nicholas anoon leet flee[5] a fart
As greet as it hadde been a thonder-dent°   *thunderbolt*
700 That with the strook he was almost yblent,°   *blinded*
And he was redy with his iren hoot,°   *hot*
And Nicholas amidde the ers he smoot:°   *smote*
Of° gooth the skin an hande-brede° aboute;   *off / handsbreadth*
The hote cultour brende so his toute°   *buttocks*
705 That for the smert° he wende for to[6] die;   *pain*
As he were wood° for wo he gan to crye,   *crazy*
"Help! Water! Water! Help, for Goddes herte!"
　　This carpenter out of his slomber sterte,
And herde oon cryen "Water!" as he were wood,
710 And thoughte, "Allas, now cometh Noweles[7] flood!"
He sette him up[8] withoute wordes mo,
And with his ax he smoot the corde atwo,
And down gooth al: he foond neither to selle
Ne breed ne ale til he cam to the celle,[9]
715 Upon the floor, and ther aswoune° he lay.   *in a faint*

---

1. Or gold coins all uncounted in a bag.
2. Foe, i.e., Satan.
3. I.e., wager.
4. Improve on.
5. Let fly.
6. Thought he would.

7. The carpenter is confusing Noah and Noel
(Christmas).
8. Got up.
9. He found time to sell neither bread nor ale
until he arrived at the foundation, i.e., he did not
take time out.

Up sterte hire[1] Alison and Nicholay,
And criden "Out" and "Harrow" in the streete.
The neighebores, bothe smale and grete,
In ronnen for to gauren° on this man   gape
720 That aswoune lay bothe pale and wan,
For with the fal he brosten° hadde his arm;   broken
But stonde he moste° unto his owene harm,   must
For whan he spak he was anoon bore down[2]
With° hende Nicholas and Alisoun: by
725 They tolden every man that he was wood—
He was agast so of Noweles flood,
Thurgh fantasye, that of his vanitee°   folly
He hadde ybought him kneeding-tubbes three,
And hadde hem hanged in the roof above,
730 And that he prayed hem, for Goddes love,
To sitten in the roof, *par compaignye.*[3]
    The folk gan laughen at his fantasye.
Into the roof they kiken° and they cape,°   peer / gape
And turned al his harm unto a jape,°   joke
735 For what so that this carpenter answerde,
It was for nought: no man his reson° herde;   argument
With othes grete he was so sworn adown,
That he was holden° wood in al the town,   considered
For every clerk anoonright heeld with other:
740 They saide, "The man was wood, my leve brother,"
And every wight gan laughen at this strif.°   fuss
Thus swived[4] was the carpenteres wif
For al his keeping° and his jalousye,   guarding
And Absolon hath kist hir nether° yë,   lower
745 And Nicholas is scalded in the toute:
This tale is doon, and God save al the route!° company

1. Started.
2. Refuted.
3. For company's sake.
4. The vulgar verb for having sexual intercourse.

The Man of Law's Epilogue

The Reeve has taken *The Miller's Tale* personally and retaliates with a fabliau about a miller whose wife and daughter are seduced by two clerks. Next the Cook begins yet another fabliau, which breaks off after fifty-five lines, thereby closing Fragment I of *The Canterbury Tales.* Chaucer may never have settled on a final order for the tales he completed, but all modern editors, following many manuscripts, agree in putting *The Man of Law's Tale* next. The Man of Law tells a long moralistic tale about the many trials of a heroine called Constance for the virtue she personifies. This tale is finished, but Fragment II shows that *The Canterbury Tales* reaches us as a work in progress, which Chaucer kept revising, creating many problems for its scribes and editors. In the link that introduces him, the Man of Law says he will tell a tale in prose, but the story of Constance turns out to be in a seven-line stanza called rhyme royal. That inconsistency has led to speculation that at one time the Man of Law was assigned a long prose allegory, which Chaucer later reassigned to his own pilgrim persona. In thirty-five manuscripts *The Man of Law's Tale* is followed by an *Epilogue* omitted in twenty-two of the manuscripts that contain more or less complete versions of *The Canterbury Tales.* The often-missing link begins with the Host praising the *Man of Law's Tale* and calling upon the Parson to tell another uplifting tale. The Parson, however, rebukes the Host for swearing. The Host angrily accuses the Parson of being a "Lollard," a derogatory term for followers of the reformist polemicist John Wycliffe. This is Chaucer's only overt reference to an important religious and political controversy that anticipates the sixteenth-century English Reformation.

A third speaker, about whose identity the manuscripts disagree (six read "Summoner"; twenty-eight, "Squire"; one, "Shipman"), interrupts with the promise to tell a merry tale. Several modern editions, including the standard one used by scholars, print *The Man of Law's Epilogue* at the end of Fragment II, and begin Fragment III with *The Wife of Bath's Prologue.* Because the third speaker in the former *sounds* like the Wife, an argument has been made that she is the pilgrim who refers to "My joly body" (line 23), who at one time told a fabliau tale in which the narrator speaks of married women in the first person plural ("we," "us," "our"). Chaucer, so the argument goes, later gave that story to the Shipman. If in fact the Wife of Bath did once tell what is now *The Shipman's Tale,* that would be an indication of the exciting new possibilities he discovered in the literary form he had invented.

	Oure Host upon his stiropes stood anoon	
	And saide, "Goode men, herkneth everichoon,	
	This was a thrifty° tale for the nones,°	*proper / occasion*
	Sire parissh Preest," quod he, "for Goddes bones,	
5	Tel us a tale as was thy forward° yore.°	*agreement / earlier*
	I see wel that ye lerned men in lore°	*teaching*
	Can° muche good, by Goddes dignitee."	*know*
	The Person him answerde, "Benedicite,°	*bless me*
	What aileth the man so sinfully to swere?"	
10	Oure Host answerede, "O Jankin, be ye there?[1]	
	I smelle a lollere[2] in the wind," quod he.	
	"Now, goode men," quod oure Hoste, "herkneth me:	
	Abideth, for Goddes digne° passioun,	*worthy*
	For we shal have a predicacioun.°	*sermon*
15	This lollere here wol prechen us somwhat."	
	"Nay, by my fader soule that shal he nat,"	
	Saide the [Wif of Bathe],[3] "here shal he nat preche:	
	He shal no gospel glosen[4] here ne teche.	
	We leven° alle in the grete God," quod [she].	*believe*
20	"He wolde sowen som difficultee	
	Or sprengen cokkel in oure clene corn.[5]	
	And therfore, Host, I warne thee biforn,	
	My joly body shal a tale telle	
	And I shal clinken you so merye a belle	
25	That I shal waken al this compaignye.	
	But it shal nat been of philosophye,	
	Ne physlias[6] ne termes quainte of lawe:	
	There is but litel Latin in my mawe."°	*stomach*

---

1. Is that where you're coming from? "Jankin": Johnny; derogatory name for a priest.
2. Contemptuous term for a religious reformer considered radical; a heretic.
3. On the speaker here, see the discussion in the headnote, above.

4. Gloss, with the sense of distorting the meaning of scripture.
5. Sow tares (impure doctrine) in our pure wheat.
6. No such word exists. The speaker is coining what sounds like a professional term in philosophy, law, or medicine.

The Wife of Bath's Prologue and Tale

The Wife of Bath. Illumination from the Ellesmere Manuscript of *The Canterbury Tales,* ca. 1400–1405. Note the whip and the spurs.

In creating the Wife of Bath, Chaucer drew upon a centuries-old tradition of misogynist writing that was particularly nurtured by the medieval Church. In their conviction that the rational, intellectual, spiritual, and, therefore, higher side of human nature predominated in men, whereas the irrational, material, earthly, and, therefore, lower side of human nature predominated in women, St. Paul and the early Church fathers exalted celibacy and virginity above marriage, although they were also obliged to concede the necessity and sanctity of matrimony. In the fourth century, a monk called Jovinian wrote a tract in which he apparently presented marriage as a positive good rather than as a necessary evil. That tract is known only through St. Jerome's extreme attack upon it. Jerome's diatribe and other antifeminist and antimatrimonial literature provided Chaucer with a rich body of bookish male "auctoritee" (authority) against which the Wife of Bath asserts her female "experience" and defends her rights and justifies her life as a five-time married woman. In her polemical wars with medieval clerks and her matrimonial wars with her five husbands, the last of whom was once a clerk of Oxenford, the Wife of Bath seems ironically to confirm the accusations of the clerks, but at the same time she succeeds in satirizing the shallowness of the stereotypes of women and marriage in antifeminist writings and in demonstrating how much the largeness and complexity of her own character rise above that stereotype.

The Prologue

Experience, though noon auctoritee	
Were in this world, is right ynough for me	
To speke of wo that is in mariage:	
For lordinges,° sith I twelf yeer was of age—	*gentlemen*
5 Thanked be God that is eterne on live—	
Housbondes at chirche dore¹ I have had five	
(If I so ofte mighte han wedded be),	
And alle were worthy men in hir degree.	
But me was told, certain, nat longe agoon is,	
10 That sith that Crist ne wente nevere but ones°	*once*
To wedding in the Cane² of Galilee,	
That by the same ensample° taughte he me	*example*
That I ne sholde wedded be but ones.	
Herke eek,° lo, which° a sharp word for the nones,³	*also / what*
15 Biside a welle, Jesus, God and man,	
Spak in repreve° of the Samaritan:	*reproof*

1. The actual wedding ceremony was celebrated at the church door, not in the chancel.

2. Cana (see John 2.1).
3. To the purpose.

"Thou hast yhad five housbondes," quod he,
"And that ilke° man that now hath thee   *same*
Is nat thyn housbonde." Thus saide he certain.
20 What that he mente therby I can nat sayn,
But that I axe° why the fifthe man   *ask*
Was noon housbonde to the Samaritan?[4]
How manye mighte she han in mariage?
Yit herde I nevere tellen in myn age
25 Upon this nombre diffinicioun.°   *definition*
Men may divine° and glosen° up and down,   *guess / interpret*
But wel I woot,° expres,° withouten lie,   *know / expressly*
God bad us for to wexe[5] and multiplye:
That gentil text can I wel understonde.
30   Eek wel I woot° he saide that myn housbonde   *know*
Sholde lete° fader and moder and take to me,[6]   *leave*
But of no nombre mencion made he—
Of bigamye or of octogamye:[7]
Why sholde men thanne speke of it vilainye?
35   Lo, here the wise king daun° Salomon: *master*
I trowe° he hadde wives many oon,[8]   *believe*
As wolde God it leveful° were to me   *permissible*
To be refresshed half so ofte as he.
Which yifte[9] of God hadde he for alle his wives!
40 No man hath swich° that in this world alive is.   *such*
God woot this noble king, as to my wit,°   *knowledge*
The firste night hadde many a merye fit°   *bout*
With eech of hem, so wel was him on live.[1]
Blessed be God that I have wedded five,
45 Of whiche I have piked out the beste,[2]
Bothe of hir nether purs[3] and of hir cheste.°   *money box*
Diverse scoles maken parfit° clerkes,   *perfect*
And diverse practikes[4] in sondry werkes
Maken the werkman parfit sikerly:°   *certainly*
50 Of five housbondes scoleying° am I.   *schooling*
Welcome the sixte whan that evere he shal![5]
For sith I wol nat kepe me chast° in al,   *celibate*
Whan my housbonde is fro the world agoon,
Som Cristen man shal wedde me anoon.°   *right away*
55 For thanne th'Apostle[6] saith that I am free
To wedde, a Goddes half, where it liketh me.[7]
He saide that to be wedded is no sinne:
Bet is to be wedded than to brinne.[8]

4. Christ was actually referring to a sixth man who was not married to the Samaritan woman (cf. John 4.6ff.).
5. I.e., increase (see Genesis 1.28).
6. See Matthew 19.5.
7. I.e., of two or even eight marriages. The Wife of Bath is referring to successive, rather than simultaneous, marriages.
8. Solomon had seven hundred wives and three hundred concubines (1 Kings 11.3).
9. What a gift.
1. I.e., so pleasant a life he had.

2. Whom I have cleaned out of everything worth while.
3. Lower purse, i.e., testicles.
4. Practical experiences.
5. I.e., shall come along.
6. St. Paul.
7. I please. "A Goddes half": on God's behalf.
8. "It is better to marry than to burn" (1 Corinthians 7.9). Many of the Wife's citations of St. Paul are from this chapter, often secondhand from St. Jerome's tract *Against Jovinian*.

What rekketh me[9] though folk saye vilainye

60 Of shrewed° Lamech[1] and his bigamye?   cursed

I woot wel Abraham was an holy man,

And Jacob eek, as fer as evere I can,°   know

And eech of hem hadde wives mo than two,

And many another holy man also.

65   Where can ye saye in any manere age

That hye God defended° mariage   prohibited

By expres word? I praye you, telleth me.

Or where comanded he virginitee?

I woot as wel as ye, it is no drede,°   doubt

70 Th'Apostle, whan he speketh of maidenhede,°   virginity

He saide that precept therof hadde he noon:

Men may conseile a womman to be oon,°   single

But conseiling nis° no comandement.   is not

He putte it in oure owene juggement.

75 For hadde God comanded maidenhede,

Thanne hadde he dampned° wedding with the deede;[2]   condemned

And certes, if there were no seed ysowe,

Virginitee, thanne wherof sholde it growe?

Paul dorste nat comanden at the leeste

80 A thing of which his maister yaf° no heeste.°   gave / command

The dart[3] is set up for virginitee:

Cacche whoso may, who renneth° best lat see.   runs

But this word is nought take of[4] every wight,°   person

But ther as[5] God list° yive it of his might.   it pleases

85 I woot wel that th'Apostle was a maide,°   virgin

But nathelees, though that he wroot and saide

He wolde that every wight were swich° as he,   such

Al nis but conseil to virginitee;

And for to been a wif he yaf me leve

90 Of indulgence; so nis it no repreve°   disgrace

To wedde me[6] if that my make° die,   mate

Withouten excepcion of bigamy[7]—

Al° were it good no womman for to touche[8]   although

(He mente as in his bed or in his couche,

95 For peril is bothe fir° and tow° t'assemble—   fire / flax

Ye knowe what this ensample may resemble).[9]

This al and som,[1] he heeld virginitee

More parfit than wedding in freletee.°   frailty

(Freletee clepe I but if[2] that he and she

100 Wolde leden al hir lif in chastitee.)

I graunte it wel, I have noon envye

Though maidenhede preferre° bigamye:°   excel / remarriage

It liketh hem to be clene in body and gost.°   spirit

---

9. What do I care.

1. The first man whom the Bible mentions as having two wives (Genesis 4.19–24); he is cursed, however, not for his marriages but for murder.

2. I.e., at the same time.

3. I.e., prize in a race.

4. Understood for, i.e., applicable to.

5. Where.

6. For me to marry.

7. I.e., without there being any legal objection on the score of remarriage.

8. "It is good for a man not to touch a woman" (1 Corinthians 7.1).

9. I.e., what this metaphor may apply to.

1. This is all there is to it.

2. Frailty I call it unless.

Of myn estaat ne wol I make no boost;
105 For wel ye knowe, a lord in his houshold
Ne hath nat every vessel al of gold:
Some been of tree,° and doon hir lord servise.   *wood*
God clepeth° folk to him in sondry wise,   *calls*
And everich hath of God a propre yifte,[3]
110 Som this, som that, as him liketh shifte.°   *ordain*
Virginitee is greet perfeccioun,
And continence eek with devocioun,
But Crist, that of perfeccion is welle,°   *source*
Bad nat every wight he sholde go selle
115 Al that he hadde and yive it to the poore,
And in swich wise folwe him and his fore:°[4]   *footsteps*
He spak to hem that wolde live parfitly°—   *perfectly*
And lordinges, by youre leve, that am nat I.
I wol bistowe the flour of al myn age
120 In th'actes and in fruit of mariage.
        Telle me also, to what conclusioun°   *end*
Were membres maad of generacioun
And of so parfit wis a wrighte ywrought?[5]
        Trusteth right wel, they were nat maad for nought.
125 Glose° whoso wol, and saye bothe up and down   *interpret*
That they were maked for purgacioun
Of urine, and oure bothe thinges smale
Was eek° to knowe a femele from a male,   *also*
And for noon other cause—saye ye no?
130 Th'experience woot it is nought so.
So that the clerkes be nat with me wrothe,
I saye this, that they been maad for bothe—
That is to sayn, for office° and for ese°   *use / pleasure*
Of engendrure,° ther we nat God displese.   *procreation*
135 Why sholde men elles in hir bookes sette
That man shal yeelde[6] to his wif hir dette?°   *(marital) debt*
Now wherwith sholde he make his payement
If he ne used his sely° instrument?   *innocent*
Thanne were they maad upon a creature
140 To purge urine, and eek for engendrure.
But I saye nought that every wight is holde,°   *bound*
That hath swich harneis° as I to you tolde,   *equipment*
To goon and usen hem in engendrure:
Thanne sholde men take of chastitee no cure.°   *heed*
145 Crist was a maide° and shapen as a man,   *virgin*
And many a saint sith that the world bigan,
Yit lived they evere in parfit chastitee.
I nil° envye no virginitee: *will not*
Lat hem be breed° of pured° whete seed,   *bread / refined*
150 And lat us wives hote° barly breed—   *be called*
And yit with barly breed, Mark telle can,

---

3. See 1 Corinthians 7.7.
4. Matthew 19.21.

5. And wrought by so perfectly wise a maker.
6. I.e., pay. See 1 Corinthians 7.4–5.

Oure Lord Jesu refresshed many a man.[7]
In swich estaat as God hath cleped us
I wol persevere: I nam nat precious.°   *fastidious*
155 In wifhood wol I use myn instrument
As freely° as my Makere hath it sent.   *generously*
If I be daungerous,[8] God yive me sorwe:
Myn housbonde shal it han both eve and morwe,°   *morning*
     Whan that him list[9] come forth and paye his dette.
160 An housbonde wol I have, I wol nat lette,[1]
Which shal be bothe my dettour° and my thral,°   *debtor / slave*
And have his tribulacion withal°   *as well*
Upon his flessh whil that I am his wif.
I have the power during al my lif
165 Upon his propre° body, and nat he: *own*
Right thus th'Apostle tolde it unto me,
And bad oure housbondes for to love us weel.
Al this sentence° me liketh everydeel.°   *sense / entirely*

[AN INTERLUDE]

     Up sterte° the Pardoner and that anoon:°   *started / at once*
170 "Now dame," quod he, "by God and by Saint John,
Ye been a noble prechour in this cas.
I was aboute to wedde a wif: allas,
What° sholde I bye° it on my flessh so dere?   *why / purchase*
Yit hadde I levere° wedde no wif toyere."°   *rather / this year*
175   "Abid," quod she, "my tale is nat bigonne.
Nay, thou shalt drinken of another tonne,°   *tun, barrel*
Er° that I go, shal savoure wors than ale.   *before*
And whan that I have told thee forth my tale
Of tribulacion in mariage,
180 Of which I am expert in al myn age—
This is to saye, myself hath been the whippe—
Thanne maistou chese° wheither thou wolt sippe   *choose*
Of thilke° tonne that I shal abroche;°   *this same / open*
Be war of it, er thou too neigh approche,
185 For I shal telle ensamples mo than ten.
'Whoso that nil° be war by othere men,   *will not*
By him shal othere men corrected be.'
Thise same wordes writeth Ptolomee:
Rede in his *Almageste* and take it there."[2]
190   "Dame, I wolde praye you if youre wil it were,"
Saide this Pardoner, "as ye bigan,
Telle forth youre tale; spareth for no man,
And teche us yonge men of youre practike."°   *mode of operation*
     "Gladly," quod she, "sith it may you like;°   *please*

7. In the descriptions of the miracle of the loaves and fishes, it is actually John, not Mark, who mentions barley bread (John 6.9).
8. In romance *dangerous* is a term for disdainfulness with which a woman rejects a lover. The Wife means she will not withhold sexual favors, in emulation of God's generosity (line 156).
9. When he wishes to.
1. I will not leave off, desist.
2. "He who will not be warned by the example of others shall become an example to others." The *Almagest*, an astronomical work by the Greek astronomer and mathematician Ptolemy (2nd century C.E.), contains no such aphorism.

195 But that I praye to al this compaignye,
If that I speke after my fantasye,[3]
As taketh nat agrief° of that I saye,   *amiss*
For myn entente nis but for to playe."

[THE WIFE CONTINUES]

Now sire, thanne wol I telle you forth my tale.
200 As evere mote I drinke win or ale,
I shal saye sooth: tho° housbondes that I hadde,   *those*
As three of hem were goode, and two were badde.
The three men were goode, and riche, and olde;
Unnethe° mighte they the statut holde   *scarcely*
205 In which they were bounden unto me—
Ye woot wel what I mene of this, pardee.
As help me God, I laughe whan I thinke
How pitously anight I made hem swinke;°   *work*
And by my fay,° I tolde of it no stoor:[4]   *faith*
210 They hadde me yiven hir land and hir tresor;
Me needed nat do lenger diligence
To winne hir love or doon hem reverence.
They loved me so wel, by God above,
That I ne tolde no daintee of[5] hir love.
215 A wis womman wol bisye hire ever in oon[6]
To gete hire love, ye, ther as she hath noon.
But sith I hadde hem hoolly in myn hand,
And sith that they hadde yiven me al hir land,
What° sholde I take keep° hem for to plese,   *why / care*
220 But it were for my profit and myn ese?
I sette hem so awerke,° by my fay,   *awork*
That many a night they songen° wailaway.   *sang*
The bacon was nat fet° for hem, I trowe,   *brought back*
That some men han in Essexe at Dunmowe.[7]
225 I governed hem so wel after° my lawe   *according to*
That eech of hem ful blisful was and fawe°   *glad*
To bringe me gaye thinges fro the faire;
They were ful glade whan I spak hem faire,
For God it woot, I chidde° hem spitously.°   *chided / cruelly*
230 Now herkneth how I bar me° proprely: *bore myself, behaved*
Ye wise wives, that conne understonde,
Thus sholde ye speke and bere him wrong on honde[8]—
For half so boldely can ther no man
Sweren and lyen as a woman can.
235 I saye nat this by wives that been wise,
But if it be whan they hem misavise.[9]
A wis wif, if that she can hir good,[1]

---

3. If I speak according to my fancy.
4. I set no store by it.
5. Set no value on.
6. Busy herself constantly.
7. At Dunmow, a side of bacon was awarded to the couple who after a year of marriage could

claim no quarrels, no regrets, and the desire, if freed, to remarry one another.
8. Accuse him falsely.
9. Unless it happens that they make a mistake.
1. If she knows what's good for her.

Shal bere him on hande the cow is wood,[2]
And take witnesse of hir owene maide
240 Of hir assent.[3] But herkneth how I saide:
"Sire olde cainard,° is this thyn array?[4]   *sluggard*
Why is my neighebores wif so gay?
She is honoured overal° ther she gooth: *wherever*
I sitte at hoom; I have no thrifty° cloth.   *decent*
245 What doostou at my neighebores hous?
Is she so fair? Artou so amorous?
What rounce° ye with oure maide, benedicite.[5]   *whisper*
Sire olde lechour, lat thy japes° be.   *tricks, intrigues*
And if I have a gossib° or a freend   *confidant*
250 Withouten gilt, ye chiden as a feend,
If that I walke or playe unto his hous.
Thou comest hoom as dronken as a mous,
And prechest on thy bench, with yvel preef.[6]
Thou saist to me, it is a greet mischief°   *misfortune*
255 To wedde a poore womman for costage.[7]
And if that she be riche, of heigh parage,°   *descent*
Thanne saistou that it is a tormentrye
To suffre hir pride and hir malencolye.°   *bad humor*
And if that she be fair, thou verray knave,
260 Thou saist that every holour° wol hire have: *lecher*
She may no while in chastitee abide[8]
That is assailed upon eech a side.
 "Thou saist som folk desiren us for richesse,
Som[9] for oure shap, and som for oure fairnesse,
265 And som for she can outher° singe or daunce,   *either*
And som for gentilesse and daliaunce,°   *flirtatiousness*
Som for hir handes and hir armes smale°—   *slender*
Thus gooth al to the devel by thy tale![1]
Thou saist men may nat keepe[2] a castel wal,
270 It may so longe assailed been overal.°   *everywhere*
And if that she be foul,° thou saist that she   *ugly*
Coveiteth° every man that she may see;   *desires*
For as a spaniel she wol on him lepe,
Til that she finde som man hire to chepe.°   *bargain for*
275 Ne noon so grey goos gooth ther in the lake,
As, saistou, wol be withoute make;°   *mate*
And saist it is an hard thing for to weelde°   *possess*
A thing that no man wol, his thankes, heelde[3]
Thus saistou, lorel,° whan thou goost to bedde,   *wretch*
280 And that no wis man needeth for to wedde,
Ne no man that entendeth° unto hevene—   *aims*
With wilde thonder-dint° and firy levene°   *thunderbolt / lightning*

---

2. Shall persuade him the chough has gone crazy.
The chough, a talking bird, was popularly supposed to tell husbands of their wives' infidelity.
3. And call as a witness her maid, who is on her side.
4. I.e., is this how you behave?
5. The Lord bless you.
6. I.e., (may you have) bad luck.

7. Because of the expense.
8. Remain faithful to her husband.
9. "Som," in this and the following lines, means "one."
1. I.e., according to your story.
2. I.e., keep safe.
3. No man would willingly hold.

Mote thy welked nekke be tobroke!⁴

Thou saist that dropping° houses and eek smoke — *leaking*

285 And chiding wives maken men to flee

Out of hir owene hous: a, benedicite,

What aileth swich an old man for to chide?

Thou saist we wives wil oure vices hide

Til we be fast,⁵ and thanne we wol hem shewe—

290 Wel may that be a proverbe of a shrewe!° — *rascal*

Thou saist that oxen, asses, hors,° and houndes, — *horses*

They been assayed° at diverse stoundes;° — *tried out / times*

Bacins, lavours,° er that men hem bye,° — *washbowls / buy*

Spoones, stooles, and al swich housbondrye,° — *household goods*

295 And so be° pottes, clothes, and array°— — *are / clothing*

But folk of wives maken noon assay

Til they be wedded—olde dotard shrewe!

And thanne, saistou, we wil oure vices shewe.

Thou saist also that it displeseth me

300 But if° that thou wolt praise my beautee, — *unless*

And but thou poure° alway upon my face, — *gaze*

And clepe me 'Faire Dame' in every place,

And but thou make a feeste on thilke day

That I was born, and make me fressh and gay,

305 And but thou do to my norice° honour, — *nurse*

And to my chamberere within my bowr,⁶

And to my fadres folk, and his allies⁷—

Thus saistou, olde barel-ful of lies.

And yit of our apprentice Janekin,

310 For his crispe° heer, shining as gold so fin, — *curly*

And for° he squiereth me bothe up and down, — *because*

Yit hastou caught a fals suspecioun;

I wil° him nat though thou were deed° tomorwe. — *want / dead*

"But tel me this, why hidestou with sorwe⁸

315 The keyes of thy cheste° away fro me? — *money box*

It is my good° as wel as thyn, pardee. — *property*

What, weenestou° make an idiot of oure dame?⁹ — *do you think to*

Now by that lord that called is Saint Jame,

Thou shalt nought bothe, though thou were wood,° — *furious*

320 Be maister of my body and of my good:

That oon thou shalt forgo, maugree thine yën.¹

"What helpeth it of me enquere° and spyen? — *inquire*

I trowe thou woldest loke° me in thy cheste. — *lock*

Thou sholdest saye, 'Wif, go wher thee leste.° — *it may please*

325 Taak youre disport²—I nil leve° no tales: — *believe*

I knowe you for a trewe wif, dame Alis.'

We love no man that taketh keep or charge³

Wher that we goon: we wol been at oure large.⁴

4. May thy withered neck be broken!
5. Tightly conjoined, i.e., married.
6. And to my chambermaid within my bedroom.
7. Relatives by marriage.
8. I.e., with sorrow to you.
9. I.e., me, the mistress of the house.

1. Despite your eyes, i.e., despite anything you can do about it.
2. Enjoy yourself.
3. Notice or interest.
4. I.e., liberty.

Of alle men yblessed mote he be
330 The wise astrologen° daun Ptolomee,   *astronomer*
That saith this proverbe in his *Almageste*:
'Of alle men his wisdom is the hyeste
That rekketh° nat who hath the world in honde.'[5]   *cares*
By this proverbe thou shalt understonde,
335 Have thou[6] ynough, what thar° thee rekke or care   *need*
How merily that othere folkes fare?
For certes, olde dotard, by youre leve,
Ye shal han queinte[7] right ynough at eve:
He is too greet a nigard that wil werne°   *refuse*
340 A man to lighte a candle at his lanterne;
He shal han nevere the lasse° lighte, pardee.   *less*
Have thou ynough, thee thar nat plaine thee.[8]
    "Thou saist also that if we make us gay
With clothing and with precious array,
345 That it is peril of oure chastitee,
And yit, with sorwe, thou moste enforce thee,[9]
And saye thise wordes in th' Apostles[1] name:
'In habit° maad with chastitee and shame   *clothing*
Ye wommen shal apparaile you,' quod he,
350 'And nat in tressed heer[2] and gay perree,°   *jewelry*
As perles, ne with gold ne clothes riche.'[3]
After thy text, ne after thy rubriche,[4]
I wol nat werke as muchel as a gnat.
Thou saidest this, that I was lik a cat:
355 For whoso wolde senge° a cattes skin,   *singe*
Thanne wolde the cat wel dwellen in his in;°   *lodging*
And if the cattes skin be slik° and gay,   *sleek*
She wol nat dwelle in house half a day,
But forth she wol, er any day be dawed,[5]
360 To shewe her skin and goon a-caterwawed.°   *caterwauling*
This is to saye, if I be gay, sire shrewe,
I wol renne° out, my borel° for to shewe.   *run / clothing*
Sir olde fool, what helpeth[6] thee t'espyen?
Though thou praye Argus with his hundred yën[7]
365 To be my wardecors,° as he can best,   *bodyguard*
In faith, he shal nat keepe° me but me lest:[8]   *guard*
Yit coude I make his beerd,[9] so mote I thee.°   *prosper*
    "Thou saidest eek that ther been thinges three,
The whiche thinges troublen al this erthe,
370 And that no wight may endure the ferthe.°   *fourth*
O leve° sire shrewe, Jesu shorte° thy lif!   *dear / shorten*
Yit prechestou and saist an hateful wif

---

5. Who rules the world.
6. If you have.
7. Elegant, pleasing thing; a euphemism for sexual enjoyment.
8. I.e., you need not complain.
9. Strengthen your position.
1. I.e., St. Paul's.
2. I.e., elaborate hairdo.
3. See 1 Timothy 2.9.

4. Rubric, i.e., direction.
5. Has dawned.
6. What does it help.
7. Argus was a monster whom Juno set to watch over one of Jupiter's mistresses. Mercury put all one hundred of his eyes to sleep and slew him.
8. Unless I please.
9. I.e., deceive him.

Yrekened° is for oon of thise meschaunces.[1]   *is counted*
Been ther nat none othere resemblaunces
375 That ye may likne youre parables to,[2]
But if° a sely° wif be oon of tho?   *unless / innocent*
  "Thou liknest eek wommanes love to helle,
To bareine° land ther water may nat dwelle;   *barren*
Thou liknest it also to wilde fir—
380 The more it brenneth,° the more it hath desir   *burns*
To consumen every thing that brent° wol be;   *burned*
Thou saist right° as wormes shende° a tree,   *just / destroy*
Right so a wif destroyeth hir housbonde—
This knowen they that been to wives bonde."°   *bound*
385 Lordinges, right thus, as ye han understonde,
Bar I stifly mine olde housbondes on honde[3]
That thus they saiden in hir dronkenesse—
And al was fals, but that I took witnesse
On Janekin and on my nece also.
390 O Lord, the paine I dide hem and the wo,
Ful giltelees, by Goddes sweete pine!°   *suffering*
For as an hors I coude bite and whine;°   *whinny*
I coude plaine° and° I was in the gilt,   *complain / if*
Or elles often time I hadde been spilt.°   *ruined*
395 Whoso that first to mille comth first grint.°   *grinds*
I plained first: so was oure werre stint.[4]
They were ful glade to excusen hem ful blive°   *quickly*
Of thing of which they nevere agilte hir live.[5]
Of wenches wolde I beren hem on honde,[6]
400 Whan that for sik[7] they mighte unnethe° stonde,   *scarcely*
Yit tikled I his herte for that he
Wende° I hadde had of him so greet cheertee.°   *thought / affection*
I swoor that al my walking out by nighte
Was for to espye wenches that he dighte.[8]
405 Under that colour[9] hadde I many a mirthe.
For al swich wit is yiven us in oure birthe:
Deceite, weeping, spinning God hath yive
To wommen kindely° whil they may live.   *naturally*
And thus of oo thing I avaunte me:[1]
410 At ende I hadde the bet° in eech degree,   *better*
By sleighte or force, or by som manere thing,
As by continuel murmur° or grucching;°   *complaint / grumbling*
Namely° abedde hadden they meschaunce: *especially*
Ther wolde I chide and do hem no plesaunce;[2]
415 I wolde no lenger in the bed abide
If that I felte his arm over my side,
Til he hadde maad his raunson° unto me;   *ransom*
Thanne wolde I suffre him do his nicetee.°   *foolishness (sex)*

---

1. For the other three misfortunes, see Proverbs
30.21–23.
2. Are there no other (appropriate) similitudes
to which you might draw analogies?
3. I rigorously accused my old husbands.
4. Our war brought to an end.
5. Of which they were never guilty in their lives.

6. Falsely accuse them.
7. I.e., sickness.
8. Had intercourse with.
9. I.e., pretense.
1. Boast.
2. Give them no pleasure.

And therfore every man this tale I telle:
420 Winne whoso may, for al is for to selle;
With empty hand men may no hawkes lure.
For winning° wolde I al his lust endure,   *profit*
And make me a feined° appetit—   *pretended*
And yit in bacon³ hadde I nevere delit.
425 That made me that evere I wolde hem chide;
For though the Pope hadde seten° hem biside,   *sat*
I wolde nought spare hem at hir owene boord.°   *table*
For by my trouthe, I quitte° hem word for word.   *repaid*
As help me verray God omnipotent,
430 Though I right now sholde make my testament,
I ne owe hem nat a word that it nis quit.
I broughte it so aboute by my wit
That they moste yive it up as for the beste,
Or elles hadde we nevere been in reste;
435 For though he looked as a wood° leoun,   *furious*
Yit sholde he faile of his conclusioun.°   *object*
    Thanne wolde I saye, "Goodelief, taak keep,⁴
How mekely looketh Wilekin,⁵ oure sheep!
Com neer my spouse, lat me ba° thy cheeke—   *kiss*
440 Ye sholden be al pacient and meeke,
And han a sweete-spiced° conscience,   *mild*
Sith ye so preche of Jobes pacience;
Suffreth alway, sin ye so wel can preche;
And but ye do, certain, we shal you teche
445 That it is fair to han a wif in pees.
Oon of us two moste bowen, doutelees,
And sith a man is more resonable
Than womman is, ye mosten been suffrable.°   *patient*
What aileth you to grucche° thus and grone?   *grumble*
450 Is it for ye wolde have my queinte° allone?   *sexual organ*
Why, taak it al—lo, have it everydeel.°   *all of it*
Peter,⁶ I shrewe° you but ye° love it weel.   *curse / if you don't*
For if I wolde selle my bele chose,⁷
I coude walke as fressh as is a rose;
455 But I wol keepe it for youre owene tooth.°   *taste*
Ye be to blame. By God, I saye you sooth!"°   *the truth*
Swiche manere° wordes hadde we on honde.   *kind of*
Now wol I speke of my ferthe° housbonde.   *fourth*
    My ferthe housbonde was a revelour°   *reveler*
460 This is to sayn, he hadde a paramour°   *mistress*
And I was yong and ful of ragerye,°   *passion*
Stibourne° and strong and joly as a pie:°   *untamable / magpie*
How coude I daunce to an harpe smale,°   *gracefully*
And singe, ywis,° as any nightingale,   *indeed*
465 Whan I hadde dronke a draughte of sweete win.
Metellius, the foule cherl, the swin,

---

3. I.e., old meat.
4. Good friend, take notice.
5. I.e., Willie.

6. By St. Peter.
7. French for "beautiful thing"; a euphemism for
sexual organs.

That with a staf birafte° his wif hir lif   *deprived*
For° she drank win, though I hadde been his wif,   *because*
Ne sholde nat han daunted° me fro drinke;   *frightened*
470 And after win on Venus moste° I thinke,   *must*
For also siker° as cold engendreth hail,   *sure*
A likerous° mouth moste han a likerous° tail: *greedy / lecherous*
In womman vinolent° is no defence—   *who drinks*
This knowen lechours by experience.
475   But Lord Crist, whan that it remembreth me[8]
Upon my youthe and on my jolitee,
It tikleth me aboute myn herte roote—
Unto this day it dooth myn herte boote°   *good*
That I have had my world as in my time.
480 But age, allas, that al wol envenime,°   *poison*
Hath me biraft[9] my beautee and my pith°—   *vigor*
Lat go, farewel, the devel go therwith!
The flour is goon, ther is namore to telle:
The bren° as I best can now moste I selle;   *bran*
485 But yit to be right merye wol I fonde.°   *strive*
Now wol I tellen of my ferthe housbonde.
    I saye I hadde in herte greet despit
That he of any other hadde delit,
But he was quit,° by God and by Saint Joce: *paid back*
490 I made him of the same wode a croce[1]—
Nat of my body in no foul manere—
But, certainly, I made folk swich cheere[2]
That in his owene grece I made him frye,
For angre and for verray jalousye.
495 By God, in erthe I was his purgatorye,
For which I hope his soule be in glorye.
For God it woot, he sat ful ofte and soong°   *sang*
Whan that his sho ful bitterly him wroong.°   *pinched*
Ther was no wight save God and he that wiste°   *knew*
500 In many wise how sore I him twiste.
He deide whan I cam fro Jerusalem,
And lith ygrave under the roode-beem,[3]
Al° is his tombe nought so curious[4]   *although*
As was the sepulcre of him Darius,
505 Which that Apelles wroughte subtilly:[5]
It nis but wast to burye him preciously.°   *expensively*
Lat him fare wel, God yive his soule reste;
He is now in his grave and in his cheste.°   *coffin*
    Now of my fifthe housbonde wol I telle—
510 God lete his soule nevere come in helle—
And yit he was to me the moste shrewe:[6]
That feele I on my ribbes al by rewe,[7]

8. When I look back.
9. Has taken away from me.
1. I made him a cross of the same wood. The proverb has much the same sense as the one quoted in line 493.
2. Pretended to be in love with others.
3. And lies buried under the rood beam (the cru- cifix beam running between nave and chancel).
4. Carefully wrought.
5. Accordingly to medieval legend, the artist Apelles decorated the tomb of Darius, king of the Persians.
6. Worst rascal.
7. In a row.

And evere shal unto myn ending day.
But in oure bed he was so fressh and gay,
515 And therwithal so wel coulde he me glose°   *flatter, coax*
Whan that he wolde han my bele chose,
That though he hadde me bet° on every boon,°   *beaten / bone*
He coude winne again my love anoon.°   *immediately*
I trowe I loved him best for that he
520 Was of his love daungerous[8] to me.
We wommen han, if that I shal nat lie,
In this matere a quainte fantasye:[9]
Waite what[1] thing we may nat lightly° have,   *easily*
Therafter wol we crye al day and crave;
525 Forbede us thing, and that desiren we;
Preesse on us faste, and thanne wol we flee.
With daunger oute we al oure chaffare:[2]
Greet prees° at market maketh dere° ware,   *crowd / expensive*
And too greet chepe is holden at litel pris.[3]
530 This knoweth every womman that is wis.
      My fifthe housbonde—God his soule blesse!—
Which that I took for love and no richesse,
He somtime was a clerk at Oxenforde,
And hadde laft° scole and wente at hoom to boorde   *left*
535 With my gossib,° dwelling in oure town   *confidante*
God have hir soule!—hir name was Alisoun;
She knew myn herte and eek my privetee°   *secrets*
Bet° than oure parissh preest, as mote I thee.°   *better / prosper*
To hire biwrayed° I my conseil° al,   *disclosed / secrets*
540 For hadde myn housbonde pissed on a wal,
Or doon a thing that sholde han cost his lif,
To hire,° and to another worthy wif,   *her*
And to my nece which I loved weel,
I wolde han told his conseil everydeel;°   *entirely*
545 And so I dide ful often, God it woot,
That made his face often reed° and hoot°   *red / hot*
For verray shame, and blamed himself for he
Hadde told to me so greet a privetee.
      And so bifel that ones° in a Lente—   *once*
550 So often times I to my gossib wente,
For evere yit I loved to be gay,
And for to walke in March, Averil, and May,
From hous to hous, to heere sondry tales—
That Janekin clerk and my gossib dame Alis
555 And I myself into the feeldes wente.
Myn housbonde was at London al that Lente:
I hadde the better leiser for to playe,
And for to see, and eek for to be seye°   *seen*
Of lusty folk—what wiste I wher my grace°   *luck*
560 Was shapen° for to be, or in what place?   *destined*

8. I.e., he played hard to get.
9. Strange fancy.
1. Whatever.

2. (Meeting) with reserve, we spread out our merchandise.
3. Too good a bargain is held at little value.

Therfore I made my visitaciouns
To vigilies[4] and to processiouns,
To preching eek, and to thise pilgrimages,
To playes of miracles and to mariages,
565 And wered upon[5] my gaye scarlet gites°—   *gowns*
Thise wormes ne thise motthes ne thise mites,
Upon my peril[6] frete° hem neveradeel: *ate*
And woostou why? For they were used weel.
   Now wol I tellen forth what happed me.
570 I saye that in the feeldes walked we,
Til trewely we hadde swich daliaunce,°   *flirtation*
This clerk and I, that of my purveyaunce°   *foresight*
I spak to him and saide him how that he,
If I were widwe, sholde wedde me.
575 For certainly, I saye for no bobaunce,°   *boast*
Yit was I nevere withouten purveyaunce
Of mariage n'of othere thinges eek:
I holde a mouses herte nought worth a leek
That hath but oon hole for to sterte° to,   *run*
580 And if that faile thanne is al ydo.[7]
I bar him on hand[8] he hadde enchaunted me
(My dame° taughte me that subtiltee);   *mother*
And eek I saide I mette° of him al night: *dreamed*
He wolde han slain me as I lay upright,°   *on my back*
585 And al my bed was ful of verray blood—
"But yit I hope that ye shul do me good;
For blood bitokeneth° gold, as me was taught."   *signifies*
And al was fals, I dremed of it right naught,
But as I folwed ay my dames° lore°   *mother's / teaching*
590 As wel of that as othere thinges more.
But now sire—lat me see, what shal I sayn?
Aha, by God, I have my tale again.
   Whan that my ferthe housbonde was on beere,°   *funeral bier*
I weep,° algate,° and made sory cheere,   *wept / anyhow*
595 As wives moten,° for it is usage,°   *must / custom*
And with my coverchief covered my visage;
But for I was purveyed° of a make.°   *provided / mate*
I wepte but smale, and that I undertake.°   *guarantee*
   To chirche was myn housbonde born amorwe;[9]
600 With neighebores that for him maden sorwe,
And Janekin oure clerk was oon of tho.
As help me God, whan that I saw him go
After the beere, me thoughte he hadde a paire
Of legges and of feet so clene[1] and faire,
605 That al myn herte I yaf unto his hold.°   *possession*
He was, I trowe,° twenty winter old,   *believe*
And I was fourty, if I shal saye sooth—
But yit I hadde alway a coltes tooth:[2]

4. Evening service before a religious holiday.
5. Wore.
6. On peril (to my soul), an oath.
7. I.e., the game is up; it's all over.

8. I pretended to him.
9. In the morning.
1. I.e., neat.
2. I.e., youthful appetites.

Gat-toothed[3] was I, and that bicam me weel;
610 I hadde the prente[4] of Sainte Venus seel.°   seal
As help me God, I was a lusty oon,
And fair and riche and yong and wel-bigoon,°   well-situated
And trewely, as mine housbondes tolde me,
I hadde the beste quoniam[5] mighte be.
615 For certes I am al Venerien
In feeling, and myn herte is Marcien:[6]
Venus me yaf my lust, my likerousnesse,°   amorousness
And Mars yaf me my sturdy hardinesse.
Myn ascendent was Taur[7] and Mars therinne—
620 Allas, allas, that evere love was sinne!
I folwed ay° my inclinacioun   ever
By vertu of my constellacioun;[8]
That made me I coude nought withdrawe
My chambre of Venus from a good felawe.
625 Yit have I Martes° merk upon my face,   Mars's
And also in another privee place.
For God so wis° be my savacioun,°   surely / salvation
I loved nevere by no discrecioun,°   moderation
But evere folwede myn appetit,
630 Al were he short or long or blak or whit;
I took no keep,° so that he liked° me,   heed / pleased
How poore he was, ne eek of what degree.
What sholde I saye but at the monthes ende
This joly clerk Janekin that was so hende°   courteous, nice
635 Hath wedded me with greet solempnitee,°   splendor
And to him yaf I al the land and fee°   property
That evere was me yiven therbifore—
But afterward repented me ful sore:
He nolde suffre no thing of my list.°   wish
640 By God, he smoot° me ones on the list°   struck / ear
For that I rente° out of his book a leef,   tore
That of the strook° myn ere weex° al deef.   blow / grew
Stibourne° I was as is a leonesse,   stubborn
And of my tonge a verray jangleresse,°   chatterbox
645 And walke I wolde, as I hadde doon biforn,
From hous to hous, although he hadde it[9] sworn;
For which he often times wolde preche,
And me of olde Romain geestes° teche,   stories
How he Simplicius Gallus lafte° his wif,   left
650 And hire forsook for terme of al his lif,
Nought but for open-heveded he hire sey[1]
Looking out at his dore upon a day.
    Another Romain tolde he me by name
That, for his wif was at a someres° game   summer's

---

3. Gap-toothed women were considered to be amorous.
4. Print, i.e., a birthmark.
5. Latin for "because"; another euphemism for a sexual organ.
6. Influenced by Mars. "Venerien": astrologically influenced by Venus.
7. My birth sign was the constellation Taurus, a sign in which Venus is dominant.
8. I.e., horoscope.
9. I.e., the contrary.
1. Just because he saw her bareheaded.

655 Withouten his witing,° he forsook hire eke;   *knowledge*
And thanne wolde he upon his Bible seeke
That ilke proverbe of Ecclesiaste²
Where he comandeth and forbedeth faste°   *strictly*
Man shal nat suffre his wif go roule° aboute;   *roam*
660 Thanne wolde he saye right thus withouten doute:
"Whoso that buildeth his hous al of salwes,°   *willow sticks*
And priketh° his blinde hors over the falwes,³   *rides*
And suffreth° his wif to go seeken halwes,°   *allows / shrines*
Is worthy to be hanged on the galwes."°   *gallows*
665 But al for nought—I sette nought an hawe⁴
Of his proverbes n'of his olde sawe;
N' I wolde nat of him corrected be:
I hate him that my vices telleth me,
And so doon mo, God woot, of us than I.
670 This made him with me wood al outrely:°   *entirely*
I nolde nought forbere° him in no cas.   *submit to*
      Now wol I saye you sooth, by Saint Thomas,
Why that I rente° out of his book a leef,   *tore*
For which he smoot me so that I was deef.
675 He hadde a book that gladly night and day
For his disport° he wolde rede alway.   *entertainment*
He cleped it *Valerie⁵ and Theofraste*,
At which book he lough° alway ful faste;   *laughed*
And eek ther was somtime a clerk at Rome,
680 A cardinal, that highte Saint Jerome,
That made a book⁶ again° Jovinian;   *against*
In which book eek ther was Tertulan,
Crysippus, Trotula, and Helouis,⁷
That was abbesse nat fer fro Paris;
685 And eek the Parables of Salomon,
Ovides *Art*,⁸ and bookes many oon—
And alle thise were bounden in oo volume.
And every night and day was his custume,
Whan he hadde leiser and vacacioun°   *free time*
690 From other worldly occupacioun,
To reden in this book of wikked wives.
He knew of hem mo legendes and lives
Than been of goode wives in the Bible.
For trusteth wel, it is an impossible°   *impossibility*
695 That any clerk wol speke good of wives,
But if it be of holy saintes lives,
N'of noon other womman nevere the mo—

2. Ecclesiasticus (25.25).
3. Plowed land.
4. I did not rate at the value of a hawthorn berry.
5. *"Valerie"*: i.e., the *Letter of Valerius Concerning Not Marrying*, by Walter Map; *"Theofraste"*: Theophrastus's *Book Concerning Marriage*. Medieval manuscripts often contained a number of different works, sometimes, as here, dealing with the same subject.

6. St. Jerome's misogynist *Against Jovinian*.
7. "Tertulan": i.e., Tertullian, author of treatises on sexual modesty. "Crysippus": mentioned by Jerome as an antifeminist. "Trotula": a female doctor whose presence here is unexplained. "Helouis": i.e., Eloise, whose love affair with the great scholar Abelard was a medieval scandal.
8. Ovid's *Art of Love*. "Parables of Salomon": the biblical Book of Proverbs.

Who painted the leon, tel me who?[9]
By God, if wommen hadden writen stories,
700 As clerkes han within hir oratories,°   *chapels*
They wolde han writen of men more wikkednesse
Than al the merk[1] of Adam may redresse.
The children of Mercurye and Venus[2]
Been in hir werking° ful contrarious:°   *operation / opposed*
705 Mercurye loveth wisdom and science,
And Venus loveth riot° and dispence;°   *revelry / spending*
And for hir diverse disposicioun
Each falleth in otheres exaltacioun,[3]
And thus, God woot, Mercurye is desolat
710 In Pisces wher Venus is exaltat,[4]
And Venus falleth ther Mercurye is raised:
Therfore no womman of no clerk is praised.
The clerk, whan he is old and may nought do
Of Venus werkes worth his olde sho,°   *shoe*
715 Thanne sit° he down and writ° in his dotage   *sits / writes*
That wommen can nat keepe hir mariage.
    But now to purpose why I tolde thee
That I was beten for a book, pardee:
Upon a night Janekin, that was our sire,[5]
720 Redde on his book as he sat by the fire
Of Eva first, that for hir wikkednesse
Was al mankinde brought to wrecchednesse,
For which that Jesu Crist himself was slain
That boughte° us with his herte blood again—   *redeemed*
725 Lo, heer expres of wommen may ye finde
That womman was the los° of al mankinde.[6]   *ruin*
    Tho° redde he me how Sampson loste his heres: *then*
Sleeping his lemman° kitte° it with hir sheres,   *lover / cut*
Thurgh which treson loste he both his yën.
730   Tho redde he me, if that I shal nat lien,
Of Ercules and of his Dianire,[7]
That caused him to sette himself afire.
No thing forgat he the sorwe and wo
That Socrates hadde with his wives two—
735 How Xantippa caste pisse upon his heed:
This sely° man sat stille as he were deed;   *poor, hapless*
He wiped his heed, namore dorste° he sayn   *dared*
But "Er that thonder stinte,° comth a rain."   *stops*
    Of Pasipha[8] that was the queene of Crete—
740 For shrewednesse° him thoughte the tale sweete—   *malice*
Fy, speek namore, it is a grisly thing

---

9. In one of Aesop's fables, the lion, shown a picture of a man killing a lion, asked who painted the picture. Had a lion been the artist, of course, the roles would have been reversed.
1. Mark, sex.
2. I.e., clerks and women, astrologically ruled by Mercury and Venus, respectively.
3. Because of their contrary positions (as planets), each one descends (in the belt of the zodiac) as the other rises, hence one loses its power as

the other becomes dominant.
4. I.e., Mercury is deprived of power in Pisces (the sign of the Fish), where Venus is most powerful.
5. My husband.
6. The stories of wicked women Chaucer drew mainly from St. Jerome and Walter Map.
7. Deianira unwittingly gave Hercules a poisoned shirt, which hurt him so much that he committed suicide by fire.
8. Pasiphaë, who had intercourse with a bull.

Of hir horrible lust and hir liking.°   *pleasure*
Of Clytermistra[9] for hir lecherye
That falsly made hir housbonde for to die,
745   He redde it with ful good devocioun.
He tolde me eek for what occasioun
Amphiorax[1] at Thebes loste his lif:
Myn housbonde hadde a legende of his wif
Eriphylem, that for an ouche° of gold   *trinket*
750   Hath prively unto the Greekes told
Wher that hir housbonde hidde him in a place,
For which he hadde at Thebes sory grace.
Of Livia tolde he me and of Lucie:[2]
They bothe made hir housbondes for to die,
755   That oon for love, that other was for hate;
Livia hir housbonde on an even late
Empoisoned hath for that she was his fo;
Lucia likerous° loved hir housbonde so   *lecherous*
That for° he sholde alway upon hire thinke,   *in order that*
760   She yaf him swich a manere love-drinke
That he was deed er it were by the morwe.[3]
And thus algates° housbondes han sorwe.   *in every way*
Thanne tolde he me how oon Latumius
Complained unto his felawe Arrius
765   That in his garden growed swich a tree,
On which he saide how that his wives three
Hanged hemself for herte despitous.[4]
"O leve° brother," quod this Arrius,   *dear*
"Yif me a plante of thilke blessed tree,
770   And in my gardin planted shal it be."
Of latter date of wives hath he red
That some han slain hir housbondes in hir bed
And lete hir lechour dighte[5] hire al the night,
Whan that the cors° lay in the floor upright;°   *corpse / on his back*
775   And some han driven nailes in hir brain
Whil that they sleepe, and thus they han hem slain;
Some han hem yiven poison in hir drinke.
He spak more harm than herte may bithinke,°   *imagine*
And therwithal he knew of mo proverbes
780   Than in this world ther growen gras or herbes:
"Bet° is," quod he, "thyn habitacioun   *better*
Be with a leon or a foul dragoun
Than with a womman using° for to chide."   *accustomed*
"Bet is," quod he, "hye in the roof abide
785   Than with an angry wif down in the hous:
They been so wikked° and contrarious,   *perverse*
They haten that hir housbondes loveth ay."

---

9. Clytemnestra, who, with her lover, Aegisthus, slew her husband, Agamemnon.
1. Amphiaraus, betrayed by his wife, Eriphyle, and forced to go to the war against Thebes.
2. Livia murdered her husband on behalf of her lover, Sejanus. "Lucie": i.e., Lucilla, who was said to have poisoned her husband, the poet Lucretius, with a potion designed to keep him faithful.
3. He was dead before it was near morning.
4. For malice of heart.
5. Have intercourse with.

He saide, "A womman cast° hir shame away   casts
When she cast of° hir smok,"⁶ and ferthermo,   off
790 "A fair womman, but she be chast also,
Is like a gold ring in a sowes nose."
Who wolde weene,° or who wolde suppose   think
The wo that in myn herte was and pine?°   suffering
     And whan I sawgh he wolde nevere fine°   end
795 To reden on this cursed book al night,
Al sodeinly three leves have I plight°   snatched
Out of his book right as he redde, and eke
I with my fist so took⁷ him on the cheeke
That in oure fir he fil° bakward adown.   fell
800 And up he sterte as dooth a wood° leoun,   raging
And with his fist he smoot me on the heed°   head
That in the floor I lay as I were deed.°   dead
And whan he sawgh how stille that I lay,
He was agast, and wolde have fled his way,
805 Til atte laste out of my swough° I braide:°   swoon / started
"O hastou slain me, false thief?" I saide,
"And for my land thus hastou mordred° me?   murdered
Er I be deed yit wol I kisse thee."
And neer he cam and kneeled faire adown,
810 And saide, "Dere suster Alisoun,
As help me God, I shal thee nevere smite.
That I have doon, it is thyself to wite.°   blame
Foryif it me, and that I thee biseeke."°   beseech
And yit eftsoones° I hitte him on the cheeke,   another time
815 And saide, "Thief, thus muchel am I wreke.°   avenged
Now wol I die: I may no lenger speke."
     But at the laste with muchel care and wo
We fille⁸ accorded by us selven two.
He yaf me al the bridel° in myn hand,   bridle
820 To han the governance of hous and land,
And of his tonge and his hand also;
And made⁹ him brenne° his book anoonright tho.   burn
And whan that I hadde geten unto me
By maistrye° al the sovereinetee,°   skill / dominion
825 And that he saide, "Myn owene trewe wif,
Do as thee lust° the terme of al thy lif;   it pleases
Keep thyn honour, and keep eek myn estat,"
After that day we hadde nevere debat.
God help me so, I was to him as kinde
830 As any wif from Denmark unto Inde,°   India
And also trewe, and so was he to me.
I praye to God that sit° in majestee,   sits
So blesse his soule for his mercy dere.
Now wol I saye my tale if ye wol heere.

6. Undergarment.   8. I.e., became.
7. I.e., hit.   9. I.e., I made.

[ANOTHER INTERRUPTION]

835   The Frere lough° whan he hadde herd all this: *laughed*
       "Now dame," quod he, "so have I joye or blis,
       This is a long preamble of a tale."
       And whan the Somnour herde the Frere gale,°   *exclaim*
       "Lo," quod the Somnour, "Goddes armes two,
840   A frere wol entremette him¹ everemo!
       Lo, goode men, a flye and eek a frere
       Wol falle in every dissh and eek matere.
       What spekestou of preambulacioun?
       What, amble or trotte or pisse or go sitte down!
845   Thou lettest° oure disport in this manere."   *hinder*
          "Ye, woltou so, sire Somnour?" quod the Frere.
       "Now by my faith, I shal er that I go
       Telle of a somnour swich a tale or two
       That al the folk shal laughen in this place."
850   'Now elles, Frere, I wol bishrewe° thy face,"   *curse*
       Quod this Somnour, "and I bishrewe me,
       But if I telle tales two or three
       Of freres, er I come to Sidingborne,²
       That I shal make thyn herte for to moorne°—   *mourn*
855   For wel I woot thy pacience is goon."
          Oure Hoste cride, "Pees, and that anoon!"
       And saide, "Lat the womman telle hir tale:
       Ye fare as folk that dronken been of ale.
       Do, dame, tel forth youre tale, and that is best."
860   "Al redy, sire," quod she, "right as you lest°—   *it pleases*
       If I have licence of this worthy Frere."
       "Yis, dame," quod he, "tel forth and I wol heere."

The Tale

As was suggested in the headnote to *The Man of Law's Epilogue*, Chaucer may have
originally written the fabliau that became *The Shipman's Tale* for the Wife of Bath.
If so, then he replaced it with a tale that is not simply appropriate to her character
but that develops it even beyond the complexity already revealed in her *Prologue*.
The story survives in two other versions in which the hero is Sir Gawain, whose
courtesy contrasts sharply with the behavior of the knight in the Wife's tale. (For
excerpts from *The Marriage of Sir Gawain and Dame Ragnell*, see "King Arthur"
in the NAEL Archive.) As Chaucer has the Wife tell it, the tale expresses her views
about the relations of the sexes, her wit and humor, and her fantasies. Like Marie de
France's lay *Lanval* (see p. 171), the Wife's tale is about a fairy bride who seeks out
and tests a mortal lover.

       In th'olde dayes of the King Arthour,
       Of which that Britouns speken greet honour,
865   Al was this land fulfild of faïrye:³
       The elf-queene° with hir joly compaignye   *queen of the fairies*
       Daunced ful ofte in many a greene mede°—   *meadow*

---

1. Intrude himself.
2. Sittingbourne (a town forty miles from
London).
3. I.e., filled full of supernatural creatures.

This was the olde opinion as I rede;
I speke of many hundred yeres ago.
870 But now can no man see none elves mo,
For now the grete charitee and prayeres
Of limitours,[4] and othere holy freres,
That serchen every land and every streem,
As thikke as motes° in the sonne-beem,   dust particles
875 Blessing halles, chambres, kichenes, bowres,
Citees, burghes,° castels, hye towres,   townships
Thropes, bernes, shipnes,[5] dayeries—
This maketh that ther been no fairies.
For ther as wont to walken was an elf
880 Ther walketh now the limitour himself,
In undermeles° and in morweninges,°   afternoons / mornings
And saith his Matins and his holy thinges,
As he gooth in his limitacioun.[6]
Wommen may go saufly° up and down: safely
885 In every bussh or under every tree
Ther is noon other incubus[7] but he,
And he ne wol doon hem but[8] dishonour.
      And so bifel it that this King Arthour
Hadde in his hous a lusty bacheler,°   young knight
890 That on a day cam riding fro river,[9]
And happed° that, allone as he was born,   it happened
He sawgh a maide walking him biforn;
Of which maide anoon, maugree hir heed,[1]
By verray force he rafte° hir maidenheed;   deprived her of
895 For which oppression° was swich clamour,   rape
And swich pursuite° unto the King Arthour,   petitioning
That dampned was this knight for to be deed[2]
By cours of lawe, and sholde han lost his heed—
Paraventure° swich was the statut tho—   perchance
900 But that the queene and othere ladies mo
So longe prayeden the king of grace,
Til he his lif him graunted in the place,
And yaf him to the queene, al at hir wille,
To chese° wheither she wolde him save or spille.[3]   choose
905 The queene thanked the king with al hir might,
And after this thus spak she to the knight,
Whan that she saw hir time upon a day:
"Thou standest yit," quod she, "in swich array°   condition
That of thy lif yit hastou no suretee.°   guarantee
910 I graunte thee lif if thou canst tellen me
What thing it is that wommen most desiren:
Be war and keep thy nekke boon° from iren.   bone
And if thou canst nat tellen me anoon,°   right away

---

4. Friars licensed to beg in a certain territory.
5. Thorps (villages), barns, stables.
6. I.e., the friar's assigned area. His "holy thinges" are prayers.
7. An evil spirit that seduces mortal women.
8. "Ne . . . but": only.
9. Hawking, usually carried out on the banks of a stream.
1. Despite her head, i.e., despite anything she could do.
2. This knight was condemned to death.
3. Put to death.

Yit wol I yive thee leve for to goon
915 A twelfmonth and a day to seeche° and lere°   search / learn
An answere suffisant° in this matere,   satisfactory
And suretee wol I han er that thou pace,°   pass
Thy body for to yeelden in this place."
    Wo was this knight, and sorwefully he siketh.°   sighs
920 But what, he may nat doon al as him liketh,
And atte laste he chees° him for to wende,   chose
And come again right at the yeres ende,
With swich answere as God wolde him purveye,°   provide
And taketh his leve and wendeth forth his waye.
925 He seeketh every hous and every place
Wher as he hopeth for to finde grace,
To lerne what thing wommen love most.
But he ne coude arriven in no coost⁴
Wher as he mighte finde in this matere
930 Two creatures according in fere.⁵
    Some saiden wommen loven best richesse;
Some saide honour, some saide jolinesse;°   pleasure
Some riche array, some saiden lust abedde,
And ofte time to be widwe and wedde.
935 Some saide that oure herte is most esed
Whan that we been yflatered and yplesed—
He gooth ful neigh the soothe, I wol nat lie:
A man shal winne us best with flaterye,
And with attendance° and with bisinesse°   attention / solicitude
940 Been we ylimed,° bothe more and lesse.   ensnared
    And some sayen that we loven best
For to be free, and do right as us lest,°   it pleases
And that no man repreve° us of oure vice,   reprove
But saye that we be wise and no thing nice.°   foolish
945 For trewely, ther is noon of us alle,
If any wight wol clawe° us on the galle,°   rub / sore spot
That we nil kike° for° he saith us sooth: kick / because
Assaye° and he shal finde it that so dooth.   try
For be we nevere so vicious withinne,
950 We wol be holden° wise and clene of sinne.   considered
    And some sayn that greet delit han we
For to be holden stable and eek secree,⁶
And in oo° purpos stedefastly to dwelle,   one
And nat biwraye° thing that men us telle—   disclose
955 But that tale is nat worth a rake-stele.°   rake handle
Pardee,° we wommen conne no thing hele:°   by God / conceal
Witnesse on Mida.° Wol ye heere the tale?   Midas
    Ovide, amonges othere thinges smale,
Saide Mida hadde under his longe heres,
960 Growing upon his heed, two asses eres,
The whiche vice° he hidde as he best mighte   defect
Ful subtilly from every mannes sighte,

4. I.e., country.   6. Reliable and also close-mouthed.
5. Agreeing together.

That save his wif ther wiste° of it namo.   *knew*
He loved hire most and trusted hire also.
965 He prayed hire that to no creature
She sholde tellen of his disfigure.°   *deformity*
    She swoor him nay, for al this world to winne,
She nolde do that vilainye or sinne
To make hir housbonde han so foul a name:
970 She nolde nat telle it for hir owene shame.
But nathelees, hir thoughte that she dyde°   *would die*
That she so longe sholde a conseil° hide;   *secret*
Hire thoughte it swal° so sore about hir herte   *swelled*
That nedely som word hire moste asterte,[7]
975 And sith she dorste nat telle it to no man,
Down to a mareis° faste° by she ran—   *marsh / close*
Til she cam there hir herte was afire—
And as a bitore bombleth[8] in the mire,
She laide hir mouth unto the water doun:
980 "Biwray° me nat, thou water, with thy soun,"°   *betray / sound*
Quod she. "To thee I telle it and namo:°   *to no one else*
Myn housbonde hath longe asses eres two.
Now is myn herte al hool,[9] now is it oute.
I mighte no lenger keep it, out of doute."
985 Here may ye see, though we a time abide,
Yit oute it moot:° we can no conseil hide.   *must*
The remenant of the tale if ye wol heere,
Redeth Ovide, and ther ye may it lere.[1]
    This knight of which my tale is specially,
990 Whan that he sawgh he mighte nat come thereby—
This is to saye what wommen loven most—
Within his brest ful sorweful was his gost,°   *spirit*
But hoom he gooth, he mighte nat sojourne:°   *delay*
The day was come that hoomward moste° he turne.   *must*
995 And in his way it happed him to ride
In al this care under° a forest side,   *by*
Wher as he sawgh upon a daunce go
Of ladies foure and twenty and yit mo;
Toward the whiche daunce he drow ful yerne,[2]
1000 In hope that som wisdom sholde he lerne.
But certainly, er he cam fully there,
Vanisshed was this daunce, he niste° where.   *knew not*
No creature sawgh he that bar° lif,   *bore*
Save on the greene he sawgh sitting a wif°—   *woman*
1005 A fouler wight ther may no man devise.°   *imagine*
Again[3] the knight this olde wif gan rise,
And saide, "Sire knight, heer forth lith° no way.°   *lies / road*
Telle me what ye seeken, by youre fay.°   *faith*
Paraventure it may the better be:
1010 Thise olde folk conne° muchel thing," quod she.   *know*

7. Of necessity some word must escape her.
8. Makes a booming noise. "Bitore": bittern, a
heron.
9. I.e., sound.
1. Learn. The reeds disclosed the secret by
whispering *"aures aselli"* (ass's ears). Cf. Ovid,
Metamorphoses 11.174–93.
2. Drew very quickly.
3. I.e., to meet.

"My leve moder,"° quod this knight, "certain,   *mother*
I nam but deed but if that I can sayn
What thing it is that wommen most desire.
Coude ye me wisse,° I wolde wel quite youre hire."⁴   *teach*
1015   "Plight° me thy trouthe here in myn hand," quod she,   *pledge*
"The nexte thing that I requere° thee,   *require of*
Thou shalt it do, if it lie in thy might,
And I wol telle it you er it be night."
    "Have heer my trouthe," quod the knight. "I graunte."
1020   "Thanne," quod she, "I dar me wel avaunte°   *boast*
Thy lif is sauf,° for I wol stande therby.   *safe*
Upon my lif the queene wol saye as I.
Lat see which is the pruddeste° of hem alle   *proudest*
That wereth on⁵ a coverchief or a calle°   *headdress*
1025 That dar saye nay of that I shal thee teche.
Lat us go forth withouten lenger speeche."
Tho rouned° she a pistel° in his ere,   *whispered / message*
And bad him to be glad and have no fere.
    Whan they be comen to the court, this knight
1030 Saide he hadde holde his day as he hadde hight,°   *promised*
And redy was his answere, as he saide.
Ful many a noble wif, and many a maide,
And many a widwe—for that they been wise—
The queene hirself sitting as justise,
1035 Assembled been this answere for to heere,
And afterward this knight was bode° appere.   *bidden to*
To every wight comanded was silence,
And that the knight sholde telle in audience°   *open hearing*
What thing that worldly wommen loven best.
1040 This knight ne stood nat stille as dooth a best,°   *beast*
But to his question anoon answerde
With manly vois that al the court it herde.
    "My lige° lady, generally," quod he,   *liege*
"Wommen desire to have sovereinetee°   *dominion*
1045 As wel over hir housbonde as hir love,
And for to been in maistrye him above.
This is youre moste desir though ye me kille.
Dooth as you list:° I am here at youre wille."   *please*
    In al the court ne was ther wif ne maide
1050 Ne widwe that contraried° that he saide,   *contradicted*
But saiden he was worthy han° his lif.   *to have*
    And with that word up sterte° that olde wif,   *started*
Which that the knight sawgh sitting on the greene;
"Mercy," quod she, "my soverein lady queene,
1055 Er that youre court departe, do me right.
I taughte this answere unto the knight,
For which he plighte me his trouthe there
The firste thing I wolde him requere°   *require*
He wolde it do, if it laye in his might.
1060 Bifore the court thanne praye I thee, sire knight,"

4. Repay your trouble.   5. That wears.

Quod she, "that thou me take unto thy wif,
For wel thou woost that I have kept° thy lif.   *saved*
If I saye fals, say nay, upon thy fay."
   This knight answerde, "Allas and wailaway,
1065 I woot right wel that swich was my biheeste.°   *promise*
For Goddes love, as chees° a newe requeste: *choose*
Taak al my good and lat my body go."
   "Nay thanne," quod she, "I shrewe° us bothe two.   *curse*
For though that I be foul and old and poore,
1070 I nolde for al the metal ne for ore
That under erthe is grave° or lith° above,   *buried / lies*
But if thy wif I were and eek thy love."
   "My love," quod he. "Nay, my dampnacioun!°   *damnation*
Allas, that any of my nacioun[6]
1075 Sholde evere so foule disparaged° be."   *degraded*
But al for nought, th'ende is this, that he
Constrained was: he needes moste hire wedde,
And taketh his olde wif and gooth to bedde.
   Now wolden some men saye, paraventure,
1080 That for my necligence I do no cure[7]
To tellen you the joye and al th'array
That at the feeste was that ilke day.
To which thing shortly answere I shal:
I saye ther nas no joye ne feeste at al;
1085 Ther nas but hevinesse and muche sorwe.
For prively he wedded hire on morwe,[8]
And al day after hidde him as an owle,
So wo was him, his wif looked so foule.
   Greet was the wo the knight hadde in his thought:
1090 Whan he was with his wif abedde brought,
He walweth° and he turneth to and fro.   *tosses*
His olde wif lay smiling everemo,
And saide, "O dere housbonde, benedicite,°   *bless me*
Fareth° every knight thus with his wif as ye?   *behaves*
1095 Is this the lawe of King Arthures hous?
Is every knight of his thus daungerous?°   *standoffish*
I am youre owene love and youre wif;
I am she which that saved hath youre lif;
And certes yit ne dide I you nevere unright.
1100 Why fare ye thus with me this firste night?
Ye faren like a man hadde lost his wit.
What is my gilt? For Goddes love, telle it,
And it shal been amended if I may."
   "Amended!" quod this knight. "Allas, nay, nay,
1105 It wol nat been amended neveremo.
Thou art so lothly° and so old also,   *hideous*
And therto comen of so lowe a kinde,°   *lineage*
That litel wonder is though I walwe and winde.°   *turn*

6. I.e., family.
7. I do not take the trouble.
8. In the morning.

So wolde God myn herte wolde breste!"°   *break*
1110   "Is this," quod she, "the cause of youre unreste?"
"Ye, certainly," quod he. "No wonder is."
"Now sire," quod she, "I coude amende al this,
If that me liste, er it were dayes three,
So° wel ye mighte bere you⁹ unto me.   *provided that*
1115   "But for ye speken of swich gentilesse°   *nobility*
As is descended out of old richesse—
That therfore sholden ye be gentilmen—
Swich arrogance is nat worth an hen.
Looke who that is most vertuous alway,
1120   Privee and apert,¹ and most entendeth° ay°   *tries / always*
To do the gentil deedes that he can,
Taak him for the gretteste° gentilman.   *greatest*
Crist wol° we claime of him oure gentilesse,   *desires that*
Nat of oure eldres for hir 'old richesse.'
1125   For though they yive us al hir heritage,
For which we claime to been of heigh parage,°   *descent*
Yit may they nat biquethe for no thing
To noon of us hir vertuous living,
That made hem gentilmen ycalled be,
1130   And bad² us folwen hem in swich degree.
    "Wel can the wise poete of Florence,
That highte Dant,³ spoken in this sentence;°   *topic*
Lo, in swich manere rym is Dantes tale:
'Ful selde° up riseth by his braunches⁴ smale   *seldom*
1135   Prowesse° of man, for God of his prowesse   *excellence*
Wol that of him we claime oure gentilesse.'
For of oure eldres may we no thing claime
But temporel thing that man may hurte and maime.
Eek every wight woot this as wel as I,
1140   If gentilesse were planted natureelly
Unto a certain linage down the line,
Privee and apert, thanne wolde they nevere fine°   *cease*
To doon of gentilesse the faire office°—   *function*
They mighte do no vilainye or vice.
1145   "Taak fir and beer° it in the derkeste hous   *bear*
Bitwixe this and the Mount of Caucasus,
And lat men shette° the dores and go thenne,°   *shut / thence*
Yit wol the fir as faire lye° and brenne°   *blaze / burn*
As twenty thousand men mighte it biholde:
1150   His° office natureel ay wol it holde,   *its*
Up° peril of my lif, til that it die.   *upon*
Heer may ye see wel how that genterye°   *gentility*
Is nat annexed° to possessioun,⁵   *related*
Sith folk ne doon hir operacioun
1155   Alway, as dooth the fir, lo, in his kinde.°   *nature*

---

9. Behave.
1. Privately and publicly.
2. I.e., they bade.

3. Dante (1265–1321), *Convivio*, Book 4.
4. I.e., by the branches of a man's family tree.
5. I.e., inheritable property.

For God it woot, men may wel often finde
A lordes sone do shame and vilainye;
And he that wol han pris of his gentrye,[6]
For he was boren° of a gentil° hous,   *born / noble*
1160 And hadde his eldres noble and vertuous,
And nil himselven do no gentil deedes,
Ne folwen his gentil auncestre that deed° is,   *dead*
He nis nat gentil, be he duk or erl—
For vilaines sinful deedes maken a cherl.
1165 Thy gentilesse[7] nis but renomee°   *renown*
Of thine auncestres for hir heigh bountee,° *magnanimity*
Which is a straunge° thing for thy persone.   *external*
For gentilesse[8] cometh fro God allone.
Thanne comth oure verray gentilesse of grace:
1170 It was no thing biquethe us with oure place.
Thenketh how noble, as saith Valerius,[9]
Was thilke Tullius Hostilius
That out of poverte° roos to heigh noblesse.   *poverty*
Redeth Senek° and redeth eek Boece:° *Seneca / Boethius*
1175 Ther shul ye seen expres that no drede° is   *doubt*
That he is gentil that dooth gentil deedes.
And therfore, leve housbonde, I thus conclude:
Al° were it that mine auncestres weren rude,[1]   *although*
Yit may the hye God—and so hope I—
1180 Graunte me grace to liven vertuously.
Thanne am I gentil whan that I biginne
To liven vertuously and waive° sinne.   *avoid*
  "And ther as ye of poverte me repreve,°   *reprove*
The hye God, on whom that we bileve,
1185 In wilful° poverte chees° to live his lif; *voluntary / chose*
And certes every man, maiden, or wif
May understonde that Jesus, hevene king,
Ne wolde nat chese° a vicious living.   *choose*
Glad poverte is an honeste° thing, certain; *honorable*
1190 This wol Senek and othere clerkes sayn.
Whoso that halt him paid of[2] his poverte,
I holde him riche al hadde he nat a sherte.°   *shirt*
He that coveiteth[3] is a poore wight,
For he wolde han that is nat in his might;
1195 But he that nought hath, ne coveiteth° have, *desires to*
Is riche, although we holde him but a knave.° *peasant*
Verray° poverte it singeth proprely.° *true / appropriately*
Juvenal saith of poverte, 'Merily
The poore man, whan he gooth by the waye,
1200 Biforn the theves he may singe and playe.'
Poverte is hateful good, and as I gesse,
A ful greet bringere out of bisinesse;[4]

6. Have credit for his noble birth.
7. I.e., the gentility you claim.
8. I.e., true gentility.
9. A Roman historian.

1. I.e., low born.
2. Considers himself satisfied with.
3. I.e., suffers desires.
4. I.e., remover of cares.

A greet amendere eek of sapience°   *wisdom*
To him that taketh it in pacience;
1205 Poverte is thing, although it seeme elenge,°   *wretched*
Possession that no wight wol chalenge;[5]
Poverte ful often, whan a man is lowe,
Maketh[6] his God and eek himself to knowe;
Poverte a spectacle° is, as thinketh me, *pair of spectacles*
1210 Thurgh which he may his verray° freendes see. *true*
And therfore, sire, sin that I nought you greve,
Of my poverte namore ye me repreve.°   *reproach*
  "Now sire, of elde° ye repreve me: *old age*
And certes sire, though noon auctoritee
1215 Were in no book, ye gentils of honour
Sayn that men sholde an old wight doon favour,
And clepe him fader for youre gentilesse—
And auctours[7] shal I finde, as I gesse.
  "Now ther ye saye that I am foul° and old: *ugly*
1220 Thanne drede you nought to been a cokewold,° *cuckold*
For filthe° and elde, also mote I thee,[8]   *ugliness*
Been grete wardeins° upon chastitee.   *guardians*
But nathelees, sin I knowe your delit,
I shal fulfille youre worldly appetit.
1225 "Chees° now," quod she, "oon of thise thinges twaye: *choose*
To han me foul and old til that I deye
And be to you a trewe humble wif,
And nevere you displese in al my lif,
Or elles ye wol han me yong and fair,
1230 And take youre aventure° of the repair[9]   *chance*
That shal be to youre hous by cause of me—
Or in some other place, wel may be.
Now chees youreselven wheither° that you liketh." *whichever*
  This knight aviseth him[1] and sore siketh;° *sighs*
1235 But atte laste he saide in this manere:
"My lady and my love, and wif so dere,
I putte me in youre wise governaunce:
Cheseth° youreself which may be most plesaunce° *choose / pleasure*
And most honour to you and me also.
1240 I do no fors the wheither[2] of the two,
For as you liketh it suffiseth° me."   *satisfies*
  "Thanne have I gete° of you maistrye," quod she, *got*
"Sin I may chese and governe as me lest?"° *it pleases me*
  "Ye, certes, wif," quod he. "I holde it best."
1245 "Kisse me," quod she. "We be no lenger wrothe.
For by my trouthe, I wol be to you bothe—
This is to sayn, ye, bothe fair and good.
I praye to God that I mote sterven wood.[3]

---

5. Claim as his property.
6. I.e., makes him.
7. I.e., authorities.
8. So may I prosper.

9. I.e., visits.
1. Considers.
2. I do not care whichever.
3. Die mad.

But° I to you be al so good and trewe   *unless*
1250 As evere was wif sin that the world was newe.
      And but I be tomorn° as fair to seene   *tomorrow morning*
      As any lady, emperisse, or queene,
      That is bitwixe the eest and eek the west,
      Do with my lif and deeth right as you lest:
1255 Caste up the curtin,⁴ looke how that it is."
          And whan the knight sawgh verraily al this,
      That she so fair was and so yong therto,
      For joye he hente° hire in his armes two;   *took*
      His herte bathed in a bath of blisse;
1260 A thousand time arewe° he gan hire kisse,   *in a row*
      And she obeyed him in every thing
      That mighte do him plesance or liking.°   *pleasure*
      And thus they live unto hir lives ende
      In parfit° joye. And Jesu Crist us sende   *perfect*
1265 Housbondes meeke, yonge, and fresshe abedde—
      And grace t'overbide° hem that we wedde.   *outlive*
      And eek I praye Jesu shorte° hir lives   *shorten*
      That nought wol be governed by hir wives,
      And olde and angry nigardes° of dispence°—   *misers / spending*
1270 God sende hem soone a verray° pestilence!   *veritable*

4. The curtain around the bed.

The Pardoner's Prologue and Tale

As with *The Wife of Bath's Prologue* and *Tale*, *The Pardoner's Prologue* and *Tale* develop in profound and surprising ways the portrait sketched in *The General Prologue*. In his *Prologue* the Pardoner boasts to his fellow pilgrims about his own depravity and the ingenuity with which he abuses his office and extracts money from poor and ignorant people.

The medieval pardoner's job was to collect money for the charitable enterprises, such as hospitals, supported by the church. In return for donations, he was licensed by the pope to award token remission of punishment for sins that the donor should have repented and confessed. By canon law pardoners were permitted to work only in a prescribed area; within that area they might visit churches during Sunday service, briefly explain their mission, receive contributions, and in the pope's name issue indulgence, which was not considered to be a sale but a gift from the infinite treasury of Christ's mercy made in return for a gift of money. In practice, pardoners ignored the restrictions on their office, made their way into churches at will, preached emotional sermons, and claimed extraordinary power for their pardons.

The Pardoner's Tale is a bombastic sermon against gluttony, gambling, and swearing, which he preaches to the pilgrims to show off his professional skills. The sermon is framed by a narrative that is supposed to function as an *exemplum* (that is, an illustration) of the scriptural text, the one on which the Pardoner, as he tells the pilgrims, always preaches: *"Radix malorum est cupiditas"* (Avarice is the root of evil).

The Introduction

Oure Hoste gan to swere as he were wood°   *insane*
"Harrow,"° quod he, "by nailes and by blood,[1]   *help*
This was a fals cherl and a fals justise.[2]
As shameful deeth as herte may devise
5   Come to thise juges and hir advocats.
Algate° this sely° maide is slain, allas!   *at any rate / innocent*
Allas, too dere boughte she beautee!
Wherfore I saye alday° that men may see   *always*
The yiftes of Fortune and of Nature
10 Been cause of deeth to many a creature.
As bothe yiftes that I speke of now,
Men han ful ofte more for harm than prow.°   *benefit*
   "But trewely, myn owene maister dere,
This is a pitous tale for to heere.
15 But nathelees, passe over, is no fors:[3]
I praye to God to save thy gentil cors,°   *body*
And eek thine urinals and thy jurdones,[4]
Thyn ipocras and eek thy galiones,[5]
And every boiste° ful of thy letuarye°—   *box / medicine*
20 God blesse hem, and oure lady Sainte Marye.
So mote I theen,[6] thou art a propre man,
And lik a prelat, by Saint Ronian![7]
Saide I nat wel? I can nat speke in terme.[8]
But wel I woot, thou doost° myn herte to erme°   *make / grieve*
25 That I almost have caught a cardinacle.[9]
By corpus bones,[1] but if° I have triacle,°   *unless / medicine*
Or elles a draughte of moiste° and corny° ale,   *fresh / malty*
Or but I here anoon° a merye tale,   *at once*
Myn herte is lost for pitee of this maide.
30   "Thou bel ami,[2] thou Pardoner," he saide,
"Tel us som mirthe or japes° right anoon."   *jokes*
   "It shal be doon," quod he, "by Saint Ronion.
But first," quod he, "here at this ale-stake[3]
I wol bothe drinke and eten of a cake."°   *flat loaf of bread*
35   And right anoon thise gentils gan to crye,
"Nay, lat him telle us of no ribaudye.°   *ribaldry*
Tel us som moral thing that we may lere,°   *learn*
Som wit,[4] and thanne wol we gladly heere."

---

1. I.e., God's nails and blood.
2. The Host has been affected by the Physician's sad tale of the Roman maiden Virginia, whose great beauty caused a judge to attempt to obtain her person by means of a trumped-up lawsuit in which he connived with a "churl" who claimed her as his slave; in order to preserve her chastity, her father killed her.
3. I.e., never mind.
4. Jordans (chamberpots): the Host is somewhat confused in his endeavor to use technical medical terms. "Urinals": vessels for examining urine.
5. A medicine, probably invented on the spot by the Host, named after Galen. "Ipocras": a medicinal drink named after Hippocrates.
6. So might I prosper.
7. St. Ronan or St. Ninian, with a possible play on "runnion" (sexual organ).
8. Speak in technical idiom.
9. Apparently a cardiac condition, confused in the Host's mind with a cardinal.
1. An illiterate oath, mixing "God's bones" with *corpus dei* (Latin for "God's body").
2. Fair friend (French).
3. Sign of a tavern.
4. I.e., something with significance.

"I graunte, ywis,"° quod he, "but I moot thinke *certainly*
40 Upon som honeste° thing whil that I drinke." *decent*

The Prologue

Lordinges—quod he—in chirches whan I preche,
I paine me[5] to han° an hautein° speeche, *have / loud*
And ringe it out as round as gooth a belle,
For I can al by rote[6] that I telle.
45 My theme is alway oon,[7] and evere was:
Radix malorum est cupiditas.[8]
First I pronounce whennes° that I come, *whence*
And thanne my bulles shewe I alle and some:[9]
Oure lige lordes seel on my patente,[1]
50 That shewe I first, my body to warente,° *keep safe*
That no man be so bold, ne preest ne clerk,
Me to destourbe of Cristes holy werk.
And after that thanne telle I forth my tales[2]—
Bulles of popes and of cardinales,
55 Of patriarkes and bisshopes I shewe,
And in Latin I speke a wordes fewe,
To saffron with[3] my predicacioun,° *preaching*
And for to stire hem to devocioun.
 Thanne shewe I forth my longe crystal stones,° *jars*
60 Ycrammed ful of cloutes° and of bones *rags*
Relikes been they, as weenen° they eechoon. *suppose*
Thanne have I in laton° a shulder-boon *brass*
Which that was of an holy Jewes sheep.
"Goode men," I saye, "take of my wordes keep:° *notice*
65 If that this boon be wasshe° in any welle, *dipped*
If cow, or calf, or sheep, or oxe swelle,
That any worm hath ete or worm ystonge,[4]
Take water of that welle and wassh his tonge,
And it is hool[5] anoon. And ferthermoor,
70 Of pokkes° and of scabbe and every soor° *pox, pustules / sore*
Shal every sheep be hool that of this welle
Drinketh a draughte. Take keep eek° that I telle: *also*
If that the goode man that the beestes oweth° *owns*
Wol every wike,° er° that the cok him croweth, *week / before*
75 Fasting drinken of this welle a draughte—
As thilke° holy Jew oure eldres taughte— *that same*
His beestes and his stoor° shal multiplye. *stock*
 "And sire, also it heleth jalousye:
For though a man be falle in jalous rage,
80 Lat maken with this water his potage,° *soup*

5. Take pains.
6. I know all by heart.
7. I.e., the same. "Theme": biblical text on which the sermon is based.
8. Avarice is the root of evil (1 Timothy 6.10).
9. Each and every one. "Bulles": papal bulls, official documents.

1. I.e., the pope's or bishop's seal on my papal license.
2. I go on with my yarn.
3. To add spice to.
4. That has eaten any worm or been bitten by any snake.
5. I.e., sound.

And nevere shal he more his wif mistriste,°   *mistrust*
Though he the soothe of hir defaute wiste,[6]
Al hadde she[7] taken preestes two or three.
    "Here is a mitein° eek that ye may see: *mitten*
85 He that his hand wol putte in this mitein
He shal have multiplying of his grain,
Whan he hath sowen, be it whete or otes—
So that he offre pens or elles grotes.[8]
    "Goode men and wommen, oo thing warne I you:
90 If any wight be in this chirche now
That hath doon sinne horrible, that he
Dar nat for shame of it yshriven° be,   *confessed*
Or any womman, be she yong or old,
That hath ymaked hir housbonde cokewold,°   *cuckold*
95 Swich° folk shal have no power ne no grace   *such*
To offren to[9] my relikes in this place;
And whoso findeth him out of swich blame,
He wol come up and offre in Goddes name,
And I assoile° him by the auctoritee   *absolve*
100 Which that by bulle ygraunted was to me."
    By this gaude° have I wonne, yeer by yeer,   *trick*
An hundred mark[1] sith° I was pardoner.   *since*
I stonde lik a clerk in my pulpet,
And whan the lewed° peple is down yset,   *ignorant*
105 I preche so as ye han herd bifore,
And telle an hundred false japes° more.   *tricks*
Thanne paine I me[2] to strecche forth the nekke,
And eest and west upon the peple I bekke°   *nod*
As dooth a douve,° sitting on a berne;°   *dove / barn*
110 Mine handes and my tonge goon so yerne°   *fast*
That it is joye to see my bisinesse.
Of avarice and of swich cursednesse°   *sin*
Is al my preching, for to make hem free°   *generous*
To yiven hir pens, and namely° unto me,   *especially*
115 For myn entente is nat but for to winne,[3]
And no thing for correccion of sinne:
I rekke° nevere whan that they been beried°   *care / buried*
Though that hir soules goon a-blakeberied.[4]
For certes, many a predicacioun°   *sermon*
120 Comth ofte time of yvel entencioun:
Som for plesance of folk and flaterye,
To been avaunced° by ypocrisye,   *promoted*
And som for vaine glorye, and som for hate;
For whan I dar noon otherways debate,°   *fight*
125 Thanne wol I stinge him[5] with my tonge smerte°   *sharply*
In preching, so that he shal nat asterte°   *escape*

---

6. Knew the truth of her infidelity.
7. Even if she had.
8. Pennies, groats, coins.
9. To make gifts in reverence of.
1. Marks (pecuniary units).

2. I take pains.
3. My intent is only to make money.
4. Go blackberrying, i.e., go to hell.
5. An adversary critical of pardoners.

To been defamed falsly, if that he
Hath trespassed to my bretheren[6] or to me.
For though I telle nought his propre name,
130 Men shal wel knowe that it is the same
By signes and by othere circumstaunces.
Thus quite° I folk that doon us displesaunces;[7]   *pay back*
Thus spete° I out my venim under hewe°   *spit / false colors*
Of holinesse, to seeme holy and trewe.
135 But shortly myn entente I wol devise:°   *explain*
I preche of no thing but for coveitise;°   *covetousness*
Therfore my theme is yit and evere was
Radix malorum est cupiditas.
      Thus can I preche again that same vice
140 Which that I use, and that is avarice.
But though myself be gilty in that sinne,
Yit can I make other folk to twinne°   *separate*
From avarice, and sore to repente—
But that is nat my principal entente:
145 I preche no thing but for coveitise.
Of this matere it oughte ynough suffise.
      Thanne telle I hem ensamples[8] many oon
Of olde stories longe time agoon,
For lewed° peple loven tales olde—   *ignorant*
150 Swiche° thinges can they wel reporte and holde.[9]   *such*
What, trowe° ye that whiles I may preche,   *believe*
And winne gold and silver for° I teche,   *because*
That I wol live in poverte wilfully?°   *voluntarily*
Nay, nay, I thoughte° it nevere, trewely,   *intended*
155 For I wol preche and begge in sondry landes;
I wol nat do no labour with mine handes,
Ne make baskettes and live therby,
By cause I wol nat beggen idelly.[1]
I wol none of the Apostles countrefete:°   *imitate*
160 I wol have moneye, wolle,° cheese, and whete,   *wool*
Al were it[2] yiven of the pooreste page,
Or of the pooreste widwe in a village—
Al sholde hir children sterve[3] for famine.
Nay, I wol drinke licour of the vine
165 And have a joly wenche in every town.
But herkneth, lordinges, in conclusioun,
Youre liking° is that I shal telle a tale: *pleasure*
Now have I dronke a draughte of corny ale,
By God, I hope I shal you telle a thing
170 That shal by reson been at youre liking;
For though myself be a ful vicious man,
A moral tale yit I you telle can,

6. Injured my fellow pardoners.
7. Make trouble for us.
8. Exempla (stories illustrating moral principles).
9. Repeat and remember.

1. I.e., without profit.
2. Even though it were.
3. Even though her children should die.

Which I am wont to preche for to winne.
Now holde youre pees, my tale I wol biginne.

The Tale

175	In Flandres whilom° was a compaignye	once
	Of yonge folk that haunteden° folye—	practiced
	As riot, hasard, stewes,[4] and tavernes,	
	Wher as with harpes, lutes, and giternes°	guitars
	They daunce and playen at dees° bothe day and night,	dice
180	And ete also and drinke over hir might,[5]	
	Thurgh which they doon the devel sacrifise	
	Within that develes temple in cursed wise	
	By superfluitee° abhominable.	overindulgence
	Hir othes been so grete and so dampnable	
185	That it is grisly for to heere hem swere:	
	Oure blessed Lordes body they totere[6]—	tore
	Hem thoughte that Jewes rente° him nought ynough.	
	And eech of hem at otheres sinne lough.°	laughed
	And right anoon thanne comen tombesteres,°	dancing girls
190	Fetis° and smale,° and yonge frutesteres,[7]	shapely / slender
	Singeres with harpes, bawdes,° wafereres[8]—	pimps
	Whiche been the verray develes officeres,	
	To kindle and blowe the fir of lecherye	
	That is annexed unto glotonye:[9]	
195	The Holy Writ take I to my witnesse	
	That luxure° is in win and dronkenesse.	lechery
	Lo, how that dronken Lot[1] unkindely°	unnaturally
	Lay by his doughtres two unwitingly:	
	So dronke he was he niste° what he wroughte.°	didn't know / did
200	Herodes, who so wel the stories soughte,[2]	
	Whan he of win was repleet° at his feeste,	filled
	Right at his owene table he yaf his heeste°	command
	To sleen° the Baptist John, ful giltelees.	slay
	Senek[3] saith a good word doutelees:	
205	He saith he can no difference finde	
	Bitwixe a man that is out of his minde	
	And a man which that is dronkelewe,°	drunken
	But that woodnesse, yfallen in a shrewe,[4]	
	Persevereth lenger than dooth dronkenesse.	
210	O glotonye, ful of cursednesse!°	wickedness
	O cause first of oure confusioun!°	downfall
	O original of oure dampnacioun,°	damnation
	Til Crist hadde bought° us with his blood again!	redeemed
	Lo, how dere, shortly for to sayn,	

---

4. Wild parties, gambling, brothels.
5. Beyond their capacity.
6. Tear apart (a reference to oaths sworn by parts of His body, such as "God's bones!" or "God's teeth!").
7. Fruit-selling girls.
8. Girl cake vendors.

9. I.e., closely related to gluttony.
1. See Genesis 19.30–36.
2. For the story of Herod and St. John the Baptist, see Mark 6.17–29. "Who so . . . soughte": i.e., whoever looked it up in the Gospel would find.
3. Seneca, the Roman Stoic philosopher.
4. But that madness, occurring in a wicked man.

215 Abought° was thilke° cursed vilainye;   *paid for / that same*
Corrupt was al this world for glotonye:
Adam oure fader and his wif also
Fro Paradis to labour and to wo
Were driven for that vice, it is no drede.°   *doubt*
220 For whil that Adam fasted, as I rede,
He was in Paradis; and whan that he
Eet° of the fruit defended° on a tree,   *ate / forbidden*
Anoon he was out cast to wo and paine.
O glotonye, on thee wel oughte us plaine!°   *complain*
225   O, wiste a man[5] how manye maladies
Folwen of excesse and of glotonies,
He wolde been the more mesurable°   *moderate*
Of his diete, sitting at his table.
Allas, the shorte throte, the tendre mouth,
230 Maketh that eest and west and north and south,
In erthe, in air, in water, men to swinke,°   *work*
To gete a gloton daintee mete° and drinke.   *food*
Of this matere, O Paul, wel canstou trete:
"Mete unto wombe,° and wombe eek unto mete,   *belly*
235 Shal God destroyen bothe," as Paulus saith.[6]
Allas, a foul thing is it, by my faith,
To saye this word, and fouler is the deede
Whan man so drinketh of the white and rede[7]
That of his throte he maketh his privee°   *toilet*
240 Thurgh thilke cursed superfluitee.°   *overindulgence*
   The Apostle[8] weeping saith ful pitously,
"Ther walken manye of which you told have I—
I saye it now weeping with pitous vois—
They been enemies of Cristes crois,°   *cross*
245 Of whiche the ende is deeth—wombe is hir god!"[9]
O wombe,° O bely, O stinking cod,°   *belly / bag*
Fulfilled° of dong° and of corrupcioun!   *filled full / dung*
At either ende of thee foul is the soun.°   *sound*
How greet labour and cost is thee to finde!°   *provide for*
250 Thise cookes, how they stampe° and straine and grinde,   *pound*
And turnen substance into accident[1]
To fulfillen al thy likerous° talent!°   *greedy / appetite*
Out of the harde bones knokke they
The mary,° for they caste nought away   *marrow*
255 That may go thurgh the golet[2] softe and soote.°   *sweetly*
Of spicerye° of leef and bark and roote   *spices*
Shal been his sauce ymaked by delit,
To make him yit a newer appetit.
But certes, he that haunteth swiche delices°   *pleasures*
260 Is deed° whil that he liveth in tho° vices.   *dead / those*

---

5. If a man knew.
6. See 1 Corinthians 6.13.
7. I.e., white and red wines.
8. I.e., St. Paul.
9. See Philippians 3.18.

1. A philosophic joke, depending on the distinction between inner reality (substance) and outward appearance (accident).
2. Through the gullet.

A lecherous thing is win, and dronkenesse
Is ful of striving° and of wrecchednesse. — *quarreling*
O dronke man, disfigured is thy face!
Sour is thy breeth, foul artou to embrace!
265 And thurgh thy dronke nose seemeth the soun
As though thou saidest ay,° "Sampsoun, Sampsoun." — *always*
And yit, God woot,° Sampson drank nevere win.[3] — *knows*
Thou fallest as it were a stiked swin;° — *stuck pig*
Thy tonge is lost, and al thyn honeste cure,[4]
270 For dronkenesse is verray sepulture° — *burial*
Of mannes wit° and his discrecioun. — *intelligence*
In whom that drinke hath dominacioun
He can no conseil° keepe, it is no drede.° — *secrets / doubt*
Now keepe you fro the white and fro the rede—
275 And namely° fro the white win of Lepe[5] — *particularly*
That is to selle in Fisshstreete or in Chepe:[6]
The win of Spaine creepeth subtilly
In othere wines growing faste° by, — *close*
Of which ther riseth swich fumositee° — *heady fumes*
280 That whan a man hath dronken draughtes three
And weeneth° that he be at hoom in Chepe, — *supposes*
He is in Spaine, right at the town of Lepe,
Nat at The Rochele ne at Burdeux town;[7]
And thanne wol he sayn, "Sampsoun, Sampsoun."
285 But herkneth, lordinges, oo° word I you praye, — *one*
That alle the soverein actes,[8] dar I saye,
Of victories in the Olde Testament,
Thurgh verray God that is omnipotent,
Were doon in abstinence and in prayere:
290 Looketh° the Bible and ther ye may it lere.° — *behold / learn*
Looke Attila, the grete conquerour,[9]
Deide° in his sleep with shame and dishonour, — *died*
Bleeding at his nose in dronkenesse:
A capitain sholde live in sobrenesse.
295 And overal this, aviseth you[1] right wel
What was comanded unto Lamuel[2]—
Nat Samuel, but Lamuel, saye I—
Redeth the Bible and finde it expresly,
Of win-yiving° to hem that har[3] justise: — *wine-serving*
300 Namore of this, for it may wel suffise.
And now that I have spoken of glotonye,
Now wol I you defende° hasardrye:° — *prohibit / gambling*
Hasard is verray moder° of lesinges,° — *mother / lies*

---

3. Before Samson's birth an angel told his mother
that he would be a Nazarite throughout his life;
persons who took this vow took no strong drink.
4. Care for self-respect.
5. A town in Spain.
6. Fishstreet and Cheapside in the London market district.
7. The Pardoner is joking about the illegal custom of adulterating fine wines of Bordeaux and
La Rochelle with strong Spanish wine.
8. Distinguished deeds.
9. Attila was the leader of the Huns who almost
captured Rome in the 5th century.
1. Consider.
2. Lemuel's mother told him that kings should
not drink (Proverbs 31.4–5).
3. I.e., administer.

And of deceite and cursed forsweringes,°   *perjuries*
305 Blaspheme of Crist, manslaughtre, and wast° also   *waste*
Of catel° and of time; and ferthermo,   *property*
It is repreve° and contrarye of honour   *disgrace*
For to been holden a commune hasardour,°   *gambler*
And evere the hyer he is of estat
310 The more is he holden desolat.[4]
If that a prince useth hasardrye,
In alle governance and policye
He is, as by commune opinioun,
Yholde the lasse° in reputacioun.   *less*
315   Stilbon, that was a wis embassadour,
Was sent to Corinthe in ful greet honour
Fro Lacedomye° to make hir alliaunce,   *Sparta*
And whan he cam him happede° parchaunce   *it happened*
That alle the gretteste° that were of that lond   *greatest*
320 Playing at the hasard he hem foond,°   *found*
For which as soone as it mighte be
He stal him[5] hoom again to his contree,
And saide, "Ther wol I nat lese° my name,   *lose*
N'I wol nat take on me so greet defame°   *dishonor*
325 You to allye unto none hasardours:
Sendeth othere wise embassadours,
For by my trouthe, me were levere[6] die
Than I you sholde to hasardours allye.
For ye that been so glorious in honours
330 Shal nat allye you with hasardours
As by my wil, ne as by my tretee."°   *treaty*
This wise philosophre, thus saide he.
   Looke eek that to the king Demetrius
The King of Parthes,° as the book[7] saith us,   *Parthians*
335 Sente him a paire of dees° of gold in scorn,   *dice*
For he hadde used hasard therbiforn,
For which he heeld his glorye or his renown
At no value or reputacioun.
Lordes may finden other manere play
340 Honeste° ynough to drive the day away.   *honorable*
   Now wol I speke of othes false and grete
A word or two, as olde bookes trete:
   Greet swering is a thing abhominable,
And fals swering is yit more reprevable.°   *reprehensible*
345 The hye God forbad swering at al—
Witnesse on Mathew.[8] But in special
Of swering saith the holy Jeremie,[9]
"Thou shalt swere sooth thine othes and nat lie,
And swere in doom° and eek in rightwisnesse,°   *equity / righteousness*
350 But idel swering is a cursednesse."°   *wickedness*

---

4. I.e., dissolute.
5. He stole away.
6. I had rather.
7. The book that relates this and the previous incident is the *Policraticus* of the 12th-century Latin writer John of Salisbury.
8. "But I say unto you, Swear not at all" (Matthew 5.34).
9. Jeremiah 4.2.

Biholde and see that in the firste Table[1]
Of hye Goddes heestes° honorable   commandments
How that the seconde heeste of him is this:
"Take nat my name in idel or amis."
355   Lo, rather° he forbedeth swich swering   sooner
Than homicide, or many a cursed thing.
I saye that as by ordre thus it stondeth—
This knoweth that[2] his heestes understondeth
How that the seconde heeste of God is that.
360   And fertherover,° I wol thee telle al plat°   moreover / plain
That vengeance shal nat parten° from his hous   depart
That of his othes is too outrageous.
"By Goddes precious herte!" and "By his nailes!"°   fingernails
And "By the blood of Crist that is in Hailes,[3]
365   Sevene is my chaunce,° and thyn is cink and traye!"[4]   winning number
"By Goddes armes, if thou falsly playe
This daggere shal thurghout thyn herte go!"
This fruit cometh of the bicche bones[5] two—
Forswering, ire, falsnesse, homicide.
370   Now for the love of Crist that for us dyde,°   died
Lete° youre othes bothe grete and smale.   leave
But sires, now wol I telle forth my tale.
        Thise riotoures° three of whiche I telle,   revelers
Longe erst er prime[6] ronge of any belle,
375   Were set hem in a taverne to drinke,
And as they sat they herde a belle clinke
Biforn a cors° was caried to his grave.   corpse
That oon of hem gan callen to his knave:°   servant
Go bet,"[7] quod he, "and axe° redily°   ask / promptly
380   What cors is this that passeth heer forby,
And looke° that thou reporte his name weel."°   be sure / well
        "Sire," quod this boy, "it needeth neveradeel.[8]
It was me told er ye cam heer two houres.
He was, pardee,° an old felawe of youres,   by God
385   And sodeinly he was yslain tonight,°   last night
Fordronke° as he sat on his bench upright;   very drunk
Ther cam a privee° thief men clepeth° Deeth,   stealthy / call
That in this contree al the peple sleeth,°   slays
And with his spere he smoot his herte atwo,
390   And wente his way withouten wordes mo.
He hath a thousand slain this° pestilence.   during this
And maister, er ye come in his presence,
Me thinketh that it were necessarye
For to be war of swich an adversarye;
395   Beeth redy for to meete him everemore:
Thus taughte me my dame.° I saye namore."   mother
        "By Sainte Marye," saide this taverner,

---

1. I.e., the first four of the Ten Commandments,
which specify duties humankind owes to God.
2. I.e., he that.
3. An abbey in Gloucestershire supposed to possess some of Christ's blood.

4. Five and three.
5. I.e., damned dice.
6. Long before 9:00 a.m.
7. Better, i.e., quick.
8. It isn't a bit necessary.

"The child saith sooth, for he hath slain this yeer,
Henne° over a mile, within a greet village,   *hence*
400 Bothe man and womman, child and hine[9] and page.
I trowe° his habitacion be there.   *believe*
To been avised° greet wisdom it were   *wary*
Er that he dide a man a dishonour."
    "Ye, Goddes armes," quod this riotour,
405 "Is it swich peril with him for to meete?
I shal him seeke by way and eek by streete,[1]
I make avow to Goddes digne° bones.   *worthy*
Herkneth, felawes, we three been alle ones:°   *of one mind*
Lat eech of us holde up his hand to other
410 And eech of us bicome otheres brother,
And we wol sleen this false traitour Deeth.
He shal be slain, he that so manye sleeth,
By Goddes dignitee, er it be night."
    Togidres han thise three hir trouthes plight[2]
415 To live and dien eech of hem with other,
As though he were his owene ybore° brother.   *born*
And up they sterte,° al dronken in this rage,   *started*
And forth they goon towardes that village
Of which the taverner hadde spoke biforn,
420 And many a grisly ooth thanne han they sworn,
And Cristes blessed body they torente:°   *tore apart*
Deeth shal be deed° if that they may him hente.°   *dead / catch*
    Whan they han goon nat fully half a mile,
Right as they wolde han treden° over a stile,   *stepped*
425 An old man and a poore with hem mette;
This olde man ful mekely hem grette,°   *greeted*
And saide thus, "Now lordes, God you see."[3]
    The pruddeste° of thise riotoures three   *proudest*
Answerde again, "What, carl° with sory grace,   *fellow*
430 Why artou al forwrapped° save thy face?   *muffled up*
Why livestou so longe in so greet age?"
    This olde man gan looke in his visage,
And saide thus, "For° I ne can nat finde   *because*
A man, though that I walked into Inde,°   *India*
435 Neither in citee ne in no village,
That wolde chaunge his youthe for myn age;
And therefore moot° I han myn age stille,   *must*
As longe time as it is Goddes wille.
    "Ne Deeth, allas, ne wol nat have my lif.
440 Thus walke I lik a restelees caitif,°   *wretch*
And on the ground which is my modres° gate   *mother's*
I knokke with my staf bothe erly and late,
And saye, 'Leve° moder, leet me in: *dear*
Lo, how I vanisshe, flessh and blood and skin.
445 Allas, whan shal my bones been at reste?
Moder, with you wolde I chaunge° my cheste[4]   *exchange*

9. Farm laborer.
1. By highway and byway.
2. Pledged their words of honor.

3. May God protect you.
4. Chest for one's belongings, used here as the symbol for life—or perhaps a coffin.

That in my chambre longe time hath be,
Ye, for an haire-clour[5] to wrappe me.'
But yit to me she wol nat do that grace,
450 For which ful pale and welked° is my face.   *withered*
But sires, to you it is no curteisye
To speken to an old man vilainye,°   *rudeness*
But° he trespasse° in word or elles in deede. *unless / offend*
In Holy Writ ye may yourself wel rede,
455 'Agains[6] an old man, hoor° upon his heed,   *hoar*
Ye shall arise.'[7] Wherfore I yive you reed,° *advice*
Ne dooth unto an old man noon harm now,
Namore than that ye wolde men dide to you
In age, if that ye so longe abide.[8]
460 And God be with you wher ye go° or ride: *walk*
I moot go thider as I have to go."
  "Nay, olde cherl, by God thou shalt nat so,"
Saide this other hasardour anoon.
"Thou partest nat so lightly,° by Saint John!   *easily*
465 Thou speke° right now of thilke traitour Deeth, *spoke*
That in this contree alle oure freendes sleeth:
Have here my trouthe, as thou art his espye,°   *spy*
Tel wher he is, or thou shalt it abye,°   *pay for*
By God and by the holy sacrament!
470 For soothly thou art oon of his assent[9]
To sleen us yonge folk, thou false thief."
  "Now sires," quod he, "if that ye be so lief°   *anxious*
To finde Deeth, turne up this crooked way,
For in that grove I lafte° him, by my fay,°   *left / faith*
475 Under a tree, and ther he wol abide:
Nat for youre boost° he wol him no thing hide.   *boast*
See ye that ook?° Right ther ye shal him finde.   *oak*
God save you, that boughte again[1] mankinde,
And you amende." Thus saide this olde man.
480   And everich of thise riotoures ran
Til he cam to that tree, and ther they founde
Of florins° fine of gold ycoined rounde   *coins*
Wel neigh an eighte busshels as hem thoughte—
Ne lenger thanne after Deeth they soughte,
485 But eech of hem so glad was of the sighte,
For that the florins been so faire and brighte,
That down they sette hem by this precious hoord.
The worste of hem he spak the firste word:
  "Bretheren," quod he, "take keep° what that I saye: *heed*
490 My wit is greet though that I bourde° and playe.   *joke*
This tresor hath Fortune unto us yiven
In mirthe and jolitee oure lif to liven,
And lightly° as it cometh so wol we spende.   *easily*
Ey, Goddes precious dignitee, who wende[2]

5. Haircloth, for a winding sheet.   9. I.e., one of his party.
6. In the presence of.   1. Redeemed.
7. Cf. Leviticus 19.32.   2. Who would have supposed.
8. I.e., if you live so long.

495 Today that we sholde han so fair a grace?
But mighte this gold be caried fro this place
Hoom to myn hous—or elles unto youres—
For wel ye woot that al this gold is oures—
Thanne were we in heigh felicitee.

500 But trewely, by daye it mighte nat be:
Men wolde sayn that we were theves stronge,°   *flagrant*
And for oure owene tresor doon us honge.³
This tresor moste ycaried be by nighte,
As wisely and as slyly as it mighte.

505 Therefore I rede° that cut° amonges us alle   *advise / straws*
Be drawe, and lat see wher the cut wol falle;
And he that hath the cut with herte blithe
Shal renne° to the town, and that ful swithe,°   *run / quickly*
And bringe us breed and win ful prively;

510 And two of us shal keepen° subtilly   *guard*
This tresor wel, and if he wol nat tarye,
Whan it is night we wol this tresor carye
By oon assent wher as us thinketh best."
That oon of hem the cut broughte in his fest°   *fist*

515 And bad hem drawe and looke wher it wol falle;
And it fil° on the yongeste of hem alle,   *fell*
And forth toward the town he wente anoon.
And also° soone as that he was agoon,°   *as / gone away*
That oon of hem spak thus unto that other:

520 "Thou knowest wel thou art my sworen brother;
Thy profit wol I telle thee anoon:
Thou woost wel that oure felawe is agoon,
And here is gold, and that ful greet plentee,
That shall departed° been among us three.   *divided*

525 But nathelees, if I can shape° it so   *arrange*
That it departed were among us two,
Hadde I nat doon a freendes turn to thee?"
That other answerde, "I noot⁴ how that may be:
He woot that the gold is with us twaye.

530 What shal we doon? What shal we to him saye?"
"Shal it be conseil?"⁵ saide the firste shrewe.°   *villain*
"And I shal telle in a wordes fewe
What we shul doon, and bringe it wel aboute."
"I graunte," quod that other, "out of doute,

535 That by my trouthe I wol thee nat biwraye."°   *expose*
"Now," quod the firste, "thou woost wel we be twaye,
And two of us shal strenger° be than oon: *stronger*
Looke whan that he is set that right anoon
Aris as though thou woldest with him playe,

540 And I shal rive° him thurgh the sides twaye,   *pierce*
Whil that thou strugelest with him as in game,
And with thy daggere looke thou do the same;
And thanne shal al this gold departed be,

3. Have us hanged.   5. A secret.
4. Don't know.

My dere freend, bitwixe thee and me.
545 Thanne we may bothe oure lustes° al fulfille,   *desires*
And playe at dees° right at oure owene wille."   *dice*
And thus accorded been thise shrewes twaye
To sleen the thridde, as ye han herd me saye.
     This yongeste, which that wente to the town,
550 Ful ofte in herte he rolleth up and down
The beautee of thise florins newe and brighte.
"O Lord," quod he, "if so were that I mighte
Have al this tresor to myself allone,
Ther is no man that liveth under the trone°   *throne*
555 Of God that sholde live so merye as I."
And at the laste the feend oure enemy
Putte in his thought that he sholde poison beye,°   *buy*
With which he mighte sleen his felawes twaye—
Forwhy° the feend° foond him in swich livinge   *because / devil*
560 That he hadde leve° him to sorwe bringe:[6]   *permission*
For this was outrely° his fulle entente,   *plainly*
To sleen hem bothe, and nevere to repente.
     And forth he gooth—no lenger wolde he tarye—
Into the town unto a pothecarye,°   *apothecary*
565 And prayed him that he him wolde selle
Som poison that he mighte, his rattes quelle,°   *kill*
And eek ther was a polcat[7] in his hawe°   *yard*
That, as he saide, his capons hadde yslawe,°   *slain*
And fain he wolde wreke him[8] if he mighte
570 On vermin that destroyed him[9] by nighte.
     The pothecarye answerde, "And thou shalt have
A thing that, also° God my soule save,   *as*
In al this world there is no creature
That ete or dronke hath of this confiture°   *mixture*
575 Nat but the mountance° of a corn° of whete—   *amount / grain*
That he ne shal his lif anoon forlete.°   *lose*
Ye, sterve° he shal, and that in lasse° while   *die / less*
Than thou wolt goon a paas[1] nat but a mile,
The poison is so strong and violent."
580 This cursed man hath in his hand yhent°   *taken*
This poison in a box and sith° he ran   *then*
Into the nexte streete unto a man
And borwed of him large botels three,
And in the two his poison poured he—
585 The thridde he kepte clene for his drinke,
For al the night he shoop him[2] for to swinke°   *work*
In carying of the gold out of that place.
And whan this riotour with sory grace
Hadde filled with win his grete botels three,
590 To his felawes again repaireth he.
     What needeth it to sermone of it more?

---

6. Christian doctrine teaches that the devil may not tempt people except with God's permission.
7. A weasel-like animal.
8. He would gladly avenge himself.
9. I.e., were ruining his farming.
1. Take a walk.
2. He was preparing.

For right as they had cast° his deeth bifore,   *plotted*
Right so they han him slain, and that anoon.
And whan that this was doon, thus spak that oon:
595 "Now lat us sitte and drinke and make us merye,
And afterward we wol his body berye."°   *bury*
And with that word it happed him par cas[3]
To take the botel ther the poison was,
And drank, and yaf his felawe drinke also,
600 For which anoon they storven° bothe two.   *died*
     But certes I suppose that Avicen
Wroot nevere in no canon ne in no *fen*[4]
Mo wonder signes[5] of empoisoning
Than hadde thise wrecches two er hir ending:
605 Thus ended been thise homicides two,
And eek the false empoisonere also.
     O cursed sinne of alle cursednesse!
O traitours homicide, O wikkednesse!
O glotonye, luxure,° and hasardrye!   *lechery*
610 Thou blasphemour of Crist with vilainye
And othes grete of usage° and of pride!   *habit*
Allas, mankinde, how may it bitide
That to thy Creatour which that thee wroughte,
And with his precious herte blood thee boughte,°   *redeemed*
615 Thou art so fals and so unkinde,° allas?   *unnatural*
     Now goode men, God foryive you youre trespas,
And ware° you fro the sinne of avarice: *guard*
Myn holy pardon may you alle warice°—   *save*
So that ye offre nobles or sterlinges,[6]
620 Or elles silver brooches, spoones, ringes.
Boweth your heed under this holy bulle!
Cometh up, ye wives, offreth of youre wolle!°   *wool*
Youre name I entre here in my rolle: anoon
Into the blisse of hevene shul ye goon.
625 I you assoile° by myn heigh power—   *absolve*
Ye that wol offre—as clene and eek as cleer
As ye were born. —And lo, sires, thus I preche.
And Jesu Crist that is oure soules leeche°   *physician*
So graunte you his pardon to receive,
630 For that is best—I wol you nat deceive.

The Epilogue

    "But sires, oo word forgat I in my tale:
I have relikes and pardon in my male°   *bag*
As faire as any man in Engelond,
Whiche were me yiven by the Popes hond.
635 If any of you wol of devocioun
Offren and han myn absolucioun,

3. By chance.
4. The *Canon of Medicine*, by Avicenna, an 11th-century Arabic philosopher, was divided into sections called "fens."
5. More wonderful symptoms.
6. "Nobles" and "sterlinges" were valuable coins.

Come forth anoon, and kneeleth here adown,
And mekely receiveth my pardoun,
Or elles taketh pardon as ye wende,°   *ride along*
640 Al newe and fressh at every miles ende—
So that ye offre alway newe and newe[7]
Nobles or pens whiche that be goode and trewe.
It is an honour to everich° that is heer   *everyone*
That ye have a suffisant° pardoner   *competent*
645 T'assoile you in contrees as ye ride,
For aventures° whiche that may bitide: *accidents*
Paraventure ther may falle oon or two
Down of his hors and breke his nekke atwo;
Looke which a suretee° is it to you alle   *safeguard*
650 That I am in youre felaweshipe yfalle
That may assoile you, bothe more and lasse,[8]
Whan that the soule shal fro the body passe.
I rede° that oure Hoste shal biginne,   *advise*
For he is most envoluped° in sinne.   *involved*
655 Com forth, sire Host, and offre first anoon,
And thou shalt kisse the relikes everichoon,°   *each one*
Ye, for a grote: unbokele° anoon thy purs."   *unbuckle*
  "Nay, nay," quod he, "thanne have I Cristes curs!
Lat be," quod he, "it shal nat be, so theech!°   *may I prosper*
660 Thou woldest make me kisse thyn olde breech°   *breeches*
And swere it were a relik of a saint,
Though it were with thy fundament° depeint.°   *anus / stained*
But, by the crois which that Sainte Elaine foond,[9]
I wolde I hadde thy coilons° in myn hond,   *testicles*
665 In stede of relikes or of saintuarye.°   *relic-box*
Lat cutte hem of: I wol thee helpe hem carye.
They shal be shrined in an hogges tord."°   *turd*
  This Pardoner answerde nat a word:
So wroth he was no word ne wolde he saye.
670 "Now," quod oure Host, "I wol no lenger playe
With thee, ne with noon other angry man."
  But right anoon the worthy Knight bigan,
Whan that he sawgh that al the peple lough,°   *laughed*
"Namore of this, for it is right ynough.
675 Sire Pardoner, be glad and merye of cheere,
And ye, sire Host that been to me so dere,
I praye you that ye kisse the Pardoner,
And Pardoner, I praye thee, draw thee neer,
And as we diden lat us laughe and playe."
680 Anoon they kiste and riden forth hir waye.

---

7. Over and over.
8. Both high and low (i.e., everybody).
9. I.e., by the cross that St. Helena found. Hel-

ena, mother of Constantine the Great, was reputed to have found the cross on which Christ was crucified.

The Nun's Priest's Tale

In the framing story, *The Nun's Priest's Tale* is linked to a dramatic exchange that follows *The Monk's Tale*. The latter consists of brief tragedies, the common theme of which is the fall of famous men and one woman, most of whom are rulers, through the reversals of Fortune. Like *The Knight's Tale*, this was probably an earlier work of Chaucer's, one that he never finished. As the Monk's tragedies promise to go on and on monotonously, the Knight interrupts and politely tells the Monk that his tragedies are too painful. The Host chimes in to say that the tragedies are "nat worth a botterflye" and asks the Monk to try another subject, but the Monk is offended and refuses. The Host then turns to the Nun's Priest, that is, the priest who is accompanying the Prioress. The three priests said in *The General Prologue* to have been traveling with her have apparently been reduced to one.

The Nun's Priest's Tale is an example of the literary genre known as the "animal fable," familiar from the fables of Aesop, in which animals, behaving like human beings, point to a moral. In the Middle Ages, fables often functioned as elementary texts to teach boys Latin. Marie de France's fables in French are the earliest known vernacular translations. This particular fable derives from an episode in the French *Roman de Renard*, a "beast epic," which satirically represents a feudal animal society ruled over by Noble the Lion. Reynard the Fox is a wily trickster hero who is constantly preying upon and outwitting the other animals, although sometimes Reynard himself is outwitted by one of his victims.

In *The Nun's Priest's Tale*, morals proliferate: both the priest-narrator and his hero, Chauntecleer the rooster, spout examples, learned allusions, proverbs, and sententious generalizations, often in highly inflated rhetoric. The simple beast fable is thus inflated into a delightful satire of learning and moralizing and of the pretentious rhetoric by which medieval writers sometimes sought to elevate their works. Among them, we may include Chaucer himself, who in this tale seems to be making affectionate fun of some of his own works, like the tragedies which became *The Monk's Tale*.

	A poore widwe somdeel stape° in age	*advanced*
	Was whilom° dwelling in a narwe[1] cotage,	*once upon a time*
	Biside a grove, stonding in a dale:	
	This widwe of which I telle you my tale,	
5	Sin thilke° day that she was last a wif,	*that same*
	In pacience ladde° a ful simple lif.	*led*
	For litel was hir catel° and hir rente,°	*property / income*
	By housbondrye° of swich as God hire sente	*economy*
	She foond° hirself and eek hir doughtren two.	*provided for*
10	Three large sowes hadde she and namo,	
	Three kin,° and eek a sheep that highte° Malle.	*cows / was called*
	Ful sooty[2] was hir bowr° and eek hir halle.	*bedroom*
	In which she eet ful many a sclendre° meel;	*scanty*
	Of poinant° sauce hire needed neveradeel:°	*pungent / not a bit*
15	No daintee morsel passed thurgh hir throte—	
	Hir diete was accordant to hir cote.°	*cottage*
	Repleccioun° ne made hire nevere sik:	*overeating*
	Attempre° diete was al hir physik,°	*moderate / medicine*
	And exercise and hertes suffisaunce.°	*contentment*

---

1. Narrow, small.
2. I.e., her cottage lacked a chimney.

20   The goute lette hire nothing for to daunce,[3]
     N'apoplexye shente° nat hir heed.°   *hurt / head*
     No win ne drank she, neither whit ne reed:°   *red*
     Hir boord° was served most with whit and blak,[4]   *table*
     Milk and brown breed, in which she foond no lak;° *found no fault*
25   Seind° bacon, and somtime an ey° or twaye,   *Broiled / egg*
     For she was as it were a manere daye.[5]
     A yeerd° she hadde, enclosed al withoute   *yard*
     With stikkes, and a drye dich aboute,
     In which she hadde a cok heet° Chauntecleer: *named*
30   In al the land of crowing nas° his peer.   *was not*
     His vois was merier than the merye orgon
     On massedayes that in the chirche goon;[6]
     Wel sikerer[7] was his crowing in his logge°   *dwelling*
     Than is a clok or an abbeye orlogge;°   *timepiece*
35   By nature he knew eech ascensioun
     Of th'equinoxial[8] in thilke town:
     For whan degrees fifteene were ascended,
     Thanne crew° he that it mighte nat been amended.° *crowed / improved*
     His comb was redder than the fin coral,
40   And batailed° as it were a castel wal;   *battlemented*
     His bile° was blak, and as the jeet° it shoon;   *bill / jet*
     Like asure[9] were his legges and his toon;°   *toes*
     His nailes whitter° than the lilye flowr,   *whiter*
     And lik the burned° gold was his colour.   *burnished*
45   This gentil° cok hadde in his governaunce   *noble*
     Sevene hennes for to doon al his plesaunce,°   *pleasure*
     Whiche were his sustres and his paramours,[1]
     And wonder like to him as of colours;
     Of whiche the faireste hewed° on hir throte   *colored*
50   Was cleped° faire damoisele Pertelote: *called*
     Curteis she was, discreet, and debonaire,°   *meek*
     And compaignable,° and bar° hirself so faire, *companionable / bore*
     Sin thilke day that she was seven night old,
     That trewely she hath the herte in hold
55   Of Chauntecleer, loken° in every lith.°   *locked / limb*
     He loved hire so that wel was him therwith.[2]
     But swich a joye was it to heere hem singe,
     Whan that the brighte sonne gan to springe,
     In sweete accord *My Lief is Faren in Londe*[3]—
60   For thilke time, as I have understonde,
     Beestes and briddes couden speke and singe.
       And so bifel that in a daweninge,
     As Chauntecleer among his wives alle
     Sat on his perche that was in the halle,

---

3. The gout didn't hinder her at all from dancing.
4. I.e., milk and bread.
5. I.e., a kind of dairywoman.
6. I.e., is played.
7. More reliable.
8. I.e., he knew by instinct each step in the progression of the celestial equator. The celestial equator was thought to make a 360° rotation around the earth every twenty-four hours; therefore, a progression of 15° would be equal to the passage of an hour (line 37).
9. Blue (lapis lazuli).
1. His sisters and his mistresses.
2. That he was well contented.
3. "My Love Has Gone Away," a popular song of the time. See p. 534.

65 And next him sat this faire Pertelote,
This Chauntecleer gan gronen in his throte,
As man that in his dreem is drecched° sore.   *troubled*
   And whan that Pertelote thus herde him rore,°   *roar*
She was agast, and saide, "Herte dere,
70 What aileth you to grone in this manere?
Ye been a verray slepere,[4] fy, for shame!"
   And he answerde and saide thus, "Madame,
I praye you that ye take it nat agrief.°   *amiss*
By God, me mette I was in swich meschief[5]
75 Right now, that yit myn herte is sore afright.
Now God," quod he, "my swevene recche aright,[6]
And keepe my body out of foul prisoun!
Me mette° how that I romed up and down   *dreamed*
Within oure yeerd, wher as I sawgh a beest,
80 Was lik an hound and wolde han maad arrest[7]
Upon my body, and han had me deed.[8]
His colour was bitwixe yelow and reed,
And tipped was his tail and bothe his eres
With blak, unlik the remenant° of his heres;°   *rest / hairs*
85 His snoute smal, with glowing yën twaye.
Yit of his look for fere almost I deye:°   *die*
This caused me my groning, doutelees."
   "Avoi,"° quod she, "fy on you, hertelees!°   *fie / coward*
Allas," quod she, "for by that God above,
90 Now han ye lost myn herte and al my love!
I can nat love a coward, by my faith.
For certes, what so any womman saith,
We alle desiren, if it mighte be,
To han housbondes hardy, wise, and free,°   *generous*
95 And secree,° and no nigard,° ne no fool,   *discreet / miser*
Ne him that is agast of every tool,°   *weapon*
Ne noon avauntour.° By that God above,   *boaster*
How dorste° ye sayn for shame unto youre love   *dare*
That any thing mighte make you aferd?
100 Have ye no mannes herte and han a beerd?°   *beard*
Allas, and conne° ye been agast of swevenes?°   *can / dreams*
No thing, God woot, but vanitee[9] in swevene is!
Swevenes engendren of replexiouns,[1]
And ofte of fume° and of complexiouns,°   *gas / bodily humors*
105 Whan humours been too habundant in a wight.[2]
Certes, this dreem which ye han met° tonight   *dreamed*
Comth of the grete superfluitee
Of youre rede colera,[3] pardee,
Which causeth folk to dreden° in hir dremes   *fear*
110 Of arwes,° and of fir with rede lemes,°   *arrows / flames*

---

4. Sound sleeper.
5. I dreamed that I was in such misfortune.
6. Interpret my dream correctly (i.e., in an auspicious manner).
7. Would have laid hold.
8. I.e., killed me.
9. I.e., empty illusion.

1. Dreams have their origin in overeating.
2. I.e., when humors (bodily fluids) are too abundant in a person. Pertelote's diagnosis is based on the familiar concept that an excess of one of the bodily humors in a person affected his or her temperament (see p. 271, n. 8).
3. Red bile.

Of rede beestes, that they wol hem bite,
Of contek,° and of whelpes grete and lite⁴—   *strife*
Right° as the humour of malencplye⁵   *just*
Causeth ful many a man in sleep to crye
115 For fere of blake beres° or boles° blake,   *bears / bulls*
Or elles blake develes wol hem take.
Of othere humours coude I tell also
That werken many a man in sleep ful wo,
But I wol passe as lightly° as I can.   *quickly*
120 Lo, Caton,⁶ which that was so wis a man,
Saide he nat thus? 'Ne do no fors of⁷ dremes.'
Now, sire," quod she, "whan we flee fro the bemes,⁸
For Goddes love, as take som laxatif.
Up° peril of my soule and of my lif,   *upon*
125 I conseile you the beste, I wol nat lie,
That bothe of colere and of malencolye
Ye purge you; and for° ye shal nat tarye,   *in order that*
Though in this town is noon apothecarye,
I shal myself to herbes techen you,
130 That shal been for youre hele° and for youre prow,°   *health / benefit*
And in oure yeerd tho° herbes shal I finde,   *those*
The whiche han of hir propretee by kinde°   *nature*
To purge you binethe and eek above.
Foryet° nat this, for Goddes owene love.   *forget*
135 Ye been ful colerik° of complexioun;   *bilious*
Ware° the sonne in his ascencioun   *beware that*
Ne finde you nat repleet° of humours hote;°   *filled / hot*
And if it do, I dar wel laye° a grote   *bet*
That ye shul have a fevere terciane,⁹
140 Or an agu° that may be youre bane.°   *ague / death*
A day or two ye shul han digestives
Of wormes, er° ye take youre laxatives   *before*
Of lauriol, centaure, and fumetere,¹
Or elles of ellebor° that groweth there,   *hellebore*
145 Of catapuce, or of gaitres beries,²
Of herb-ive° growing in oure yeerd ther merye is³—   *herb ivy*
Pekke hem right up as they growe and ete hem in.
Be merye, housbonde, for youre fader° kin!   *father's*
Dredeth no dreem: I can saye you namore."
150   "Madame," quod he, "graunt mercy of youre lore,⁴
But nathelees, as touching daun° Catoun,   *master*
That hath of wisdom swich a greet renown,
Though that he bad no dremes for to drede,
By God, men may in olde bookes rede
155 Of many a man more of auctoritee°   *authority*
Than evere Caton was, so mote I thee,°   *prosper*

---

4. And of big and little dogs.
5. I.e., black bile.
6. Dionysius Cato, supposed author of a book of maxims used in elementary education.
7. Pay no attention to.
8. Fly down from the rafters.
9. Tertian (recurring every other day).

1. Of laureole, centaury, and fumitory. These, and the herbs mentioned in the next lines, were all common medieval medicines used as cathartics.
2. Of caper berry or of gaiter berry.
3. Where it is pleasant.
4. Many thanks for your instruction.

That al the revers sayn of his sentence,°   *opinion*
And han wel founden by experience
That dremes been significaciouns
160 As wel of joye as tribulaciouns
That folk enduren in this lif present.
Ther needeth make of this noon argument:
The verray preve[5] sheweth it in deede.
    "Oon of the gretteste auctour[6] that men rede
165 Saith thus, that whilom two felawes wente
On pilgrimage in a ful good entente,
And happed so they comen in a town,
Wher as ther was swich congregacioun
Of peple, and eek so strait of herbergage,[7]
170 That they ne founde as muche as oo cotage
In which they bothe mighte ylogged° be;   *lodged*
Wherfore they mosten° of necessitee   *must*
As for that night departe° compaignye.   *part*
And eech of hem gooth to his hostelrye,
175 And took his logging as it wolde falle.°   *befall*
That oon of hem was logged in a stalle,
Fer° in a yeerd, with oxen of the plough;   *far away*
That other man was logged wel ynough,
As was his aventure° or his fortune,   *lot*
180 That us governeth alle as in commune.
And so bifel that longe er it were day,
This man mette° in his bed, ther as he lay,   *dreamed*
How that his felawe gan upon him calle,
And saide, 'Allas, for in an oxes stalle
185 This night I shal be mordred° ther I lie!   *murdered*
Now help me, dere brother, or I die!
In alle haste com to me,' he saide.
    "This man out of his sleep for fere abraide,°   *started up*
But whan that he was wakened of his sleep,
190 He turned him and took of this no keep:°   *heed*
Him thoughte his dreem nas but a vanitee.°   *illusion*
Thus twies in his sleeping dremed he,
And atte thridde time yit his felawe.
Cam, as him thoughte, and saide, 'I am now slawe:°   *slain*
195 Bihold my bloody woundes deepe and wide.
Axis up erly in the morwe tide,[8]
And atte west gate of the town,' quod he,
'A carte ful of dong° ther shaltou see,   *dung*
In which my body is hid ful prively:
200 Do thilke carte arresten boldely.[9]
My gold caused my mordre, sooth to sayn'
—And tolde him every point how he was slain,
With a ful pitous face, pale of hewe.
And truste wel, his dreem he foond° ful trewe,   *found*
205 For on the morwe° as soone as it was day,   *morning*

5. Actual experience.
6. I.e., one of the greatest authors (perhaps Cicero or Valerius Maximus).
7. And also such a shortage of lodging.
8. In the morning.
9. Boldly have this same cart seized.

To his felawes in° he took the way,   *lodging*
And whan that he cam to this oxes stalle,
After his felawe he bigan to calle.
   "The hostiler° answerde him anoon,   *innkeeper*
210 And saide, 'Sire, youre felawe is agoon:°   *gone away*
As soone as day he wente out of the town.'
   "This man gan fallen in suspecioun,
Remembring on his dremes that he mette;°   *dreamed*
And forth he gooth, no lenger wolde he lette,°   *tarry*
215 Unto the west gate of the town, and foond
A dong carte, wente as it were to donge° lond,   *put manure on*
That was arrayed in that same wise
As ye han herd the dede° man devise;   *dead*
And with an hardy herte he gan to crye,
220 'Vengeance and justice of this felonye!
My felawe mordred is this same night,
And in this carte he lith° gaping upright!°   *lies / on his back*
I crye out on the ministres,' quod he,
'That sholde keepe and rulen this citee.
225 Harrow,° allas, here lith my felawe slain!'   *help*
What sholde I more unto this tale sayn?
The peple up sterte° and caste the carte to grounde,   *started*
And in the middel of the dong they founde
The dede man that mordred was al newe.[1]
230   "O blisful God that art so just and trewe,
Lo, how that thou biwrayest° mordre alway!   *disclose*
Mordre wol out, that see we day by day:
Mordre is so wlatsom° and abhominable   *loathsome*
To God that is so just and resonable,
235 That he ne wol nat suffre it heled° be,   *concealed*
Though it abide a yeer or two or three.
Mordre wol out: this my conclusioun.
And right anoon ministres of that town
Han hent° the cartere and so sore him pined,[2]   *seized*
240 And eek the hostiler so sore engined,°   *racked*
That they biknewe° hir wikkednesse anoon,   *confessed*
And were anhanged° by the nekke boon.   *hanged*
Here may men seen that dremes been to drede.[3]
   "And certes, in the same book I rede—
245 Right in the nexte chapitre after this—
I gabbe° nat, so have I joye or blis—   *lie*
Two men that wolde han passed over see
For certain cause into a fer contree,
If that the wind ne hadde been contrarye
250 That made hem in a citee for to tarye,
That stood ful merye upon an haven° side—   *harbor's*
But on a day again° the even-tide   *toward*
The wind gan chaunge, and blewe right as hem leste:[4]
Jolif° and glad they wenten unto reste,   *merry*

1. Recently.   3. Worthy of being feared.
2. Tortured.   4. Just as they wished.

255 And casten° hem ful erly for to saile.   *determined*
    "But to that oo man fil° a greet mervaile;   *befell*
That oon of hem, in sleeping as he lay,
Him mette⁵ a wonder dreem again the day:
Him thoughte a man stood by his beddes side,
260 And him comanded that he sholde abide,
And saide him thus, 'If thou tomorwe wende,
Thou shalt be dreint:° my tale is at an ende.'   *drowned*
    "He wook and tolde his felawe what he mette,
And prayed him his viage° to lette;°   *voyage / delay*
265 As for that day he prayed him to bide.
    "His felawe that lay by his beddes side
Gan for to laughe, and scorned him ful faste.°   *hard*
'No dreem,' quod he, 'may so myn herte agaste°   *terrify*
That I wol lette for to do my thinges.°   *business*
270 I sette nat a straw by thy dreminges,⁶
For swevenes been but vanitees and japes:⁷
Men dreme alday° of owles or of apes,⁸   *constantly*
And of many a maze° therwithal—   *delusion*
Men dreme of thing that nevere was ne shal.⁹
275 But sith I see that thou wolt here abide,
And thus forsleuthen° wilfully thy tide,°   *waste / time*
God woot, it reweth me,¹ and have good day.'
And thus he took his leve and wente his way.
But er that he hadde half his cours ysailed—
280 Noot I nat why ne what meschaunce it ailed—
But casuelly the shippes botme rente,²
And ship and man under the water wente,
In sighte of othere shippes it biside,
That with hem sailed at the same tide.
285 And therfore, faire Pertelote so dere,
By swiche ensamples olde maistou lere°   *learn*
That no man sholde been too recchelees°   *careless*
Of dremes, for I saye thee doutelees
That many a dreem ful sore is for to drede.
290   "Lo, in the lif of Saint Kenelm³ I rede—
That was Kenulphus sone, the noble king
Of Mercenrike°—how Kenelm mette a thing   *Mercia*
A lite° er he was mordred on a day.   *little*
His mordre in his avision° he sey.°   *dream / saw*
295 His norice° him expounded everydeel°   *nurse / every bit*
His swevene, and bad him for to keepe him⁴ weel
For traison, but he nas but seven yeer old,
And therfore litel tale hath he told
Of any dreem,⁵ so holy was his herte.
300 By God, I hadde levere than my sherte⁶

---

5. He dreamed.
6. I don't care a straw for your dreamings.
7. Dreams are but illusions and frauds.
8. I.e., of absurdities.
9. I.e., shall be.
1. I'm sorry.
2. I don't know why nor what was the trouble

with it—but accidentally the ship's bottom split.
3. Kenelm succeeded his father as king of Mercia at the age of seven, but was slain by his aunt (in 821).
4. Guard himself.
5. Therefore he has set little store by any dream.
6. I.e., I'd give my shirt.

That ye hadde rad° his legende as have I.   *read*
   "Dame Pertelote, I saye you trewely,
Macrobeus,[7] that writ the *Avisioun*
In Affrike of the worthy Scipioun,
305 Affermeth° dremes, and saith that they been   *confirms*
Warning of thinges that men after seen.
   "And ferthermore, I praye you looketh wel
In the Olde Testament of Daniel,
If he heeld° dremes any vanitee.[8]   *considered*
310   "Rede eek of Joseph[9] and ther shul ye see
Wher° dremes be somtime—I saye nat alle—   *whether*
Warning of thinges that shul after falle.
   "Looke of Egypte the king daun Pharao,
His bakere and his botelere° also,   *butler*
315 Wher they ne felte noon effect in dremes.[1]
Whoso wol seeke actes of sondry remes°   *realms*
May rede of dremes many a wonder thing.
   "Lo Cresus, which that was of Lyde° king,   *Lydia*
Mette° he nat that he sat upon a tree,   *dreamed*
320 Which signified he sholde anhanged° be?   *hanged*
   "Lo here Andromacha, Ectores° wif,   *Hector's*
That day that Ector sholde lese° his lif,   *lose*
She dremed on the same night biforn
How that the lif of Ector sholde be lorn,°   *lost*
325 If thilke° day he wente into bataile;   *that same*
She warned him, but it mighte nat availe:°   *do any good*
He wente for to fighte nathelees,
But he was slain anoon° of Achilles.   *right away*
But thilke tale is al too long to telle,
330 And eek it is neigh day, I may nat dwelle.
Shortly I saye, as for conclusioun,
That I shal han of this avisioun[2]
Adversitee, and I saye ferthermoor
That I ne telle of[3] laxatives no stoor,
335 For they been venimes,° I woot it weel: *poisons*
I hem defye, I love hem neveradeel.°   *not a bit*
   "Now lat us speke of mirthe and stinte° al this.   *stop*
Madame Pertelote, so have I blis,
Of oo thing God hath sente me large grace:
340 For whan I see the beautee of youre face—
Ye been so scarlet reed° aboute youre yën—   *red*
It maketh al my drede for to dien.
For also siker° as *In principio*,[4]   *certain*
Mulier est hominis confusio,[5]
345 Madame, the sentence° of this Latin is,   *meaning*
'Womman is mannes joye and al his blis.'

---

7. Macrobius wrote a famous commentary on Cicero's account in *De Republica* of the dream of Scipio Africanus Minor; the commentary came to be regarded as a standard authority on dream lore.
8. See Daniel 7.
9. See Genesis 37.
1. See Genesis 39–41.

2. Divinely inspired dream (as opposed to the more ordinary "swevene" or "dreem").
3. Set by.
4. Beginning of the Gospel of St. John that gives the essential premises of Christianity: "In the beginning was the Word" (Latin).
5. Woman is man's ruination (Latin).

For whan I feele anight youre softe side—
Al be it that I may nat on you ride,
For that oure perche is maad so narwe, allas—
350   I am so ful of joye and of solas°   *delight*
That I defye bothe swevene and dreem."
And with that word he fleigh° down fro the beem,   *flew*
For it was day, and eek his hennes alle,
And with a "chuk" he gan hem for to calle,
355   For he hadde founde a corn° lay in the yeerd.   *grain*
Real° he was, he was namore aferd:°   *regal / afraid*
He fethered[6] Pertelote twenty time,
And trad hire as ofte er it was prime.[7]
He looketh as it were a grim leoun,
360   And on his toes he rometh up and down:
Him deined[8] nat to sette his foot to grounde.
He chukketh whan he hath a corn yfounde,
And to him rennen° thanne his wives alle.   *run*
Thus royal, as a prince is in his halle,
365   Leve I this Chauntecleer in his pasture,
And after wol I telle his aventure.
     Whan that the month in which the world bigan,
That highte° March, whan God first maked man,   *is called*
Was compleet, and passed were also,
370   Sin March biran,° thritty days and two,[9]   *passed by*
Bifel that Chauntecleer in al his pride,
His sevene wives walking him biside,
Caste up his yën to the brighte sonne,
That in the signe of Taurus hadde yronne
375   Twenty degrees and oon and somwhat more,
And knew by kinde,° and by noon other lore,   *nature*
That it was prime, and crew with blisful stevene.°   *voice*
"The sonne," he saide, "is clomben[1] up on hevene
Fourty degrees and oon and more, ywis.°   *indeed*
380   Madame Pertelote, my worldes blis,
Herkneth thise blisful briddes° how they singe,   *birds*
And see the fresshe flowers how they springe:
Ful is myn herte of revel and solas."
But sodeinly him fil° a sorweful cas,°   *befell / chance*
385   For evere the latter ende of joye is wo—
God woot that worldly joye is soone ago,
And if a rethor° coude faire endite,°   *rhetorician / compose*
He in a cronicle saufly° mighte it write,   *safely*
As for a soverein notabilitee.[2]
390   Now every wis man lat him herkne me:
This storye is also° trewe, I undertake,   *as*
As is the book of *Launcelot de Lake*,[3]
That wommen holde in ful greet reverence.
Now wol I turne again to my sentence.°   *main point*

---

6. I.e., embraced.
7. 9:00 a.m. "Trad": trod, copulated with.
8. He deigned.
9. The rhetorical time telling yields May 3.

1. Has climbed.
2. Indisputable fact.
3. Romances of the courteous knight Lancelot of the Lake were very popular.

395   A colfox[4] ful of sly iniquitee,
       That in the grove hadde woned° yeres three,   *dwelled*
       By heigh imaginacion forncast,[5]
       The same night thurghout the hegges° brast°   *hedges / burst*
       Into the yeerd ther Chauntecleer the faire
400   Was wont, and eek his wives, to repaire;
       And in a bed of wortes° stille he lay   *cabbages*
       Til it was passed undren° of the day,   *midmorning*
       Waiting his time on Chauntecleer to falle,
       As gladly doon thise homicides alle,
405   That in await liggen to mordre[6] men.
       O false mordrour, lurking in thy den!
       O newe Scariot! Newe Geniloun![7]
       False dissimilour!° O Greek Sinoun,[8]   *dissembler*
       That broughtest Troye al outrely° to sorwe!   *utterly*
410   O Chauntecleer, accursed be that morwe°   *morning*
       That thou into the yeerd flaugh° fro the bemes!   *flew*
       Thou were ful wel ywarned by thy dremes
       That thilke day was perilous to thee;
       But what that God forwoot° moot° needes be,   *foreknows / must*
415   After° the opinion of certain clerkes: *according to*
       Witnesse on him that any parfit° clerk is   *perfect*
       That in scole is greet altercacioun
       In this matere, and greet disputisoun,°   *disputation*
       And hath been of an hundred thousand men.
420   But I ne can nat bulte it to the bren,[9]
       As can the holy doctour Augustin,
       Or Boece, or the bisshop Bradwardin[1]—
       Wheither that Goddes worthy forwiting°   *foreknowledge*
       Straineth me nedely[2] for to doon a thing
425   ("Nedely" clepe I simple necessitee),
       Or elles if free chois be graunted me
       To do that same thing or do it naught,
       Though God forwoot° it er that I was wrought;   *foreknew*
       Or if his wiring° straineth neveradeel,   *knowledge*
430   But by necessitee condicionel[3]—
       I wol nat han to do of swich matere:
       My tale is of a cok, as ye may heere,
       That took his conseil of his wif with sorwe,
       To walken in the yeerd upon that morwe
435   That he hadde met° the dreem that I you tolde.   *dreamed*
       Wommenes conseils been ful ofte colde,[4]
       Wommanes conseil broughte us first to wo,

4. Fox with black markings.
5. Having planned with great cunning.
6. That lie in ambush to murder.
7. I.e., Ganelon, who betrayed Roland to the Saracens (in the medieval French epic *The Song of Roland*). "Scariot": Judas Iscariot.
8. Sinon, who persuaded the Trojans to take the Greeks' wooden horse into their city—with, of course, the result that the city was destroyed.
9. Sift it to the bran, i.e., get to the bottom of it.

1. St. Augustine, Boethius (6th-century Roman philosopher, whose *Consolation of Philosophy* was translated by Chaucer), and Thomas Bradwardine (archbishop of Canterbury, d. 1349) were all concerned with the interrelationship between people's free will and God's foreknowledge.
2. Constrains me necessarily.
3. Boethius's "conditional necessity" permitted a large measure of free will.
4. I.e., baneful.

And made Adam fro Paradis to go,
Ther as he was ful merye and wel at ese.
440 But for I noot° to whom it mighte displese   *don't know*
If I conseil of wommen wolde blame,
Passe over, for I saide it in my game°—   *sport*
Rede auctours where they trete of swich matere,
And what they sayn of wommen ye may heere—
445 Thise been the cokkes wordes and nat mine:
I can noon harm of no womman divine.°   *guess*
    Faire in the sond° to bathe hire merily   *sand*
Lith° Pertelote, and alle hir sustres by,   *lies*
Again° the sonne, and Chauntecleer so free°   *in / noble*
450 Soong° merier than the mermaide in the see—   *sang*
For Physiologus[5] saith sikerly
How that they singen wel and merily.
    And so bifel that as he caste his yë
Among the wortes on a boterflye,°   *butterfly*
455 He was war of this fox that lay ful lowe.
No thing ne liste him[6] thanne for to crowe,
But cride anoon "Cok cok!" and up he sterte,°   *started*
As man that[7] was affrayed in his herte—
For naturelly a beest desireth flee
460 Fro his contrarye[8] if he may it see,
Though he nevere erst° hadde seen it with his yë.   *before*
This Chauntecleer, whan he gan him espye,
He wolde han fled, but that the fox anoon
Saide, "Gentil sire, allas, wher wol ye goon?
465 Be ye afraid of me that am youre freend?
Now certes, I were worse than a feend
If I to you wolde° harm or vilainye.   *meant*
I am nat come youre conseil° for t'espye,   *secrets*
But trewely the cause of my cominge
470 Was only for to herkne how ye singe:
For trewely, ye han as merye a stevene°   *voice*
As any angel hath that is in hevene.
Therwith ye han in musik more feelinge
Than hadde Boece,[9] or any that can singe.
475 My lord your fader—God his soule blesse!—
And eek youre moder, of hir gentilesse,°   *gentility*
Han in myn hous ybeen, to my grete ese.
And certes sire, ful fain° wolde I you plese.   *gladly*
    "But for men speke of singing, I wol saye,
480 So mote I brouke[1] wel mine yën twaye,
Save ye, I herde nevere man to singe
As dide youre fader in the morweninge.
Certes, it was of herte° al that he soong.°   *heartfelt / sang*
And for to make his vois the more strong,

---

5. Supposed author of a bestiary, a book of moralized zoology describing both natural and supernatural animals (including mermaids).
6. He wished.
7. Like one who.
8. I.e., his natural enemy.
9. Boethius also wrote a treatise on music.
1. So might I enjoy the use of.

485 He wolde so paine him[2] that with bothe his yën
He moste winke,[3] so loude wolde he cryen;
And stonden on his tiptoon therwithal,
And strecche forth his nekke long and smal;
And eek he was of swich discrecioun
490 That ther nas no man in no regioun
That him in song or wisdom mighte passe.
I have wel rad° in *Daun Burnel the Asse*[4]   *read*
Among his vers how that ther was a cok,
For a preestes sone yaf him a knok[5]
495 Upon his leg whil he was yong and nice,°   *foolish*
He made him for to lese° his benefice.[6]   *lose*
But certain, ther nis no comparisoun
Bitwixe the wisdom and discrecioun
Of youre fader and of his subtiltee.[7]
500 Now singeth, sire, for sainte° charitee!   *holy*
Lat see, conne° ye youre fader countrefete?"°   *can / imitate*
    This Chauntecleer his winges gan to bete,
As man that coude his traison nat espye,
So was he ravisshed with his flaterye.
505   Allas, ye lordes, many a fals flatour°   *flatterer*
Is in youre court, and many a losengeour°   *deceiver*
That plesen you wel more, by my faith,
Than he that soothfastnesse° unto you saith!   *truth*
Redeth Ecclesiaste[8] of flaterye.
510 Beeth war, ye lordes, of hir trecherye.
    This Chauntecleer stood hye upon his toos,
Strecching his nekke, and heeld his yën cloos,
And gan to crowe loude for the nones;°   *occasion*
And daun Russel the fox sterte° up atones,   *jumped*
515 And by the gargat° hente° Chauntecleer,   *throat / seized*
And on his bak toward the wode him beer,°   *bore*
For yit ne was ther no man that him sued.°   *followed*
        O destinee that maist nat been eschued!°   *eschewed*
Allas that Chauntecleer fleigh° fro the bemes!   *flew*
520 Allas his wif ne roughte nat of[9] dremes!
And on a Friday fil° al this meschaunce!   *befell*
        O Venus that art goddesse of plesaunce,
Sin that thy servant was this Chauntecleer,
And in thy service dide al his power—
525 More for delit than world[1] to multiplye—
Why woldestou suffre him on thy day[2] to die?
        O Gaufred,[3] dere maister soverein,
That, whan thy worthy king Richard was slain

---

2. Take pains.
3. He had to shut his eyes.
4. Master Brunellus, a discontented donkey, was the hero of a 12th-century satirical poem by Nigel Wireker.
5. Because a priest's son gave him a knock.
6. The offended cock neglected to crow so that his master, now grown to manhood, overslept, missing his ordination and losing his benefice.

7. His (the cock in the story) cleverness.
8. The Book of Ecclesiasticus, in the Apocrypha.
9. Didn't care for.
1. I.e., population.
2. Friday is Venus's day.
3. Geoffrey of Vinsauf, a famous medieval rhetorician, who wrote a lament on the death of Richard I in which he scolded Friday, the day on which the king died.

With shot,[4] complainedest his deeth so sore,
530 Why ne hadde I now thy sentence and thy lore,[5]
The Friday for to chide as diden ye?
For on a Friday soothly slain was he.
Thanne wolde I shewe you how that I coude plaine°   *lament*
For Chauntecleres drede and for his paine.
535   Certes, swich cry ne lamentacioun
Was nevere of ladies maad when Ilioun°   *Ilium, Troy*
Was wonne, and Pyrrus[6] with his straite° swerd,   *drawn*
Whan he hadde hent° King Priam by the beerd   *seized*
And slain him, as saith us *Eneidos*,[7]
540 As maden alle the hennes in the cloos,°   *yard*
Whan they hadde seen of Chauntecleer the sighte.
But sovereinly° Dame Pertelote shrighte°   *supremely / shrieked*
Ful louder than dide Hasdrubales[8] wif
Whan that hir housbonde hadde lost his lif,
545 And that the Romains hadden brend° Cartage: *burned*
She was so ful of torment and of rage°   *madness*
That wilfully unto the fir she sterte,°   *jumped*
And brende hirselven with a stedefast herte.
O woful hennes, right so criden ye
550 As, whan that Nero brende the citee
Of Rome, criden senatoures wives
For that hir housbondes losten alle hir lives:[9]
Withouten gilt this Nero hath hem slain.
Now wol I turne to my tale again.
555   The sely° widwe and eek hir doughtres two   *innocent*
Herden thise hennes crye and maken wo,
And out at dores sterten° they anoon,   *leapt*
And sien° the fox toward the grove goon,   *saw*
And bar upon his bak the cok away,
560 And criden, "Out, harrow,° and wailaway,   *help*
Ha, ha, the fox," and after him they ran,
And eek with staves many another man;
Ran Colle oure dogge, and Talbot and Gerland,[1]
And Malkin with a distaf in hir hand,
565 Ran cow and calf, and eek the verray hogges,
Sore aferd° for berking of the dogges   *frightened*
And shouting of the men and wommen eke.
They ronne° so hem thoughte hir herte breke;[2]   *ran*
They yelleden as feendes doon in helle;
570 The dokes° criden as men wolde hem quelle;°   *ducks / kill*
The gees for fere flowen° over the trees;   *flew*
Out of the hive cam the swarm of bees;
So hidous was the noise, a, benedicite,°   *bless me*

---

4. I.e., a missile.
5. Thy wisdom and thy learning.
6. Pyrrhus was the Greek who slew Priam, king of Troy.
7. As the *Aeneid* tells us.
8. Hasdrubal was king of Carthage when it was

destroyed by the Romans.
9. According to the legend, Nero not only set fire to Rome (in 64 C.E.) but also put many senators to death.
1. Two other dogs.
2. Would break.

Certes, he Jakke Straw[3] and his meinee°　　　　　　　　*company*
575　Ne made nevere shoutes half so shrille
Whan that they wolden any Fleming kille,
As thilke day was maad upon the fox:
Of bras they broughten bemes° and of box,°　　　*trumpets / boxwood*
Of horn, of boon,° in whiche they blewe and pouped,°　　*bone / tooted*
580　And therwithal they skriked° and they houped°—　　*shrieked / whooped*
It seemed as that hevene sholde falle.
　　Now goode men, I praye you herkneth alle:
Lo, how Fortune turneth° sodeinly　　　　　　*reverses, overturns*
The hope and pride eek of hir enemy.
585　This cok that lay upon the foxes bak,
In al his drede unto the fox he spak,
And saide, "Sire, if that I were as ye,
Yit sholde I sayn, as wis° God helpe me,　　　　　　　　*surely*
'Turneth ayain, ye proude cherles alle!
590　A verray pestilence upon you falle!
Now am I come unto this wodes side,
Maugree your heed,[4] the cok shal here abide.
I wol him ete, in faith, and that anoon.'"
　　The fox answerde, "In faith, it shal be doon."
595　And as he spak that word, al sodeinly
The cok brak from his mouth deliverly,°　　　　　　　　*nimbly*
And hye upon a tree he fleigh° anoon.　　　　　　　　　*flew*
　　And whan the fox sawgh that he was agoon,
"Allas," quod he, "O Chauntecleer, allas!
600　I have to you," quod he, "ydoon trespas,
In as muche as I maked you aferd
Whan I you hente° and broughte out of the yeerd.　　　*seized*
But sire, I dide it in no wikke° entente:　　　　　　　*wicked*
Come down, and I shal telle you what I mente.
605　I shal saye sooth to you, God help me so."
　　"Nay thanne," quod he, "I shrewe° us bothe two:　　*curse*
But first I shrewe myself, bothe blood and bones,
If thou bigile me ofter than ones;
Thou shalt namore thurgh thy flaterye
610　Do° me to singe and winken with myn yë.　　　　　　*cause*
For he that winketh° whan he sholde see,　　　*closes both eyes*
Al wilfully, God lat him nevere thee."°　　　　　　　　*prosper*
　　"Nay," quod the fox, "but God yive him meschaunce
That is so undiscreet of governaunce°　　　　　　*self-control*
615　That jangleth° whan he sholde holde his pees."　　*chatters*
　　Lo, swich it is for to be reccheless°　　　　　　　*careless*
And necligent and truste on flaterye.
But ye that holden this tale a folye
As of a fox, or of a cok and hen,
620　Taketh the moralitee, goode men.
For Saint Paul saith that al that writen is

---

3. One of the leaders of the Uprising of 1381,　　4. Despite your head—i.e., despite anything you
which was partially directed against the Flem-　　can do.
ings living in London.

To oure doctrine° it is ywrit, ywis:[5]   *teaching*
Taketh the fruit, and lat the chaf be stille.[6]
Now goode God, if that it be thy wille,
625   As saith my lord, so make us alle goode men,
And bringe us to his hye blisse. Amen.

---

5. See Romans 15.4.
6. The "fruit" refers to the kernel of moral or doctrinal meaning; the "chaf," or husk, is the nar-rative containing that meaning. The metaphor was commonly applied to scriptural interpretation.

Close of *The Canterbury Tales*

At the end of *The Canterbury Tales*, Chaucer invokes a common allegorical theme, that life on earth is a pilgrimage. As Chaucer puts it in his moral ballade *Truth* (p. 362), "*Here* in noon home . . . / Forth, pilgrim, forth!" In the final fragment, he makes explicit a metaphor that has been implicit all along in the journey to Canterbury. The pilgrims never arrive at the shrine of St. Thomas, but in *The Parson's Tale*, and in its short introduction and in the "Retraction" that follows it, Chaucer seems to be making an end for two pilgrimages that had become one, that of his fiction and that of his life.

In the introduction to the tale we find the twenty-nine pilgrims moving through a nameless little village as the sun sinks to within twenty-nine degrees of the horizon. The atmosphere contains something of both the chill and the urgency of a late autumn afternoon, and we are surprised to find that the pilgrimage is almost over, that there is need for haste to make that "good end" that every medieval Christian hoped for. This delicately suggestive passage, rich with allegorical overtones, introduces an extremely long penitential treatise, translated by Chaucer from Latin or French sources. Although often assumed to be an earlier work, it may well have been written by Chaucer to provide the ending for *The Canterbury Tales.*

In the "Retraction" that follows *The Parson's Tale*, Chaucer acknowledges, lists, revokes, and asks forgiveness for his "giltes" (that is, his sins), which consist of having written most of the works on which his reputation as a great poet depends. He thanks Christ and Mary for his religious and moral works. One need not take this as evidence of a spiritual crisis or conversion at the end of his life. The "Retraction" seems to have been written to appear at the end of *The Canterbury Tales*, without censoring any of the tales deemed to be sinful. At the same time, one need not question Chaucer's sincerity. A readiness to deny his own reality before the reality of his God is implicit in many of Chaucer's works, and the placement of the "Retraction" within or just outside the border of the fictional pilgrimage suggests that although Chaucer finally rejected his fictions, he recognized that he and they were inseparable.

From The Parson's Tale

The Introduction

By that[1] the Manciple hadde his tale al ended,
The sonne fro the south line[2] was descended
So lowe, that he has nat to my sighte
Degrees nine and twenty as in highte.
5   Four of the clokke it was, so as I gesse,
For elevene foot, or litel more or lesse,

---

1. By the time that.
2. I.e., the line that runs some 28° to the south of the celestial equator and parallel to it.

My shadwe was at thilke time as there,
Of swich feet as° my lengthe parted° were   *as if / divided*
In six feet equal of proporcioun.[3]
10 Therwith the moones exaltacioun[4]—
I mene Libra—always gan ascende,
As we were entring at a thropes° ende.   *village's*
For which oure Host, as he was wont to gie°   *lead*
As in this caas oure joly compaignye,
15 Saide in this wise, "Lordinges everichoon,
Now lakketh us no tales mo than oon:
Fulfild is my sentence° and my decree;   *purpose*
I trowe° that we han herd of ech degree;   *believe*
Almost fulfild is al myn ordinaunce.
20 I praye to God, so yive him right good chaunce
That telleth this tale to us lustily.
Sire preest," quod he, "artou a vicary,°   *vicar*
Or arte a Person? Say sooth, by thy fay.°   *faith*
Be what thou be, ne breek° thou nat oure play,   *break*
25 For every man save thou hath told his tale.
Unbokele and shew us what is in thy male!°   *bag*
For trewely, me thinketh by thy cheere°   *expression*
Thou sholdest knitte up wel a greet matere.
Tel us a fable anoon, for cokkes bones!"[5]
30   This Person answerde al atones,°   *immediately*
"Thou getest fable noon ytold for me,
For Paul, that writeth unto Timothee,
Repreveth° hem that waiven soothfastnesse,[6]   *reproves*
And tellen fables and swich wrecchednesse.
35 Why sholde I sowen draf° out of my fest,°   *chaff / fist*
Whan I may sowen whete if that me lest?[7]
For which I saye that if you list to heere
Moralitee and vertuous matere,
And thanne that ye wol yive me audience,
40 I wol ful fain,° at Cristes reverence,   *gladly*
Do you plesance leveful° as I can.   *lawful*
But trusteth wel, I am a southren man:
I can nat geeste Rum-Ram-Ruf by lettre[8]—
Ne, God woot, rym holde° I but litel bettre.   *consider*
45 And therfore, if you list—I wol nat glose[9]—
I wol you telle a merye tale in prose
To knitte up al this feeste and make an ende.
And Jesu for his grace wit me sende
To shewe you the way in this viage°   *journey*
50 Of thilke parfit glorious pilgrimage
That highte° Jerusalem celestial.   *is called*
And if ye vouche sauf, anoon I shal
Biginne upon my tale, for which I praye

3. This detailed analysis merely says that the shadows are lengthening.
4. I.e., the astrological sign in which the moon's influence was dominant.
5. Cock's bones, a euphemism for God's bones.
6. Depart from truth (see 1 Timothy 1.4).

7. It pleases me.
8. I.e., I cannot tell stories in the alliterative measure (without rhyme): this form of poetry was not common in southeastern England.
9. I.e., speak in order to please.

Telle youre avis:° I can no bettre saye. *opinion*
55 But nathelees, this meditacioun
I putte it ay under correccioun
Of clerkes, for I am nat textuel:[1]
I take but the sentence,° trusteth wel. *meaning*
Therefore I make protestacioun° *public acknowledgment*
60 That I wol stonde to correccioun."
    Upon this word we han assented soone,
For, as it seemed, it was for to doone[2]
To enden in som vertuous sentence,° *doctrine*
And for to yive him space° and audience; *time*
65 And bede[3] oure Host he sholde to him saye
That alle we to telle his tale him praye.
    Oure Hoste hadde the wordes for us alle:
"Sire preest," quod he, "now faire you bifalle:
Telleth," quod he, "youre meditacioun.
70 But hasteth you; the sonne wol adown.
Beeth fructuous,° and that in litel space,° *fruitful / time*
And to do wel God sende you his grace.
Saye what you list, and we wol gladly heere."
And with that word he saide in this manere.

Chaucer's Retraction

Here taketh the makere of this book his leve[4]

Now praye I to hem alle that herkne this litel tretis[5] or rede, that if ther be any thing in it that liketh[6] hem, that therof they thanken oure Lord Jesu Crist, of whom proceedeth al wit[7] and al goodnesse. And if ther be any thing that displese hem, I praye hem also that they arrette it to the defaute of myn unconning,[8] and nat to my wil, that wolde ful fain[9] have said bettre if I hadde had conning. For oure book saith, "Al that is writen is writen for oure doctrine,"[1] and that is myn entente. Wherfore I biseeke[2] you mekely, for the mercy of God, that ye praye for me that Crist have mercy on me and foryive me my giltes, and namely of my translacions and enditinges[3] of worldly vanitees, the whiche I revoke in my retraccions: as is the *Book of Troilus*; the Book also of *Fame*; the *Book of the Five and Twenty Ladies*;[4] the *Book of the Duchesse*; the *Book of Saint Valentines Day of the Parlement of Briddes*; the *Tales of Canterbury*, thilke that sounen into[5] sinne; the *Book of the Leon*;[6] and many another book, if they were in my remembrance, and many a song and many a leccherous lay:[7] that Crist for his grete mercy foryive me the sinne. But of the translacion of Boece[8] *De Consolatione*, and othere bookes of legendes of

---

1. Literal, faithful to the letter.
2. Necessary to be done.
3. I.e., we bade.
4. "Chaucer's Retraction" is the title given to this passage by modern editors. The heading, "Here . . . leve," which does appear in all manuscripts, may be by Chaucer himself or by a scribe.
5. Hear this little treatise, i.e., *The Parson's Tale*.
6. Pleases.
7. Understanding.

8. Ascribe it to the defect of my lack of skill.
9. Gladly.
1. Romans 15.4.
2. Beseech.
3. Compositions. "Namely": especially.
4. I.e., the *Legend of Good Women*.
5. Those that tend toward.
6. The *Book of the Lion* has not been preserved.
7. Lyric poem.
8. Boethius.

saintes, and omelies,[9] and moralitee, and devocion, that thanke I oure Lord
Jesu Crist and his blisful Moder and alle the saintes of hevene, biseeking hem
that they from hennes[1] forth unto my lives ende sende me grace to biwaile my
giltes and to studye to the salvacion of my soule, and graunte me grace of verray[2] penitence, confession, and satisfaccion to doon in this present lif, thurgh
the benigne grace of him that is king of kinges and preest over alle preestes,
that boughte[3] us with the precious blood of his herte, so that I may been oon
of hem at the day of doom[4] that shulle be saved. *Qui cum patre et Spiritu
Sancto vivit et regnas Deus per omnia saecula.*[5] Amen.

1386–1400

9. Homilies.
1. Hence.
2. True.
3. Redeemed.

4. Judgment.
5. Who with the Father and the Holy Spirit
[thou] livest and reignest God forever (Latin).

LYRICS AND OCCASIONAL VERSE

In addition to his narrative verse, Chaucer wrote lyric poetry on the models of
famous French and Italian poets who made lyric into a medieval art form aimed at
learned and aristocratic audiences, an audience that included fellow poets. Chaucer also embedded lyric in narrative poetry. As an example of courtly lyric, we print
a "song" that Troilus, the hero of Chaucer's romance *Troilus and Criseyde*, makes up
about his violent and puzzling emotions after falling in love. The "song" is actually
Chaucer's translation into rhyme royal of one of Petrarch's sonnets, more than a
century before Sir Thomas Wyatt introduced the sonnet form itself to England. In
the fifteenth century, Troilus's song was sometimes excerpted and included in
anthologies of lyric poetry.

Chaucer also wrote homiletic ballades, one of which is entitled *Truth* by modern
editors and called "ballade de bon conseil" (ballade of good advice) in some manuscripts. A ballade is a verse form of three or more stanzas, each with an identical
rhyme scheme and the same last line, the refrain. Often a ballade ends with a shorter
final stanza called an *envoy* in which the poem is addressed or sent to a friend or
patron, or, conventionally, to a "prince" or "princes" in general. The good advice of
Truth is to abandon worldly pursuits of wealth and power and to concentrate on the
pilgrimage that leads to our true home in heaven. There are many copies of *Truth*
with only this heartfelt advice. The one printed below contains a unique humorous
envoy, addressed to a "Vache" (French for "cow"), who is probably Sir Philip de la
Vache.

A single stanza *To His Scribe Adam* comically conveys Chaucer's exasperation
at the sloppy work of a professional copyist. The *Complaint to His Purse* is a parody
of a lover's complaint to his lady: Ladies, like coins, should be golden, and, like
purses, they should not be "light" (i.e., fickle). *Purse* survives both without and with
an *envoy*. The addressee in the latter case is the recently crowned Henry IV, who is
being wittily implored to restore payment of Chaucer's annuity, which had been
interrupted by the new king's deposition of Richard II.

Troilus's Song[1]

If no love is, O God, what feele I so?
And if love is, what thing and which is he?
If love be good, from whennes cometh my wo?
If it be wikke,° a wonder thinketh° me,   *miserable / it seems to*
5 Whan every torment and adversitee
 That cometh of him may to me savory° thinke,°   *pleasant / seem*
 For ay° thurste I, the more that ich° drinke.   *always / I*

 And if that at myn owene lust° I brenne,°   *desire / burn*
 From whennes cometh my wailing and my plainte?° *complaint*
10 If harm agree° me, wherto plaine° I thenne? *agrees with / complain*
 I noot,° ne why unwery° that I fainte.   *know not / not weary*
 O quikke° deeth, O sweete harm so quainte,°   *living / strange*
 How may° of thee in me swich quantitee,   *can there be*
 But if° that I consente that it be?   *unless*

15 And if that I consente, I wrongfully
 Complaine: ywis,° thus possed° to and fro   *indeed / tossed*
 All stereless° within a boot° am I   *rudderless / boat*
 Amidde the see, bitwixen windes two,
 That in contrarye stonden everemo.
20 Allas, what is this wonder maladye?
 For hoot° of cold, for cold of hoot I die.   *hot*

Truth[1]

Flee fro the prees° and dwelle with soothfastnesse; *crowd*
Suffise unto° thy thing, though it be smal;   *be content with*
For hoord hath[2] hate, and climbing tikelnesse;°   *insecurity*
Prees hath envye, and wele° blent° overal. *prosperity / blinds*
5 Savoure° no more than thee bihoove shal;   *relish*
 Rule wel thyself that other folk canst rede:°   *advise*
 And Trouthe thee shal delivere,[3] it is no drede.° *doubt*

Tempest thee nought al crooked to redresse[4]
In trust of hire[5] that turneth as a bal;
10 Muche wele stant in litel bisinesse;[6]
 Be war therfore to spurne ayains an al[7]

1. *Troilus and Criseyde*, Book 1, lines 400–420.
A translation of Petrarch's Sonnet 132, "S'amor
non è."
1. Taking as his theme Christ's words to his disciples (in John 8.32), "And ye shall know the truth,
and the truth shall make you free," Chaucer plays
on the triple meaning that the Middle English word
trouthe seems to have had for him: the religious
truth of Christianity, the moral virtue of integrity,
and the philosophical idea of reality. By maintain-
ing one's faith and one's integrity, one rises superior
to the vicissitudes of this world and comes eventually to know reality—which is not, however, of this
world.
2. Hoarding causes.
3. I.e., truth shall make you free.
4. Do not disturb yourself to straighten all that's
crooked.
5. Fortune, who turns like a ball in that she is
always presenting a different aspect to people.
6. Peace of mind stands in little anxiety.
7. Awl, i.e., "don't kick against the pricks,"
wound yourself by kicking a sharp instrument.

Strive nat as dooth the crokke° with the wal.   *pot*
Daunte° thyself that dauntest otheres deede: *master*
And Trouthe thee shal delivere, it is no drede.

15 That° thee is sent, receive in buxomnesse;°   *what / obedience*
The wrastling for the world axeth° a fal;   *asks for*
Here is noon hoom, here nis° but wildernesse: *is not*
Forth, pilgrim, forth! Forth, beest, out of thy stal!
Know thy countree, looke up, thank God of al.
20 Hold the heigh way and lat thy gost° thee lede: *spirit*
And Trouthe thee shal delivere, it is no drede.

Envoy

Therfore, thou Vache,[8] leve thyn olde wrecchednesse
Unto the world; leve° now to be thral.   *i.e., cease*
Crye him mercy° that of his heigh goodnesse   *beg him for mercy*
25 Made thee of nought, and in especial
Draw unto him, and pray in general,
For thee and eek for othere, hevenelich meede:[9]
And Trouthe thee shal delivere, it is no drede.

To His Scribe Adam[1]

Adam scrivain,° if evere it thee bifalle   *scribe*
Boece or *Troilus*[2] for to writen newe,
Under thy longe lokkes thou moste[3] have the scalle,°   *scurf*
But after my making thou write more trewe,[4]
5 So ofte a day I moot° thy werk renewe,   *must*
It to correcte, and eek to rubbe and scrape:
And al is thurgh thy necligence and rape.°   *haste*

Complaint to His Purse

To you, my purs, and to noon other wight,°   *person*
Complaine I, for ye be my lady dere.
I am so sory, now that ye be light,
For certes, but if° ye make me hevy cheere,   *unless*
5 Me were as lief[1] be laid upon my beere;°   *bier*
For which unto youre mercy thus I crye:
Beeth hevy again, or elles moot° I die.   *must*

8. Probably Sir Philip de la Vache, with a pun on
the French for "cow."
9. Reward, with a pun on *meadow.*
1. Chaucer had fair copies of longer works made
by a professional scribe. This humorous complaint about Adam's sloppy work is written in the
verse form of Chaucer's great poem *Troilus and*

Criseyde.
2. *Troilus and Criseyde.* "Boece": i.e., Chaucer's
translation of Boethius's *De Consolatione.*
3. I.e., may you.
4. Unless you write more accurately what I've
composed.
1. I'd just as soon.

Now voucheth sauf° this day er° it be night   *grant / before*
That I of you the blisful soun may heere,
10   Or see youre colour, lik the sonne bright,
That of yelownesse hadde nevere peere.°   *equal*
Ye be my life, ye be myn hertes steere,°   *rudder, guide*
Queene of confort and of good compaignye:
Beeth hevy again, or elles moot I die.

15   Ye purs, that been to me my lives light
And saviour, as in this world down here,
Out of this towne[2] helpe me thurgh your might,
Sith that ye wol nat be my tresorere;°   *treasurer*
For I am shave as neigh as any frere.[3]
20   But yit I praye unto youre curteisye:
Beeth hevy again, or elles moot I die.

Envoy to Henry IV

O conquerour of Brutus Albioun,[4]
Which that by line° and free eleccioun   *lineage*
Been verray° king, this song to you I sende: *true*
25   And ye, that mowen° alle oure harmes amende,   *may*
Have minde upon my supplicacioun.

2. Probably Westminster, where Chaucer had rented a house.
3. Shaved as close as any (tonsured) friar, an expression for being broke.

4. Britain (Albion) was supposed to have been founded by Brutus, the grandson of Aeneas, the founder of Rome.

JOHN GOWER
ca. 1330–1408

Of Gower's life relatively little is known: he was certainly a landowner in Kent, and from about 1377 he seems to have been resident in Southwark, just over the River Thames from the City of London. He had close relations with Chaucer, who sent *Troilus and Criseyde* (ca. 1385) to "moral Gower" for "correction" (5.1856). Indeed, as the co-initiator of a new tradition of English poetry, his reputation throughout the fifteenth century was very nearly on a par with that of Chaucer. He was himself more concerned than Chaucer for his own literary posterity, since he took care that texts of his work would be transmitted in finished, stable form. No contemporary poet matches him for linguistic virtuosity, since Gower wrote in three languages. His main poetic works are as follows: the *Mirour de l'omme* (Mirror of Man) (finished 1376–78), written in Anglo-Norman (the dialect of French spoken in England); the Latin *Vox Clamantis* (Voice of the Crier), written substantially before 1386; and the English *Confessio Amantis* (The Lover's Confession), first published in 1390. The *Mirour* (the last major work written in Anglo-Norman in England) was addressed primarily to an upper-class audience capable of reading both French and English, while the Latin *Vox* was clearly directed to a highly educated audience. The first version of the *Confessio* was dedicated to Richard II. By the time of the third recension (1392–93), Richard had been replaced by Henry Bolingbroke, the future Henry IV, as the poem's dedicatee. Despite these dedications to specific and powerful readers, Gower in fact addressed the *Confessio* to all educated readers, both men and women.

Vox Clamantis refers to the saint whose name Gower bore, John the Baptist, whom all four gospels refer to as "the voice of one crying out in the wilderness" (Matthew 3.3, Mark 1.3, Luke 3.4, John 1.23) who will prepare the way for the Lord, fulfilling the prophecy of Isaiah 40.3. Gower thus identifies himself with the prophetic voice of John the Baptist as well as the apocalyptic voice of John the Evangelist in the Book of Revelation. In keeping with this posture, the *Mirour* and the *Vox* are examples of estates satire, a genre of satire in which the writer addresses and berates each main occupational grouping of society in turn. (For more information on estates satire, go to "Medieval Estates and Orders" in the NAEL Archive, where there are translations of excerpts from the *Mirour* and *Vox*.) In the *Vox*, for example, Gower vigorously attacks the peasantry for their part in the English Uprising of 1381.

While Gower wrote as moralist and satirist in the *Mirour* and the *Vox*, he changed tack in the *Confessio Amantis*. To be sure, the poem is structured as a moral discourse: the Confessor figure Genius hears the confession of the penitent Amans, as if enacting the procedures of the Church's sacrament of penance (one part of which was a formal, confidential confession to a priest). In seven of the poem's eight books, Genius hears Amans's confession concerning a different Deadly Sin (respectively Pride, Envy, Anger, Sloth, Greed, Gluttony, and Lechery). The very names of penitent and confessor themselves suggest, however, that this is no ordinary confession. For Amans (literally "one who loves") is heard by a "genial" aspect of the psyche, Genius, who is the priest of Venus. Far from condemning Amans for his hopeless subjection to erotic desire, Genius as often as not encourages Amans in his passion, or so it would seem initially. The eighty or so stories Genius tells by way of "correcting" Amans are drawn not from penitential treatises; they are rather, on the whole, drawn from secular, classical sources, and often from the poetry of Ovid, the classical poet of erotic love.

As the *Confessio* progresses, however, Genius increasingly registers the social and political disasters that result from solipsistic pursuit of sexual desire. While never abandoning his "genial" perspective altogether, and while never wishing wholly to repress sexual passion, Genius finally brings Amans around, to the point where Amans reintegrates with the psyche of which he is ideally a part. He finally regains his full identity as "John Gower." This recovery of identity involves a very moving self-recognition scene in the poem's finale, in which an aged Gower recognizes his position as a lover, a citizen, and a Christian. The poem is not only about one individual, however: Gower's sexual governance is linked to political governance of the kingdom. Just as Gower must rule yet recognize the proper demands of his body, so too must the king rule and recognize his kingdom.

Many of Genius's narratives relate stories whose violence entirely overshadows the often pathetic and always hopeless pursuit of Amans for his lady. The narrative of Tereus and Philomela ("Philomene" in Gower's narrative), drawn from Ovid, *Metamorphoses* (6.426–676), is one such frightening text. It tells a story of unremitting domestic violence, relating the "greediness" of rape to the larger concept of greed, the sin treated by Genius in Book 5 of the *Confessio*. A husband (Tereus) rapes and cuts out the tongue of his sister-in-law (Philomela); his wife (Procne) and her sister take their vengeance by murdering and cooking the rapist's child (Itys). Philomela's concern is as much for *publication* of the rape as for vengeance: with her excised tongue, she relies on weaving as a means of writing to communicate the terror of her experience, just as, transformed into a chattering bird at the end of the story, she continues to remind humans of Tereus's disgrace. When Chaucer had recounted the same story in *The Legend of Good Women* (ca. 1386), he omitted the most hair-raising episodes of the Ovidian source. Gower, by contrast, follows the lineaments of Ovid's narrative fairly closely and does not turn aside from the transformation of suffering women into terrible avengers, as Procne (here "Progne") murders and butchers her own child. Nor does he fail to register the horror of rape, as Philomela feels the inescapable weight of Tereus upon her (lines 96–101).

From The Lover's Confession[1]

The Tale of Philomene and Tereus

GENIUS:

Now list,° my Sone, and thou shalt heere,	*listen*
So as it hath befalle er° this	*before*
In loves cause how that it is	
A man to take be° ravine°	*seize by / rape*
5 The preie° that is femeline.	*prey*
Ther was a real° noble king,	*royal*
And riche of alle worldes thing,	
Which of his propre° inheritance	*own*
Athenes hadde in governance,	
10 And who so° thenke thereupon,	*whoever*
His name was king Pandion.	
Two doughtres° hadde he be his wif,	*daughters*
The whiche he lovede as his lif;	
The firste doughter Progne highte,°	*was called*
15 And the secounde, as she wel mighte,	
Was cleped° faire Philomene,	*called*
To whom fell after° muchel tene.°	*afterward / grief*
The fader of his purveance°	*forethought*
His daughter Progne wolde avance°	*advance*
20 And yaf° hire unto marriage	*gave*
A worthy king of hye lignage,°	*high lineage*
A noble knight eke° of his hond,[2]	*also*
So was he kid° in every lond,	*known*
Of Trace[3] he highte Tereus;	
25 The clerk Ovide[4] telleth thus.	
This Tereus his wif hoom ladde,	
A lusty° lif with hire he hadde;	*agreeable*
Til it befell upon a tide,°	*certain time*
This Progne, as she lay him beside,	
30 Bethoughte hire° how it mighte be	*considered*
That she hir suster mighte see,	
And to hir lord hir will she saide,	
With goodly wordes and him prayde	

1. The text is drawn from *The English Works of John Gower*, edited by G. C. Macaulay, Early English Text Society, extra series 81–82 (London: Oxford University Press, 1900–1901).
2. With respect to himself (in addition to his high lineage).
3. Thrace.
4. Gower's source is the Roman poet Ovid's *Metamorphoses* 4.424–674.

That she to hire mighte go:

35 And if it liked him noght° so,   *if it did not displease him*

That than he wolde himselve wende,°   *go*

Or elles be° some other sende,   *by*

Which mighte hir deere suster greete

And shape° how that they mighten meete.   *arrange*

40 Hir lord anon° to that he herde   *immediately*

Yaf his acord, and thus answerde:

"I wol," he saide, "for thy sake

The way after thy suster take

Myself, and bring hire, if I may."

45 And she with that, ther as he lay,

Began him in hir armes clippe,°   *embrace*

And kist him with hir softe lippe,

And saide, "Sire, grant mercy."°   *thank you*

And he soone° after was redy,   *right away*

50 And took his leve forto go;

In sory° time dide he so.   *sorrowful*

  This Tereus gooth forth to shipe

With him and with his felaweshipe;

By see the righte course he nam,°   *took*

55 Into the contree til he cam,

Wher Philomene was dwellinge,

And of hir suster the tidinge°   *news*

He tolde, and tho° they weren glade,   *then*

And muchel joy of him they made.

60 The fader and the moder bothe

To leve hir doughter weren lothe,

But if they weren in presence⁵

And natheles at reverence°   *with due respect*

Of him, that wolde himself travaile,°   *take the trouble*

65 They wolden noght he sholde faile

Of that he prayed, and yive hire leve:

And she, that wolde noght beleve,°   *remain*

In alle haste made hire yare°   *ready*

Toward hir suster forto fare°   *travel*

70 With Tereus and forth she wente.

And he withal his hool entente,°   *mind*

Whan she was from hir frendes go,

Assoteth° of hir love so,   *is besotted*

His yë° myghte he noght withholde,   *eye*

75 That he ne moste on hire beholde;⁶

And with the sighte he gan desire,

And set his owene herte on fire;

And fir, whan it to tow° aprocheth,   *flax*

To him° anon the strengthe acrocheth,°   *it / draws*

80 Til with his° hete it be devoured,   *its*

The tow ne may noght be socoured.°   *preserved*

And so that tyrant raviner,

Whan that she was in his power,

---

5. Unless they should be present.   6. Could not keep from looking at her.

And he therto saugh time and place,
85 As he that lost hath alle grace,
Foryat he was a wedded man,
And in a rage on hire he ran,
Right as a wolf which takth[7] his preye.
And she began to crye and praye,
90 "O fader, o mi moder deere,
Now help!" But they ne mighte it heere,
And she was of to litel might
Defense again° so rude° a knight   against / rough
To make, whan he was so wood°   mad
95 That he no reson understood,
But held hire under in such wise,
That she ne myghte noght arise,
But lay oppressed and disesed,°   distressed
As if a goshawk hadde sesed°   seized
100 A brid° which dorste noght for fere°   bird / fear
Remue°: and thus this tyrant there   escape
Beraft° hire such thing as men sayn   deprived
May neveremore be yolde° again,   restored
And that was the virginitee:
105 Of such ravine it was pitee.
    But whan she to hirselven cam,
And of hir meschief heede nam,°   took heed of her misfortune
And knew how that she was no maide,
With wofull herte thus she saide:
110 "O thou of alle men the worste,
Wher was ther evere man that dorste
Do such a dede as thou hast do?
That day shal falle, I hope so,
That I shal telle out al my fille,[8]
115 And with my speeche I shal fulfille
The wide world in brede° and lengthe.   breadth
That° thou hast do to me be strengthe,   that which
If I among the peple dwelle,
Unto the peple I shal it telle;
120 And if I be withinne wall
Of stones closed, than I shal
Unto the stones clepe° and crye,   call
And tellen hem thy felonye;
And if I to the woodes wende,
125 Ther shal I tellen tale and ende,°   the whole story
And crye it to the briddes oute,
That they shul heer it al aboute.
For I so loude it shal reherse,°   repeat
That my vois shal the hevene perce,°   pierce
130 That it shal soune° in goddes ere.   resound
Ha, false man, where is thy fere?°   fear (of the gods)
O more cruel than any beste,

---

7. Gower frequently contracts the third-person
present singular of verbs (takth = taketh).

8. I.e., have my fill of telling, tell all.

How hast thou holden thy biheste°   *promise*
Which thou unto my suster madest?
135 O thou, which alle love ungladest,
And art ensample of alle untrewe,
Now wolde God my suster knewe,
Of thin untrouthe, how that it stood!"
And he than as a lion wood°   *mad*
140 With his unhappy handes stronge
Hire caughte be the tresses longe,
With which he bond ther bothe hir armes—
That was a fieble° deed of armes—   *feeble, cowardly*
And to the grounde anon hire caste,
145 And out he clippeth also faste
Hir tonge with a paire of sheres,°   *shears*
So what with blood and what with teres
Out of hir yë and of hir mouth,
He made hir faire face uncouth:°   *unfamiliar, distorted*
150 She lay swounende° unto the deeth,   *fainting*
Ther was unnethes° any breeth;   *scarcely*
But yit whan he hir tonge refte,
A litel part therof belefte,°   *was left*
But she with al no word may soune,°   *utter*
155 But chitre° as a brid jargoune.°   *twitter / chatters*
And natheles that woode hound
Hir body hent° up fro the ground,   *seized*
And sente hire ther as be his wille
She sholde abide in prison stille
160 For everemo: but now take heede
What after fell of this misdeede.
Whan al this meschief was befalle,
This Tereus, that foule him falle,
Unto his contree hoom he tye;°   *traveled*
165 And whan he com his paleis nye,
His wif al redy ther him kepte.°   *awaited*
Whan he hire sih,° anon he wepte,   *saw*
And that he dide for deceite,
For she began to axe° him streite,°   *ask / directly*
170 "Wher is my suster?" And he saide
That she was deed; and Progne abraide,°   *started violently*
As she that was a woful wif,°   *woman*
And stood between hir deeth and lif,
Of that she herde such tidinge:
175 But for she sih° hir lord wepinge,   *saw*
She wende° noght but alle trouthe,   *thought*
And hadde wel the more routhe.°   *pity*
The perles weren tho forsake
To hire,⁹ and blake clothes take;
180 As she that was gentil and kinde,
In worshipe° of hir sustres minde°   *respect / memory*
She made a riche enterement,°   *funeral*

_____
9. I.e., she gave up jewelry.

For she fond non amendement°   *betterment*
To sighen or to sobbe more:
185 So was ther guile under gore.[1]
  Now leve we this king and queene,
And torne again to Philomene,
As I began to tellen erst.°   *before*
Whan she cam into prison ferst,
190 It thoghte° a kinges doughter straunge *seemed to*
To maken so sodein a chaunge
Fro welthe unto so greet a wo;
And she began to thenke tho,
Thogh she be mouthe nothing prayde,
195 Withinne hir herte thus she saide:
"O thou, almighty Jupiter,
That hye sits and lookest fer,
Thou suffrest many a wrong doinge,
And yit it is noght thy willinge.
200 To thee ther may nothing been hid,
Thou woost how it is me betid:
I wolde I hadde noght be bore,°   *born*
For thanne I hadde noght forlore°   *lost*
My speeche and my virginitee.
205 But, goode lord, al is in thee,
Whan thou therof wolt do° vengeance *wish to do*
And shape my deliverance."
And evere among this lady wepte,
And thoghte that she nevere kepte°   *cared*
210 To been a worldes womman more,
And that she wisheth everemore.
But ofte unto hir suster deere
Hir herte spekth in this manere,
And saide, "Ha, Suster, if ye knewe
215 Of myn estat, ye wolde rewe,
I trowe,° and my deliverance   *believe*
Ye wolde shape, and do vengeance
On him that is so fals a man:
And natheles, so as I can,
220 I wol you sende some tokeninge,°   *token*
Whereof ye shul have knowlechinge
Of thing I woot, that shal you lothe,° *make sick*
The which you toucheth and me bothe."
And tho withinne a while als tit°   *as quickly*
225 She waf° a cloth of silk al whit   *wove*
With lettres and ymagerye,
In which was al the felonye
Which Tereus to hire hath do;
And lappede° it togidre tho   *wrapped*
230 And sette hir signet° therupon   *seal*
And sende it unto Progne anon.

---

1. I.e., deceit under cover. "Gore" is a kind of cloak; the expression is probably proverbial for "deception."

The messager which forth it bar,
What it amounteth° is noght war;   *means*
And natheles to Progne he goth
235 And prively takth hire the cloth,
And wente again right as he cam,
The court of him non heede nam.
    Whan Progne of Philomene herde,
She wolde knowe how that it ferde,
240 And openeth that the man hath broght,
And woot therby what hath be wroght
And what meschief ther is befalle.
In swoune° tho she gan doun falle,   *faint*
And eft° aroos and gan to stonde,   *again*
245 And eft she takth the cloth on honde,
Beheld the lettres and thymages;
But atte laste, "Of such outrages,"
She sayth, "weeping is noght the boote,"°   *remedy*
And swerth, if that she live moote,
250 It shal be venged otherwise.
And with that she gan hire avise°   *consider*
How ferst she mighte unto hire winne°   *get*
Hir suster, that noman withinne,
But only they that were swore,°   *sworn (to silence)*
255 It sholde knowe, and shoop° therefore   *arranged*
That Tereus nothing it wiste;°   *knew*
And yit right as hirselven liste,°   *desired*
Hir suster was delivered soone
Out of prison, and be the moone
260 To Progne she was broght be nighte.
    Whan ech of other hadde a sighte,
In chambre, ther they were al one,
They maden many a pitous mone;°   *moaning*
But Progne most of sorwe made,
265 Which sih° hir suster pale and fade°   *saw / wan*
And speecheles and deshonoured,
Of that she hadde be defloured;
And eke upon hir lord she thoughte,
Of that he so untrewely wroghte
270 And hadde his espousaile broke.
She makth a vow it shal be wroke,°   *avenged*
And with that word she kneleth doun
Weeping in greet devocioun:
Unto Cupide and to Venus
275 She prayde, and saide thanne thus:
"O ye, to whom nothing asterte°   *escapes*
Of love may, for every herte
Ye knowe, as ye that been above
The god and goddesse of love;
280 Ye witen wel that evere yit
With al my will and al my wit,
Sith ferst ye shoopen me to wedde,
That I lay with my lord abedde,

I have be trewe in my degree,
285 And evere thoghte forto be,
And nevere love in other place,
But al only the king of Trace,
Which is my lord and I his wif.
But now allas this wofull strif!
290 That I him thus againward° finde   *on the contrary*
The most untrewe and most unkinde°   *unnatural*
That evere in lady armes lay.
And wel I woot that he ne may
Amende his wrong, it is so greet;
295 For he to litel of me leet,°   *prized*
Whan he myn owne suster took,
And me that am his wif forsook."
   Lo, thus to Venus and Cupide
She prayed, and furthermore she cryde
300 Unto Appollo the higheste,
And saide, "O mighty god of reste,
Thou do vengeance of this debat.
My suster and al hir estat
Thou woost, and how she hath forlore°   *lost*
305 Hir maidenhood, and I therfore
In al the world shal bere a blame
Of that my suster hath a shame,
That Tereus to hire I sente:
And wel thou woost that myn entente
310 Was al for worship and for goode.
O lord, that yifst° the lives foode   *gives*
To every wight, I pray thee here
Thes wofull sustres that been here,
And let us noght to thee been lothe;°   *hateful*
315 We been thyn owne wommen bothe."
   Thus plaineth Progne and axeth wreche,°   *vengeance*
And thogh hir suster lacke speeche,
To him that alle thinges woot
Hir sorwe is noght the lasse hoot:°   *hot*
320 But he that thanne had herd hem two,
Him oughte have sorwed everemo
For sorwe which was hem betweene.
With signes plaineth Philomene,
And Progne sayth, "It shal be wreke,°   *avenged*
325 That al the world therof shal speke."
And Progne tho° siknesse feineth,   *then*
Wherof unto hir lord she plaineth,
And prayth she most hir chambres keepe,
And as hire liketh wake and sleepe.
330 And he hire granteth to be so;
And thus togidre been they two,
That wolde him but a litel good.
Now herk herafter how it stood
Of wofull auntres° that befelle: *chances*
335 Thes sustres, that been bothe felle°—   *fiercely cunning*

And that was noght on hem along,°   *natural*
But onliche on° the greete wrong   *on account of*
Which Tereus hem hadde do—
They shoopen forto venge hem tho.
340   This Tereus be Progne his wif
A sone hath, which as his lif
He loveth, and Ithis he highte:
His moder wiste wel she mighte
Do Tereus no more grief
345 Than slee this child, which was so lief.°   *dear*
Thus she, that was, as who sayth, mad
Of wo, which hath hir overlad,°   *overborne*
Withoute insighte of moderheede
Foryat pitee and loste dreede,
350 And in hir chambre prively
This child withouten noise or cry
She slou° and hewe° him al to pieces.   *slew / cut*
And after with diverse spices
The flessh, whan that it was tohewe,°   *all cut up*
355 She takth, and makth therof a sewe,°   *stew*
With which the fader at his mete°   *meal*
Was served, til he hadde him ete;
That he ne wiste how it stood,
But thus his owene flessh and blood
360 Himself devoureth again kinde,°   *contrary to nature*
As he that was tofore unkinde.
And thanne, er that he were arise,
For that he sholde been agrise,°   *horrified*
To shewen him the child was deed,
365 This Philomene took the heed
Between two dishes, and al wrothe°   *angry*
Tho comen forth the sustres bothe,
And setten it upon the bord.
And Progne tho began the word,
370 And saide, "O werste of alle wicke,
Of conscience whom no pricke
May stere,° lo, what thou hast do!   *disturb*
Lo, here been now we sustres two;
O raviner, lo here thy preie,°   *prey*
375 With whom so falsliche on the waye
Thou hast thy tyrannye wroght.
Lo, now it is somdel aboght,°   *somewhat repaid*
And bet° it shal, for of thi deede   *better*
The world shal evere singe and rede
380 In remembrance of thy defame:
For thou to love hast do such shame,
That it shal nevere be foryete."
With that he sterte up fro the mete,
And shoof° the bord unto the floor,   *pushed*
385 And caughte a swerd anon and swoor
That they sholde of his handes dye
And they unto the goddess crye

Begunne with so loude a stevene,°   *voice*
That they were herd unto the hevene;
390   And in a twinklinge of an yë
The goddes, that the meschief syë,
Hir formes chaungen alle three.
Echoon of hem in his degree
Was torned into briddes kinde;
395   Diverseliche as men may finde,
After thestat that they were inne,
Hir formes were set atwinne.[2]
And as it telleth in the tale,
The ferst into a nightingale
400   Was shape, and that was Philomene,
Which in the winter is noght sene,
For thanne been the leves falle
And naked been the bushes alle.
For after that she was a brid,
405   Hir will was evere to been hid,
And forto dwelle in privee place,
Than noman sholde seen hir face
For shame which may noght be lassed,°   *diminished*
Of thing that was tofore passed,
410   Whan that she loste hir maidenhede:
For evere upon hir wommanhede,
Thogh that the goddes wolde hire chaunge,
She thenkth, and is the more straunge,
And halt hire cloos[3] the winters day.
415   But whan the winter gooth away,
And that Nature the goddesse
Wole of hir owene free° largesse   *generous*
With herbes and with flowres bothe
The feldes and the medwes° clothe   *meadows*
420   And eke the woodes and the greves°   *groves*
Been heled° al with greene leves,   *covered*
So that a brid hire hide may,
Between Averil° and March and May,   *April*
She that the winter held hire cloos,
425   For pure shame and noght aroos,
Whan that she seeth the bowes thikke,
And that ther is no bare stikke,
But al is hid with leves greene,
To woode comth this Philomene
430   And makth hir ferste yeres flight;
Wher as she singeth day and night,
And in hir song al openly
She makth hir plainte and sayth, "O why,
O why ne were I yit a maide?"°   *virgin*
435   For so these olde wise saide,
Which understooden what she mente,

---

2. I.e., their forms as birds differed from one another as they had in their human estate or condition.
3. Keeps herself concealed.

Hir notes been of such entente.°   *meaning*
And eke they saide how in hir song
She makth greet joye and mirthe among,
440 And sayth, "Ha, now I am a brid,
Ha, now my face may been hid:
Though I have lost my maidenhede,
Shal noman see my cheekes rede."
Thus medleth° she with joye wo   *mixes*
445 And with hir sorwe mirthe also,
So that of loves maladye
She makth diverse melodye,
And sayth love is a wofull blisse,
A wisdom which can noman wisse,°   *instruct*
450 A lusty° fevere, a wounde softe: *healthy*
This note she reherseth ofte
To hem, whiche understonde hir tale.
Now have I of this nightingale,
Which erst was cleped Philomene,
455 Told al that evere I wolde mene,
Bothe of hir forme and of hir note,
Wherof men may the storye note.°   *remember*
    And of hir suster Progne I finde,
How she was torned° out of kinde   *transformed*
460 Into a swalwe° swift of winge,   *swallow*
Which eke in winter lith swouninge,°   *lies fainting*
Ther as she may nothing be sene:
But whan the world is woxe° greene   *grown*
And comen is the somertide,
465 Than fleth she forth and ginth° to chide,   *begins*
And chitreth out in hir langage
What falshood is in marriage,
And telleth in a maner speeche
Of Tereus spousebreeche.°   *adultery*
470 She wol noght in the woodes dwelle,
For she wolde openliche telle;
And eke for that she was a spouse,
Among the folk she comth to house,
To do these wives understonde
475 The falshood of hir housbonde,
That they of hem be war also,
For ther been many untrewe of tho.°   *those*
Thus been the sustres briddes bothe,
And been toward the men so lothe,
480 That they ne wole of pure shame
Unto no mannes hand be tame;
For evere it dwelleth in hir minde
Of that they founde a man unkinde,
And that was false Tereus.
485 If such oon be amonges us
I noot,° but his condicioun   *do not know*
Men sayn in every regioun
Withinne toune and eke withoute

Now regneth communliche aboute.
490 And natheles in remembrance
I wol declare what vengeance
The goddess hadden him ordained,
Of that the sustres hadden plained:
For anon after he was chaunged
495 And from his owene kinde straunged,°   *estranged*
A lappewinge made he was,
And thus he hoppeth on the gras,
And on his heed ther stant upright
A creste in tokne he was a knight;
500 And yit unto this day men sayth,
A lappewinge hath lore° his faith   *lost*
And is the brid falseste of alle.
    Bewar my sone, er thee so falle;
For if thou be of such covine,°   *treachery*
505 To get of love be ravine
Thy lust,° it may thee falle thus,   *desire*
As it befell of Tereus.

AMANS:
My fader, goddes forebode!°   *forbid*
Me were levere be fortrode°   *trodden*
515 With wilde hors and be todrawe,°   *drawn*
Er I again love and his lawe
Dide any thing or loude or stille,
Which were noght my lady wille.
Men sayn that every love hath drede;
520 So folweth it that I hire drede,
For I hire love, and who so dredeth,
To plese his love and serve him needeth.
Thus may ye knowen be this skile°   *argument*
That no ravine doon I wille
525 Again hir will be such a waye;
But while I live, I wol obeye
Abidinge on hir courtesye,
If any mercy wolde hir plye.°   *persuade*
Forthy, my fader, as of this
530 I woot noght I have doon amis:
But furthermore I you beseeche,
Some other point that ye me teche
And axeth forth, if ther be ought,°   *anything*
That I may be the bettre taught.

1390

THOMAS HOCCLEVE
ca. 1367–1426

"Debate is now noon bitwix me and my wit," declares the first-person narrator, one "Thomas," in line 247 of Thomas Hoccleve's poem *My Complaint* (1419–20), telling his readers that he is now recovered from mental instability. The text as a whole, however, tells a much more painful story: Hoccleve's problem is less mental instability and more the fact that his friends think him unstable. Thomas acknowledges that he had a nervous breakdown of sorts five years ago, but now, feeling fully recovered, he remains tortured by his friends' lack of trust. He's so distressed by their distrust, in fact, that it is driving him insane.

The real Thomas Hoccleve corresponds closely to the "Thomas" as represented in Hoccleve's poetry. Hoccleve was a civil servant, working as a skilled clerk in the office of the Privy Seal. In addition to his bureaucratic tasks, he produced poetic texts of a high order, notably the *Regement of Princes* (1410–13) and the so-called *Series* (ca. 1419–21), a compilation of which *My Complaint* is the first part. He also wrote occasional poems, both subtle petitionary texts (asking for payment) and poetry voicing official policy. He seems to have experienced a period of mental instability in 1414. The detailed evidence for this inference derives only from the *Series*, although it might be relevant that Hoccleve was not paid in Michaelmas 1414.

Hoccleve represents himself in sometimes amusingly, more often painfully, vulnerable ways. He is English poetry's first alienated urban bureaucrat, intellectual, and poet, alienated from his work (for which he is underpaid and paid late, if paid at all) and alienated from his patrons, readers, and friends.

Being thought less than fully sane is a tricky challenge for both a human being and an author. Staying away from company so as to avoid suspicion merely provokes further suspicion: Thomas's friends will, he reasonably surmises, think him "fallen in again" (line 182). Out in public he overhears the voices of those commenting on his bizarre physical mannerisms; but back home, he retreats to his mirror and searches for signs of instability that he might rectify. In public or alone with his mirror image, Thomas is bounced back and forth by the "peoples imagination" (line 380), what others think or say about him, his public image, subject as it is to the "social media" conditions of early-fifteenth-century London. Maybe reading books of consolation is the answer, books that anchor identity in God, not in society. So ends *My Complaint*, but, interestingly, Thomas never gets to the end of that book, and besides, his apparent acceptance of its

Patronage. Thomas Hoccleve, *Regement of Princes*, 1412. Hoccleve presents his poem to Prince Henry. The author is on his knees to his patron, even if the book he presents is less subservient than the image might suggest.

advice is belied by the complex time sequence of *My Complaint*: he claims to have been pacified by the spiritual book *before* the time of bursting out with the complaint. Only Hoccleve's own text might do the trick here, by reintegrating him with his readers, unless of course they examine his work diagnostically, looking for signs in his poetry of uncured madness.

My Complaint is a searing expression of, and attempted self-therapy for, melancholia. This is the "thoughtful maladye" (line 21), or what we might call depression. Hoccleve represents the author in the act of dying, his voice invaded by the distrustful voices of his readers and so-called friends. The painful predicament of the outsider in the claustrophobic society of late-medieval court society points forward to early-modern court satire. It might also point us to that other striking misfit in late-medieval English writing, Hoccleve's contemporary Margery Kempe, whose distinctiveness is either saintly or sad.

My Complaint[1]

After that harvest° inned° had his sheaves,	*autumn / brought in*
And that the brown season of Michelmesse[2]	
Was come, and gan° the trees rob of her° leaves,	*proceeded / their*
That green had been and in lusty° fresshnesse,	*pleasing*
5 And hem into color of yelownesse	
Had dyed° and down throwen underfoote,	*died*
That chaunge sank into myn herte° roote.	*heart's*
For freshly brought it to my remembrance	
That stableness in this worlde is ther none.	
10 Ther is nothing but change and variance.°	*alteration*
How wealthy a man be or wel begun,°	*prosperous*
Endure it shall not. He shall it forgoon.°	*lose*
Death underfoot shall him thruste adown.°	*thrust down*
That is every wightes° conclusion,	*person's*
15 Which for to weyve° is in no mannes might,	*avoid*
How° rich he be, strong, lusty,° fresh and gay.	*however / vigorous*
And in the end of November, upon a night,	
Sighinge° sore, as I in my bed lay,	*sighing*
For this and other thoughtes which many a day,	
20 Before I took, sleep cam noon in myn eye,	
So vexed me the thoughtful maladye.°	*i.e., melancholia*
I saw well, sithen° I with sickness last	*since*
Was scourged, cloudy hath been the favor	
That shone on me full bright° in times past.	*very brightly*
25 The sun abated,° and the darke° shower	*diminished / dark*
Hilded° down right on me, and in langor°	*poured / depression*

1. The text is drawn from Thomas Hoccleve, "*My Compleinte*" *and Other Poems*, edited by Roger Ellis, Exeter Medieval Texts and Studies (Exeter: University of Exeter Press, 2001). Obsolete letter forms have been modernized. Spelling has also been modernized so as to facilitate sense, wherever this does not interfere with meter or rhyme.

Ellis's glosses have been preserved, with some modification. Readers should aim to produce an iambic pentameter for each line. Some lines demand variation on that default pattern.
2. Michaelmas falls on September 29. Note the melancholy inversion of the opening of Chaucer's *Canterbury Tales*.

Me made swim, so that my spirit
To live no lust° had, ne no delight.   *pleasure*

30 The grief about myn heart so sore swal°   *swelled*
And bolned° ever to and to° so sore   *swelled / more and more*
That nedes° oute° I muste therwithal.° *necessarily / burst out / with it*
I thought I nolde° kepe it close° no more, *would not / secret*
Ne let it in me for to elde° and hore,°   *age / grow gray*
And for to preve° I cam° of a woman,   *prove / was born*
35 I burst out on the morrow° and thus began.   *next day*

Here endeth my prologue and foloweth my compleint.

Almighty God, as liketh° his goodnesse,   *pleases*
Visiteth° folk alday,° as men may see, *visits / continually*
With loss of good and bodily sicknesse,
And among other,° he forgot not me.   *others*
40 Witness upon the wild infirmity
Whiche that I had, as many a man well knew,
And which me out of myself cast and threw.

It was so knowen to the peple and couthe°   *familiar*
That counseil° was it noon, ne not be might.   *secret*
45 How it with me stood was in every mannes mouthe,
And that ful sore° my friends affright.° *sorely / frightened*
They for myn health pilgrimages hight,°   *promised*
And sought hem, some on horse and some on foot,
God yeld it hem,° to gete me my boot.° *reward them for it / health*

50 But although the substance of my memory
Went to play as for a certain space,°   *for a time*
Yet° the lord of virtue, the king of glory,   *although*
Of his high might and his benigne grace,
Made it for to return into the place
55 Whence it came,° whiche at Alle Hallowmess³ *went out*
Was five year,° neither more ne less.   *five years ago*

And ever sithen,° thanked be God our Lord   *since*
Of° his good and gracious reconciliation,   *for*
My wit and I have been of such accord° *as well agreed*
60 As we were or° the alteration   *before*
Of it was, but by my salvation,
Sith° that time have I been sore set on fire   *since*
And lived in great torment and martire.°   *suffering*

For though that my wit were home come again,
65 Men would it not so understand or take.°   *accept*
With me to deal hadden they disdain.°   *scorn*
A riotous° person I was and forsake.° *dissolute / abandoned*
Min olde frendship was al overshake.°   *shaken off*
No wight° with me list make daliance.° *person / pleased to converse*

3. All Hallowmas, or All Saints Day, falls on November 1.

<table>
<tr><td>70</td><td>The world me made a strange countinance,°</td><td>the face of a stranger</td></tr>
</table>

70 The world me made a strange countinance,°   *the face of a stranger*
    Which that myn herte sore gan to torment,
    For ofte whan I in Westminster Halle,
    And eke° in London, among the press° went,   *also / crowd*
    I saw the cheer abaten° and apalle°   *faces grow dejected / pale*
75 Of hem° that weren wont° me for to call   *those / accustomed*
    To company.° Her° head they cast awry,°   *to join them / their / aside*
    Whan I hem met, as° they not me sy.°   *as if / saw*

    As said is in the Psalter might I sey,
    'They that me saw, fledden away from me.'[4]
80 Forgotten I was all out of mind away,
    As he that dead was from° heart's charity.°   *far from / love*
    To a lost vessel likened might I be,
    For many a wight° aboute me dwelling°   *person / in my vicinity*
    Heard I me blame and put in dispraising.°   *and censure*

85 Thus spake many one and said by° me: *about*
    'Although from him his sickeness savage°   *wild*
    Withdrawn and passed as for a time be,
    Resort° it will, namely° in such age   *return / especially*
    As he is of,' and thanne my visage°   *face*
90 Began to glow° for the woe and fear.   *burn*
    Tho° wordes, hem unwar,° came to myn ear.   *those / without their knowledge*

    'Whan passing° heat is,' quod they, 'trusteth° this,   *extreme / believe*
    Assail him will again that malady.'
    And yet, parde,° they token hem amiss.°   *by heaven / were wrong*
95 None effect at all took her prophecy.°   *their prophecy was wrong*
    Many summers been° passed sithen° remedy   *are / since*
    Of that God of his grace° me purveyed.°   *by his grace / provided with*
    Thanked be God, it shoop° not as they seyd.   *happened*

    What° falle shal,° what men so deem°   *whatever / shall happen / judge*
       or guess,
100 To him that woot° every hertes secree,°   *knows / secret*
    Reserved is. It is a lewednesse°   *an ignorance*
    Men wiser hem pretende° than they be,   *to pretend themselves*
    And no wight° knoweth, be it he or she,   *person*
    Whom, how, ne when God will him visite.°   *visit*
105 It happeth often when men wene° it lite.°   *expect / not at all*

    Sometime I wende° as lite° as any man   *thought / little*
    For to han fall° into that wildenesse,   *to have fallen*
    But God, whan him liste,° may, will and can   *it pleases*
    Health withdraw and send a wight° sicknesse.   *person*
110 Though man be wel this day, no sikernesse°   *certainty*
    To him bihight° is that it shall endure.   *promised*
    God hurt now can, and nowe heal and cure.

---

4. From Psalm 31; a Psalter is a book of Psalms and perhaps other devotional material.

He suffreth° long but at the last he smit.°　　*endures / smites*
Whan that a man is in prosperity,
115　To dread a fall coming it is a wit.°　　*mark of wisdom*
Whoso° that taketh heed oft may see　　*whoever*
This worldes change and mutability
In sundry wise,° how nedeth not expresse.°　　*different ways / to declare*
To my matter straight° will I me dresse.°　　*immediately / address myself*

120　Men seiden I loked° as a wilde steer,°　　*looked like / ox*
And so my look about I gan to throw.°　　*cast*
Myn head to high, another said, I beer.°　　*carried*
'Full buckissh° is his brain, well may I trow.'°　　*very like a buck / believe*
And said the third, 'And apt is° in the row°　　*(he) is fit / (i.e., company)*
125　To sit of hem that a reasonless reed°　　*senseless piece of advice*
Can give: no sadness° is in his heed.'　　*soundness*

Changed had I my pace,° some seiden eke,°　　*step / moreover*
For here and there forth stirte° I as a roe,°　　*started / roebuck*
None abode,° none arrest,° but al brainseke.°　　*resting / stopping / brainsick*
130　Another spake and of° me said also,　　*concerning*
My feet weren ay waving° to and fro,　　*moving*
When that I stonde° should and with men talke,　　*stand (still)*
And that myn eyen° soughten° every halke.°　　*eyes / sought / corner (of room)*

I leide an ear ay to° as I by went　　*gave an ear to this constantly*
135　And herde al, and thus in myn heart I caste:°　　*reflected*
'Of long abidinge here I may me repent.
Lest that of hastiness I at the laste
Answer amiss, best is hence hie faste,°　　*to depart quickly*
For if I in this press° amiss me gye,°　　*crowd / misbehave myself*
140　To harm wole it me turn and to folie.'°　　*and (make me) a laughingstock*

And this I deemed° well and knew well eke,°　　*judged / also*
Whatso° that ever I should answer or seie,°　　*whatever / say*
They wolden not han holde° it worth a leke.°　　*considered / leek*
Forwhy,° as° I had lost my tounges keie,°　　*therefore / as if / tongue's key*
145　Kepte I me close,° and trussed me my weie,°　　*private / took myself off*
Dropping° and heavy and all woe bistad.°　　*drooping / woebegone*
Small cause had I, methoughte, to be glad.

My spirits laboureden ever ful busily
To painte countenance,° cheer and look,°　　*appearance / face*
150　For° that men spake of me so wondringly,　　*because*
And for the very shame and fear I qwook.°　　*shook*
Though° myn herte had be dippid° in the brook　　*even if / been plunged*
It wet and moist was ynow° of my swoot,°　　*enough / with my sweat*
Which was now frosty cold, nowe fiery hoot.°　　*hot as fire*

155　And in my chamber at home whan that I was
Myself alone I in this wise° wrought.°　　*way / did*
I straight° unto my mirror and my glass,　　*went directly*
To look how that me of my chere thought,°　　*my expression seemed to me*

If any° other° were it than it ought,   *in any way / different*
160 For fain° would I, if it not had been right,   *gladly*
    Amended° it to my cunning° and might   *improved / according to my skill*

    Many a saut° made I to this mirror,   *leap*
    Thinking, 'If that I look in this manere
    Amonge folk as I now do, noon° error   *no*
165 Of suspect° look may in my face appere.   *suspicious*
    This countenance,° I am sure, and this chere,°   *appearance / expression*
    If I it forth° use, is nothing° reprevable°   *abroad / not / objectionable*
    To hem that han conceites° resonable.'   *understanding*

    And therwithal° I thoughte thus anoon:°   *thereupon / at once*
170 'Men in her° owne cas° been blind alday,°   *their / situations / continually*
    As I have herde seie many a day agoon,°   *before this*
    And in that same plight° I stonde may.   *danger*
    How shall I do? Which is the beste way
    My troubled spirit for to bring in rest?
175 If I wiste° how, fain° would I do the best.'   *knew / gladly*

    Sithen° I recovered was, have I full oft   *since*
    Cause had of anger and impacience,
    Where I borne have it easily° and soft,°   *calmly / gently*
    Suffring° wrong be done to me, and offence,   *enduring*
180 And not answered again,° but kept silence,   *back*
    Lest that men of me deem° would, and sein,   *judge*
    'See how this man is fallen in° again.'°   *(to his sickness) / again*

    As that I ones° from Westminster[4] cam,   *once*
    Vexed full grievously with thoughtful hete,°   *burning thought*
185 Thus thought I, 'A greet fool I am,
    This pavement adaies° thus to bete,°   *daily / beat (upon)*
    And in and out° laboure fast and swete,°   *everywhere / sweat*
    Wondringe° and heavinesse to purchase,°   *uncertainty / gain*
    Sithen° I stand out of all favor and grace.'   *since*

190 And than thought I on that other side,
    'If that I not be seen among the press,°   *throng*
    Men deme° will that I myn hede° hide,   *judge / head*
    And am worse than I am, it is no lees.'°   *lie*
    O Lorde, so my spirit was restelees.
195 I soughte reste and I not it fonde,°   *found*
    But ay° was trouble ready at myn honde.   *always*

    I may not let° a man to imagine°   *prevent / from imagining*
    Far above the moon, if that him liste.°   *pleases*
    Thereby the soth° he may not determine,   *truth*
200 But by the preef° been thinges known and wiste.°   *proof / understood*
    Many a doom° is wrapped in° the miste.   *judgment / hidden (as) in*
    Man by his dedes° and not by his lookes   *deeds*
    Shall known be. As it is written in bookes,

---

4. Westminster, a city separate from London proper; Hoccleve's workplace as a royal bureaucrat.

By taste of fruit men may wel wite° and knowe   *understand*
205 What that it is. Other preef° is ther none.   *proof*
Every man woote° well that, as that I trowe.°   *knows / believe*
Right so, they that deemen° my wit is gone,   *judge*
As yet this day there deemeth many one°   *many a one*
I am not well, may, as I by hem go,
210 Taste and assay° if it be so or no.   *test*

Uppon a look is° harde men hem to ground°   *it is / for men to determine*
What a man is. Therby the soth° is hid.   *truth*
Whether his wittes° sick been° or sound,   *wits / are*
By countenance is it not wist° ne kid.°   *known / made public*
215 Though a man hard have once been bitid,°   *has once experienced hardship*
God shield° it should on him continue alway.   *forbid*
By communinge° is the best assay.°   *conversation / test*

I mene, to commune° of thinges mene,°   *converse / ordinary*
For I am but right lewed,° doubteless,   *uneducated*
220 And ignorant. My cunning° is ful lene.°   *knowledge / very slight*
Yet homely reason° know I neveretheless.   *ordinary reasoning*
Not hope° I founden be° so reasonless°   *think / to be found / foolish*
As men deemen.° Marie,° Crist forbede!°   *judge / St. Mary / forbid*
I can° no more. Preve° may the dede.°   *know / prove this / deed*

225 If a man once falle in drunkenesse,
Shall he continue therein everemo°?   *evermore*
Nay, though a man do in drinking excesse   *drink to excess*
So ferforth° that not speak he ne can, ne go,   *far*
And his wits well nigh been refte° him fro,   *are almost all taken*
230 And buried in the cup; he afterward
Cometh to himself again, else were it° hard.   *otherwise it would be*

Right so, though that my wit were a pilgrim,
And wente fer° from home, he cam° again.   *far / returned*
God me devoided° of the grievous venim   *emptied*
235 That had infected and wilded° my brain.   *maddened*
See how the courteous leche° most sovereign   *doctor*
Unto the sike yeveth° medicine   *sick man gives*
In need, and him releveth of his grievous pine.°   *torment*

Now let this pass. God woot,° many a man   *knows*
240 Semeth ful wise by countenance° and chere°   *appearance / expression*
Which, and° he tasted° were what he can,°   *if / tested / knows*
Men mighten liken° him to a fooles pere,°   *compare / mate*
And some man looketh in foltisshe manere°   *like a fool*
As to the outward doom° and jugement,   *external estimation*
245 That, at the prefe,° discreet° is and prudent.   *when tested / rational*

But algates,° how so° be my countenance,   *all the same / however*
Debate° is now noon bitwix° me and my wit,   *disagreement / between*
Although that there were a disseverance,°   *separation*
As for a time, bitwixe me and it.

250 The greater harme is myn, that never yit°   *yet*
  Was I wel lettred,° prudent and discreet.° *educated / deliberative*
  Ther never stood yet wise man on my feet.

  The soth° is this, suche conceit° as I had   *truth / thoughts*
  And understanding, al° were it but° small,   *although / only*
255 Before that my wittes weren unsad,°   *unstable*
  Thanked be our Lorde Jhesu Christ of all,°   *for all*
  Such have I now, but blow° is nigh overall° *blown / nearly everywhere*
  The reverse, wherethrough° much is my   *through which*
    mourning,
  Which causeth me thus sigh in complaining.

260 Sithen° my good fortune hath changed hir cheer,° *since / look*
  High tyme is me° to creep into my grave.   *for me*
  To live joylees,° what do I here?   *joyless*
  I in myn herte can no gladness have.
  I may but small say but if° men deem° I rave. *unless / judge*
265 Sithen° other thing than woe may I noon gripe,° *since / grasp*
  Unto° my sepulcher am I now ripe.°   *for / ready*

  My wele,° adieu, farewell, my good fortune.   *wealth*
  Oute of youre tables me planed° han ye.   *removed*
  Sithen welnigh any wight° for to commune°   *person / talk*
270 With me loathe is, farewell prosperity.
  I am no longer of your livery.
  Ye have me put out of your retenance.°   *retinue*
  Adieu, my good aventure° and good chaunce.° *fortune / luck*

  And aswith° after, thus bithought I me:° *immediately / reflected*
275 'If that I in this wise me despair,
  It is purchase of more adversity.
  What nedeth it° my feeble wit appair,° *need is there / to weaken*
  Sith° God hath made myn healthe home repair,° *since / return*
  Blessed be he. And what° men deem° and speke, *whatever / judge*
280 Suffer° it think I and me not on me wreke.'° *to endure / to avenge*

  But somdel° had I rejoysing amonge,° *somewhat / between whiles*
  And a gladness also in my spirite,
  That though the people took hem° miss° and *judged / amiss*
    wronge,°   *wrongly*
  Me deeming° of my sicknesse not quite,°   *judging / freed*
285 Yet for they complained° the heavy plite° *regretted / plight*
  That they had seen me in with tenderness
  Of hertes cherte,° my grief was the less.   *love*

  In hem putte I no default° but oon.° *found no fault / one*
  That I was whole, they not ne deme° coude,° *judge / could*
290 And day by day they saw me by hem goon°   *go*
  In heat and cold, and neither still or lowde° *silent or speaking*
  Knew they me do suspectly.° A derke° clowde *to act suspiciously / dark*

Hir° sight obscured withinne and withoute,   *their*
And for all that were° ay° in such a doute.°   *they were / always / uncertainty*

295 Axed° han they full oftesith,° and freined°   *asked / often / inquired*
Of my fellowes of the Privy Seel,[5]
And prayed hem to telle hem with heart unfained,°   *sincere*
How it stood with me, whether evil or well.
And they the sothe° tolde hem every del,°   *truth / completely*
300 But they helden her° wordes not but lees.°   *reckoned their / nothing but lies*
They mighten as well have holden her peace.°   *kept their peace*

This troubly° life hath all too long endured.   *troublesome*
Not have I wist° how in my skin to tourne.   *known*
But now myself to myself have ensured°   *guaranteed*
305 For no such wondring° after this to mourne.°   *puzzlement / to be fretful*
As long as my life shall in me sojourne°   *remain*
Of such imagining I not ne recche.°   *care*
Let hem deem° as hem list° and speak   *judge / please*
     and drecche.°   *speculate*

This other day a lamentacioun
310 Of a wooful man in a book[6] I sy,°   *saw*
To whom wordes of consolacioun
Reason yaf° speking effectuelly,°   *gave / to good effect*
And well eased myn herte was thereby,°   *by it*
For when I had a while in the book read,
315 With the speech of Reason was I well fed.°   *nourished*

The heavy° man woeful and anguishous°   *depressed / anguished*
Complained in this wise, and thus said he:
'My life is unto me full encombrous,°   *burdensome*
For whither or unto what place I flee,
320 My wickednesses evere followen me,
As men may see the shadow a body sue,°   *follow*
And in no manner I may hem eschewe.°   *avoid*

'Vexation of spirit and torment
Lack I right none. I have of hem plenty.
325 Wonderly° bitter is my taste and scent.°   *amazingly / smell*
Woe° be the time of my nativity.   *accursed*
Unhappy man, that ever should I be.
O death, thy stroke a salve° is of sweetnesse   *ointment*
To hem that liven in such wrecchednesse.

330 'Greater plesance were it me° to die,   *pleasure would it be for me*
By many fold° than for to live so.   *many times over*
Sorrows so many in me multiplye

---

5. Hoccleve was a clerk in the Office of the Privy Seel, one of three great bureaucratic offices, responsible for the production and issuing of many kinds of official documents. Hoccleve himself pro- duced a set, or "Formulary," of almost 900 model Privy Seal documents.
6. The book can be identified as the *Synonyma* of Isidore of Seville (d. 636).

That my life is to me a very foe.
Comforted may I not be of my woe.
335 Of my distresse see none end I can.
No force° how soon I stinte° to be a man.'   *matter / cease*

Thanne spake Reason, 'What meneth all this fare?°   *behavior*
Though wealth be not friendly to thee, yit°   *yet*
Out of thine herte voide° woe and care.'   *cast*
340 'By what skill,° how, and by what reed° and wit,'°   *strategem / counsel / skill*
Said this woeful man, 'might I doon° it?'   *do*
'Wrestle,' quod Resoun, 'ayein° heavynesse°   *against / sadnesses*
Of the worlde, troubles, suffringe and duresse.°   *hardships*

'Biholde how many a man suffreth disease,
345 As great as thou and alaway° grettere,   *continually*
And though it hem° pinche sharply and sieze,   *them*
Yet patiently they it suffer and bere.°   *bear*
Think hereon and the less it shall thee dere.°   *injure*
Such suffrance is of mannes guilt cleansing,°   *purification*
350 And hem enableth to° joy everlasting.   *enables them to attain*

'Woe, heaviness and tribulation
Common aren° to men all, and profitable.   *are*
Though grievous be mannes temptation,
It sleeth° man not. To hem that° ben suffrable°   *kills / those who / are patient*
355 And to whom Goddes stroke is acceptable
Purveyed° joy is, for God woundeth tho°   *ordained / those*
That he ordeined hath to bliss to go.

'Gold purged° is, thou seest, in the furneis,°   *purified / furnace*
For the finer and cleaner° it shall be.   *purer*
360 Of thy disease the weighte and the peis°   *burden*
Bear lightly,° for God, to prove° thee,   *easily / test*
Scourged thee hath with sharpe adversite.
Not grouche° and say, "Why sustain I this?"   *complain*
For if thou do, thou thee takest amiss.°   *act wrongly*

365 'But thus thou shouldest thinke in thine herte,
And say, "To thee, lord God, I have aguilte°   *done wrong*
So sore° I moot° for myn offences smerte,°   *grievously / must / suffer*
As I am worthy.° O Lorde I am spilte,°   *as I deserve / destroyed*
But° thou to me thy mercy grante wilte.   *unless*
370 I am ful sure thou mayst it not deny.
Lord, I me repent, and I thee mercy cry.'"°   *beg mercy of you*

Longer I thought read have° in this book,   *to have read*
But so it shope° that I ne might naught.°   *happened / not*
He that it oughte° again it to him took,   *owned*
375 Me of his haste unware.° Yet have I caught°   *unaware / taken*
Some of the doctrine by Reason taught
To the man, as above have I said.
Well thereof° I holde me full well apaid,°   *with it / satisfed*

For evere sithen° set have I the less   *since*
380   By the peoples imagination,
Talkinge this and that of my sickness
Which came of° Goddes visitation.   *from*
Might I have be° found in probation°   *been / when tested*
Not grouching° but han take it in souffrance,° *complaining / patience*
385   Wholesome and wise had be° my   *would have been*
   governance.°   *self-control*

Farewell my sorrow, I cast it to the cock.
With patience I henceforth think unpick°   *to undo*
Of such thoughtful disease° and woe the lock, *i.e., melancholia*
And let hem° out that han me made to sike.° *them (my thoughts) / sigh*
390   Hereafter our Lorde God may, if him like,°   *please*
Make all myn old affeccioun° resort,°   *feeling / return*
And in hope of that will I me comfort.

Thorugh° Godes just doom° and his jugement *through / sentence*
And for my best,° now I take and deeme,° *my greatest profit / reckon*
395   Gave that good lorde me my punishment.
In wealth I took of him none heed or yeme,°   *attention*
Him for to please and him honor and queme,°   *gratify*
And he me gave a bone on for to gnawe,
Me to correct and of him to have awe.

400   He gave wit and he took it away
When that he saw that I it misdispente,°   *used it amiss*
And gave again when it was to his pay°   *profit*
He granted me my guiltes to repente,
And hence forward to sette myn entente°   *intention*
405   Unto his deity to do plesaunce,°   *to please his godhead*
And to amend my sinful governaunce.°   *way of life*

Laud° and honor and thank unto thee be,   *praise*
Lord God, that salve art to all heavinesse.°   *sadness*
Thank of° my wealth and myn adversity.   *thanks for*
410   Thank of myn elde° and of my sicknesse.°   *age / sickness*
And thank be to thine infinite goodnesse
And thy giftes and benefices° alle,   *benefits*
And unto thy mercy and grace I calle.

WILLIAM LANGLAND
ca. 1330–1388

William Langland is agreed by most scholars to be the sole author of a long religious allegory in alliterative verse known as *The Vision of Piers Plowman* or more simply *Piers Plowman*, which survives in at least three distinct versions that scholars refer to as the A-, B-, and C-texts. The first, about twenty-four hundred lines long, breaks off at a rather inconclusive point in the action; the second (from which all but one of the selections here have been drawn) is a revision of the first plus an extension of more than four thousand lines; and the third is a revision of the second. About Langland we know hardly anything except what can be inferred from the poem itself. He came from the west of England and was probably a native of the Malvern Hills area in which the opening of the poem is set. We can never identify the persona of the narrator of a medieval text positively or precisely with its author, especially when we are dealing with allegory. Nevertheless, a passage that was added to the C-text, the last of the selections printed here, gives the strong impression of being at one and the same time an allegory in which the narrator represents willful Mankind as well as a poignantly ironic self-portrait of the stubborn-willed poet who occasionally plays on his own name: "I have lived in *land* . . . my name is *Long Will*" (15.152). In this new episode the narrator tries to defend his shiftless way of life against Conscience and Reason, presumably his own conscience and reason. Conscience dismisses his specious argument that a clerical education has left him no "tools" to support himself with except for his prayer book and the Psalms with which he prays for the souls of those from whom he begs alms. The entire work conforms well with the notion that its author was a man who was educated to enter the Church but who, through marriage and lack of preferment, was reduced to poverty and may well have wandered in his youth like those "hermits" he scornfully describes in the prologue.

Piers Plowman has the form of a dream vision, a common medieval type in which the author presents the story under the guise of having dreamed it. The dream vision generally involves allegory, not only because one expects from a dream the unrealistic, the fanciful, but also because people have always suspected that dreams relate the truth in disguised form—that they are natural allegories. Through a series of such visions it traces the Dreamer-narrator's tough-minded, persistent, and passionate search for answers to his many questions, especially the question he puts early in the poem to Lady Holy Church: "How I may save my soul." Langland's theme is nothing less than the history of Christianity as it unfolds both in the world of the Old and New Testaments and in the life and heart of an individual fourteenth-century Christian—two seemingly distinct realms between which the poet's allegory moves with dizzying rapidity.

Within the larger sequence of the poem, from its beginning until the end of *Passus* 7, the following selections form a thematically coherent narrative. In the Prologue (the first selection), Langland's narrator falls asleep and witnesses a compact vision of the whole of late fourteenth-century English society. Poised between two stark and static possibilities of heaven and hell, an intensely active, mobile earthly life is concentrated into a "field full of folk." Some ideal practitioners of earthly occupations are surrounded and undermined by a much larger set of very energetic social types who exploit their occupations for entirely selfish ends. Langland practices an estates satire, which surveys and excoriates each worldly occupation (cf. Chaucer's very different example of estates satire in the *General Prologue* to the

Between Heaven and Hell. Hieronymus Bosch, *Haywain Triptych*, ca. 1490–95. The calm scene atop the haystack is perilously perched between heaven and hell, and above the furious activity of the world.

Canterbury Tales; for other examples, see "Medieval Estates and Orders" in the NAEL Archive.) He reserves his especial anger for those who abuse ecclesiastical authority, and for the wealthy, pitiless laity (i.e., non-ecclesiastical figures).

Passus, Latin for "step," is the word used for the poem's basic divisions. Passus 1 (the second selection) promises to give some intellectual and moral purchase on the teeming energies of the Prologue. Holy Church instructs the poem's narrator and dreamer Will in the proper relation of material wealth and spiritual health. In particular, she accentuates the value of the "best treasure," *truthe*, one of Langland's key words: *truthe* is the justice that flows from God; it manifests itself in the exercise of earthly justice and fidelity, and in the correlative poetic value of truthtelling. Will recognizes the force of Holy Church's sermon, but still needs to know it by an interior form of knowledge, grounded in the depths of the self.

It would seem that the rest of the poem is devoted to the discovery of that internalized truth. The first of the poem's large-scale narratives (Passus 2–4) represents the attempt of earthly justice to control the disruptive energies of the profit economy. That economy is here represented by the personification "Lady Mede," meaning "reward beyond deserving." After this sequence concerning earthly justice, the poem then turns to the deeper, more personal mechanisms of spiritual justice. In Passus 5, accordingly, the seven Deadly Sins confess in turn, before the poem's ideal earthly representative of justice, Piers Plowman, offers to lead a spiritual pilgrimage to the shrine of St. Truthe (Passus 5.507–642, the third selection).

The ideal of *truthe* takes a local habitation, then, in the model of society that Piers establishes for the conduct of his "pilgrimage." The truest form of pilgrimage is no pilgrimage at all; instead, all classes of society should stay at home and work harmoniously for the production of material food by agricultural workers, with knights helping plowmen and protecting the Church, while priests pray for both workers and knights. This ideal scene is pictured in Passus 6 (the fourth selection).

Langland's poem might seem, thus far, to be a deeply conservative one, whereby justice is manifest only in a manorial society, within which each person knows his or

Sin. Hieronymus Bosch, *The Seven Deadly Sins*, ca. 1500. The violence of sin springs from no abstract source but is embedded in the precise social practices and material fabric of this world.

her place, and works harmoniously and obediently with the others. There is, however, a problem with this model: it collapses. In Passus 6 the ideal society put into action by Piers fails entirely; workers simply refuse to work, abuse the authority of knights, and respond only to the terrible pressure of Hunger, a punishing, Gargantuan figure who graphically evokes the ravages of famine in the fourteenth century.

In Passus 7 (the fifth selection) the limitations of the *truthe* model become dramatically visible. A pardon sent from God, as *Truthe*, promises no pardon at all, but only retribution for those who fail to meet the standards of God's justice, and reward for those who do not so fail. As the plowing has demonstrated, however, all fail. Such a "pardon" promises nothing but universal damnation. In an exceptionally powerful, dramatic, and enigmatic moment, Piers actually tears this pardon in two, as he disputes with a priest about its force. Earlier in the poem it had seemed that all Will had to do was to absorb Holy Church's understanding of *Truthe*; once Piers tears the pardon, however, we realize that the search for *Truthe* modifies the goal. We realize, that is, that *Truthe* cannot be the whole truth. The shortcomings of *Truthe* propel Will to a more urgent search for God's love and forgiveness, beyond justice, in the deepest resources of his own self. This search climaxes in the vision of Christ's Atonement (Passus 18; see the selection in this volume, pp. 415–26).

In the last selection from the C-text, Langland presents a more moving, if less passionate and conflicted, scene than the tearing of *Truthe's* pardon. In a passage often regarded as autobiographical, Will argues with Conscience and Reason (principles of law, but also, doubtless, Will's own conscience and reason). They reproach him for his way of life in a poor district of London, where Will barely supports his family with alms he gets by praying for the souls of wealthy burghers.

A large number of manuscripts and two sixteenth-century editions show that *Piers Plowman* was avidly read and studied by a great many people from the end of the fourteenth century to the reign of Elizabeth I. Some of these readers have left a record of their engagement with the poem in marginal comments. Almost from the first, it was a controversial text. Within four years of the writing of the second version—which scholars have good evidence to date 1377, the year of Edward III's death and Richard II's accession to the throne—it had become so well known that the leaders of the Uprising of 1381 used phrases borrowed from it as part of the rhetoric of the rebellion (for an example of such rhetoric, see the letter by John Ball, "The Uprising of 1381," in "Medieval Estates and Orders" in the NAEL Archive). Langland's sympathy with the sufferings of the poor and his indignant satire of corruption in Church and State undoubtedly made his poem popular with the rebels. Although he may not have sympathized with the violence of the rebels and their leaders, he recognized that for the Church to be preserved, it needed profound reform. The passionate sympathy for the commoner, idealized in *Piers Plowman*, also appealed to reformers who felt that true religion was best represented not by the ecclesiastical hierarchy but by the humblest orders of society. Many persons reading his poem in the sixteenth century (it was first printed in 1550) saw in *Piers Plowman* a prophecy and forerunner of the English Reformation. Immersed as it is in thorny political and theological controversies of its own day, *Piers Plowman* is arguably the most difficult and, at times, even the most frustrating of Middle English texts, but its poetic, intellectual, and moral complexity and integrity also make it one of the most rewarding.

From The Vision of Piers Plowman[1]

From *The Prologue*

[THE FIELD OF FOLK]

In a summer season when the sun was mild
I clad myself in clothes as I'd become a sheep;
In the habit of a hermit unholy of works,[2]
Walked wide in this world, watching for wonders.
5   And on a May morning, on Malvern Hills,
There befell me as by magic a marvelous thing:
I was weary of wandering and went to rest
At the bottom of a broad bank by a brook's side,
And as I lay lazily looking in the water
10 I slipped into a slumber, it sounded so pleasant.
There came to me reclining there a most curious dream
That I was in a wilderness, nowhere that I knew;
But as I looked into the east, up high toward the sun,
I saw a tower on a hill-top, trimly built,
15 A deep dale beneath, a dungeon tower in it,
With ditches deep and dark and dreadful to look at.
A fair field full of folk I found between them,
Of human beings of all sorts, the high and the low,
Working and wandering as the world requires.
20   Some applied themselves to plowing, played very rarely,

---

1. The translation is by E. T. Donaldson (1990) and is based on *Piers Plowman: The B Version*, edited by George Kane and E. T. Donaldson (1975).

2. For Langland's opinion of hermits, see lines 28–30 and 53–57. The sheep's clothing may suggest the habit's physical resemblance to sheep's wool as well as a false appearance of innocence.

Sowing seeds and setting plants worked very hard;
Won what wasters gluttonously consume.
And some pursued pride, put on proud clothing,
Came all got up in garments garish to see.
25 To prayers and penance many put themselves,
All for love of our Lord lived hard lives,
Hoping thereafter to have Heaven's bliss—
Such as hermits and anchorites that hold to their cells,
Don't care to go cavorting about the countryside,
30 With some lush livelihood delighting their bodies.
And some made themselves merchants—they managed better,
As it seems to our sight that such men prosper.
And some make mirth as minstrels can
And get gold for their music, guiltless, I think.
35 But jokers and word jugglers, Judas' children,[3]
Invent fantasies to tell about and make fools of themselves,
And have whatever wits they need to work if they wanted.
What Paul preaches of them I don't dare repeat here:
Qui loquitur turpiloquium[4] is Lucifer's henchman.
40 Beadsmen[5] and beggars bustled about
Till both their bellies and their bags were crammed to the brim;
Staged flytings[6] for their food, fought over beer.
In gluttony, God knows, they go to bed
And rise up with ribaldry, those Robert's boys.°   *i.e., robbers*
45 Sleep and sloth pursue them always.
      Pilgrims and palmers[7] made pacts with each other
To seek Saint James[8] and saints at Rome.
They went on their way with many wise stories,
And had leave to lie all their lives after.
50 I saw some that said they'd sought after saints:
In every tale they told their tongues were tuned to lie
More than to tell the truth—such talk was theirs.
A heap of hermits with hooked staffs
Went off to Walsingham,[9] with their wenches behind them.
55 Great long lubbers that don't like to work
Dressed up in cleric's dress to look different from other men
And behaved as they were hermits, to have an easy life.
I found friars there—all four of the orders[1]—
Preaching to the people for their own paunches' welfare,
60 Making glosses° of the Gospel that would look good for   *interpretations*
      themselves;
Coveting copes,[2] they construed it as they pleased.
Many of these Masters[3] may clothe themselves richly,

---

3. Minstrels who deceive with jokes and fantastic stories are regarded as descendants of Christ's betrayer, Judas.
4. Who speaks filthy language (Latin). Cf. Ephesians 5.3–4 and 11–12.
5. Prayer sayers, i.e., people who offered to say prayers, sometimes counted on the beads of the rosary, for the souls of those who gave them alms.
6. Contests in which the participants took turns insulting each other, preferably in verse.
7. Virtually professional pilgrims who took advantage of the hospitality offered them to go on traveling year after year (see p. 261, n. 6).
8. I.e., his shrine at Compostela in Spain.
9. English town, site of a famous shrine to the Virgin Mary.
1. In Langland's day there were four orders of friars in England: Franciscans, Dominicans, Carmelites, and Augustinians.
2. Monks', friars', and hermits' capes.
3. I.e., masters of divinity.

For their money and their merchandise[4] march hand in hand.
Since Charity[5] has proved a peddler and principally shrives lords,
65 Many marvels have been manifest within a few years.
Unless Holy Church and friars' orders hold together better,
The worst misfortune in the world will be welling up soon.
    A pardoner[6] preached there as if he had priest's rights,
Brought out a bull[7] with bishop's seals,
70 And said he himself could absolve them all
Of failure to fast, of vows they'd broken.
Unlearned men believed him and liked his words,
Came crowding up on knees to kiss his bulls.
He banged them with his brevet and bleared their eyes,[8]
75 And raked in with his parchment-roll rings and brooches.
Thus you give your gold for gluttons' well-being,
And squander it on scoundrels schooled in lechery.
If the bishop were blessed and worth both his ears,
His seal should not be sent out to deceive the people.
80 —It's nothing to the bishop that the blackguard preaches,
And the parish priest and the pardoner split the money
That the poor people of the parish would have but for them.
    Parsons and parish priests complained to the bishop
That their parishes were poor since the pestilence-time,[9]
85 Asked for license and leave to live in London,
And sing Masses there for simony,[1] for silver is sweet.

* * *

    Yet scores of men stood there in silken coifs
Who seemed to be law-sergeants[2] that served at the bar,
Pleaded cases for pennies and impounded[3] the law,
And not for love of our Lord once unloosed their lips:
215 You might better measure mist on Malvern Hills
Than get a "mum" from their mouths till money's on the table.
Barons and burgesses[4] and bondmen also
I saw in this assemblage, as you shall hear later;
Bakers and brewers and butchers aplenty.
220 Weavers of wool and weavers of linen,
Tailors, tinkers, tax-collectors in markets,
Masons, miners, many other craftsmen.
Of all living laborers there leapt forth some,

4. The "merchandise" sold by the friars for money is shrift, i.e., confession and remission of sins, which by canon law cannot be sold.
5. The ideal of the friars, as stated by St. Francis, was simply love, i.e., charity.
6. An official empowered to pass on from the pope temporal indulgence for the sins of people who contributed to charitable enterprises—a function frequently abused.
7. Papal license to act as a pardoner, endorsed with the local bishop's seals.
8. I.e., pulled the wool over their eyes. "Brevet": pardoner's license.
9. Since 1349 England had suffered a number of epidemics of the plague, the Black Death, which had caused famine and depopulated the countryside.

1. Buying and selling the functions, spiritual powers, or offices of the church. Wealthy persons, especially in London, set up foundations to pay priests to sing masses for their souls and those of their relatives (see the portrait of Chaucer's Parson, pp. 273–74, lines 479–530).
2. Important lawyers (see The General Prologue to The Canterbury Tales, p. 269, lines 311ff.). "Coifs": a silk scarf was a lawyer's badge of office.
3. Detained in legal custody. Pennies were fairly valuable coins in medieval England.
4. Town dwellers who had full rights as the citizens of a municipality. In contrast, barons were members of the upper nobility, and bondmen were peasants who held their land from a lord in return for customary services or rent.

Such as diggers of ditches that do their jobs badly,
225 And dawdle away the long day with *"Dieu save dame Emme."*[5]
Cooks and their kitchen-boys crying, "Hot pies, hot!
Good geese and pork! Let's go and dine!"
Tavern-keepers told them a tale of the same sort:
"White wine of Alsace and wine of Gascony,
230 Of the Rhine and of La Rochelle, to wash the roast down with."
All this I saw sleeping, and seven times more.

From *Passus 1*

[THE TREASURE OF TRUTH]

What this mountain means, and the murky dale,
And the field full of folk I shall clearly tell you.
A lady lovely of look, in linen clothes,
Came down from the castle and called me gently,
5 And said, "Son, are you asleep? Do you see these people,
How busy they're being about the maze?
The greatest part of the people that pass over this earth,
If they have well-being in this world, they want nothing more:
For any heaven other than here they have no thought."
10 I was afraid of her face, fair though she was,
And said, "Mercy, madam, what may this mean?"
"The tower on the hill-top," she said, "Truth[6] is within it,
And would have you behave as his words teach.
For he is father of faith, formed you all
15 Both with skin and with skull, and assigned you five senses
To worship him with while you are here.
And therefore he ordered the earth to help each one of you
With woolens, with linens, with livelihood at need,
In a moderate manner to make you at ease;
20 And of his kindness declared three things common to all:
None are necessary but these, and now I will name them
And rank them in their right order—you repeat them after.
The first is vesture to defend you from the cold;
The second is food at fit times to fend off hunger,
25 And drink when you're dry—but don't drink beyond reason
Or you will be the worse for it when you've work to do.
For Lot in his lifetime because he liked drink
Did with his daughters what the Devil found pleasing,
Took delight in drink as the Devil wished,
30 And lechery laid hold on him and he lay with them both,
Blamed it all on the wine's working, that wicked deed.
    Let us make him drunk with wine, and let us lie with him,
        that we may preserve seed of our father.[7]
By wine and by women there Lot was overcome
And there begot in gluttony graceless brats.

---

5. "God save Dame Emma," presumably a popular song.
6. Langland plays on three meanings of the term "Truth": (1) fidelity, integrity—as in modern "troth"; (2) reality, actuality, conformity with what is; (3) God, the ultimate truth.
7. Genesis 19.32.

Therefore dread delicious drink and you'll do the better:
35 Moderation is medicine no matter how you yearn.
It's not all good for your ghost[8] that your gut wants
Nor of benefit to your body that's a blessing to your soul.
Don't believe your body for it does the bidding of a liar:
That is this wretched world that wants to betray you;
40 For the Fiend and your flesh both conform to it,
And that besmirches your soul: set this in your heart,
And so that you should yourself be wary I'm giving this advice."
    "Ah, madam, mercy," said I, "your words much please me.
But the money minted on earth that men are so greedy for,
45 Tell me to whom that treasure belongs?"
"Go to the Gospel," she said, "that God himself spoke
When the people approached him with a penny in the temple
And asked whether they should worship[9] with it Caesar the king.
And he asked them to whom the inscription referred
50 'And the image also that is on the coin?'
'Caesaris,'[1] they said, 'we can all see it clearly.'
'Reddite Caesari,' said God, 'what Caesari belongs,[2]
And quae sunt Dei Deo, or else you do wrong.'
For rightfully Reason[3] should rule you all,
55 And Kind Wit be keeper to take care of your wealth
And be guardian of your gold to give it out when you need it,
For economy[4] and he are of one accord."
    Then I questioned her courteously, in the Creator's name,
"The dungeon in the dale that's dreadful to see,
60 What may it mean, madam, I beseech you?"
"That is the Castle of Care: whoever comes into it
Will be sorry he was ever born with body and soul.
The captain of the castle is called Wrong,
Father of falsehood, he founded it himself.
65 Adam and Eve he egged to evil,
Counseled Cain to kill his brother;
He made a joke out of Judas with Jewish silver,[5]
And afterwards on an elder tree hanged him high.
He's a molester of love, lies to every one;
70 Those who trust in his treasure are betrayed soonest."
    Then I wondered in my wits what woman it might be
Who could show from Holy Scripture such wise words,
And I conjured her in the high name, ere she went away,
To say who she really was that taught me so well.
75 "I am Holy Church," she said, "you ought to know me:
I befriended you first and taught the faith to you.

---

8. Spirit.
9. "Worship" in Middle English often means religious celebration, but the worship of God is only one instance of showing the appropriate honor and respect to someone or something; the word can therefore be used about objects other than God.
1. Caesar's (Latin).
2. "Render unto Caesar" (Latin); "to Caesar." In the next line the Latin clause means "What are God's unto God." See Matthew 22.15–21.
3. Langland distinguishes the role of reason, as

the distinctive human capacity to reach truth by discursive reasoning, from the functions of a number of other related mental processes and sources of truth, e.g., Kind Wit (next line): natural intelligence, common sense.
4. I.e., prudent management.
5. For the fall of Adam and Eve, see Genesis 3; for Cain's murder of Abel, see Genesis 4. In the next lines, for Judas's betrayal of Jesus, see Matthew 26.14–16; for his death (line 68), see Matthew 27.3–6.

You gave me gages[6] to be guided by my teaching
And to love me loyally while your life lasts."
Then kneeling on my knees I renewed my plea for grace,
80 Prayed piteously to her to pray for my sins,
And advise me how I might find natural faith[7] in Christ,
That I might obey the command of him who made me man.
"Teach me of no treasure, but tell me this one thing,
How I may save my soul, sacred as you are?"
85 "When all treasures are tried, Truth is the best.
I call on *Deus caritas*[8] to declare the truth.
It's as glorious a love-gift as dear God himself.
For whoever is true of his tongue, tells nothing untrue,
Does his work with truth, wishes no man ill,
90 He is a god by the Gospel, on ground and aloft.
And also like our Lord by Saint Luke's words.[9]
Clerks who've been taught this text should tell it all about,
For Christians and non-Christians lay claim to it both.
To keep truth kings and knights are required by reason,
95 And to ride out in realms about and beat down wrong-doers,
Take *transgressores*[1] and tie them up tight
Until Truth has determined their trespass in full.
For David in his days when he dubbed knights[2]
Made them swear on their swords to serve Truth forever.
100 That is plainly the profession that's appropriate for knights,
And not to fast one Friday in five score winters,
But to hold with him and with her who ask for truth,
And never leave them for love nor through a liking for presents,
And whoever passes that point is an apostate to his order.
105 For Christ, King of Kings, created ten orders,[3]
Cherubim and seraphim, seven such and another.
Gave them might in his majesty—the merrier they thought it—
And over his household he made them archangels,
Taught them through the Trinity how Truth may be known,
110 And to be obedient to his bidding—he bade nothing else.
Lucifer with his legions learned this in Heaven,
And he was the loveliest of light after our Lord
Till he broke obedience—his bliss was lost to him
And he fell from that fellowship in a fiend's likeness
115 Into a deep dark hell, to dwell there forever,
And more thousands went out with him than any one could count,
Leaping out with Lucifer in loathly shapes,
Because they believed Lucifer who lied in this way:
I shall set my foot in the north and I shall be like the most high.[4]

---

6. I.e., pledges (at baptism).
7. The Middle English phrase is "kynde knowynge."
8. "God [is] love" (Latin): 1 John 4.8.
9. Not Luke, but see 1 John 4.16 and cf. Psalms 81.6. The phrase "a god by the Gospel" is Langland's; what he means by it will be a recurrent theme.
1. Transgressors: the Latin word appears in Isaiah 53.12.
2. Behind the idea that King David created knighthood probably lies his selection of officers for his army (1 Chronicles 12.18) translated into

chivalric terms; like other heroes, he was typically portrayed in the Middle Ages as a chivalric figure, just as God's creation of the angels, below, is pictured in terms of a medieval aristocratic household.
3. I.e., ten orders of heavenly beings; seraphim, cherubim, thrones, dominions, virtues, powers, principalities, archangels, angels, and the nameless order that fell with Lucifer.
4. Cf. Isaiah 14.13–14, which has "throne" (*sedem*) where Langland has "foot" (*pedem*).

120 And all that hoped it might be so, no Heaven could hold them,
But they fell out in fiend's likeness fully nine days together,
Till God of his goodness granted that Heaven settle,
Become stationary and stable, and stand in quiet.
When these wicked ones went out they fell in wondrous wise,
125 Some in air, some on earth, some deep in hell,
But Lucifer lies lowest of them all.
For pride that puffed him up his pain has no end.
And all that work with wrong will surely make their way
After their death-day to dwell with that wretch.
130 But those who wish to work well, as holy words direct,
And who end, as I said earlier, in Truth that is the best
May be certain that their souls will ascend to Heaven
Where Truth is in Trinity, bestowing thrones on all who come.
Therefore I say as I said before, by the sense of these texts
135 When all treasures are tried, Truth is the best.
Let unlearned men be taught this, for learned men know it,
That Truth is the trustiest treasure on earth."
  "Yet I've no natural knowledge,"[5] said I, "you must teach me more
    clearly
Through what force faith is formed in my body and where."
140 "You doting dolt," said she, "dull are your wits:
Too little Latin you learned, lad, in your youth.
    Alas, I repine for a barren youth was mine.[6]
It's a natural knowledge that's nurtured in your heart
To love your Lord more dearly than you love yourself,
To do no deadly sin though you should die for it.
145 This I trust is truth: whoever can teach you better,
Look to it that you let him speak, and learn it after.
For thus his word witnesses: do your work accordingly.
For Truth tells us that love is the trustiest medicine in Heaven.
No sin may be seen on him by whom that spice is used.
150 And all the deeds he pleased to do were done with love.
And he[7] taught it to Moses as a matchless thing, and most like Heaven,
And also the plant of peace, most precious of virtues.
For Heaven might not hold it,[8] so heavy it seemed,
Till it had with earth alloyed itself.
155 And when it had of this earth taken flesh and blood,
Never was leaf upon linden lighter thereafter,
And portable and piercing as the point of a needle:
No armor might obstruct it, nor any high walls.
Therefore Love is leader of the Lord's people in Heaven,
160 And an intermediary as the mayor is between community and king.
Just so Love is a leader by whom the law's enforced
Upon man for his misdeeds—he measures the fine.
And to know this naturally, it's nourished by a power
That has its head in the heart, and its high source.

---

5. Instinctive or experiential knowledge; Langland's phrase, a recurrent and important one, is "kynde knowynge."
6. Proverbial.

7. I.e., Truth.
8. I.e., love, which, as the passage goes on, becomes embodied in Christ.

165 For a natural knowledge in the heart is nourished by a power
That's let fall by the Father who formed us all,
Looked on us with love and let his son die
Meekly for our misdeeds, to amend us all.
Yet he[9] did not ask harm on those who hurt him so badly,
170 But with his mouth meekly made a prayer for mercy—
For pity for those people who so painfully killed him.
Here you may see examples in himself alone,
How he was mighty and meek, and bade mercy be granted
To those who hanged him high and pierced his heart.

* * *

Love is Life's doctor, and next[1] our Lord himself,
205 And also the strait[2] street that goes straight to Heaven.
Therefore I say as I said before, by the sense of these texts,
When all treasures are tried, Truth is the best.
Now that I've told you what Truth is—there's no treasure better—
I may delay no longer now: our Lord look after you."

From *Passus 5*

[PIERS PLOWMAN SHOWS THE WAY TO SAINT TRUTH]

Then Hope took hold of a horn of *Deus tu conversus vivificabis nos*[3]
And blew it with *Beati quorum remissae sunt iniquitates*,[4]
So that all the saints sang for sinners at once,
"*Men and animals thou shalt save inasmuch as thou hast multiplied thy
        mercy, O God.*"[5]
510 A thousand men then thronged together,
Cried upward to Christ and to his clean mother
To have grace to go to Truth—God grant they might!
But there was no one so wise as to know the way thither,
But they blundered forth like beasts over banks and hills
515 Till they met a man, many hours later,
Appareled like a pagan[6] in pilgrims' manner.
He bore a stout staff with a broad strap around it,
In the way of woodbine wound all about.
A bowl and a bag he bore by his side.
520 A hundred holy water phials were set on his hat,
Souvenirs of Sinai and shells of Galicia,
And many a Cross on his cloak and keys of Rome,
And the vernicle in front so folk should know
By seeing his signs what shrines he'd been to.[7]

9. I.e., Christ, not the Father as in the sentence
before. In such slippery transitions from one
subject to another, Langland takes advantage of
the greater flexibility of Middle English syntax;
and usually, as here, the transition reflects an
important connection of ideas, in this case the
relationship between God's action and Christ's.
1. Next to.
2. I.e., narrow; see Matthew 7.13–14.
3. O God, you will turn and give us life (from
the Latin Mass).

4. Blessed [are they] whose transgressions are
forgiven (Latin; Psalms 32.1).
5. Psalms 36.6–7.
6. I.e., outlandishly. (Langland's word *paynym* was
especially associated with Saracens, i.e., Arabs.)
7. A pilgrim to Canterbury collected a phial of holy
water from St. Thomas's shrine; collecting another
every time one passed through Canterbury was a
mark of a professional pilgrim. "Sinai": souvenirs
from the Convent of St. Katharine on Sinai.
"Shells": the emblem of St. James at Compostela,

525 These folk asked him fairly from whence he came.
"From Sinai," he said, "and from the Holy Sepulchre.
Bethlehem, Babylon, I've been to both;
In Armenia, in Alexandria,[8] in many other places.
You can tell by the tokens attached to my hat
530 That I've walked far and wide in wet and in dry
And sought out good saints for my soul's health."
"Did you ever see a saint," said they, "that men call Truth?
Could you point out a path to where that person lives?"
"No, so God save me," said the fellow then.
535 "I've never known a palmer° with knapsack or staff   *pilgrim*
To ask after him ere now in this place."
    "Peter!"[9] said a plowman, and put forth his head.
"We're as closely acquainted as a clerk and his books.
Conscience and Kind Wit[1] coached me to his place
540 And persuaded me to swear to him I'd serve him forever,
Both to sow and set plants so long as I can work.
I have been his follower all these forty winters,
Both sowed his seed and overseen his cattle,
Indoors and outdoors taken heed for his profit,
545 Made ditches and dikes, done what he bids.
Sometimes I sow and sometimes I thresh,
In tailor's craft and tinker's, whatever Truth can devise.
I weave wool and wind it and do what Truth says.
For though I say it myself, I serve him to his satisfaction.
550 I get good pay from him, and now and again more.
He's the promptest payer that poor men know.
He withholds no worker's wages so he's without them by evening.
He's as lowly as a lamb and lovely of speech.
And if you'd like to learn where that lord dwells,
555 I'll direct you on the road right to his palace."
"Yes, friend Piers,"[2] said these pilgrims, and proffered him pay.
"No, by the peril of my soul!" said Piers, and swore on oath:
"I wouldn't take a farthing's fee for Saint Thomas's shrine.[3]
Truth would love me the less a long time after.
560   But you that are anxious to be off, here's how you go:
You must go through Meekness, both men and women,
Till you come into Consciences[4] that Christ knows the truth
That you love our Lord God of all loves the most,
And next to him your neighbors—in no way harm them,
565 Otherwise than you'd have them behave to you.

---

in Galicia. "Many a cross": commemorating trips to the Holy Land. "Keys": the sign of St. Peter's keys, from Rome. "Vernicle": a copy of the image of Christ's face preserved on a cloth, another famous relic from Rome. It was believed to have appeared after Veronica gave her head cloth to Christ, as he was going to execution, to wipe his face on.
8. "Babylon": near Cairo, where there was a church on the site where Mary lived during the Flight into Egypt. "Armenia": presumably to visit Mount Ararat, where the Ark is said to have landed. "Alexandria": the site of the martyrdom of St. Catherine and St. Mark.
9. I.e., an oath "By St. Peter!"
1. Moral sense and natural intelligence (common sense).
2. I.e., Peter, hence the particular appropriateness of his swearing by St. Peter (line 537), a connection that Langland will exploit in a variety of ways.
3. The shrine of St. Thomas at Canterbury was famous for the gold and jewels offered by important pilgrims.
4. Consciousness, moral awareness, related to but not identical with the moral sense personified in line 539.

And so follow along a brook's bank, Be-Modest-Of-Speech,
Until you find a ford, Do-Your-Fathers-Honor;
 Honor thy father and thy mother, etc.[5]
Wade in that water and wash yourselves well there
And you'll leap the lighter all your lifetime.
570 So you shall see Swear-Not-Unless-It-Is-For-Need-
And-Namely-Never-Take-In-Vain-The-Name-Of-God-Amighty.
Then you'll come to a croft,[6] but don't come into it:
The croft is called Covet-Not-Men's-Cattle-Nor-Their-Wives-
And-None-Of-Your-Neighbor's-Serving-Men-So-As-To-Harm-Them.
575 See that you break no boughs there unless they belong to you.
Two wooden statues stand there, but don't stop for them:
They're called Steal-Not and Slay-Not: stay away from both;
Leave them on your left hand and don't look back.
And hold well your holiday until the high evening.[7]
580 Then you shall blench at a barrow,[8] Bear-No-False-Witness:
It's fenced in with florins and other fees aplenty.
See that you pluck no plant there for peril of your soul.
Then you shall see Speak-The-Truth-So-It-Must-Be-Done-
And-Not-In-Any-Other-Way-Not-For-Any-Man's-Asking.
585 Then you shall come to a castle shining clear as the sun.
The moat is made of mercy, all about the manor;
And all the walls are of wit° to hold will out.   *reason*
The crenelations° are of Christendom to save Christiankind, *battlements*
Buttressed with Believe-So-Or-You-Won't-Be-Saved;
590 And all the houses are roofed, halls and chambers,
Not with lead but with Love-And-Lowness-As-Brothers-Of-
 One-Womb.
The bridge is of Pray-Properly-You-Will-Prosper-The-More.
Every pillar is of penance, of prayers to saints;
The hooks are of almsdeeds that the gates are hanging on.
595 The gate-keeper's name is Grace, a good man indeed;
His man is called Amend-Yourself, for he knows many men.
Say this sentence to him: 'Truth sees what's true;
I performed the penance the priest gave me to do
And I'm sorry for my sins and shall be so always
600 When I think thereon, though I were a pope.'
Pray Amend-Yourself mildly to ask his master once
To open wide the wicket-gate that the woman shut
When Adam and Eve ate unroasted apples.
 Through Eve it was closed to all and through the Virgin
  Mary it was opened again.[9]
605 For he keeps the latchkey though the king sleep.
And if Grace grants you to go in in this way
You shall see in yourself Truth sitting in your heart

---

5. Exodus 20.12. Beginning in lines 563–64 with the two "great" commandments (Matthew 22.37–39), Piers's directions include most of the commandments of Exodus 20.
6. A small enclosed field, or a small agricultural holding worked by a tenant.
7. A holiday (i.e., a holy day) lasted until sunset ("high evening"); it was not supposed to be used for work, and drinking and games were forbidden, at least until after attendance at church services.
8. A low hillock or a burial mound.
9. From a service commemorating the Virgin Mary.

In a chain of charity as though you were a child again,[1]
To suffer your sire's will and say nothing against it."

* * *

630 "By Christ," cried a pickpocket, "I have no kin there."
"Nor I," said an ape-trainer, "for anything I know."
"God knows," said a cake-seller, "if I were sure of this,
I wouldn't go a foot further for any friar's preaching."
"Yes!" said Piers Plowman, and prodded him for his good.
635 "Mercy is a maiden there that has dominion over them all,
And she is sib to all sinners, and her son as well,
And through the help of these two—think nothing else—
You might get grace there if you go in time."
"By Saint Paul!" said a pardoner, "possibly I'm not known there;
640 I'll go fetch my box with my brevets and a bull with bishop's letters."
"By Christ!" said a common woman,[2] "I'll keep you company.
You shall say I am your sister." I don't know what became of them.

Passus 6

[THE PLOWING OF PIERS'S HALF-ACRE]

"This would be a bewildering way unless we had a guide
Who could trace our way foot by foot": thus these folk complained.
Said Perkin[3] the Plowman, "By Saint Peter of Rome!
I have a half-acre to plow by the highway;
5 If I had plowed this half-acre and afterwards sowed it,
I would walk along with you and show you the way to go."
"That would be a long delay," said a lady in a veil.
"What ought we women to work at meanwhile?"
"Some shall sew sacks to stop the wheat from spilling.
10 And you lovely ladies, with your long fingers,
See that you have silk and sendal to sew when you've time
Chasubles[4] for chaplains for the Church's honor.
Wives and widows, spin wool and flax;
Make cloth, I counsel you, and teach the craft to your daughters.
15 The needy and the naked, take note how they fare:
Keep them from cold with clothing, for so Truth wishes.
For I shall supply their sustenance unless the soil fails
As long as I live, for the Lord's love in Heaven.
And all sorts of folk that feed on farm products,
20 Busily abet him who brings forth your food."
    "By Christ!" exclaimed a knight then, "your counsel is the best.
But truly, how to drive a team has never been taught me.
But show me," said the knight, "and I shall study plowing."

---

1. Cf. Mark 10.15: "whosoever shall not receive the kingdom of God as a little child, he shall not enter therein." This childlike quality is here envisaged as total submissiveness. "In a chain of charity": either Truth is bound by (that is, constrained by) *caritas* (love) or Truth is enthroned, adorned with *caritas* like a chain of office.
2. Prostitute. "Brevets": pardoner's credentials.
3. A nickname for Piers, or Peter.
4. Garments worn by priests to celebrate Mass. "Sendal": a thin, rich form of silk.

"By Saint Paul," said Perkin, "since you proffer help so humbly,
25   I shall sweat and strain and sow for us both,
And also labor for your love all my lifetime,
In exchange for your championing Holy Church and me
Against wasters and wicked men who would destroy me.
And go hunt hardily hares and foxes,
30   Boars and bucks that break down my hedges,
And have falcons at hand to hunt down the birds
That come to my croft° and crop my wheat."   small enclosed field
Thoughtfully the knight then spoke these words:
"By my power, Piers, I pledge you my word
35   To uphold this obligation though I have to fight.
As long as I live I shall look after you."
"Yes, and yet another point," said Piers, "I pray you further:
See that you trouble no tenant unless Truth approves,
And though you may amerce⁵ him, let Mercy set the fine,
40   And Meekness be your master no matter what Meed° does.   bribery
And though poor men proffer you presents and gifts,
Don't accept them for it's uncertain that you deserve to have them.
For at some set time you'll have to restore them
In a most perilous place called purgatory.
45   And treat no bondman badly—you'll be the better for it;
Though here he is your underling, it could happen in Heaven
That he'll be awarded a worthier place, one with more bliss:
        Friend, go up higher.⁶
For in the charnelhouse⁷ at church churls are hard to distinguish,
Or a knight from a knave: know this in your heart.
50   And see that you're true of your tongue, and as for tales—hate them
Unless they have wisdom and wit for your workmen's instruction.
Avoid foul-mouthed fellows and don't be friendly to their stories,
And especially at your repasts shun people like them,
For they tell the Fiend's fables—be very sure of that."
55   "I assent, by Saint James," said the knight then,
"To work by your word while my life lasts."
"And I shall apparel myself," said Perkin, "in pilgrims' fashion
And walk along the way with you till we find Truth."
He donned his working-dress, some darned, some whole,
60   His gaiters and his gloves to guard his limbs from cold,
And hung his seed-holder behind his back instead of a knapsack:
"Bring a bushel of bread-wheat for me to put in it,
For I shall sow it myself and set out afterwards
On a pilgrimage as palmers do to procure pardon.
65   And whoever helps me plow or work in any way
Shall have leave, by our Lord, to glean my land in harvest-time,
And make merry with what he gets, no matter who grumbles.
And all kinds of craftsmen that can live in truth,
I shall provide food for those that faithfully live,
70   Except for Jack the juggler and Jonette from the brothel,
And Daniel the dice-player and Denot the pimp,

5. Punish with a fine the amount of which is at   7. A house for dead bodies connected to a
the discretion of the judge.   church graveyard.
6. Luke 14.10.

And Friar Faker and folk of his order,
And Robin the ribald for his rotten speech.
Truth told me once and bade me tell it abroad:
75 *Deleantur de libro viventium:*[8] I should have no dealings with them,
For Holy Church is under orders to ask no tithes[9] of them.
    For let them not be written with the righteous.[1]
Their good luck has left them, the Lord amend them now."
    Dame-Work-When-It's-Time-To was Piers's wife's name;
His daughter was called Do-Just-So-Or-Your-Dame-Will-Beat-You;
80 His son was named Suffer-Your-Sovereigns-To-Have-Their-Will-
Condemn-Them-Not-For-If-You-Do-You'll-Pay-A-Dear-Price-
Let-God-Have-His-Way-With-All-Things-For-So-His-Word-Teaches.
"For now I am old and hoary and have something of my own,
To penance and to pilgrimage I'll depart with these others;
85 Therefore I will, before I go away, have my will written:
'*In Dei nomine, amen,*[2] I make this myself.
He shall have my soul that has deserved it best,
And defend it from the Fiend—for so I believe—
Till I come to his accounting, as my Creed teaches me—
90 To have release and remission I trust in his rent book.
The kirk° shall have my corpse and keep my bones,   *church*
For of my corn and cattle it craved the tithe:
I paid it promptly for peril of my soul;
It is obligated, I hope, to have me in mind
95 And commemorate me in its prayers among all Christians.
My wife shall have what I won with truth, and nothing else,
And parcel it out among my friends and my dear children.
For though I die today, my debts are paid;
I took back what I borrowed before I went to bed.'
100 As for the residue and the remnant, by the Rood of Lucca,[3]
I will worship Truth with it all my lifetime,
And be his pilgrim at the plow for poor men's sake.
My plowstaff shall be my pikestaff and push at the roots
And help my coulter to cut and cleanse the farrows."
105   Now Perkin and the pilgrims have put themselves to plowing.
Many there helped him to plow his half-acre.
Ditchers and diggers dug up the ridges;
Perkin was pleased by this and praised them warmly.
There were other workmen who worked very hard:
110 Each man in his manner made himself a laborer,
And some to please Perkin pulled up the weeds.
At high prime[4] Piers let the plow stand
To oversee them himself; whoever worked best

8. Let them be blotted out of the book of the living (Psalms 69.28).
9. Because the money they make is not legitimate income or increase derived from the earth; therefore, they do not owe the tithes, or 10 percent taxes, due the church.
1. Psalms 69.28.
2. "In the name of God, amen" (Latin), customary beginning of a will.
3. An ornate crucifix at Lucca in Italy was a popular object of pilgrimage. "Residue and remnant":

land had to be left to one's natural heirs, although up to one-third of personal property (the "residue and remnant") could be left to the church for Masses for the testator or other purposes; the other two-thirds had to go to the family, one to the widow and the other to the children. Piers's arrangements seem to leave the wife considerably more latitude.
4. 9:00 a.m., or after a substantial part of the day's work has been done, because laborers start so early.

Should be hired afterward, when harvest-time came.
115 Then some sat down and sang over ale
And helped plow the half-acre with "Ho! trolly-lolly!"[5]
"Now by the peril of my soul!" said Piers in pure wrath,
"Unless you get up again and begin working now,
No grain that grows here will gladden you at need,
120 And though once off the dole you die, let the Devil care!"
Then fakers were afraid and feigned to be blind;
Some set their legs askew as such loafers can
And made their moan to Piers, how they might not work:
"We have no limbs to labor with, Lord, we thank you;
125 But we pray for you, Piers, and for your plow as well,
That God of his grace make your grain multiply,
And reward you for whatever alms you will give us here,
For we can't strain and sweat, such sickness afflicts us."
     "If what you say is so," said Piers, "I'll soon find out.
130 I know you're ne'er-do-wells, and Truth knows what's right,
And I'm his sworn servant and so should warn him
Which ones they are in this world that do his workmen harm.
You waste what men win with toil and trouble.
But Truth shall teach you how his team should be driven,
135 Or you'll eat barley bread and use the brook for drink;
Unless you're blind or broken-legged, or bolted° with iron—   braced
Those shall eat as well as I do, so God help me,
Till God of his goodness gives them strength to arise.
But you could work as Truth wants you to and earn wages and bread
140 By keeping cows in the field, the corn from the cattle,
Making ditches or dikes or dinging on sheaves,
Or helping make mortar, or spreading muck afield.
You live in lies and lechery and in sloth too,
And it's only for suffrance that vengeance has not fallen on you.
145 But anchorites and hermits that eat only at noon
And nothing more before the morrow, they shall have my alms,
And buy copes[6] at my cost—those that have cloisters and churches.
But Robert Runabout shall have no rag from me,
Nor 'Apostles' unless they can preach and have the bishop's
       permission.
150 They shall have bread and boiled greens and a bit extra besides,
For it's an unreasonable religious life that has no regular meals."
     Then Waster waxed angry and wanted to fight;
To Piers the Plowman he proffered his glove.
A Breton, a braggart, he bullied Piers too,
155 And told him to go piss with his plow, peevish wretch.
"Whether you're willing or unwilling, we will have our will
With your flour and your flesh, fetch it when we please,
And make merry with it, no matter what you do."
Then Piers the Plowman complained to the knight
160 To keep him safe, as their covenant was, from cursed rogues,
"And from these wolfish wasters that lay waste the world,

5. Presumably the refrain of a popular song
(note similarly musical loafers in the *Prologue*,
lines 224–25).
6. Capes that signify religious callings.

For they waste and win nothing, and there will never be
Plenty among the people while my plow stands idle."
Because he was born a courteous man the knight spoke kindly to
  Waster
165 And warned him he would have to behave himself better:
"Or you'll pay the penalty at law, I promise, by my order!"
"It's not my way to work," said Waster, "I won't begin now!"
And made light of the law and lighter of the knight,
And said Piers wasn't worth a pea or his plow either,
170 And menaced him and his men if they met again.
  "Now by the peril of my soul!" said Piers, "I'll punish you all."
And he whooped after Hunger who heard him at once.
"Avenge me on these vagabonds," said he, "that vex the whole world."
Then Hunger in haste took hold of Waster by the belly
175 And gripped him so about the guts that his eyes gushed water.
He buffeted the Breton about the cheeks
That he looked like a lantern all his life after.
He beat them both so that he almost broke their guts.
Had not Piers with a pease loaf[7] prayed him to leave off
180 They'd have been dead and buried deep, have no doubt about it.
"Let them live," he said, "and let them feed with hogs,
Or else on beans and bran baked together."
Fakers for fear fled into barns
And flogged sheaves with flails from morning till evening,
185 So that Hunger wouldn't be eager to cast his eye on them.
For a potful of peas that Piers had cooked
A heap of hermits laid hands on spades
And cut off their copes and made short coats of them
And went like workmen to weed and to mow,
190 And dug dirt and dung to drive off Hunger.
Blind and bedridden got better by the thousand;
Those who sat to beg silver were soon healed,
For what had been baked for Bayard[8] was boon to many hungry,
And many a beggar for beans obediently labored,
195 And every poor man was well pleased to have peas for his wages,
And what Piers prayed them to do they did as sprightly as
  sparrowhawks.
And Piers was proud of this and put them to work,
And gave them meals and money as they might deserve.
  Then Piers had pity and prayed Hunger to take his way
200 Off to his own home and hold there forever.
"I'm well avenged on vagabonds by virtue of you.
But I pray you, before you part," said Piers to Hunger,
"With beggars and street-beadsmen[9] what's best to be done?
For well I know that once you're away, they will work badly;
205 Misfortune makes them so meek now,
And it's for lack of food that these folk obey me.
And they're my blood brothers, for God bought° us all.   *redeemed*

7. A cheap and coarse grade of bread, the food of those who cannot get better.
8. Generic name for a horse; a bread made of beans and bran, the coarsest category of bread, was used to feed horses and hounds, but was eaten by people when need was great.
9. Paid prayer sayers.

Truth taught me once to love them every one
And help them with everything after their needs.
210 Now I'd like to learn, if you know, what line I should take
And how I might overmaster them and make them work."
"Hear now," said Hunger, "and hold it for wisdom:
Big bold beggars that can earn their bread,
With hounds' bread and horses' bread hold up their hearts,
215 And keep their bellies from swelling by stuffing them with beans—
And if they begin to grumble, tell them to get to work,
And they'll have sweeter suppers once they've deserved them.
And if you find any fellow-man that fortune has harmed
Through fire or through false men, befriend him if you can.
220 Comfort such at your own cost, for the love of Christ in Heaven;
Love them and relieve them—so the law of Kind° directs.   Nature
     Bear ye one another's burdens[1]
And all manner of men that you may find
That are needy or naked and have nothing to spend,
With meals or with money make them the better.
225 Love them and don't malign them; let God take vengeance.
Though they behave ill, leave it all up to God
     Vengeance is mine and I will repay.[2]
And if you want to gratify God, do as the Gospel teaches,
And get yourself loved by lowly men: so you'll unloose his grace."
     Make to yourselves friends of the mammon of unrighteousness.[3]
     "I would not grieve God," said Piers, "for all the goods on earth!
230 Might I do as you say without sin?" said Piers then.
"Yes, I give you my oath," said Hunger, "or else the Bible lies:
Go to Genesis the giant, engenderer of us all:[4]
In sudore[5] and slaving you shall bring forth your food
And labor for your livelihood, and so our Lord commanded.
235 And Sapience says the same—I saw it in the Bible.
Piger propter frigus[6] would plow no field;
He shall be a beggar and none abate his hunger.
Matthew with man's face[7] mouths these words:
'Entrusted with a talent, *servus nequam*[8] didn't try to use it,
240 And earned his master's ill-will for evermore after,
And he took away his talent who was too lazy to work,
And gave it to him in haste that had ten already;
And after he said so that his servants heard it,
He that has shall have, and help when he needs it,
245 And he that nothing has shall nothing have and no man help him,
And what he trusts he's entitled to I shall take away.'
Kind Wit wants each one to work,

---

1. Galatians 6.2.
2. Romans 12.19.
3. Luke 16.9.
4. This puzzling epithet has been explained on the grounds that Genesis is the longest book (except for Psalms) in the Bible and that it recounts the creation of humankind.
5. In the sweat [of thy face shalt thou eat bread] (Latin, Genesis 3.19).
6. The sluggard [will not plow] by reason of the cold (Latin; Proverbs 20.4). "Sapience": the bibli-

cal "Wisdom Books" attributed to Solomon.
7. Each of the four Evangelists had his traditional pictorial image, derived partly from the faces of the four creatures in Ezekiel's vision (Ezekiel 1.5–12) and partly from those of the four beasts of the Apocalypse (Revelation 4.7): Matthew was represented as a winged man; Mark, a lion; Luke, a winged ox; and John, an eagle.
8. The wicked servant (Latin; Luke 19.22; see 17–27). "Talent": valuable coin.

Either in teaching or tallying or toiling with his hands,
Contemplative life or active life; Christ wants it too.
250 The Psalter says in the Psalm of *Beati omnes,*[9]
The fellow that feeds himself with his faithful labor,
He is blessed by the Book in body and in soul."
    The labors of thy hands, etc.[1]
    "Yet I pray you," said Piers, "*pour charité,*° if you know   *for charity*
Any modicum of medicine, teach me it, dear sir.
255 For some of my servants and myself as well
For a whole week do no work, we've such aches in our stomachs."
"I'm certain," said Hunger, "what sickness ails you.
You've munched down too much: that's what makes you groan,
But I assure you," said Hunger, "if you'd preserve your health,
260 You must not drink any day before you've dined on something.
Never eat, I urge you, ere Hunger comes upon you
And sends you some of his sauce to add savor to the food;
And keep some till suppertime, and don't sit too long;
Arise up ere Appetite has eaten his fill.
265 Let not Sir Surfeit sit at your table;
Love him not for he's a lecher whose delight is his tongue,
And for all sorts of seasoned stuff his stomach yearns.
And if you adopt this diet, I dare bet my arms
That Physic for his food will sell his furred hood
270 And his Calabrian[2] cloak with its clasps of gold,
And be content, by my troth, to retire from medicine
And learn to labor on the land lest livelihood fail him.
There are fewer physicians than frauds—reform them, Lord!—
Their drinks make men die before destiny ordains."
275 "By Saint Parnel,"[3] said Piers, "these are profitable words.
This is a lovely lesson; the Lord reward you for it!
Take your way when you will—may things be well with you always!"
    "My oath to God!" said Hunger, "I will not go away
Till I've dined this day and drunk as well."
280 "I've no penny," said Piers, "to purchase pullets,
And I can't get goose or pork; but I've got two green cheeses,
A few curds and cream and a cake of oatmeal,
A loaf of beans and bran baked for my children.
And yet I say, by my soul, I have no salt bacon
285 Nor any hen's egg, by Christ, to make ham and eggs,
But scallions aren't scarce, nor parsley, and I've scores of cabbages,
And also a cow and a calf, and a cart-mare
To draw dung to the field while the dry weather lasts.
By this livelihood I must live till Lammass[4] time
290 When I hope to have harvest in my garden.
Then I can manage a meal that will make you happy."
All the poor people fetched peasepods;[5]

9. Blessed [are] all [who] (Latin; Psalms 128.1).
1. Psalms 128.2. Thou shalt eat the labor of thine hands: happy shalt thou be, and it shall be well with thee.
2. Of gray fur (a special imported squirrel fur).
3. Who St. Parnel was is obscure; other manuscripts and editions read "By Saint Paul."

4. The harvest festival, August 1 (the name derived from Old English *hlaf,* "loaf"), when a loaf made from the first wheat of the season was offered at Mass.
5. Peas in the pod. These, like most foods in the next lines, are early crops.

Beans and baked apples they brought in their skirts,
Chives and chervils and ripe cherries aplenty,
295 And offered Piers this present to please Hunger with.
Hunger ate this in haste and asked for more.
Then poor folk for fear fed Hunger fast,
Proffering leeks and peas, thinking to appease him.
And now harvest drew near and new grain came to market.[6]
300 Then poor people were pleased and plied Hunger with the best;
With good ale as Glutton taught they got him to sleep.
Then Waster wouldn't work but wandered about,
And no beggar would eat bread that had beans in it,
But the best bread or the next best, or baked from pure wheat,
305 Nor drink any half-penny ale[7] in any circumstances,
But of the best and the brownest that barmaids sell.
Laborers that have no land to live on but their hands
Deign not to dine today on last night's cabbage.
No penny-ale can please them, nor any piece of bacon,
310 But it must be fresh flesh or else fried fish,
And that *chaud* or *plus chaud*[8] so it won't chill their bellies.
Unless he's hired at high wages he will otherwise complain;
That he was born to be a workman he'll blame the time.
Against Cato's counsel he commences to murmur:
315 *Remember to bear your burden of poverty patiently.*[9]
He grows angry at God and grumbles against Reason,
And then curses the king and all the council after
Because they legislate laws that punish laboring men.[1]
But while Hunger was their master there would none of them
    complain
320 Or strive against the statute,[2] so sternly he looked.
But I warn you workmen, earn wages while you may,
For Hunger is hurrying hitherward fast.
With waters he'll awaken Waster's chastisement;
Before five years are fulfilled such famine shall arise.
325 Through flood and foul weather fruits shall fail,
And so Saturn[3] says and has sent to warn you:
When you see the moon amiss and two monks' heads,
And a maid have the mastery, and multiply by eight,[4]
Then shall Death withdraw and Dearth be justice,
330 And Daw the diker[5] die for hunger,
Unless God of his goodness grants us a truce.

---

6. Presumably as the new harvest approaches, merchants who have been holding grain for the highest prices release it for sale, because prices are about to tumble.
7. Weak ale diluted with water; in line 309, laborers are too fussy and will no longer accept even penny ale.
8. "Hot" or "very hot" (French).
9. From Cato's *Distichs*, a collection of pithy phrases used to teach Latin to beginning students.
1. Like so many governments, late-14th-century England responded to inflation and the bargain-ing power of the relatively scarce laborers with wage and price freezes, which had their usual lack of effect. One way landowners, desperate to obtain enough laborers, tried to get around the wage laws was by offering food as well as cash.
2. I.e., anti-inflationary legislation.
3. Planet thought to influence the weather, generally perceived as hostile.
4. This cryptic prophecy has never been satisfactorily explained; the basic point is that it is Apocalyptic.
5. A laborer who digs dikes and ditches.

From *Passus* 7

[PIERS TEARS TRUTH'S PARDON]

Truth heard tell of this and sent word to Piers
To take his team and till the earth,
And procured him a pardon *a poena et a culpa*,[6]
For him and for his heirs for evermore after;
5 And bade him hold at home and plow his land,
And any one who helped him plow or sow,
Or any kind of craft that could help Piers,
Pardon with Piers Plowman Truth has granted.

* * *

"Piers," said a priest then, "your pardon must I read,
For I'll explain each paragraph to you and put it in English."
And Piers unfolds the pardon at the priest's prayer,
110 And I behind them both beheld all the bull.[7]
In two lines it lay, and not a letter more,
And was worded this way in witness of truth:
They that have done good shall go into life everlasting;
And they that have done evil into everlasting fire.[8]
115 "Peter!" said the priest then, "I can find no pardon here—
Only 'Do well, and have well,' and God will have your soul,
And 'Do evil, and have evil,' and hope nothing else
But that after your death-day the Devil will have your soul."
And Piers for pure wrath pulled it in two
120 And said, "*Though I walk in the midst of the shadow of death*
I will fear no evil; for thou art with me.[9]
I shall cease my sowing and not work so hard,
Nor be henceforth so busy about my livelihood.
My plow shall be of penance and of prayers hereafter,
125 And I'll weep when I should work, though wheat bread fails me.
The prophet[1] ate his portion in penance and sorrow
As the Psalter says, and so did many others.
Who loves God loyally, his livelihood comes easy.
My tears have been my bread day and night.[2]
And unless Luke lies, he finds another lesson for us
130 In birds that are not busy about their belly-joy:
'*Ne soliciti sitis*,'[3] he says in the Gospel,
And shows us examples by which to school ourselves.

---

6. This pardon has remained one of the most controversial elements of the poem. "From punishment and from guilt" is a formula indicating an absolute pardon. Strictly speaking, remissions obtained by pilgrimages (and pardons dispensed by pardoners in return for donations) could remit only the *punishment* for sin; note that even Truth's pardon does both only for some people. Christ alone, through the Atonement, had the power to absolve repentant sinners from the *guilt* and delegated it to St. Peter and to the Church through the apostolic succession to be dispensed in the sacrament of confession and in penance. (This pardon also covers, according to another legal formula in the next line, Piers's heirs, which ordinary pardons could not.) The belief, however, that indulgences (especially those obtained from the pope himself) absolved guilt as well as punishment was widespread.
7. A document issued by the pope and sealed with his *bulla*, or seal.
8. From the Athanasian Creed, based on Matthew 25.31–46.
9. Psalms 23.4.
1. David, whose Psalm is quoted below.
2. Psalms 42.3.
3. "Take no thought [for your life]" (Latin): Matthew 6.25; also Luke 12.22.

The fowls in the firmament, who feeds them in winter?
When the frost freezes they forage for food,
135 They have no granary to go to, but God feeds them all."
"What!" said the priest to Perkin, "Peter, it would seem
You are lettered a little. Who lessoned you in books?"
"Abstinence the abbess taught me my a b c,
And Conscience came after and counseled me better."
140 "If you were a priest, Piers," said he, "you might preach when you
    pleased
As a doctor of divinity, with *Dixit insipiens*,[4] as your text."
"Unlearned lout!" said Piers, "you know little of the Bible;
Solomon's sayings are seldom your reading."
    *Cast out the scorners and contentions with them, lest they
        increase.*[5]
    The priest and Perkin opposed each other,
145 And through their words I awoke and looked everywhere about,
And saw the sun sit due south at that time.
Meatless and moneyless on Malvern Hills,
Musing on my dream, I walked a mile-way.

From *The C-Text*

[THE DREAMER MEETS CONSCIENCE AND REASON][6]

Thus I awoke, as God's my witness, when I lived in Cornhill,[7]
Kit and I in a cottage, clothed like a loller,[8]
And little beloved, believe you me,
Among lollers of London and illiterate hermits.
5 For I wrote rhymes of those men as Reason taught me.
For as I came by Conscience I met with Reason,
In a hot harvest time when I had my health,
And limbs to labor with, and loved good living,
And to do no deed but to drink and sleep.
10 My body sound, my mind sane, a certain one accosted me;
Roaming in remembrance, thus Reason upbraided me:
    "Can you serve," he said, "or sing in a church?
Or cock hay with my hay-makers, or heap it on the cart,
Mow it or stack what's mown or make binding for sheaves?
15 Or have a horn and be a hedge-guard and lie outdoors at night,
And keep my corn in my field from cattle and thieves?
Or cut cloth or shoe-leather, or keep sheep and cattle,
Mend hedges, or harrow, or herd pigs or geese,

---

4. "The fool hath said [in his heart, There is no God]" (Latin): Psalms 14.1.
5. Proverbs 22.10.
6. In the C-text, the last of the three versions of *Piers Plowman*, Langland prefixed to the "Confession of the Seven Deadly Sins" (Passus 5 of the B-text) an apology by the Dreamer, "Long Will," who is at once long (or tall) and long on willing (or, arguably, willful). Although there is no conclusive historical evidence for doing so, readers of *Piers Plowman* have generally regarded this passage as a source of information about the real author, about whom we otherwise know so little.

7. An area of London associated with vagabonds, seedy clerics, and people at loose ends.
8. Idler, vagabond. The term was eventually applied to the proto-Protestant followers of John Wycliffe. "Kit": refers to "Kit my wife and Calote [i.e., Colette] my daughter" (B-text, 18.426). The Dreamer seems to be someone with clerical training who has received consecration into minor clerical orders (such as that of deacon) but who is not a priest. Lesser clerics could marry, although marriage blocked their further advancement in the church.

Or any other kind of craft that the commons needs,
20 So that you might be of benefit to your bread-providers?"
    "Certainly!" I said, "and so God help me,
I am too weak to work with sickle or with scythe,
And too long,[9] believe me, for any low stooping,
Or laboring as a laborer to last any while."
25 "Then have you lands to live by," said Reason, "or relations with
        money
To provide you with food? For you seem an idle man,
A spendthrift who thrives on spending, and throws time away.
Or else you get what food men give you going door to door,
Or beg like a fraud on Fridays[1] and feastdays in churches.
30 And that's a loller's life that earns little praise
Where Rightfulness rewards men as they really deserve.
    He shall reward every man according to his works.[2]
Or are you perhaps lame in your legs or other limbs of your body,
Or maimed through some misadventure, so that you might be
        excused?"
    "When I was young, many years ago,
35 My father and my friends provided me with schooling,
Till I understood surely what Holy Scripture meant,
And what is best for the body as the Book tells,
And most certain for the soul, if so I may continue.
And, in faith, I never found, since my friends died,
40 Life that I liked save in these long clothes.[3]
And if I must live by labor and earn my livelihood,
The labor I should live by is the one I learned best.
    [Abide] in the same calling wherein you were called.[4]
And so I live in London and upland[5] as well.
The tools that I toil with to sustain myself
45 Are Paternoster and my primer, *Placebo* and *Dirige*,[6]
And sometimes my Psalter and my seven Psalms.
These I say for the souls of such as help me.
And those who provide my food vouchsafe, I think,
To welcome me when I come, once a month or so,
50 Now with him, now with her, and in this way I beg
Without bag or bottle but my belly alone.
    And also, moreover, it seems to me, sir Reason,
No clerk should be constrained to do lower-class work.
For by the law of Leviticus[7] that our Lord ordained
55 Clerks with tonsured crowns should, by common understanding,
Neither strain nor sweat nor swear at inquests,
Nor fight in a vanguard and defeat an enemy:
    Do not render evil for evil.[8]

9. I.e., tall, perhaps a pun on "willfulness." The
Dreamer is called "Long Will" in B-text, 15.152.
1. Fast days, because Christ was crucified on a
Friday.
2. Matthew 16.27; cf. Psalms 62.12.
3. The long dress of a cleric, not limited to
actual priests.
4. 1 Corinthians 7.20, with variations.
5. North of London, in rural country.
6. "I will please [the Lord]" and "Make straight

[my way]" (Latin; Psalms 116.9 and 5.8, respectively). *Placebo* and *Dirige* are the first words of
hymns based on two of the seven "penitential"
Psalms that were part of the regular order of
personal prayer. "Paternoster": the Lord's Prayer
("Our father" in Latin). The "primer" was the
basic collection of private prayers for laypeople.
7. Leviticus 21 sets restrictions on members of
the priesthood.
8. 1 Thessalonians 5.15, with variations.

For they are heirs of Heaven, all that have the tonsure,
And in choir and in churches they are Christ's ministers.
    The Lord is the portion of my inheritance. And elsewhere,
      Mercy does not constrain.[9]
60 It is becoming for clerks to perform Christ's service,
And untonsured boys be burdened with bodily labor.
For none should acquire clerk's tonsure unless he claims descent
From franklins[1] and free men and folk properly wedded.
Bondmen and bastards and beggars' children—
65 These belong to labor; and lords' kin should serve
God and good men as their degree requires,
Some to sing Masses or sit and write,
Read and receive what Reason ought to spend.
But since bondmen's boys have been made bishops,
70 And bastards' boys have been archdeacons,
And shoemakers and their sons have through silver become knights,
And lords' sons their laborers whose lands are mortgaged to them—
And thus for the right of this realm they ride against our enemies
To the comfort of the commons and to the king's honor—
75 And monks and nuns on whom mendicants must depend
Have had their kin named knights and bought knight's-fees,[2]
And popes and patrons have shunned poor gentle blood
And taken the sons of Simon Magus[3] to keep the sanctuary,
Life-holiness and love have gone a long way hence,
80 And will be so till this is all worn out or otherwise changed.
Therefore proffer me no reproach, Reason, I pray you,
For in my conscience I conceive what Christ wants me to do.
Prayers of a perfect man and appropriate penance
Are the labor that our Lord loves most of all.
85   "*Non de solo,*" I said, "forsooth *vivit homo,*
Nec in pane et in pabulo;[4] the Paternoster witnesses
Fiat voluntas Dei[5]—that provides us with everything."
    Said Conscience, "By Christ, I can't see that this lies;°   *is pertinent*
But it seems no serious perfectness to be a city-beggar,
90 Unless you're licensed to collect for prior or monastery."
    "That is so," I said, "and so I admit
That at times I've lost time and at times misspent it;
And yet I hope, like him who has often bargained
And always lost and lost, and at the last it happened
95 He bought such a bargain he was the better ever,
That all his loss looked paltry in the long run,
Such a winning was his through what grace decreed.

---

9. I.e., "mercy is not restricted," source unknown. The quotation above is from Psalms 16.5.

1. Freemen. By this date, the term did not just mean nonserfs but designated landowners who were becoming members of the gentry class yet were not knights. The distinction Langland seems to make in this line between franklins and freemen may reflect the rising status of certain families of "freedmen," the original meaning of the word *franklins.*

2. The estate a knight held from his overlord in return for military service was called his "fee."

3. Priests who obtained office through bribery or "simony," a term derived from Simon Magus, a magician who offered the apostles money for their power to perform miracles through the Holy Spirit (see Acts 8).

4. "Not solely [by bread] doth man live, neither by bread nor by food" (Latin); the verse continues, "but by every word that proceedeth out of the mouth of God": Matthew 4.4, with variations; cf. Deuteronomy 8.3.

5. "God's will be done" (Latin). The Lord's Prayer reads, "Thy will be done" (Matthew 6.10).

> *The kingdom of Heaven is like unto treasure hidden in a field.*
> *The woman who found the piece of silver, etc.*[6]
> So I hope to have of him that is almighty
> A gobbet of his grace, and begin a time
100 That all times of my time shall turn into profit."
> "And I counsel you," said Reason, "quickly to begin
> The life that is laudable and reliable for the soul."
> "Yes, and continue," said Conscience, and I came to the church.[7]

6. Matthew 13.44, Luke 15.9–10. Both passages come from parables that compare finding the kingdom of heaven to risking everything you have to get the one thing that matters most.
7. The four lines that follow this passage connect it to the beginning of the second dream (B-text, 5): "And to the church I set off, to honor God; before the Cross, on my knees, I beat my breast, sighing for my sins, saying my Paternoster, weeping and wailing until I fell asleep."

CHRIST'S HUMANITY

The literary and visual representation of the godhead is necessarily, in any religion, a powerful index of religious culture. In some religions, indeed, visual representation of God is such a sensitive issue that it is forbidden altogether. Christian culture has experienced moments of severe hostility to visual representation (for example, in the Reformation period of the sixteenth century), but has, in general, permitted images of God (and especially of God-become-man, Christ). In the later Middle Ages in Europe, the bodily representation of Christ became a central preoccupation for writers, readers, and visual artists.

In the late eleventh century, St. Anselm of Canterbury (1033–1099) developed a new conception of the Atonement ("at-one-ment"), the act whereby humans are reconciled with God after the separation caused by Original Sin. An earlier theory had posited that the Atonement was the solution to a dispute between God and the Devil concerning property rights over mankind. In his tract *Why Did Christ Become Man?* Anselm argued instead that the real center of the Atonement was mankind's moral responsibility to pay God back. Humanity needed to repay God for the sin committed, but was unable to do so. Faced with this impasse, God could either simply abolish the debt, or else *become human*, in order to repay himself, as it were. God chose this latter route, allowing Christ to suffer and die as a human in order to clear the debt.

Earlier representations of the Crucifixion had tended to place the accent on Christ as impassive king, standing erect on the Cross, come to claim his property of mankind. In *The Dream of the Rood* (see pp. 34–37), for example, Christ's suffering is for the most part absorbed by the Cross itself, while Christ is represented as a conquering, royal hero. Later medieval representations of Christ, by contrast, accentuate the suffering, sagging, lacerated body of a very human God. In this newly conceived theology, Christ's suffering humanity takes center stage. The artistic significance of this massively influential development was itself massive. Certainly the older tradition survived in vital form: compare, for example, the triumphalist lyric "What is he, this lordling, that cometh from the fight?" with the quiet suffering of "Ye that pasen by the weye." Langland's Christ, too, comes to claim his property as a conquering hero. It was, nonetheless, the tradition of Christ suffering in his humanity that dominated literary and visual art from the thirteenth century until the Reformation began in 1517.

These theological developments had forceful artistic and stylistic consequences. Because the theology was best expressed through visual or verbal images, it fed readily into both painting and a highly pictorial literature. In both painting and literature, a humble style, focusing on the particularities of bodily pain and grief, became the bearer of high theological significance. The painting of Giotto (1266?–1337), for example, broke with a prior tradition of painting that represented an elegant Christ against a splendid gold background; Giotto's inelegant and crucified Christ suffers under the pull of his own weight. Spiritual experience was, in the first instance, something *seen* more than something *thought*. It was also a spirituality rooted in the dramatic present: as one saw Christ, one saw him in the here and now. Thus works in this almost cinematic mode foreshorten historical and geographical distance: such texts encourage readers, that is, to imagine that they are physically and emotionally present at the crucial scenes of Christ's life. In some examples of the tradition, viewers are encouraged to imagine those around Christ (especially Romans and Jews) as wholly responsible for the infliction of pain; in others, viewers are made to realize that they are themselves responsible for the continued suffering of Christ.

As deployed by the Church, this movement discouraged abstract thought. It did nevertheless have the effect of widening access to spiritual experience, and, in ways unforeseen by official sponsors of such piety, could be the springboard for sophisticated theology. As the Church attempted to deepen the spiritual literacy of its members from the late twelfth century on, emphasis on Christ's humanity in art and literature opened powerful spiritual experience to a much wider audience of readers and viewers. To engage in this spirituality, a public did not need to be versed in detailed matters of doctrine. Instead, a reader or viewer had to develop the capacity for sympathetic response to physical suffering. Such spirituality gained official impetus through the foundation of the Franciscan order of friars (1223), who promoted earthly poverty in imitation of, and emotional response to, Christ's sufferings. The centrality of Christ's living presence in the liturgy was, furthermore, reaffirmed and extended with the establishment, throughout Christendom, of the Feast of Corpus Christi (the Feast of the Body of Christ), first proclaimed by the pope in 1264 and again in 1311. This feast celebrated the Eucharistic host, or wafer, as Christ's body. It grew steadily in popularity and came to involve outdoor processions depicting the biblical foreshadowings of the Eucharist, as a prelude to display of the Eucharist itself. In some medieval English cities this was the day also chosen for the performance of cycle plays, sometimes known as the plays of Corpus Christi.

Female readers in particular, who had been excluded from the Latin-based, textual traditions of theology, discovered fertile ground in this tradition of so-called affective, or emotional, piety. Through such emotive imagining, one gained an apparently unmediated, and potentially authoritative, relation with Christ. Women working in this tradition did not necessarily remain, however, within its visual, imaginative terms: Julian of Norwich is, for example, capable of developing subtle and abstract thought, holding the incarnate image in view all the while.

This powerfully emotional piety also provoked wider social applications of the Christian narrative. Whereas "The Parable of the Christ Knight" in the *Ancrene Wisse* presents a suffering Christ as an aristocratic lover for a select spiritual elite of women, the Christ of Margery Kempe is very much the "homely" husband of a bourgeois woman (see in particular Book I, Chapter 36). On a much larger scale, the mystery plays mark the moment in which urban institutions represent Christ for themselves. In these dramas, both Old and New Testament narrative is inflected by the trials of domestic and urban experience (on the origins, civic sponsorship, and production of these plays, see the introduction to "Mystery Plays," p. 465).

WILLIAM LANGLAND

For full information about William Langland, see the headnote on pages 388–91. The following passage (Passus 18 of *Piers Plowman*) both completes the selections from Langland and serves as the first text of "Christ's Humanity."

Passus 18 describes the central event of Christianity, the Crucifixion, followed by an account of Christ's descent into hell, traditionally called the "Harrowing of Hell." The Dreamer has come a long way in his personal search for truth, and this vision is the most immediate and fulfilling answer to the questions he addressed to Holy Church, although not a final answer, for in Langland's poem the search has no end in this life. Piers, who had assumed aspects of Adam, Moses, and the Good Samaritan (while never ceasing to be the ideal plowman), is now partially identified with Christ. The terms of this identification are rooted in the material necessity of food: Christ has come to fetch the "fruit" of Piers Plowman (lines 20 and 33). The "food" that Christ seeks has now become the souls of the patriarchs and prophets, and of all mankind, which must be redeemed from the devil's power. And just as the earthly Piers becomes Christ-like, so too does Christ, in his bodily manifestation, become intensely human. He jousts in the arms (i.e., no arms at all, but the unprotected flesh) of Piers Plowman (line 25); he comes to earth precisely in order to *know* what being human is like (lines 220–25); and he does so precisely because of his co-natural, sympathetic kinship with suffering humanity (lines 400–401).

For all that, Langland does not focus here for long on the grievous suffering of Christ. On the contrary, he addresses the terms of the Atonement through intellectual debate, first through the Four Daughters of God (personifications taken from Psalm 85.10), and then through Christ's direct encounter with Lucifer. Against powerful legal and written evidence to the contrary, first Mercy and Peace and then Christ himself reveal a divine curiosity and sympathy with imprisoned humanity. This mercy is anterior to, and more powerful than, the law of strict *Truthe* or justice, by which mankind appears to have been irredeemably damned. So far from being a wounded, suffering Christ, Langland's Christ is at once spiritually triumphant and a delighted trickster, by whose divine guile the devil has been fooled.

The Vision of Piers Plowman

Passus 18

[THE CRUCIFIXION AND HARROWING OF HELL]

Wool-chafed[1] and wet-shoed I went forth after
Like a careless creature unconscious of woe,
And trudged forth like a tramp, all the time of my life,
Till I grew weary of the world and wished to sleep again,
5 And lay down till Lent, and slept a long time,

---

1. Scratchy wool was worn next to the body as an act of penance.

Rested there, snoring roundly, till *Ramis-Palmarum.*[2]
    I dreamed chiefly of children and cheers of *"Gloria, laus!"*
And how old folk to an organ sang *"Hosanna!"*
And of Christ's passion and pain for the people he had reached for.

10 One resembling the Samaritan[3] and somewhat Piers the Plowman
Barefoot on an ass's back bootless came riding
Without spurs or spear: sprightly was his look,
As is the nature of a knight that draws near to be dubbed,
To get himself gilt spurs and engraved jousting shoes.

15 Then was Faith watching from a window and cried, *"A, fill David!"*
As does a herald of arms when armed men come to joust.
Old Jews of Jerusalem joyfully sang,
    "Blessed is he who cometh in the name of the Lord."
And I asked Faith to reveal what all this affair meant,
And who was to joust in Jerusalem. "Jesus," he said,

20 "And fetch what the Fiend claims, the fruit of Piers the Plowman."
"Is Piers in this place?" said I; and he pierced me with his look:
"This Jesus for his gentleness will joust in Piers's arms,
In his helmet and in his hauberk, *humana natura,*[4]
So that Christ be not disclosed here as *consummatus Deus.*[5]

25 In the plate armor of Piers the Plowman this jouster will ride,
For no dint will do him injury as *in deitate Patris.*[6]
"Who shall joust with Jesus," said I, "Jews or Scribes?"[7]
"No," said Faith, "but the Fiend and False-Doom°-To-Die.   *sentence*
Death says he will undo and drag down low

30 All that live or look upon land or water.
Life says that he lies, and lays his life in pledge
That for all that Death can do, within three days he'll walk
And fetch from the Fiend the fruit of Piers the Plowman,
And place it where he pleases, and put Lucifer in bonds,

35 And beat and bring down burning death forever.
    O death, I will be thy death."[8]
    Then Pilate came with many people, *sedens pro tribunali,*[9]
To see how doughtily Death should do, and judge the rights of both.
The Jews and the justice were joined against Jesus,
And all the court cried upon him, *"Crucifige!"*[1] loud.

40 Then a plaintiff appeared before Pilate and said,
"This Jesus made jokes about Jerusalem's temple,
To have it down in one day and in three days after
Put it up again all new[2]—here he stands who said it—

<hr>

2. Palm Sunday (literally, "branches of palms" in Latin): the background of this part of the poem is the biblical account of Christ's entry into Jerusalem on this day, when the crowds greeted him crying, "Hosanna (line 8) to the son of David (line 15): Blessed is he that cometh in the name of the Lord (line 17a); Hosanna in the highest" (see Matthew 21.9). *"Gloria, laus"* (line 7) are the first words of a Latin anthem, "Glory, praise, and honor," that was sung by children in medieval religious processions on Palm Sunday.

3. In the previous vision, the Dreamer has encountered Abraham, or Faith (mentioned in lines 15, 18, 28, and 92); Moses, or Hope; and the Good Samaritan, or Charity, who was riding toward a "jousting in Jerusalem" and who now appears as an aspect of Christ.

4. Human nature (Latin), which Christ assumed in order to redeem humanity. "Hauberk": coat of mail.

5. The perfect (three-personed) God (Latin).

6. In the godhead of the Father (Latin): as God, Christ could not suffer but as man, he could.

7. People who made a very strict, literal interpretation of the Old Law and hence rejected teaching of the New.

8. Cf. Hosea 13.14.

9. Sitting as a judge (Latin; cf. Matthew 27.19).

1. Crucify him! (Latin; John 19.15).

2. See John 2.19–21 and Mark 14.58–59.

And yet build it every bit as big in all dimensions,
45 As long and as broad both, above and below."
"*Crucifige!*" said a sergeant, "he knows sorcerer's tricks."
"*Tolle! tolle!*"[3] said another, and took sharp thorns
And began to make a garland out of green thorn,
And set it sorely on his head and spoke in hatred,
50 "*Ave, Rabbi,*" said that wretch, and shot reeds[4] at him;
They nailed him with three nails naked on a Cross,
And with a pole put a potion up to his lips
And bade him drink to delay his death and lengthen his days,
And said, "If you're subtle, let's see you help yourself.
55 If you are Christ and a king's son, come down from the Cross!
Then we'll believe that Life loves you and will not let you die."
    "*Consummatum est,*"[5] said Christ and started to swoon,
Piteously and pale like a prisoner dying.
The Lord of Life and of Light then laid his eyelids together.
60 The day withdrew for dread and darkness covered the sun;
The wall wavered and split and the whole world quaked.
Dead men for that din came out of deep graves
And spoke of why that storm lasted so long:
"For a bitter battle," the dead body said;
65 "Life and Death in this darkness, one destroys the other.
No one will surely know which shall have the victory
Before Sunday about sunrise"; and sank with that to earth.
Some said that he was God's son that died so fairly:
    Truly this was the Son of God.[6]
And some said he was a sorcerer: "We should see first
70 Whether he's dead or not dead before we dare take him down."
Two thieves were there that suffered death that time
Upon crosses beside Christ; such was the common law.
A constable came forth and cracked both their legs
And the arms afterward of each of those thieves.
75 But no bastard was so bold as to touch God's body there;
Because he was a knight and a king's son, Nature decreed that time
That no knave should have the hardiness to lay hand on him.
    But a knight with a sharp spear was sent forth there
Named Longeus[7] as the legend tells, who had long since lost his sight;
80 Before Pilate and the other people in that place he waited on his horse.
For all that he might demur, he was made that time
To joust with Jesus, that blind Jew Longeus.
For all who watched there were unwilling, whether mounted or afoot,
To touch him or tamper with him or take him down from the Cross,
85 Except this blind bachelor° that bore him through the heart.   *knight*
The blood sprang down the spear and unsparred[8] his eyes.
The knight knelt down on his knees and begged Jesus for mercy.

---

3. Away with him, away with him! (Latin; John 19.15).
4. Arrows, probably small ones intended to hurt rather than to kill. "*Ave, Rabbi*": "Hail, master" (Latin; Matthew 26.49): these are actually Judas's words when he kissed Christ in order to identify him to the arresting officers.
5. It is finished (Latin; John 19.30).

6. Matthew 27.54.
7. Longeus (usually Longinus) appears in the apocryphal Gospel of Nicodemus, which provided Langland with the material for much of his account of Christ's despoiling of hell.
8. Opened; in the original there is a play on words with "spear."

"It was against my will, Lord, to wound you so sorely."
He sighed and said, "Sorely I repent it.
90 For what I here have done, I ask only your grace.
Have mercy on me, rightful Jesu!" and thus lamenting wept.
    Then Faith began fiercely to scorn the false Jews,[9]
Called them cowards, accursed forever.
"For this foul villainy, may vengeance fall on you!
95 To make the blind beat the dead, it was a bully's thought.
Cursed cowards, no kind of knighthood was it
To beat a dead body with any bright weapon.
Yet he's won the victory in the fight for all his vast wound,
For your champion jouster, the chief knight of you all,
100 Weeping admits himself worsted and at the will of Jesus.
For when this darkness is done, Death will be vanquished,
And you louts have lost, for Life shall have the victory;
And your unfettered freedom has fallen into servitude;
And you churls and your children shall achieve no prosperity,
105 Nor have lordship over land or have land to till,
But be all barren and live by usury,
Which is a life that every law of our Lord curses.
Now your good days are done as Daniel prophesied;
When Christ came their kingdom's crown should be lost:
    When the Holy of Holies comes your anointing shall cease."[1]
110 What for fear of this adventure and of the false Jews
I withdrew in that darkness to *Descendit-ad-Inferna*,[2]
And there I saw surely *Secundum Scripturas*[3]
Where out of the west a wench,[4] as I thought,
Came walking on the way—she looked toward hell.
115 Mercy was that maid's name, a meek thing withal,
A most gracious girl, and goodly of speech.
Her sister as it seemed came softly walking
Out of the east, opposite, and she looked westward,
A comely creature and cleanly: Truth was her name.
120 Because of the virtue that followed her, she was afraid of nothing.
When these maidens met, Mercy and Truth,
Each of them asked the other about this great wonder,
And of the din and of the darkness, and how the day lowered,
And what a gleam and a glint glowed before hell.
125   "I marvel at this matter, by my faith," said Truth,
"And am coming to discover what this queer affair means."
    "Do not marvel," said Mercy, "it means only mirth.
A maiden named Mary, and mother without touching
By any kind of creature, conceived through speech
130 And grace of the Holy Ghost; grew great with child;

---

9. The references in this passage (lines 92–110) and in lines 258–60 appear to reflect a blind anti-Semitism all too prevalent in late-medieval art and literature, brought out especially in portrayals of the Passion. Elsewhere Langland exhibits a more enlightened attitude—for instance, in a passage in which he holds up Jewish charity as an example to Christians. In the present passage he may intend a distinction between those who betrayed and condemned Jesus and the "old Jews of Jerusalem" who welcomed him in the Palm Sunday procession (lines 7–17).

1. Daniel 9.24.
2. He descended into hell (Latin; from the Apostles' Creed).
3. According to the Scriptures (Latin).
4. The word is Langland's and had much the same connotations in his time as it has in ours.

With no blemish to her woman's body brought him into this world.
And that my tale is true, I take God to witness,
Since this baby was born it has been thirty winters,[5]
Who died and suffered death this day about midday.

135 And that is the cause of this eclipse that is closing off the sun,
In meaning that man shall be removed from darkness
While this gleam and this glow go to blind Lucifer.
For patriarchs and prophets have preached of this often
That man shall save man through a maiden's help,

140 And what a tree took away a tree shall restore,[6]
And what Death brought down a death shall raise up."
    "What you're telling," said Truth, "is just a tale of nonsense.
For Adam and Eve and Abraham and the rest,
Patriarchs and prophets imprisoned in pain,

145 Never believe that yonder light will lift them up,
Or have them out of hell—hold your tongue, Mercy!
Your talk is mere trifling. I, Truth, know the truth,
For whatever is once in hell, it comes out never.
Job the perfect patriarch disproves what you say:
    Since in hell there is no redemption."[7]

150   Then Mercy most mildly uttered these words:
"From observation," she said, "I suppose they shall be saved,
Because venom destroys venom, and in that I find evidence
That Adam and Eve shall have relief.
For of all venoms the foulest is the scorpion's:

155 No medicine may amend the place where it stings
Till it's dead and placed upon it—the poison is destroyed,
The first effect of the venom, through the virtue it possesses.
So shall this death destroy—I dare bet my life—
All that Death did first through the Devil's tempting.

160 And just as the beguiler with guile beguiled man first,
So shall grace that began everything make a good end
And beguile the beguiler—and that's a good trick:
    A trick by which to trick trickery."[8]
    "Now let's be silent," said Truth. "It seems to me I see
Out of the nip[9] of the north, not far from here,

165 Righteousness come running—let's wait right here,
For she knows far more than we—she was here before us both."
    "That is so," said Mercy, "and I see here to the south
Where Peace clothed in patience[1] comes sportively this way.
Love has desired her long: I believe surely

170 That Love has sent her some letter, what this light means
That hangs over hell thus: she will tell us what it means."
When Peace clothed in patience approached near them both,
Righteousness did her reverence for her rich clothing

---

5. See Luke 3.23.
6. The first tree bore the fruit that Adam and Eve ate, thereby damning humankind; the second tree is the cross on which Christ was crucified, thereby redeeming humankind.
7. Cf. Job 7.9.
8. From a medieval Latin hymn.
9. The word is Langland's and the sense obscure; it probably meant "coldness" to him, although an Old English word similar to *nip* meant "gloom."
1. What Langland envisioned clothes of patience to look like, aside from their "richness" (line 173), it is impossible to say; to him any abstraction could become a concrete allegory without visual identification.

And prayed Peace to tell her to what place she was going,
175 And whom she was going to greet in her gay garments.
    "My wish is to take my way," said she, "and welcome them all
Whom many a day I might not see for murk of sin.
Adam and Eve and the many others in hell,
Moses and many more will merrily sing,
180 And I shall dance to their song: sister, do the same.
Because Jesus jousted well, joy begins to dawn.
    Weeping may endure for a night, but joy cometh in the morning.[2]
Love who is my lover sent letters to tell me
That my sister Mercy and I shall save mankind,
And that God has forgiven and granted me, Peace, and Mercy
185 To make bail for mankind for evermore after.
Look, here's the patent," said Peace: "*In pace in idipsum:*
And that this deed shall endure, *dormiam et requiescam.*"[3]
    "What? You're raving," said Righteousness. "You must be really
      drunk.
Do you believe that yonder light might unlock hell
190 And save man's soul? Sister, don't suppose it.
At the beginning God gave the judgment himself
That Adam and Eve and all that followed them
Should die downright and dwell in torment after
If they touched a tree and ate the tree's fruit.
195 Adam afterwards against his forbidding
Fed on that fruit and forsook as it were
The love of our Lord and his lore too,
And followed what the Fiend taught and his flesh's will
Against Reason. I, Righteousness, record this with Truth,
200 That their pain should be perpetual and no prayer should help them,
Therefore let them chew as they chose, and let us not chide, sisters,
For it's misery without amendment, the morsel they ate."
    "And I shall prove," said Peace, "that their pain must end,
And in time trouble must turn into well-being;
205 For had they known no woe, they'd not have known well-being;
For no one knows what well-being is who was never in woe,
Nor what is hot hunger who has never lacked food.
If there were no night, no man, I believe,
Could be really well aware of what day means.
210 Never should a really rich man who lives in rest and ease
Know what woe is if it weren't for natural death.
So God, who began everything, of his good will
Became man by a maid for mankind's salvation
And allowed himself to be sold to see the sorrow of dying.
215 And that cures all care and is the first cause of rest,
For until we meet *modicum,*° I may well avow it,   *small quantity*
No man knows, I suppose, what 'enough' means.
Therefore God of his goodness gave the first man Adam
A place of supreme ease and of perfect joy,

---

2. Psalms 30.5.
3. The "patent" or "deed" is a document conferring authority: this one consists of Latin phrases from
Psalms 4.8: "In peace in the selfsame"; "I will sleep and find rest."

220 And then he suffered him to sin so that he might know sorrow,
And thus know what well-being is—to be aware of it naturally.
And afterward God offered himself, and took Adam's nature,
To see what he had suffered in three separate places,
Both in Heaven and on earth, and now he heads for hell,

225 To learn what all woe is like who has learned of all joy.
So it shall fare with these folk: their folly and their sin
Shall show them what sickness is—and succor from all pain.
No one knows what war is where peace prevails,
Nor what is true well-being till 'Woe, alas!' teaches him."

230   Then was there a wight° with two broad eyes: creature, person
Book was that beaupere's⁴ name, a bold man of speech.
"By God's body," said this Book, "I will bear witness
That when this baby was born there blazed a star
So that all the wise men in the world agreed with one opinion

235 That such a baby was born in Bethlehem city
Who should save man's soul and destroy sin.
And all the elements," said the Book, "hereof bore witness.
The sky first revealed that he was God who formed all things:
The hosts in Heaven took *stella comata*⁵

240 And tended her like a torch to reverence his birth.
The light followed the Lord into the low earth.
The water witnessed that he was God for he walked on it;
Peter the Apostle perceived his walking
And as he went on the water knew him well and said,
    '*Bid me come unto thee on the water.*'⁶

245 And lo, how the sun locked her light in herself
When she saw him suffer that made sun and sea.
The earth for heavy heart because he would suffer
Quaked like a quick° thing and the rock cracked all to pieces.   living
Lo, hell might not hold, but opened when God suffered,

250 And let out Simeon's sons⁷ to see him hang on Cross.
And now shall Lucifer believe it, loath though he is,
For Jesus like a giant with an engine⁸ comes yonder
To break and beat down all that may be against him,
And to have out of hell every one he pleases.

255 And I, Book, will be burnt unless Jesus rises to life
In all the mights of a man and brings his mother joy,
And comforts all his kin, and takes their cares away,
And all the joy of the Jews disjoins and disperses;
And unless they reverence his Rood and his resurrection

260 And believe on a new law be lost body and soul."
    "Let's be silent," said Truth, "I hear and see both
A spirit speaks to hell and bids the portals be opened."

---

4. Fine fellow (French). The book's two broad eyes suggest the Old and New Testaments.
5. Hairy star (Latin), i.e., comet.
6. Matthew 14.28.
7. Simeon, who was present at the presentation of the infant Jesus in the temple, had been told by the Holy Ghost that "he should not see death" before he had seen "the Lord's Christ"

(Luke 2.26). The Apocryphal Gospel of Nicodemus echoes the incident in reporting that Simeon's sons were raised from death at the time of Jesus's crucifixion.
8. A device, probably thought of as a gigantic slingshot, although, of course, Christ needs nothing to break down his enemies but his own authority.

Lift up your gates.[9]
A voice loud in that light cried to Lucifer,
"Princes of this place, unpin and unlock,
265 For he comes here with crown who is King of Glory."
Then Satan[1] sighed and said to hell,
"Without our leave such a light fetched Lazarus away:[2]
Care and calamity have come upon us all.
If this King comes in he will carry off mankind
270 And lead it to where Lazarus is, and with small labor bind me.
Patriarchs and prophets have long prated of this,[3]
That such a lord and a light should lead them all hence."
"Listen," said Lucifer, "for this lord is one I know;
Both this lord and this light, it's long ago I knew him.
275 No death may do this lord harm, nor any devil's trickery,
And his way is where he wishes—but let him beware of the perils.
If he bereaves me of my right he robs me by force.
For by right and by reason the race that is here
Body and soul belongs to me, both good and evil.
280 For he himself said it who is Sire of Heaven,
If Adam ate the apple, all should die
And dwell with us devils: the Lord laid down that threat.
And since he who is Truth himself said these words,
And since I've possessed them seven thousand winters,
285 I don't believe law will allow him the least of them."
"That is so," said Satan, "but I'm sore afraid
Because you took them by trickery and trespassed in his garden,
And in the semblance of a serpent sat upon the apple tree
And egged them to eat, Eve by herself,
290 And told her a tale with treasonous words;
And so you had them out, and hither at the last."
"It's an ill-gotten gain where guile is at the root,
For God will not be beguiled," said Goblin, "nor tricked.
We have no true title to them, for it was by treason they were
    damned."
295 "Certainly I fear," said the Fiend,[4] "lest Truth fetch them out.
These thirty winters, as I think, he's gone here and there and
    preached.
I've assailed him with sin, and sometimes asked
Whether he was God or God's son: he gave me short answer.
And thus he's traveled about like a true man these two and thirty
    winters.
300 And when I saw it was so, while she slept I went

9. The first words of Psalms 24.9, which reads in the Latin version, "Lift up your gates, O princes, and be ye lift up, ye everlasting doors, and the King of Glory shall come in."
1. Langland, following a tradition also reflected in Milton's *Paradise Lost*, pictures hell as populated by a number of devils: Satan; Lucifer (line 273 ff.), who began the war in heaven and tempted Eve; Goblin (line 293); Belial (line 321); and Ashtoreth (line 404). Lucifer the rebel angel naturally became identified with Satan, a word that in the Old Testament had originally meant an evil adversary; many of the other devils are displaced gods of pagan religions.
2. For Christ's raising of Lazarus from the dead, see John 11.
3. E.g., Psalms 68.18, as interpreted in Ephesians 4.8–10.
4. Here and in line 309, "the Fiend" is presumably Lucifer's most articulate critic, Satan, whom Christ names as his tempter in Matthew 4.10.

To warn Pilate's wife what sort of man was Jesus,[5]
For some hated him and have put him to death.
I would have lengthened his life, for I believed if he died
That his soul would suffer no sin in his sight.
305 For the body, while it walked on its bones, was busy always
To save men from sin if they themselves wished.
And now I see where a soul comes descending hitherward
With glory and with great light; God it is, I'm sure.
My advice is we all flee," said the Fiend, "fast away from here.
310 For we had better not be at all than abide in his sight.
For your lies, Lucifer, we've lost all our prey.
Through you we fell first from Heaven so high:
Because we believed your lies we all leapt out.
And now for your latest lie we have lost Adam,
315 And all our lordship, I believe, on land and in hell."
    Now shall the prince of this world be cast out.[6]
  Again the light bade them unlock, and Lucifer answered,
    "Who is that?[7]
What lord are you?" said Lucifer. The light at once replied,
    "The King of Glory.
The Lord of might and of main and all manner of powers:
    The Lord of Powers.
Dukes of this dim place, at once undo these gates
320 That Christ may come in, the Heaven-King's son."
And with that breath hell broke along with Belial's bars;
For° any warrior or watchman the gates wide opened.   *in spite of*
Patriarchs and prophets, *populus in tenebris*,[8]
Sang Saint John's song, *Ecce agnus Dei*.[9]
325 Lucifer could not look, the light so blinded him.
And those that the Lord loved his light caught away,
And he said to Satan, "Lo, here's my soul in payment
For all sinful souls, to save those that are worthy.
Mine they are and of me—I may the better claim them.
330 Although Reason records, and right of myself,
That if they ate the apple all should die,
I did not hold out to them hell here forever.
For the deed that they did, your deceit caused it;
You got them with guile against all reason.
335 For in my palace Paradise, in the person of an adder,
You stole by stealth something I loved.
Thus like a lizard with a lady's face[1]
Falsely you filched from me; the Old Law confirms
That guilers be beguiled, and that is good logic:

---

5. In Matthew 27.19, Pilate's wife warns Pilate to "have nothing to do with that just man [Jesus]," for she has been troubled by a dream about him. Langland has the Fiend admit to having caused the dream so that Pilate's wife should persuade her husband not to harm Jesus and thus keep him safe on earth and not come to visit hell and despoil it.
6. John 12.31. "Prince of this world" is a title for the devil.
7. This and the next two phrases translated from

the Latin are from Psalms 24.8, following immediately on the words quoted in line 262a.
8. "People in darkness"; the phrase is from Matthew 4.16, citing Isaiah 9.2: "The people that walked in darkness have seen a great light."
9. Behold the Lamb of God (Latin; John 1.36).
1. In medieval art, the devil tempting Eve was sometimes represented as a snake (see the "serpent" of line 288) and sometimes as a lizard with a female human face and standing upright.

A tooth for a tooth and an eye for an eye.[2]

340 *Ergo*[3] soul shall requite soul and sin revert to sin,
And all that man has done amiss, I, man, will amend.
Member for member was amends in the Old Law,
And life for life also, and by that law I claim
Adam and all his issue at my will hereafter.

345 And what Death destroyed in them, my death shall restore
And both quicken° and requite what was quenched   revitalize
    through sin.
And that grace destroy guile is what good faith requires.
So don't believe it, Lucifer, against the law I fetch them,
But by right and by reason here ransom my liegemen.
    I have not come to destroy the law but to fulfill it.[4]

350 You fetched mine in my place unmindful of all reason
Falsely and feloniously; good faith taught me
To recover them by reason and rely on nothing else.
So what you got with guile through grace is won back.
You, Lucifer, in likeness of a loathsome adder

355 Got by guile those whom God loved;
And I, in likeness of a mortal man, who am master of Heaven,
Have graciously requited your guile: let guile go against guile!
And as Adam and all died through a tree
Adam and all through a tree return to life,[5]

360 And guile is beguiled and grief has come to his guile:
    And he is fallen into the ditch which he made.[6]
And now your guile begins to turn against you,
And my grace to grow ever greater and wider.
The bitterness that you have brewed, imbibe it yourself
Who are doctor[7] of death, the drink you made.

365   For I who am Lord of Life, love is my drink
And for that drink today I died upon earth.
I struggled so I'm thirsty still for man's soul's sake.
No drink may moisten me or slake my thirst
Till vintage time befall in the Vale of Jehoshaphat,[8]

370 When I shall drink really ripe wine, *Resurrectio mortuorum.*[9]
And then I shall come as a king crowned with angels
And have out of hell all men's souls.
Fiends and fiendkins shall stand before me
And be at my bidding, where best it pleases me.

375 But to be merciful to man then, my nature requires it.
For we are brothers of one blood, but not in baptism all.
And all that are both in blood and in baptism my whole brothers
Shall not be damned to the death that endures without end.
    Against thee only have I sinned, etc.[1]

---

2. See Matthew 5.38 citing Exodus 21.24.
3. Therefore. The Latin conjunction was used in formal debate to introduce the conclusion derived from a number of propositions.
4. See Matthew 5.17.
5. See 1 Corinthians 15.21–22.
6. Psalms 7.15.
7. The ironic use of the word carries the sense both of "physician" and of "one learned in a discipline."

8. On the evidence of Joel 3.2, 12, the site of the Last Judgment was thought to be the Vale of Jehoshaphat.
9. The resurrection of the dead (from the Nicene Creed).
1. Psalms 51.4. The psalm is understood to assign the sole power of judging the sinner to God, because it is only against God that the sinner has acted.

It is not the custom on earth to hang a felon
380   Oftener than once, even though he were a traitor.
And if the king of the kingdom comes at that time
When a felon should suffer death or other such punishment,
Law would he give him life if he looks upon him.[2]
And I who am King of Kings shall come in such a time
385   Where doom to death damns all wicked,
And if law wills I look on them, it lies in my grace
Whether they die or do not die because they did evil.
And if it be any bit paid for, the boldness of their sins,
I may grant mercy through my righteousness and all my true words;
390   And though Holy Writ wills that I wreak vengeance on those
        that wrought evil,
        No evil unpunished, etc.[3]
They shall be cleansed and made clear and cured of their sins,
In my prison purgatory till *Parce!*° says 'Stop!'   *Spare!*
And my mercy shall be shown to many of my half-brothers,
For blood-kin may see blood-kin both hungry and cold,
395   But blood-kin may not see blood-kin bleed without his pity:
        I heard unspeakable words which it is not lawful for a man
            to utter.[4]
But my righteousness and right shall rule all hell
And mercy rule all mankind before me in Heaven.
For I'd be an unkind king unless I gave my kin help,
And particularly at such a time when help was truly needed.
        Enter not into judgment with thy servant.[5]
400   Thus by law," said our Lord, "I will lead from here
Those I looked on with love who believed in my coming;
And for your lie, Lucifer, that you lied to Eve,
You shall buy it back in bitterness"—and bound him with chains.
Ashtoreth and all the gang hid themselves in corners;
405   They dared not look at our Lord, the least of them all,
But let him lead away what he liked and leave what he wished.
      Many hundreds of angels harped and sang,
        Flesh sins, flesh redeems, flesh reigns as God of God.[6]
Then Peace piped a note of poetry:
        As a rule the sun is brighter after the biggest clouds; After
          hostilities love is brighter.
"After sharp showers," said Peace, "the sun shines brightest;
410   No weather is warmer than after watery clouds;
Nor any love lovelier, or more loving friends,
Than after war and woe when Love and peace are masters.
There was never war in this world nor wickedness so sharp

---

2. I.e., "Law dictates that the king pardon the felon if the king sees him."

3. [He is a just judge who leaves] no evil unpunished [and no good unrewarded]. Not from the Bible but from Pope Innocent III's tract *Of Contempt for the World* (1195).

4. In 2 Corinthians 12.4, St. Paul tells how in a vision he was snatched up to heaven where he heard things that may not be repeated among men. Langland is apparently invoking a similar mystic experience when he puts into Christ's mouth a promise to spare many of his half-brothers, the unbaptized. The orthodox theology of the time taught that all the unbaptized were irredeemably damned, a proposition Langland refused to accept: in his vision he has heard words to the contrary that might not be held among men, because they would be held heretical.

5. Psalms 143.2.

6. From a medieval Latin hymn. The source of the two Latin verses immediately below is Alain of Lille, a late-12th-century poet and philosopher.

That Love, if he liked, might not make a laughing matter.
415 And peace through patience puts an end to all perils."
"Truce!" said Truth, "you tell the truth, by Jesus!
Let's kiss in covenant, and each of us clasp other."
"And let no people," said Peace, "perceive that we argued;
For nothing is impossible to him that is almighty."
420 "You speak the truth," said Righteousness, and reverently kissed her,
Peace, and Peace her, *per saecula saeculorum:*[7]

> Mercy and Truth have met together; Righteousness and Peace
> have kissed each other.[8]

Truth sounded a trumpet then and sang *Te Deum Laudamus,*[9]
And then Love strummed a lute with a loud note:

> Behold how good and how pleasant, etc.[1]

Till the day dawned these damsels caroled.
425 When bells rang for the Resurrection, and right then I awoke
And called Kit my wife and Calote my daughter:

> "Arise and go reverence God's resurrection,
> And creep to the Cross on knees, and kiss it as a jewel,

For God's blessed body it bore for our good,
430 And it frightens the Fiend, for such is its power
That no grisly ghost may glide in its shadow."

---

7. For ever and ever (the Latin liturgical formula).
8. Psalms 85.10.

9. We praise thee, O Lord (Latin).
1. Psalms 133.1. The verse continues, "it is for brothers to dwell together in unity."

MIDDLE ENGLISH INCARNATION AND CRUCIFIXION LYRICS

Many religious lyrics were written down and preserved. These were mostly written by anonymous clerics, but in rare instances we know at least the name of an author. Seventeen poems by the Franciscan William Herebert are collected in a single manuscript. In his dramatic lyric printed here, the main speaker is the Christ-knight, returning from the Crucifixion, which is treated as a battle the way it is in *The Dream of the Rood* and in Passus 18 of *Piers Plowman*. The famous image from Isaiah 63.2 of the figure treading grapes in a winepress is compared to Christ in his blood-stained garments.

The religious lyrics are for the most part devotional poems that depend on the Latin Bible and liturgy of the Church. "What is he, this lordling . . .," the passage from Isaiah adapted by Herebert, was part of a lesson in a mass performed during Holy Week. But the diction of that poem, though there are a few French loan words, is predominantly of English origin. Many of the poems, like Herebert's, contain an element of drama: "Ye That Pasen by the Weye" is spoken by Christ from the Cross to all wayfarers; similar verses are spoken by the crucified Christ to the crowd (as well as to the audience) in the mystery plays of the Crucifixion.

Among the most beautiful and tender lyrics are those about the Virgin Mary, who is the greatest of all queens and ladies. They celebrate Mary's joys, sorrows, and the mystery of her virgin motherhood. "Sunset on Calvary," a tableau of Mary at the foot of the Cross, contains an implicit play upon English "sun," which is setting, and the "son," who is dying but, like the sun, will rise again. Like love songs, the Marian lyrics often celebrate the mysteries of the natural world and thus defy any simple division of medieval lyric into "secular" or "religious" poetry. "I Sing of a Maiden" visualizes the conception of Jesus in terms of the falling dew, and he steals silently to her bower like a lover. "Adam Lay Bound" cheerfully treats the original sin as though it were a child's theft of an apple, which had the happy result of making Mary the Queen of Heaven. "The Corpus Christi Carol" has the form of a lullaby but penetrates by stages to the heart of a mystery similar to the Holy Grail, the chalice that contained Christ's blood, which continues to flow, as it does in this carol, for humanity's salvation.

What is he, this lordling, that cometh from the fight[1]

"What is he, this lordling,[2] that cometh from the fight
With blood-rede wede so grislich ydight,[3]
So faire ycointised,° so semelich in sight,[4]   *appareled*
So stiflich he gangeth,[5] so doughty° a knight?"   *valiant*

5   "Ich° it am, ich it am, that ne speke but right,[6]   *I*
Champioun to helen° mankinde in fight."   *save*

"Why then is thy shroud rede, with blood al ymeind,
As troddares in wringe with must al bespreind?"[7]

"The wring ich have ytrodded al myself one°   *alone*
10   And of° al mankinde was none other wone.°   *for / hope*
Ich hem[8] have ytrodded in wrathe and in grame,°   *anger*
And al my wede is bespreind with here blood ysame,[9]
And al my robe yfouled° to here grete shame.   *soiled*
The day of th'ilke wreche[1] liveth in my thought;

15   The yeer of medes yelding ne foryet ich nought.[2]
Ich looked al aboute some helping mon;[3]
Ich soughte al the route,[4] but help nas ther non.
It was mine owne strengthe that this bote° wrought,   *remedy*
Mine owne doughtinesse that help ther me brought."[5]
20   Ich have ytrodded the folk in wrathe and in grame,
Adreint al with shennesse, ydrawe down with shame."[6]

1. The poem, by William Herebert (d. 1333), paraphrases Isaiah 63.1–7, in which the "lordling" (lord's son) is a messianic figure returning from battle against the Edomites.
2. Who is this lord's son?
3. With blood-red garment, so terribly arrayed.
4. So fair to behold.
5. So boldly he goes.
6. Who speaks only what is right.
7. Why then is thy garment red, all stained with blood, like treaders in the winepress all spattered with must (the juice of the grapes).

8. Them, i.e., humankind symbolized by the grapes in the press. Cf. line 20.
9. And my garment is all spattered with their blood together.
1. That same vengeance (perhaps Judgment Day).
2. I do not forget the year of paying wages.
3. I looked all around for some man to help (me).
4. I searched the whole crowd.
5. My own valor brought help to me there.
6. All drowned with ignominy, pulled down with shame.

"On Godes milsfulnesse° ich wil bethenche me,[7]   mercy
And herien° him in alle thing that he yeldeth° me."   praise / gives

Ye That Pasen by the Weye

Ye that pasen by the weye,
Abidet a little stounde.°   while
Beholdet, all my felawes,
Yif° any me lik is founde.[8]   if
5   To the tre with nailes thre
Wol° fast I hange bounde;   very
With a spere all thoru my side
To mine herte is made a wounde.

Sunset on Calvary

Now gooth sunne under wode:[9]
Me reweth,[1] Marye, thy faire rode.°   face
Now gooth sunne under tree:
Me reweth, Marye, thy sone and thee.

I Sing of a Maiden

I sing of a maiden
    That is makelees:[2]
King of alle kinges
    To° her sone she chees.°   as / chose

5   He cam also° stille   as
    Ther° his moder° was   where / mother
As dewe in Aprille
    That falleth on the gras.

He cam also stille
10   To his modres bowr
As dewe in Aprille
    That falleth on the flowr.

He cam also stille
    Ther his moder lay
15   As dewe in Aprille
    That falleth on the spray.

7. I will bethink myself.
8. Lines 1–4 paraphrase Lamentations 1.1–2.
9. Both the woods and the wooden Cross.

1. I pity.
2. Spotless, matchless, and mateless—a triple pun.

Moder and maiden
   Was nevere noon but she:
Wel may swich° a lady   *such*
20   Godes moder be.

Adam Lay Bound

Adam lay ybounden, bounden in a bond,
Four thousand winter thoughte he not too long;
And al was for an apple, an apple that he took,
As clerkes finden writen, writen in hire book.
5 Ne hadde° the apple taken been, the apple taken been,   *had not*
Ne hadde nevere Oure Lady ybeen hevene Queen.
Blessed be the time that apple taken was:
Therfore we mown° singen *Deo Gratias.*[3]   *may*

The Corpus Christi Carol

Lully, lullay, lully, lullay,
The faucon° hath borne my make° away.   *falcon / mate*

He bare him up, he bare him down,
He bare him into an orchard brown.

5 In that orchard ther was an hall
That was hanged with purple and pall.°   *black velvet*

And in that hall ther was a bed:
It was hanged with gold so red.

And in that bed ther lith° a knight,   *lies*
10   His woundes bleeding by day and night.

By that beddes side ther kneeleth a may,°   *maid*
And she weepeth both night and day.

And by that beddes side ther standeth a stoon°   *stone*
Corpus Christi[4] writen thereon.

---

3. Thanks be to God (Latin).   4. Body of Christ (Latin).

JULIAN OF NORWICH
1342–ca. 1416

The "Showings," or "Revelations" as they are also called, were sixteen mystical visions received by the woman known as Julian of Norwich. The name may be one that she adopted when she became an anchoress in a cell attached to the church of St. Julian that still stands in that city in East Anglia, then one of the most important English cities. An anchorite (m.) or anchoress (f.) is a religious recluse confined to an enclosure, which he or she has vowed never to leave. At the time of such an enclosing the burial service was performed, signifying that the enclosed person was dead to the world and that the enclosure corresponded to a grave. The point of this confinement was, of course, to pursue more actively the contemplative or spiritual life.

Julian may well have belonged to a religious order at the time that her visions led her to choose the life of an anchoress. We know little about her except what she tells us in her writings. She is, however, very precise about the date of her visions. They occurred, she tells us, at the age of thirty and a half on May 13, 1373. Four extant wills bequeath sums for Julian's maintenance in her anchorage. The most important document witnessing her life is *The Book of Margery Kempe*. Kempe asked Julian whether there might be any deception in Kempe's own visions, "for the anchoress," she says, "was expert in such things." Kempe's description of Julian's conversation accords well with the doctrines and personality that emerge from Julian's own book.

A *Book of Showings* survives in a short and a long version. The longer text, from which the following excerpts are taken, was the product of fifteen and more years of meditation on the meaning of the visions in which much had been obscure to Julian. Apparently the mystical experiences were never repeated, but through constant study and contemplation the showings acquired a greater clarity, richness, and profundity as they continued to be turned over in a mind both gifted with spiritual insight and learned in theology. Her editors document her extensive use of the Bible and her familiarity with medieval religious writings in both English and Latin.

Julian's sixteen revelations are each treated in uneven numbers of Chapters; these groupings of chapters form an extended meditation on a given vision. Each vision is treated with an unpredictable combination of visual description of what Julian saw, the words she was offered, and the meanings she "saw." Her visions are, in her words, "ghostly" (that is, spiritual), "bodily," and subtle combinations of the two. They embrace powerful visual phenomena such as blood drops running from the crown of thorns and revelations that take place in pure mind. All are, nevertheless, "seen"; the spiritualized meanings do not render bodily sights redundant.

Of the selections here, Chapters 3 and 86 are from the opening and closing sequences of the work; Chapters 4, 5, and 7 are from the First Vision; Chapter 27 from the Thirteenth Vision; and Chapters 58, 59, 60, and 61 from the great Fourteenth Vision.

Julian's First Vision is rooted in, but moves beyond, the tradition of affective piety described in the headnote to this section on pages 413–14. The vision is provoked by Julian's own bodily approximation to the bodily pains of Christ, as she thinks she is dying. The crucifix offered for her comfort provokes a kinetic, fresh response, as it seems to move into life, bleeding and persuading Julian that the vision is God's unmediated gift to her. Julian moves well beyond this initial sight, however; she sees a sequence of created things: the Virgin Mary as the best creature that God made, and, lower down the scale, the entire world in her palm, "the quantity of an hazelnut." Such a vision might lead away from created things altogether into a realm of pure essence; significantly, it does not, precisely because Julian never leaves the sight of the wounded, bodily Christ, whose physical suffering is somehow simultaneous with these almost immaterial visions. Julian strains the tradition of affective piety to its limits, but ends by transforming rather than rejecting it.

The serene optimism Julian's visions express for the material, created world and for fallen creatures extends into the most daring and surprising realms of speculation. "Sin is behovely": these are (Julian's) Christ's own words. They are expressed in the Thirteenth Vision for the first time (Chapter 27), but only in the extended, daring meditation of the Fourteenth Vision (not included in the shorter version of

Reading and Vision. *The Hours of Mary of Burgundy,* ca. 1475. This extraordinary and utterly impossible view makes perfect sense as a vision of what the woman envisions from her reading.

The Book of Showings) are they given their deepest sense. At the heart of Julian's profoundly optimistic theology is a transformative understanding of Christ's humanity. She develops, without ever mentioning it explicitly, the idea of the *felix culpa*: the notion that, given its happy consequence in Christ's redemption of mankind, Adam's sin, or *culpa*, was somehow "happy" (*felix*). Christ is so much a part of us, by Julian's account, that he is "the ground of our kind [natural/kind] making" (Chapter 59). He is our mother, who strains and suffers as he gives birth to our salvation. Julian's concept of Jesus as mother has antecedents in both Old and New Testaments, in medieval theology, and in the writings of medieval mystics (both men and women), but nowhere else in Middle English writing is the concept so subtly and resonantly explored.

Julian was clearly aware of the dangers of expressing such high mysteries as a woman writer. She participates, it is true, in a late-medieval tradition of visionary writing, often by women, such as the *Dialogue* of Catherine of Siena (translated into Middle English as the *Orchard of Syon*) and the *Revelations* of St. Bridget of Sweden (also translated into Middle English). Julian, however, does not refer to these figures; instead, she negotiates the difficulties and dangers of writing as a woman with enormous tact and shrewdness, both disclaiming and creating exceptional authority. Part of her strategy is to write with calm lucidity; part is to claim that the vision is not particular to her alone. Precisely by virtue of a common humanity, the visions are common property: "We are all one, and I am sure I saw it for the profit of many other."

From A Book of Showings to the Anchoress
Julian of Norwich[1]

Chapter 3

[JULIAN'S BODILY SICKNESS AND THE WOUNDS OF CHRIST]

And when I was thirty year old and a half, God sent me a bodily sickness in the which I lay three days and three nights; and on the fourth night I took all my rites of holy church, and went[2] not to have liven till day. And after this I lay two days and two nights; and on the third night I weened[3] oftentimes to have passed,[4] and so weened they that were with me. And yet in this I felt a great loathsomeness[5] to die, but for nothing that was on earth that me liketh to live for, ne[6] for no pain that I was afraid of, for I trusted in God of his mercy. But it was for I would have lived to have loved God better and longer time, that I might by the grace of that living have the more knowing and loving of God in the bliss of heaven. For me thought[7] all that time that I had lived here so little and so short in regard of[8] that endless bliss, I thought: Good Lord, may my living no longer be to thy worship?[9] And I understood by my reason and by the feeling of my pains that I should die; and I assented fully with all the will of my heart to be at God's will.

Thus I endured till day, and by then was my body dead from the middes downward, as to my feeling.[1] Then was I holpen[2] to be set upright, underset[3] with help, for to have the more freedom of my heart to be at God's will, and thinking on God while my life lasted. My curate was sent for to be at my ending, and before he came I had set up my eyen[4] and might not speak. He set the cross before my face and said: "I have brought the image of thy savior; look thereupon and comfort thee therewith." Me thought I was well, for my eyen was set upright into heaven, where I trusted to come by the mercy of God; but nevertheless I assented to set my eyen in the face of the crucifix, if I might, and so I did, for me thought I might longer dure to look even forth than right up.[5] After this my sight began to fail. It waxed as dark about me in the chamber as if it had been night, save in the image of the cross, wherein held a common light; and I wist[6] not how. All that was beside the cross was ugly and fearful to me as[7] it had been much occupied with fiends.

After this the over[8] part of my body began to die so farforth that unneth[9] I had any feeling. My most pain was shortness of breath and failing of life. Then went[1] I verily to have passed. And in this suddenly all my pain was taken from me, and I was as whole, and namely in the over part of my body, as ever I was before. I marvelled of this sudden change, for me thought that it was a privy working of God, and not of kind;[2] and yet by feeling of this

---

1. The text is based on that given by Edmund Colledge, O.S.A., and James Walsh, S.J., for the Pontifical Institute of Mediaeval Studies, Toronto (1978), but it has been freely edited and modern spelling has been used where possible.
2. Thought.
3. Supposed.
4. Died.
5. Reluctance.
6. Nor.
7. I thought, [it] thought me.
8. In comparison with.

9. Glory.
1. As it felt to me.
2. Helped.
3. Supported.
4. Eyes.
5. Endure to look straight ahead than straight up.
6. Knew.
7. As if.
8. Upper.
9. To the extent that scarcely.
1. Thought.
2. Nature.

ease I trusted never more to have lived, ne the feeling of this ease was no full ease to me, for me thought I had liever[3] have been delivered of this world, for my heart was willfully set thereto.

Then came suddenly to my mind that I should desire the second wound of our Lord's gift and of his grace, that my body might be fulfilled with mind and feeling of his blessed passion, as I had before prayed,[4] for I would that his pains were my pains, with compassion and afterward longing to God. Thus thought me that I might with his grace have the wounds that I had before desired; but in this I desired never no bodily sight ne no manner showing of God, but compassion as me thought that a kind soul might have with our Lord Jesu, that for love would become a deadly[5] man. With him I desired to suffer, living in my deadly body, as God would give me grace.

Chapter 4

[CHRIST'S PASSION AND INCARNATION]

And in this suddenly I saw the red blood running down from under the garland, hot and freshly, plenteously and lively, right as it was in the time that the garland of thorns was pressed on his blessed head. Right so, both God and man, the same that suffered for me, I conceived truly and mightily that it was himself that shewed it me without any mean.[6]

And in the same showing suddenly the Trinity fulfilled my heart most of joy, and so I understood it shall be in heaven without end to all that shall come there. For the Trinity is God, God is the Trinity. The Trinity is our maker, the Trinity is our keeper, the Trinity is our everlasting lover, the Trinity is endless joy and our bliss, by our Lord Jesu Christ, and in our Lord Jesu Christ. And this was showed in the first sight and in all, for where Jesu appeareth, the blessed Trinity is understand, as to my sight.[7] And I said, "Benedicite dominum."[8] This I said for reverence in my meaning,[9] with a mighty voice, and full greatly was I astoned[1] for wonder and marvel that I had, that he that is so reverend and so dreadful[2] will be so homely[3] with a sinful creature living in this wretched flesh.

Thus I took it for that time that our Lord Jesu of his courteous love would show me comfort before the time of my temptation; for me thought it might well be that I should by the sufferance of God and with his keeping be tempted of[4] fiends before I should die. With this sight of his blessed passion, with the godhead that I saw in my understanding, I knew well that it was strength enough to me, yea, and to all creatures living that should be saved, against all the fiends of hell, and against all ghostly[5] enemies.

In this he brought our Lady Saint Mary to my understanding; I saw her ghostly in bodily likeness, a simple maiden and a meek, young of age, a little waxen above a child,[6] in the stature as she was when she conceived. Also God

---

3. Rather.
4. Julian had prayed for three gifts: direct experience of Christ's passion, mortal sickness, and the wounds of true contrition, loving compassion, and a willed desire for God.
5. Mortal.
6. Intermediary.
7. Is understood, as I see it.
8. Bless be the Lord (Latin).

9. Intention.
1. Astonished.
2. Awe-inspiring.
3. Familiar, intimate (the quality of being "at home").
4. By.
5. Spiritual.
6. Grown a little older than a child.

showed me in part the wisdom and the truth of her soul, wherein I understood the reverend beholding, that she beheld her God, that is her maker, marvelling with great reverence that he would be born of her that was a simple creature of his making. And this wisdom and truth, knowing the greatness of her maker and the littlehead[7] of herself that is made, made her to say full meekly to Gabriel: "Lo me here, God's handmaiden."[8] In this sight I did understand verily that she is more than all that God made beneath her in worthiness and in fullhead;[9] for above her is nothing that is made but the blessed manhood of Christ, as to my sight.

Chapter 5

[ALL CREATION AS A HAZELNUT]

In this same time that I saw this sight of the head bleeding, our good Lord showed a ghostly sight of his homely loving. I saw that he is to us all thing that is good and comfortable to our help. He is our clothing that for love wrappeth us and windeth us, halseth us[1] and all becloses us, hangeth about us for tender love that[2] he may never leave us. And so in this sight I saw that he is all thing that is good, as to my understanding.

And in this he showed a little thing, the quantity of an hazelnut, lying in the palm of my hand, as me seemed, and it was as round as a ball. I looked thereon with the eye of my understanding, and thought: What may this be? And it was answered generally thus: It is all that is made. I marvelled how it might last, for me thought it might suddenly have fallen to nought for[3] littleness. And I was answered in my understanding: It lasteth and ever shall, for God loveth it; and so hath all thing being by the love of God.

In this little thing I saw three properties. The first is that God made it, the second that God loveth it, the third that God keepeth[4] it. But what beheld I therein? Verily, the maker, the keeper, the lover. For till I am substantially united to him[5] I may never have full rest ne very[6] bliss; that is to say that I be so fastened to him that there be right nought that is made between my God and me.

This little thing that is made, me thought it might have fallen to nought for littleness. Of this needeth us to have knowledge, that us liketh nought all thing that is made, for to love and have God that is unmade.[7] For this is the cause why we be not all in ease of heart and of soul, for we seek here rest in this thing that is so little, where no rest is in, and we know not our God, that is almighty, all wise and all good, for he is very rest. God will be known, and him liketh that we rest us in him; for all that is beneath him suffiseth not to us. And this is the cause why that no soul is in rest till it is noughted of all things that is made.[8] When she is wilfully[9] noughted for love, to have him that is all, then is she able to receive ghostly rest.

---

7. Littleness.
8. See Luke 1.38.
9. Perfection.
1. Envelops us and embraces us.
2. So that.
3. Because of.
4. Looks after.
5. Joined to him in "substance," which Julian

regards as the eternal essence of being.
6. True.
7. I.e., we need to know that we should not be attracted to earthly things, which are made, to love and possess God, who is not made, who exists eternally.
8. Emptied of (its attachment to) all created things.
9. Of its free will.

And also our good Lord showed that it is full great pleasance to him that a sely[1] soul come to him naked, plainly and homely. For this is the kind[2] yearning of the soul by the touching of the Holy Ghost, as by the understanding that I have in this showing: God of thy goodness gave me thyself, for thou art enough to me, and I may ask nothing that is less that may be full worship to thee. And if I ask any thing that is less, ever me wanteth;[3] but only in thee I have all.

And these words of the goodness of God be full lovesome to the soul and full near touching the will of our Lord, for his goodness fulfilleth all his creatures and all his blessed works and overpasseth[4] without end. For he is the endlesshead and he made us only to himself and restored us by his precious passion,[5] and ever keepeth us in his blessed love; and all this is of his goodness.

*　*　*

Chapter 7

[CHRIST AS HOMELY AND COURTEOUS]

And in all that time that he showed this that I have now said in ghostly sight, I saw the bodily sight lasting of the plenteous bleeding of the head. The great drops of blood fell down fro under the garland like pellets, seeming as it had come out of the veins. And in the coming out they were brown red, for the blood was full thick; and in the spreading abroad they were bright red. And when it came at the brows, there they vanished; and not withstanding the bleeding continued till many things were seen and understanded. Nevertheless the fairhead and livelihead continued in the same beauty and liveliness.

The plenteoushead is like to the drops of water that fall of the evesing[6] of an house after a great shower of rain, that fall so thick that no man may number them with no bodily wit.[7] And for the roundness they were like to the scale of herring in the spreading of the forehead.

These three things came to my mind in the time: pellets for the roundhead[8] in the coming out of the blood, the scale of the herring for the roundhead in the spreading, the drops of the evesing of a house for the plenteoushead unnumerable. This showing was quick[9] and lively and hideous and dreadful and sweet and lovely; and of all the sight that I saw this was most comfort to me, that our good Lord, that is so reverend and dreadful, is so homely and so courteous, and this most fulfilled me with liking and sickerness[1] in soule.

And to the understanding of this he showed this open example. It is the most worship[2] that a solemn king or a great lord may do to a poor servant if he will be homely with him; and namely if he show it himself of a full true meaning[3] and with a glad cheer both in private and openly. Then thinketh this poor creature thus: "Lo, what might this noble lord do more worship and joy to me than to show to me that am so little this marvelous homeliness? Verily, it is more joy and liking to me than if he gave me great gifts and

1. Innocent.
2. Natural.
3. I am forever lacking.
4. Surpasses.
5. Suffering.
6. Eaves.

7. Intelligence.
8. Roundness.
9. Vivid.
1. Security.
2. Honor.
3. Intent.

were himself strange in manner." This bodily example was showed so high that this man's heart might be ravished and almost forget himself for joy of this great homeliness.

Thus it fareth by our Lord Jesu and by us, for verily it is the most joy that may be, as to my sight, that he that is highest and mightiest, noblest and worthiest, is lowest and meekest, homeliest and courteousest. And truly and verily this marvelous joy shall he show us all when we shall see him. And this will our good Lord that we believe and trust, joy and like, comfort us and make solace as we may with his grace and with his help, into[4] the time that we see it verily. For the most fullhead of joy that we shall have, as to my sight, is this marvelous courtesy and homeliness of our fader, that is our maker, in our Lord Jesu Christ, that is our brother and oure saviour. But this marvelous homeliness may no man know in this life, but if he have it by special showing of our Lord, or of great plenty of grace inwardly given of the Holy Ghost. But faith and belief with charity deserve the meed,[5] and so it is had by grace. For in faith with hope and charity our life is grounded. The showing is made to whom that God will, plainly teacheth the same opened and declared, with many privy points belonging to our faith and belief which be worshipful to be known. And when the showing which is given for a time is passed and hid, then faith keepeth it by grace of the Holy Ghost into our life's end. And thus by the showing it is none other than the faith, ne less ne more, as it may be seen by our Lord's meaning in the same matter, by then[6] it come to the last end.

Chapter 27

[SIN IS FITTING]

And after this our Lord brought to my mind the longing that I had to him before; and I saw nothing letted[7] me but sin, and so I beheld generally in us all, and me thought that if sin had not been, we should all have been clean[8] and like to our Lord as he made us. And thus in my folly before this time often I wondered why, by the great foreseeing wisdom of God, the beginning of sin was not letted.[9] For then thought me that all should have been well.

This stering[1] was much to be forsaken; and nevertheless mourning and sorrow I made therefore without reason and discretion. But Jesu that in this vision informed me of all that me needed answered by this word and said: "Sin is behovely[2] but all shall be well, and all manner of thing shall be well."[3] In this naked word "Sin," our Lord brought to my mind generally all that is not good, and the shameful despite[4] and the uttermost tribulation that he bore for us in this life, and his dying and all his pains, and passion[5] of all his creatures ghostly and bodily. For we be all in part troubled, and we shall be troubled, following our master Jesu, till we be fully purged of our deadly[6] flesh which be not very good.

4. Until.
5. Reward. "Charity": love. See 1 Corinthians 13.13.
6. By the time that.
7. Hindered.
8. Pure.
9. Prevented.
1. Fretting.

2. Fitting.
3. T. S. Eliot quotes this statement, versions of which appear several times in the *Showings*, in the last movement of his *Four Quartets*.
4. Spite.
5. Suffering.
6. Mortal.

And with the beholding of this, with all the pains that ever were or ever shall be, I understood the passion of Christ for the most pain and overpassing.[7] And with all, this was showed in a touch, readily passed over into comfort. For our good Lord would not that the soul were afeared of this ugly sight. But I saw not sin, for I believe it had no manner of substance, ne no part of being,[8] ne it might not be known but by the pain that is caused thereof. And this pain is something, as to my sight, for a time, for it purgeth and maketh us to know ourself and ask mercy; for the passion of our Lord is comfort to us against all this, and so is his blessed will. And for the tender love that our good Lord hath to all that shall be saved, he comforteth readily and sweetly, meaning thus: It is true that sin is cause of all this pain, but all shall be well, and all manner of thing shall be well.

These words were showed full tenderly, showing no manner of blame to me ne to none that shall be safe.[9] Then were it great unkindness of me to blame or wonder on God of my sin, sithen[1] he blameth not me for sin. And in these same words I saw an high marvelous privity[2] hid in God, which privity he shall openly make and shall be known to us in heaven. In which knowing we shall verily see the cause why he suffered sin to come, in which sight we shall endlessly have joy.

Chapters 58, 59, 60, 61

[JESUS AS MOTHER]

From Chapter 58

God the blessedful Trinity, which is everlasting being, right as he is endless fro without beginning,[3] right so it was in his purpose endless to make mankind,[4] which fair kind[5] first was dight to[6] for his own son, the second person; and when he would,[7] by full accord of all the Trinity he made us all at once.[8] And in our making he knit us and oned[9] us to himself, by which oneing we be kept as clean[1] and as noble as we were made. By the virtue of that ilke[2] precious oneing we love our maker and like[3] him, praise and thank him, and endlessly enjoy[4] in him. And this is the working which is wrought continually in each soul that shall be saved, which is the godly will before said.

And thus in our making God almighty is our kindly[5] father, and god all wisdom is our kindly mother, with the love and the goodness of the Holy Ghost, which is all one God, one Lord. And in the knitting and in the oneing he is our very true spouse and we his loved wife[6] and his fair maiden, with which wife he was never displeased. For he sayeth: "I love thee and thou lovest me, and our love shall never part in two."

7. Exceeding (pain).
8. On "substance" and "being," see chapter 5, p. 434, n. 5.
9. Saved.
1. Since.
2. Secret.
3. I.e., eternal.
4. I.e., his purpose to make humankind is also eternal.
5. Nature.
6. Prepared for.
7. Wanted to.

8. All of us at one and the same time.
9. United. Julian sustains the idea of oneness in the verb *oned* and the noun *oneing*.
1. Pure.
2. Same.
3. Please.
4. Rejoice.
5. Both "kind" and "natural."
6. The relationship between God and humanity is also conceived as a mystical marriage in which Christ is the bridegroom and the human soul his spouse.

I beheld the working of all the blessed Trinity, in which beholding I saw and understood these three properties: The property of the fatherhood, and the property of the motherhood, and the property of the lordship in one God. In our father almighty we have our keeping[7] and our bliss as anemptis[8] our kindly substance which is to us by our making fro without beginning.[9] And in the second person in wit[1] and wisdom we have our keeping as anemptis our sensuality[2] our restoring and our saving, for he is our mother, brother and savior. And in our good lord the Holy Ghost we have our rewarding and our yielding[3] for our living and our travail,[4] and endlessly overpassing[5] all that we desire in his marvelous courtesy of his high plenteous grace. For all our life is in three: in the first we have our being, and in the second we have our increasing, and in the third we have our fulfilling. The first is kind,[6] the second is mercy, the third is grace.

For the first[7] I saw and understood that the high might of the Trinity is our father, and the deep wisdom of the Trinity is our mother, and the great love of the Trinity is our lord; and all these have we in kind and in our substantial making. And furthermore I saw that the second person, which is our mother, substantially the same dearworthy person,[8] is now become our mother sensual,[9] for we be double of God's making, that is to say substantial and sensual. Our substance is the higher part, which we have in our father God almighty; and the second person of the Trinity is our mother in kind in our substantial making, in whom we be grounded and rooted, and he is our mother of mercy in our sensual taking.[1]

* * *

From *Chapter 59*

* * *

And thus is Jesu our very[2] mother in kind of our first making, and he is our very mother in grace by taking of our kind made. All the fair working and all the sweet kindly offices of dearworthy motherhood is impropered to[3] the second person, for in him we have this goodly will, whole and safe without end, both in kind and in grace, of his own proper goodness.

I understood three manner of beholdings of motherhood in God. The first is ground of our kind making, the second is taking of our kind, and there beginneth the motherhood of grace, the third is motherhood in working.[4] And therein is a forthspreading[5] by the same grace of length and breadth, of high and of deepness without end. And all is one love.

Chapter 60

But now me behooveth to say a little more of this forthspreading, as I understood, in the meaning of our Lord: how that we be brought again by the motherhood of mercy and grace into our kindly stead, where that we were in,[6] made by the motherhood of kind love, which kind love never leaveth us.

Our kind mother, our gracious mother (for he would[7] all wholly become our mother in all thing) he took the ground of his work full low[8] and full mildly in the maiden's womb. And that showed he first, where he brought that meek maiden before the eye of my understanding, in the simple stature as she was when she conceived;[9] that is to say our high god, the sovereign wisdom of all, in this low place he arrayed him and dight him[1] all ready in our poor flesh, himself to do the service, he and the office of motherhood in all thing. The mother's service is nearest, readiest, and surest: nearest for it is most of kind, readiest for it is most of love, and sikerest[2] for it is most of truth. This office ne might nor could never none doon to the full but he alone. We wit[3] that all our mothers bear us to pain and to dying. Ah, what is that? But our very Mother Jesu, he alone beareth us to joy and to endless living, blessed moot[4] he be. Thus he sustaineth us within him in love and travail, into the full time that he would suffer the sharpest thorns and grievous pains that ever were or ever shall be, and died at the last. And when he had done, and so borne us to bliss, yet might not all this make aseeth[5] to his marvelous love. And that showed he in these high overpassing words of love: "If I might suffer more I would suffer more."[6] He might no more die, but he would not stint[7] working.

Wherefore him behooveth to find[8] us, for the dearworthy love of motherhood hath made him debtor to us.[9] The mother may give her child sucken her milk, but our precious mother Jesu, he may feed us with himself, and doth full courteously and full tenderly with the blessed sacrament, that is precious food of very life; and with all the sweet sacraments he sustaineth us full mercifully and graciously, and so meant he in these blessed words, where he said: "I it am that holy church preacheth thee and teacheth thee." That is to say: All the health and the life of sacraments, all the virtue and the grace of my word, all the goodness that is ordained in holy church to thee, I it am.

The mother may lay her child tenderly to her breast, but our tender mother Jesu, he may homely lead us into his blessed breast by his sweet open side,[1] and show us therein in party of[2] the godhead and the joys of heaven with ghostly sureness of endless bliss. And that showed he in the tenth revelation, giving the same understanding in this sweet word where he sayeth: "Lo, how I love thee." * * *

This fair lovely word "Mother," it is so sweet and so kind in itself that it may not verily be said of none ne to none but of him and to him[3] that is very mother of life and of all. To the property of motherhood longeth[4] kind love, wisdom, and knowing, and it is God. For though it be so that our bodily forthbringing be but little, low, and simple in regard[5] of our ghostly forth-

---

6. The natural condition, i.e., the state of grace, that we were in originally.
7. Because he wanted to.
8. I.e., he laid the groundwork for his mission in a very humble place.
9. The appearance of the Virgin in Julian's first vision. See chapter 4, p. 433.
1. Arrayed and dressed himself.
2. Surest.
3. Know.
4. May.
5. Bring satisfaction.
6. I.e., If I could suffer more, I would [wish to]

suffer more. These and other quotations refer to Julian's earlier revelations.
7. Stop.
8. Nourish, feed.
9. As any mother is obligated to look after her child.
1. The wound inflicted by a soldier in John 19.34.
2. A part of.
3. Other manuscripts read "her," with reference to the Virgin.
4. Belongs.
5. In comparison with.

bringing, yet it is he that doth it in the creatures by whom that it is done. The kind loving mother that woot and knoweth the need of her child, she keepeth it full tenderly as the kind and condition of motherhood will. And ever as it waxeth[6] in age and in stature, she changeth her works but not her love. And when it is waxed of more age, she suffereth it that it be chastised in breaking down of vices to make the child receive virtues and grace. This working with all that be fair and good, our Lord doth it in hem by whom it is done. Thus he is our mother in kind by the working of grace in the lower party for love of the higher. And he will[7] that we know it, for he will have all our love fastened to him; and in this I saw that all debt that we owe by God's bidding to fatherhood and motherhood is fulfilled in true loving of God, which blessed love Christ worketh in us. And this was showed in all, and namely in the words where he sayeth: "I it am that thou lovest."

Chapter 61

And in our ghostly forthbringing he useth more tenderness in keeping without any comparison, by as much as our soul is of more price in his sight. He kindleth our understanding, he prepareth our ways, he easeth our conscience, he comforteth our soul, he lighteth our heart and giveth us in party knowing and loving in his blessedful godhead, with gracious mind in his sweet manhood and his blessed passion, with courteous marveling in his high overpassing goodness, and maketh us to love all that he loveth for his love, and to be well apaid[8] with him and with all his works. And when we fall, hastily he raiseth us by his lovely becleping[9] and his gracious touching. And when we be strengthened by his sweet working, then we wilfully[1] choose him by his grace to be his servants and his lovers, lastingly without end.

And yet after this he suffereth some of us to fall more hard and more grievously than ever we did before, as us thinketh. And then ween[2] we (that be not all wise) that all were nought that we have begun. But it is not so, for it needeth us to fall, and it needeth us to see it; for if we fell not, we should not know how feeble and how wretched we be of ourself, nor also we should not so fulsomely[3] know the marvelous love of our maker.

For we shall verily see in heaven without end that we have grievously sinned in this life; and notwithstanding this we shall verily see that we were never hurt in his love, nor we were never the less of price in his sight. And by the assay of this falling we shall have an high and a marvelous knowing of love in God without an end. For hard and marvelous is that love which may not nor will not be broken for[4] trespass.

And this was one understanding of profit; and other[5] is the lowness and meekness that we shall get by the sight of our falling, for thereby we shall highly be raised in heaven, to which rising we might never have come without that meekness. And therefore it needed us to see it; and if we see it not, though we fell it should not profit us. And commonly first we fall and sithen[6] we see it; and both is of the mercy of God.

---

6. Grows.
7. Wants.
8. Pleased.
9. Calling (to us).
1. Gladly.

2. Suppose.
3. Fully.
4. Because of.
5. Another.
6. Then.

The mother may suffer the child to fall sometime and be diseased[7] in diverse manner, for its own profit, but she may never suffer that any manner of peril come to her child for love. And though our earthly mother may suffer her child to perish, our heavenly mother Jesu may never suffer us that be his children to perish, for he is all mighty, all wisdom, and all love, and so is none but he, blessed mote he be.

But oft times when our falling and our wretchedness is showed to us, we be so sore adread and so greatly ashamed of ourself that unnethes[8] we wit where that we may hold us. But then will not our courteous mother that we flee away, for him were nothing loather;[9] for then he will that we use[1] the condition of a child. For when it is diseased and afeared, it runneth hastily to the mother; and if it may do no more, it crieth on the mother for help with all the might. So will he that we do as the meek child, saying thus: "My kind mother, my gracious mother, my dearworthy mother, have mercy on me. I have made myself foul and unlike to thee, and I may not nor can amend it but with thine help and grace."

And if we feel us not then eased, as soon be we sure that he useth[2] the condition of a wise mother. For if he see that it be for profit to us to mourn and to weep, he suffereth with ruth[3] and pity, into the best time,[4] for love. And he will then that we use the property of a child that ever more kindly trusteth to the love of the mother in weal and in woe. And he will that we take us mightily to the faith of holy church and find there our dearworthy mother in solace and true understanding with all the blessed common.[5] For one singular person may oftentimes be broken, as it seemeth to the self, but the whole body of holy church was never broken, nor never shall be without end. And therefore a sure thing it is, a good and a gracious, to willen meekly and mightily been fastened and oned to our mother holy church, that is Christ Jesu. For the flood of his mercy that is his dearworthy blood and precious water is plenteous to make us fair and clean. The blessed wounds of our savior be open and enjoy[6] to heal us. The sweet gracious hands of our mother be ready and diligent about us; for he in all this working useth the very office of a kind nurse that hath not else to do but to entend[7] the salvation of her child.

It is his office to save us, it is his worship to do it, and it is his will we know it; for he will we love him sweetly and trust in him meekly and mightily. And this showed he in these gracious words: "I keep thee full surely."

Chapter 86

[CHRIST'S MEANING]

This book is begun by God's gift and his grace, but it is not yet performed,[8] as to my sight. For charity, pray we all together with God's working, thanking, trusting, enjoying, for thus will our good Lord be prayed, but the understanding that I took in all his own meaning, and in the sweet words where he sayeth full merrily: "I am ground of thy beseeching." For truly I saw and understood in our Lord's meaning that he showed it for he will have it known

7. Unhappy.
8. Scarcely.
9. Nothing would be more hateful to him.
1. He wants us to experience.
2. Right away we are sure he is practicing.
3. Compassion.

4. Until the right time.
5. Community.
6. Rejoice.
7. Be busy about.
8. Completed.

more than it is. In which knowing he will give us grace to love him and cleave to him, for he beheld his heavenly treasure with so great love on earth that he will give us more light, and solace in heavenly joy, in drawing of our hearts fro sorrow and darkness which we are in.

And fro the time that it was showed, I desired oftentimes to wit[9] in what was our Lord's meaning. And fifteen year after and more, I was answered in ghostly understanding, saying thus: "What, wouldst thou wit thy Lord's meaning in this thing? Wit it well, love was his meaning. Who showeth it thee? Love. What showed he thee? Love. Wherefore showeth he it thee? For love. Hold thee therein, thou shalt wit more in the same. But thou shalt never wit therein other withouten end."

Thus was I learned,[1] that love is our Lord's meaning. And I saw full surely in this and in all, that ere God made us he loved us, which love was never slaked[2] ne never shall. And in this love he hath done all his works, and in this love he hath made all things profitable to us, and in this love our life is everlasting. In our making we had beginning, but the love wherein he made us was in him fro without beginning. In which love we have our beginning, and all this shall we see in God withouten end.

Deo gracias. Explicit liber revelacionum Julyane anacorite Norwyche, cuius anime propicietur deus.[3]

ca. 1390

---

9. Know.
1. Taught.
2. Abated.

3. Thanks be to God. Here ends the book of revelations of Julian, anchorite of Norwich, on whose soul may God have mercy (Latin).

MARGERY KEMPE
ca. 1373–1438

The Book of Margery Kempe is the spiritual autobiography of a medieval laywoman, telling of her struggles to carry out instructions for a holy life that she claimed to have received in personal visions from Christ and the Virgin Mary. The assertion of such a mission by a married woman, the mother of fourteen children, was in itself sufficient grounds for controversy; in addition, Kempe's outspoken defense of her visions as well as her highly emotional style of religious expression embroiled her with fellow citizens and pilgrims and with the Church, although she also won both lay and clerical supporters. Ordered by the archbishop of York to swear not to teach in his diocese, she courageously stood up for her freedom to speak her conscience.

Margery Kempe was the daughter of John Burnham, five-time mayor of King's Lynn, a thriving commercial town in Norfolk. At about the age of twenty she married John Kempe, a well-to-do fellow townsman. After the traumatic delivery of her first child—the rate of maternal mortality in childbirth was high—she sought to confess to a priest whose harsh, censorious response precipitated a mental breakdown, from which she eventually recovered through the first of her visions. Her subsequent conversion and strict religious observances generated a good deal of domestic strife, but she continued to share her husband's bed until, around the age of forty, she negotiated a vow of celibacy with him, which was confirmed before the bishop and left her free to undertake a pilgrimage to the Holy Land. There she experienced visions of Christ's passion and of the sufferings of the Virgin. These visions recurred during the rest of her life, and her noisy weeping at such times made her the object of much scorn and hostility. Her orthodoxy was several times examined, but her unquestioning acceptance of the Church's doctrines and authority, and perhaps also her status as a former mayor's daughter, shielded her against charges of heresy.

Kempe was unable to read or write, but acquired her command of Scripture and theology from sermons and other oral sources. Late in her life, she dictated her story in two parts to two different scribes; the latter of these was a priest who revised the whole text. Nevertheless, it seems likely that the work retains much of the characteristic form and expression of its author.

Kempe's text offers a perspective on the tradition of "affective piety" unlike any other: here that visionary tradition comes to life in the context of vividly realized, often painful psychological and bodily experience. Kempe's own marriage, and her often troubled worldly relations, inform and are informed by her "homely" and sometimes erotic spiritual relations. Her imitation of Christ moves her to travel vast distances to be present at the scenes of Christ's suffering, just as she sees Christ present in male babies or good-looking young men. She sees the living divine presence in the Eucharistic host. "Sir," she says to a skeptic, "His death is as fresh to me as He had died this same day." This form of intensely sympathetic vision has, however, its negative obverse. As in Chaucer's *Prioress's Tale*, where tender feeling for the Blessed Virgin is complemented by hatred for the "cursed Jewes," Christian pathos produces an anti-Semitic reflex (Book 1.79).

From The Book of Margery Kempe[1]

[THE BIRTH OF HER FIRST CHILD AND HER FIRST VISION]

[**Book 1.1**] When this creature[2] was twenty years of age or somewhat more, she was married to a worshipful[3] burgess and was with child within a short time, as nature would. And, after she had conceived, she was labored with great attacks of illness until the child was born, and then, what for the labor she had in childing and for the sickness going before, she despaired of her life, thinking she might not live. And then she sent for her ghostly father,[4] for she had a thing in conscience which she had never shown before that time in all her life. For she was ever hindered by her enemy, the devil, evermore saying to her that, while she was in good health, she needed no confession but could do penance by herself alone, and all should be forgiven, for God is merciful enough. And therefore this creature oftentimes did great penance in fasting on bread and water and other deeds of alms with devout prayers, except she would not show this sin in confession. And, when she was at any time sick or troubled, the devil said in her mind that she should be damned, for she was not shriven[5] of that sin. Wherefore, after her child was born, she, not trusting her life, sent for her ghostly father, as was said before, in full will to be shrive of all her lifetime as nearly as she could. And,

---

1. The text is based on the unique manuscript, first discovered in 1934, edited by Lynn Staley. Spelling and inflexional forms have in many cases been modernized. Some archaic words have also been silently translated.
2. Throughout the book Kempe refers to herself in the third person as "this creature," a standard way of saying "this person, a being created by God."
3. Worthy.
4. Spiritual father; i.e., a priest.
5. Confessed and then absolved.

when she came to the point to say that thing which she had so long concealed, her confessor was a little too hasty and began sharply to reprove her before she had fully said her intent, and so she would no more say for aught he might do.

And anon, for the dread she had of damnation on the one side and his sharp reproving on that other side, this creature went out of her mind and was wonderfully vexed and labored with spirits for half a year, eight weeks and some odd days. And in this time she saw, as she thought, devils open their mouths, all inflamed with burning flames of fire as if they should have swallowed her in, sometimes menacing her, sometimes threatening her, sometimes pulling her and hailing her both night and day during the foresaid time. And also the devils cried upon her with great threats and bade her that she should forsake her Christianity, her faith, and deny her God, his mother, and all the saints in heaven, her good works and all good virtues, her father, her mother, and all her friends. And so she did. She slandered her husband, her friends and her own self; she spoke many a reproving word and many a harsh word; she knew no virtue nor goodness; she desired all wickedness; just as the spirits tempted her to say and do, so she said and did. She would have killed herself many a time because of her stirrings and have been damned with them in hell. And as a witness thereof she bit her own hand so violently that it was seen all her life afterward. And also she tore the skin on her body against her heart grievously with her nails, for she had no other instruments, and worse she would have done, save she was bound and kept with strength both day and night so that she might not have her will.

And, when she had long been labored in these and many other temptations, so that men thought she should never have escaped nor lived, then on a time, as she lay alone and her keepers were away from her, our merciful Lord Christ Jesus, ever to be trusted, worshiped be his name, never forsaking his servant in time of need, appeared to his creature, who had forsaken him, in likeness of a man, most seemly, most beautiful, and most amiable that ever might be seen with man's eye, clad in a mantle of purple silk, siting upon her bedside, looking upon her with so blessed a countenance that she was strengthened in all her spirits, said to her these words: "Daughter, why have you forsaken me, and I forsook never you?"

And anon, as soon as he had said these words, she saw verily how the air opened as bright as any lightning, and he rose up into the air, not right hastily and quickly, but fairly and easily so that she might well behold him in the air until it was closed again. And anon the creature was stabled in her wits and in her reason as well as ever she was before, and prayed her husband, as soon as he came to her, that she might have the keys of the buttery[6] in order to take her meat and drink as she had done before.

* * *

[MARGERY AND HER HUSBAND REACH A SETTLEMENT]

* * *

[Book 1.11] It befell upon a Friday on Midsummer Eve in right hot weather, as this creature was coming from York bearing a bottle with beer in her hand and

---

6. Pantry.

her husband a loaf in his bosom, he asked his wife this question, "Margery, if there came a man with a sword and would smite off my head unless I should common naturally with you as I have done before, tell me the truth from your conscience—for you say you will not lie—whether would you suffer my head to be smote off or else suffer me to meddle with you again, as I did at one time?"

"Alas, sir," she said, "why move you this matter, and have we been chaste these eight weeks?"

"For I will know the truth of your heart."

And then she said with great sorrow, "Forsooth I had rather see you be slain than we should turn again to our uncleanness."

And he said in reply, "You are no good wife."

And then she asked her husband what was the cause that he had not meddled with her eight weeks before, since she lay with him every night in his bed. And he said he was so made afraid when he would have touched her that he dared do no more.

"Now, good sir, amend yourself and ask God mercy, for I told you nearly three years since that you should be slain suddenly, and now is this the third year, and yet I hope I shall have my desire. Good sir, I pray you grant me what I shall ask, and I shall pray for you that you shall be saved through the mercy of our Lord Jesus Christ, and you shall have more reward in heaven than if you wore a hair cloth or a jacket of mail. I pray you, suffer me to make a vow of chastity in whatever bishop's hand that God will."

"No," he said, "that will I not grant you, for now may I use you without deadly sin and then might I not so."

Then she said again, "If it be the will of the Holy Ghost to fulfill what I have said, I pray God you may consent thereto; and, if it be not the will of the Holy Ghost, I pray God you never consent thereto."

Then went they forth toward Bridlington in right hot weather, the aforesaid creature having great sorrow and great dread for her chastity. And, as they came by a cross, her husband set himself down under the cross, calling his wife unto him and saying these words unto her, "Margery, grant me my desire, and I shall grant you your desire. My first desire is that we shall lie still together in one bed as we have done before; the second, that you shall pay my debts before you go to Jerusalem; and the third, that you shall eat and drink with me on Fridays as you were wont to do."[7]

"No, sir," she said, "to break the Friday I will never grant you while I live."

"Well," he said, "then shall I meddle you again."

She prayed him that he would give her leave to make her prayers, and he granted it well. Then she kneeled down beside a cross in the field and prayed in this manner with great abundance of tears, "Lord God, you know all things; you know what sorrow I have had to be chaste in my body to you all these three years, and now might I have my wish, and I dare not for love of you. For, if I would break that manner of fasting which you commanded me, to keep the Friday without food or drink, I should now have my desire. But, blessed Lord, you know I will not go against your will, and great now is my sorrow unless I find comfort in you. Now, blessed Jesus, make your will known to me, unworthy, so that I may follow thereafter and fulfill it with all my might."

---

7. Christ had told her that keeping a strict Friday fast would allow her to have her wish to end further sexual relations with her husband.

And then our Lord Jesus Christ with great sweetness spoke to this creature, commanding her to go again to her husband and pray him to grant her what she desired. "And he shall have what he desires. For, my worthy daughter, this was the cause that I bade you to fast, for you should the sooner obtain and get your desire, and now it is granted you. I wish no longer for you to fast, therefore I bid you in the name of Jesus eat and drink as your husband does."

Then this creature thanked our Lord Jesus Christ for his grace and his goodness, then rose up and went to her husband, saying unto him, "Sir, if it pleases you, you shall grant me my desire, and you shall have your desire. Grant me that you shall not come in my bed, and I grant you to requite your debts before I go to Jerusalem. And make my body free to God so that you never challenge me by asking the debt of matrimony after this day while you live, and I shall eat and drink on the Friday at your bidding."

Then said her husband again to her, "As free may your body be to God as it has been to me."

This creature thanked God greatly, rejoicing that she had her desire, praying her husband that they should say three Our Father's in the worship of the Trinity for the great grace that he had granted them. And so they did, kneeling under a cross, and afterward they ate and drank together in great gladness of spirit. This was on a Friday on Midsummer Eve.

* * *

[MARGERY SEES THE HOST[8] FLUTTER AT MASS]

* * *

[Book 1.20] One day as this creature was hearing her Mass, a young man and a good priest holding up the sacrament[9] in his hands over his head, the sacrament shook and flickered to and fro as a dove flickers with her wings. And, when he held up the chalice with the precious sacrament, the chalice moved to and fro as though it should have fallen out of his hands. When the consecration was done, this creature had great marvel about the stirring and moving of the blessed sacrament, desiring to see more consecrations, looking if it would do so again. Then said our Lord Jesus Christ to the creature, "You shall no more see it in this manner, therefore thank God that you have seen. My daughter, Bridget[1] saw me never in this manner."

Then said this creature in her thought, "Lord, what does this betoken?"

"It betokens vengeance."

"A, good Lord, what vengeance?"

Then said our Lord in reply to her, "There shall be an earthquake; tell it to whom you wish in the name of Jesus. For I tell you forsooth, right as I spoke to Saint Bridget, right so I speak to you, daughter, and I tell you truly it is true, every word that is written in Bridget's book, and by you it shall be known for very truth. And you shall fare well, daughter, in spite of all your enemies. The more envy they have for you because of my grace, the better shall I love you. I were not a rightful God unless I proved you, for I know

---

8. I.e., the Eucharistic wafer consumed in the sacrament of Communion.
9. A metonymy for the Eucharistic wafer, strictly one of the seven sacraments.

1. Saint Bridget of Sweden (ca. 1303–1373), to whose *Revelations* Margery refers in Book 1.17 and 1.58.

you better than you know yourself, whatever men say of you. You say I have great patience for the sin of the people, and you say the truth, but, if you saw the sin of the people as I do, you would have much more marvel in my patience and much more sorrow in the sin of the people than you have."

Then the creature said, "Alas, worthy Lord, what shall I do for the people?"

Our Lord answered, "It is enough for you to do as you do."

Then she prayed, "Merciful Lord Christ Jesus, in you is all mercy and grace and goodness. Have mercy, pity, and compassion for them. Show your mercy and your goodness upon them. Help them; send them very contrition, and let them never die in their sin."

Our merciful Lord said, "I may no more, daughter, for my rightfulness, do for them than I do. I send them preaching and teaching, pestilence and battles, hunger and famine, loss of their goods with great sickness, and many other tribulations, and they will not believe my words, nor will they know my visitation. And therefore I shall say to them that I made my servants to pray for you, and you despised their works and their living."

* * *

[PILGRIMAGE TO JERUSALEM]

* * *

[**Book 1.28**] And so they[2] went forth into the Holy Land till they might see Jerusalem. And, when this creature saw Jerusalem, riding on an ass, she thanked God with all her heart, praying him for his mercy that, as he had brought her to see this earthly city Jerusalem, he would grant her grace to see the blissful city Jerusalem above, the city of heaven. Our Lord Jesus Christ, answering to her thought, granted her to have her desire. Then, for joy that she had and the sweetness that she felt in the dalliance of our Lord, she was in point to have fallen off her ass, for she might not bear the sweetness and grace that God wrought in her soul. Then two German pilgrims went to her and kept her from falling, of which one was a priest. And he put spices in her mouth to comfort her, thinking she had been sick. And so they helped her forth to Jerusalem.

And, when she came there, she said, "Sirs, I pray you be not displeased though I weep sorely in this holy place where our Lord Jesus Christ was quick[3] and dead."

Then went they to the Temple[4] in Jerusalem, and they were let in on the one day at evensong time and abided therein till the next day at evensong time.

Then the friars lifted up a cross and led the pilgrims about from one place to another where our Lord had suffered his pains and his passions, every man and woman bearing a wax candle in their hand. And the friars always, as they went about, told them what our Lord suffered in every place. And the foresaid creature wept and sobbed so plenteously as though she had seen our Lord with her bodily eye suffering his Passion at that time. Before her in her soul she saw him verily by contemplation, and that caused her to have compassion. And when they came up onto the Mount of Calvary, she fell down so that she might not stand or kneel but wallowed and twisted with her body,

---

2. The company of pilgrims.
3. Living.

4. The Church of the Holy Sepulcher, site of Christ's crucifixion, death, and burial.

spreading her arms abroad, and cried with a loud voice as though her heart should have burst asunder, for in the city of her soul she saw verily and freshly how our Lord was crucified. Before her face she heard and saw in her ghostly sight the mourning of our Lady, of Saint John and Mary Magdalene,[5] and of many others who loved our Lord. And she had so great compassion and so great pain to see our Lord's pain that she might not keep herself from crying and roaring though she should have died from it.

And this was the first cry that ever she cried in any contemplation. And this manner of crying endured many years after this time for aught that any man might do, and therefore suffered she much despite and much reproof. The crying was so loud and so wonderful that it made the people astonished unless they had heard it before or else they knew the cause of the crying. And she had them so often that they made her right[6] weak in her bodily mights, and, namely, if she heard of our Lord's Passion. And sometimes, when she saw the crucifix, or if she saw a man or a beast, whether[7] it were, had a wound or if a man beat a child before her or smote a horse or another beast with a whip, if she might see it or hear it, she thought she saw our Lord being beaten or wounded just as she saw in the man or in the beast, as well in the field as in the town, and by herself alone, as well as among the people.

First when she had her cryings at Jerusalem, she had them often times, and in Rome also. And, when she came home into England, first at her coming home it came but seldom, as it were once in a month, afterward once in the week, afterward daily, and once she had fourteen on one day, and another day she had seven, and so as God would visit her, sometime in the church, sometime in the street, sometime in the chamber, sometime in the field when God would send them, for she knew never time nor hour when they should come. And they came never without passing great sweetness of devotion and high contemplation.

And, as soon as she perceived that she should cry, she would keep it in as much as she might, so that the people should not have heard it, for it annoyed them. For some said it was a wicked spirit vexed her; some said it was a sickness; some said she had drunk too much wine; some banned her; some wished she had been in the harbor; some would she had been in the sea in a bottomless boat; and so each man as he thought. Other ghostly men loved her and favored her the more. Some great clerks said our Lady cried never so, nor no saint in heaven, but they knew full little what she felt, nor would they not believe that she might have abstained from crying if she wished.

※ ※ ※

[MARGERY'S MARRIAGE TO AND INTIMACY WITH CHRIST]

※ ※ ※

[Book 1.35] As this creature was in the Apostle's Church at Rome on St. John Lateran's Day,[8] the Father of Heaven said to her, "Daughter, I am well pleased with you, inasmuch as you believe in all the sacraments of Holy Church and in all faith that pertains to it, and specially because you believe in the man-

---

5. Mary, St. John, and Mary Magdalene are traditionally portrayed at the foot of the Cross in medieval art. See John 19.25.

6. Especially.
7. Whichever.
8. Saint John Lateran's Day, November 9.

hood of my son and because of the great compassion that you have for his bitter Passion."

Also the Father said to this creature, "Daughter, I will have you wedded to my Godhead, for I shall show you my secrets and my counsels,[9] for you shall dwell with me without end."

Then the creature kept silence in her soul and answered not thereto, for she was full sore afraid of the Godhead, and she had no knowledge of the dalliance of the Godhead, for all her love and all her affection was set on the manhood of Christ and thereof had she good knowledge, and she would for no thing have parted therefrom. She was so much affected by the manhood of Christ that when she saw women in Rome bearing children in their arms, if she might learn that there were any men children, she should then cry, roar, and weep as though she had seen Christ in his childhood. And, if she might have had her will, oftentimes she would have taken the children out from the mother's arms and have kissed them in the place of Christ. And, if she saw a handsome man, she had great pain to look on him in case she might have seen him who was both God and man. And therefore she cried many times and often when she met a seemly man and wept and sobbed full sorely in the manhood of Christ as she went in the streets at Rome, so that those who saw her wondered full much on her, for they knew not the cause.

And therefore it was no wonder if she were silent and answered not the Father of Heaven when he told her that she should be wedded to his Godhead. Then said the second person, Christ Jesus, whose manhood she loved so much, to her, "What say you, Margery, daughter, to my Father of these words that he speaks to you? Are you well pleased that it is so?"

And then she would not answer the second person but wept wonder sore, desiring to have still himself and in no way to be parted from him.

Then the second person in the Trinity answered to his Father for her and said, "Father, have her excused, for she is yet but young and not fully instructed as to how she should answer."

And then the Father took her by the hand in her soul before the Son and the Holy Ghost and the Mother of Jesus and all the twelve apostles and Saint Katherine and Saint Margaret and many other saints and holy virgins, with a great multitude of angels, saying to her soul, "I take you, Margery, for my wedded wife, for fairer, for fouler, for richer, for poorer, as long as you be buxom[1] and obedient to do what I bid you do. For, daughter, there was never a child so buxom to the mother as I shall be to you, both in well and in woe, to help you and comfort you. And thereto I make you surety."

And then the Mother of God and all the saints that were there present in her soul prayed that they might have much joy together. And then the creature with high devotion, with great plenty of tears, thanked God for this ghostly[2] comfort, considering herself in her own feeling right unworthy of any such grace as she felt, for she felt many great comforts, both ghostly comforts and bodily comforts. Sometimes she felt sweet smells with her nose; it was sweeter, she thought, than ever was any sweet earthly thing that she smelled before, nor might she ever tell how sweet it was, for she thought she might have lived thereby if they would have lasted.

9. Private deliberations.
1. Submissive.

2. Spiritual.

Sometimes she heard with her bodily ears such sounds and melodies that she might not well hear what a man said to her in that time unless he spoke the louder. These sounds and melodies had she heard nearly every day for the term of twenty-five years when this book was written, and especially when she was in devout prayer, also many times while she was at Rome and in England both.

She saw with her bodily eye many white things flying all about her on every side, as thick in a manner as motes[3] in the sun; they were right delicate and comfortable, and the brighter that the sun shone, the better she might see them. She saw them many different times and in many different places, both in church and in her chamber, at her meal and in her prayers, in field and in town, both going and sitting. And many times she was afraid what they might be, for she saw them as well in nights in darkness as in daylight. Then, when she was afraid of them, our Lord said unto her, "By this token, daughter, believe it is God that speaks in you, for whereso God is, heaven is, and where God is there are many angels, and God is in you and you are in him. And therefore be not afraid, daughter, for this betokens that you have many angels about you to keep you both day and night so that no devil shall have power over you nor no evil man harm you."

Then from that time forward she used to say when she saw them come, "*Benedictus qui venit in nomine domini*."[4]

Also our Lord gave her another token, which endured about sixteen years, and it increased ever more and more, and that was a flame of fire wonderfully hot and delectable and right comfortable, not wasting but ever increasing of flame, for, though the weather was never so cold, she felt the heat burning in her breast and at her heart, as verily as a man should feel the material fire if he put his hand or his finger therein.

When she felt first the fire of love burning in her breast, she was afraid thereof, and then our Lord answered to her mind and said, "Daughter, be not afraid, for this heat is the heat of the Holy Ghost, which shall burn away all your sins, for the fire of love quenches all sins. And you shall understand by this token that the Holy Ghost is in you, and you know well wherever the Holy Ghost is, there is the Father, and where the Father is, there is the Son, and so you have fully in your soul all the Holy Trinity. Therefore you have great cause to love me right well, and yet you shall have greater cause than ever you had to love me, for you shall hear what you never heard, and you shall see what you never saw, and you shall feel what you never felt.

For, daughter, you are sure of the love of God as God is God. Your soul is more sure of the love of God than of your own body, for your soul shall part from your body, but God shall never part from your soul, for they are joined together without end. Therefore, daughter, you have as great cause to be merry as any lady in this world, and, if you knew, daughter, how much you please me when you suffer me willfully to speak in you, you should never do otherwise, for this is a holy life, and the time is right well spent. For, daughter, this life pleases me more than wearing of the jacket of mail or of the hair shirt or fasting on bread and water, for, if you said every day a thou-

---

3. Specks of dust.
4. "Blessed is he who comes in the name of the

Lord" (Latin; Matthew 21.9). A blessing used in the mass as part of the consecration.

sand Pater Nosters[5] you should not please me as well as you do when you are in silence and suffer me to speak in your soul.

[Book 1.36] "Fasting, daughter, is good for young beginners and discreet penance, especially that which their ghostly father gives them or enjoins them to do. And to bid many beads,[6] it is good to those who can do no better, and yet it is not perfect. But it is a good way toward perfection. For I tell you, daughter, those who are great fasters and great doers of penance, they desire that it should be considered the best life; also those who give themselves to say many devotions, they would have that the best life, and those who give many alms, they would that that was held the best life. And I have oftentimes, daughter, told you that thinking, weeping, and high contemplation is the best life on earth. And you shall have more merit in heaven for one year of thinking in your mind than for a hundred years of praying with your mouth, and yet you will not believe me, for you will bid many beads whether I will or not.

"And yet, daughter, I will not be displeased with you whatever you think, say, or speak, for I am always pleased with you. And, if I were on earth as bodily as I was before I died on the cross, I should not be ashamed of you as many other men are, for I should take you by the hand among the people and make you great welcome so that they should well know that I loved you right well. For it is suitable for the wife to be homely with her husband. Be he never so great a lord and she so poor a woman when he wedded her, yet they must lie together and rest together in joy and peace. Right so must it be between you and me, for I take no heed what you have been but what you wish to be. And oftentimes have I told you that I have clean forgiven you all your sins. Therefore must I needs be homely with you and lie in your bed with you. Daughter, you desire greatly to see me, and you may boldly, when you are in your bed, take me to you as your wedded husband, as your most worthy darling, and as your sweet son, for I will be loved as a son should be loved by the mother and will that you love me, daughter, as a good wife ought to love her husband. And therefore you may boldly take me in the arms of your soul and kiss my mouth, my head, and my feet as sweetly as you will.

"And, as often as you think on me or would do any good deed to me, you shall have the same reward in heaven as if you did it to my own precious body which is in heaven, for I ask no more of you but your heart to love what loves you, for my love is ever ready for you."

Then she gave thanks and praise to our Lord Jesus Christ for the high grace and mercy that he showed unto her, an unworthy wretch.

This creature had divers tokens in her bodily hearing. One was a manner of sound as if it had been a pair of bellows blowing in her ear. She, being confounded thereof, was warned in her soul no fear to have, for it was the sound of the Holy Ghost. And then our Lord turned that sound into the voice of a dove, and afterward he turned it into the voice of a little bird which is called a red breast that sang full merrily oftentimes in her right ear. And then should she evermore have great grace after she heard such a token. And she had been used to such tokens about twenty-five years at the writing of this book.

---

5. "Our Father" (Latin), i.e., the Lord's Prayer.
6. Prayers (the original sense of the word "bedes," applied by association to beads in a rosary).

Then our Lord Jesus Christ said to his creature, "By these tokens may you well know that I love you, for you are to me a very mother, and to all the world, because of that great charity that is in you, and yet I myself am the cause of that charity, and you shall have great reward therefore in Heaven."

[MARGERY'S REACTION TO A PIETÀ[7]]

* * *

[**Book 1.60**] The good priest, of whom it is written before, who was her reader,[8] fell into great sickness, and she was stirred in her soul to take care of him in God's service. And, when she lacked such as was needful for him, she went about to good men and good women and got such thing as was necessary unto him. He was so sick that men trusted nothing for his life, and his sickness was long continuing. Then on a time, as she was in the church hearing her mass and prayed for the same priest, our Lord said to her that he should live and fare right well. Then was she stirred to go to Norwich to Saint Stephen's Church where is buried the good vicar,[9] who died but little before that time, for whom God showed high mercy to his people, and thank him for the recovery of his priest.

She took leave of her confessor, going forth to Norwich. When she came in the churchyard of Saint Stephen's, she cried, she roared, she wept, she fell down to the ground, so fervently the fire of love burnt in her heart. Afterward she rose up again and went forth weeping into the church to the high altar, and there she fell down with violent sobbing, weepings, and loud cries beside the grave of the good vicar, all ravished with spiritual comfort in the goodness of our Lord who wrought so great grace for his servant who had been her confessor and many times heard her confession of all her living,[1] and administered to her the precious sacrament of the altar at divers times. And in so much was her devotion the more increased in that she saw our Lord work such special grace for such a creature as she had been conversant with in his lifetime. She had such holy thoughts and such holy visions that she might not control her weeping nor her crying. And therefore the people had great marvel of her, supposing that she had wept for some fleshly or earthly affection, and said unto her, "What ails you, woman? Why do you fare thus with yourself? We knew him as well as you."

Then were there priests in the same place who knew her manner of working, and they full charitably led her to a tavern and made her drink and made her full high and goodly comfort. Also there was a lady who desired to have the said creature to a meal. And therefore, as good manners required, she went to the church where the lady heard her service, where this creature saw a fair image of our Lady called a *pity*. And through the beholding of that *pity*, her mind was all wholly occupied in the Passion of our Lord Jesus Christ and in the compassion of our Lady, Saint Mary, by which she was compelled to cry full loudly and weep full sorely, as though she should have died.

---

7. An image, painted or sculpted, of the dead Christ laid across the Virgin's lap.
8. Book 1.58 relates how a priest newly arrived in King's Lynn read to Margery across seven or eight

years, from the Bible and from visionary texts.
9. Richard of Caister (d. 1429), who had a reputation for sanctity.
1. Of (sins committed in) her entire life.

Then came to her the lady's priest, saying, "Damsel, Jesus is dead long since."

When her crying was ceased, she said to the priest, "Sir, his death is as fresh to me as if he had died this same day, and so I think it ought to be to you and to all Christian people. We ought ever to have mind of his kindness and ever think of the doleful death that he died for us."

Then the good lady, hearing her communication, said, "Sir, it is a good example to me, and to other men also, the grace that God works in her soul."

And so the good lady was her advocate and answered for her. Afterward she had her home with her to meat and showed her full glad and goodly comfort as long as she would abide there. And soon after, she came home again to Lynn, and the foresaid priest, for whom she went most specially to Norwich, who had read to her for about seven years, recovered and went about where he wished, thanked be almighty God for his goodness.

*   *   *

[MARGERY NURSES HER HUSBAND IN HIS OLD AGE]

*   *   *

[Book 1.76] It happened on a time that the husband of the said creature, a man of great age passing three score years,[2] as he would have come down from his chamber barefoot and bare-leg, he slithered or else failed of his footing and fell down to the ground from the steps, with his head under him grievously broken and bruised, insomuch that he had in his head five rolls of soft material in the wounds for many days while his head was healing. And, as God would, it was known to some of his neighbors how he had fallen down the steps, perhaps through the din and the rushing of his falling. And so they came to him and found him lying with his head under him, half on life, all streaked with blood, never likely to have spoken with priest nor with clerk unless by high grace and miracle.[3] Then the said creature, his wife, was sent for, and so she came to him. Then was he taken up and his head was sewn, and he was sick a long time after, so that men thought that he should have been dead. And then the people said, if he died, his wife was worthy to be hanged for his death, forasmuch as she might have kept him and did not.

They dwelled not together; they lay not together, for, as is written before, they both with one assent and with free will of the other had made a vow to live chaste. And therefore to avoid all perils they dwelled and so journed in divers places where no suspicion should be had of their incontinence, for first they dwelled together after they had made their vow, and then the people slandered them and said they used their lust and their liking as they did before their vow-making. And, when they went out on pilgrimage or to see and speak with other ghostly creatures, many evil folk whose tongues were their own, lacking the dread and love of our Lord Jesus Christ, thought and said that they went rather to woods, groves, or valleys to use the lust of their bodies so that the people should not espy it nor know it. They, having knowledge how prone the people were to think evil of them, desiring to avoid all occasion, inasmuch as they might goodly, by their good will and

2. Sixty years.
3. I.e., unlikely to have confessed to a priest and received rites except by grace.

their mutual consent, they parted asunder as touching their board and their chambers, and went to board in divers places. And this was the cause that she was not with him and also that she should not be hindered from her contemplation.

And therefore, when he had fallen and grievously was hurt, as is said before, the people said, if he died, it was worthy that she answer for his death. Then she prayed to our Lord that her husband might live a year and she delivered from slander if it were his pleasure. Our Lord said to her mind, "Daughter, you shall have your boon, for he shall live, and I have wrought a great miracle for you that he was not dead. And I bid you take him home and keep him for my love."

She said, "No, good Lord, for I shall then not tend to you as I do now."

"Yes, daughter," said our Lord, "you shall have as much reward for keeping him and helping him in his need at home as if you were in church to make your prayers. And you have said many times that you would fain keep me. I pray you now keep him for the love of me, for he has sometime fulfilled your will and my will both, and he has made your body free to me so that you should serve me and live chaste and clean, and therefore I will that you be free to help him at his need in my name."

"A, Lord," said she, "for your mercy grant me grace to obey your will and fulfill your will and let never my ghostly enemies have any power to hinder me from fulfilling your will."

Then she took home her husband with her and kept him years after, as long as he lived, and had full much labor with him, for in his last days he turned childish again and lacked reason so that he could not do his own easement by going to a stool, or else he would not, but, as a child, voided his natural digestion in his linen clothes where he sat by the fire or at the table, wherever it might be, he would spare no place. And therefore was her labor much the more in washing and wringing and her expense in making fires and hindered her full much from her contemplation, so that many times she should have been irked at her labor save she bethought herself of how she in her young age had full many delectable thoughts, fleshly lusts, and inordinate loves for his body. And therefore she was glad to be punished with the same person and took it much the more easily and served him and helped him, as she thought, as she would have done Christ himself.

* * *

[MARGERY'S VISION OF THE PASSION SEQUENCE[4]]

* * *

[Book 1.79] Then she beheld in the sight of her soul our blissful Lord Christ Jesus coming toward his Passion, and, before he went, he kneeled down and took his mother's blessing. Then she saw his mother falling down in swooning before her son, saying unto him, "Alas, my dear Son, how shall I suffer this sorrow and have no joy in all this world but you alone. A, dear Son, if you will die anyway, let me die before you and let me never suffer this day of sorrow, for I may never bear this sorrow that I shall have for your

---

4. Margery experiences this vision while participating in a Palm Sunday mass.

death. I would, Son, that I might suffer death for you so that you should not die, if man's soul might so be saved. Now, dear son, if you have no pity on yourself, have pity on your mother, for you know full well there can no man in all this world comfort me but you alone."

Then our Lord took up his mother in his arms and kissed her full sweetly and said to her, "A, blessed mother, be of a good cheer and of a good comfort, for I have told you full often that I must needs suffer death, otherwise no man should be saved nor ever come into bliss. And mother, it is my father's will that it be so, and therefore I pray you let it be your will also, for my death shall bring me great honor and you and all mankind great joy and profit, for whomever trusts in my passion and works thereafter. And therefore, blessed mother, you must abide here after me, for in you shall rest all the faith of Holy Church, and by your faith Holy Church shall increase in her faith. And therefore I pray you, worthy mother, cease from your sorrowing, for I shall not leave you comfortless. I shall leave here with you John, my cousin, to comfort you instead of me; I shall send my holy angels to comfort you on earth; and I shall comfort you in your soul my own self, for, mother, you know well I have promised you the bliss of heaven and that you are sure thereof. A, worthy mother, what would you better than where I am king you be queen, and all angels and saints shall be obedient to your will?

"And what grace you ask me I shall not deny your desire. I shall give you power over the devils so that they shall be afraid of you and you not of them. And also, my blessed mother, I have said to you beforetime that I shall come for you my own self when you shall pass out of this world with all my angels and all my saints that are in heaven and bring you before my father with all manner of music, melody, and joy. And there shall I set you in great peace and rest without end. And there shall you be crowned as Queen of Heaven, as lady of all the world, and as Empress of Hell. And therefore, my worthy mother, I pray you bless me and let me go do my father's will, for therefore I came into this world and took flesh and blood from you."

When the said creature beheld this glorious sight in her soul and saw how he blessed his mother and his mother him, and then his blessed mother might not speak one word more to him but fell down to the ground, and so they parted asunder, his mother lying still as if she had been dead, then the said creature thought she took our Lord Jesus Christ by the clothes and fell down at his feet, praying him to bless her, and therewith she cried full loudly and wept right sorely, saying in her mind, "A, Lord, what shall become of me? I had far rather that you would slay me than let me abide in the world without you, for without you I may not abide here, Lord."

Then answered our Lord to her, "Be still, daughter, and rest with my mother here, and comfort you in her, for she who is my own mother must suffer this sorrow. But I shall come again, daughter, to my mother and comfort her and you both and turn all your sorrow into joy."

And then she thought our Lord went forth his way, and she went to our Lady and said, "A, blessed Lady, rise up and let us follow your blessed son as long as we may see him so that I may look enough upon him before he dies. A, dear Lady, how may your heart last and see your blissful son see all this woe? Lady, I may not endure it, and yet am I not his mother."

Then our Lady answered and said, "Daughter, you hear well it will not otherwise be, and therefore I must needs suffer it for my son's love."

And then she thought that they followed forth after our Lord and saw how he made his prayers to his father in the Mount of Olives[5] and heard the goodly answer that came from his father and the goodly answer that he gave his father in reply. Then she saw how our Lord went to his disciples and bade them wake; his enemies were near. And then came a great multitude of people with much light and many armed men with staves, swords, and pole-axes to seek our Lord Jesus Christ. Our merciful Lord as a meek lamb saying unto them, "Whom seek you?"

They answered with a sharp spirit, "Jesus of Nazareth."

Our Lord said in reply, "*Ego sum.*"[6]

And then she saw the Jews fall down on the ground; they might not stand for dread, but anon they rose again and sought as they had done before. And our Lord asked, "Whom seek you?"

And they said again, "Jesus of Nazareth."

Our Lord answered, "I it am."

And then anon she saw Judas come and kiss our Lord, and the Jews laid hands upon him full violently.

Then had our Lady and she much sorrow and great pain to see the lamb of innocence so contemptibly be held and drawn by his own people that he was specially sent unto. And immediately the said creature beheld with her spiritual eye the Jews putting a cloth before our Lord's eye, beating him and buffeting him in the head and striking him before his sweet mouth, crying full cruelly unto him, "Tell us now who smote you."

They spared not to spit in his face in the most shameful way that they could. And then our Lady and she her unworthy handmaiden for the time wept and sighed full sorely, for the Jews acted so foully and so venomously with her blissful Lord. And they would not spare to pull his blissful ears and pull the hair of his beard. And anon after she saw them draw off his clothes and make him all naked and then draw him forth before them as if he had been the greatest malefactor in all the world. And he went forth full meekly before them, all mother-naked as he was born, to a pillar of stone and spoke no word against them but let them do and say what they would. And there they bound him to the pillar as straight as they could and beat him on his fair white body with switches, with whips, and with scourges. And then she thought our Lady wept wonderfully sorely. And therefore the said creature must needs weep and cry when she saw such ghostly sights in her soul as freshly and as verily as if it had been done in deed in her bodily sight, and she thought that our Lady and she were always together to see our Lord's pains, such ghostly sights had she every Palm Sunday and every Good Friday, and in many other ways for many years together. And therefore cried she and wept full sorely and suffered full much despite and reproof in many a country.

And then our Lord said to her soul, "Daughter, these sorrows and many more suffered I for your love, and divers pains, more than any man can tell on earth. Therefore, daughter, you have great cause to love me right well, for I have bought your love full dearly."

* * *

1436–38

5. For Christ's betrayal on the Mount of Olives, see Luke 22.39–54 and John 18.3–12. 6. "I am He" (Latin; John 18.4–8).

THE YORK PLAY OF THE CRUCIFIXION
ca. 1425

The climax of the mystery cycles (see the introduction to "Mystery Plays," pp. 465–67) is reached with a sequence of plays about the passion, or suffering, of Christ. Everything in each cycle leads up to the Crucifixion, the turning point in human history, when the original sin of Adam and Eve is paid for by Christ's suffering and death. No cycle has a more dramatic series of passion plays than that performed at York, the longest of the four extant English cycles. Records of the York mystery plays begin to appear in the last quarter of the fourteenth century when York was, next to London, England's most populous and prosperous city. Richard II came to see the cycle in 1397. Sometime after 1415 the plays of the passion sequence were extensively revised by a gifted playwright referred to by scholars as the York Realist. The *Crucifixion*, although not written in that author's distinctive alliterative style, has sometimes been attributed to him, and is, in any case, a powerful example of late-medieval dramatic art. It is also an especially powerful example of the representation of Christ in his suffering humanity that was characteristic of late-medieval spirituality.

The York plays leading up to the *Crucifixion* are especially cruel: a silent Jesus is vilified, scourged, crowned with thorns, battered, and mocked in a sadistic game of blind man's bluff. Much of the York *Crucifixion* revolves around the mechanical difficulties the soldiers encounter in nailing Jesus to the Cross. The play focuses on the soldiers; they are villains, to be sure, but ordinary men engaged in what they see as ordinary work. They are not monsters.

The gory details, part of the play's "realism," create a shudder, but the play has larger designs on its audience. While the soldiers are hard at work, the audience see only them, complaining of bad workmanship by those who bored the nail holes too far apart, necessitating the stretching of Christ's arms. Only when Christ is raised does the audience recognize the full extent to which both soldiers and audience have been shielded from the pain inflicted by the soldiers' work. When the Cross is finally raised, the actor-Christ speaks to "All men that walk by way or street" (cf. the lyric "Ye That Pasen by the Weye," derived from Lamentations 1.12). He thereby addresses the spectators in the streets of York as though *they* were representing the crowd around the Cross on Calvary, directly involving and implicating them in the drama and its theme of salvation. The soldiers may concentrate on their "work" of nailing Christ to the Cross, but the audience is prompted to reflect on the relation between daily labor and the "works" of mercy incumbent upon each Christian. The meaning of Christ's words is, however, lost on the soldiers, who truly "know not what they do" and proceed to quarrel about possession of Christ's cloak.

The York Play of the Crucifixion

Cast of Characters

JESUS   FOUR SOLDIERS

[*Calvary*]

1ST SOLDIER	Sir knights, take heed hither in hie,°	*haste*
	This deed on dergh we may not draw[1]	
	Ye woot° yourself as well as I	*know*
	How lords and leaders of our law	
5	Has given doom that this dote° shall die.	*fool*
2ND SOLDIER	Sir, all their counsel well we know.	
	Sen° we are comen to Calvary,	*since*
	Let ilk° man help now as him awe.°	*each / ought*
3RD SOLDIER	We are all ready, lo,	
10	This forward° to fulfill.	*agreement*
4TH SOLDIER	Let hear how we shall do,	
	And go we tite theretill.[2]	
1ST SOLDIER	It may not help here for to hone,°	*delay*
	If we shall any worship° win.	*honor*
15 2ND SOLDIER	He must be dead needlings° by noon.	*of necessity*
3RD SOLDIER	Then is good time that we begin.	
4TH SOLDIER	Let ding° him down, then is he done:	*strike*
	He shall not dere° us with his din.	*annoy*
1ST SOLDIER	He shall be set and learned soon[3]	
20	With care° to him and all his kin.	*sorrow*
2ND SOLDIER	The foulest dead° of all	*death*
	Shall he die for his deeds.	
3RD SOLDIER	That means cross° him we shall.	*crucify*
4TH SOLDIER	Behold, so right he reads.°	*speaks*
25 1ST SOLDIER	Then to this work us must take heed,	
	So that our working be not wrang.°	*wrong*
2ND SOLDIER	None other note to neven is need,[4]	
	But let us haste him for to hang.	
3RD SOLDIER	And I have gone for gear good speed,°	*quickly*
30	Both hammers and nails large and lang.°	*long*
4TH SOLDIER	Then may we boldly do this deed.	
	Come on, let kill this traitor strong.°	*flagrant*
1ST SOLDIER	Fair might ye fall in fere[5]	
	That has wrought on this wise.	
35 2ND SOLDIER	Us needs not for to lear°	*learn*
	Such faitours° to chastise.	*fakers*

---

1. We may not delay the time of this deed.
2. And let's get to it quickly.
3. He'll be put in his place and taught quickly.
4. There is no need to mention any other business.
5. May you all have good luck together.

3RD SOLDIER	Sen ilk a thing is right arrayed,	
	The wiselier° now work may we.	*more skillfully*
4TH SOLDIER	The cross on ground is goodly graid,°	*prepared*
40	And bored[6] even as it ought to be.	
1ST SOLDIER	Look that the lad on length be laid,	
	And made be fest° unto this tree.[7]	*fastened*
2ND SOLDIER	For all his fare he shall be flayed:°	*beaten*
	That on assay[8] soon shall ye see.	
45 3RD SOLDIER	Come forth, thou cursed knave,	
	Thy comfort soon shall keel.°	*grow cold*
4TH SOLDIER	Thine hire here shall thou have.	
1ST SOLDIER	Walk on, now work we weel.°	*well*

JESUS	Almighty God, my Father free,°	*noble*
50	Let these matters be made in mind:	
	Thou bade that I should buxom° be,	*obedient*
	For Adam° plight for to be pined.°	*Adam's / tortured*
	Here to dead° I oblige me[9]	*death*
	Fro° that sin for to save mankind,	*from*
55	And sovereignly beseek I thee,[1]	
	That they for me may favor find.	
	And from the Fiend them fend,°	*defend*
	So that their souls be safe,	
	In wealth° withouten end.	*welfare*
60	I keep° nought else to crave.	*care*

1ST SOLDIER	We,[2] hark, sir knights, for Mahound's[3] blood.	
	Of Adam-kind° is all his thought!	*mankind*
2ND SOLDIER	The warlock waxes worse than wood.[4]	
	This doleful dead° ne dreadeth he nought.	*death*
65 3RD SOLDIER	Thou should have mind, with main and mood,[5]	
	Of wicked works that thou hast wrought.	
4TH SOLDIER	I hope° that he had been as good°	*think / well off*
	Have ceased of saws that he up sought.[6]	
1ST SOLDIER	Those saws° shall rue° him sore	*sayings / repent*
70	For all his sauntering[7] soon.	
2ND SOLDIER	I'll speed them that him spare[8]	
	Till he to dead° be done.	*death*

3RD SOLDIER	Have done belive,° boy, and make thee boun°	*at once / ready*
	And bend thy back unto this tree.	
	[JESUS *lies down.*]	

6. I.e., bored with holes for the nails, which were probably wooden.
7. I.e., the Cross. "Fare": behavior.
8. I.e., in actual experience.
9. Render myself liable.
1. And above all I beseech thee.
2. "We": an exclamation of surprise or displeasure.
3. Muhammad's; the sacred figures of other religions were considered devils by Christians in the Middle Ages; the soldier is swearing by the Devil.
4. This devil grows worse than crazy.
5. You should think, with all your strength and wits.
6. I.e., to have ceased of the sayings that he thought up.
7. Behaving like a saint.
8. Bad luck to them that spare him.

75	4TH SOLDIER	Behold, himself has laid him down,	
		In length and breadth as he should be.	
	1ST SOLDIER	This traitor here tainted° of treasoun,	*convicted*
		Go fast and fetch him then, ye three.	
		And sen he claimeth kingdom with crown,	
80		Even as a king here hang shall he.	
	2ND SOLDIER	Now certes I shall not fine°	*stop*
		Ere his right hand be fest.°	*fastened*
	3RD SOLDIER	The left hand then is mine:	
		Let see who bears him⁹ best.	
85	4TH SOLDIER	His limbs on length then shall I lead,°	*stretch*
		And even unto the bore° them bring.	*hole*
	1ST SOLDIER	Unto his head I shall take heed,	
		And with my hand help him to hing.°	*hang*
	2ND SOLDIER	Now sen we four shall do this deed,	
90		And meddle° with this unthrifty° thing,	*deal / unrewarding*
		Let no man spare for special speed,¹	
		Till that we have made ending.	
	3RD SOLDIER	This forward° may not fail,	*agreement*
		Now are we right arrayed.°	*set up*
95	4TH SOLDIER	This boy here in our bail°	*control*
		Shall bide° full bitter braid.°	*abide / treatment*
	1ST SOLDIER	Sir knights, say, how work we now?	
	2ND SOLDIER	Yes, certes, I hope° I hold this hand.	*think*
		And to the bore I have it brought,	
100		Full buxomly° withouten band.°	*effortlessly / cord*
	1ST SOLDIER	Strike on then hard, for him thee bought.²	
	2ND SOLDIER	Yes, here is a stub° will safely stand:	*nail*
		Through bones and sinews it shall be sought.°	*driven*
		This work is well, I will warrand.°	*warrant*
105	1ST SOLDIER	Say, sir, how do we thore?°	*there*
		This bargain may not blin.³	
	3RD SOLDIER	It fails° a foot and more,	*falls short*
		The sinews are so gone in.°	*shrunken*
	4TH SOLDIER	I hope that mark° amiss be bored.	*hole*
110	2ND SOLDIER	Then must he bide° in bitter bale.°	*wait / woe*
	3RD SOLDIER	In faith, it was over-scantly scored.⁴	
		That makes it foully° for to fail.	*badly*
	1ST SOLDIER	Why carp° ye so? Fast° on a cord	*complain / fasten*
		And tug him to, by top and tail.⁵	
115	3RD SOLDIER	Yea, thou commands lightly° as a lord:	*readily*
		Come help to haul, with ill hail.⁶	

9. Handles himself.
1. Let nobody slacken because of his own welfare.
2. Drive the nail in hard, for him who redeemed thee (a splendidly anachronistic oath).
3. This arrangement may not fail; the arrange-ment is of the four soldiers at the four ends of the cross.
4. It was too carelessly bored.
5. And stretch him to it, head and toe.
6. With bad luck to you.

	IST SOLDIER	Now certes° that shall I do	certainly
		Full snelly° as a snail.	quickly
	3RD SOLDIER	And I shall tach° him to	attach
120		Full nimbly with a nail.	

		This work will hold, that dare I heet,°	promise
		For now are fest° fast both his hend.°	fastened / hands
	4TH SOLDIER	Go we all four then to his feet:	
		So shall our space° be speedly° spend.	time / well
125	2ND SOLDIER	Let see, what bourd his bale might beet.[7]	
		Thereto my back now will I bend.	
	4TH SOLDIER	Ow! this work is all unmeet:°	wrongly done
		This boring must be all amend.	
	IST SOLDIER	Ah, peace, man, for Mahound,°	Mohammed
130		Let no man woot° that wonder,	know
		A rope shall rug° him down,	jerk
		If all his sinews go asunder.	

	2ND SOLDIER	That cord full kindly can I knit,°	knot
		The comfort of this carl° to keel.°	knave / cool
135	IST SOLDIER	Fest on then fast that all be fit.	
		It is no force° how fell° he feel.	matter / badly
	2ND SOLDIER	Lug on, ye both, a little yit,°	yet
	3RD SOLDIER	I shall not cease, as I have seel.[8]	
	4TH SOLDIER	And I shall fond° him for to hit.	try
140	2ND SOLDIER	Ow, hail!°	pull
	4TH SOLDIER	Ho, now I hold° it weel.°	think / well
	IST SOLDIER	Have done, drive in that nail	
		So that no fault be found.	
	4TH SOLDIER	This working would not fail	
		If four bulls here were bound.	

145	IST SOLDIER	These cords have evil° increased his pains	badly
		Ere° he were till° the borings brought.	before / to
	2ND SOLDIER	Yea, asunder are both sinews and veins	
		On ilk a side, so have we sought.°	afflicted
	3RD SOLDIER	Now all his gauds° nothing him gains:	tricks
150		His sauntering shall with bale be bought.[9]	
	4TH SOLDIER	I will go say to our sovereigns	
		Of all these works how we have wrought.	
	IST SOLDIER	Nay, sirs, another thing	
		Falls first to you and me:[1]	
155		They bade we should him hing°	hang
		On height that men might see.	

| | 2ND SOLDIER | We woot well so their words were, | |
| | | But sir, that deed will do us dere.° | harm |

---

7. Let's see, what trick could increase his suffering.
8. As I may have good luck.
9. His acting like a saint (?) shall be paid for

with pain.
1. You and I must do first.

1ST SOLDIER	It may nought mend° for to moot° more:		*improve / argue*
160	This harlot° must be hanged here.		*rascal*
2ND SOLDIER	The mortise[2] is made fit° therefore.		*ready*
3RD SOLDIER	Fast on your fingers then, in fere.[3]		
4TH SOLDIER	I ween° it will never come there.		*think*
	We four raise it not right to°-year.		*this*
165 1ST SOLDIER	Say, man, why carps thou so?		
	Thy lifting was but light.°		*easy*
2ND SOLDIER	He means there must be mo°		*more*
	To heave him up on height.		

3RD SOLDIER	Now certes I hope it shall not need
170	To call to us more company.
	Methink we four should do this deed,
	And bear him to yon hill on high.

1ST SOLDIER	It must be done withouten dread:°		*doubt*
	No more, but look ye be ready,		
175	And this part shall I lift and lead.°		*carry*
	On length he shall no longer lie.		
	Therefore now make you boun:°		*ready*
	Let bear him to yon hill.		
4TH SOLDIER	Then will I bear here down,		
180	And tent his toes untill.[4]		

2ND SOLDIER	We two shall see till either side,		
	For else this work will wry° all wrang.°		*turn out / wrong*
3RD SOLDIER	We are ready.		
4TH SOLDIER	Good sirs, abide,		
	And let me first his feet up fang.°		*take*
185 2ND SOLDIER	Why tent ye so to tales this tide?[5]		
1ST SOLDIER	Lift up!		

[*All lift the cross together.*]

4TH SOLDIER	Let see!		
2ND SOLDIER	Ow! Lift along!		
3RD SOLDIER	From all this harm he should him hide°		*protect*
	And° he were God.		*if*
4TH SOLDIER	The Devil him hang!		
1ST SOLDIER	For great harm° I have hent:°		*injury / received*
190	My shoulder is in sunder.		
2ND SOLDIER	And certes I am near shent,°		*ruined*
	So long have I born under.[6]		

3RD SOLDIER	This cross and I in two must twin°—		*separate*
	Else breaks my back in sunder soon.		
195 4TH SOLDIER	Lay down again and leave° your din.		*cease*
	This deed for us will never be done.		

2. A hole in the ground shaped to receive the cross.
3. Fasten your fingers on it, all together.
4. Then I'll carry the part down here and attend to his toes.

5. Why are you so intent on talking at a time like this?
6. So long have I borne it up.

	[*They lay it down.*]		
1ST SOLDIER	Assay,° sirs, let see if any gin°	*try / trick*
	May help him up, withouten hone.°	*delay*
	For here should wight° men worship win,	*strong*
200	And not with gauds° all day to gone.	*pranks*
2ND SOLDIER	More wighter° men than we	*stronger*
	Full few I hope° ye find.	*think*
3RD SOLDIER	This bargain° will not be,°	*arrangement / work*
	For certes me wants wind.	
205 4TH SOLDIER	So will° of work never we wore.°	*at a loss / were*
	I hope this carl some cautels cast.[7]	
2ND SOLDIER	My burden sat° me wonder sore:	*vexed*
	Unto the hill I might not last.	
1ST SOLDIER	Lift up and soon he shall be thore.°	*there*
210	Therefore fest° on your fingers fast.	*fasten*
3RD SOLDIER	Ow, lift!	
1ST SOLDIER	We, lo!	
4TH SOLDIER	A little more!	
2ND SOLDIER	Hold then!	
1ST SOLDIER	How now?	
2ND SOLDIER	The worst is past.	
3RD SOLDIER	He weighs a wicked weight.	
2ND SOLDIER	So may we all four say,	
215	Ere he was heaved on height	
	And raised on this array.°	*way*

4TH SOLDIER	He made us stand as any stones,	
	So boistous° was he for to bear.	*bulky*
1ST SOLDIER	Now raise him nimbly for the nones,[8]	
220	And set him by this mortise here;	
	And let him fall in all at once,	
	For certes that pain shall have no peer.°	*equal*
3RD SOLDIER	Heave up!	
4TH SOLDIER	Let down, so all his bones	
	Are asunder now on sides sere.[9]	
	[*The cross is raised.*]	
225 1ST SOLDIER	That falling was more fell°	*cruel*
	Than all the harms he had.	
	Now may a man well tell°	*count*
	The least lith° of this lad.	*joint*

3RD SOLDIER	Methinketh this cross will not abide	
230	Nor stand still in this mortise yit.°	*yet*
4TH SOLDIER	At the first was it made overwide:	
	That makes it wave, thou may well wit.°	*learn*

7. I think this knave cast some spells.   9. Are pulled apart on every side.
8. For the purpose.

	1ST SOLDIER	It shall be set on ilk a side,	
		So that it shall no further flit.°	*move*
235		Good wedges shall we take this tide,°	*time*
		And fast° the foot, then is all fit.	*fasten*
	2ND SOLDIER	Here are wedges arrayed°	*prepared*
		For that, both great and small.	
	3RD SOLDIER	Where are our hammers laid	
240		That we should work withal?	

	4TH SOLDIER	We have them here even at our hand.	
	2ND SOLDIER	Give me this wedge, I shall it in drive.	
	4TH SOLDIER	Here is another yit ordand.°	*ready*
	3RD SOLDIER	Do take° it me hither belive.°	*give / quickly*
240	1ST SOLDIER	Lay on then fast.	
	3RD SOLDIER	Yes. I warrand.°	*guarantee*
		I thring them sam, so mote I thrive.[1]	
		Now will this cross ful stably stand:	
		All if he rave they will not rive.[2]	
	1ST SOLDIER	Say, sir, how likes thou now	
250		The work that we have wrought?	
	4TH SOLDIER	We pray you, say us how	
		Ye feel, or faint ye aught?[3]	

	JESUS	All men that walk by way or street,	
		Take tent—ye shall no travail tine[4]—	
255		Behold mine head, mine hands, my feet,	
		And fully feel now ere ye fine°	*cease*
		If any mourning may be meet	
		Or mischief° measured unto mine.	*injury*
		My Father, that all bales may bete,[5]	
260		Forgive these men that do me pine.°	*torment*
		What they work woot° they nought:	*know*
		Therefore my Father I crave	
		Let never their sins be sought,°	*searched*
		But see their souls to save.	

265	1ST SOLDIER	We, hark! he jangles like a jay.	
	2ND SOLDIER	Methink he patters like a pie.°	*magpie*
	3RD SOLDIER	He has been doand° all this day,	*doing so*
		And made great mening° of mercy.	*talk*
	4TH SOLDIER	Is this the same that gun° us say	*did*
270		That he was God's son almighty?[6]	
	1ST SOLDIER	Therefore he feels full fell affray,[7]	
		And doomed this day was for to die.	
	2ND SOLDIER	Vath! *qui destruis templum!*[8]	

1. I press them together, so may I thrive.
2. Even if he struggles, they will not budge.
3. Or do you feel somewhat faint?
4. Take heed, you shall not lose your labor.
5. My father, who may remedy all evils.
6. That he was the son of almighty God.
7. For that he suffers a full cruel assault.
8. In Faith thou who destroys the temple (Latin; cf. Mark 14.58, John 2.19).

	3RD SOLDIER	His saws° were so, certain.	*sayings*
275	4TH SOLDIER	And, sirs, he said to some	
		He might raise it again.	
	1ST SOLDIER	To muster° that he had no might,	*exhibit*
		For all the cautels° that he could cast;	*charms*
		All if he were in word so wight,[9]	
280		For all his force now is he fast.	
		All Pilate deemed is done and dight:°	*accomplished*
		Therefore I read° that we go rest.	*advise*
	2ND SOLDIER	This race must be rehearsed right[1]	
		Through the world both east and west.	
285	2ND SOLDIER	Yea, let him hang here still	
		And make mows on the moon.[2]	
	4TH SOLDIER	Then may we wend° at will.	*go away*
	1ST SOLDIER	Nay, good sirs, not so soon.	
		For certes us needs another note:[3]	
290		This kirtle would I of you crave.	
	2ND SOLDIER	Nay, nay, sir, we will look° by lot	*see*
		Which of us four falls° it to have.	*chances*
	3RD SOLDIER	I read° we draw cut° for this coat.	*advise / lots*
		Lo, see now soon, all sides to save.[4]	
295	4TH SOLDIER	The short cut° shall win, that well ye woot,	*straw*
		Whether it fall to knight or knave.	
	1ST SOLDIER	Fellows, ye thar not flite,[5]	
		For this mantle is mine.	
	2ND SOLDIER	Go we then hence tite,°	*quickly*
300		This travail here we tine.[6]	

9. Even though he was so clever in words.
1. This course of action must be repeated correctly.
2. And make faces at the moon.
3. For surely we have another piece of business

to settle.
4. See now straightway, to protect all parties.
5. Fellows, you don't need to quarrel.
6. We're wasting our time here.

MYSTERY PLAYS

The increasing prosperity and importance of the towns was shown by performances of the mystery plays—a sequence or "cycle" of plays based on the Bible and produced by the city guilds, the organizations representing the various trades and crafts. The cycles of several towns are lost. Those of York and Chester have been preserved, the latter in a post-Reformation form. The Towneley plays, sometimes connected with Wakefield (Yorkshire), and those that constitute the so-called N-town plays from East Anglia treat comparable material, as do fragmentary survivals from elsewhere.

Medieval mystery plays had an immensely confident reach in both space and time. In York, for example, the theatrical space and time of this urban, amateur drama was that of the entire city, lasting from sunrise throughout the entire long summer holiday. The time represented ran from the Fall of the Angels and the Creation of the World right through to the end of time, in the Last Judgment. Between these extremities of the beginning and end of time, each cycle presents key episodes of Old Testament narrative, such as the Fall and the Flood, before presenting a concentrated sequence of freely interpreted New Testament plays focused on the life and passion of Christ.

The Church had its own drama in Latin, dating back to the tenth century, which developed through the dramatization and elaboration of the liturgy—the regular service—for certain holidays, the Easter morning service in particular. The vernacular drama was once thought to have evolved from the liturgical, passing by stages from the church into the streets of the town. However, even though the vernacular plays at times echo their Latin counterparts and although their authors may have been clerics, the mysteries represent an old and largely independent tradition of vernacular religious drama. As early as the twelfth century, a *Play of Adam* in Anglo-Norman French was performed in England—a dramatization of the Fall with highly sophisticated dialogue, characterization, and stagecraft.

During the late fourteenth and the fifteenth centuries, the great English mystery cycles were formed in provincial yet increasingly powerful and independent cities. They were the production of the city itself, with particular responsibility for staging and performance devolving onto the city guilds. A guild was also known as a "mystery," from Latin *ministerium*, whence the phrase "mystery plays." A guild combined the functions of modern trade union, club, religious society, and political action group. The performance and staging required significant investments of time and money from amateur performers, the status of whose mystery might be at stake in the quality of their performance. Often the subject of the play corresponded to the function of the guild (thus the Pinners, or nail-makers, performed the York Crucifixion, for example).

Most of our knowledge of the plays, apart from the texts themselves, comes through municipal and guild records, which tell us a great deal about the evolution, staging, and all aspects of the production of the cycles. In some of the cities each guild had a wagon that served as a stage. The wagon proceeded from one strategic point in the city to another, and the play would be performed a number of times on the same day. In other towns, plays were probably acted out in sequence on a platform erected at a single location such as the main city square.

The cycles were performed every year at the time of one of two great early summer festivals—Whitsuntide, the week following the seventh Sunday after Easter, or Corpus Christi, a week later (falling somewhere between May 21 and June 24). They served as both religious instruction and entertainment for wide audiences, including unlearned folk like the carpenter in *The Miller's Tale* (lines 405–74), who recalls from them the trouble Noah had getting his wife aboard the ark, but also educated laypeople and clerics, who besides enjoying the sometimes boisterous comedy would find the plays acting out traditional interpretations of Scripture such as the ark as a type, or prefiguration, of the Church.

Thus the cycles were public spectacles watched by every layer of society, and they paved the way for the professional theater in the age of Elizabeth I. The rainbow in *Noah's Flood* (one of the Chester mystery plays) and the Angel's *Gloria* in the *Shepherds' Play*, with their messages of mercy and hope, unite actors and audience in a common faith. Yet the first shepherd's opening speech, complaining of taxation and the insolent exploitation of farmers by "gentlery-men," shows how the plays also served as vehicles of social criticism and reveal many of the rifts and tensions in the late-medieval social fabric.

The particular intersection of religious and civic institutions that made the cycles possible was put under strain from the beginning of the Reformation in England from the 1530s. Given the strength of civic institutions, the cycles survived into the reign of Elizabeth, but partly because they were identified with the Catholic Church, they were suppressed by local ecclesiastical (by then Protestant) pressures in each city in the late 1560s and 1570s. The last performance of the York Cycle in 1569 is nearly coincident with the opening of the first professional theater in Whitechapel (London) in 1567.

On the morality play—the other major form of theater that flourished in England in the fifteenth century and continued on into the sixteenth—see the headnote to *Everyman* (p. 558).

The Wakefield Second Shepherds' Play

In putting on the stage biblical shepherds and soldiers, medieval playwrights inevitably and often quite deliberately gave them the appearance and characters of contemporary men and women. No play better illustrates this aspect of the drama than the *Second Shepherds' Play*, included in the Towneley collection of mystery plays and imaginatively based on scriptural material typical of the cycles. As the play opens, the shepherds complain about the cold, the taxes, and the high-handed treatment they get from the gentry— evils closer to shepherds on the Yorkshire moors than to those keeping their flocks near Bethlehem. The sophisticated dramatic intelligence at work in this and several other of the Wakefield plays belonged undoubtedly to one individual, who probably revised older, more traditional plays sometime during the last quarter of the fifteenth century. His identity is not known, but because of his achievement scholars refer to him as the Wakefield Master. He was probably a highly educated cleric stationed in the vicinity of Wakefield. The Wakefield Master had a genius for combining comedy, including broad farce, with religion in ways that make them enhance one another. In the *Second Shepherds' Play*, by linking the comic subplot of Mak and Gill with the solemn story of Christ's nativity, the Wakefield Master has produced a dramatic parable of what the Nativity means in Christian history and in Christian hearts. No one will fail to observe the parallels between the stolen sheep, ludicrously disguised as Mak's latest heir, lying in the cradle, and the real Lamb of God, born in the stable among beasts. A complex of relationships based on this relationship suggests itself. But perhaps the most important point is that the charity twice shown by the shepherds—in the first instance to the supposed son of Mak and in the second instance to Mak and Gill when they decide to let them off with only the mildest of punishments—is rewarded when they are invited to visit the Christ Child, the embodiment of charity. The bleak beginning of the play, with its series of individual complaints, is ultimately balanced by the optimistic ending, which sees the shepherds once again singing together in harmony.

The *Second Shepherds' Play* is exceptional among the mystery plays in its development of plot and character. There is no parallel to its elaboration of the comic subplot and no character quite like Mak, who has doubtless been imported into religious drama from popular farce. Mak is perhaps the best humorous character outside of Chaucer's works in this period. A braggart of the worst kind, he has something of Falstaff's charm, and he resembles Falstaff also in his grotesque attempts to maintain the last shreds of his dignity when he is caught in a lie. Most readers will be glad that the shepherds do not carry out their threat to have the death penalty invoked for his crime.

Following the 1994 edition of the Early English Text Society, the stanza, traditionally printed as nine lines (with an opening quatrain of four long lines, the first halves of which rhyme with one another) is rendered here as "thirteeners," rhyming *a b a b a b a b c d d d c*.

The Second Shepherds' Play[1]

CAST OF CHARACTERS

COLL	GILL
GIB	ANGEL
DAW	MARY
MAK	

[*A field.*]

[*Enter* COLL.]

COLL   Lord, how this weather is cold,
And I am ill wrapped;
I am numb with cold
So long have I napped;

5   My legs they fold,
My fingers are chapped.
It is not as I would,
For I am all lapped
      In sorrow:

10   In storms and tempest,
Now in the east, now in the west,
Woe is him that never has rest
      Midday nor morrow!

But we hapless husbands°   *farmers*
15   Who walk on the moor,
In faith we are nearhands°   *almost*
Out of the door.°   *homeless*
No wonder, as it stands
If we be poor,

20   For the earth of our lands
Lies fallow as the floor,[2]
      As you ken.°   *know*
We are so hammed,
Fortaxed, and rammed,

25   We are made hand-tamed
      By these gentlery-men.

Thus they rob us our rest—
Our Lady them harry

1. The text is distantly based on the (1994) edition by A. C. Cawley and Martin Stevens, but it has been significantly altered so as to facilitate comprehension and performance. Non–rhyme words have been frequently substituted by modern equivalents; some rhyme words have been modernized where the rhyme can be preserved. Spelling has been normalized except where rhyme makes changes impossible. The result is a text that retains the flavor of the original while being readily intelligible to a reader of modern English. The text presented here could be performed for a modern audience. The original text does not signal changes of scene, of which there are many. The original does supply four stage directions, in Latin (these are identified in the notes). The text presented here signals scene changes and adds stage directions where appropriate.
2. Fifteenth- and sixteenth-century English landowners converted arable land to pasture for more profitable wool production (the so-called enclosure movement). Book One of Thomas More's *Utopia* underlines the brutal social results of this movement.

These lords' men are pests,
30 Who cause the plow tarry.
What men say is for the best—
We find it contrary.
Thus are farmers oppressed
In point to miscarry
35   In life.
Thus hold they us under,
Thus they bring us in blunder,
It were a great wonder
If ever should we thrive.

40 For may he get a paint-sleeve[3]
Or brooch nowadays,
Woe is him that him grieves
Or once gainsays.
Dare no man tell him leave
45 With whatever force that he may.°   may use
And yet may no man believe
One word that he says,
No letter.
He can make purveyance[4]
50 With boast and bragance,
And all is through maintenance[5]
Of men that are greater.

There shall come a swain°   fellow
As proud as a po:°   peacock
55 He must borrow my wain,°   wagon
My plow also;
Then I am full fain°   glad
To grant ere he go.
Thus live we in pain,
60 Anger, and woe,
By night and by day.
He must have if he wants it,
Even if I should forgo it.
I were better be hanged
65   Than once say him nay.

It does me good, as I walk
Thus by mine own
Of this world for to talk
In manner of moan.
70 To my sheep I will stalk,
And hearken anon,

3. A decorated sleeve, a sign of the livery worn by
the landlord's aggressive officers.
4. Appropriation (of private property).

5. The widespread late medieval practice of
building aggressive private militias.

There abide on a balk,[6]
Or sit on a stone,
   Full soon;
75   For I think pardie,°   *by God*
True men if they be,
We get more company
   Ere it be noon.

        [*Enter* GIB, *who initially does not see* COLL.]

GIB   Bensté Dominus,[7]
80   What may this mean?
Why fares this world thus?
Oft have we not seen.
Lord, these weathers aren't piteous
And the winds are full keen,
85   And the frosts so hideous
They water mine eien,°   *eyes*
   No lie.
Now in dry, now in wet,
Now in snow, now in sleet,
90   When my shoes freeze to my feet
   It is not all easy.

But as far as I ken,°   *see*
Or yet as I go,
We poor married men
95   Suffer much woe;
We have sorrow then and then—
It falls oft so.
Silly Copple, our hen,[8]
Both to and fro
100   She cackles;
But begin she to croak,
To groan or to cluck,
Woe is him, our cock,
   For he is in shackles.

105   These men that are wed
Have not all their will:
When they are full hard stead°   *placed*
They sigh full still;
God knows they are led
110   Full hard and full ill;
In bower nor in bed
They speak not their will.

---

6. An elevated line of grassland forming a boundary.
7. A Latin phrase effectively meaning "Bless us, Lord," the learned form of which has been changed through aural reception by the unlearned.
8. I.e., Gib's wife.

This tide°   *time*
My part have I found
115   I know my lesson:
Woe is him that is bound,
    For he must abide.

But now late in our lives—
A marvel to me,
120   That I think my heart rives°   *splits*
Such wonders to see;
What that destiny drives
It must so be—
Some men will have two wives,
125   And some men three
    In store.[9]
Some are sad that has any,
But so far as know I,
Woe is him that has many,
130   For he feels sore.

But young men awooing,
For God that you bought,°   *redeemed*
Be well ware of wedding
And think in your thought:
135   "Had I known" is a thing
That serves of nought.
Much secret mourning
Has wedding home brought,
    And griefs,
140   With many a sharp shower,°   *dispute*
For you may catch in an hour
That will vex you full sour
    As long as you live.

For as ever read in 'pistle,[1]
145   I have one by my fire
As sharp as a thistle,
As rough as a briar.
She is browed like a bristle,
With a sourpuss cheer;
150   Had she once wet her whistle
She could sing full clear
    Her Pater Noster.[2]
She is great as a whale;
She has a gallon of gall:
155   By him that died for us all,
    I would I had run till I'd lost her.

---

9. I.e., by marrying again.
1. Epistle (i.e., a New Testament epistle, as read in church); an expression meaning "truly."
2. "Our Father" (Latin), i.e. the Lord's Prayer.

COLL   God look over the row!
   [*to* GIB] Full deafly you stand!
GIB   Yea, the devil in your maw°   *guts*
160   So standing around!
    Saw you anywhere Daw?
COLL   Yea, on feedland
    Heard I him blow.
    He comes here at hand,
165   Not far.
    Stand still.
GIB   Why?
COLL   For he comes, think I.
GIB   He will make us both a lie
    Unless we be ware.

      [*Enter* the boy DAW, *who does not see the two older shepherds.*]

170 DAW   Christ's cross me speed
    And Saint Nicholas!
    Thereof had I need:
    It is worse than it was.
    Whoso could take heed
175   And let the world pass,
    It is ever in dread
    And brittle as glass,
      And slide.°   *slips away*
    This world was never so,
180   With marvels more and more,
    Now in weal, now in woe,
      And no thing abides.

    Was never since Noah's flood
    Such waters seen,
185   Winds and rains so rude
    And storms so keen:
    Some stammered, some stood
    In fear as I deem
    Now God turn all to good!
190   I say as I mean.
      For ponder:
    These floods so they drown
    Both in fields and in town,
    And bears all down,
195   And that is a wonder

    We that walk on the nights
    Our cattle to keep,
    We see sudden sights
    When other men sleep.

200 Yet methink my heart lights:
I see rascals peep.

[*He sees the others, but does not greet them.*]

You are two tall wights.°   *creatures*
I will give my sheep
   A turn.
205 But full ill have I meant:[3]
As I walk on this bent°   *field*
I may quickly repent,
   My toes if I spurn.°   *stub*

Ah, sir, God you save,
210 And master mine!
A drink would I have,
And somewhat to dine.
COLL   Christ's curse, my knave,
You're a lazy child!
215 GIB   What, the boy's set to rave!
Abide for a while
   We have eaten it.°   *had dinner*
Ill thrift on thy pate![4]
Though the rascal came late
220 Yet is he in state
   To dine—if he had it.

DAW   Such servants as I,
Who sweat and swink,°   *toil*
Eat our bread full dry,
225 And that me forthinks°   *makes me regret*
We are oft wet and weary
When master-men wink,°   *sleep*
Yet comes full lately
Both dinners and drink.
230   But nately°   *quickly*
Both our dame and our sire,
When we have run in the mire,
They can nip at our hire,
   And pay us full lately.

235 But here my oath, master,
For the food that ye make
I shall earn thereafter:
Work as I take.
I shall do a little, sir,
240 And between times lake,°   *play*

3. But it's a bad idea (to give the sheep a walk).   4. Bad fortune on your head!

For too much supper
Lay never on my stomach
   In fields.
Whereto should I threap?°   *haggle*
245   With my staff can I leap,
And men say, "Bargaining cheap
   Poor return yields."

COLL   You'd be an ill lad
Yourself to defend
250   With a man that had
But little to spend.
GIB   Peace, boy, I bade—
No more to this end,
Or I shall make thee full rad,°   *quickly (stop)*
255   By the heaven's King!
   With thy gauds°—   *tricks*
Where are our sheep, boy?—we scorn.[5]
DAW   This same day at morn
I left them in the corn
260   When they rang Lauds.[6]

They have pasture good,
They cannot go wrong.
COLL   That is right. By the rood,°   *cross*
These nights are long!
265   Yet I would, ere we yode,°   *went*
Come, give us a song.
GIB   So I thought as I stood,
To cheer us among.°   *meanwhile*
DAW   I grant.
270   COLL   Let me sing the tenory.°   *tenor*
GIB   And I the treble so hee.°   *high*
DAW   Then the mean falls to me.
   Let see how you chant.

    [*They sing.*]

    [*Enter* MAK, *cloaked.*][7]

MAK   Now, Lord, for thy names seven,
275   That made both moon and stars
Well more than I can neven,°   *name*
Thy will, Lord, now me mars.
I am all uneven—
That moves oft my harns.°   *brains*
280   Now would God I were in heaven,

---

5. We are not impressed by your tricks.
6. The earliest church service of the day.

7. The original manuscript has this stage direction.

For there weep no barns°   *children*
  Ever still.
COLL   Who is that pipes so poor?
MAK [*aside*] Would God you knew how I foor!°   *fared*
285   [*aloud*] Lo, a man that walks on the moor
  And has not all his will.

GIB   Mak, where have you gone?
  Tell us tidings.
DAW   Is he come? Then each one
290   Take heed to his things.[8]

     [*Snatches the cloak off him.*]

MAK   What! Ich[9] be a yeoman,
  I tell you, of the king,
  The self and the same,
  Sent by a great lording
295   And sich.°   *suchlike*
  Fie on you! Go hence
  Out of my presence:
  I must have reverence.
    Why, who be ich?

300 COLL   Why make ye it so quaint?°   *fancy*
  Mak, ye do wrong.
GIB   But, Mak, why play the saint?
  Why keep it up so long?
DAW   I think the rascal can paint°—   *act the part*
305   The devil might him hang!
MAK   Ich shall make complaint
  And make you all to thwang°   *be whipped*
    At a word,
  And tell just how ye doth.
310 COLL   But Mak, is that sooth?
  Now take out that Southern tooth,[1]
    And set it in turd!

GIB   Mak, the devil in your ee!°   *eye*
  A stroke would I give you!
315 DAW   Mak, know ye not me?
  By God, I could irk you.
MAK   God protect you all three:
  I thought I had seen you.
  You are a fair company.
320 COLL   You now remember it's you?[2]

---

8. Possessions (in case Mak should steal them).
The stage direction below is in the manuscript.
9. I (a southern dialect form). The Yorkshire
shepherds speak in a northern dialect. Mak pretends to be a southener, and of high social rank.
1. I.e., drop the southern accent.
2. Can you now remember (who you are)?

GIB Crook, peep!° *watch out!*
   Thus late as it goes,
   What will men suppose?
   And you have an ill nose° *reputation*
325   Of stealing sheep.

MAK And I am true as steel,
   All men know
   But a sickness I feel
   That holds me full low:
330   My belly fares not well,
   It is out of estate.
DAW Seldom lies the devil
   Dead by the gate.[3]
MAK Therefore
335 Full sore am I and ill
   If I stand stone-still,
   I eat not a needle,
      This month and more.

COLL How fares thy wife? By my hood,
340   How fares sho?° *she*
MAK Lies sprawling, by the rood,° *cross*
   By the fire, lo!
   And a house full of brood.
   She drinks well, too:
345 That's the only good
   That she will do!
      But sho
   Eats as fast as she can;
   And each year that comes to man
350 She brings forth a bairn° *baby*
      And some years two.

   But were I now more prosperous
   And richer by far,
   I'd still be eaten out of house
355 And of harbar.° *home*
   Yet is she a foul douce,° *sweetheart*
   If you come nar:° *near*
   There is none that trows° *imagines*
   Nor knows a war° *worse*
360   Than know I.
   Now will you see what I proffer:
   To give all in my coffer
   Tomorrrow I'd offer
      Her head-mass penny.[4]

---

3. Road, i.e., the devil is always on the move.
4. The money paid for a mass for her soul; i.e., I wish she were dead.

365 GIB   I know so forwaked°   *exhausted*
    Is none in this shire.
    I would sleep if° I taked   *even if*
    Less to my hire.
  DAW   I am cold and naked
370   And would have a fire.
  COLL   I am weary forraked°   *from walking*
    And run in the mire.
    The guard is you!°   *you keep watch*

[*Lies down.*]

  GIB   Nay, I will lie down by,
375   For I must sleep, truly.

[*Lies down beside him.*]

  DAW   As good a man's son was I
    As any of you.

[*Lies down and signals to* MAK *to lie between them.*]

    But Mak, come hither, between
    Shall you lie down.
380 MAK   Then might I stop your team
    Of what you would rown,°   *whisper together*
    No dread.°   *doubt*

[*Lies down and prays.*]

    From my top to my toe,
    Manus tuas commendo
385   *Pontio Pilato*[5]
    Christ's cross me speed!°   *help*

[*He rises as the others sleep and speaks.*][6]

    Now were time for a man
    That lacks what he wold°   *wants*
    To stalk privily then
390   Unto a fold,
    And nimbly to work than,
    And be not too bold,
    For he might pay dear the bargain
    If it were told
395   At the end.
    Now were time for to reel:°   *move fast*
    But he needs good counsel

---

5. "Thy hands I commend to Pontius Pilate" (Latin). A parody of Luke 23.46, "Into thy hands I commend my spirit."
6. One of the original stage directions.

That fain would fare well
    And has but little to spend.

[He draws a magic circle around the shepherds and utters a spell.]

400 But about you a circle
    As round as a moon,
Til I have done what I will,
Till that it be noon,
That ye lie stone-still
405 Until that I have done;
And I shall say theretill°   *in addition*
    Of good words a foon:°   *few*
    "On hight,°   *high*
Over your heads my hand I lift.
410 Out go your eyes! Block your sight!"
But yet I must make better shift
    If it's to be right.

Lord, how they sleep hard—
    That may you all hear.
415 Was I never a shepherd,
But now will I lear.°   *learn*
The flock may be scared,
    Yet shall I nip near.

[He grabs one.]

How! Draw hitherward!
420 Now mends our cheer
    From sorrow.
A fat sheep, I dare say!
A good fleece, dare I lay!
Repay when I may,
425   But this will I borrow.

[Goes with the sheep to his cottage and calls from outside.]

How, Gill, art you in?
Get us some light.
GILL *[inside]* Who makes such a din
    This time of the night?
430 I am set for to spin;
There's no way I might
Rise, a penny to win.
I curse them on height!°   *aloud*
    So fares
435 A housewife that has been
Harried thus between:
Here may no reward be seen
    For such small chares.°   *chores*

MAK   Good wife, open the hek!°   *hatch*
440   Don't you see what I bring?
       GILL   Just draw the sneck.°   *latch*
       Ah, come in, my darling.
       MAK   Yea, no need to reck°   *care*
       About keeping me standing.

       [*She opens the door.*]

445   GILL   By the naked neck
       Are you like for to hang.
       MAK   No way!
       I deserve my meat,
       For in a pinch I can get
450   More than they that sweat
           All the long day.

       Thus it fell to my lot,
       Gill, I had such grace.
       GILL   It were a foul blot
455   To be hanged for the case.
       MAK   I have escaped, Jelot,°   *Gill*
       From as hard a glase.°   *blow*
       GILL   But "So long goes the pot
       To the water," men says,
460   "At last
       Comes it home broken."
       MAK   Well know I the token,°   *saying*
       But let it never be spoken!
           But come and help fast.

465   I would it were flain,°   *skinned*
       I sure wish to eat:
       This twelvemonth was I not so fain
       Of one sheep-meat.
       GILL   Come they ere it be slain,
470   And hear the sheep bleat—
       MAK   Then might I be ta'en°—   *taken*
       That were a cold sweat!
           Go spar°   *fasten*
       The street-door.
475   GILL   Yes, Mak,
       For if they come at thy back—
       MAK   Then might I pay, for all the pack,
       The devil of the war.°   *worse bargain*

       GILL   A good ploy have I spied,
480   Since you have none.
       Here shall we him hide
       Till they be gone,
       In my cradle. Abide!

Let me alone,
485 And I shall lie beside
In childbed and groan.
MAK   Get you red,°   *get ready*
And I shall say you were light°   *delivered*
Of a boy-child this night.
490 GILL   Now well is the day bright
That ever I was bred.°   *born*

This is a good guise°   *deception*
And a far-cast:°   *clever trick*
Yet a woman's advice
495 Helps at the last.
I know never who spies:
To it, go fast.
MAK   Unless I come ere they rise,
There blows a cold blast.
500 I will go sleep.

[*Returns to the sleeping shepherds.*]

Yet sleeps all this meny,°   *company*
And I shall go stalk privily,
As it had never been I
That carried their sheep.

[*Lies down between them.*]

[*The shepherds are waking up.*]

505 COLL   *Resurrex a mortruus!*[7]
Have hold my hand!
Judas carnas dominus![8]
I may not well stand.
My foot sleeps, by Jesus,
510 And I totter fastand.°   *(from) fasting*
I thought we had laid us
Full near England.
GIB   Ah, yea?
Lord, how I have slept well!
515 As fresh as an eel,
As light I me feel
As leaf on a tree.

DAW   Bensté° be herein!   *(God's) blessing*
So my body quakes,
520 My heart is out of skin,
Whatever it makes.°   *causes*
Who makes all this din?
So my skin blakes°   *turns pale*

7. A mangled form of *resurrexit a mortuis* (Latin   Creed.
for "he arose from the dead"), from the Apostles'   8. More mangled Latin: Judas, (in?)carnate lord.

To the door will I win.[9]
525 Hark, fellows, wakes!
　　We were four:
　　See ye anywhere of Mak now?
COLL　We were up ere you.
GIB　Man, I give God avow
530 Yet went he naw're.°　　　　　　　　　　　　　　*nowhere*

DAW　Methought he was lapped
　　In a wolfskin.
COLL　So are many happed°　　　　　　　　　　　*clad*
　　Now, especially within.
535 DAW　When we had long napped,
　　Methought with a gin°　　　　　　　　　　　*snare*
　　A fat sheep he trapped,
　　But he made no din.
GIB　Be still!
540 Thy dream makes thee wood.°　　　　　　　*crazy*
　　It is but phantom, by the rood.°　　　　　*cross*
COLL　Now God turn all to good,
　　If it be his will.

[*They wake up* MAK, *who pretends to have been asleep.*]

GIB　Rise, Mak, for shame!
545 You lie right long.
MAK　Now Christ's holy name
　　Be us among!
　　What is this? For Saint Jame,
　　I may not well be gone.
550 I think I be the same.
　　Ah, my neck has lain wrong.

[*One of them twists his neck.*]

　　Enough!
　　Much thank! Since yestereven
　　Now, by Saint Stephen,
555 I was flayed with a sweven°—　　　　　　　*dream*
　　My heart out of slough.[1]

　　I thought Gill began to croak
　　And labor full sad,°　　　　　　　　　　　*hard*
　　Well-near at the first cock,
560 Of a young lad,
　　For to grow our flock—
　　Then be I never glad:
　　I have tow on my rock[2]

9. I'll go to the door. Half-asleep, Daw thinks
he's inside.
1. My heart leapt out of my skin.

2. Flax on my distaff (i.e., demands, mouths to
feed).

More than ever I had.
565   Ah, my head!
A house full of young tharms!°   *bellies*
The devil knock out their harns!°   *brains*
Woe is him has many barns,°   *children*
    And thereto little bread.

570   I must go home, by your leave,
To Gill, as I thought.°   *intended*
I pray you look to my sleeve,
    That I steal nought.
I am loath you to grieve
575   Or from you take aught.
DAW   Go forth! Ill might thou chieve!°   *prosper*
Now would I we sought
    This morn,
That we had all our store.°   *stock*
580 COLL   But I will go before.
    Let us meet.
GIB   Whore?°   *where*
DAW   At the crooked thorn.

[MAK's *house.* MAK *is at the door.*]

MAK   Undo this door!
585 GILL   Who is here?
MAK   How long shall I stand?
GILL   Who makes such a stir?
    Now walk in the weniand!°   *waning of the moon (i.e., in poor light)*
MAK   Ah, Gill, what cheer?
590   It is I, Mak, your husband.
GILL   Then may we see here
The devil in a band,³
    Sir Guile!
Lo, he comes with a lote°   *sound*
595 As° he were held by the throat: *as if*
I may not sit at my note°   *work*
    A short while.

MAK   Will you hear what fuss she makes
To get her a glose?°   *an excuse*
600 And does nought but lakes°   *plays*
And scratches her toes?
GILL   Why, who wanders? Who wakes?
Who comes? Who goes?
Who brews? Who bakes?
605 What makes me thus hoarse?
    And then

---

3. In a noose. Gill knows that sheep stealing is a hanging offense.

It is ruth to behold,
Now in hot, now in cold,
Full woeful is the household
610   That lacks a woman.

But what end have you made
With the shepherds, Mak?
MAK   The last word that they said
When I turned my back,
615 They would look that they had
Their sheep all the pack.
I don't think they'll be well paid°   *pleased*
When they their sheep lack.
     Pardie!°   *by God*
620 But how-so the game goes,
It's me they'll suppose,°   *suspect*
And make a foul noise,
     And cry out upon me.

But you must do as you hight.°   *promised*
625 GILL   I accord me theretill.°   *with that*
I shall swaddle him right
In my cradill.

       [*She enfolds the sheep and puts it in the cradle.*]

If it were a greater sleight,°   *trick*
Yet could I help still.
630 I will lie down straight.°   *immediately*
Come cover me.
MAK   I will.
        [*Covers her.*]
GILL   Behind
Come Coll and his marrow,[4]
635   They will nip us full narrow.
MAK   But I may cry "Out, harrow,"[5]
     The sheep if they find.

GILL   Hearken ay when they call—
They will come anon.
640 Come and make ready all,
And sing by your own.
Sing "lullay"° you shall,   *a lullaby*
For I must groan
And cry out by the wall
645 On Mary and John
     For sore.°   *pain*
Sing "lullay" on fast

---

4. Coll and his companion are following your tracks.   5. An expression of distress.

When you hear them at last,
And if I don't play a false cast,°   *trick*
650   Trust me no more.

       [*The shepherds meet again.*]

DAW   Ah, Coll, good morn.
    Why sleep you not?
COLL   Alas, that ever I was born!
    We have a foul blot:
655   A fat wether° have we lorn.°   *ram / lost*
DAW   Marry, God's forbot!°   *God forbid*
GIB   Who should do us that scorn?
    That were a foul spot!°   *disgrace*
COLL   Some shrew.°   *knave*
660   I have sought with my dogs
    All Horbury[6] shrogs,°   *thickets*
    And of fifteen hogs
      I found only a ewe.[7]

DAW   Now believe me, if you will,
665   By Saint Thomas of Kent,
    Either Mak or Gill
    Was of that assent.
COLL   Peace, man, be still!
    I saw when he went.
670   You slander him ill—
    You ought to repent
      With speed.
GIB   Now as ever might I thee,°   *prosper*
    If I should even here dee,°   *die*
675   I would say it were he
      That did that same deed.

DAW   Go we thither, I read,°   *advise*
    And run on our feet.
    Shall I never eat bread
680   The truth till I weet.°   *know*
COLL   Nor drink in my head,
    With him till I meet.
GIB   I will rest in no stead°   *place*
    Till that I him greet,
685   My brother.
    One thing I hight:°   *promise*
    Till I see him in sight
    Shall I never sleep one night
      Where I do in another.

6. A village near Wakefield.   7. I.e., the ram was absent.

[*The shepherds outside* MAK's *house.* MAK *and* GILL *are inside;* GILL
lies in bed, groaning; MAK *sings a lullaby.*]

690 DAW   Will you hear how they hack?[8]
　　　Our sire wants to croon.
　　COLL   Heard I never none crack°　　　　　　　　　　　　　*sing*
　　　So clear out of tune.
　　　Call on him.
695 GIB   Mak!
　　　Undo your door soon!°　　　　　　　　　　　　　　　*at once*
　　MAK   Who is that spake,
　　　As if it were noon,
　　　　On loft?°　　　　　　　　　　　　　　　　　　　*so loudly*
700 　Who is that, I say?
　　DAW   Good fellows, if it were day.[9]
　　MAK   As far as you may,
　　　[*opening*] Good, men speak soft

　　　Over a sick woman's head
705 　That is at malease.°　　　　　　　　　　　　　　　*suffering*
　　　I had rather be dead
　　　Ere she had any disease.°　　　　　　　　　　　　　*distress*
　　GILL   Go to another stead!°　　　　　　　　　　　　　*place*
　　　I may not well wheeze:°　　　　　　　　　　　　　*breathe*
710 　Each foot that ye tread
　　　Goes through my nese.°　　　　　　　　　　*nose (i.e., head)*
　　　　So, hee!°　　　　　　　　　　　　　　　　　　　*loudly*
　　COLL   Tell us, Mak, if you may,
　　　How fare you, I say?
715 MAK   But are you in this town° today?　　　　　*neighborhood*
　　　Now how fare ye?

　　　You have run in the mire
　　　And are wet yit.
　　　I shall make you a fire
720 　If you will sit.
　　　A nurse would I hire.
　　　Think you on yit?[1]
　　　Well quit is my hire—
　　　My dream this is it—
725 　　A season.[2]
　　　I have babes, if ye knew,
　　　Wel more than enew:°　　　　　　　　　　　　　　*enough*
　　　But we must drink as we brew,
　　　　And that is but reason.

730 　I would you dined ere you yode.°　　　　　　　　　*went*
　　　Methink that you sweat.

8. I.e., Sing (here badly).
9. I.e., not friends, since the sun has not risen.
1. Do you remember the dream I recounted?

2. My season's wage is paid—my dream (that Gill
was giving birth) has come to pass.

GIB Nay, neither amends our mood,
  Drink nor meat.° *food*
MAK Why sir, ails you aught but good?³
735 DAW Yea, our sheep that we get° *watch over*
  Are stolen as they yode:° *wandered*
  Our loss is great.
MAK Sirs, drinks!
  Had I been there,
740 Some should have suffered full sore.
COLL Marry, some men think that you were,
  And that us forthinks.° *displeases*

GIB Mak, some men trows,° *suspect*
  That it should be ye.
745 DAW Either you or your spouse,
  So say we.
MAK Now if you have suspouse° *suspicion*
  To Gill or to me,
  Come and ransack the house
750 And then may you see
    Who had her⁴—
  If I any sheep fot,° *stole*
  Either cow or stot⁵—
  And Gill my wife rose not
755 Here since she laid her.° *lay down*

As I am true and leal,° *honest*
  To God here I pray
  That this be the first meal
  That I shall eat this day.
760 COLL Mak, as I have sele,⁶
  Advise thee, I say:
  He learned timely to steal
  That could not say nay.⁷

  [*They begin to search.*]

GILL I swelt!° *die*
765 Out, thieves, from my wones!° *dwelling*
  You come to rob us for the nones.° *right now*
MAK Hear you not how she groans?
  Your hearts should melt.

GILL Out, thieves, my barn!° *child*
770 Approach him not thore!° *there*
MAK If you knew how she'd farn,° *fared*
  Your hearts would be sore.

3. Does anything other than good vex you?
4. I.e., the sheep.
5. Of either sex.

6. As I hope to be saved.
7. Proverbial.

You do wrong, I you warn,
That thus come before°   *in the presence*
775   To a woman that has farn°—   *been in labor*
But I say no more.
GILL   Ah, my middle!
I pray to God so mild,
If ever I you beguiled,
780   That I'll eat this child
That lies in this cradle.

MAK   Peace, woman, for God's pain,
And cry not so!
You're harming your brain
785   And make me full woe.
GIB   I think our sheep is slain.
What find you two?
DAW   All work we in vain;
As well may we go.
790   But hatters!⁸
I can find no flesh,
Hard nor nesh,°   *soft*
Salt nor fresh,
But two empty platters.

795   Live creatures but this,°   *(i.e., the baby)*
Tame nor wild,
None, as I have bliss,
As bad as he smelled.

[*Approaches the cradle.*]

GILL   No, so God me bless,
800   And give me joy of my child!
COLL   We have aimed amiss—
I judge us beguiled.
GIB   Sir, don!°   *totally*
[*to* MAK] Sir—Our Lady him save!—
805   Is your child a knave?°   *boy*
MAK   Any lord might him have,
This child, as his son.⁹

When he wakens he kips,°   *grabs*
That joy is to see.
810   DAW   In good time to his hips,
And in sely.¹
But who were his gossips,°   *godparents*
So soon ready?

8. An expression of unpleasant surprise.   ing of *knave* as "lowborn").
9. Boy (although Mak evokes an alternate mean-   1. Good luck and joy to him.

MAK   So fair fall their lips[2]—
815 COLL   Hark, now, a lee,°   *lie*
MAK   So God them thank,
     Perkin, and Gibbon Waller, I say,
     And gentle John Horne, in good fay°—   *faith*
     He made all the garray°   *quarrel*
820   With the great shank.[3]

GIB   Mak, friends will we be,
     For we are all one.°   *in accord*
MAK   We? Now I hold for me,°   *take care of myself*
     For amends get I none.
825 Farewell all three,
     We'd be glad were you gone.
DAW   Fair words may there be,
     But love is there none
          This year.

               [*They go out the door.*]

830 COLL   Gave ye the child anything?
GIB   I trow not one farthing.
DAW   Fast again will I fling.°   *dash in*
     Abide ye me there.

               [*He returns quickly.*]

     Mak, take it no grief
835 If I come to your barn.°   *child*
MAK   Nay, thou does me great reprief,°   *shame*
     And foul° has thou farn.°   *ill / acted*
DAW   The child it will not grief,
     That little day-starn.°   *day star*
840 Mak, with your leave,
     Let me give your barn
          But sixpence.
MAK   Nay, do way! He sleeps.
DAW   Methinks he peeps.
845 MAK   When he wakens he weeps.
     I pray you go hence.

          [*The other shepherds come back into the cottage.*]

DAW   Give me leave him to kiss,
     And lift up the clout.°   *cover*
          [*Raises the cover.*]
     What the devil is this?
850 He has a long snout!

2. May they enjoy good luck.
3. An allusion to a dispute among the shepherds in the author's *First Shepherds' Play.*

COLL He is shaped amiss.
There's ill about.
GIB Ill-spun weft, ywis,
Ay comes foul out.[4]

855   Aye, so!
He is like to our sheep.
DAW How, Gib, may I peep?
COLL I trow kind will creep
Where it may not go.[5]

860 GIB This was a quaint gaud
And a far-cast.[6]
It was high fraud.
DAW Yea, sirs, was't.
Let's burn this bawd°   *evildoer*
865 And bind her fast.
A false scold
Should hang at the last:
So shall thou.
Will you see how they swaddle
870 His four feet in the middle?
Saw I never in the cradle
A horned lad ere now.

MAK Peace bid I! What,
Let be your fare!°   *commotion*
875 I am he that him gat.°   *begot*
And yond woman him bare.
COLL What devil shall he hat?[7]
Lo, God, Mak's heir!
GIB Let be all that!
880 Now God give him care°—   *grief*
I saw.
GILL A pretty child is he
As sits on a woman's knee,
A dillydown,° pardie,°   *darling / by God*
885   To make a man laugh.

DAW I know him by the earmark—
That is a good token.
MAK I tell you, sirs, hark,
His nose was broken.
890 Then told me a clerk
That he was forspoken.°   *bewitched*
COLL This is a false work.
I would fain be wroken.°   *avenged*

---

4. An ill-spun fabric, indeed, always comes out
badly (proverbial).
5. Nature will creep where it can't walk (proverbial);
i.e., nature will reveal itself one way or another.

6. This was an elaborate trick and a clever
deception.
7. What the devil shall he be called?

Get weapon.
895 GILL He was taken by an elf[8]
I saw it myself—
When the clock struck twelf
Was he forshapen.°   *transformed*

GIB You two are well feft°   *equipped*
900 Together in a stead.°   *place*
DAW Since they maintain their theft,
Put them to death.
MAK If I trespass eft,°   *again*
Cut off my head.
905 With you will I be left.[9]
COLL Sirs, do my read:°   *advice*
For this trespass
We will neither curse nor flite,°   *quarrel*
Fight nor chide,
910 But have done as tite,°   *quickly*
And cast him in canvas.

[*They toss* MAK *in a blanket.*]

[*The fields.*]

COLL Lord, how I am sore,
In point for to burst!
In faith, I may no more—
915 Therefore will I rest.
GIB As a sheep of seven score[1]
He weighed in my fist:
For to sleep anywhere
Methink that I list.°   *want*
920 DAW Now I pray you
Lie down on this green.
COLL On the thieves yet I mean.°   *think*
DAW Whereto should ye teen?°   *be angry*
Do as I say you.

[*They lie down.*]

[*An* ANGEL *sings* Gloria in Excelsis *and then speaks.*][2]

925 ANGEL Rise, herdmen hend,°   *gracious*
For now is he born
That shall take from the fiend
That Adam had lorn;°   *lost*
That devil to shend,°   *destroy*

8. I.e., the baby is a changeling.
9. I stand entirely at your mercy.
1. I.e., 140 pounds.

2. An original stage direction; "Glory [to God] in the highest" (Latin; see Luke 2.14).

930 This night is he born.
    God is made your friend
    Now at this morn,
       He behestys.°   *promises*
    At Bedlem° go see: *Bethlehem*
935 There lies that free,°   *noble one*
    In a crib full poorly,
       Betwixt two bestys.°   *beasts*

      [*The* ANGEL *retires.*]

COLL   This was a strange steven°   *voice*
    That ever yet I heard.
940 It is a marvel to neven°   *tell of*
    Thus to be scared.
GIB Of God's Son of heaven
    He spake upward.°   *on high*
    All the woods on a leven°   *by a flash of lightning*
945 Methought that he gard°   *made*
       Appear.
DAW He spake of a barn°   *child*
    In Bedlem, I you warn.°   *tell*
COLL   That betokens yond starn.°   *star*
950   Let us seek him there.

GIB Say, what was his song?
    Heard ye not how he cracked it?°   *trilled it*
    Three breves° to a long?   *in triple rhythm*
DAW Yea, marry, he hacked it.
955 Was no crochet[3] wrong,
    Nor nothing that lacked it.°   *was missing*
COLL   For to sing us among,
    Right as he knacked it,
       I can.°   *know how*
960 GIB Let see how ye croon!
    Can ye bark at the moon?
DAW Hold your tongues! Have done!
COLL Hark after, than!

      [*Sings.*]

GIB To Bedlem he bade
965 That we should gang:°   *go*
    I am full fard°   *afraid*
    That we tarry too lang.°   *long*
DAW Be merry and not sad;
    Of mirth is our sang:
970 Everlasting glad°   *joy*
    Our reward may we fang.°   *get*

---

3. A short musical note, requiring skillful control to sing.

COLL   Without noise
   Hie° we thither forthy°   *hurry / therefore*
   To that child and that lady;
975   Though we be wet and weary,
     We have it not to lose.[4]

GIB   We find by the prophecy—
   Let be your din!—
   Of David and Isaiah,
980   And more than I mention
   That prophesied by clergy°   *learning*
   That in a virgin
   Should he alight and lie,
   To quench our sin
985   And relieve it,
   Humankind from woe,
   For Isaiah said so:
   Ecce virgo
    Concipiet[5] a child that is naked.

990 DAW   Full glad may we be
   If we abide that day
   That lovely lad to see,
   That all mights may.°   *who is almighty*
   Lord, well were me
995   For once and for ay°   *always*
   Might I kneel on my knee,
   Some word for to say
    To that child.
   But the angel said
1000   In a crib was he laid,
   He was poorly arrayed,
    Both humble and mild.

COLL   Patriarchs that has been,
   And prophets beforn,°   *before (our time)*
1005   That desired to have seen
   This child that is born,
   They are gone full clean—
   That have they lorn.°[6]   *lost*
   We shall see him, I ween,°   *think*
1010   Ere it be morn,
    To token.°   *as a sign*
   When I see him and feel,
   Then know I full well
   It is true as steel
1015   What prophets have spoken:

4. We must not lose the opportunity.
5. Behold, a virgin shall conceive (Latin; Isaiah 7.14).
6. See Matthew 13.17.

To so poor as we are
That he would appear,
First find and declare°   *announce (himself)*
By his messenger.
1020 GIB Go we now, let us fare,
The place is us near.
  DAW I am ready and yare;°   *eager*
Go we in fere°   *together*
  To that bright.°   *glorious one*
1025 Lord, if thy will be—
We are unlettered all three—
Grant us some glee
  To comfort your wight.°   *child*

  [*They go to Bethlehem and enter the stable.*]

  COLL Hail, comely and clean!°   *pure*
1030 Hail, young child!
Hail Maker, as I mean,°   *believe*
Of a virgin so mild!   *born of*
You have cursed I ween,°   *think*
The warlock° so wild.   *devil*
1035 The false guiler of teen,°   *pain*
Now goes he beguiled.
  Lo, he merries!°   *is merry*
Lo, he laughs, my sweeting!
A well fair meeting!
1040 I have holden my heting:°   *promise*
  Have a bob° of cherries.   *bunch*

  GIB Hail, sovereign Saviour,
For you has us sought!
Hail freely food° and flour,°   *noble child / flower*
1045 That all thing has wrought!°   *created*
Hail, full of favour,
That made all of nought!
Hail! I kneel and I cower.°   *crouch*
A bird have I brought
1050   To my barn.°   *child*
Hail, little tiny mop!°   *baby*
Of our creed thou art crop.°   *head*
I would drink on thy cup,
  Little day-starn.°   *day star*

1055 DAW Hail, darling dear,
Full of Godhead!
I pray you be near
When that I have need.
Hail, sweet is thy cheer°—   *face*
1060 My heart would bleed

To see you sit here
In so poor weed,°   *clothing*
   With no pennies.
Hail, put forth your dall!°   *hand*
1065 I bring you but a ball:
Have and play thee withal,
   And go to the tennis.

MARY The Father of heaven,
God omnipotent,
1070 That set all on seven,°   *seven days*
His Son has he sent.
My name could he neven,°   *utter*
And light ere he went.[7]
I conceived him full even
1075 Through might as he meant.°   *intended*
   And now is he born.
May he keep you from woe!
I shall pray him so.
Tell forth as you go,
1080   And think on this morn.

COLL Farewell, lady,
So fair to behold,
   With your child on your knee.
GIB But he lies full cold.
1085 Lord, well is me.
Now we go, you behold.
DAW Forsooth, already
   It seems to be told
     Full oft.
1090 COLL What grace we have fun!°   *received*
GIB Come forth, now are we won!°   *redeemed*
DAW To sing are we bun:°   *bound*
   Let's take on loft.[8]

   [*They sing.*]

---

7. And descended (into me) before he departed (cf. Luke 1.28).
8. Let's sing loudly.

TALKING ANIMALS

Literature written in Britain between the twelfth and the sixteenth centuries is crowded with animals. Of course writers of encyclopedias and moralists also focused on animals as sources of, respectively, knowledge about the natural world and ethical instruction for humans. Literary animals, by contrast, tell us something very different—much funnier, more skeptical, and more daring.

Medieval literature tells us little of serious interest about the reality of the natural world, and neither for the most part does it pretend to. Even if they do not offer plausible zoology, many works of literature about animals do seem superficially to use animals in the same way moralists use them, as prompts to ideal ethical behavior for humans. In fact, however, the ethics prompted by animal literature tends to be much more daring than that of the moralists, and much more candid than the moralists are about the powerful challenges humans face as they attempt to live ethically. The animal literature frankly confesses, for example, that humans experience sexual desire, that many of us eat other animals, and that we are likely to ignore ethical advice when we are hungry. The literature frankly recognizes, that is, that we too are animals.

In addition to thinking adventurously about ethics, animal literature also prompts us to think about politics. The need for collective action is all the more urgent and all the more difficult to achieve when considered through the lens of the animal "kingdom." Much late-medieval animal literature is not about animals so much as about us; it uses animals to think with, and it thinks daring, often refreshing, if sometimes uncomfortable thoughts.

Above all, animals talk in late-medieval animal literature. When they talk, they obviously blur the boundary between animals and humans, underlining the fact that talking animals point to linguistically gifted human counterparts. They therefore often speak in heightened and learned rhetoric, as in, for example, Henryson's "The Cock and the Jasper" (pp. 555–58), or Chaucer's *Nun's Priest's Tale* (pp. 344–58). Precisely as they speak in specifically human ways, however, authors will take care to remind readers that these are animals talking, that humans are animals too, and that, therefore, human pretension to elevated philosophical, ethical, and political discourse might be vulnerable in precisely the ways it is vulnerable when voiced by animals. The same vulnerability attends the rhetorically elevated ways in which narrators describe animal action: if it is ridiculous to describe animals as exemplary of higher human aspirations, then maybe it is no less ridiculous to describe humans in that way.

The main genre of medieval literary animal story is the animal fable. Animal fables claim Aesop (ca. sixth century B.C.E.) as their source. They are small narratives in which animals act and speak, with even smaller morals tacked on at the end. They involve many animals (e.g., frogs, mice, lambs, foxes, birds, wolves, and lions). Such stories were used to teach schoolboys both Latin and some commonsense morality into the bargain (e.g., don't overeat; don't overreach; save up for the hard times; justice can be rough and ready, so keep clear of the predators). In the hands of great literary artists such as Chaucer and Henryson, however, these narratives express mordant comedy and truths whose force extends well beyond the elementary classroom.

Beast epic is a much later offshoot from the ancient animal fable tradition. It appears in Europe for the first time in the tenth century in Latin, and in the twelfth century in vernacular languages. Beast epics are groups of interconnected narratives, set in the court of the lion; their single (anti-)hero is Reynard the Fox. Beast epic presents narratives of dark but vital humor that repeat the same narrative with many variations: its rhetorically brilliant fox Reynard almost always outwits all comers by manipulating their greed or vanity. No matter how tight the corner into which Reynard has been backed, we know he'll escape. He'll escape through brilliant narrative control and intimate, intuitive knowledge of his enemies' weaknesses. He exposes the arrogance of the greedy, but also, even more damagingly, the hypocrisy of the "civilized" order. Chaucer's *Nun's Priest's Tale* is excerpted from larger narratives of this kind, even if the fox in that tale is finally unsuccessful.

Late-medieval writers reach for animals in many other genres, too. A great tradition of late-medieval, Neoplatonic philosophical poetry attempted to express the ecological balance of the cosmos, placing the microcosm of humans within the macrocosm of the natural world and planets. Humans were definitely at the center of that vision, but were in no way conceived as transcendent above the natural world: in order to understand ourselves, these texts tell us, humans need to understand how we are a compact amalgam of the forces and matter that govern the universe. Humans share with the rest of nature the tense balance of the natural energies that constitute natural systems. We can understand nature because we are made of the same stuff, but for that reason we are dangerously prone to place appetite above understanding. Animals naturally figure powerfully in philosophical fictions such as Bernard Silvestris's *Cosmographia* (1140s) and Alan of Lille's *Complaint of Nature* (1160s). Vernacular poems such as Chaucer's *Parliament of Birds* (1370s) rework and question this Latin tradition.

In all the traditions so far considered, humans are humans and animals are animals, even if they are talking animals. Medieval literature also has examples of interspecies crossing, of humans provisionally and painfully locked into animal form. Derived ultimately from the tradition of Ovid's *Metamorphoses* (finished before 8 C.E.), these stories are said to be taken from folk culture and the cultural margins, thereby permitting weird, unscientific, but wonderfully penetrating accounts of human/animal overlaps. Because they merge animal and human, they permit and provoke reflection across the species divide: what might it be like to be an animal? Marie de France's lay *Bisclavret* (late twelfth century) is an especially rich example of this genre.

All these traditions involve narrative and literary surprises, not to say shocks. Animals fail to observe the rules of social or literary decorum that govern human actors. These surprises can be amusing or dark, but they are always revealing about the full scope of what it is to be human.

MARIE DE FRANCE

For the full headnote on Marie de France (fl. ca. 1180), see pages 159–60.

The Germanic word *werewolf* (in this tale "garwaf" [l. 4]) is a compound word with two equally balanced, juxtaposed elements: *wer*, meaning "man," and *wolf*. Marie de France's *Bisclavret* tests the degree to which these species categories are indeed balanced.

Romances (see pp. 158–59) always involve a narrative movement from civilization to wild place, and from wild back to a reformed, strengthened civilization. The wisdom embedded in that narrative structure is that civilization is not a unitary concept; on the contrary, for the civilized order to maintain its balance, it must have commerce with all that threatens it. In testing that claim, romances rarely involve a species shift from human to animal. *Bisclavret* not only involves that shift, but does so at an extreme limit: the human morphs into one of the most brutal and savage of animals, the wolf. *Bisclavret* therefore tests the binary civilizational claim of romance narrative at an extreme, limited case. Can the human survive transformation into a wolf? Or, even further, *must* the human have commerce with its wolf counterpart to maintain its balance?

Binary romance narratives, always moving between tame and wild, express and disguise a shameful secret: civilization *needs* the wild. The story structure might pretend otherwise, as it returns the protagonist to, and reconfirms the values of, civilization at its end. That story structure has, however, secretly confessed civilization's dependence on the wild. Romances cannot be explicit about the need for the untamed;

rather, the need is implicit in the story structure. In this story, the husband clearly needs to be a wolf, for three whole days a week. His marriage is stable as long as this need is *not* articulated by the couple. Once articulated, the structure of the marriage collapses, since the wife wants nothing to do with the man-wolf, and repudiates him.

One might expect a savage, civilization-destroying narrative from here on. And indeed, that expectation is in part confirmed: the wolf is condemned to his wild state; twice he attacks humans; and he is twice on the point of being torn apart as a wild animal. Savagery is not, however, the whole story: the wolf "speaks," his attacks are targeted, and he otherwise observes court propriety with extreme delicacy. Even when he can retrieve his human form through his clothes, he refuses to do so in public. Through his wildness he prompts the mechanisms of human justice. Sometimes the bad manners of a wolf attack in the court itself are necessary to prompt justice.

That is one way of reading *Bisclavret*, from the wolf-man's perspective. From that angle, however, structures of heterosexual marriage turn out to be disposable. The wife is attacked and tortured, and she ends up banished, without a nose, and becomes the ancestor of noseless offspring. The husband ends up kissing and hugging the king in the king's bed. "Civilization," "justice," and "human," then, turn out to have more-restricted referents in this story by a woman author.

Bisclavret[1]

In crafting lays, I won't forget
—I mustn't—that of Bisclavret;
Bisclavret: so named in Breton;
But *Garwaf* in the Norman tongue.[2]

5   One used to hear, in times gone by
—it often happened, actually—
men became werewolves, many men,
and in the forest made their den.
A werewolf is a savage beast;
10   in his blood-rage, he makes a feast
of men, devours them, does great harms,
and in vast forests lives and roams.
Well, for now, let us leave all that;
I want to speak of Bisclavret.

15   In Brittany there lived a lord
—wondrous, the praise of him I've heard—
a good knight, handsome, known to be
all that makes for nobility.
Prized, he was, much, by his liege lord;

1. Lycanthropy—belief in werewolves—was an intensely popular belief in the Middle Ages, and it figures frequently in folklore and also in literature: lays, romances, fabliaux, and beast fables. Versions of this story appear as early as in Roman works by Pliny (*Natural History*) and Petronius (*The Satyricon*). Marie's story may well have contributed to later versions in the thirteenth and fourteenth centuries, such as the *Roman de Reynart le Contrefait*, where the hero is called Bisclarel and the king is Arthur. The text is derived from

the translation of Dorothy Gilbert (2015). The notes derive from the same edition, though they are much reduced.
2. Alfred Ewert derives the name *bisclavret* from the Breton *bleis lauaret*, "speaking wolf" (*Marie de France, Lais*, 172). Jean Rychner, in his perhaps even more authoritative edition, mentions as well an alternative opinion, in which the form *bisclavret* may derive from *bisc lavret*, which suggests a wolf in pants or breeches, a different human characteristic.

20 by all his neighbors was adored.
He'd wed a wife, a worthy soul,
most elegant and beautiful;
he loved her, and she loved him, too.
One thing she found most vexing, though.
25 During the week he'd disappear
for three whole days, she knew not where;
what happened to him, where he went.
His household, too, was ignorant.
He returned home again one day;
30 high-spirited and happy. She
straightway proceeded to inquire:
    "My fair sweet friend," she said, "fair sire,
if I just dared, I'd ask of you
a thing I dearly wish to know,
35 except that I'm so full of fear
of your great anger, husband dear."
    When he had heard this, he embraced her,
drew her to him, clasped and kissed her.
    "Lady," he said, "come, ask away!
40 Nothing you wish, dear, certainly
I will not tell you, that I know."
    "Faith!" she said, "you have cured me so!
But I have such anxiety,
sire, on those days you part from me,
45 my heart is full of pain. I fear
so much that I will lose you, dear.
Oh, reassure me, hastily!
If you do not, I soon will die.
Tell me, dear husband; tell me, pray,
50 What do you do? Where do you stay?
It seems to me you've found another!
You wrong me, if you have a lover!"
    "Lady," he said, "have mercy, do!
I'll have much harm in telling you.
55 I'd lose your love, if I should tell
and be lost to myself, as well."
    Now when the wife was thus addressed,
it seemed to her to be no jest.
Oftimes she begged, with all her skill,
60 coaxing and flattering, until
at last he told her all he did,
the tale entire; kept nothing hid.
    "Dame, I become a bisclavret.
in the great forest I'm afoot,
65 in deepest woods, near thickest trees,
and live on prey I track and seize."
    When he had told the whole affair,
she persevered; she asked him where
his clothes were; was he naked there?
70   "Lady," he said, "I go all bare."
    "Tell me, for God's sake, where you put your clothes!"

"Oh, I'll not tell you that:
I would be lost, you must believe,
75 if it were seen just how I live.
Bisclavret would I be, forever;
never could I be helped then, never,
till I got back my clothes, my own;
that's why their cache must not be known."
80   "Sire," said his lady in reply,
"more than all earth I love you. Why
hide, why have secrets in your life?
Why, why mistrust your own dear wife?
That does not seem a loving thought.
85 What have I done? What sin, what fault
has caused your fear, in any way?
You must be fair! You have to say!"
    So she harassed and harried him
so much, he finally gave in.
90   "Lady," he said, "just by the wood,
just where I enter, by the road,
there's an old chapel. Now, this place
has often brought me help and grace.
There is a stone there, in the brush,
95 hollow and wide, beneath a bush.
In brush and under bush, I store
my clothes, till I head home once more."
    The lady was amazed to hear:
She blushed deep red, from her pure fear.
100 Terror, she felt, at this strange tale.
She thought what means she could avail
herself of how to leave this man.
She could not lie with him again.

    In these parts lived a chevalier
105 who had long been in love with her.
Much did he pray and sue, and give
largesse in service to his love;
she had not loved him, nor had she
granted him any surety
110 that she, too, loved; but now she sent
this knight the news of her intent.
    "Friend," she wrote him, "rejoice, and know
that for which you have suffered so,
I grant you now without delay;
115 I'll not hold back in any way.
My body and my love I grant;
make me your mistress, if you want!"
    Kindly he thanked her, and her troth
accepted; she received his oath.
120 She told her lover how her lord
went to the wood, and what he did,
what he became, once he was there.
She told in detail how and where

to find the road and clothing cache;
125 and then she sent him for the stash.
 Thus was Bisclavret trapped for life;
ruined, betrayed, by his own wife.
Because his absences were known,
people assumed he'd really gone,
130 this time, for good. They searched around,
enough, but he could not be found,
for all their inquiries. At last
everyone let the matter rest.
The lady wed the chevalier
135 who'd been so long in love with her.

 A whole year, after this event,
thus passed. The king went out to hunt,
went to the forest straightaway,
there where the bisclavret now lay.
140 The hunting dogs were now unleashed
and soon they found the changeling beast.
All day they flung themselves at him,
all day pursued, both dogs and men;
they almost had him. Now they'd rend
145 and tear him; now he'd meet his end.
His eye, distinguishing, could see
the king; to beg his clemency
he seized the royal stirrup, put
a kiss upon the leg and foot.
150 The king, observing, felt great fear.
Calling his men, he cried, "Come here!"
"Lords!" he said, "Come and look at this!
See what a marvel is this kiss,
this humble, gracious gesturing!
155 That's a man's mind; it begs the king
for mercy. Now, drive back the hounds!
See that none strike or give it wounds.
This beast has mind; it has intent.
Come, hurry up! It's time we went.
160 I'll give protection for this beast.
And for today, the hunt has ceased."[3]

 The king had turned around, at that;
following him, the bisclavret
close by; he would not lose the king,
165 abandon him, for anything.
The king then led the beast, to bring
it to the castle, marveling,

---

3. Cf. the famous story of Actaeon as told by the Roman poet Ovid in his *Metamorphoses* (3.138–252), an immensely popular and influential work in the Middle Ages and the Renaissance. In that tale the unfortunate hunter Actaeon happens to see—by *aventure*, as Marie would say—the goddess Diana bathing naked, which enrages her; she turns him into a stag, and he is mauled to death by his hounds. He has a human mind in a stag's body but no opportunity to prove it and thus be recognized as human and saved. This story would certainly have been well known to Marie and her original audience, and the knowledge might well have added suspense to Marie's episode.

rejoicing at it, for he'd never
seen such a wondrous creature, ever.
170 He loved the wolf and held it dear
and he charged every follower
that, for his love, they guard it well
and not mistreat the animal.
No one must strike it; and, he'd said,
175 it must be watered and well fed.
Gladly his men now guarded it.
Among the knights, the bisclavret
now lived, and slept close by the king;
everyone loved it, cherishing
180 its noble bearing and its charm.
It never wanted to do harm,
and where the king might walk or ride,
there it must be, just at his side,
wherever he might go or move;
185 so well it showed its loyal love.

What happened after that? Now, hear.
The king held court; he had appear
all barons, vassals; gave commands
to all who held from him their lands,
190 to help a festival take place,
serving with elegance and grace.
Among those chevaliers was he
—so richly dressed, so splendidly!—
who'd wed the wife of Bisclavret.
195 Little he knew or thought just yet
that he would find his foe so near!
Soon as he came, this chevalier,
to court, and Bisclavret could see
the man, he ran up furiously,
200 sank in his teeth, and dragged him close.
Many the injuries and woes
he would have suffered, but the king
called out commands, while brandishing
his staff. The beast rushed, twice, that day,
205 to bite the man; all felt dismay,
for none had seen the beast display
toward anyone, in any way,
such viciousness. There must be reason,
the household said, for him to seize on
210 the knight, who must have done him wrong;
the wish for vengeance seemed so strong.
And so they let the matter rest
till the conclusion of the feast.
The barons took their leave, each one,
215 each to his castle and his home.
All my good judgment counsels me
he who was first to leave was he
set upon by the bisclavret.
Small wonder the beast had such hate!

220   Not too long after this occurred
—such is my thought, so I have heard—
into the forest went the king
—so noble and so wise a being—
where he'd first found the bisclavret.
225   The animal was with him yet.
The night of this return, the king
took, in this countryside, lodging.
And this the wife of Bisclavret
well knew. Dressed fetchingly, she set
230   out to have speech with him next day;
rich gifts were part of her display.
Bisclavret saw her come. No man
had strength to hold him as he ran
up to his wife in rage and fury.
235   Hear of his vengeance! Hear the story!
He tore her nose off, then and there.
What worse could he have done to her?
From all sides now, and full of threat
men ran and would have killed him, but
240   a wise man expeditiously
spoke to the king. "Listen to me!
He's been with you, this animal;
there is not one man of us all
who has not, long since, had to see
245   and travel with him, frequently,
and he has harmed no one, not once
shown viciousness nor violence
save just now, as you saw him do.
And by the faith I owe to you,
250   he has some bitter quarrel with her
and with her husband, her seigneur.
She was wife to that chevalier
whom you so prized, and held so dear,
who disappeared some time ago.
255   What happened, no one seems to know.
Put her to torture. She may state
something, this dame, to indicate
why the beast feels for her such hate.
Force her to speak! She'll tell it straight.
260   We've all known marvels, chanced to see
strange events, here in Brittany."
The king thought this advice was fair;
and he detained the chevalier.
The lady, too, he held; and she
265   he put to pain and agony.
Part out of pain, part out of fear,
she made her former lord's case clear:
how she had managed to betray
her lord, and take his clothes away;
270   the story he had told to her,
what he became, and how, and where;

and how, when once his clothes were gone
—stolen—he was not seen again.
She gave her theory and her thought:
275 Surely this beast was Bisclavret.
These spoils, these clothes, the king demanded;
whether she would or no, commanded
that she go back and find them, get
and give them to the bisclavret.

280   When they were put in front of him
he didn't seem to notice them.
The king's wise man spoke up once more
—the one who'd counselled him before—
"Fair sire, this will not do at all!
285 We can't expect this animal,
in front of you, sire, to get dressed
and change his semblance of a beast.
You don't grasp what this means, my king!
—or see his shame and suffering.
290 Into your room have led this beast;
with him, his clothes. Let him get dressed;
For quite some time, leave him alone.
If he's a man, that is soon known!"
   The king himself led the bisclavret;
295 and on him all the doors were shut.
They waited. And then finally
two barons, with the king, all three,
entered. What a discovery!
There on the king's bed, they could see
300 asleep, the knight. How the king ran
up to the bed, to embrace his man,
kiss him, a hundred times and more!
   Quickly he acted to restore
his lands, as soon as possible;
305 more he bestowed than I can tell.
His wife was banished. She was chased
out of the country, and disgraced,
and chased out, travelling with her,
her mate and co-conspirator.

310   Quite a few children had this dame,
who in their way achieved some fame
for looks, for a distinctive face;
numbers of women of her race
—it's true—were born without a nose.
315 Noseless they lived, the story goes.

And this same story you have heard
truly occurred; don't doubt my word.
I made this *lai* of Bisclavret
so no one, ever, will forget.

GEOFFREY CHAUCER

F or the full headnote on Geoffrey Chaucer (ca. 1343–1400), see pages 256–59.

Chaucer's *Parliament of Birds* is deeply indebted to two classic texts, but a servant to neither. For in both cases, dreaming, desire, and the birds take over.

Chaucer's narrator starts reading a text by the Roman lawyer and politician Marcus Tullius Cicero (106–43 B.C.E.), Book 6 of his *Republic* (51 B.C.E.), known in the medieval period as *The Dream of Scipio*. The Latin text relates the dream of the Roman general Scipio (d. 129 B.C.E.), who dreams that his grandfather Scipio Africanus takes him on an astral voyage to understand how service to the state will be rewarded in the afterlife, and how pursuit of sensual desire must instead be repressed by servants of the state as they pursue the Roman military conquest of North Africa.

Later in the poem, the narrator mentions another Latin philosophical text, the late-medieval *Complaint of Nature* (1160s) by Alan of Lille. In this text the goddess Nature, whose gown is splendidly embroidered with images of every species of bird, explains to the narrator why human desire, especially homosexual desire, alone in nature deviates from the ideal, fertile, and productive models of the natural order. The poem ends with the excommunication of homosexual love.

How are these severe Latin texts received in Chaucer's vernacular poem? They enter the dream world and are there rewritten by the desire of the narrator's dreaming psyche. He enters the walled garden of Nature, there to replay Cicero's "common profit," or political good as the collective "good" of sexual desire as expressed in Nature's parliament, where birds choose their mates on Valentine's Day. And the birds embroidered on the outer garment of Alan's goddess Nature come to life here, irrepressibly debating, singing, and quacking their way to a collective, ecological resolution of desire. And whereas Alan's natural order is ideally a hierarchical one ruled by cosmic reason, here the hierarchy is invoked only to be questioned in many ways. The aristocratic birds (revealingly, they are birds of prey) may, for example, be sophisticated in their pursuit of a refined and courtly love, but it's the lower birds who, for all their comic, no-nonsense quacking, are better serving the common profit of Nature's ecological order by choosing their mates with admirable dispatch. And when it comes to advising the young aristocratic female bird about the male lover she should should choose among the three offering themselves, Nature refuses to recognize the "natural" hierarchy of birth: "If I *were* Reson, certes, than wolde I / Counseyle yow the royal tercel take" (lines 632–33, emphasis added). With this single subjunctive, Chaucer opens up a significant difference between himself and his Neoplatonic poetic and philosophical frames: passionate love may not be rational, but it *is* natural. And natural love can cross the class boundaries of birth, thereby revealing that those boundaries are not in fact natural at all. In this poem, bonding is a matter of election.

This, then, is an account of a new and largely joyous ecology, with immediate implications for humans and human society. Chaucer's Latin source texts promote cosmic, philosophical reason as expressed by patrician figures; his own vernacular poem takes its cue rather from the parliament (literally "the speaking") of birds of all classes.

Parliament of Birds[1]

The lyf so short, the craft so long to lerne,[2]
Thassay° so sharp, so hard° the conqueringe,   *the attempt / difficult*
The dredful° joy, that alwey slit so yerne,[3]   *fearful*
Al this mene I by love,[4] that my felinge°   *emotional state*
5   Astonyeth° with his wonderful worching   *is bewildered*
So sore[5] ywis,° that whan I on him thinke,   *indeed*
Nat wot[6] I wel wher that I flete° or sinke.   *float*

For al be° that I knowe nat love in dede,   *although*
Ne wot° how that he quyteth folk hir hyre,[7]   *know*
10 Yet happeth me ful ofte in bokes rede
Of his miracles, and his cruel yre;°   *ire*
Ther rede I wel he wol be lord and syre,
I dar not seyn, his strokes been so sore,°   *severe*
But God save swich a lord! I can no more.

15 Of usage,[8] what for luste what for lore,[9]
On bokes rede I ofte, as I yow tolde.
But wherfor° that I speke al this? not yore   *why*
Agon,° it happed me for to beholde   *not long ago*
Upon a boke, was write with lettres olde;
20 And therupon, a certeyn thing to lerne,
The longe day ful faste° I radde and yerne.°   *diligently / very intently*

For out of olde feldes, as men sey,
Cometh al this newe corn fro yeer to yere;
And out of olde bokes, in good fey,°   *faith*
25 Cometh al this newe science° that men lere.   *knowledge*
But now to purpos as of this matere[1]—
To rede forth so gan me to delyte,
That al that day me thoughte but a lyte.[2]

This book of which I make of mencioun,
30 Entitled was al thus, as I shal telle,
"Tullius of the dreme of Scipion."[3]

---

1. The text has been edited afresh by James Simpson with help from Michelle de Groot.
2. Middle English rendering of a Latin proverb (*Ars longa, vita brevis*). Chaucer probably encountered it the Roman Stoic Seneca's essay "On the Brevity of Life" (1.1), but Seneca himself was quoting the Greek physician Hippocrates' *Aphorisms* (1). Chaucer's translation, "craft," makes explicit the classical and medieval conception of poetic art as a skill comparable to practical skills like medicine or carpentry.
3. Passes so quickly.
4. I.e., all this refers to love.
5. I.e., so intensely.
6. I do not know.
7. Pays people for their service.
8. I.e., habitually.
9. Both for enjoyment and edification.
1. I.e., to come to the point.

2. I.e., the day seemed brief.
3. *The Dream of Scipio* is the closing episode of Marcus Tullius Cicero's *De re publica*, composed in 51 B.C.E. It is told from the point of view of Publius Cornelius Scipio Africanus the Younger, who traveled to Carthage in North Africa as part of his duties as a military tribune. There, he visits King Masinissa, an old friend of his grandfather, Publius Cornelius Scipio Africanus the Elder (Chaucer calls him "African" here). During his visit, Scipio's grandfather visits him in a dream. Taking him up into the sky, Scipio the Elder shows his grandson the nine planetary spheres of classical cosmography and exhorts him to stoic civic virtue. The *Dream* was known in the Middle Ages through an influential late 4th-century commentary by Macrobius, which uses the Ciceronian text to discourse on a number of topics in natural history, astronomy, and dream theory.

Chapitres seven it hadde, of hevene and helle,
And erthe, and soules that therin dwelle,
Of whiche, as shortly as I can it trete,°   *deal with it*
35   Of his sentence° I wol you seyn the grete.°   *teaching / gist*

First telleth it, whan Scipion was come
In Afrik,° how he met Massinisse,   *Africa*
That him for joye in armes hath ynome.°   *taken*
Than telleth it hir° speche and al the blisse   *their*
40   That was betwix° hem, til the day gan misse;   *between*
And how his auncestre, African so dere,
Gan in his slepe that night to him appere.

Than telleth it, that fro a sterry place,
How African hath him Cartage° shewed,   *Carthage*
45   And warned him beforn° of al his grace,°   *in advance / fortune*
And seyde him, what man, lered° other lewed,°   *learned / unlearned*
That loveth comun profit,[4] wel ythewed,°   *virtuous*
He shuld unto a blisful place wende,°   *go*
Ther as joye is that last withouten ende.

50   Than asked he, if folk that now ben dede
Have lyf and dwelling in another place;
And African seyde, "Ye, withouten drede,"[5]
And that our present worldes lyves space[6]
Nis but a maner° deth, what wey we trace,[7]   *a type of*
55   And rightful folk shal go, after they dye,
To heven; and shewed him the galaxye.

Than shewed he him the litel erthe, that heer is,
At regard of[8] the hevenes quantite;
And after shewed he him the nyne speres,°   *spheres*
60   And after that the melodye herde he
That cometh of thilke° speres thryes° three,[9]   *those same / thrice*
That welle° is of musyk and melodye   *source*
In this world here, and cause of armonye.°   *harmony*

Than bad° he him, sin erthe was so lyte,°   *bade / insignificant*
65   And ful of torment and of harde grace,°   *misfortune*
That he ne shulde him in the world delyte.
Than tolde he him, in certeyn yeres space,[1]
That every sterre shulde come into his place
Ther it was first; and al shulde out of minde[2]

70   That in this worlde is don of° al mankinde.   *by*
Than prayde him Scipioun to telle him al
The wey to come into that hevene blisse;

4. The common good.
5. Yes, certainly.
6. I.e., lifetime.
7. Whatever way we go.
8. In comparison to.
9. According to classical and medieval cosmog- raphy, the earth sat at the center of nine plane- tary spheres, each of which turned at a different rate. Their rotation was believed to generate ethereal music.
1. I.e., in time.
2. I.e., be forgotten.

And he seyde, "Know thyself first immortal,[3]
And loke ay besily thou werke and wisse°   teach
75 To comun profit, and thou shalt not misse°   fail
To comen swiftly to that place dere,°   joyous
That ful of blisse is and of soules clere.°   pure

But brekers of the lawe, soth° to seyne,°   truth / say
And lykerous° folk, after that they be dede,   lecherous
80 Shul alwey whirle aboute the erthe in peyne,
Til many a world be passed,[4] out of drede,[5]
And than, foryeven° alle hir wikked dede,°   forgiven / deeds
Than shul they come unto that blisful place,
To which to comen god thee sende his grace!"

85 The day gan failen, and the derke night,
That reveth° bestes° from her besinesse,°   takes / beasts / activity
Berafte° me my book for lakke of light,   deprived me of
And to my bedde I gan me for to dresse,°   prepare
Fulfild° of thought and besy hevinesse;°   full / anxious perplexity
90 For bothe I hadde thing which that I nolde,°   did not want
And eek I ne hadde that thing that I wolde.°   wanted

But fynally my spirit, at the laste,
Forwery of° my labour al the day,   exhausted from
Took rest, that made me to slepe faste,
95 And in my slepe I mette,° as that° I lay,   dreamed / while
How African, right in the selfe° aray   same
That Scipioun him saw before that tyde,[6]
Was come and stood right at my bedes syde.

The wery hunter, slepinge in his bed,
100 To wode° ayein his minde goth anoon;   the woods
The juge dremeth how his plees° ben sped;   cases
The carter dremeth how his cart is goon;
The riche, of gold; the knight fight with his foon;°   foes
The seke° met he drinketh of the tonne;°   sick man / cask
105 The lover met he hath his lady wonne.[7]

Can I nat seyn if that the cause were
For I had red° of African beforn,   read
That made me to mete° that he stood there;   dream
But thus seyde he, "Thou hast thee so wel born
110 In loking of myn olde book totorn,°   tattered
Of which Macrobie roghte° nat a lyte,   concerned himself with
That somdel° of thy labour wolde I quyte!"°—   some / repay

3. I.e., know first of all that you are immortal. A
version of the Delphic maxim, "Know thyself."
4. I.e., a long time.
5. I.e., quite certainly.
6. I.e., in the past.
7. Chaucer is alluding to Macrobius's theory of
dreams put forth in his commentary on *The
Dream of Scipio*. Macrobius proposes that nightmares (*insomnia*) are a category of dream that
contain no prophetic significance and instead
result from mental reactions to the events of the

day. Another category of dream that Macrobius
describes is the oracle (*oraculum*) in which a
trusted authority figure appears and offers advice.
The Dream of Scipio is an oracular dream. Chaucer is also aware of a more refined, 12th-century
categorization of non-predictive dreams, the
so-called animal dream, according to which many
dreams simply replicate what the dreamer has
been doing during the day. Chaucer here is equivo-
cating about what kind of dream the *Parliament
of Birds* might be.

Citherea!⁸ thou blisful lady swete,
That with thy fyrbrand° dauntest whom thee lest,°   *torch / like*
115 And madest me this sweven° for to mete,°   *dream / dream*
Be thou my help in this, for thou mayst best;
As wisly° as I saw thee north-north-west,   *surely*
When I began my sweven for to wryte,⁹
So yif me might to ryme and ek tendyte!°   *compose*

120 This forseid African me hente° anoon,°   *laid hold of / at once*
And forth with him unto a gate broghte
Right of a parke, walled of grene stoon;
And over the gate, with lettres large ywroghte,°   *made*
Ther weren vers ywriten, as me thoghte,
125 On eyther halfe, of ful gret difference,
Of which I shal yow sey the pleyn sentence.°   *meaning*

"Thorgh me men goon into that blisful place
Of hertes hele° and dedly woundes cure;   *health*
Thorgh me men goon unto the welle of Grace,
130 Ther grene and lusty° May shal ever endure;   *pleasant*
This is the wey to al good aventure;°   *fortune*
Be glad, thou reder, and thy sorwe ofcaste,
Al open am I; passe in, and sped the faste!"¹

"Thorgh me men goon," than spak that other syde,
135 "Unto the mortal strokes of the spere,
Of which Disdayn and Daunger° is the gyde,°   *haughtiness / wielder*
Ther tre shal never fruyt ne leves bere.
This streem yow ledeth to the
    sorwful were,°   *obstruction in a stream to catch fish*
Ther as° the fish in prison is al drye;°   *where / dried out*
140 Theschewing° is only the remedye."²   *the avoidance*

Thise vers of gold and blak ywriten were,
Of whiche I gan astouned° to beholde,   *bewildered*
For with that oon encresed ay my fere,
And with that other gan myn herte bolde;°   *embolden*
145 That oon me hette,° that other did me colde,°   *heated / made me cold*
No wit had I, for errour,° for to chese   *confusion*
To entre or flee, or me to save or lese.°   *lose*

Right as, betwixen adamauntes° two   *lodestones*
Of even might, a pece of iren yset,
150 That hath no might to meve° to ne fro—   *move*
For what that on may hale,° that other let°—   *pull / hinders*
Ferde° I; that niste whether me was bet,³   *fared*
To entre or leve, til African my gyde
Me hente,° and shoof° in at the gates wyde,   *took hold of / shoved*

---

8. Cytherea, another name for Venus, the Roman goddess of love.
9. Probably an astronomical reference to the position of the planet Venus in the sky when Chaucer began to compose the poem.

1. I.e., prosper.
2. The contradictory inscriptions on the gate are reminescent of the words on the gates to hell in Dante's *Inferno* 3.1–9.
3. I knew not whether it would be better for me.

155 And seyde, "It stondeth writen in thy face,
Thyn errour, though thou telle it not to me;
But dred the nat to come into this place,
For this wryting nys nothing ment by thee,[4]
Ne by noon,[5] but° he Loves servant be;   *unless*
160 For thou of love hast lost thy tast,° I gesse,   *appreciation*
As seek° man hath of swete and bitternesse.   *sick*

But natheles, although that thou be dulle,°   *apathetic*
Yit that thou canst not do, yit mayst thou see;
For many a man that may not stonde a pulle,°   *a wrestling hold*
165 Yit lyketh him° at wrastling for to be,   *it pleases him*
And demeth yit wher he do bet or he;[6]
And if thou haddest cunning° for tendyte,°   *skill / to compose*
I shal thee shewen mater of° to wryte."   *matter about which*

With that my hond he took in his anoon,
170 Of which I comfort caughte, and went in faste;°   *immediately*
But, lord! so I was glad and wel begoon!°   *well placed*
For overal, wher I myn eyen caste,
Were trees clad with leves that ay shal laste,
Eche in his kinde, of colour fresh and grene
175 As emeraude, that joye was to sene.

The bilder° ook,° and eek the hardy asshe;   *builder / oak*
The piler° elm, the cofre° unto careyne;°   *pillar / coffer / corpse*
The boxtree piper;° holm° to whippes lasshe;   *for pipes / holly*
The sayling° fir; the cipres,° deth to   *for masts / cypress*
   pleyne;°   *lament*
180 The sheter ew,° the asp° for shaftes°   *yew for bows / aspen / arrows*
   pleyne;°   *straight*
The olyve of pees,° and eek the drunken vyne,   *peace*
The victor palm, the laurer° to devyne.°[7]   *laurel / foretell the future*

A gardyn saw I, ful of blosmy bowes,°   *branches*
Upon a river, in a grene mede,
185 Ther as swetnesse evermore ynow° is,   *in abundance*
With floures whyte, blewe, yelowe, and rede;
And colde welle-stremes, nothing dede,°   *stagnant*
That swommen ful of smale fisshes lighte,
With finnes rede and scales silver-brighte.

190 On every bough the briddes° herde I singe,   *birds*
With voys of aungel in hir armonye,
Som besyed hem[8] hir briddes forth to bringe;
The litel conyes° to hir pley gunne hye.[9]   *rabbits*

---

4. I.e., does not refer to you.
5. Nor to anyone.
6. I.e., still judges which wrestler does better.
7. These lines associate species of trees with their uses in human crafts. Thus, oaks and ash are described as useful for construction; elm as appropriate for support pillars and coffins; boxwood for making musical pipes; holly for making whips; fir for ships' timbers; cypresses for mourning; ewe and aspen for making bows and arrows; olive trees as symbols of peace; grapevines for the production of wine; palm leaves as symbols of victory; and laurels as useful in divination.
8. I.e., strove.
9. I.e., hurried themselves to their play.

And further al aboute I gan espye
195 The dredful° roo,° the buk, the hert and hinde,   *timid / roe*
Squerels, and bestes smale of gentil kinde.

Of instruments of strenges in accord
Herde I so pleye° and ravisshing swetnesse,   *play*
That god, that maker is of al and lord,
200 Ne herde never better, as I gesse;
Therwith° a wind, unnethe it might be lesse,[1]   *in addition*
Made in the leves grene a noise so softe
Acordaunt to° the briddes songe onlofte.°   *in harmony with / on high*

The air of that place so attempre° was   *temperate*
205 That never was grevaunce of hoot ne cold;
Ther wex° eek every holsum spyce and gras,   *grew*
Ne no man may ther wexe seek° ne old;   *sick*
Yet was ther joye more than a thousand fold
Than man can telle; ne never wolde it nighte,°   *become night*
210 But ay° cleer day to any mannes sighte.   *forever*

Under a tree, besyde a welle, I say°   *saw*
Cupyde[2] our lord his arwes° forge and fyle;°   *arrows / sharpen*
And at his fete his bowe al redy lay,
And Will° his doghter tempred al this whyle   *Desire*
215 The hedes in the welle, and with hir fyle
She couched hem[3] after as they shulde serve,
Some for to slee,° and some to wounde and kerve.°   *slay / cut*

Tho was I war of Plesaunce° anonright,   *sensual pleasure*
And of Aray,° and Lust,[4] and Curtesye,   *sartorial splendor*
220 And of the Craft that can and hath the might
To doon by force a wight° to do folye—   *person*
Disfigurat was she, I nil not[5] lye;
And by himself, under an oke, I gesse,
Saw I Delyt, that stood with
    Gentilnesse.°   *nobility (of birth, character, or manners)*

225 I saw Beautee, withouten any atyr,°   *clothing*
And Youthe, ful of game and jolyte,
Foolhardinesse, Flatery, and Desyr,
Messagerye,° and Mede,° and other three—   *sending of messages / reward*
Hir names shul noght here be told for me—
230 And upon pilers grete of jasper longe
I saw a temple of bras yfounded stronge.°   *well founded*

Aboute the temple daunceden alway
Wommen ynowe,° of whiche some ther were   *many*
Faire of hemself,[6] and somme of hem were gay;

---

1. It hardly could have been lighter.
2. Cupid, Roman god of love, son of Venus.
3. I.e., laid them out. The Italian poet Boccaccio describes this scene in the *Teseida* (7.50–66).

4. Desire. The word did not always have the pejorative connotation that it does today.
5. I will not.
6. I.e., by nature.

235 In kirtels,[7] al disshevele,° wente they there—   *with hair unbound*
That was hir office° alway, yeer by yere—   *duty*
And on the temple, of doves whyte and faire
Saw I sittinge many a hundred paire.

Before the temple dore ful soberly
240 Dame Pees° sat, with a curteyn in hir hond: *Peace*
And by hir syde, wonder discretly,°   *subtly*
Dame Pacience sitting ther I fond
With face pale, upon an hille of sond;°   *sand*
And aldernext,° within and eek withoute,   *nearest of all*
245 Behest° and Art,° and of hir folke a   *vow / rituals of courtly love*
    route.°   *retinue*

Within the temple, with syghes° hote as fyr   *sighs*
I herde a swogh° that gan aboute renne;[8]   *rushing sound*
Which syghes were engendred with[9] desyr,
That maden every auter° for to brenne°   *altar / burn*
250 Of° newe flaume; and wel aspyed I thenne   *with*
That al the cause of sorwe° that they drye°   *sorrow / suffer*
Cam of the bitter goddesse Jalousye.

The god Priapus[1] saw I, as I wente,
Within the temple, in soverayn place stonde,
255 In swich aray° as whan the asse him shente°   *state / put him to shame*
With crye by night, and with ceptre° in honde;   *scepter*
Ful besily men gunne assaye° and fonde°   *attempt / strive*
Upon his hede to sette, of sondry hewe,
Garlondes ful of floures fresshe newe.

260 And in a privee corner, in disporte,
Fond I Venus and hir porter Richesse,°   *wealth*
That was ful noble and hauteyn° of hir porte;°   *proud / bearing*
Derk was that place, but afterward lightnesse
I saw a lyte, unnethe° it might be lesse,   *hardly*
265 And on a bed of golde she lay to reste,
Til that the hote sonne gan to weste.°   *set in the West*

Hir gilte° heres with a golden threde   *golden*
Ybounden were, untressed° as she lay,   *loose*
And naked fro the breste up to the hede
270 Men might hir see; and, sothly for to say,
The remenant was wel kevered to my pay°   *satisfaction*
Right with a subtil° kerchef of Valence,[2]   *delicate*
Ther was no thikker cloth of no defence.[3]

---

7. Kirtel, a garment for women or girls, often an outer garment, sometimes worn over a smock or under a mantle, gown, or cloak.
8. I.e., that filled the place.
9. Begotten by.
1. Priapus, a Roman fertility god represented iconographically as a small man with a comically large penis. Chaucer refers to a story in Ovid's *Fasti* (1.415–40), in which Priapus is thwarted in his

plans to rape a sleeping nymph when a donkey brays and wakes her. She runs away, and her compatriots, now aware of the situation, mock Priapus and his erection. Boccaccio also recounts the story in the *Teseida* (7.60).
2. Thin, fine, openwork cloth from Valence (in southern France) or Valenciennes (in northern France), both towns known for fine clothmaking.
3. I.e., there was no thicker cloth to provide defense.

The place yaf° a thousand savours swote,°   *exuded / sweet*
275 And Bachus,[4] god of wyn, sat hir besyde,
And Ceres[5] next, that doth of hunger bote;[6]
And, as I seide, amiddes lay Cipryde,[7]
To whom on knees two yonge folkes there cryde
To ben hir help; but thus I leet° hir lye,   *let*
280 And ferther in the temple I gan espye

That, in dispyte of Diane the chaste,[8]
Ful many a bowe ybroke° heng on the wal   *broken*
Of maydens, suche as gunne hir tymes waste
In hir servyse; and peynted over al
285 Ful many a story, of which I touche shal
A fewe, as of Calixte[9] and Athalaunte,[1]
And many a mayde, of which the name I wante;°   *lack*

Semyramus,[2] Candace,[3] and Ercules,[4]
Biblis,[5] Dido,[6] Thisbe, and Piramus,[7]
290 Tristram, Isoude,[8] Paris,[9] and Achilles,[1]
Eleyne, Cleopatre,[2] and Troilus,[3]
Silla,[4] and eek the moder of Romulus[5]—
Alle these were peynted on that other syde,
And al hir love, and in what plyte° they dyde.   *predicament*

---

4. Bacchus, Roman god of wine.
5. Ceres, Roman goddess of the harvest.
6. I.e., cures hunger.
7. Another name for Venus.
8. In order to spite Diana the chaste. Diana, Roman goddess of the hunt, archery, and the moon, was associated with strict virginity. She was said to have a retinue of virginal huntresses.
9. Callisto, a member of Diana's retinue of huntresses. She was raped by Jove and became pregnant; when Diana discovered this, she banished her. Meanwhile, Juno, Jove's wife, turned her and her son into bears. To save them, Jove swept them into the sky, where they became the constellations Ursa Major and Ursa Minor. See Ovid, *Metamorphoses* 2.409–507.
1. Atalanta, a gifted runner who vowed she would never marry unless a man bested her in a footrace. With Venus's help, Hippomenes tricked Atalanta by distracting her during the race with golden apples and so married her. See Ovid, *Metamorphoses* 10.560–707.
2. Semiramis, an Assyrian queen, believed to have built Babylon and an emblem of sexual perversion in the Middle Ages. See Ovid, *Metamorphoses* 4.59, and Dante, *Inferno* 5.52–60.
3. Probably Canace, the daughter of the Roman god of wind, Aeolus, whom he forced to commit suicide after she became pregnant by her brother. See Ovid, *Heroides* 11.
4. Hercules. While famous for his twelve labors, he died when his wife, attempting to regain his affection, sent him a cloak soaked in the blood of a centaur he had killed, not knowing he had killed the creature with a poisoned arrow. He died in agony when he put on the poison-soaked cloak. See Ovid, *Metamorphoses* 9.198–238.

5. Byblis, a classical figure who fell in love with her brother and went insane when he rejected her. See Ovid, *Metamorphoses* 9.454–655.
6. Dido, queen of Carthage. She fell in love with Aeneas and committed suicide when he abandoned her to fulfill his destiny as the founder of Rome. See Virgil, *Aeneid* 4, and Ovid, *Heroides* 7.
7. Piramus and Thisbe, tragic lovers on whom the story of *Romeo and Juliet* is based. See Ovid, *Metamorphoses* 4.55–106.
8. Tristram and Isoude, tragic adulterous lovers in Arthurian legend. See, for instance, Thomas, *Le Roman de Tristan* (12th century), pp. 138–43.
9. Paris and Helen (here spelled "Eleyne") famously set off the Trojan War when they eloped. See Ovid, *Heroides* 16 and 17.
1. Achilles, famous in the Middle Ages for dying of love for Polyxena. See Chaucer, *Book of the Duchess*, lines 1067–71.
2. Cleopatra, queen of Egypt. She had love affairs first with Julius Caesar and then with Mark Anthony; she committed suicide after Mark Anthony's death. See Shakespeare, *Antony and Cleopatra*.
3. Troilus, the hero of Chaucer's major poem *Troilus and Criseyde*, died after he was betrayed by his lover Criseyde during the Trojan War.
4. Scylla, daughter of Nisus, king of Megara. When King Minos of Crete besieged the city, she betrayed Megara for the love of him. When Minos discovered what she had done, he spurned her in disgust at her unfilial behavior. She was then transformed into a bird.
5. Rhea Silvia. Romulus was the founder of Rome, who, according to Ovid, was fathered by Mars. She was killed by her uncle after giving birth. See Ovid, *Fasti* 3.9–45.

295 Whan I was come ayen° unto the place   *again*
That I of spak, that was so swote° and grene,   *sweet*
Forth walked I, myselven to solace.
Tho was I war wher that ther sat a queen
That, as of light the somer sonne shene°   *bright*
300 Passeth the sterre, right so over mesure
She fairer was than any creature.

And in a launde,° upon an hille of floures,   *glade*
Was set this noble goddesse of Nature;
Of braunches were hir halles and hir boures,°   *bowers*
305 Ywrought° after° hir caste° and hir   *crafted / according to / design*
    mesure;°   *plan*
Ne ther nas foul° that cometh of engendrure,°   *bird / procreation*
That they ne were al prest° in hir presence,   *ready*
To take hir doom° and yeve hir audience.[6]   *judgment*

For this was on seynt Valentynes day,[7]
310 Whan every bryd° cometh ther to chese° his   *bird / choose*
    make,°   *mate*
Of every kinde, that men thenke may;
And that so huge a noyse gan they make,
That erthe and air, and tree, and every lake
So ful was, that unnethe° was ther space   *barely*
315 For me to stonde, so ful was al the place.

And right as Aleyn, in the Pleynt of Kinde,[8]
Devyseth° Nature in aray° and face,   *describes / clothing*
In swich aray men mighten hir ther finde.
This noble emperesse, ful of grace,
320 Bad every foul° to take his owne place,   *fowl*
As they were wont alwey fro yeer to yere,
Seynt Valentynes day, to stonden there.

That is to seyn, the foules of ravine[9]
Were hyest set; and thanne foules smale,
325 That eten as hem° nature wolde enclyne,   *them*
As worm or thing of whiche I telle no tale;[1]
And water-foul sat loweste in the dale;°   *glen*
But foul that liveth by seed sat on the grene,
And that so fele,° that wonder was to sene.   *many*

330 There mighte men the royal egle finde,
That with his sharpe look perceth the sonne;

6. Give her audience. i.e., listen to her.
7. Saint Valentine's Day, February 14. Saint Valentine was an early Christian martyr, and the modern association between Valentine's Day and romantic love almost certainly begins with this poem.
8. Alan of Lille, in *The Complaint of Nature*. The 12th-century Latin poem describes Nature allegorically as a goddess of luminous and sensual (though modest) beauty, wearing a golden crown with jewels representing the constellations of the zodiac and the seven planetary spheres. She is dressed in a finely woven garment with shifting colors (representing air) that resolve into images of birds, a mantle representing water covered with images of aquatic animals, and a tunic representing earth with images of land animals, including humankind.
9. I.e., birds of prey.
1. I.e., which I do not deign to mention.

And other egles of a lower kinde,
Of which that clerkes wel devysen cunne.[2]
Ther was the tyraunt with his fethres dunne°   *brown*
335 And greye, I mene the goshauk,° that doth   *a type of hawk*
        pyne°   *injury*
    To briddes for° his outrageous°   *on account of / violent*
        ravyne.°   *predation*

    The gentil° faucoun, that with his feet distreyneth°   *noble / holds fast*
    The kinges hond; the hardy sperhauk° eke,   *sparrow hawk*
    The quayles foo; the merlion° that payneth   *merlin*
340 Himself ful ofte, the larke for to seke;
    Ther was the douve, with hir eyen meke;
    The jalous swan, ayens° hir deth that singeth;   *in preparation for*
    The oule° eek, that of dethe the bode° bringeth;   *owl / message*

    The crane geaunt,° with his trompes soune;   *gigantic*
345 The theef, the chogh;° and eek the jangling°   *jackdaw / chattering*
        pye°   *magpie*
    The scorning jay; the eles foo,° heroune;   *eel's foe*
    The false lapwing, ful of trecherye;
    The starlyng, that the counseyl° can bewreye;°   *secret / divulge*
    The tame ruddok;° and the coward kyte;   *robin*
350 The cok, that orloge° is of thorpes° lyte;°   *clock / villages / little*

    The sparow, Venus sone; the nightingale,
    That clepeth° forth the grene leves newe;   *calls*
    The swalow, mordrer of the flyes smale
    That maken hony of floures fresshe of hewe;
355 The wedded turtel,° with hir herte trewe;   *turtledove*
    The pecok, with his aungels fethres brighte;
    The fesaunt, scorner of the cok by nighte;

    The waker° goos;° the cukkow most unkinde;[3]   *active / goose*
    The popiniay, ful of delicasye;°   *love of luxury*
360 The drake, stroyer° of his owne kinde;   *destroyer*
    The stork, the wreker° of avouterye;°   *avenger / adultery*
    The hote cormeraunt of glotonye;
    The raven wys, the crow with vois of care;
    The throstel° olde; the frosty feldefare.°   *song thrush / fieldfare (thrush)*

365 What shulde I seyn? of foules every kinde
    That in this world han fethres and stature,°   *shape*
    Men mighten in that place assembled finde
    Before the noble goddesse of Nature,
    And everich of hem did his besy cure
370 Benignely° to chese or for to take,   *with good will*
    By hir acord, his formel° or his make.°   *female bird / mate*

---

2. I.e., which scholars have the knowledge to describe.
3. Unnatural. The cuckoo was often a symbol during the Middle Ages for unfaithfulness, fickleness, or dishonesty, due in part to its habit of laying eggs in other birds' nests.

But to the poynt—Nature held on hir hond
A formel egle, of shap the gentileste
That ever she among hir werkes fonde,
375 The moste benigne° and the goodlieste;   *gentle*
In hir was every vertu at his reste,
So ferforth, that Nature hirself had blisse
To loke on hir, and ofte hir bek° to kisse.   *beak*

Nature, the vicaire[4] of thalmighty lorde,
380 That hoot, cold, hevy, light, and moist and dreye
Hath knit with even noumbre of acorde,[5]
In esy vois gan for to speke and seye,
"Foules, tak hede of my sentence,° I preye,   *teaching*
And, for your ese, in furthering of your nede,
385 As faste as I may speke, I wol me spede.[6]

Ye knowe wel how, seynt Valentynes day,
By my statut and through my governaunce,
Ye come for to chese—and flee your way—
Your makes,° as I prik° yow with plesaunce.°   *partners / incite / desire*
390 But natheles, my rightful ordenaunce
May I not breke, for al this world to winne,
That he that most is worthy shal beginne.

The tercel egle, as that ye know ful wel,
The foul royal above yow in degree,
395 The wyse and worthy, secree,° trewe as stel,°   *able to keep secrets / steel*
The which I formed have, as ye may see,
In every part as it best lyketh me,[7]
It nedeth noght his shap yow to devyse,°   *describe*
He shal first chese and speken in his gyse.°   *in his manner*

400 And after him, by order shul ye chese,
After your kinde, everich as yow lyketh,
And, as your hap° is, shul ye winne or lese;   *luck*
But which of yow that love most entryketh,°   *ensnares*
God sende him hir that sorest for him syketh."°   *sighs*
405 And therwithal the tercel gan she calle,
And seyde, "My sone, the choys is to yow falle.

But natheles, in this condicioun
Mot be the choys of everich that is here,
That she agree to his eleccioun,°   *choice*
410 Whatso he be that shulde be hir fere;°   *spouse*
This is our usage alwey, fro yeer to yere;
And who so may at this time have his grace,
In blisful tyme he cam into this place."

---

4. Vicar, or representative. The word has priestly
connotations.
5. I.e., in balance.

6. I.e., I will speak as quickly as I can.
7. As is most pleasing to me.

With hed enclyned and with ful humble chere°   *facial expression*
415 This royal tercel spak and taried nought:
"Unto my sovereyn lady, and noght my fere,[8]
I chese, and chese with wille and herte and thought,
The formel on your hond so wel ywrought,°   *formed*
Whos I am al and ever wol hir serve,
420 Do what hir list,[9] to do° me live or sterve.°   *cause / die*

Beseching hir of mercy and of grace,
As she that is my lady sovereyne;
Or let me dye present° in this place.   *immediately*
For certes, long I may not live in peyne;
425 For in myn herte is corven° every veyne;   *cut*
Having reward only to my trouthe,[1]
My dere herte, have on my wo som routhe.°   *pity*

And if that I to hir be founde untrewe,
Disobeysaunt, or wilful negligent,
430 Avauntour,° or in proces[2] love a newe,   *braggart*
I pray to you this be my jugement,
That with° these foules I be al torent,°   *by / torn to pieces*
That ilke° day that ever she me finde   *same*
To hir untrewe, or in my gilte° unkinde.   *offense*

435 And sin that hire lovyth noon so wel as I,[3]
Al be she never of love me behette,[4]
Than oghte she be myn thourgh hir mercy,
For other bond° can I noon on hir knette.°   *obligation / fasten*
For never, for no wo, ne shal I lette°   *cease*
440 To serven hir, how fer so that she wende;[5]
Sey what yow list, my tale° is at an ende."   *speech*

Right as the fresshe, rede rose newe
Ayen° the somer sonne coloured is,   *matchingly with*
Right so for shame° al wexen gan hire hewe   *modesty*
445 Of this formel, whan she herde al this;
She neyther answerde wel, ne seyde amis,
So sore abasshed was she, til that Nature
Seyde, "Doghter, drede yow noght, I yow assure."

Another tercel egle spak anoon
450 Of lower kinde, and seyde, "That shal nat be;
I love hir bet than ye do, by seynt John,
Or atte leste I love as wel as ye;
And lenger have hir served, in my degree,[6]
And if she shulde have loved for long loving,
455 To me allone had been the guerdoninge.°   *reward*

---

8. Wife. The contrast here is between a sovereign lady, above the speaker in rank, and an espoused wife, who was seen as theologically as well as socially subordinate to her husband.
9. Regardless of what she does.
1. Having regard only to my fidelity.

2. I.e., eventually.
3. And since no one loves her as well as I do.
4. Even though she never vowed her love to me.
5. However far she goes.
6. I.e., according to my rank.

I dar eek° seyn, if she me finde fals,   *also*
Unkinde, or jangler,° or rebel in any wyse,   *gossip*
Or jalous, do me hongen by the hals!°   *neck*
And but I bere me in hir servyse
460 As wel as that my wit can me suffyse,
From poynt to poynt, hir honour for to save,
Tak she my lyf, and al the good° I have."   *property*

The thridde° tercel egle answerde tho°   *third / then*
"Now, sirs, ye seen the litel leyser° here;   *time*
465 For every foul cryeth out to been ago°   *begone*
Forth with his make, or with his lady dere;
And eek Nature hirself ne wol nought here,°   *hear*
For tarying° here, noght half that I wolde seye; *the delay*
And but I speke, I mot for sorwe deye.[7]

470 Of long servyse avaunte I me nothing,[8]
But as possible is me to dye today
For wo, as he that hath ben languisshing
Thise twenty winter, and wel happen may
A man may serven bet and more to pay[9]
475 In half a yere, although it were no more,
Than som man doth that hath served ful yore.

I ne sey not this by me, for I ne can
Do no servyse that may my lady plese;
But I dar seyn, I am hir trewest man
480 As to my dome,[1] and feynest wolde hir ese;[2]
At shorte wordes,° til that deth me sese,   *in short*
I wol ben hires, whether I wake or winke,°   *sleep*
And trewe in al that herte may bethinke."

Of al my lyf, sin° that day I was born,   *since*
485 So gentil plee° in love or other thing   *plea*
Ne herde never no man me beforn,
Whoso that hadde leyser and cunning°   *skill*
For to reherse° hir chere° and hir speking; *report / mien*
And from the morwe° gan this speche laste   *morning*
490 Til dounward drow the sonne wonder faste.

The noyse of foules for to ben delivered
So loude rong, "Have doon and let us wende!"°   *depart*
That wel wende I the wode had al toshivered.[3]
"Come of!"[4] they cryde, "Allas! ye wil us shende!° *ruin*
495 Whan shal your cursed pleding have an ende?
How shulde a juge eyther party leve,°   *believe*
For yee or nay, withouten any preve?"°   *proof*

---

7. And unless I speak, I must die of sorrow.
8. I.e., I do not brag.
9. I.e., more pleasingly.
1. According to my judgment.

2. I.e., most eager to please her.
3. That I really thought the wood would have
splintered into pieces.
4. I.e., finish up.

The goos, the cokkow, and the doke also
So cryden, "kek, kek!" "kukkow!" "quek, quek!" hye,
500 That thorgh myn eres the noyse wente tho.
The goos seyde, "Al this nis not worth a flye!
But I can shape hereof a remedye,
And I wol sey my verdit° faire and swythe°   verdict / swiftly
For water-foul, whoso be wrooth or blythe."°   glad

505 "And I for worm-foul," quod the fool° cukkow,   foolish
"And I wol, of myn owne auctorite,°   authority
For comune profit, take the charge° now,   responsibility
For to delivere us is gret charite."
"Ye may abyde a whyle yet, parde!"°   by God
510 Quod the turtel,° "If it be your wille   dove
A wight⁵ may speke, him were as good be stille.

I am a seed-foul, oon the unworthieste,
That wot° I wel, and litel of kunninge;°   know / understanding
But bet is that a wightes tonge reste
515 Than entermeten him⁶ of such doinge
Of which he neyther rede° can nor singe.   advise
And whoso doth, ful foule himself acloyeth,°   burdens
For office uncommitted° ofte   not bestowed
    anoyeth."°   causes annoyance

Nature, which that alway had an ere
520 To murmour of the lewednes behinde,⁷
With facound° voys seide, "Hold your tonges there!   eloquent
And I shal sone, I hope, a counseyl finde
You to delivere, and fro this noyse unbinde;
I juge, of every folk° men shal oon calle   species
525 To seyn the verdit° for you foules alle."   verdict

Assented were to this conclusioun
The briddes alle; and foules of ravyne
Han chosen first, by pleyn eleccioun,
The tercelet of the faucon,⁸ to diffyne°   state
530 Al hir sentence,° and as him list,⁹   opinions
    termyne;°   render a final judgment
And to Nature him gonnen to presente,
And she accepteth him with glad entente.

The tercelet seide than in this manere:
"Ful hard were it to preve by resoun¹
535 Who loveth best this gentil formel here;
For everich hath swich replicacioun,°   a rejoinder
That noon by skilles° may be broght adoun;   arguments
I can not seen that argumentes avayle;
Than semeth it ther moste be batayle."

---

5. A man (i.e., an impersonal "one"). Here, of course, the speaker is technically a bird.
6. I.e., interfere with.
7. For the grumbling of the ignorant (ones) in the back.
8. I.e., a male falcon.
9. I.e., as seems best to him.
1. I.e., by rights.

540 "Al redy!" quod these egles tercels tho.
"Nay, sirs!" quod he, "if that I dorste it seye,
Ye doon me wrong, my tale is not ydo!°   *finished*
For sirs, ne taketh noght agref,° I preye,   *amiss*
It may noght gon, as ye wolde, in this weye;
545 Oures is the voys that han the charge on honde,
And to the juges dome ye moten° stonde;°   *must / submit*

"And therfor, pees! I seye, as to my wit,
Me wolde thinke how that the worthieste
Of knighthode, and lengest hath used it,
550 Moste of estat,° of blode the gentileste,   *rank*
Were sittingest° for hir, if that hir leste;²   *most fitting*
And of these three she wot° hirself, I trowe,°   *knows / believe*
Which that he be, for it is light° to knowe."   *easy*

The water-foules han her hedes leyd
555 Togedre, and of° a short avysement,°   *after / consultation*
Whan everich had his large golee° seyd,   *throatful*
They seyden sothly, al by oon assent,
How that "the goos, with hir facounde° so gent,°   *eloquence / graceful*
That so desyreth to pronounce our nede,
560 Shal telle our tale," and preyde "god hir spede."

And for these water-foules tho began
The goos to speke, and in hir cakelinge
She seyde, "Pees! now tak kepe every man,
And herkeneth which a reson° I shal bringe;   *principle*
565 My wit is sharp, I love no taryinge;
I seye, I rede° him, though he were my brother,   *advise*
But° she wol love him, lat him take another!"   *unless*

"Lo here! a parfit reson° of a goos!"   *process of reasoning*
Quod the sperhauk; "never mot° she thee!°   *may / prosper*
570 Lo, swich it is to have a tonge loos!°   *loose*
Now parde, fool, yet were it bet for thee
Have holde thy pees, than shewen thy nycete!°   *foolishness*
It lyth not in his wit nor in his wille,
But sooth is seyd, 'a fool can noght be stille.'"

575 The laughtre aroos of gentil foules alle,
And right anoon° the seed-foul chosen hadde   *immediately*
The turtel trewe, and gunne hir to hem calle,
And preyden hir to seye the sothe sadde³
Of this matere, and asked what she radde;°   *advised*
580 And she answerde, that pleynly hir entente
She wolde it shewe, and sothly° what she mente.   *truly*

"Nay, god forbede a lover shulde chaunge!"
The turtle seyde, and wex° for shame al reed;°   *grew / red*
"Thogh that his lady evermore be straunge,°   *aloof*

---

2. I.e., if she wishes.   3. I.e., the settled truth.

585   Yet let him serve hir, til that he be deed;
   For sothe, I preyse noght the gooses reed;°   *advice*
   For thogh she deyed, I wolde° non other make,°   *would want / mate*
   I wol ben hires, til that the deth me take."

   "Wel bourded!"° quod the doke, "by my hat!   *well joked*
590   That men shulde loven alwey, causeles,
   Who can a reson finde or wit in that?
   Daunceth he mury° that is mirtheles?   *merrily*
   Who shulde recche° of him that is reccheles?"°   *care about / careless*
   "Quek, quek!" yit seith the doke, ful wel and faire,
595   "There been mo sterres,° god wot, than a paire!"°   *stars / two*

   "Now fy, cherl!"[4] the gentil tercelet,
   "Out of the dunghil com that word ful right,
   Thou canst noght see what thing is wel beset:[5]
   Thou farest by° love as oules° doon by light,   *in / owls*
600   The day hem blent,° but wel they see by night;   *blinds*
   Thy kind is of so lowe a wrechednesse,
   That what love is, thou canst nat see ne gesse."

   Tho gan the cukkow putte him forth in prees[6]
   For foul that eteth worm, and seide blyve,°   *at once*
605   "So I," quod he, "may have my make° in pees,   *companion*
   I recche not how longe that ye stryve;
   Lat ech of hem be soleyn° al hir lyve,   *alone*
   This is my reed,° sin they may not acorde;   *opinion*
   This shorte lesson nedeth noght recorde."[7]

610   "Ye! have the glotoun fild ynogh his paunche,[8]
   Than are we wel!" seyde then a merlioun;
   "Thou mordrer° of the heysugge° on the   *murderer / hedge sparrow*
      braunche
   That broghte thee forth, thou rewthelees° glotoun!   *pitiless*
   Live thou soleyn,° wormes corrupcioun!   *alone*
615   For no fors is of lakke of thy nature;[9]
   Go, lewed° be thou, whyl the world may dure!"°   *ignorant / last*

   "Now pees," quod Nature, "I comaunde here;
   For I have herd al your opinioun,
   And in effect yet be we not the nere;°   *any nearer (to a solution)*
620   But fynally, this is my conclusioun,
   That she hirself shal han° the eleccioun   *have*
   Of whom hir list,° whoso be wrooth or   *she likes*
      blythe,°   *angry or happy*
   Him that she cheest,° he shal hir have as swythe.°   *chooses / at once*

---

4. Churl or boor, associated with the lower classes as opposed to aristocratic, or "gentle," classes.
5. I.e., well done.
6. I.e., came forward in the crowd.
7. I.e., to enter in the official written account of proceedings.
8. Yes! If the glutton has sufficiently filled his belly.
9. (It would be) no matter if there were none of your kind.

For sith it may not here discussed° be — *determined*
625 Who loveth hir best, as seide the tercelet,
Than wol I doon hir this favour, that she
Shal have right him on whom hir herte is set,
And he hir that his herte hath on hir knet.° — *knitted*
Thus juge I, Nature, for I may not lye;
630 To noon estat I have non other ye.[1]

But as for counseyl for to chese a make,° — *partner*
If I were Reson, certes, than wolde I
Counseyle yow the royal tercel take,
As seide the tercelet ful skilfully,° — *wisely*
635 As for the gentilest° and most worthy, — *noblest*
Which I have wroght so wel to my plesaunce;° — *liking*
That to yow oghte to been a suffisaunce."° — *enough*

With dredful° vois the formel hir answerde, — *reverent*
"My rightful lady, goddesse of Nature,
640 Soth is that I am ever under your yerde,[2]
As is everiche other creature,
And moot be youres whyl that my lyf may dure;
And therfor graunteth me my firste bone,° — *request*
And myn entente that wol I sey wel sone."

645 "I graunte it you," quod she; and right anon
This formel egle spak in this degree,
"Almighty quene, unto° this yeer be gon — *until*
I aske respit for to avysen me.[3]
And after that to have my choys al free;
650 This al and sum, that I wol speke and seye;
Ye gete no more, although ye do me deye.° — *kill me*

I wol noght serven Venus ne Cupyde
For sothe as yet, by no manere wey."
"Now sin it may non other wyse betyde,"° — *happen*
655 Quod tho° Nature, "here is no more to sey; — *then*
Than wolde I that these foules were awey
Ech with his make, for° tarying lenger here"— — *instead of*
And seyde hem thus, as ye shul after here.

"To you speke I, ye tercelets," quod Nature,
660 "Beth of good herte and serveth, alle three;
A yeer is not so longe to endure,
And ech of yow peyne him,[4] in his degree,
For to do wel; for, god wot, quit[5] is she
Fro yow this yeer; what after so befalle,
665 This entremes° is dressed° for you alle." — *interval of time / arranged*

1. I.e., I have no concern with any other condition (than love).
2. Scepter (i.e., authority).
3. I.e., to consider the issue.
4. I.e., take pains.
5. Excused from obligation (a legal term)

And whan this werk al broght was to an ende,
To every foule Nature yaf° his make   *gave*
By even acorde,[6] and on hir wey they wende.
But lord! the blisse and joye that they make!
670   For ech gan other in his winges take,
And with hir nekkes ech gan other winde,
Thanking alwey the noble queen of kinde.°   *nature*

But first were chosen foules for to singe,
As yeer by yere was alwey the usaunce
675   To singe a roundel[7] at hir departinge,
To do to Nature honour and plesaunce.
The note,° I trowe, ymaked was in Fraunce;   *melody*
The wordes wer swich as ye may heer finde,
The nexte vers, as I now have in minde.

680   "Now welcom somer, with thy sonne softe,°   *gentle*
That hast this wintres weders overshake,°   *dispersed*
And driven awey the longe nightes blake!

"Saynt Valentyn, that art ful hy° onlofte;—   *high*
Thus singen smale foules for thy sake—
685   Now welcom somer, with thy sonne softe,
That hast this wintres weders overshake.°   *driven away*

"Wel han they cause for to gladen° ofte,   *rejoice*
Sith ech of hem recovered hath his make;
Ful blisful may they singen whan they wake;
690   Now welcom somer, with thy sonne softe,
That hast this wintres weders overshake,
And driven away the longe nightes blake."

And with the showting,° whan the song was do,°   *clamor of birds / done*
That foules maden at hir flight away,
695   I wook,° and other bokes took me to   *woke*
To rede upon, and yet° I rede alway;   *still*
In hope, ywis, to rede so som day
That I shal mete[8] som thing for to fare
The bet;[9] and thus to rede I nil not spare.

---

6. I.e., by mutual agreement.
7. A short poem on two rhymes, with the opening line(s) serving as refrain in the middle and at the end. The form originated in France and was often set to music.

8. Chaucer puns here on the double meaning of "mete" (both "to meet" and "to dream").
9. That I shall find (or dream) something so that I may fare better.

ROBERT HENRYSON

For the full headnote on Robert Henryson (ca. 1425–ca. 1490), see pages 554–55.

The Preaching of the Swallow simultaneously urges prudential wisdom upon us, even as it recognizes the uselessness of such urging. It promotes a learned understanding of the pattern of the universe, even as it recognizes that the truly wise person knows that wisdom will be ignored. The processional pattern of the poem, moving through the cosmos and across the seasons as it does, finally prepares us for the defeat of prudence, from the example of thoughtless larks.

The text belongs to a collection of fables, Henryson's Moral Fables (ca. 1470s). The structure of each fable represents a basic cognitive division between reading and interpreting: each is clearly divided, that is, into a narrative sequence (relating an animal story), and a moral (the moralitas) (see Talking Animals, pp. 494–96). That division might suggest that we are dealing with two separate things: animal action, on the one hand, and wise, abstract human interpretation on the other. The division between story and interpretation also suggests that we can learn something from animal stories.

The Preaching of the Swallow refuses to observe both these common features of a fable. The swallow already interprets and moralizes the action from within the narrative. And the failure of the swallow's teaching suggests that no one ever learns anything much of practical moral value from the official sources of wisdom.

The failure of wisdom is powerfully presented in both the tale and the moral. Fundamental resources of natural philosophy are marshaled in the tale, so as to use not just animals, but the entire cosmos—planets, plants, all creatures—as the occasion to understand that nature can lead us to wise, detached understanding of the way of the divinely ruled natural world. The beautiful procession of the seasons manifests a cosmos ruled by a beneficent order, whose pattern can be understood in self-protective ways. Once the bird narrative starts, the swallow plays the part of prudential counselor, advising the larks to understand the very pattern of seasonal movement and its consequences, through which we as readers have just moved. And if natural wisdom is approached prospectively within the narrative, specifically Christian moral theology reinforces that wisdom retrospectively from outside the tale in the moral, by looking back to the narrative we have just witnessed.

All that wisdom, however, as made available to the larks, gains no traction whatsoever. The bird world continues to be ruled by appetite and by self-destructively foreshortened temporal units. Whereas the swallow speaks with long perspectives in generous philosophical language, the larks use practical proverbs to block the swallow's prudential wisdom. The story of wisdom's delivery and transmission ends with a shocking scene of carnage, as the fowler piteously clubs the helpless larks.

All this would suggest that this is a narrative underwritten by profound elitism and skepticism: wisdom remains the preserve of the wise; any effort to transmit it to a broader public will end badly. It is no accident that the preceding fable in Henryson's collection should start with the poet Aesop refusing to tell a story, since, as he says, what's the point of telling an allegorical animal tale when holy preaching itself gets nowhere?

Perhaps, however, Henryson as poet is less skeptical and less elitist than the obvious emphases of this narrative might suggest. Perhaps poetry, combining philosophy, moral theology, and simple but forceful animal narrative might be more effective than pure philosophy or theology. The story of the poor larks is more powerful and memorable than the abstract philosophy, however beautifully that philosophy is presented. We as readers are not only rational, but we are also animals, subject to the same appetites and failings as the larks. It's their story that affects us more powerfully than the preaching of the eloquent swallow.

The Preaching of the Swallow[1]

<blockquote>

God's great wisdom and his marvellous workings,
The deep insight of the Omnipotent,
Are in themselves so perfect and discerning
They far excel our merely human judgement,
5 All things for Him being ever present,
As they are now and at all times shall be
In the full sight of His divinity.[2]

Because our soul, imprisoned in the body,
Is bound and fettered by the sensual
10 We may not clearly understand or see
God as he is, or things celestial.
Our murky, gross, death-bound material
Blindfolds the operation of the spirit
Like a prisoner shut in darkness and chained up.

15 In his *Metaphysics* Aristotle says
The soul of man resembles a bat's eye,
The bat that hides daylong from the sun's rays,
Then in the gloaming ventures forth to fly—
Her eyes are weak, the sun she must not see.[3]
20 Soul's vision too is faulty and unsure,
Missing true things manifest in Nature.

For God is in His power infinite,
Man's soul feeble, diminutively small,
Weak in understanding and unfit
25 To comprehend the One who contains all.
None should presume by their own natural
Reason to unravel the Trinity.
They should have firm faith and let reason be.

Nevertheless we may gain comprehension
30 Of God almighty and learn from His creatures
That He is just, good, wise, and most benign.[4]
Take, for example, the loveliness of flowers,
Their rich, sweet smells, the pleasure of their colors,
Some green, some blue, some purple, white, and red—
35 Their variety the gift of His Godhead.

</blockquote>

---

1. The translation is by Seamus Heaney, *The Testament of Cresseid & Seven Fables* (2009).
2. Cf. Ecclesiasticus 39.19–20.

3. Aristotle, *Metaphysics* 2.1.3.
4. Cf. Romans 1.20.

The firmament, star-stippled sheer and clear,
From east to west rolling round and round;
Every planet in its proper sphere
And motion making harmony and sound;
40 The fire, the air, the water, and the ground—
They should suffice to demonstrate to us
The intelligence of God in all his works.

Consider well the fish that swim the sea,
Consider too the beasts that dwell on land,
45 Birds in their strength and beauty as they fly
Cleaving the air with large or small wingspan,
Consider then His last creation, man
Made in His image and similitude:[5]
By these we know that God is just and good.

50 He created all things for man's benefit,
For his subsistence and his preservation
Upon the earth, beneath it, and above it,
In weight, in number, and correct proportion;
Differentiating time and every season
55 To our advantage and convenience—
As is daily evident from experience.

Summer comes in his garment green and cheerful,
Every hem and pleating flounced with flowers,
Which Flora, queen and goddess bountiful,
60 Has lent that lord for his due season's hours,
And Phoebus with his golden beams and glamours
And heat and moisture hazing from the sky
Has decked and dyed with colours pleasantly.[6]

Next then warm autumn when the goddess Ceres[7]
65 Heaps the barn floors high with her abundance,
And Bacchus, god of wine, replenishes
Her casks for her in Italy and France
With heady wines and liquors that entrance;
And the plenty of the season fills that horn
70 Of plenty never filled with wheat or corn.

Then gloomy winter, when stern Aeolus,
God of the wind, with his bleak northern blasts
Tears open, rends, and rips into small pieces
The green and glorious garment summer sports.
75 Now fairest flowers must fade and fall to frosts
And the nearly perished songbirds modulate
Their sweet notes to lament the snow and sleet.

5. Cf. Genesis 1.26.
6. Compare the description of the passage of the seasons in *Sir Gawain and the Green Knight*

(pp. 204–56), lines 500–530.
7. Roman goddess of the harvest.

The dales are flooded deep with dirty puddles,
Hills and hedges covered with hoar frost,
80 The sheltering bough is stripped and shrinks and shudders
In cruel winds as winter does its worst.
All creatures of the wild withdraw perforce
From blasted farmlands to hole up and cower
Against the cold in burrow, den, or lair.

85 Then when winter's gone there comes the spring—
Summer's secretary, bearing his seal—
When columbine peeps out after hiding
Her fearful head beneath the frosty field.
The thrushes and the blackbirds sing their fill.
90 The lark on high, soaring far up yonder,
Is seen again, and other little songsters.

That same season, one mild and pleasant morning,
Delighted that the bitter blasts were gone,
I walked in woods to see the flowers blooming
95 And hear the thrush and songbirds at their song,
And as I walked and looked and wandered on
Enjoyed the prospect of the vernal soil
Ready for seed, in good heart, fresh and fertile.

Free and easy like that, on I go,
100 Happy watching labourers at their tasks,
Some digging ditches, some behind the plough,
Some in full stride, sowing the seed broadcast,
The harrow hopping off the ground they'd paced.
For one who loved the corn crop, it was joy
105 To see them at their work there, late and early.

Then as I stood beneath a bank to rest,
Heartened and elated by the scene,
There swooped into the hedge in sudden haste
And quickly lit and roosted on the green
110 Leaves of the hawthorn bush that was my screen
A flock of small birds, everywhere at once,
Innumerable, amazing, marvellous.

Among them next I heard a swallow cry
From where she perched on the top branch of the thorn,
115 "You birds there on your branches, hear, O hear me,
And be instructed; understand and learn.
When dangers loom or when perils threaten
The wise course is to foresee and take care:
Plan, make provision, think, forestall, and store."

120 The lark laughed and then answered, "Lady Swallow,
What have you seen that's making you afraid?"
"Do you see," she said, "yon fellow with his plough
Sowing—look—hemp and lint, broadcasting seed?

In no time at all the lint will braird°   *sprout*
125 And when it's grown that churl will make a net
And already plots to snare us under it.

"So my advice is this: when he is gone
This evening we descend and with our claws
Scrape every seed out of the earth and then
130 Eat it immediately, for if it grows
We'll surely rue the day—and with good cause.
Thus straightway we shall remedy our case
Since the one who takes precautions suffers less.

"For scholars say it is not sufficient
135 To consider only things that you can see,
Prudence being an inner discipline
That causes one to look ahead and be
Aware what good or evil end is likely,
Which course of action better guarantees
140 Our safety in the last analysis."

The lark laughed at the swallow then for scorn
And said she fished before she'd found a net—
"The baby's easy dressed before it's born.
What grows is never all that has been set;
145 It's time enough to bend and bare the neck
When the blow is aimed; most fated's like to fall."
And so they scorned the swallow, one and all.

Despising thus her salutary lesson
The birds departed in a sudden flurry;
150 Some whirled across the fields in quick commotion,
Some to the greenwood in a panicked hurry.
Left on my own then, out there in the country,
I took my staff and headed back for home
In wonderment, as in a waking dream.

155 Time passed, then came the pleasant month of June
When seeds that had been sown earlier
Grew high round corncrakes[8] craking out their tune
And hiding places of the leaping hare.
So again one morning I went roving where
160 I found that same hedge and green hawthorn tree
Which held those birds I've spoken of already.

And as I stood there, by the strangest chance,
Those same birds you have heard me talk about—
Maybe because it was one of their haunts,
165 A safer, maybe, or a lonelier spot—
They lighted down and when they had alit
The swallow cheeped, still harping on her theme:
"Woe to the one who won't beware in time.

8. Birds that live among standing corn

"You birds, so blinded and so negligent,
170 Unmindful of your own prosperity,
Lift up your eyes, see clearly what has happened:
Look at the lint now growing on yon lea.
That is the stuff I argued once that we
Should uproot, while it was seed, from the earth.
175 Now it's a crop, young stalks, a sprouting braird.

"While it's still tender, immature, and small,
Go, stop it growing. Pull it up this minute.
It makes my heart beat fast and my flesh crawl,
It gives me nightmares just to think of it."
180 The other birds then cried out and protested,
And told the swallow: "That lint will do us good.
Is linseed not our little fledglings' food?

"When the flax is grown and the seed-pods ripe
We'll feast and take our fill then of the seed,
185 And sing and swing on it and peep and pipe.
Who cares about the farmer?" "So be it,"
The swallow said, "But I am sore afraid
You'll find things bitter that now seem so sweet
When you're scorched and skewered on yon fellow's spit.

190 "The owner of that lint field is a fowler,
A stealthy hunter, full of craft and guile,
We'll all be prey for him, birds of a feather,
Unless we watch and match him, wile for wile.
Our kith and kin he has been wont to kill:
195 He spilled their blood for sport, most casually.
God and his holy cross save and preserve me."

These little birds who hardly gave a thought
To dangers that might fall by misadventure
Ignored the swallow; they set her words at nought
200 As they rose up and flew away together,
Some to the wood, some to the heather moor.
Noontime was approaching; I took my staff
And bearing all in mind I headed off.

The flax grew ripe, the farmer pulled it green,
205 Combed and dressed the seed-heads, stooked°   *set up in sheaves*
    the beets,
Then buried it and steeped° it in the burn,°   *soaked / fountain*
Spread and dried it, beetled° the stalks to bits,   *threshed*
And scutched° and heckled° all to tow°   *prepared / straightened / fiber*
    in plaits.
His wife then spun a linen thread from it
210 Which the fowler took and wove into a net.

The winter came, the freezing wind did blow,
Green woods wilted in the weltering wet,

Hoar frosts hardened over hill and hollow,
Glens and gullies were slippery with sleet.
215 The frail and famished birds fell off their feet—
Useless to try to shelter on bare boughs,
So they hied them° to the haggard° and   *hurried / storehouse*
    outhouses.

Some to the barn, some to the stacks of corn
Fly for shelter and settle themselves in.
220 The fowler sees them coming and has sworn
He'll catch and make them pay for pilfering.
He spreads his nets and in preparation
Clears a space, shovels the surface snow off,
Then tops it level with a layer of chaff.

225 The small birds saw the chaff and were distracted.
Believing it was corn they lighted down.
The net was the last thing they suspected.
They set to work to scrape and grub for grain
With no thought of the fowler's cunning plan.
230 The swallow on a little branch nearby,
Fearing a trick, shouted this warning cry:

"Scrape in that chaff until your nails are bleeding,
You're won't find any corn, no matter what.
Do you think yon churl's the sort who would be feeding
235 Birds out of pity? No, that chaff is bait.
I'm warning you, away, or you'll get caught.
The nets are set and ready for their prey.
Beware in time therefore, or rue the day.

"Only a fool is going to risk life
240 And honor on a useless enterprise;
Only a fool persists when he's warned off
And continues to ignore all good advice.
Only a fool fails to take cognizance
Of what the future holds and thinks the present
245 Forever stable, safe, and permanent."

These little birds, half-dead from hunger now
And foraging for dear life for their food,
Paid no heed to the preaching of the swallow
Although their grubbing did them little good.
250 That was the moment when she understood
Their foolish hearts and minds were obdurate
And as she fled the fowler drew his net.

Alas, it was heartbreaking then to see him
Butcher those little songbirds out of hand
255 And hear, when they understood their hour had come,
How grievously they sang their last and mourned.
Some he hit with his stick and left there stunned,

Some he beheaded, on some he broke the neck,
Some he just stuffed alive into his sack.

260 And when the swallow saw that they were dead,
"Behold," she said, "the fate that often follows
Those who won't take counsel or pay heed
To words of prudent men or wisest scholars.
Three times and more I warned them of the perils.
265 Now they are dead. I am saddened and heartsore."
She flew off and I saw her then no more.

Moralitas°   *Moral*

Lo, worthy people, that noble scholar Aesop,[9]
A poet worthy to be laureate,
When he relaxed from more exacting work
270 Wrote this fable and other fables like it
Which at this moment serve to educate
And edify, because they have a meaning
That furthers good and accords with reason.

This tenant churl, this mean ignoble peasant
275 Sowing chaff, making small birds his prey,
He is the fiend in exile from high heaven,
An angel cast down by the deity,
Ever unrelenting and unweary,
Apt to poison man's thought and his soul
280 Which Christ redeemed most dearly for us all.

And when the soul (figured as seed in earth)
Yields to the flesh and sensual temptation,
Then wickedness begins to bloom and braird
As mortal sin, which issues in damnation.
285 Reason is thus blindfolded by passion
And carnal lust springs green and takes deep root
Daily and deliciously through habit.

Thus practised and confirmed, habituated,
Sin ripens and all shame is cast aside.
290 The fiend cross-weaves and webs his cruel net
And lurks in secret under pleasure's bed.
Then on the field he sows chaff far and wide—
Lusts of the flesh, insubstantial, empty,
Will-o'-the-wisps and vacuous vanity.

295 These hungry birds stand for those poor wretches
Grubbing in the world for goods and gain,
Busy rooting round for earthly riches
Which, like the chaff, are insubstantial, vain,

---

9. Aesop, putative author of Aesop's fables.

Of no real value, fleeting, false, a bane—
300 As dust whipped up and whisked before the wind
Flung in poor wretches' faces makes them blind.

This swallow, who escaped free from the snare,
May signify in turn the holy preacher
Warning his flock to watch and still beware
305 The wicked fiend, our cruel fowler-netter—
Devious, unsleeping, vigilant, ever
Ready as wretches scrape in the world's chaff
To draw the net and spit them on his gaff.°   *iron hook*

Alas what grief, what weeping and what woes
310 There will be when the body's reft from soul.
Down to the worms' kitchen body goes,
Soul to the fire, to everlasting dole.°   *suffering*
What help's your chaff then, will your goods console
When Lucifer has you captured in his sack
315 And brought to hell, to hang there by the neck?

Therefore let us pray while we're alive
For these four things: the first is to shun sin;
The second is to cease from war and strife;
The third to practice charity and love;
320 The fourth, and the most crucial, is to win
Heavenly bliss, and hence our lives to hallow.°   *sanctify*
And so concludes the preaching of the swallow.

MIDDLE ENGLISH LYRICS

I t was only late in the fourteenth century that English began to develop the kinds
of aristocratic, formal, learned, and literary types of lyric that had long been cultivated on the Continent by the Troubador poets in the south of France, the Min-
nesänger in Germany (German *Minne* corresponds to French *fine amour*—that is,
refined or aristocratic love), or the Italian poets whose works Dante characterized
as the *dolce stil nuovo* (the sweet new style). Chaucer, under the influence of French
poets, wrote lovers' complaints, homiletic poetry, and verse letters in the form of
ballades, roundels, and other highly stylized lyric types. In the fifteenth century,
John Lydgate, Thomas Hoccleve, and others following Chaucer wrote lyrics of this
sort, which were praised for embellishing the English language, and these along with
Chaucer's were collected in manuscript anthologies that were produced commercially
for well-to-do buyers.

   Chaucer, his courtly predecessors, and their followers were of course familiar with
and influenced by an ancient tradition of popular song from which only a small fraction
survives. With one exception, the Middle English lyrics included in this section are the
work of anonymous poets and are difficult to date with any precision. Some of these

survive in only a single manuscript, especially in anthologies of religious poetry and prose. The topics and language in these poems are highly conventional, yet the lyrics often seem remarkably fresh and spontaneous. Many are marked by strong accentual rhythms with a good deal of alliteration. Their pleasure does not come from originality or lived experience but from variations of expected themes and images. Some were undoubtedly set to music, and in a few cases the music has survived. Perhaps the earliest of those printed here, "The Cuckoo Song," is a canon or round in which the voices follow one another and join together echoing the joyous cry, "Cuckou." The rooster and hen in *The Nun's Priest's Tale* sing "My Lief Is Faren in Londe" in "sweet accord." "I Am of Ireland" was undoubtedly accompanied by dancing as well as music.

The joyous return of spring (the *reverdie*, spring song, or, literally, "regreening") is the subject of many lyrics. In love lyrics the mating of birds and animals in wild nature often contrasts with the melancholy of unrequited or forsaken lovers. These lovers are usually male. We know that some women wrote troubador and court poetry, but we do not know whether women composed popular lyrics; women certainly sang popular songs, just as they are portrayed doing in narrative poetry.

The Cuckoo Song

Sumer is ycomen in,
Loude sing cuckou!
Groweth seed and bloweth meed[1]
And springth the wode° now.   *wood*
5   Sing cuckou!

Ewe bleteth after lamb,
Loweth after calve cow,
Bulloc sterteth,° bucke verteth,°   *leaps / farts*
Merye sing cuckou!
10   Cuckou, cuckou,
Wel singest thou cuckou:
Ne swik° thou never now!   *cease*

Foweles in the Frith

Foweles° in the frith,°   *birds / forest*
The fisses° in the flod,°   *fishes / sea*
And I mon° waxe wod:°   *must / go mad*
Mulch sorw° I walke with   *much sorrow*
For beste[1] of bon and blod°   *bone and blood*

1. Most obviously "best," but note possible pun on Middle English "beste," meaning "beast." So one might translate as "creature."

1. The meadow blossoms.

Alison

	Bitweene° Merch and Averil,	*in the seasons of*
	When spray biginneth to springe,	
	The litel fowl hath hire wil°	*pleasure*
	On hire leod[1] to singe.	
5	Ich° libbe° in love-longinge	*I / live*
	For semlokest° of alle thinge.	*seemliest, fairest*
	Heo° may me blisse bringe:	*she*
	Ich am in hire baundoun.°	*power*
	An hendy hap ich habbe yhent,[2]	
10	Ichoot° from hevene it is me sent:	*I know*
	From alle[3] wommen my love is lent,°	*removed*
	And light° on Alisoun.	*alights*
	On hew° hire heer° is fair ynough,	*hue / hair*
	Hire browe browne, hire yë° blake;	*eye*
15	With lossum cheere heo on me lough;[4]	
	With middel smal and wel ymake.	
	But° heo me wolle to hire take	*unless*
	For to been hire owen make,°	*mate*
	Longe to liven ichulle° forsake,	*I will*
20	And feye° fallen adown.	*dead*
	An hendy hap, etc.	
	Nightes when I wende° and wake,	*turn*
	Forthy° mine wonges° waxeth wan:	*therefore / cheeks*
	Levedy,° al for thine sake	*lady*
25	Longinge is ylent me on.[5]	
	In world nis noon so witer° man	*clever*
	That al hire bountee° telle can;	*excellence*
	Hire swire° is whittere° than the swan,	*neck / whiter*
	And fairest may° in town.	*maid*
30	An hendy, etc.	
	Ich am for wowing° al forwake,°	*wooing / worn out from waking*
	Wery so° water in wore.[6]	*as*
	Lest any reve me° my make	*deprive me*
	Ich habbe y-yerned yore.[7]	
35	Bettere is tholien° while° sore	*to endure / for a time*
	Than mournen evermore.	
	Geinest under gore,[8]	
	Herkne to my roun:°	*song*
	An hendy, etc.	

1. In her language.
2. A gracious chance I have received.
3. I.e., all other.
4. With lovely face she on me smiled.

5. Longing has come upon me.
6. Perhaps "millpond."
7. I have been worrying long since.
8. Fairest beneath clothing.

My Lief Is Faren in Londe

My lief is faren in londe[9]—
Allas, why is she so?
And I am so sore bonde°   bound
I may nat come her to.
5   She hath myn herte in holde
Wherever she ride or go°—   walk
With trewe love a thousand folde.

Western Wind

Westron wind, when will thou blow?
The small rain down can rain.
Christ, that my love were in my arms,
And I in my bed again.

I Am of Ireland

Ich am of Irlonde,
And of the holy londe
Of Irlonde.
Goode sire, praye ich thee,
5   For of° sainte charitee,   sake of
Com and dance with me
In Irlonde.

9. My beloved has gone away.

SIR THOMAS MALORY
ca. 1415–1471

*M*orte Darthur (Death of Arthur) is the title that William Caxton, the first English printer, gave to Malory's volume, which Caxton described more accurately in his Preface as "the noble histories of King Arthur and of certain of his knights." The volume begins with the mythical story of Arthur's birth. King Uther Pendragon falls in love with the wife of one of his barons. Merlin's magic transforms Uther into the likeness of her husband, and Arthur is born of this union. The volume ends with the destruction of the Round Table and the deaths of Arthur, Queen Guinevere, and Sir Lancelot, who is Arthur's best knight and the queen's lover. The bulk of the work is taken up with the separate adventures of the knights of the Round Table.

On the evolution of the Arthurian legend, see the headnote to "The Myth of Arthur's Return," p. 136. During the thirteenth century, the stories about Arthur and his knights had been turned into a series of enormously long prose romances in French, and it was these that, as Caxton informed his readers, "Sir Thomas Malory did take out of certain books of French and reduced into English." For Caxton's Preface, see "King Arthur" in the NAEL Archive.

Little was known about the author until the early twentieth century when scholars began to unearth the criminal record of a Sir Thomas Malory of Newbold Revell in Warwickshire. In 1451 he was arrested for the first time to prevent his doing injury—presumably further injury—to a priory in Lincolnshire, and shortly thereafter he was accused of a number of criminal acts. These included escaping from prison after his first arrest, twice breaking into and plundering the Abbey of Coombe, extorting money from various persons, and committing rape. Malory pleaded innocent of all charges. The Wars of the Roses—in which Malory, like the formidable earl of Warwick (the "kingmaker"), whom he seems to have followed, switched sides from Lancaster to York and back again—may account for some of his troubles with the law. After a failed Lancastrian revolt, the Yorkist king, Edward IV, specifically excluded Malory from four amnesties he granted to the Lancastrians.

The identification of this Sir Thomas Malory (there is another candidate with the same name) as the author of the *Morte* was strengthened by the discovery in 1934 of a manuscript that differed from Caxton's text, the only version previously known. The manuscript contained eight separate romances. Caxton, in order to give the impression of a continuous narrative, had welded these together into twenty-one books, subdivided into short chapters with summary chapter headings. Caxton suppressed all but the last of the personal remarks the author had appended to individual tales in the manuscript. At the very end of the book Malory asks "all gentlemen and gentlewomen that readeth this book pray for me while I am alive that God send me good deliverance." The discovery of the manuscript revealed that at the close of the first tale he had written: "this was drawyn by a knight presoner Sir Thomas Malleoré, that God sende him good recover." There is strong circumstantial evidence, therefore, that the book from which the Arthurian legends were passed on to future generations to be adapted in literature, art, and film was written in prison by a man whose violent career might seem at odds with the chivalric ideals he professes.

Such a contradiction—if it really is one—should not be surprising. Nostalgia for an ideal past that never truly existed is typical of much historical romance. Like the slave-owning plantation society of Margaret Mitchell's *Gone with the Wind*, whose southern gentlemen cultivate chivalrous manners and respect for gentlewomen, Malory's Arthurian world is a fiction. In our terms, it cannot even be labeled "historical," although the distinction between romance and history is not one that Malory would have made. Only rarely does he voice skepticism about the historicity of his tale; one such example is his questioning of the myth of Arthur's return. Much of the tragic power of his romance lies in his sense of the irretrievability of past glory in comparison with the sordidness of his own age.

The success of Malory's retelling owes much to his development of a terse and direct prose style, especially the naturalistic dialogue that keeps his narrative close to earth. And both he and many of his characters are masters of understatement who express themselves, in moments of great emotional tension, with a bare minimum of words.

In spite of its professed dedication to service of women, Malory's chivalry is primarily devoted to the fellowship and competitions of aristocratic men. Fighting consists mainly of single combats in tournaments, chance encounters, and battles, which

Malory never tires of describing in professional detail. Commoners rarely come into view; when they do, the effect can be chilling—as when pillagers by moonlight plunder the corpses of the knights left on the field of Arthur's last battle. Above all, Malory cherishes an aristocratic male code of honor for which his favorite word is "worship." Men win or lose "worship" through their actions in war and love.

The most "worshipful" of Arthur's knights is Sir Lancelot, the "head of all Christian knights," as he is called in a moving eulogy by his brother, Sir Ector. But Lancelot is compromised by his fatal liaison with Arthur's queen and torn between the incompatible loyalties that bind him as an honorable knight, on the one hand, to his lord Arthur and, on the other, to his lady Guinevere. Malory loves his character Lancelot even to the point of indulging in the fleeting speculation, after Lancelot has been admitted to the queen's chamber, that their activities might have been innocent, "for love that time was not as love is nowadays." But when the jealousy and malice of two wicked knights force the affair into the open, nothing can avert a mighty civil war; the breaking up of the fellowship of the Round Table; and the death of Arthur himself, which Malory relates with somber magnificence as the passing of a great era.

From Morte Darthur[1]

[THE CONSPIRACY AGAINST LANCELOT AND GUINEVERE]

In May, when every lusty[2] heart flourisheth and burgeoneth, for as the season is lusty to behold and comfortable,[3] so man and woman rejoiceth and gladdeth of summer coming with his fresh flowers; for winter with his rough winds and blasts causeth lusty men and women to cower and to sit fast by the fire—so this season it befell in the month of May a great anger and unhap that stinted not[4] till the flower of chivalry of all the world was destroyed and slain. And all was long upon two unhappy[5] knights which were named Sir Agravain and Sir Mordred that were brethren unto Sir Gawain.[6] For this Sir Agravain and Sir Mordred had ever a privy[7] hate unto the Queen, Dame Guinevere, and to Sir Lancelot, and daily and nightly they ever watched upon Sir Lancelot.

So it misfortuned Sir Gawain and all his brethren were in King Arthur's chamber, and then Sir Agravain said thus openly, and not in no counsel,[8] that many knights might hear: "I marvel that we all be not ashamed both to see and to know how Sir Lancelot lieth daily and nightly by the Queen. And all we know well that it is so, and it is shamefully suffered of us all[9] that we should suffer so noble a king as King Arthur is to be shamed."

Then spoke Sir Gawain and said, "Brother, Sir Agravain, I pray you and charge you, move no such matters no more afore[1] me, for wit you well, I will not be of your counsel."[2]

---

1. The selections here are from the section that Caxton called book 20, chaps. 1–4, 8–10, and book 21, chaps. 3–7, 10–12, with omissions. In the Winchester manuscript this section is titled "The Most Piteous Tale of the Morte Arthur Saunz Guerdon" (i.e., the death of Arthur without reward or compensation). The text is based on Winchester, with some readings introduced from the Caxton edition; spelling has been modernized and modern punctuation added.
2. Merry.
3. Pleasant.

4. Misfortune that ceased not.
5. On account of two ill-fated.
6. Gawain and Agravain are sons of King Lot of Orkney and his wife, Arthur's half-sister Morgause. Mordred is the illegitimate son of Arthur and Morgause.
7. Secret.
8. Secret manner.
9. Put up with by all of us.
1. Before. "Move": propose.
2. On your side. "Wit you well": know well, i.e., give you to understand.

"So God me help," said Sir Gaheris and Sir Gareth,[3] "we will not be known of your deeds."[4]

"Then will I!" said Sir Mordred.

"I lieve[5] you well," said Sir Gawain, "for ever unto all unhappiness, sir, ye will grant.[6] And I would that ye left all this and make you not so busy, for I know," said Sir Gawain, "what will fall of it."[7]

"Fall whatsoever fall may," said Sir Agravain, "I will disclose it to the King."

"Not by my counsel," said Sir Gawain, "for and[8] there arise war and wrack betwixt[9] Sir Lancelot and us, wit you well, brother, there will many kings and great lords hold with Sir Lancelot. Also, brother, Sir Agravain," said Sir Gawain, "ye must remember how often times Sir Lancelot hath rescued the King and the Queen. And the best of us all had been full cold at the heart-root[1] had not Sir Lancelot been better than we, and that has he proved himself full oft. And as for my part," said Sir Gawain, "I will never be against Sir Lancelot for[2] one day's deed, when he rescued me from King Carados of the Dolorous[3] Tower and slew him and saved my life. Also, brother, Sir Agravain and Sir Mordred, in like wise Sir Lancelot rescued you both and three score and two[4] from Sir Tarquin. And therefore, brother, methinks such noble deeds and kindness should be remembered."

"Do as ye list,"[5] said Sir Agravain, "for I will layne[6] it no longer."

So with these words came in Sir Arthur.

"Now, brother," said Sir Gawain, "stint your noise."[7]

"That will I not," said Sir Agravain and Sir Mordred.

"Well, will ye so?" said Sir Gawain. "Then God speed you, for I will not hear of your tales, neither be of your counsel."

"No more will I," said Sir Gaheris.

"Neither I," said Sir Gareth, "for I shall never say evil by[8] that man that made me knight." And therewithal they three departed making great dole.[9]

"Alas!" said Sir Gawain and Sir Gareth, "now is this realm wholly destroyed and mischieved,[1] and the noble fellowship of the Round Table shall be disparbeled."[2]

So they departed, and then King Arthur asked them what noise[3] they made. "My lord," said Sir Agravain, "I shall tell you, for I may keep[4] it no longer. Here is I and my brother Sir Mordred broke[5] unto my brother Sir Gawain, Sir Gaheris, and to Sir Gareth—for this is all, to make it short—how that we know all that Sir Lancelot holdeth your queen, and hath done long; and we be your sister[6] sons, we may suffer it no longer. And all we woot[7] that ye should be above Sir Lancelot, and ye are the king that made him knight, and therefore we will prove it that he is a traitor to your person."

---

3. Sons of King Lot and Gawain's brothers.
4. A party to your doings.
5. Believe.
6. You will consent to all mischief.
7. Come of it.
8. If.
9. Strife between.
1. Would have been dead.
2. On account of.
3. Dismal.
4. I.e., sixty-two.
5. You please.

6. Conceal.
7. Stop making scandal.
8. About.
9. Lamentation.
1. Put to shame.
2. Dispersed.
3. Rumor.
4. Conceal.
5. Revealed.
6. Sister's.
7. Know.

"If it be so," said the King, "wit[8] you well, he is none other. But I would be loath to begin such a thing but[9] I might have proofs of it, for Sir Lancelot is an hardy knight, and all ye know that he is the best knight among us all. And but if he be taken with the deed,[1] he will fight with him that bringeth up the noise, and I know no knight that is able to match him. Therefore, and[2] it be sooth as ye say, I would that he were taken with the deed."

For, as the French book saith, the King was full loath that such a noise should be upon Sir Lancelot and his queen. For the King had a deeming[3] of it, but he would not hear of it, for Sir Lancelot had done so much for him and for the Queen so many times that, wit you well, the King loved him passingly[4] well.

"My lord," said Sir Agravain, "ye shall ride tomorn[5] on hunting, and doubt ye not, Sir Lancelot will not go with you. And so when it draweth toward night, ye may send the Queen word that ye will lie out all that night, and so may ye send for your cooks. And then, upon pain of death, that night we shall take him with the Queen, and we shall bring him unto you, quick[6] or dead."

"I will well,"[7] said the King. "Then I counsel you to take with you sure fellowship."

"Sir," said Sir Agravain, "my brother, Sir Mordred, and I will take with us twelve knights of the Round Table."

"Beware," said King Arthur, "for I warn you, ye shall find him wight."[8]

"Let us deal!"[9] said Sir Agravain and Sir Mordred.

So on the morn King Arthur rode on hunting and sent word to the Queen that he would be out all that night. Then Sir Agravain and Sir Mordred got to them[1] twelve knights and hid themself in a chamber in the castle of Carlisle. And these were their names: Sir Colgrevance, Sir Mador de la Porte, Sir Guingalen, Sir Meliot de Logres, Sir Petipace of Winchelsea, Sir Galeron of Galway, Sir Melion de la Mountain, Sir Ascamore, Sir Gromore Somyr Jour, Sir Curselayne, Sir Florence, and Sir Lovell. So these twelve knights were with Sir Mordred and Sir Agravain, and all they were of Scotland, or else of Sir Gawain's kin, or well-willers[2] to his brother.

So when the night came, Sir Lancelot told Sir Bors[3] how he would go that night and speak with the Queen.

"Sir," said Sir Bors, "ye shall not go this night by my counsel."

"Why?" said Sir Lancelot.

"Sir," said Sir Bors, "I dread me[4] ever of Sir Agravain that waiteth upon[5] you daily to do you shame and us all. And never gave my heart against no going that ever ye went[6] to the queen so much as now, for I mistrust[7] that the King is out this night from the Queen because peradventure he hath lain[8] some watch for you and the Queen. Therefore, I dread me sore of some treason."

"Have ye no dread," said Sir Lancelot, "for I shall go and come again and make no tarrying."

---

8. Know.
9. Unless
1. Unless he is caught in the act.
2. If.
3. Suspicion.
4. Exceedingly.
5. Tomorrow.
6. Alive.
7. Readily agree.
8. Strong.

9. Leave it to us.
1. Gathered to themselves.
2. Partisans.
3. Nephew and confidant of Sir Lancelot.
4. I am afraid.
5. Lies in wait.
6. Never misgave my heart against any visit you made.
7. Suspect.
8. Perhaps he has set.

"Sir," said Sir Bors, "that me repents,[9] for I dread me sore that your going this night shall wrath[1] us all."

"Fair nephew," said Sir Lancelot, "I marvel me much why ye say thus, sithen[2] the Queen hath sent for me. And wit you well, I will not be so much a coward, but she shall understand I will[3] see her good grace."

"God speed you well," said Sir Bors, "and send you sound and safe again!"

So Sir Lancelot departed and took his sword under his arm, and so he walked in his mantel,[4] that noble knight, and put himself in great jeopardy. And so he passed on till he came to the Queen's chamber, and so lightly he was had[5] into the chamber. And then, as the French book saith, the Queen and Sir Lancelot were together. And whether they were abed or at other manner of disports, me list[6] not thereof make no mention, for love that time[7] was not as love is nowadays.

But thus as they were together there came Sir Agravain and Sir Mordred with twelve knights with them of the Round Table, and they said with great crying and scaring[8] voice: "Thou traitor, Sir Lancelot, now are thou taken!" And thus they cried with a loud voice that all the court might hear it. And these fourteen knights all were armed at all points, as[9] they should fight in a battle.

"Alas!" said Queen Guinevere, "now are we mischieved[1] both!"

"Madam," said Sir Lancelot, "is there here any armor within your chamber that I might cover my body withal? And if there be any, give it me, and I shall soon stint[2] their malice, by the grace of God!"

"Now, truly," said the Queen, "I have none armor neither helm, shield, sword, neither spear, wherefore I dread me sore our long love is come to a mischievous end. For I hear by their noise there be many noble knights, and well I woot they be surely[3] armed, and against them ye may make no resistance. Wherefore ye are likely to be slain, and then shall I be burned! For and[4] ye might escape them," said the Queen, "I would not doubt but that ye would rescue me in what danger that ever I stood in."

"Alas!" said Sir Lancelot, "in all my life thus was I never bestead[5] that I should be thus shamefully slain for lack of mine armor."

But ever in one[6] Sir Agravain and Sir Mordred cried: "Traitor knight, come out of the Queen's chamber! For wit thou well thou art beset so that thou shalt not escape."

"Ah, Jesu mercy!" said Sir Lancelot, "this shameful cry and noise I may not suffer, for better were death at once than thus to endure this pain." Then he took the Queen in his arms and kissed her and said, "Most noblest Christian queen, I beseech you, as ye have been ever my special good lady, and I at all times your poor knight and true unto[7] my power, and as I never failed you in right nor in wrong sithen the first day King Arthur made me knight, that ye will pray for my soul if that I be slain. For well I am assured that Sir Bors, my nephew, and all the remnant of my kin, with Sir Lavain and Sir Urry,[8] that they will not fail you to rescue you from the fire. And

---

9. I regret.
1. Cause injury to.
2. Since.
3. Wish to.
4. Cloak. Lancelot goes without armor.
5. Quickly he was received.
6. I care. "Disports": pastimes.
7. At that time.
8. Terrifying.
9. Completely, as if.

1. Come to grief.
2. Stop.
3. Securely.
4. If.
5. Beset.
6. In unison.
7. To the utmost of.
8. The brother of Elaine, the Fair Maid of Astolat, and a knight miraculously healed of his wound by Sir Lancelot. "Remnant": rest.

therefore, mine own lady, recomfort yourself,[9] whatsoever come of me, that ye go with Sir Bors, my nephew, and Sir Urry and they all will do you all the pleasure that they may, and ye shall live like a queen upon my lands."

"Nay, Sir Lancelot, nay!" said the Queen. "Wit thou well that I will not live long after thy days. But and[1] ye be slain I will take my death as meekly as ever did martyr take his death for Jesu Christ's sake."

"Well, Madam," said Sir Lancelot, "sith it is so that the day is come that our love must depart,[2] wit you well I shall sell my life as dear as I may. And a thousandfold," said Sir Lancelot, "I am more heavier[3] for you than for myself! And now I had liefer[4] than to be lord of all Christendom that I had sure armor upon me, that men might speak of my deeds ere ever I were slain."

"Truly," said the Queen, "and[5] it might please God, I would that they would take me and slay me and suffer[6] you to escape."

"That shall never be," said Sir Lancelot. "God defend me from such a shame! But, Jesu Christ, be Thou my shield and mine armor!" And therewith Sir Lancelot wrapped his mantel about his arm well and surely; and by then they had gotten a great form[7] out of the hall, and therewith they all rushed at the door. "Now, fair lords," said Sir Lancelot, "leave[8] your noise and your rushing, and I shall set open this door, and then may ye do with me what it liketh you."[9]

"Come off,[1] then," said they all, "and do it, for it availeth thee not to strive against us all. And therefore let us into this chamber, and we shall save thy life until thou come to King Arthur."

Then Sir Lancelot unbarred the door, and with his left hand he held it open a little, that but one man might come in at once. And so there came striding a good knight, a much[2] man and a large, and his name was called Sir Colgrevance of Gore. And he with a sword struck at Sir Lancelot mightily. And he put aside[3] the stroke and gave him such a buffet[4] upon the helmet that he fell groveling dead within the chamber door. Then Sir Lancelot with great might drew the knight within[5] the chamber door. And then Sir Lancelot, with help of the Queen and her ladies, he was lightly[6] armed in Colgrevance's armor. And ever stood Sir Agravain and Sir Mordred, crying, "Traitor knight! Come forth out of the Queen's chamber!"

"Sirs, leave[7] your noise," said Sir Lancelot, "for wit you well, Sir Agravain, ye shall not prison me this night. And therefore, and[8] ye do by my counsel, go ye all from this chamber door and make you no such crying and such manner of slander as ye do. For I promise you by my knighthood, and ye will depart and make no more noise, I shall as tomorn appear afore you all and before the King, and then let it be seen which of you all, other else ye all,[9] that will deprove[1] me of treason. And there shall I answer you, as a knight should, that hither I came to the Queen for no manner of mal engine,[2] and that will I prove and make it good upon you with my hands."

---

9. Take heart again.
1. If.
2. Come to an end.
3. More grieved.
4. Rather.
5. If.
6. Allow.
7. Bench.
8. Stop.
9. Pleases you.
1. Go ahead.

2. Big.
3. Fended off.
4. Blow.
5. Inside.
6. Quickly.
7. Stop.
8. If.
9. Or else all of you.
1. Accuse.
2. Evil design.

"Fie upon thee, traitor," said Sir Agravain and Sir Mordred, "for we will have thee malgré thine head[3] and slay thee, and we list.[4] For we let thee wit we have the choice of[5] King Arthur to save thee other slay thee."

"Ah, sirs," said Sir Lancelot, "is there none other grace with you? Then keep[6] yourself!" And then Sir Lancelot set all open the chamber door and mightily and knightly he strode in among them. And anon[7] at the first stroke he slew Sir Agravain, and after twelve of his fellows. Within a little while he had laid them down cold to the earth, for there was none of the twelve knights might stand Sir Lancelot one buffet.[8] And also he wounded Sir Mordred, and therewithal he fled with all his might.

And then Sir Lancelot returned again unto the Queen and said, "Madam, now wit you well, all our true love is brought to an end, for now will King Arthur ever be my foe. And therefore, Madam, and it like you[9] that I may have you with me, I shall save you from all manner adventurous[1] dangers."

"Sir, that is not best," said the Queen, "me seemeth, for[2] now ye have done so much harm, it will be best that ye hold you still with this. And if ye see that as tomorn they will put me unto death, then may ye rescue me as ye think best."

"I will well,"[3] said Sir Lancelot, "for have ye no doubt, while I am a man living I shall rescue you." And then he kissed her, and either of them gave other a ring, and so there he left the Queen and went until[4] his lodging.

[WAR BREAKS OUT BETWEEN ARTHUR AND LANCELOT][5]

Then said King Arthur unto Sir Gawain, "Dear nephew, I pray you make ready in your best armor with your brethren, Sir Gaheris and Sir Gareth, to bring my Queen to the fire, there to have her judgment and receive the death."

"Nay, my most noble king," said Sir Gawain, "that will I never do, for wit you well I will never be in that place where so noble a queen as is my lady Dame Guinevere shall take such a shameful end. For wit you well," said Sir Gawain, "my heart will not serve me for to see her die, and it shall never be said that ever I was of your counsel for her death."

"Then," said the King unto Sir Gawain, "suffer[6] your brethren Sir Gaheris and Sir Gareth to be there."

"My lord," said Sir Gawain, "wit you well they will be loath to be there present because of many adventures[7] that is like to fall, but they are young and full unable to say you nay."

Then spake Sir Gaheris and the good knight Sir Gareth unto King Arthur: "Sir, ye may well command us to be there, but wit you well it shall be sore against our will. But and[8] we be there by your strait commandment,

3. In spite of you.
4. If we please.
5. From.
6. Defend.
7. Right away.
8. I.e., withstand (even) one blow (from) Sir Lancelot.
9. If it please you.
1. Perilous.
2. Because.
3. Agree.
4. To.

5. Lancelot and Sir Bors mobilize their friends for the rescue of Guinevere. In the morning Mordred reports the events of the night to Arthur who, against Gawain's strong opposition, condemns the queen to be burned, for "the law was such in those days that whatsoever they were, of what estate or degree, if they were found guilty of treason there should be none other remedy but death."
6. Allow.
7. Chance occurrences.
8. If.

ye shall plainly[9] hold us there excused—we will be there in peaceable wise and bear none harness of war[1] upon us."

"In the name of God," said the King, "then make you ready, for she shall have soon[2] her judgment."

"Alas," said Sir Gawain, "that ever I should endure[3] to see this woeful day." So Sir Gawain turned him and wept heartily, and so he went into his chamber.

And then the Queen was led forth without[4] Carlisle, and anon she was dispoiled into[5] her smock. And then her ghostly father[6] was brought to her to be shriven of her misdeeds.[7] Then was there weeping and wailing and wringing of hands of many lords and ladies, but there were but few in comparison that would bear any armor for to strengthen[8] the death of the Queen.

Then was there one that Sir Lancelot had sent unto that place, which went to espy what time the Queen should go unto her death. And anon as[9] he saw the Queen dispoiled into her smock and shriven, then he gave Sir Lancelot warning. Then was there but spurring and plucking up[1] of horses, and right so they came unto the fire. And who[2] that stood against them, there were they slain—there might none withstand Sir Lancelot. So all that bore arms and withstood them, there were they slain, full many a noble knight. * * * And so in this rushing and hurling, as Sir Lancelot thrang[3] here and there, it misfortuned him[4] to slay Sir Gaheris and Sir Gareth, the noble knight, for they were unarmed and unwares.[5] As the French book saith, Sir Lancelot smote Sir Gaheris and Sir Gareth upon the brain-pans, wherethrough[6] that they were slain in the field, howbeit[7] Sir Lancelot saw them not. And so were they found dead among the thickest of the press.[8]

Then when Sir Lancelot had thus done, and slain and put to flight all that would withstand him, then he rode straight unto Queen Guinevere and made a kirtle[9] and a gown to be cast upon her, and then he made her to be set behind him and prayed her to be of good cheer. Now wit you well the Queen was glad that she was escaped from death, and then she thanked God and Sir Lancelot.

And so he rode his way with the Queen, as the French book saith, unto Joyous Garde,[1] and there he kept her as a noble knight should. And many great lords and many good knights were sent him, and many full noble knights drew unto him. When they heard that King Arthur and Sir Lancelot were at debate,[2] many knights were glad, and many were sorry of their debate.

Now turn we again unto King Arthur, that when it was told him how and in what manner the Queen was taken away from the fire, and when he heard of the death of his noble knights, and in especial Sir Gaheris and Sir Gareth, then he swooned for very pure[3] sorrow. And when he awoke of his swoon, then he said: "Alas, that ever I bore crown upon my head! For now

---

9. Openly; "strait": strict.
1. Armor.
2. Right away.
3. Live.
4. Outside.
5. Undressed down to.
6. Spiritual father, i.e., her priest.
7. For her to be confessed of her sins.
8. Secure.
9. As soon as.
1. Urging forward.

2. Whoever.
3. Pressed. "Hurling": turmoil.
4. He had the misfortune.
5. Unaware.
6. Through which.
7. Although.
8. Crowd.
9. Petticoat.
1. Lancelot's castle in England.
2. Strife.
3. Sheer.

have I lost the fairest fellowship of noble knights that ever held Christian king[4] together. Alas, my good knights be slain and gone away from me. Now within these two days I have lost nigh forty knights and also the noble fellowship of Sir Lancelot and his blood,[5] for now I may nevermore hold them together with my worship.[6] Alas, that ever this war began!

"Now, fair fellows," said the King, "I charge you that no man tell Sir Gawain of the death of his two brethren, for I am sure," said the King, "when he heareth tell that Sir Gareth is dead, he will go nigh out of his mind. Mercy Jesu," said the King, "why slew he Sir Gaheris and Sir Gareth? For I dare say, as for Sir Gareth, he loved Sir Lancelot above all men earthly."[7]

"That is truth," said some knights, "but they were slain in the hurling,[8] as Sir Lancelot thrang in the thickest of the press. And as they were unarmed, he smote them and wist[9] not whom that he smote, and so unhappily[1] they were slain."

"Well," said Arthur, "the death of them will cause the greatest mortal war that ever was, for I am sure that when Sir Gawain knoweth hereof that Sir Gareth is slain, I shall never have rest of him[2] till I have destroyed Sir Lancelot's kin and himself both, other else he to destroy me. And therefore," said the King, "wit you well, my heart was never so heavy as it is now. And much more I am sorrier for my good knights' loss[3] than for the loss of my fair queen; for queens I might have enough, but such a fellowship of good knights shall never be together in no company. And now I dare say," said King Arthur, "there was never Christian king that ever held such a fellowship together. And alas, that ever Sir Lancelot and I should be at debate. Ah, Agravain, Agravain!" said the King, "Jesu forgive it thy soul, for thine evil will that thou and thy brother Sir Mordred haddest unto Sir Lancelot hath caused all this sorrow." And ever among these complaints the King wept and swooned.

Then came there one to Sir Gawain and told him how the Queen was led away with[4] Sir Lancelot, and nigh a four-and-twenty knights slain. "Ah, Jesu, save me my two brethren!" said Sir Gawain. "For full well wist I," said Sir Gawain, "that Sir Lancelot would rescue her, other else he would die in that field. And to say the truth he were not of worship but if he had[5] rescued the Queen, insomuch as she should have been burned for his sake. And as in that," said Sir Gawain, "he hath done but knightly, and as I would have done myself and I had stood in like case. But where are my brethren?" said Sir Gawain. "I marvel that I hear not of them."

Then said that man, "Truly, Sir Gaheris and Sir Gareth be slain."

"Jesu defend!"[6] said Sir Gawain. "For all this world I would not that they were slain, and in especial my good brother Sir Gareth."

"Sir," said the man, "he is slain, and that is great pity."

"Who slew him?" said Sir Gawain.

"Sir Lancelot," said the man, "slew them both."

"That may I not believe," said Sir Gawain, "that ever he slew my good brother Sir Gareth, for I dare say my brother loved him better than me and all

4. That Christian king ever held.
5. Kin.
6. Keep both them and my dignity.
7. Earthly men.
8. Turmoil.
9. Knew.

1. Unluckily.
2. He will never give me any peace.
3. The loss of my good knights.
4. By.
5. Of honor if he had not.
6. Forbid.

his brethren and the King both. Also I dare say, an[7] Sir Lancelot had desired my brother Sir Gareth with him, he would have been with him against the King and us all. And therefore I may never believe that Sir Lancelot slew my brethren."

"Verily, sir," said the man, "it is noised[8] that he slew him."

"Alas," said Sir Gawain, "now is my joy gone." And then he fell down and swooned, and long he lay there as he had been dead. And when he arose out of his swoon, he cried out sorrowfully and said, "Alas!" And forthwith he ran unto the King, crying and weeping, and said, "Ah, mine uncle King Arthur! My good brother Sir Gareth is slain, and so is my brother Sir Gaheris, which were two noble knights."

Then the King wept and he both, and so they fell on swooning. And when they were revived, then spake Sir Gawain and said, "Sir, I will go and see my brother Sir Gareth."

"Sir, ye may not see him," said the King, "for I caused him to be interred and Sir Gaheris both, for I well understood that ye would make overmuch sorrow, and the sight of Sir Gareth should have caused your double sorrow."

"Alas, my lord," said Sir Gawain, "how slew he my brother Sir Gareth? Mine own good lord, I pray you tell me."

"Truly," said the King, "I shall tell you as it hath been told me—Sir Lancelot slew him and Sir Gaheris both."

"Alas," said Sir Gawain, "they bore none arms against him, neither of them both."

"I woot not how it was," said the King, "but as it is said, Sir Lancelot slew them in the thickest of the press and knew them not. And therefore let us shape a remedy for to revenge their deaths."

"My king, my lord, and mine uncle," said Sir Gawain, "wit you well, now I shall make you a promise which I shall hold by my knighthood, that from this day forward I shall never fail[9] Sir Lancelot until that one of us have slain the other. And therefore I require you, my lord and king, dress[1] you unto the wars, for wit you well, I will be revenged upon Sir Lancelot; and therefore, as ye will have my service and my love, now haste you thereto and assay[2] your friends. For I promise unto God," said Sir Gawain, "for the death of my brother Sir Gareth I shall seek Sir Lancelot throughout seven kings' realms, but I shall slay him, other else he shall slay me."

"Sir, ye shall not need to seek him so far," said the King, "for as I hear say, Sir Lancelot will abide me and us all within the castle of Joyous Garde. And much people draweth unto him, as I hear say."

"That may I right well believe," said Sir Gawain, "but my lord," he said, "assay your friends and I will assay mine."

"It shall be done," said the King, "and as I suppose I shall be big[3] enough to drive him out of the biggest tower of his castle."

So then the King sent letters and writs throughout all England, both the length and the breadth, for to summon all his knights. And so unto King Arthur drew many knights, dukes, and earls, that he had a great host, and when they were assembled the King informed them how Sir Lancelot had

---

7. If.
8. Reported.
9. Give up the pursuit of.

1. Prepare.
2. Appeal to.
3. Strong.

bereft him his Queen. Then the King and all his host made them ready to lay siege about Sir Lancelot where he lay within Joyous Garde.

[THE DEATH OF ARTHUR][4]

So upon Trinity Sunday at night King Arthur dreamed a wonderful dream, and in his dream him seemed that he saw upon a chafflet[5] a chair, and the chair was fast to a wheel, and thereupon sat King Arthur in the richest cloth of gold that might be made. And the King thought there was under him, far from him, an hideous deep black water, and therein was all manner of serpents, and worms, and wild beasts, foul and horrible. And suddenly the King thought that the wheel turned upside down, and he fell among the serpents, and every beast took him by a limb. And then the King cried as he lay in his bed, "Help, help!"

And then knights, squires, and yeomen awaked the King, and then he was so amazed[6] that he wist[7] not where he was. And then so he awaked[8] until it was nigh day, and then he fell on slumbering again, not sleeping nor thoroughly waking. So the King seemed[9] verily that there came Sir Gawain unto him with a number of fair ladies with him. So when King Arthur saw him, he said, "Welcome, my sister's son. I weened ye had been dead. And now I see thee on-live, much am I beholden unto Almighty Jesu. Ah, fair nephew and my sister's son, what been these ladies that hither be come with you?"

"Sir," said Sir Gawain, "all these be ladies for whom I have foughten for when I was man living. And all these are tho[1] that I did battle for in righteous quarrels, and God hath given them that grace, at their great prayer, because I did battle for them for their right, that they should bring me hither unto you. Thus much hath given me leave God, for to warn you of your death. For and ye fight as tomorn[2] with Sir Mordred, as ye both have assigned,[3] doubt ye not ye must be slain, and the most party of your people on both parties. And for the great grace and goodness that Almighty Jesu hath unto you, and for pity of you and many mo other good men there[4] shall be slain, God hath sent me to you of his special grace to give you warning that in no wise ye do battle as tomorn, but that ye take a treatise for a month-day.[5] And proffer you largely,[6] so that tomorn ye put in a delay. For within a month shall come Sir Lancelot with all his noble knights and rescue you worshipfully and slay Sir Mordred and all that ever will hold with him."

Then Sir Gawain and all the ladies vanished. And anon the King called upon his knights, squires, and yeomen, and charged them wightly[7] to fetch his noble lords and wise bishops unto him. And when they were come the King told them of his avision,[8] that Sir Gawain had told him and warned him that, and he fought on the morn, he should be slain. Then the King

---

4. The pope arranges a truce, Guinevere is returned to Arthur, and Lancelot and his kin leave England to become rulers of France. At Gawain's instigation Arthur invades France to resume the war against Lancelot. Word comes to the king that Mordred has seized the kingdom, and Arthur leads his forces back to England. Mordred attacks them upon their landing, and Gawain is mortally wounded and dies, although not before he has repented for insisting that Arthur fight Lancelot and has written Lancelot to come to the aid of his former lord.
5. Scaffold. "Him seemed": it seemed to him.

6. Confused.
7. Knew.
8. Lay awake.
9. It seemed to the king.
1. Those.
2. If you fight tomorrow.
3. Decided.
4. I.e., who there. "Mo": more.
5. For a month from today. "Treatise": treaty, truce.
6. Make generous offers.
7. Quickly.
8. Dream.

commanded Sir Lucan the Butler[9] and his brother Sir Bedivere the Bold, with two bishops with them, and charged them in any wise to take a treatise for a month-day[1] with Sir Mordred. "And spare not: proffer him lands and goods as much as ye think reasonable."

So then they departed and came to Sir Mordred where he had a grim host of an hundred thousand, and there they entreated[2] Sir Mordred long time. And at the last Sir Mordred was agreed for to have Cornwall and Kent by King Arthur's days,[3] and after that, all England, after the days of King Arthur.

Then were they condescended[4] that King Arthur and Sir Mordred should meet betwixt both their hosts, and everich[5] of them should bring fourteen persons. And so they came with this word unto Arthur. Then said he, "I am glad that this is done," and so he went into the field.

And when King Arthur should depart, he warned all his host that, and[6] they see any sword drawn, "Look ye come on fiercely and slay that traitor Sir Mordred, for I in no wise trust him." In like wise Sir Mordred warned his host that "And ye see any manner of sword drawn, look that ye come on fiercely, and so slay all that ever before you standeth, for in no wise I will not trust for this treatise." And in the same wise said Sir Mordred unto his host, "For I know well my father will be avenged upon me."

And so they met as their pointment[7] was and were agreed and accorded thoroughly. And wine was fetched and they drank together. Right so came an adder out of a little heath-bush, and it stung a knight in the foot. And so when the knight felt him so stung, he looked down and saw the adder. And anon he drew his sword to slay the adder, and thought[8] none other harm. And when the host on both parties saw that sword drawn, then they blew beams,[9] trumpets, and horns, and shouted grimly. And so both hosts dressed them[1] together. And King Arthur took his horse and said, "Alas, this unhappy day!" and so rode to his party, and Sir Mordred in like wise.

And never since was there never seen a more dolefuller battle in no Christian land, for there was but rushing and riding, foining[2] and striking; and many a grim word was there spoken of either to other, and many a deadly stroke. But ever King Arthur rode throughout the battle[3] of Sir Mordred many times and did full nobly, as a noble king should do, and at all times he fainted[4] never. And Sir Mordred did his devoir[5] that day and put himself in great peril.

And thus they fought all the long day, and never stinted[6] till the noble knights were laid to the cold earth. And ever they fought still till it was near night, and by then was there an hundred thousand laid dead upon the down.[7] Then was King Arthur wood-wroth[8] out of measure when he saw his people so slain from him. And so he looked about him and could see no mo[9] of all

---

9. "Butler" here is probably only a title of high rank, although it was originally used to designate the officer who had charge of wine for the king's table.
1. By any means necessary to make a treaty for the period of a month.
2. Dealt with.
3. During King Arthur's lifetime.
4. Agreed.
5. Each.
6. If.
7. Arrangement.

8. Meant.
9. A kind of trumpet.
1. Prepared to come.
2. Lunging.
3. Battalion.
4. Lost heart.
5. Knightly duty.
6. Stopped.
7. Upland.
8. Mad with rage.
9. Others.

his host, and good knights left no mo on-live, but two knights: the t'one[1] was Sir Lucan the Butler and [the other] his brother Sir Bedivere. And yet they were full sore wounded.

"Jesu, mercy," said the King, "where are all my noble knights become?[2] Alas that ever I should see this doleful day! For now," said King Arthur, "I am come to mine end. But would to God," said he, "that I wist[3] now where were that traitor Sir Mordred that has caused all this mischief."

Then King Arthur looked about and was ware where stood Sir Mordred leaning upon his sword among a great heap of dead men.

"Now give me my spear," said King Arthur unto Sir Lucan, "for yonder I have espied the traitor that all this woe hath wrought."

"Sir, let him be," said Sir Lucan, "for he is unhappy.[4] And if ye pass this unhappy day ye shall be right well revenged upon him. And, good lord, remember ye of your night's dream, and what the spirit of Sir Gawain told you tonight, and yet God of his great goodness hath preserved you hitherto. And for God's sake, my lord, leave off by this,[5] for, blessed be God, ye have won the field: for yet we been here three on-live, and with Sir Mordred is not one on-live. And therefore if ye leave off now, this wicked day of destiny is past."

"Now, tide[6] me death, tide me life," said the King, "now I see him yonder alone, he shall never escape mine hands. For at a better avail[7] shall I never have him."

"God speed you well!" said Sir Bedivere.

Then the King got his spear in both his hands and ran toward Sir Mordred, crying and saying, "Traitor, now is thy deathday come!"

And when Sir Mordred saw King Arthur he ran until him with his sword drawn in his hand, and there King Arthur smote Sir Mordred under the shield, with a foin[8] of his spear, throughout the body more than a fathom.[9] And when Sir Mordred felt that he had his death's wound, he thrust himself with the might that he had up to the burr[1] of King Arthur's spear, and right so he smote his father King Arthur with his sword holden in both his hands, upon the side of the head, that the sword pierced the helmet and the tay[2] of the brain. And therewith Sir Mordred dashed down stark dead to the earth.

And noble King Arthur fell in a swough[3] to the earth, and there he swooned oftentimes, and Sir Lucan and Sir Bedivere ofttimes heaved him up. And so, weakly betwixt them, they led him to a little chapel not far from the seaside, and when the King was there, him thought him reasonably eased. Then heard they people cry in the field. "Now go thou, Sir Lucan," said the King, "and do me to wit[4] what betokens that noise in the field."

So Sir Lucan departed, for he was grievously wounded in many places. And so as he yede[5] he saw and harkened by the moonlight how that pillers[6] and robbers were come into the field to pill and to rob many a full noble knight of brooches and bees[7] and of many a good ring and many a rich jewel. And who

---

1. That one, i.e., the first.
2. What has become of all my noble knights?
3. Knew.
4. I.e., unlucky for you.
5. I.e., with this much accomplished.
6. Betide.
7. Advantage.
8. Thrust.

9. I.e., six feet.
1. Hand guard.
2. Outer membrane.
3. Swoon.
4. Let me know.
5. Walked.
6. Plunderers.
7. Bracelets.

that were not dead all out there they slew them for their harness[8] and their riches. When Sir Lucan understood this work, he came to the King as soon as he might and told him all what he had heard and seen. "Therefore by my read,"[9] said Sir Lucan, "it is best that we bring you to some town."

"I would it were so," said the King, "but I may not stand, my head works[1] so. Ah, Sir Lancelot," said King Arthur, "this day have I sore missed thee. And alas that ever I was against thee, for now have I my death, whereof Sir Gawain me warned in my dream."

Then Sir Lucan took up the King the t'one party[2] and Sir Bedivere the other party; and in the lifting up the King swooned and in the lifting Sir Lucan fell in a swoon that part of his guts fell out of his body, and therewith the noble knight's heart burst. And when the King awoke he beheld Sir Lucan how he lay foaming at the mouth and part of his guts lay at his feet.

"Alas," said the King, "this is to me a full heavy[3] sight to see this noble duke so die for my sake, for he would have holpen[4] me that had more need of help than I. Alas that he would not complain him for[5] his heart was so set to help me. Now Jesu have mercy upon his soul."

Then Sir Bedivere wept for the death of his brother.

"Now leave this mourning and weeping, gentle knight," said the King, "for all this will not avail me. For wit thou well, and[6] I might live myself, the death of Sir Lucan would grieve me evermore. But my time passeth on fast," said the King. "Therefore," said King Arthur unto Sir Bedivere, "take thou here Excalibur[7] my good sword and go with it to yonder water's side; and when thou comest there I charge thee throw my sword in that water and come again and tell me what thou sawest there."

"My lord," said Sir Bedivere, "your commandment shall be done, and [I shall] lightly[8] bring you word again."

So Sir Bedivere departed. And by the way he beheld that noble sword, that the pommel and the haft[9] was all precious stones. And then he said to himself, "If I throw this rich sword in the water, thereof shall never come good, but harm and loss." And then Sir Bedivere hid Excalibur under a tree. And so, as soon as he might, he came again unto the King and said he had been at the water and had thrown the sword into the water.

"What saw thou there?" said the King.

"Sir," he said, "I saw nothing but waves and winds."

"That is untruly said of thee," said the King. "And therefore go thou lightly again and do my commandment; as thou art to me lief[1] and dear, spare not, but throw it in."

Then Sir Bedivere returned again and took the sword in his hand. And yet him thought[2] sin and shame to throw away that noble sword. And so eft[3] he hid the sword and returned again and told the King that he had been at the water and done his commandment.

---

8. Armor. "All out": entirely.
9. Advice.
1. Aches.
2. On one side.
3. Sorrowful.
4. Helped.
5. Because.
6. If.
7. The sword that Arthur had received as a young

man from the Lady of the Lake; it is presumably she who catches it when Bedivere finally throws it into the water.
8. Quickly.
9. Handle. "Pommel": rounded knob on the hilt.
1. Beloved.
2. It seemed to him.
3. Again.

"What sawest thou there?" said the King.

"Sir," he said, "I saw nothing but waters wap and waves wan."[4]

"Ah, traitor unto me and untrue," said King Arthur, "now hast thou betrayed me twice. Who would have weened that thou that has been to me so lief and dear, and thou art named a noble knight, and would betray me for the riches of this sword. But now go again lightly, for thy long tarrying putteth me in great jeopardy of my life, for I have taken cold. And but if thou do now as I bid thee, if ever I may see thee I shall slay thee mine[5] own hands, for thou wouldest for my rich sword see me dead."

Then Sir Bedivere departed and went to the sword and lightly took it up, and so he went to the water's side; and there he bound the girdle[6] about the hilts, and threw the sword as far into the water as he might. And there came an arm and an hand above the water and took it and clutched it, and shook it thrice and brandished; and then vanished away the hand with the sword into the water. So Sir Bedivere came again to the King and told him what he saw.

"Alas," said the King, "help me hence, for I dread me I have tarried overlong."

Then Sir Bedivere took the King upon his back and so went with him to that water's side. And when they were at the water's side, even fast[7] by the bank hoved[8] a little barge with many fair ladies in it; and among them all was a queen; and all they had black hoods, and all they wept and shrieked when they saw King Arthur.

"Now put me into that barge," said the King; and so he did softly. And there received him three ladies with great mourning, and so they set them[9] down. And in one of their laps King Arthur laid his head, and then the queen said, "Ah, my dear brother, why have ye tarried so long from me? Alas, this wound on your head hath caught overmuch cold." And anon they rowed fromward the land, and Sir Bedivere beheld all tho ladies go froward him.

Then Sir Bedivere cried and said, "Ah, my lord Arthur, what shall become of me, now ye go from me and leave me here alone among mine enemies?"

"Comfort thyself," said the King, "and do as well as thou mayest, for in me is no trust for to trust in. For I must into the vale of Avilion[1] to heal me of my grievous wound. And if thou hear nevermore of me, pray for my soul."

But ever the queen and ladies wept and shrieked that it was pity to hear. And as soon as Sir Bedivere had lost the sight of the barge he wept and wailed and so took the forest, and went[2] all that night. And in the morning he was ware betwixt two holts hoar[3] of a chapel and an hermitage.[4]

* * *

---

4. The phrase seems to mean "waters wash the shore and waves grow dark."
5. I.e., with mine.
6. Sword belt.
7. Close.
8. Waited.
9. I.e., they sat.
1. A legendary island, sometimes identified with the earthly paradise.
2. Walked. "Took": took to.

3. Ancient thickets of small trees.
4. In the passage here omitted, Sir Bedivere meets the former bishop of Canterbury, now a hermit, who describes how on the previous night a company of ladies had brought to the chapel a dead body, asking that it be buried. Sir Bedivere exclaims that the dead man must have been King Arthur and vows to spend the rest of his life there in the chapel as a hermit.

Thus of Arthur I find no more written in books that been authorized,[5] neither more of the very certainty of his death heard I never read,[6] but thus was he led away in a ship wherein were three queens: that one was King Arthur's sister, Queen Morgan la Fée,[7] the t'other[8] was the Queen of North Wales, and the third was the Queen of the Waste Lands. * * *

Now more of the death of King Arthur could I never find but that these ladies brought him to his burials,[9] and such one was buried there that the hermit bore witness that sometime was Bishop of Canterbury.[1] But yet the hermit knew not in certain that he was verily the body of King Arthur, for this tale Sir Bedivere, a Knight of the Table Round, made it to be written. Yet some men say in many parts of England that King Arthur is not dead, but had[2] by the will of our Lord Jesu into another place. And men say that he shall come again and he shall win the Holy Cross. Yet I will not say that it shall be so, but rather I will say, Here in this world he changed his life. And many men say that there is written upon his tomb this verse: *Hic iacet Arthurus, rex quondam, rexque futurus.*[3]

[THE DEATHS OF LANCELOT AND GUINEVERE][4]

And thus upon a night there came a vision to Sir Lancelot and charged him, in remission[5] of his sins, to haste him unto Amesbury: "And by then[6] thou come there, thou shalt find Queen Guinevere dead. And therefore take thy fellows with thee, and purvey them of an horse-bier,[7] and fetch thou the corse[8] of her, and bury her by her husband, the noble King Arthur. So this avision[9] came to Lancelot thrice in one night. Then Sir Lancelot rose up ere day and told the hermit.

"It were well done," said the hermit, "that ye made you ready and that ye disobey not the avision."

Then Sir Lancelot took his eight fellows with him, and on foot they yede[1] from Glastonbury to Amesbury, the which is little more than thirty mile, and thither they came within two days, for they were weak and feeble to go. And when Sir Lancelot was come to Amesbury within the nunnery, Queen Guinevere died but half an hour afore. And the ladies told Sir Lancelot that Queen Guinevere told them all ere she passed that Sir Lancelot had been priest near a twelve-month:[2] "and hither he cometh as fast as he may to fetch my corse, and beside my lord King Arthur he shall bury me." Wherefore the Queen said in hearing of them all, "I beseech Almighty God that I may never have power to see Sir Lancelot with my worldly eyes."

"And thus," said all the ladies, "was ever her prayer these two days till she was dead."

5. That have authority.
6. Tell.
7. The fairy.
8. The second.
9. Grave.
1. Of whom the hermit, who was formerly bishop of Canterbury, bore witness.
2. Conveyed.
3. "Here lies Arthur, who was once king and king will be again" (Latin).
4. Guinevere enters a convent at Amesbury, where Lancelot, returned with his companions to England, visits her, but she commands him never to see her again. Emulating her example, Lancelot joins the bishop of Canterbury and Bedivere in their hermitage, where he takes holy orders and is joined in turn by seven of his fellow knights.
5. For the remission.
6. By the time.
7. Provide them with a horse-drawn hearse.
8. Body.
9. Dream.
1. Went.
2. Nearly twelve months.

Then Sir Lancelot saw her visage, but he wept not greatly, but sighed. And so he did all the observance of the service himself, both the *dirige*[3] and on the morn he sang mass. And there was ordained[4] an horse-bier, and so with an hundred torches ever burning about the corse of the Queen, and ever Sir Lancelot with his eight fellows went about[5] the horse-bier, singing and reading many an holy orison,[6] and frankincense upon the corse incensed.[7]

Thus Sir Lancelot and his eight fellows went on foot from Amesbury unto Glastonbury, and when they were come to the chapel and the hermitage, there she had a *dirige* with great devotion.[8] And on the morn the hermit that sometime[9] was Bishop of Canterbury sang the mass of requiem with great devotion, and Sir Lancelot was the first that offered, and then als[1] his eight fellows. And then she was wrapped in cered cloth of Rennes, from the top[2] to the toe, in thirtyfold, and after she was put in a web[3] of lead, and then in a coffin of marble.

And when she was put in the earth Sir Lancelot swooned and lay long still, while[4] the hermit came and awaked him, and said, "Ye be to blame, for ye displease God with such manner of sorrow-making."

"Truly," said Sir Lancelot, "I trust I do not displease God, for He knoweth mine intent—for my sorrow was not, nor is not, for any rejoicing of sin, but my sorrow may never have end. For when I remember of her beaulté and of her noblesse[5] that was both with her king and with her,[6] so when I saw his corse and her corse so lie together, truly mine heart would not serve to sustain my careful[7] body. Also when I remember me how by my defaute and mine orgule[8] and my pride that they were both laid full low, that were peerless that ever was living of Christian people, wit you well," said Sir Lancelot, "this remembered, of their kindness and mine unkindness, sank so to mine heart that I might not sustain myself." So the French book maketh mention.

Then Sir Lancelot never after ate but little meat,[9] nor drank, till he was dead, for then he sickened more and more and dried and dwined[1] away. For the Bishop nor none of his fellows might not make him to eat, and little he drank, that he was waxen by a kibbet[2] shorter than he was, that the people could not know him. For evermore, day and night, he prayed, but sometime he slumbered a broken sleep. Ever he was lying groveling on the tomb of King Arthur and Queen Guinevere, and there was no comfort that the Bishop nor Sir Bors, nor none of his fellows could make him—it availed not.

So within six weeks after, Sir Lancelot fell sick and lay in his bed. And then he sent for the Bishop that there was hermit, and all his true fellows. Then Sir Lancelot said with dreary steven,[3] "Sir Bishop, I pray you give to me all my rights that longeth[4] to a Christian man."

3. *Dirige* (Latin source of modern "dirge"): the first word of the anthem beginning the funeral service.
4. Prepared.
5. Around.
6. Reciting many a prayer.
7. Burned frankincense over the body.
8. Earnest reverence.
9. Once.
1. Also. "Offered": made his donation.
2. Head. "Cloth of Rennes": A shroud made of fine linen smeared with wax, produced at Rennes.

3. Afterward she was put in a sheet.
4. Until.
5. Her beauty and nobility.
6. That she and her king both had.
7. Sorrowful.
8. My fault and my haughtiness.
9. Food.
1. Wasted.
2. Grown by a cubit.
3. Sad voice.
4. Pertains. "Rights": last sacrament of extreme unction.

"It shall not need you,"[5] said the hermit and all his fellows. "It is but heaviness of your blood. Ye shall be well mended by the grace of God tomorn."

"My fair lords," said Sir Lancelot, "wit you well my careful body will into the earth; I have warning more than now I will say. Therefore give me my rights."

So when he was houseled and annealed[6] and had all that a Christian man ought to have, he prayed the Bishop that his fellows might bear his body to Joyous Garde. (Some men say it was Alnwick, and some men say it was Bamborough.) "Howbeit," said Sir Lancelot, "me repenteth[7] sore, but I made mine avow sometime that in Joyous Garde I would be buried. And because of breaking[8] of mine avow, I pray you all, lead me thither." Then there was weeping and wringing of hands among his fellows.

So at a season of the night they all went to their beds, for they all lay in one chamber. And so after midnight, against[9] day, the Bishop that was hermit, as he lay in his bed asleep, he fell upon a great laughter. And therewith all the fellowship awoke and came to the Bishop and asked him what he ailed.[1]

"Ah, Jesu mercy," said the Bishop, "why did ye awake me? I was never in all my life so merry and so well at ease."

"Wherefore?" said Sir Bors.

"Truly," said the Bishop, "here was Sir Lancelot with me, with mo[2] angels than ever I saw men in one day. And I saw the angels heave[3] up Sir Lancelot unto heaven, and the gates of heaven opened against him."

"It is but dretching of swevens,"[4] said Sir Bors, "for I doubt not Sir Lancelot aileth nothing but good."[5]

"It may well be," said the Bishop. "Go ye to his bed and then shall ye prove the sooth."

So when Sir Bors and his fellows came to his bed, they found him stark dead. And he lay as he had smiled, and the sweetest savor[6] about him that ever they felt. Then was there weeping and wringing of hands, and the greatest dole they made that ever made men. And on the morn the Bishop did his mass of Requiem, and after the Bishop and all the nine knights put Sir Lancelot in the same horse-bier that Queen Guinevere was laid in tofore that she was buried. And so the Bishop and they all together went with the body of Sir Lancelot daily, till they came to Joyous Garde. And ever they had an hundred torches burning about him.

And so within fifteen days they came to Joyous Garde. And there they laid his corse in the body of the choir,[7] and sang and read many psalters[8] and prayers over him and about him. And ever his visage was laid open and naked, that all folks might behold him; for such was the custom in tho[9] days that all men of worship should so lie with open visage till that they were buried.

And right thus as they were at their service, there came Sir Ector de Maris that had seven year sought all England, Scotland, and Wales, seeking his

5. You shall not need it.
6. Given communion and extreme unction.
7. I am sorry.
8. In order not to break.
9. Toward.
1. Ailed him.
2. More.
3. Lift.

4. Illusion of dreams.
5. Has nothing wrong with him.
6. Odor. A sweet scent is a conventional sign in saints' lives of a sanctified death.
7. The center of the chancel, the place of honor.
8. Psalms.
9. Those.

brother, Sir Lancelot. And when Sir Ector heard such noise and light in the choir of Joyous Garde, he alight and put his horse from him and came into the choir. And there he saw men sing and weep, and all they knew Sir Ector, but he knew not them. Then went Sir Bors unto Sir Ector and told him how there lay his brother, Sir Lancelot, dead. And then Sir Ector threw his shield, sword, and helm from him, and when he beheld Sir Lancelot's visage, he fell down in a swoon. And when he waked, it were hard any tongue to tell the doleful complaints that he made for his brother.

"Ah, Lancelot!" he said, "thou were head of all Christian knights. And now I dare say," said Sir Ector, "thou Sir Lancelot, there thou liest, that thou were never matched of earthly knight's hand. And thou were the courteoust[1] knight that ever bore shield. And thou were the truest friend to thy lover that ever bestrode horse, and thou were the truest lover, of a sinful man,[2] that ever loved woman, and thou were the kindest man that ever struck with sword. And thou were the goodliest person that ever came among press of knights, and thou was the meekest man and the gentlest that ever ate in hall among ladies, and thou were the sternest knight to thy mortal foe that ever put spear in the rest."[3]

Then there was weeping and dolor out of measure.

Thus they kept Sir Lancelot's corse aloft fifteen days, and then they buried it with great devotion. And then at leisure they went all with the Bishop of Canterbury to his hermitage, and there they were together more than a month.

Then Sir Constantine that was Sir Cador's son of Cornwall was chosen king of England, and he was a full noble knight, and worshipfully he ruled this realm. And then this King Constantine sent for the Bishop of Canterbury, for he heard say where he was. And so he was restored unto his bishopric and left that hermitage, and Sir Bedivere was there ever still hermit to his life's end.

Then Sir Bors de Ganis, Sir Ector de Maris, Sir Gahalantine, Sir Galihud, Sir Galihodin, Sir Blamour, Sir Bleoberis, Sir Villiars le Valiant, Sir Clarrus of Clermount, all these knights drew them to their countries.[4] Howbeit[5] King Constantine would have had them with him, but they would not abide in this realm. And there they all lived in their countries as holy men.

And some English books make mention that they went never out of England after the death of Sir Lancelot—but that was but favor of makers.[6] For the French book maketh mention—and is authorized—that Sir Bors, Sir Ector, Sir Blamour, and Sir Bleoberis went into the Holy Land, thereas Jesu Christ was quick[7] and dead, and anon as they had stablished their lands;[8] for the book saith so Sir Lancelot commanded them for to do ere ever he passed out of this world. There these four knights did many battles upon the miscreaunts,[9] or Turks, and there they died upon a Good Friday for God's sake.

---

1. Most courteous.
2. Of any man born in original sin.
3. Support for the butt of the lance.
4. Withdrew themselves to their home districts.
5. However.

6. The authors' bias.
7. Living. "Thereas": where.
8. As soon as they had put their lands in order.
9. Infidels.

Here is the end of the whole book of King Arthur and of his noble knights of the Round Table, that when they were whole together there was ever an hundred and forty. And here is the end of *The Death of Arthur*.[1]

I pray you all gentlemen and gentlewomen that readeth this book of Arthur and his knights from the beginning to the ending, pray for me while I am alive that God send me good deliverance. And when I am dead, I pray you all pray for my soul.

For this book was ended the ninth year of the reign of King Edward the Fourth, by Sir Thomas Malory, knight, as Jesu help him for His great might, as he is the servant of Jesu both day and night.

1469–70   1485

---

1. By the "whole book" Malory refers to the entire work; the *Death of Arthur*, which Caxton made the title of the entire work, refers to the last part of Malory's book.

ROBERT HENRYSON
ca. 1425–ca. 1490

Robert Henryson is perhaps the greatest of a set of exceptionally accomplished late-fifteenth- and early-sixteenth-century Scots poets.

Little is known for certain about Henryson's life. Because he is spoken of as "master," he probably held a master's degree, and evidence points to his having been a schoolmaster in a grammar school founded by monks in the town of Dunfermline, just to the north of Edinburgh. He is the author of three major works: *Orpheus and Eurydice*, *Moral Fables*, and *The Testament of Cresseid*. Together, they reveal an author skilled in legal, literary, and philosophical traditions; they also reveal a great and ambitious literary artist capable of trenchant comedy within a larger vision that is dark, austere, and commanding. His intense poem *The Testament of Cresseid*, for example, is a sequel to Chaucer's *Troilus and Criseyde*. It imagines the fate of Criseyde/Cresseid as she becomes a prostitute in the Greek camp, stricken with both venereal disease and, finally, remorse. In sixteenth-century editions of Chaucer's works, this text was routinely printed at the end of *Troilus and Criseyde* as its sixth book.

As a schoolmaster, Henryson would have taught schoolboys how to read Latin; one of the texts would have been a collection of animal fables (probably the so-called late-twelfth-century elegiac *Romulus*) (see "Talking Animals," pp. 495–96). Henryson took up the challenge of these simple school texts to transform them into a work of extraordinary range, from the cute and comic, to the savagely satirical, to the philosophically dark and bleak. He drew on previous works of animal literature (especially Chaucer's *Nun's Priest's Tale*, in his *The Cock and the Fox*). His particular contribution, however, is to extend the philosophical and rhetorical range of the fables and to press their interpretive challenges to the limit. Fable traditions generally present animals as reduced and recognizable humans, designed to guide human behavior in simple ways. Not so for Henryson, and not so in this opening fable of the collection, *The Cock and the Jasper.*

Fables can be thought of as the dunghill of literature, the place of worthless scraps and sweepings. Only the moral interpretation, outside and attached to the animal narrative, invests the low story with high significance. *The Cock and the Jasper* begins in precisely the locus of the dunghill in the farmyard. Just as, however, fables might in fact hide rich literary treasure, so too does the cock find a jewel in the filth. And so far from dismissing it, the cock exercises discretion to know both what's for him and what's not (a standard kind of practical advice enjoined by fables). The cock is even a rhetorical master in his crafted apostrophe to the jasper. We might seem to have a complete fable here, since the cock would seem to have persuasively moralized the narrative from within, even before we reach the *Moralitas* in the concluding stanzas.

Animal stories are, however, full of sudden jolts as we shift from the animal to the human perspective. Henryson does not want us to settle for easy treasure and instead surprises us with an unexpected morality in the appended interpretation of the apparently wise cock. As an animal, he might be wise; as a human, he's missed the point of fables.

The Cock and the Jasper[1]

A cock one time, with feathers pert and bright,
Canty° and bold, although he was dirt poor,   *cheerful*
Rose and flew to a dunghill at first light,
An early bird, already to the fore,
5 Scraping away, when the next thing in the stour°   *flying dust*
He finds this gemstone under dust and ashes,
Swept out by chance with sweepings from the house.

Giddy young ones, with their minds on nothing
But swanking in the street and being seen
10 Have little interest in their besoming.°   *sweeping*
They birl the brush° to make the floor look clean.   *manipulate the broom*
So precious items dropped are very often
Swept from the doorstep out into the yard.
Something like that, in this case, had occurred.

15 He marvels at the stone and then says he,
'O jewel rare, O rich and noble thing,
I may have found you, but you're not for me.
You are a gemstone for a lord or king.
For you to be interred here in the dung
20 Is a great pity, down in the muck and mold,
And you so lovely and worth so much gold.

'And a pity I should find you, who could never
Make clear hues like yours more sheer and clear
Nor prove your great worth any worthier:

---

1. This translation is by Seamus Heaney, *The Testament of Cresseid & Seven Fables* (2009). Jasper is a stone, quartz or chalcedony, that may be polished and used as a gemstone.

25 Little about you gives me heart or cheer.
Let great lords cherish you and hold you dear.
Lesser things are better fit to tempt me,
Like corn or hogwash when my gizzard's empty.

'I'd rather be here scraping with my nails
30 In dust and dirt for dear life, hunting food—
The dregs and dross and little worms and snails
Or any grub at all that does me good—
I'd rather them than gems by the cartload.
While you, for your part, are uninterested
35 In anything that I desire or need.

'You don't have corn, and corn is what I covet.
Your color calms the eye and feeds the sight
But color's never going to feed my gullet.
I'm foraging from morning until night
40 And on the lookout always. But that's it!
How can I live on looks? It's food I need,
Not cooked or even hot: I'd eat dry bread.

'But where, gemstone, should be your habitation?
Where should you dwell but in a royal tower?
45 Where should you sit but on a royal crown
Exalted and installed in honor there?[2]
Arise, Sir Jasper, fairest of the fair,
Shake off this filth and go where you should be.
I was not meant for you, nor you for me.'

50 Leaving the jewel lying on the ground,
This cock went foraging upon his way.
But when or how or by whom it was found
I have no sure report, so cannot say.
But the inner point and import and idea
55 Behind the fable in the original
I shall rehearse in plain and homely style.

Moralitas°   *moral*

The properties of this fair gem are seven:
First, as to color, it is marvelous,
Like fire partly, partly like the heaven.
60 It makes a man strong and victorious,
Preserves him too when things turn dangerous.
Whoever has this stone, good luck will favor:
No need for him to fear the fire or water.

This noble jasper, with its changing hue,
65 Signifies true wisdom and true learning

2. Note the triple apostrophe, characteristic of courtly rhetoric.

Perfected by the exercise of virtue
And far excelling any earthly thing.
This is what inclines men to good living
And makes them glad to strive, and fit to conquer
70 Every vice and spiritual danger.

Who's to be wealthy, kind, courageous?
Who is immune to chance and misadventure?
Who can take charge in home, town-hall or palace
And be a know-nothing? No one, for sure.
75 Knowledge is the wealth that will endure,
That rain won't ruin, nor moth nor rust devour.[3]
To man's soul it is sustenance forever.

This cock, so obsessed with ordinary corn
He scorned a jasper, may in his ignorance
80 Be likened to a fool, who will scoff and scorn
At learning; impervious, thick, a dunce,
He takes a scunner at° wise arguments,   *is disgusted by*
The same as a sow that snotters in her gruel,
And spurns pearls in the trough, preferring swill.[4]

85 Ignoramuses are the enemy
Of knowledge and of learning, and possess
No understanding of a thing so worthy,
So noble it is past all earthly price.
The luckiest man is one who spends his days
90 In study of the knowledge of the good:
A man like that fulfils his every need.

But now, alas, this jewel is lost and hid;
No one looks for it, no one pursues
95 The study of it. We make our wealth our god[5]
And turn our souls to paupers, gain to lose.
But talk of this is like the wind that blows.
Therefore I conclude. I have said my say.
Look for the jewel who will, for there it lay.

---

3. Cf. Matthew 6.19.
4. Cf. Matthew 7.6 ("neither cast ye your pearls before swine, lest perhaps they trample them under their feet"). Henryson quietly points out that the scriptures also use animals to teach by.
5. Cf. Philippians 3.19 ("whose God is their belly").

EVERYMAN
after 1485

E veryman belongs to the midpoint of the morality play's history. The surviving examples of this genre include only a handful from the fifteenth century (e.g., the earliest, *The Pride of Life,* ca. 1400) but more than two dozen from the sixteenth century, dating as late as 1579 (*The Marriage between Wit and Wisdom*). Morality plays apparently originated side by side with the mystery plays but were composed individually rather than in cycles and were dominated by allegorical characters. Some morality plays addressed such diverse subjects as social and political satire (e.g., *All for Money,* Skelton's *Magnificence*), philosophy of education (e.g., *The Marriage of Wit and Science*), Protestant polemic (e.g., *The Conflict of Conscience*), prudential morality (e.g., *The Contention between Liberality and Prodigality*), and natural science (e.g., *The Nature of the Four Elements*). From first to last, however, the dominant theme was the struggle of good and evil for the human soul (*psychomachia*), usually depicted in the life span of a representative figure with a name like "Mankind." *Everyman,* untypically, is devoted entirely to the day of judgment that every individual human being must face eventually. The play represents allegorically the forces— both outside the protagonist and within—that can help save Everyman and those that cannot or that obstruct his salvation.

Everyman lacks the broad (even slapstick) humor of many morality plays that portray as clowns the vices that try to lure the Everyman figure away from salvation. The play does contain a certain grim humor in showing the haste with which the hero's fair-weather friends abandon him when they discover what his problem is. The play inculcates its austere lesson by the simplicity and directness of its language and of its approach. A sense of urgency builds—one by one Everyman's supposed resources fail him as time is running out. Ultimately Knowledge teaches him the lesson that every Christian must learn in order to be saved.

The play was written near the end of the fifteenth century. It is probably a translation of a Flemish play, although it is possible that the Flemish play is the translation and the English *Everyman* the original.

Everyman[1]

CAST OF CHARACTERS

MESSENGER	KNOWLEDGE
GOD	CONFESSION
DEATH	BEAUTY
EVERYMAN	STRENGTH
FELLOWSHIP	DISCRETION

1. The text is based on the earliest printing of the play (no manuscript is known) by John Skot about 1530, as reproduced by W. W. Greg (1904). The spelling has been modernized except where modernization would spoil the rhyme, and modern punctuation has been added. The stage directions have been amplified.

KINDRED   FIVE-WITS
COUSIN   ANGEL
GOODS   DOCTOR
GOOD DEEDS

HERE BEGINNETH A TREATISE HOW THE HIGH FATHER OF HEAVEN
SENDETH DEATH TO SUMMON EVERY CREATURE TO COME AND GIVE
ACCOUNT OF THEIR LIVES IN THIS WORLD, AND IS IN MANNER OF
A MORAL PLAY

[*Enter* MESSENGER.]

MESSENGER I pray you all give your audience,°		*hearing*
And hear this matter with reverence,°		*respect*
By figure° a moral play.		*in form*
The Summoning of Everyman called it is,		
5 That of our lives and ending shows		
How transitory we be all day.°		*always*
The matter is wonder precious,		
But the intent of it is more gracious		
And sweet to bear away.		
10 The story saith: Man, in the beginning		
Look well, and take good heed to the ending,		
Be you never so gay.		
You think sin in the beginning full sweet,		
Which in the end causeth the soul to weep,		
15 When the body lieth in clay.		
Here shall you see how fellowship and jollity,		
Both strength, pleasure, and beauty,		
Will fade from thee as flower in May.		
For ye shall hear how our Heaven-King		
20 Calleth Everyman to a general reckoning.		
Give audience and hear what he doth say.		

[*Exit* MESSENGER.—*Enter* GOD.]

GOD I perceive, here in my majesty,		
How that all creatures be to me unkind,°		*thoughtless*
Living without dread in worldly prosperity.		
25 Of ghostly° sight the people be so blind,		*spiritual*
Drowned in sin, they know me not for their God.		
In worldly riches is all their mind:		
They fear not of my righteousness the sharp rod;		
My law that I showed when I for them died		
30 They forget clean, and shedding of my blood red.		
I hanged between two,[2] it cannot be denied:		
To get them life I suffered to be dead.°		*allowed myself to die*
I healed their feet, with thorns hurt was my head.		
I could do no more than I did, truly—		

---

2. I.e., the two thieves between whom Christ was crucified.

35 And now I see the people do clean forsake me.
  They use the seven deadly sins damnable,
  As pride, coveitise,° wrath, and lechery³   *avarice*
  Now in the world be made commendable.
  And thus they leave of angels the heavenly company.
40 Every man liveth so after his own pleasure,
  And yet of their life they be nothing sure.
  I see the more that I them forbear,
  The worse they be from year to year:
  All that liveth appaireth° fast.   *degenerates*
45 Therefore I will, in all the haste,
  Have a reckoning of every man's person.
  For, and° I leave the people thus alone   *if*
  In their life and wicked tempests,
  Verily they will become much worse than beasts;
50 For now one would by envy another up eat.
  Charity do they all clean forgeet.
  I hoped well that every man
  In my glory should make his mansion,
  And thereto I had them all elect.°   *chosen*
55 But now I see, like traitors deject,°   *abased*
  They thank me not for the pleasure that I to° them meant,   *for*
  Nor yet for their being that I them have lent.
  I proffered the people great multitude of mercy,
  And few there be that asketh it heartily.°   *sincerely*
60 They be so cumbered° with worldly riches   *encumbered*
  That needs on them I must do justice—
  On every man living without fear.
  Where art thou, Death, thou mighty messenger?

    [*Enter* DEATH.]

DEATH Almighty God, I am here at your will,
65   Your commandment to fulfill.
GOD Go thou to Everyman,
    And show him, in my name,
    A pilgrimage he must on him take,
    Which he in no wise may escape;
70   And that he bring with him a sure reckoning
    Without delay or any tarrying.
DEATH Lord, I will in the world go run over all,°   *everywhere*
    And cruelly out-search both great and small.

    [*Exit* GOD.]

  Everyman will I beset that liveth beastly
75 Out of God's laws, and dreadeth not folly.
  He that loveth riches I will strike with my dart,

---

3. The other three deadly sins are envy, gluttony, and sloth.

His sight to blind, and from heaven to depart°   *separate*
Except that Almsdeeds be his good friend—
In hell for to dwell, world without end.
80   Lo, yonder I see Everyman walking:
Full little he thinketh on my coming;
His mind is on fleshly lusts and his treasure,
And great pain it shall cause him to endure
Before the Lord, Heaven-King.

           [*Enter* EVERYMAN.]

85   Everyman, stand still! Whither art thou going
Thus gaily? Hast thou thy Maker forgeet?°   *forgotten*
EVERYMAN   Why askest thou?
Why wouldest thou weet?°   *know*
DEATH   Yea, sir, I will show you:
90   In great haste I am sent to thee
From God out of his majesty.
EVERYMAN   What! sent to me?
DEATH   Yea, certainly.
Though thou have forgot him here,
95   He thinketh on thee in the heavenly sphere,
As, ere we depart, thou shalt know.
EVERYMAN   What desireth God of me?[4]
DEATH   That shall I show thee:
A reckoning he will needs have
100   Without any longer respite.
EVERYMAN   To give a reckoning longer leisure I crave.°   *request*
This blind° matter troubleth my wit.   *unexpected*
DEATH   On thee thou must take a long journay:
Therefore thy book of count° with thee thou bring,   *accounts*
105   For turn again thou cannot by no way.
And look thou be sure of thy reckoning,
For before God thou shalt answer and shew
Thy many bad deeds and good but a few—
How thou hast spent thy life and in what wise,
110   Before the Chief Lord of Paradise.
Have ado that we were in that way,[5]
For weet thou well thou shalt make none attornay.[6]
EVERYMAN   Full unready I am such reckoning to give.
I know thee not. What messenger art thou?
115 DEATH   I am Death that no man dreadeth,[7]
For every man I 'rest,° and no man spareth;   *arrest*
For it is God's commandment
That all to me should be obedient.
EVERYMAN   O Death, thou comest when I had thee least in mind.
120   In thy power it lieth me to save:

---

4. "What doth the Lord require of thee, but to do justly, and to love mercy, and to walk humbly with thy God?" (Micah 6.8).
5. I.e., let's get started at once.
6. I.e., none to appear in your stead.
7. That fears nobody.

Yet of my good° will I give thee, if thou will be kind,   *goods*
Yea, a thousand pound shalt thou have—
And defer this matter till another day.
DEATH   Everyman, it may not be, by no way.
125   I set nought by[8] gold, silver, nor riches,
Nor by pope, emperor, king, duke, nor princes,
For, and° I would receive gifts great,   *if*
All the world I might get.
But my custom is clean contrary:
130   I give thee no respite. Come hence and not tarry!
EVERYMAN   Alas, shall I have no longer respite?
I may say Death giveth no warning.
To think on thee it maketh my heart sick,
For all unready is my book of reckoning.
135   But twelve year and I might have a biding,[9]
My counting-book I would make so clear
That my reckoning I should not need to fear.
Wherefore, Death, I pray thee, for God's mercy,
Spare me till I be provided of remedy.
140 DEATH   Thee availeth not to cry, weep, and pray;
But haste thee lightly° that thou were gone that journay   *quickly*
And prove° thy friends, if thou can.   *test*
For weet° thou well the tide° abideth no man,   *know / time*
And in the world each living creature
145   For Adam's sin must die of nature.[1]
EVERYMAN   Death, if I should this pilgrimage take
And my reckoning surely make,
Show me, for saint° charity,   *holy*
Should I not come again shortly?
150 DEATH   No, Everyman. And° thou be once there,   *if*
Thou mayst never more come here,
Trust me verily.
EVERYMAN   O gracious God in the high seat celestial,
Have mercy on me in this most need!
155   Shall I have company from this vale terrestrial
Of mine acquaintance that way me to lead?
DEATH   Yea, if any be so hardy
That would go with thee and bear thee company.
Hie° thee that thou were gone to God's magnificence,   *hasten*
160   Thy reckoning to give before his presence.
What, weenest° thou thy life is given thee,   *suppose*
And thy worldly goods also?
EVERYMAN   I had weened so, verily.
DEATH   Nay, nay, it was but lent thee.
165   For as soon as thou art go,
Another a while shall have it and then go therefro,[2]
Even as thou hast done.

---

8. I care nothing for.
9. If I might have a delay for just twelve years.

1. Naturally. See Romans 5.12.
2. See Luke 12.19–20.

Everyman, thou art mad! Thou hast thy wits° five,   *senses*
And here on earth will not amend thy live!³
170   For suddenly I do come.
    EVERYMAN   O wretched caitiff! Whither shall I flee
    That I might 'scape this endless sorrow?
    Now, gentle Death, spare me till tomorrow,
    That I may amend me
175   With good advisement.°   *preparation*
    DEATH   Nay, thereto I will not consent,
    Nor no man will I respite,
    But to the heart suddenly I shall smite,
    Without any advisement.°   *warning*
180   And now out of thy sight I will me hie:
    See thou make thee ready shortly,
    For thou mayst say this is the day
    That no man living may 'scape away.

      [*Exit* DEATH.]

    EVERYMAN   Alas, I may well weep with sighs deep:
185   Now have I no manner of company
    To help me in my journey and me to keep.°   *guard*
    And also my writing° is full unready—   *ledger*
    How shall I do now for to excuse me?
    I would to God I had never be geet!°   *been begotten*
190   To my soul a full great profit it had be.
    For now I fear pains huge and great.
    The time passeth: Lord, help, that all wrought!
    For though I mourn, it availeth nought.
    The day passeth and is almost ago:°   *gone by*
195   I wot° not well what for to do.   *know*
    To whom were I best my complaint to make?
    What and° I to Fellowship thereof spake,   *if*
    And showed him of this sudden chance?
    For in him is all mine affiance,°   *trust*
200   We have in the world so many a day
    Be good friends in sport and play.
    I see him yonder, certainly.
    I trust that he will bear me company.
    Therefore to him will I speak to ease my sorrow.

      [*Enter* FELLOWSHIP.]

205   Well met, good Fellowship, and good morrow!
    FELLOWSHIP   Everyman, good morrow, by this day!
    Sir, why lookest thou so piteously?
    If anything be amiss, I pray thee me say,
    That I may help to remedy.

---

3. In thy life.

210 EVERYMAN   Yea, good Fellowship, yea:
     I am in great jeopardy.
     FELLOWSHIP   My true friend, show to me your mind.
     I will not forsake thee to my life's end
     In the way of good company.
215 EVERYMAN   That was well spoken, and lovingly!
     FELLOWSHIP   Sir, I must needs know your heaviness.°   *sorrow*
     I have pity to see you in any distress.
     If any have you wronged, ye shall revenged be,
     Though I on the ground be slain for thee,
220 Though that I know before that I should die.
     EVERYMAN   Verily, Fellowship, gramercy.°   *many thanks*
     FELLOWSHIP   Tush! by thy thanks I set not a stree.°   *straw*
     Show me your grief and say no more.
     EVERYMAN   If I my heart should to you break,°   *disclose*
225 And then you to turn your mind fro me,
     And would not me comfort when ye hear me speak,
     Then should I ten times sorrier be.
     FELLOWSHIP   Sir, I say as I will do, indeed.
     EVERYMAN   Then be you a good friend at need.
230 I have found you true herebefore.
     FELLOWSHIP   And so ye shall evermore.
     For, in faith, and° thou go to hell,   *if*
     I will not forsake thee by the way.
     EVERYMAN   Ye speak like a good friend. I believe you well.
235 I shall deserve° it, and° I may.   *repay / if*
     FELLOWSHIP   I speak of no deserving, by this day!
     For he that will say and nothing do
     Is not worthy with good company to go.
     Therefore show me the grief of your mind,
240 As to your friend most loving and kind.
     EVERYMAN   I shall show you how it is:
     Commanded I am to go a journay,
     A long way, hard and dangerous,
     And give a strait° count,° without delay,   *strict / accounting*
245 Before the high judge Adonai.°   *God*
     Wherefore I pray you bear me company,
     As ye have promised, in this journay.
     FELLOWSHIP   This is matter indeed! Promise is duty—
     But, and° I should take such a voyage on me,   *if*
250 I know it well, it should be to my pain.
     Also it maketh me afeard, certain.
     But let us take counsel here, as well as we can—
     For your words would fear° a strong man.   *frighten*
     EVERYMAN   Why, ye said if I had need,
255 Ye would me never forsake, quick ne dead,
     Though it were to hell, truly.
     FELLOWSHIP   So I said, certainly,
     But such pleasures° be set aside, the sooth to say.   *jokes*
     And also, if we took such a journay,

260 When should we again come?

EVERYMAN   Nay, never again, till the day of doom.

FELLOWSHIP   In faith, then will not I come there!
Who hath you these tidings brought?

EVERYMAN   Indeed, Death was with me here.

265 FELLOWSHIP   Now by God that all hath bought,°   *redeemed*
If Death were the messenger,
For no man that is living today
I will not go that loath° journay—   *loathsome*
Not for the father that begat me!

270 EVERYMAN   Ye promised otherwise, pardie.°   *by God*

FELLOWSHIP   I wot well I said so, truly.
And yet, if thou wilt eat and drink and make good cheer,
Or haunt to women the lusty company,[4]
I would not forsake you while the day is clear,
275 Trust me verily!

EVERYMAN   Yea, thereto ye would be ready—
To go to mirth, solace,° and play: *pleasure*
Your mind to folly will sooner apply°   *attend*
Than to bear me company in my long journay.

280 FELLOWSHIP   Now in good faith, I will not that way.
But, and° thou will murder or any man kill,   *if*
In that I will help thee with a good will.

EVERYMAN   O that is simple° advice, indeed!   *foolish*
Gentle fellow, help me in my necessity:
285 We have loved long, and now I need—
And now, gentle Fellowship, remember me!

FELLOWSHIP   Whether ye have loved me or no,
By Saint John, I will not with thee go!

EVERYMAN   Yet I pray thee take the labor and do so much for me,
290 To bring me forward,° for saint charity,   *escort me*
And comfort me till I come without the town.

FELLOWSHIP   Nay, and° thou would give me a new gown,   *if*
I will not a foot with thee go.
But, and° thou had tarried, I would not have left thee so.   *if*
295 And as now, God speed thee in thy journey!
For from thee I will depart as fast as I may.

EVERYMAN   Whither away, Fellowship? Will thou forsake me?

FELLOWSHIP   Yea, by my fay!° To God I betake° thee.   *faith / commend*

EVERYMAN   Farewell, good Fellowship! For thee my heart is sore.
300 Adieu forever—I shall see thee no more.

FELLOWSHIP   In faith, Everyman, farewell now at the ending:
For you I will remember that parting is mourning.

[*Exit* FELLOWSHIP.]

EVERYMAN   Alack, shall we thus depart° indeed—   *part*
Ah, Lady, help![5]—without any more comfort?

4. Or frequent the lusty company of women.   5. An appeal to the Virgin Mary.

305 Lo, Fellowship forsaketh me in my most need!
For help in this world whither shall I resort?
Fellowship herebefore° with me would merry make,   *before this*
And now little sorrow for me doth he take.
It is said, "In prosperity men friends may find
310 Which in adversity be full unkind."
Now whither for succor° shall I flee,   *aid*
Sith° that Fellowship hath forsaken me?   *since*
To my kinsmen I will, truly,
Praying them to help me in my necessity.
315 I believe that they will do so,
For kind will creep where it may not go.[6]
I will go 'say°—for yonder I see them—   *assay*
Where° be ye now my friends and kinsmen.   *whether*

[*Enter* KINDRED *and* COUSIN.]

KINDRED   Here be we now at your commandment:
320 Cousin, I pray you show us your intent
In any wise, and not spare.
COUSIN   Yea, Everyman, and to us declare
If ye be disposed to go anywhither.
For, weet° you well, we will live and die togither.   *know*
325 KINDRED   In wealth and woe we will with you hold,
For over his kin a man may be bold.[7]
EVERYMAN   Gramercy,° my friends and kinsmen kind.   *much thanks*
Now shall I show you the grief of my mind.
I was commanded by a messenger
330 That is a high king's chief officer:
He bade me go a pilgrimage, to my pain—
And I know well I shall never come again.
Also I must give a reckoning strait,°   *strict*
For I have a great enemy that hath me in wait,[8]
335 Which intendeth me to hinder.
KINDRED   What account is that which ye must render?
That would I know.
EVERYMAN   Of all my works I must show
How I have lived and my days spent;
340 Also of ill deeds that I have used
In my time sith° life was me lent,   *since*
And of all virtues that I have refused.
Therefore I pray you go thither with me
To help me make mine account, for saint° charity.   *holy*
345 COUSIN   What, to go thither? Is that the matter?
Nay, Everyman, I had liefer fast[9] bread and water
All this five year and more!

---

6. For kinship will creep where it cannot walk (i.e., kinsmen will suffer hardship for one another).
7. I.e., for a man may make demands of his kinsmen.
8. I.e., Satan lies in ambush for me.
9. I.e., rather fast on.

EVERYMAN   Alas, that ever I was bore!°   *born*
    For now shall I never be merry
350   If that you forsake me.
KINDRED   Ah, sir, what? Ye be a merry man:
    Take good heart to you and make no moan.
    But one thing I warn you, by Saint Anne,
    As for me, ye shall go alone.
355 EVERYMAN   My Cousin, will you not with me go?
COUSIN   No, by Our Lady! I have the cramp in my toe:
    Trust not to me. For, so God me speed,°   *prosper*
    I will deceive you in your most need.
KINDRED   It availeth you not us to 'tice.°   *entice*
360   Ye shall have my maid with all my heart:
    She loveth to go to feasts, there to be nice,°   *wanton*
    And to dance, and abroad to start.[1]
    I will give her leave to help you in that journey,
    If that you and she may agree.
365 EVERYMAN   Now show me the very effect° of your mind: *true bent*
    Will you go with me or abide behind?
KINDRED   Abide behind? Yea, that will I and° I may!   *if*
    Therefore farewell till another day.

      [*Exit* KINDRED.]

EVERYMAN   How should I be merry or glad?
370   For fair promises men to me make,
    But when I have most need they me forsake.
    I am deceived. That maketh me sad.
COUSIN   Cousin Everyman, farewell now,
    For verily I will not go with you;
375   Also of mine own an unready reckoning
    I have to account—therefore I make tarrying.
    Now God keep thee, for now I go.

      [*Exit* COUSIN.]

EVERYMAN   Ah, Jesus, is all come hereto?°   *to this*
    Lo, fair words maketh fools fain:°   *glad*
380   They promise and nothing will do, certain.
    My kinsmen promised me faithfully
    For to abide with me steadfastly,
    And now fast away do they flee.
    Even so Fellowship promised me.
385   What friend were best me of to provide?
    I lose my time here longer to abide.
    Yet in my mind a thing there is:
    All my life I have loved riches;
    If that my Good° now help me might,   *Goods*
390   He would make my heart full light.

---

1. To go gadding about.

I will speak to him in this distress.
Where art thou, my Goods and riches?
GOODS [*within*]   Who calleth me? Everyman? What, hast thou haste?
I lie here in corners, trussed and piled so high,
395   And in chests I am locked so fast—
Also sacked in bags—thou mayst see with thine eye
I cannot stir, in packs low where I lie.
What would ye have? Lightly° me say.   *quickly*
EVERYMAN   Come hither, Good, in all the haste thou may,
400   For of counsel I must desire thee.

    [*Enter* GOODS.]

GOODS   Sir, and° ye in the world have sorrow or adversity,[2]   *if*
That can I help you to remedy shortly.
EVERYMAN   It is another disease° that grieveth me: *distress*
In this world it is not, I tell thee so.
405   I am sent for another way to go,
To give a strait count general
Before the highest Jupiter° of all.   *God*
And all my life I have had joy and pleasure in thee:
Therefore I pray thee go with me,
410   For, peradventure, thou mayst before God Almighty
My reckoning help to clean and purify.
For it is said ever among°   *now and then*
That money maketh all right that is wrong.
GOODS   Nay, Everyman, I sing another song:
415   I follow no man in such voyages.
For, and° I went with thee,   *if*
Thou shouldest fare much the worse for me;
For because on me thou did set thy mind,
Thy reckoning I have made blotted and blind,°   *illegible*
420   That thine account thou cannot make truly—
And that hast thou for the love of me.
EVERYMAN   That would grieve me full sore
When I should come to that fearful answer.
Up, let us go thither together.
425   GOODS   Nay, not so, I am too brittle, I may not endure.
I will follow no man one foot, be ye sure.
EVERYMAN   Alas, I have thee loved and had great pleasure
All my life-days on good and treasure.
GOODS   That is to thy damnation, without leasing,°   *lie*
430   For my love is contrary to the love everlasting.
But if thou had me loved moderately during,°   *in the meanwhile*
As to the poor to give part of me,
Then shouldest thou not in this dolor be,
Nor in this great sorrow and care.
435   EVERYMAN   Lo, now was I deceived ere I was ware,
And all I may wite° misspending of time.   *blame on*

2. See John 16.33.

GOODS What, weenest° thou that I am thine?   *suppose*
EVERYMAN I had weened so.
GOODS Nay, Everyman, I say no.
440 As for a while I was lent thee;
     A season thou hast had me in prosperity.
     My condition° is man's soul to kill;   *disposition*
     If I save one, a thousand I do spill.°   *ruin*
     Weenest thou that I will follow thee?
445 Nay, from this world, not verily.
EVERYMAN I had weened otherwise.
GOODS Therefore to thy soul Good is a thief;
     For when thou art dead, this is my guise°—   *custom*
     Another to deceive in the same wise
450 As I have done thee, and all to his soul's repreef.°   *shame*
EVERYMAN O false Good, cursed thou be,
     Thou traitor to God, that hast deceived me
     And caught me in thy snare!
GOODS Marry, thou brought thyself in care,°   *sorrow*
455 Whereof I am glad:
     I must needs laugh, I cannot be sad.
EVERYMAN Ah, Good, thou hast had long my heartly° love;   *sincere*
     I gave thee that which should be the Lord's above.
     But wilt thou not go with me, indeed?
460 I pray thee truth to say.
GOODS No, so God me speed!
     Therefore farewell and have good day.

        [*Exit* GOODS.]

EVERYMAN Oh, to whom shall I make my moan
     For to go with me in that heavy° journay?   *sorrowful*
465 First Fellowship said he would with me gone:°   *go*
     His words were very pleasant and gay,
     But afterward he left me alone.
     Then spake I to my kinsmen, all in despair,
     And also they gave me words fair—
470 They lacked no fair speaking,
     But all forsake me in the ending.
     Then went I to my Goods that I loved best,
     In hope to have comfort; but there had I least,
     For my Goods sharply did me tell
475 That he bringeth many into hell.
     Then of myself I was ashamed,
     And so I am worthy to be blamed:
     Thus may I well myself hate.
     Of whom shall I now counsel take?
480 I think that I shall never speed°   *prosper*
     Till that I go to my Good Deed.
     But alas, she is so weak
     That she can neither go° nor speak.   *walk*

Yet will I venture° on her now. *gamble*
485 My Good Deeds, where be you?
GOOD DEEDS [*speaking from the ground*]   Here I lie, cold in
    the ground:
Thy sins hath me sore bound
That I cannot stear.° *stir*
EVERYMAN   O Good Deeds, I stand in fear:
490 I must you pray of counsel,
For help now should come right well.
GOOD DEEDS   Everyman, I have understanding
That ye be summoned, account to make,
Before Messiah of Jer'salem King.
495 And you do by me,[3] that journey with you will I take.
EVERYMAN   Therefore I come to you my moan to make:
I pray you that ye will go with me.
GOOD DEEDS   I would full fain,° but I cannot stand, verily. *gladly*
EVERYMAN   Why, is there anything on you fall?° *fallen*
500 GOOD DEEDS   Yea, sir, I may thank you of all:
If ye had perfectly cheered me,
Your book of count full ready had be.

[GOOD DEEDS *shows him the account book.*]

Look, the books of your works and deeds eke,° *also*
As how they lie under the feet,
505 To your soul's heaviness.° *distress*
EVERYMAN   Our Lord Jesus help me!
For one letter here I cannot see.
GOOD DEEDS   There is a blind° reckoning in time of distress! *an illegible*
EVERYMAN   Good Deeds, I pray you help me in this need,
510 Or else I am forever damned indeed.
Therefore help me to make reckoning
Before the Redeemer of all thing
That King is and was and ever shall.
GOOD DEEDS   Everyman, I am sorry of° your fall *for*
515 And fain would help you and° I were able. *if*
EVERYMAN   Good Deeds, your counsel I pray you give me.
GOOD DEEDS   That shall I do verily,
Though that on my feet I may not go;
I have a sister that shall with you also,
520 Called Knowledge, which shall with you abide
To help you to make that dreadful reckoning.

[*Enter* KNOWLEDGE.]

KNOWLEDGE   Everyman, I will go with thee and be thy guide,
In thy most need to go by thy side.
EVERYMAN   In good condition I am now in everything,

3. I.e., if you do what I say.

525 And am whole content with this good thing,
Thanked be God my Creator.
GOOD DEEDS   And when she hath brought you there
Where thou shalt heal thee of thy smart,°   *pain*
Then go you with your reckoning and your Good Deeds
together
530 For to make you joyful at heart
Before the blessed Trinity.
EVERYMAN   My Good Deeds, gramercy!°   *thanks*
I am well content, certainly,
With your words sweet.
535 KNOWLEDGE   Now go we together lovingly
To Confession, that cleansing river.
EVERYMAN   For joy I weep—I would we were there!
But I pray you give me cognition,°   *knowledge*
Where dwelleth that holy man Confession?
540 KNOWLEDGE   In the House of Salvation:
We shall us comfort, by God's grace.

[KNOWLEDGE *leads* EVERYMAN *to* CONFESSION.]

Lo, this is Confession: kneel down and ask mercy,
For he is in good conceit° with God Almighty.   *esteem*
EVERYMAN [*kneeling*]   O glorious fountain that all
uncleanness doth clarify,°   *purify*
545 Wash from me the spots of vice unclean,
That on me no sin may be seen.[4]
I come with Knowledge for my redemption,
Redempt° with heart and full contrition,   *redeemed*
For I am commanded a pilgrimage to take
550 And great accounts before God to make.
Now I pray you, Shrift,° mother of Salvation,   *confession*
Help my Good Deeds for my piteous exclamation.
CONFESSION   I know your sorrow well, Everyman:
Because with Knowledge ye come to me,
555 I will you comfort as well as I can,
And a precious jewel I will give thee,
Called Penance, voider° of adversity.   *expeller*
Therewith shall your body chastised be—
With abstinence and perseverance in God's service.
560 Here shall you receive that scourge of me,
Which is penance strong° that ye must endure,   *harsh*
To remember thy Saviour was scourged for thee
With sharp scourges,[5] and suffered it patiently.
So must thou ere thou 'scape that painful pilgrimage.
565 Knowledge, keep° him in this voyage,   *guard*
And by that time Good Deeds will be with thee.
But in any wise be secure° of mercy—   *certain*

4. See Zechariah 13.1.   5. See John 19.1.

For your time draweth fast—and ye will saved be.
Ask God mercy and he will grant, truly.
570   When with the scourge of penance man doth him° bind,   *himself*
The oil of forgiveness then shall he find.
EVERYMAN   Thanked be God for his gracious work,
For now I will my penance begin.
This hath rejoiced and lighted my heart,
575   Though the knots be painful and hard within.⁶
KNOWLEDGE   Everyman, look your penance that ye fulfill,
What pain that ever it to you be;
And Knowledge shall give you counsel at will
How your account ye shall make clearly.
580   EVERYMAN   O eternal God, O heavenly figure,
O way of righteousness, O goodly vision,
Which descended down in a virgin pure
Because he would every man redeem,
Which Adam forfeited by his disobedience;
585   O blessed Godhead, elect and high Divine,°   *divinity*
Forgive my grievous offense!
Here I cry thee mercy in this presence:
O ghostly° Treasure, O Ransomer and Redeemer,   *spiritual*
Of all the world Hope and Conduiter,°   *guide*
590   Mirror of joy, Foundator° of mercy,   *Founder*
Which enlumineth° heaven and earth thereby,   *lights up*
Hear my clamorous complaint, though it late be;
Receive my prayers, of thy benignity.
Though I be a sinner most abominable,
595   Yet let my name be written in Moses' table.⁷
O Mary, pray to the Maker of all thing
Me for to help at my ending,
And save me from the power of my enemy,
For Death assaileth me strongly.
600   And Lady, that I may by mean of thy prayer
Of your Son's glory to be partner—
By the means of his passion° I it crave.   *suffering*
I beseech you help my soul to save.
Knowledge, give me the scourge of penance:
605   My flesh therewith shall give acquittance.°   *satisfaction for sins*
I will now begin, if God give me grace.
KNOWLEDGE   Everyman, God give you time and space!°   *opportunity*
Thus I bequeath you in the hands of our Saviour:
Now may you make your reckoning sure.
610   EVERYMAN   In the name of the Holy Trinity
My body sore punished shall be:
Take this, body, for the sin of the flesh!
Also° thou delightest to go gay and fresh,   *as*
And in the way of damnation thou did me bring,

---

6. I.e., to my senses. "Knots": i.e., the knots on the scourge (whip) of penance.

7. Here, the tablet on which are recorded those who have been baptized and have done penance.

615 Therefore suffer now strokes of punishing!
Now of penance I will wade the water clear,
To save me from purgatory, that sharp fire.
GOOD DEEDS   I thank God, now can I walk and go,
And am delivered of my sickness and woe.
620 Therefore with Everyman I will go, and not spare:
His good works I will help him to declare.
KNOWLEDGE   Now, Everyman, be merry and glad:
Your Good Deeds cometh now, ye may° not be sad.   *can*
Now is your Good Deeds whole and sound,
625 Going° upright upon the ground.   *walking*
EVERYMAN   My heart is light, and shall be evermore.
Now will I smite faster than I did before.
GOOD DEEDS   Everyman, pilgrim, my special friend,
Blessed be thou without end!
630 For thee is preparate° the eternal glory.   *prepared*
Ye have me made whole and sound
Therefore I will bide by thee in every stound.°8   *trial*
EVERYMAN   Welcome, my Good Deeds! Now I hear thy voice,
I weep for very sweetness of love.
635 KNOWLEDGE   Be no more sad, but ever rejoice:
God seeth thy living in his throne above.
Put on this garment to thy behove,°   *advantage*
Which is wet with your tears—
Or else before God you may it miss
640 When ye to your journey's end come shall.
EVERYMAN   Gentle Knowledge, what do ye it call?
KNOWLEDGE   It is a garment of sorrow;
From pain it will you borrow:°   *redeem*
Contrition it is
645 That getteth forgiveness;
It pleaseth God passing° well.   *surpassingly*
GOOD DEEDS   Everyman, will you wear it for your heal?°   *welfare*
EVERYMAN   Now blessed be Jesu, Mary's son,
For now have I on true contrition.
650 And let us go now without tarrying.
Good Deeds, have we clear our reckoning?
GOOD DEEDS   Yea, indeed, I have it here.
EVERYMAN   Then I trust we need not fear.
Now friends, let us not part in twain.
655 KNOWLEDGE   Nay, Everyman, that will we not, certain.
GOOD DEEDS   Yet must thou lead with thee
Three persons of great might.
EVERYMAN   Who should they be?
GOOD DEEDS   Discretion and Strength they hight,°   *are called*
660 And thy Beauty may not abide behind.

---

8. "Blessed are the dead which die in the Lord from henceforth: yea, saith the spirit, that they may rest from their labors; and their works do follow them" (Revelation 14.13).

KNOWLEDGE   Also ye must call to mind
   Your Five-Wits° as for your counselors.   *senses*
GOOD DEEDS   You must have them ready at all hours.
EVERYMAN   How shall I get them hither?
665 KNOWLEDGE   You must call them all togither,
   And they will be here incontinent.°   *at once*
EVERYMAN   My friends, come hither and be present,
   Discretion, Strength, my Five-Wits, and Beauty!

   [*They enter.*]

BEAUTY   Here at your will we be all ready.
670   What will ye that we should do?
GOOD DEEDS   That ye would with Everyman go
   And help him in his pilgrimage.
   Advise you:° will ye with him or not in that voyage?   *take thought*
STRENGTH   We will bring him all thither,
675   To his help and comfort, ye may believe me.
DISCRETION   So will we go with him all togither.
EVERYMAN   Almighty God, loved° might thou be!   *praised*
   I give thee laud that I have hither brought
   Strength, Discretion, Beauty, and Five-Wits—lack I nought—
680   And my Good Deeds, with Knowledge clear,
   All be in my company at my will here:
   I desire no more to my business.
STRENGTH   And I, Strength, will by you stand in distress,
   Though thou would in battle fight on the ground.
685 FIVE-WITS   And though it were through the world round,
   We will not depart for sweet ne sour.
BEAUTY   No more will I, until death's hour,
   Whatsoever thereof befall.
DISCRETION   Everyman, advise you first of all:
690   Go with a good advisement° and deliberation.   *preparation*
   We all give you virtuous° monition°   *confident / prediction*
   That all shall be well.
EVERYMAN   My friends, hearken what I will tell;
   I pray God reward you in his heaven-sphere;
695   Now hearken all that be here,
   For I will make my testament,
   Here before you all present:
   In alms half my good° I will give with my hands twain,   *goods*
   In the way of charity with good intent;
700   And the other half, still° shall remain,   *which still*
   I 'queath° to be returned there it ought to be.   *bequeath*
   This I do in despite of the fiend of hell,
   To go quit out of his perel,[9]
   Ever after and this day.

---

9. In order to go free of danger from him.

705 KNOWLEDGE Everyman, hearken what I say:
Go to Priesthood, I you advise,
And receive of him, in any wise,°   *at all costs*
The holy sacrament and ointment° togither;   *extreme unction*
Then shortly see ye turn again hither:
710 We will all abide you here.
    FIVE-WITS Yea, Everyman, hie° you that ye ready were.   *haste*
There is no emperor, king, duke, ne baron,
That of God hath commission
As hath the least priest in the world being:
715 For of the blessed sacraments pure and bening°   *benign*
He beareth the keys, and thereof hath the cure°   *care*
For man's redemption—it is ever sure—
Which God for our souls' medicine
Gave us out of his heart with great pine,°   *torment*
720 Here in this transitory life for thee and me.
The blessed sacraments seven there be:
Baptism, confirmation, with priesthood° good,   *ordination*
And the sacrament of God's precious flesh and blood,
Marriage, the holy extreme unction, and penance:
725 These seven be good to have in remembrance,
Gracious sacraments of high divinity.
    EVERYMAN Fain° would I receive that holy body,   *gladly*
And meekly to my ghostly° father I will go.   *spiritual*
    FIVE-WITS Everyman, that is the best that ye can do:
730 God will you to salvation bring.
For priesthood exceedeth all other thing:
To us Holy Scripture they do teach,
And converteth man from sin, heaven to reach;
God hath to them more power given
735 Than to any angel that is in heaven.
With five words[1] he may consecrate
God's body in flesh and blood to make,
And handleth his Maker between his hands.
The priest bindeth and unbindeth all bands,[2]
740 Both in earth and in heaven.
Thou ministers° all the sacraments seven;   *administers*
Though we kiss thy feet, thou were worthy;
Thou art surgeon that cureth sin deadly;
No remedy we find under God
745 But all only priesthood.[3]
Everyman, God gave priests that dignity
And setteth them in his stead among us to be.
Thus be they above angels in degree.

      [*Exit* EVERYMAN.]

1. The five words ("For this is my body") spoken by the priest when he offers the wafer at communion.
2. A reference to the power of the keys, inherited by the priesthood from St. Peter, who received it from Christ (Matthew 16.19) with the promise that whatever St. Peter bound or loosed on earth would be bound or loosed in heaven.
3. Except from priesthood alone.

KNOWLEDGE   If priests be good, it is so, surely.

750   But when Jesu hanged on the cross with great smart,°   *pain*
      There he gave out of his blessed heart
      The same sacrament in great torment,
      He sold them not to us, that Lord omnipotent:
      Therefore Saint Peter the Apostle doth say
755   That Jesu's curse hath all they
      Which God their Saviour do buy or sell,[4]
      Or they for any money do take or tell.[5]
      Sinful priests giveth the sinners example bad:
      Their children sitteth by other men's fires, I have heard;
760   And some haunteth° women's company   *frequent*
      With unclean life, as lusts of lechery.
      These be with sin made blind.
FIVE-WITS   I trust to God no such may we find.
      Therefore let us priesthood honor,
765   And follow their doctrine for our souls' succor.
      We be their sheep and they shepherds be
      By whom we all be kept in surety.
      Peace, for yonder I see Everyman come,
      Which hath made true satisfaction.
770   GOOD DEEDS   Methink it is he indeed.

      [*Re-enter* EVERYMAN.]

EVERYMAN   Now Jesu be your alder speed![6]
      I have received the sacrament for my redemption,
      And then mine extreme unction.
      Blessed be all they that counseled me to take it!
775   And now, friends, let us go without longer respite.
      I thank God that ye have tarried so long.
      Now set each of you on this rood° your hond   *cross*
      And shortly follow me:
      I go before there° I would be. God be our guide!   *where*
775   STRENGTH   Everyman, we will not from you go
      Till ye have done this voyage long.
DISCRETION   I, Discretion, will bide by you also.
KNOWLEDGE   And though this pilgrimage be never so strong,°   *harsh*
      I will never part you fro.
785   STRENGTH   Everyman, I will be as sure by thee
      As ever I did by Judas Maccabee.[7]
EVERYMAN   Alas, I am so faint I may not stand—
      My limbs under me doth fold!
      Friends, let us not turn again to this land,
790   Not for all the world's gold.

---

4. To give or receive money for the sacraments is
simony, named after Simon, who wished to buy
the gift of the Holy Ghost and was cursed by St.
Peter. See Acts 8.20.
5. Or who, for any sacrament, take or count out

money.
6. The prosperer of you all.
7. Judas Maccabaeus was an enormously powerful warrior in the defense of Israel against the
Syrians in late Old Testament times.

For into this cave must I creep
And turn to earth, and there to sleep.
BEAUTY   What, into this grave, alas?
EVERYMAN   Yea, there shall ye consume,° more and lass.[8]   *decay*
795   BEAUTY   And what, should I smother here?
EVERYMAN   Yea, by my faith, and nevermore appear.
In this world live no more we shall,
But in heaven before the highest Lord of all.
BEAUTY   I cross out all this! Adieu, by Saint John—
800   I take my tape in my lap and am gone.[9]
EVERYMAN   What, Beauty, whither will ye?
BEAUTY   Peace, I am deaf—I look not behind me,
Not and thou wouldest give me all the gold in thy chest.

[*Exit* BEAUTY.]

EVERYMAN   Alas, whereto may I trust?
805   Beauty goeth fast away fro me—
She promised with me to live and die!
STRENGTH   Everyman, I will thee also forsake and deny.
Thy game liketh° me not at all.   *pleases*
EVERYMAN   Why then, ye will forsake me all?
810   Sweet Strength, tarry a little space.
STRENGTH   Nay, sir, by the rood of grace,
I will hie me from thee fast,
Though thou weep till thy heart tobrast.°   *break*
EVERYMAN   Ye would ever bide by me, ye said.
815   STRENGTH   Yea, I have you far enough conveyed!°   *escorted*
Ye be old enough, I understand,
Your pilgrimage to take on hand:
I repent me that I hither came.
EVERYMAN   Strength, you to displease I am to blame,[1]
820   Yet promise is debt, this ye well wot.°   *know*
STRENGTH   In faith, I care not:
Thou art but a fool to complain;
You spend your speech and waste your brain.
Go, thrust thee into the ground.

[*Exit* STRENGTH.]

825   EVERYMAN   I had weened° surer I should you have found.   *supposed*
He that trusteth in his Strength
She him deceiveth at the length.
Both Strength and Beauty forsaketh me—
Yet they promised me fair and lovingly.
830   DISCRETION   Everyman, I will after Strength be gone:
As for me, I will leave you alone.
EVERYMAN   Why Discretion, will ye forsake me?

---

8. More and less (i.e., all of you).   1. I'm to blame for displeasing you.
9. I tuck my skirts in my belt and am off.

DISCRETION   Yea, in faith, I will go from thee.
   For when Strength goeth before,
835   I follow after evermore.
EVERYMAN   Yet I pray thee, for the love of the Trinity,
   Look in my grave once piteously.
DISCRETION   Nay, so nigh will I not come.
   Farewell everyone!

     [*Exit* DISCRETION.]

840 EVERYMAN   O all thing faileth save God alone—
   Beauty, Strength, and Discretion.
   For when Death bloweth his blast
   They all run fro me full fast.
FIVE-WITS   Everyman, my leave now of thee I take.
845 I will follow the other, for here I thee forsake.
EVERYMAN   Alas, then may I wail and weep,
   For I took you for my best friend.
FIVE-WITS   I will no longer thee keep.°   *watch over*
   Now farewell, and there an end!

     [*Exit* FIVE-WITS.]

850 EVERYMAN   O Jesu, help, all hath forsaken me!
GOOD DEEDS   Nay, Everyman, I will bide with thee:
   I will not forsake thee indeed;
   Thou shalt find me a good friend at need.
EVERYMAN   Gramercy, Good Deeds! Now may I true friends see.
855 They have forsaken me every one—
   I loved them better than my Good Deeds alone.
   Knowledge, will ye forsake me also?
KNOWLEDGE   Yea, Everyman, when ye to Death shall go,
   But not yet, for no manner of danger.
860 EVERYMAN   Gramercy, Knowledge, with all my heart!
KNOWLEDGE   Nay, yet will I not from hence depart
   Till I see where ye shall be come.[2]
EVERYMAN   Methink, alas, that I must be gone
   To make my reckoning and my debts pay,
865 For I see my time is nigh spent away.
   Take example, all ye that this do hear or see,
   How they that I best loved do forsake me,
   Except my Good Deeds that bideth truly.
GOOD DEEDS   All earthly things is but vanity.
870 Beauty, Strength, and Discretion do man forsake,
   Foolish friends and kinsmen that fair spake—
   All fleeth save Good Deeds, and that am I.
EVERYMAN   Have mercy on me, God most mighty,
   And stand by me, thou mother and maid, holy Mary!

---

2. Till I see where you will come to.

875 GOOD DEEDS   Fear not: I will speak for thee.
EVERYMAN   Here I cry God mercy!
GOOD DEEDS   Short our end, and 'minish our pain.[3]
    Let us go, and never come again.
EVERYMAN   Into thy hands, Lord, my soul I commend:
880   Receive it, Lord, that it be not lost.
    As thou me boughtest,° so me defend,   *redeemed*
    And save me from the fiend's boast,
    That I may appear with that blessed host
    That shall be saved at the day of doom.
885   *In manus tuas*, of mights most,
    Forever *commendo spiritum meum.*[4]

      [EVERYMAN *and* GOOD DEEDS *descend into the grave.*]

KNOWLEDGE   Now hath he suffered that we all shall endure,
    The Good Deeds shall make all sure.
    Now hath he made ending,
890   Methinketh that I hear angels sing
    And make great joy and melody
    Where Everyman's soul received shall be.
ANGEL [*within*]   Come, excellent elect° spouse to Jesu![5]   *chosen*
    Here above thou shalt go
895   Because of thy singular virtue.
    Now the soul is taken the body fro,
    Thy reckoning is crystal clear:
    Now shalt thou into the heavenly sphere—
    Unto the which all ye shall come
900   That liveth well before the day of doom.

      [*Enter* DOCTOR.][6]

DOCTOR   This memorial° men may have in mind: *reminder*
    Ye hearers, take it of worth,° old and young,   *prize it*
    And forsake Pride, for he deceiveth you in the end.
    And remember Beauty, Five-Wits, Strength, and Discretion,
905   They all at the last do Everyman forsake,
    Save his Good Deeds there doth he take—
    But beware, for and° they be small,   *if*
    Before God he hath no help at all—
    None excuse may be there for Everyman.
910   Alas, how shall he do than?°   *then*
    For after death amends may no man make,
    For then mercy and pity doth him forsake.
    If his reckoning be not clear when he doth come,

---

3. I.e., make our dying quick and diminish our pain.

4. Into thy hands, O greatest of powers, I commend my spirit forever (Latin). Cf. Christ's dying words (Luke 23.46).

5. The soul is often referred to as the bride of Jesus.

6. The Doctor is the learned theologian who explains the meaning of the play.

God will say, *"Ite, maledicti, in ignem eternum!"*[7]
915 And he that hath his account whole and sound,
High in heaven he shall be crowned,
Unto which place God bring us all thither,
That we may live body and soul togither.
Thereto help, the Trinity!
920 Amen, say ye, for saint° charity.   *holy*

---

7. Depart, ye cursed, into everlasting fire (Latin; Matthew 25.41).

APPENDIXES

General Bibliography

This bibliography consists of a list of suggested general readings on English literature. Bibliographies for the authors in *The Norton Anthology of English Literature* are available online in the NAEL Archive (digital.wwnorton.com/englishlit10abc and digital.wwnorton.com/englishlit10def).

Suggested General Readings

Histories of England and of English Literature

Even the most distinguished of the comprehensive general histories written in past generations have come to seem outmoded. Innovative research in social, cultural, and political history has made it difficult to write a single coherent account of England from the Middle Ages to the present, let alone to accommodate in a unified narrative the complex histories of Scotland, Ireland, Wales, and the other nations where writing in English has flourished. Readers who wish to explore the historical matrix out of which the works of literature collected in this anthology emerged are advised to consult the studies of particular periods listed in the appropriate sections of this bibliography. The multivolume *Oxford History of England* and *New Oxford History of England* are useful, as are the three-volume *Peoples of the British Isles: A New History*, ed. Stanford Lehmberg, 1992; the nine-volume *Cambridge Cultural History of Britain*, ed. Boris Ford, 1992; the three-volume *Cambridge Social History of Britain, 1750–1950*, ed. F. M. L. Thompson, 1992; and the multivolume *Penguin History of Britain*, gen. ed. David Cannadine, 1996–. For Britain's imperial history, readers can consult the five-volume *Oxford History of the British Empire*, ed. Roger Louis, 1998–99, as well as *Gender and Empire*, ed. Philippa Levine, 2004. Given the cultural centrality of London, readers may find particular interest in *The London Encyclopaedia*, ed. Ben Weinreb et al., 3rd ed., 2008; Roy Porter, *London: A Social History*, 1994; and Jerry White, *London in the Nineteenth Century: "A Human Awful Wonder of God,"* 2007, and *London in the Twentieth Century: A City and Its People*, 2001.

Similar observations may be made about literary history. In the light of such initiatives as women's studies, new historicism, and postcolonialism, the range of authors deemed significant has expanded, along with the geographical and conceptual boundaries of literature in English. Attempts to capture in a unified account the great sweep of literature from *Beowulf* to the early twenty-first century have largely given way to studies of individual genres, carefully delimited time periods, and specific authors. For these more focused accounts, see the listings by period. Among the large-scale literary surveys, *The Cambridge Guide to Literature in English*, 3rd ed., 2006, is useful, as is the nine-volume *Penguin History of Literature*, 1993–94. *The Feminist Companion to Literature in English*, ed. Virginia Blain, Isobel Grundy, and Patricia Clements, 1990, is an important resource, and the editorial materials in *The Norton Anthology of Literature by Women*, 3rd ed., 2007, eds. Sandra M. Gilbert and Susan Gubar, constitute a concise history and set of biographies of women authors since the Middle Ages. *Annals of English Literature, 1475–1950*, rev. 1961, lists important publications year by year, together with the significant literary events for each year. Six volumes have been published in the *Oxford English Literary History*, gen. ed. Jonathan Bate, 2002–: Laura Ashe, *1000–1350: Conquest and Transformation*;

James Simpson, *1350–1547: Reform and Cultural Revolution*; Philip Davis, *1830–1880: The Victorians*; Chris Baldick, *1830–1880: The Modern Movement*; Randall Stevenson, *1960–2000: The Last of England?*; and Bruce King, *1948–2000: The Internationalization of English Literature*. See also *The Cambridge History of Medieval English Literature*, ed. David Wallace, 1999; *The Cambridge History of Early Medieval English Literature*, ed. Clare E. Lees, 2012; *The Cambridge History of Early Modern English Literature*, ed. David Loewenstein and Janel Mueller, 2003; *The Cambridge History of English Literature, 1660–1780*, ed. John Richetti, 2005; *The Cambridge History of English Romantic Literature*, ed. James Chandler, 2009; *The Cambridge History of Victorian Literature*, ed. Kate Flint, 2012; and *The Cambridge History of Twentieth-Century English Literature*, ed. Laura Marcus and Peter Nicholls, 2005.

Helpful treatments and surveys of English meter, rhyme, and stanza forms are Paul Fussell Jr., *Poetic Meter and Poetic Form*, rev. 1979; Donald Wesling, *The Chances of Rhyme: Device and Modernity*, 1980; Charles O. Hartman, *Free Verse: An Essay in Prosody*, 1983; John Hollander, *Rhyme's Reason: A Guide to English Verse*, rev. 1989; Derek Attridge, *Poetic Rhythm: An Introduction*, 1995; Robert Pinsky, *The Sounds of Poetry: A Brief Guide*, 1998; Mark Strand and Eavan Boland, eds., *The Making of a Poem: A Norton Anthology of Poetic Forms*, 2000; Helen Vendler, *Poems, Poets, Poetry*, 3rd ed., 2010; Virginia Jackson and Yopie Prins, eds., *The Lyric Theory Reader*, 2013; and Jonathan Culler, *Theory of the Lyric*, 2015.

On the development and functioning of the novel as a form, see Ian Watt, *The Rise of the Novel*, 1957; Gérard Genette, *Narrative Discourse: An Essay in Method*, 1980; *Theory of the Novel: A Historical Approach*, ed. Michael McKeon, 2000; McKeon, *The Origins of the English Novel, 1600–1740*, 15th anniversary ed., 2002; and *The Novel*, ed. Franco Moretti, 2 vols., 2006–07. *The Cambridge History of the English Novel*, eds. Robert L. Caserio and Clement Hawes, 2012; *A Companion to the English Novel*, eds. Stephen Arata et al., 2015; eight volumes have been published from *The Oxford History of the Novel in English*, 2011–16. On women novelists and readers, see Nancy Armstrong, *Desire and Domestic Fiction: A Political History of the Novel*, 1987; and Catherine Gallagher, *Nobody's Story: The Vanishing Acts of Women Writers in the Marketplace, 1670–1820*, 1994.

On the history of playhouse design, see Richard Leacroft, *The Development of the English Playhouse: An Illustrated Survey of Theatre Building in England from Medieval to Modern Times*, 1988. For a survey of the plays that have appeared on these and other stages, see Allardyce Nicoll, *British Drama*, rev. 1962; the eight-volume *Revels History of Drama in English*, gen. eds. Clifford Leech and T. W. Craik, 1975–83; and Alfred Harbage, *Annals of English Drama, 975–1700*, 3rd ed., 1989, rev. S. Schoenbaum and Sylvia Wagonheim; and the three volumes of *The Cambridge History of British Theatre*, eds. Jane Milling, Peter Thomson, and Joseph Donohue, 2004.

On some of the key intellectual currents that are at once reflected in and shaped by literature and contemporary literary criticism, Arthur O. Lovejoy's classic studies *The Great Chain of Being*, 1936, and *Essays in the History of Ideas*, 1948, remain valuable, along with such works as Georg Simmel, *The Philosophy of Money*, 1907; Lovejoy and George Boas, *Primitivism and Related Ideas in Antiquity*, 1935; Norbert Elias, *The Civilizing Process*, orig. pub. 1939, English trans. 1969; Simone de Beauvoir, *The Second Sex*, 1949; Frantz Fanon, *Black Skin, White Masks*, 1952, new trans. 2008; Ernst Cassirer, *The Philosophy of Symbolic Forms*, 4 vols., 1953–96; Ernst Kantorowicz, *The King's Two Bodies: A Study in Medieval Political Theology*, 1957, new ed. 1997; Hannah Arendt, *The Human Condition*, 1958; Richard Popkin, *The History of Skepticism from Erasmus to Descartes*, 1960; M. H. Abrams, *Natural Supernaturalism: Tradition and Revolution in Romantic Literature*, 1971; Michel Foucault, *Madness and Civilization: A History of Insanity in the Age of Reason*, Eng.

trans. 1965, and *The Order of Things: An Archaeology of the Human Sciences*, Eng. trans. 1970; Gaston Bachelard, *The Poetics of Space*, Eng. trans. 1969; Martin Jay, *The Dialectical Imagination: A History of the Frankfurt School and the Institute of Social Research, 1923–1950*, 1973, new ed. 1996; Hayden White, *Metahistory*, 1973; Roland Barthes, *The Pleasure of the Text*, Eng. trans. 1975; Jacques Derrida, *Of Grammatology*, Eng. trans. 1976, and *Dissemination*, Eng. trans. 1981; Richard Rorty, *Philosophy and the Mirror of Nature*, 1979; Gilles Deleuze and Félix Guattari, *A Thousand Plateaus*, 1980; Raymond Williams, *Keywords: A Vocabulary of Culture and Society*, rev. 1983; Pierre Bourdieu, *Distinction: A Social Critique of the Judgment of Taste*, Eng. trans. 1984; Michel de Certeau, *The Practice of Everyday Life*, Eng. trans. 1984; Hans Blumenberg, *The Legitimacy of the Modern Age*, Eng. trans. 1985; Jürgen Habermas, *The Philosophical Discourse of Modernity*, Eng. trans, 1987; Slavoj Žižek, *The Sublime Object of Ideology*, 1989; Homi Bhabha, *The Location of Culture*, 1994; Judith Butler, *The Psychic Life of Power: Theories in Subjection*, 1997; and Sigmund Freud, *Writings on Art and Literature*, ed. Neil Hertz, 1997.

Reference Works

The single most important tool for the study of literature in English is the *Oxford English Dictionary*, 2nd ed. 1989, 3rd ed. in process. The most current edition is available online to subscribers. The *OED* is written on historical principles: that is, it attempts not only to describe current word use but also to record the history and development of the language from its origins before the Norman conquest to the present. It thus provides, for familiar as well as archaic and obscure words, the widest possible range of meanings and uses, organized chronologically and illustrated with quotations. The *OED* can be searched as a conventional dictionary arranged a–z and also by subject, usage, region, origin, and timeline (the first appearance of a word). Beyond the *OED* there are many other valuable dictionaries, such as *The American Heritage Dictionary* (5th ed., 2016), *The Oxford Dictionary of Abbreviations*, *The Concise Oxford Dictionary of English Etymology*, *The Oxford Dictionary of English Grammar*, *A New Dictionary of Eponyms*, *The Oxford Essential Dictionary of Foreign Terms in English*, *The Oxford Dictionary of Idioms*, *The Concise Oxford Dictionary of Linguistics*, *The Oxford Guide to World English*, and *The Concise Oxford Dictionary of Proverbs*. Other valuable reference works include *The Cambridge Encyclopedia of the English Language*, 2nd ed., ed. David Crystal, 2003; *The Concise Oxford Companion to the English Language*; *Pocket Fowler's Modern English Usage*; and the numerous guides to specialized vocabularies, slang, regional dialects, and the like.

There is a steady flow of new editions of most major and many minor writers in English, along with a ceaseless outpouring of critical appraisals and scholarship. James L. Harner's *Literary Research Guide: An Annotated List of Reference Sources in English Literary Studies* (6th ed., 2009; online ed. available to subscribers at www.mlalrg.org/public) offers thorough, evaluative annotations of a wide range of sources. For the historical record of scholarship and critical discussion, *The New Cambridge Bibliography of English Literature*, ed. George Watson, 5 vols. (1969–77) and *The Cambridge Bibliography of English Literature*, 3rd ed., 5 vols. (1941–2000) are useful. The *MLA International Bibliography* (also online) is a key resource for following critical discussion of literatures in English. Ranging from 1926 to the present; it includes journal articles, essays, chapters from collections, books, and dissertations, and covers folklore, linguistics, and film. The *Annual Bibliography of English Language and Literature* (*ABELL*), compiled by the Modern Humanities Research Association, lists monographs, periodical articles, critical editions of literary works, book reviews, and collections of essays published anywhere in the world; unpublished doctoral dissertations are covered for the period 1920–99 (available online to subscribers and as part of Literature Online, http://literature. proquest.com/marketing/index.jsp).

For compact biographies of English authors, see the multivolume *Oxford Dictionary of National Biography* (*DNB*), ed. H. C. G. Matthew and Brian Harrison, 2004; since 2004 the *DNB* has been extended online with three annual updates. Handy reference books of authors, works, and various literary terms and allusions include many volumes in the *Cambridge Companion* and *Oxford Companion* series (e.g., *The Cambridge Companion to Narrative*, ed David Herman, 2007; *The Oxford Companion to English Literature*, ed. Dinah Birch, rev. 2016; *The Cambridge Companion to Allegory*, ed. Rita Copeland and Peter Struck, 2010; etc.). Likewise, *The Princeton Encyclopedia of Poetry and Poetics*, ed. Roland Greene and others, 4th ed., is available online to subscribers in ProQuest Ebook Central. Handbooks that define and illustrate literary concepts and terms are *The Penguin Dictionary of Literary Terms and Literary Theory*, ed. J. A. Cuddon and M. A. R. Habib, 5th ed., 2015; William Harmon, *A Handbook to Literature*, 12th ed., 2011; *Critical Terms for Literary Study*, ed. Frank Lentricchia and Thomas McLaughlin, rev. 1995; and M. H. Abrams and Geoffrey Harpham, *A Glossary of Literary Terms*, 11th ed., 2014. Also useful are Richard Lanham, *A Handlist of Rhetorical Terms*, 2nd ed., 2012; Arthur Quinn, *Figures of Speech: 60 Ways to Turn a Phrase*, 1995; and the *Barnhart Concise Dictionary of Etymology*, ed. Robert K. Barnhart, 1995; and George Kennedy, *A New History of Classical Rhetoric*, 2009.

On the Greek and Roman backgrounds, see *The Cambridge History of Classical Literature* (vol. 1: *Greek Literature*, 1982; vol. 2: *Latin Literature*, 1989), both available online; *The Oxford Companion to Classical Literature*, ed. M. C. Howatson, 3rd ed., 2011; Gian Biagio Conte, *Latin Literature: A History*, 1994; *The Oxford Classical Dictionary*, 4th ed., 2012; Richard Rutherford, *Classical Literature: A Concise History*, 2005; and Mark P. O. Morford, Robert J. Lenardon, and Michael Sham, *Classical Mythology*, 10th ed., 2013. The Loeb Classical Library of Greek and Roman texts is now available online to subscribers at www.loebclassics.com.

Digital resources in the humanities have vastly proliferated since the previous edition of *The Norton Anthology of English Literature* and are continuing to grow rapidly. The NAEL Archive (accessed at digital.wwnorton.com/englishlit10abc and digital .wwnorton.com/englishlit10def) is the gateway to an extensive array of annotated texts, images, and other materials especially gathered for the readers of this anthology. Among other useful electronic resources for the study of English literature are enormous digital archives, available to subscribers: Early English Books Online (EEBO), http://eebo.chadwyck.com/home; Literature Online, http://literature.proquest.com /marketing/index.jsp; and Eighteenth Century Collections Online (ECCO), www.gale .com/primary-sources/eighteenth-century-collections-online. There are also numerous free sites of variable quality. Many of the best of these are period or author specific and hence are listed in the period/author bibiliographies in the NAEL Archive. Among the general sites, one of the most useful and wide-ranging is Voice of the Shuttle (http://vos.ucsb.edu), which includes in its aggregation links to Bartleby.com and Project Gutenberg.

Literary Criticism and Theory

Nine volumes of the *Cambridge History of Literary Criticism* have been published, 1989– : *Classical Criticism*, ed. George A. Kennedy; *The Middle Ages*, ed. Alastair Minnis and Ian Johnson; *The Renaissance*, ed. Glyn P. Norton; *The Eighteenth Century*, ed. H. B. Nisbet and Claude Rawson; *Romanticism*, ed. Marshall Brown; *The Nineteenth Century ca. 1830–1914*, ed. M. A. R. Habib; *Modernism and the New Criticism*, ed. A. Walton Litz, Louis Menand, and Lawrence Rainey; *From Formalism to Poststructuralism*, ed. Raman Selden; and *Twentieth-Century Historical, Philosoph-*

ical, and Psychological Perspectives, ed. Christa Knellwolf and Christopher Norris. See also M. H. Abrams, *The Mirror and the Lamp: Romantic Theory and the Critical Tradition*, 1953; William K. Wimsatt and Cleanth Brooks, *Literary Criticism: A Short History*, 1957; René Wellek, *A History of Modern Criticism: 1750–1950*, 9 vols., 1955–93; Frank Lentricchia, *After the New Criticism*, 1980; and J. Hillis Miller, *On Literature*, 2002. Raman Selden, Peter Widdowson, and Peter Brooker have written *A Reader's Guide to Contemporary Literary Theory*, 5th ed., 2015. Other useful resources include *The Johns Hopkins Guide to Literary Theory and Criticism*, 2nd ed., 2004; *Literary Theory, an Anthology*, eds. Julie Rivkin and Michael Ryan, 1998; and *The Norton Anthology of Theory and Criticism*, 3rd ed., gen. ed. Vincent Leitch, 2018.

Modern approaches to English literature and literary theory were shaped by certain landmark works: William Empson, *Seven Types of Ambiguity*, 1930, 3rd ed. 1953, *Some Versions of Pastoral*, 1935, and *The Structure of Complex Words*, 1951; F. R. Leavis, *Revaluation*, 1936, and *The Great Tradition*, 1948; Lionel Trilling, *The Liberal Imagination*, 1950; T. S. Eliot, *Selected Essays*, 3rd ed. 1951, and *On Poetry and Poets*, 1957; Erich Auerbach, *Mimesis: The Representation of Reality in Western Literature*, 1953; William K. Wimsatt, *The Verbal Icon*, 1954; Northrop Frye, *Anatomy of Criticism*, 1957; Wayne C. Booth, *The Rhetoric of Fiction*, 1961, rev. ed. 1983; and W. J. Bate, *The Burden of the Past and the English Poet*, 1970. René Wellek and Austin Warren, *Theory of Literature*, rev. 1970, is a useful introduction to the variety of scholarly and critical approaches to literature up to the time of its publication. Jonathan Culler's *Literary Theory: A Very Short Introduction*, 1997, discusses recurrent issues and debates.

Beginning in the late 1960s, there was a significant intensification of interest in literary theory as a specific field. Certain forms of literary study had already been influenced by the work of the Russian linguist Roman Jakobson and the Russian formalist Viktor Shklovsky and, still more, by conceptions that derived or claimed to derive from Marx and Engels, but the full impact of these theories was not felt until what became known as the "theory revolution" of the 1970s and '80s. For Marxist literary criticism, see Georg Lukács, *Theory of the Novel*, 1920, trans. 1971; *The Historical Novel*, 1937, trans. 1983; and *Studies in European Realism*, trans. 1964; Walter Benjamin's essays from the 1920s and '30s represented in *Illuminations*, trans. 1986, and *Reflections*, trans. 1986; Mikhail Bakhtin's essays from the 1930s represented in *The Dialogic Imagination*, trans. 1981, and *Rabelais and His World*, 1941, trans. 1968; *Selections from the Prison Notebooks of Antonio Gramsci*, ed. and trans. Quintin Hoare and Geoffrey Smith, 1971; Raymond Williams, *Marxism and Literature*, 1977; Tony Bennett, *Formalism and Marxism*, 1979; Fredric Jameson, *The Political Unconscious: Narrative as a Socially Symbolic Act*, 1981; and Terry Eagleton, *Literary Theory: An Introduction*, 3rd ed., 2008, and *The Ideology of the Aesthetic*, 1990.

Structural linguistics and anthropology gave rise to a flowering of structuralist literary criticism; convenient introductions include Robert Scholes, *Structuralism in Literature: An Introduction*, 1974, and Jonathan Culler, *Structuralist Poetics*, 1975. Poststructuralist challenges to this approach are epitomized in such influential works as Jacques Derrida, *Writing and Difference*, 1967, trans. 1978, and Paul de Man, *Blindness and Insight: Essays in the Rhetoric of Contemporary Criticism*, 1971, 2nd ed., 1983. Poststructuralism is discussed in Jonathan Culler, *On Deconstruction*, 1982; Slavoj Žižek, *The Sublime Object of Ideology*, 1989; Fredric Jameson, *Postmodernism; or the Cultural Logic of Late Capitalism*, 1991; John McGowan, *Postmodernism and Its Critics*, 1991; and *Beyond Structuralism*, ed. Wendell Harris, 1996. A figure who greatly influenced both structuralism and poststructuralism is Roland Barthes, in *Mythologies*, trans. 1972, and *S/Z*, trans. 1974. Among other influential contributions to literary theory are the psychoanalytic approach in Harold Bloom, *The Anxiety of*

Influence, 1973; and the reader-response approach in Stanley Fish, *Is There a Text in This Class?: The Authority of Interpretive Communities*, 1980. For a retrospect on the theory decades, see Terry Eagleton, *After Theory*, 2003.

Influenced by these theoretical currents but not restricted to them, modern feminist literary criticism was fashioned by such works as Patricia Meyer Spacks, *The Female Imagination*, 1975; Ellen Moers, *Literary Women*, 1976; Elaine Showalter, *A Literature of Their Own*, 1977; and Sandra Gilbert and Susan Gubar, *The Madwoman in the Attic*, 1979. Subsequent studies include Jane Gallop, *The Daughter's Seduction: Feminism and Psychoanalysis*, 1982; Luce Irigaray, *This Sex Which Is Not One*, trans. 1985; Gayatri Chakravorty Spivak, *In Other Worlds: Essays in Cultural Politics*, 1987; Sandra Gilbert and Susan Gubar, *No Man's Land: The Place of the Woman Writer in the Twentieth Century*, 3 vols., 1988–94; Barbara Johnson, *A World of Difference*, 1989; Judith Butler, *Gender Trouble*, 1990; and the critical views sampled in Elaine Showalter, *The New Feminist Criticism*, 1985; *The Hélène Cixous Reader*, ed. Susan Sellers, 1994; *Feminist Literary Theory: A Reader*, ed. Mary Eagleton, 3rd ed., 2010; and *Feminisms: An Anthology of Literary Theory and Criticism*, eds. Robyn R. Warhol and Diane Price Herndl, 2nd ed., 1997; *The Cambridge Companion to Feminist Literary Theory*, ed. Ellen Rooney, 2006; *Feminist Literary Theory and Criticism*, ed. Sandra Gilbert and Susan Gubar, 2007; and *Feminist Literary Theory: A Reader*, ed. Mary Eagleton, 3rd ed., 2011.

Just as feminist critics used poststructuralist and psychoanalytic methods to place literature in conversation with gender theory, a new school emerged placing literature in conversation with critical race theory. Comprehensive introductions include *Critical Race Theory: The Key Writings That Formed the Movement*, eds. Kimberlé Crenshaw et al.; *The Routledge Companion to Race and Ethnicity*, ed. Stephen Caliendo and Charlton McIlwain, 2010; and *Critical Race Theory: An Introduction*, ed. Richard Delgado and Jean Stefancic, 3rd ed., 2017. For an important precursor in cultural studies, see Stuart Hall et al., *Policing the Crisis*, 1978. Seminal works include Henry Louis Gates, Jr., *The Signifying Monkey: A Theory of African-American Literature*, 1988; Patricia Williams, *The Alchemy of Race and Rights*, 1991; Toni Morrison, *Playing the Dark: Whiteness and the Literary Imagination*, 1992; Cornel West, *Race Matters*, 2001; and Gene Andrew Jarrett, *Representing the Race: A New Political History of African American Literature*, 2011. Helpful anthologies and collections of essays have emerged in recent decades, such as *The Oxford Companion to African American Literature*, eds., William L. Andrews, Frances Smith Foster, and Trudier Harris, 1997; also their *Concise Companion*, 2001; *The Cambridge Companion to Jewish American Literature*, eds. Hana Wirth-Nesher and Michael P. Kramer, 2003; *The Routledge Companion to Anglophone Caribbean Literature*, eds. Michael A. Bucknor and Alison Donnell, 2011; *The Routledge Companion to Latino/a Literature*, eds. Suzanne Bost and Frances R. Aparicio, 2013; *A Companion to African American Literature*, ed. Gene Andrew Jarrett, 2013; *The Routledge Companion to Asian American and Pacific Islander Literature*, ed. Rachel Lee, 2014; *The Cambridge Companion to Asian American Literature*, eds. Crystal Parikh and Daniel Y. Kim, 2015; and *The Cambridge Companion to British Black and Asian Literature (1945–2010)*, ed. Deirdre Osborne, 2016.

Gay literature and queer studies are represented in *Inside/Out: Lesbian Theories, Gay Theories*, ed. Diana Fuss, 1991; *The Lesbian and Gay Studies Reader*, eds. Henry Abelove, Michele Barale, and David Halperin, 1993; *The Columbia Anthology of Gay Literature: Readings from Western Antiquity to the Present Day*, ed. Byrne R. S. Fone, 1998; and by such books as Eve Sedgwick, *Between Men: English Literature and Male Homosocial Desire*, 1985, and *Epistemology of the Closet*, 1990; Diana Fuss, *Essentially Speaking: Feminism, Nature, and Difference*, 1989; Terry Castle, *The Apparitional Lesbian: Female Homosexuality and Modern Culture*, 1993; Leo Bersani, *Homos*, 1995; Gregory Woods, *A History of Gay Literature: The Male Tradition*,

1998; David Halperin, *How to Do the History of Homosexuality*, 2002; Judith Halberstam, *In a Queer Time and Place: Transgender Bodies, Subcultural Lives*, 2005; Heather Love, *Feeling Backward: Loss and the Politics of Queer History*, 2009; *The Cambridge History of Gay and Lesbian Literature*, eds. E. L. McCallum and Mikko Tuhkanen, 2014; and *The Cambridge Companion to Lesbian Literature*, ed. Jodie Medd, 2015.

New historicism is represented in Stephen Greenblatt, *Learning to Curse*, 1990; in the essays collected in *The New Historicism Reader*, ed. Harold Veeser, 1993; in *New Historical Literary Study: Essays on Reproducing Texts, Representing History*, eds. Jeffrey N. Cox and Larry J. Reynolds, 1993; and in Catherine Gallagher and Stephen Greenblatt, *Practicing New Historicism*, 2000. The related social and historical dimension of texts is discussed in Jerome McGann, *Critique of Modern Textual Criticism*, 1983; and *Scholarly Editing: A Guide to Research*, ed. D. C. Greetham, 1995. Characteristic of new historicism is an expansion of the field of literary interpretation still further in cultural studies; for a broad sampling of the range of interests, see Lawrence Grossberg, Cary Nelson, and Paula Treichler, eds., *Cultural Studies*, 1992; *The Cultural Studies Reader*, ed. Simon During, 3rd ed., 2007; and *A Cultural Studies Reader: History, Theory, Practice*, eds. Jessica Munns and Gita Rajan, 1996.

This expansion of the field is similarly reflected in postcolonial studies: see Frantz Fanon, *Black Skin, White Masks*, 1952, new trans. 2008, and *The Wretched of the Earth*, 1961, new trans. 2004; Edward Said, *Orientalism*, 1978, and *Culture and Imperialism*, 1993; *The Post-Colonial Studies Reader*, 2nd ed., 2006; and such influential books as Homi Bhabha, ed., *Nation and Narration*, 1990, and *The Location of Culture*, 1994; Robert J. C. Young, *Postcolonialism: An Historical Introduction*, 2001; Bill Ashcroft, Gareth Griffiths, and Helen Tiffin, *The Empire Writes Back: Theory and Practice in Post-Colonial Literatures*, 2nd ed. 2002; Elleke Boehmer, *Colonial and Postcolonial Literature*, 2nd ed. 2005; and *The Cambridge History of Postcolonial Literature*, ed. Ato Quayson, 2011; *The Cambridge Companion to the Postcolonial Novel*, ed. Ato Quayson, 2015; and *The Cambridge Companion to Postcolonial Poetry*, ed. Jahan Ramazani, 2017.

In the wake of the theory revolution, critics have focused on a wide array of topics, which can only be briefly surveyed here. One current of work, focusing on the history of emotion, is represented in Brian Massumi, *Parables for the Virtual*, 2002; Sianne Ngai, *Ugly Feelings*, 2005; *The Affect Theory Reader*, eds. Melissa Gregg and Gregory J. Seigworth, 2010; and Judith Butler, *Senses of the Subject*, 2015. A somewhat related current, examining the special role of traumatic memory in literature, is exemplified in Cathy Caruth, *Trauma: Explorations in Memory*, 1995; and Dominic LaCapra, *Writing History, Writing Trauma*, 2000. Work on the literary implications of cognitive science may be glimpsed in *Introduction to Cognitive Cultural Studies*, ed. Lisa Zunshine, 2010. Interest in quantitative approaches to literature was sparked by Franco Moretti, *Graphs, Maps, Trees: Abstract Models for Literary History*, 2005. For the growing field of digital humanities, see also Moretti, *Distant Reading*, 2013; *Defining Digital Humanities: A Reader*, eds. Melissa Terras, Julianne Nyhan, and Edward Vanhoutte, 2014; and *A New Companion to Digital Humanities*, eds. Susan Schreibman, Ray Siemens, and John Unsworth, 2nd ed., 2016. There has also been a flourishing of ecocriticism, or studies of literature and the environment, including *The Ecocriticism Reader: Landmarks in Literary Ecology*, eds. Cheryll Glotfelty and Harold Fromm, 1996; *Writing the Environment*, eds. Richard Kerridge and Neil Sammells, 1998; Jonathan Bate, *The Song of the Earth*, 2002; Lawrence Buell, *The Future of Environmental Criticism: Environmental Crisis and Literary Imagination*, 2005; Timothy Morton, *Ecology Without Nature*, 2009; and *The Oxford Handbook of Ecocriticism*, ed. Greg Garrard, 2014. Related are the emerging fields of animal studies and posthumanism, where key works include

Bruno Latour, *We Have Never Been Modern*, 1993; Steve Baker, *Postmodern Animal*, 2000; Jacques Derrida, *The Animal That Therefore I Am*, trans. 2008; Cary Wolfe, *Animal Rites: American Culture, the Discourse of Species, and Posthumanist Theory*, 2003, and *What is Posthumanism?* 2009; Kari Weil, *Thinking Animals: Why Animal Studies Now?* 2012; and Aaron Gross and Anne Vallely, eds. *Animals and the Human Imagination: A Companion to Animal Studies*, 2012; and *Critical Animal Studies: Thinking the Unthinkable*, ed. John Sorenson, 2014. The relationship between literature and law is central to such works as *Interpreting Law and Literature: A Hermeneutic Reader*, eds. Sanford Levinson and Steven Mailloux, 1988; *Law's Stories: Narrative and Rhetoric in the Law*, eds. Peter Brooks and Paul Gerwertz, 1998; and *Literature and Legal Problem Solving: Law and Literature as Ethical Discourse*, Paul J. Heald, 1998. Ethical questions in literature have been usefully explored by, among others, Geoffrey Galt Harpham in *Getting It Right: Language, Literature, and Ethics*, 1997, and Derek Attridge in *The Singularity of Literature*, 2004. Finally, approaches to literature, such as formalism and literary biography, that seemed superseded in the theoretical ferment of the late twentieth century, have had a powerful resurgence. A renewed interest in form is evident in Susan Stewart, *Poetry and the Fate of the Senses*, 2002; *Reading for Form*, eds. Susan J. Wolfson and Marshall Brown, 2007; and Caroline Levine, *Forms: Whole, Rhythm, Hierarchy, Network*, 2015. Interest in the history of the book was spearheaded by D. F. McKenzie's *Bibliography and the Sociology of Texts*, 1986; Jerome McGann's *The Textual Condition*, 1991; and Roger Chartier's *The Order of Books: Readers, Authors, and Libraries in Europe Between the Fourteenth and Eighteenth Centuries*, 1994. See also *The Cambridge History of the Book in Britain*, 7 vols., 1998–2017; and *The Practice and Representation of Reading in England*, eds. James Raven, Helen Small, and Naomi Tadmor, 2007; *The Book History Reader*, eds. David Finkelstein and Alistair McCleery, 2nd ed., 2006; and *The Cambridge Companion to the History of the Book*, ed. Leslie Howsam, 2014.

Anthologies representing a range of recent approaches include *Modern Criticism and Theory*, ed. David Lodge, 1988; *Contemporary Literary Criticism*, ed. Robert Con Davis and Ronald Schlieffer, 4th ed., 1998; and *The Norton Anthology of Theory and Criticism*, gen. ed. Vincent Leitch, 3rd ed., 2018.

Literary Terminology*

Using simple technical terms can sharpen our understanding and streamline our discussion of literary works. Some terms, such as the ones in section A, help us address the internal style, structure, form, and kind of works. Other terms, such as those in section B, provide insight into the material forms in which literary works have been produced.

In analyzing what they called "rhetoric," ancient Greek and Roman writers determined the elements of what we call "style" and "structure." Our literary terms are derived, via medieval and Renaissance intermediaries, from the Greek and Latin sources. In the definitions that follow, the etymology, or root, of the word is given when it helps illuminate the word's current usage.

Most of the examples are drawn from texts in this anthology.

Words **boldfaced** within definitions are themselves defined in this appendix. Some terms are defined within definitions; such words are *italicized*.

A. Terms of Style, Structure, Form, and Kind

accent (synonym "stress"): a term of **rhythm.** The special force devoted to the voicing of one syllable in a word over others. In the noun "accent," for example, the accent, or stress, is on the first syllable.

act: the major subdivision of a play, usually divided into **scenes.**

aesthetics (from Greek, "to feel, apprehend by the senses"): the philosophy of artistic meaning as a distinct mode of apprehending untranslatable truth, defined as an alternative to rational enquiry, which is purely abstract. Developed in the late eighteenth century by the German philosopher Immanuel Kant especially.

Alexandrine: a term of **meter.** In French verse a line of twelve syllables, and, by analogy, in English verse a line of six stresses. See **hexameter.**

allegory (Greek "saying otherwise"): saying one thing (the "vehicle" of the allegory) and meaning another (the allegory's "tenor"). Allegories may be momentary aspects of a work, as in **metaphor** ("John is a lion"), or, through extended metaphor, may constitute the basis of narrative, as in Bunyan's *Pilgrim's Progress*: this second meaning is the dominant one. See also **symbol** and **type.** Allegory is one of the most significant **figures of thought.**

alliteration (from Latin "litera," alphabetic letter): a **figure of speech.** The repetition of an initial consonant sound or consonant cluster in consecutive or closely positioned words. This pattern is often an inseparable part of the meter in Germanic languages, where the tonic, or accented **syllable,** is usually the first syllable. Thus all Old English poetry and some varieties of Middle English poetry use alliteration as part of their basic metrical practice. *Sir Gawain and the Green Knight*, line 1: "Sithen the sege and the assaut was sesed at Troye" (see vol. A, p. 204). Otherwise used for local effects; Stevie Smith, "Pretty," lines 4–5: "And in the pretty pool the pike stalks / He stalks his prey . . ." (see vol. F, p. 733).

*This appendix was devised and compiled by James Simpson with the collaboration of all the editors. We especially thank Professor Lara Bovilsky of the University of Oregon at Eugene, for her help.

allusion: Literary allusion is a passing but illuminating reference within a literary text to another, well-known text (often biblical or **classical**). Topical allusions are also, of course, common in certain modes, especially **satire.**

anagnorisis (Greek "recognition"): the moment of **protagonist's** recognition in a narrative, which is also often the moment of moral understanding.

anapest: a term of **rhythm.** A three-syllable foot following the rhythmic pattern, in English verse, of two unstressed (uu) syllables followed by one stressed (/). Thus, for example, "Illinois."

anaphora (Greek "carrying back"): a **figure of speech.** The repetition of words or groups of words at the beginning of consecutive sentences, clauses, or phrases. Blake, "London," lines 5–8: "In every cry of every Man, / In every Infant's cry of fear, / In every voice, in every ban . . ." (see vol. D, p. 141); Louise Bennett, "Jamaica Oman," lines 17–20: "Some backa man a push, some side-a / Man a hole him han, / Some a lick sense eena him head, / Some a guide him pon him plan!" (see vol. F, p. 860).

animal fable: a **genre.** A short narrative of speaking animals, followed by moralizing comment, written in a low style and gathered into a collection. Robert Henryson, "The Preaching of the Swallow" (see vol. A, p. 523).

antithesis (Greek "placing against"): a **figure of thought.** The juxtaposition of opposed terms in clauses or sentences that are next to or near each other. Milton, *Paradise Lost* 1.777–80: "They but now who seemed / In bigness to surpass Earth's giant sons / Now less than smallest dwarfs, in narrow room / Throng numberless" (see vol. B, p. 1514).

apostrophe (from Greek "turning away"): a **figure of thought.** An address, often to an absent person, a force, or a quality. For example, a poet makes an apostrophe to a Muse when invoking her for inspiration.

apposition: a term of **syntax.** The repetition of elements serving an identical grammatical function in one sentence. The effect of this repetition is to arrest the flow of the sentence, but in doing so to add extra semantic nuance to repeated elements. This is an especially important feature of Old English poetic style. See, for example, Caedmon's *Hymn* (vol. A, p. 31), where the phrases "heaven-kingdom's Guardian," "the Measurer's might," "his mind-plans," and "the work of the Glory-Father" each serve an identical syntactic function as the direct objects of "praise."

assonance (Latin "sounding to"): a **figure of speech.** The repetition of identical or near identical stressed vowel sounds in words whose final consonants differ, producing half-rhyme. Tennyson, "The Lady of Shalott," line 100: "His broad clear brow in sunlight glowed" (see vol. E, p. 149).

aubade (originally from Spanish "alba," dawn): a **genre.** A lover's dawn song or lyric bewailing the arrival of the day and the necessary separation of the lovers; Donne, "The Sun Rising" (see vol. B, p. 926). Larkin recasts the genre in "Aubade" (see vol. F, p. 930).

autobiography (Greek "self-life writing"): a **genre.** A narrative of a life written by the subject; Wordsworth, *The Prelude* (see vol. D, p. 362). There are subgenres, such as the spiritual autobiography, narrating the author's path to conversion and subsequent spiritual trials, as in Bunyan's *Grace Abounding.*

ballad stanza: a **verse form.** Usually a **quatrain** in alternating **iambic tetrameter** and **iambic trimeter** lines, rhyming abcb. See "Sir Patrick Spens" (vol. D, p. 36); Louise Bennett's poems (vol. F, pp. 857–61); Eliot, "Sweeney among the Nightingales" (vol. F, p. 657); Larkin, "This Be The Verse" (vol. F, p. 930).

ballade: a **verse form.** A form consisting usually of three stanzas followed by a four-line envoi (French, "send off"). The last line of the first stanza establishes a **refrain,** which is repeated, or subtly varied, as the last line of each stanza. The form was derived from French medieval poetry; English poets, from the fourteenth to the sixteenth centuries especially, used it with varying stanza forms. Chaucer, "Complaint to His Purse" (see vol. A, p. 363).

bathos (Greek "depth"): a **figure of thought.** A sudden and sometimes ridiculous descent of tone; Pope, *The Rape of the Lock* 3.157–58: "Not louder shrieks to pitying heaven are cast, / When husbands, or when lapdogs breathe their last" (see vol. C, p. 518).

beast epic: a **genre.** A continuous, unmoralized narrative, in prose or verse, relating the victories of the wholly unscrupulous but brilliant strategist Reynard the Fox over all adversaries. Chaucer arouses, only to deflate, expectations of the genre in *The Nun's Priest's Tale* (see vol. A, p. 344).

biography (Greek "life-writing"): a **genre.** A life as the subject of an extended narrative. Thus Izaak Walton, *The Life of Dr. Donne* (see vol. B, p. 976).

blank verse: a **verse form.** Unrhymed **iambic pentameter** lines. Blank verse has no stanzas, but is broken up into uneven units (verse paragraphs) determined by sense rather than form. First devised in English by Henry Howard, earl of Surrey, in his translation of two books of Virgil's *Aeneid* (see vol. B, p. 141), this very flexible verse type became the standard form for dramatic poetry in the seventeenth century, as in most of Shakespeare's plays. Milton and Wordsworth, among many others, also used it to create an English equivalent to **classical epic.**

blazon: strictly, a heraldic shield; in rhetorical usage, a **topos** whereby the individual elements of a beloved's face and body are singled out for **hyperbolic** admiration. Spenser, *Epithalamion*, lines 167–84 (see vol. B, p. 495). For an inversion of the **topos,** see Shakespeare, Sonnet 130 (vol. B, p. 736).

burlesque (French and Italian "mocking"): a work that adopts the **conventions** of a genre with the aim less of comically mocking the genre than of satirically mocking the society so represented (see **satire**). Thus Pope's *Rape of the Lock* (see vol. C, p. 507) does not mock **classical epic** so much as contemporary mores.

caesura (Latin "cut") (plural "caesurae"): a term of **meter.** A pause or breathing space within a line of verse, generally occurring between syntactic units; Louise Bennett, "Colonization in Reverse," lines 5–8: "By de hundred, by de tousan, / From country an from town, / By de ship-load, by de plane-load, / Jamaica is Englan boun" (see vol. F, p. 858), where the caesurae occur in lines 5 and 7.

canon (Greek "rule"): the group of texts regarded as worthy of special respect or attention by a given institution. Also, the group of texts regarded as definitely having been written by a certain author.

catastrophe (Greek "overturning"): the decisive turn in **tragedy** by which the plot is resolved and, usually, the **protagonist** dies.

catharsis (Greek "cleansing"): According to Aristotle, the effect of **tragedy** on its audience, through their experience of pity and terror, was a kind of spiritual cleansing, or catharsis.

character (Greek "stamp, impression"): a person, personified animal, or other figure represented in a literary work, especially in narrative and drama. The more a character seems to generate the action of a narrative, and the less he or she seems merely to serve a preordained narrative pattern, the "fuller," or more "rounded," a character is said to be. A "stock" character, common particularly in many comic genres, will perform a predictable function in different works of a given genre.

chiasmus (Greek "crosswise"): a **figure of speech.** The inversion of an already established sequence. This can involve verbal echoes: Pope, "Eloisa to Abelard," line 104, "The crime was common, common be the pain" (see vol. C, p. 529); or it can be purely a matter of syntactic inversion: Pope, *Epistle to Dr. Arbuthnot*, line 8: "They pierce my thickets, through my grot they glide" (see vol. C, p. 544).

classical, classicism, classic: Each term can be widely applied, but in English literary discourse, "classical" primarily describes the works of either Greek or Roman antiquity. "Classicism" denotes the practice of art forms inspired by classical antiquity, in particular the observance of rhetorical norms of **decorum** and balance, as opposed to following the dictates of untutored inspiration, as in Romanticism. "Classic" denotes an especially famous work within a given **canon.**

climax (Greek "ladder"): a moment of great intensity and structural change, especially in drama. Also a **figure of speech** whereby a sequence of verbally linked clauses is made, in which each successive clause is of greater consequence than its predecessor. Bacon, *Of Studies*: "Studies serve for pastimes, for ornaments, and for abilities. Their chief use for pastimes is in privateness and retiring; for ornament, is in discourse; and for ability, is in judgement" (see vol. B, p. 1223–24).

comedy: a **genre.** A term primarily applied to drama, and derived from ancient drama, in opposition to **tragedy.** Comedy deals with humorously confusing, sometimes ridiculous situations in which the ending is, nevertheless, happy. A comedy often ends in one or more marriages. Shakespeare, *Twelfth Night* (see vol. B, p. 741).

comic mode: Many genres (e.g., **romance, fabliau, comedy**) involve a happy ending in which justice is done, the ravages of time are arrested, and that which is lost is found. Such genres participate in a comic mode.

connotation: To understand connotation, we need to understand **denotation.** While many words can denote the same concept—that is, have the same basic meaning—those words can evoke different associations, or connotations. Contrast, for example, the clinical-sounding term "depression" and the more colorful, musical, even poetic phrase "the blues."

consonance (Latin "sounding with"): a **figure of speech.** The repetition of final consonants in words or stressed syllables whose vowel sounds are different. Herbert, "Easter," line 13: "Consort, both heart and lute . . ." (see vol. B, p. 1258).

convention: a repeatedly recurring feature (in either form or content) of works, occurring in combination with other recurring formal features, which constitutes a convention of a particular genre.

couplet: a **verse form.** In English verse two consecutive, rhyming lines usually containing the same number of stresses. Chaucer first introduced the **iambic pentameter** couplet into English (*Canterbury Tales*); the form was later used in many types of writing, including drama; imitations and translations of **classical epic** (thus *heroic couplet*); essays; and **satire** (see Dryden and Pope). The *distich* (Greek "two lines") is a couplet usually making complete sense; Aemilia Lanyer, *Salve Deus Rex Judaeorum*, lines 5–6: "Read it fair queen, though it defective be, / Your excellence can grace both it and me" (see vol. B, p. 981).

dactyl (Greek "finger," because of the finger's three joints): a term of **rhythm.** A three-syllable foot following the rhythmic pattern, in English verse, of one stressed followed by two unstressed syllables. Thus, for example, "Oregon."

decorum (Latin "that which is fitting"): a rhetorical principle whereby each formal aspect of a work should be in keeping with its subject matter and/or audience.

deixis (Greek "pointing"): relevant to **point of view.** Every work has, implicitly or explicitly, a "here" and a "now" from which it is narrated. Words that refer to or imply this point from which the voice of the work is projected (such as "here," "there," "this," "that," "now," "then") are examples of deixis, or "deictics." This technique is especially important in drama, where it is used to create a sense of the events happening as the spectator witnesses them.

denotation: A word has a basic, "prosaic" (factual) meaning prior to the associations it connotes (see **connotation**). The word "steed," for example, might call to mind a horse fitted with battle gear, to be ridden by a warrior, but its denotation is simply "horse."

denouement (French "unknotting"): the point at which a narrative can be resolved and so ended.

dialogue (Greek "conversation"): a **genre.** Dialogue is a feature of many genres, especially in both the **novel** and drama. As a genre itself, dialogue is used in philosophical traditions especially (most famously in Plato's *Dialogues*), as the representation of a conversation in which a philosophical question is pursued among various speakers.

diction, or **"lexis"** (from, respectively, Latin *dictio* and Greek *lexis*, each meaning "word"): the actual words used in any utterance—speech, writing, and, for our purposes here, literary works. The choice of words contributes significantly to the style of a given work.

didactic mode (Greek "teaching mode"): **Genres** in a didactic mode are designed to instruct or teach, sometimes explicitly (e.g., sermons, philosophical **discourses, georgic**), and sometimes through the medium of fiction (e.g., **animal fable, parable**).

diegesis (Greek for "narration"): a term that simply means "narration," but is used in literary criticism to distinguish one kind of story from another. In a *mimetic* story, the events are played out before us (see **mimesis**), whereas in diegesis someone recounts the story to us. Drama is for the most part *mimetic*, whereas the novel is for the most part diegetic. In novels the narrator is not, usually, part of the action of the narrative; s/he is therefore extradiegetic.

dimeter (Greek "two measure"): a term of **meter.** A two-stress line, rarely used as the meter of whole poems, though used with great frequency in single poems by Skelton, e.g., "The Tunning of Elinour Rumming" (see vol. B, p. 39). Otherwise used for single lines, as in Herbert, "Discipline," line 3: "O my God" (see vol. B, p. 1274).

discourse (Latin "running to and fro"): broadly, any nonfictional speech or writing; as a more specific genre, a philosophical meditation on a set theme. Thus Newman, *The Idea of a University* (see vol. E, p. 64).

dramatic irony: a feature of narrative and drama, whereby the audience knows that the outcome of an action will be the opposite of that intended by a **character.**

dramatic monologue (Greek "single speaking"): a **genre.** A poem in which the voice of a historical or fictional **character** speaks, unmediated by any narrator, to an implied though silent audience. See Tennyson, "Ulysses" (vol. E, p. 156); Browning, "The Bishop Orders His Tomb" (vol. E, p. 332); Eliot, "The Love Song of J. Alfred Prufrock" (vol. F, p. 654); Carol Ann Duffy, "Medusa" and "Mrs Lazarus" (vol. F, pp. 1211–13).

ecphrasis (Greek "speaking out"): a **topos** whereby a work of visual art is represented in a literary work. Auden, "Musée des Beaux Arts" (see vol. F, p. 815).

elegy: a **genre.** In **classical** literature elegy was a form written in elegiac **couplets** (a **hexameter** followed by a **pentameter**) devoted to many possible topics. In Ovidian elegy a lover meditates on the trials of erotic desire (e.g., Ovid's *Amores*). The **sonnet** sequences of both Sidney and Shakespeare exploit this genre, and, while it was still practiced in classical tradition by Donne ("On His Mistress" [see vol. B, p. 942]), by the later seventeenth century the term came to denote the poetry of loss, especially through the death of a loved person. See Tennyson, *In Memoriam* (vol. E, p. 173); Yeats, "In Memory of Major Robert Gregory" (vol. F, p. 223); Auden, "In Memory of W. B. Yeats" (see vol. F, p. 815); Heaney, "Clearances" (vol. F, p. 1104).

emblem (Greek "an insertion"): a **figure of thought.** A picture allegorically expressing a moral, or a verbal picture open to such interpretation. Donne, "A Hymn to Christ," lines 1–2: "In what torn ship soever I embark, / That ship shall be my emblem of thy ark" (see vol. B, p. 966).

end-stopping: the placement of a complete syntactic unit within a complete poetic line, fulfilling the metrical pattern; Auden, "In Memory of W. B. Yeats," line 42: "Earth, receive an honoured guest" (see vol. F, p. 817). Compare **enjambment.**

enjambment (French "striding," encroaching): The opposite of **end-stopping,** enjambment occurs when the syntactic unit does not end with the end of the poetic line and the fulfillment of the metrical pattern. When the sense of the line overflows its meter and, therefore, the line break, we have enjambment; Auden, "In Memory of W. B. Yeats," lines 44–45: "Let the Irish vessel lie / Emptied of its poetry" (see vol. F, p. 817).

epic (synonym, *heroic poetry*): a **genre.** An extended narrative poem celebrating martial heroes, invoking divine inspiration, beginning in medias res (see **order**), written in a high style (including the deployment of **epic similes;** on high style, see **register**), and divided into long narrative sequences. Homer's *Iliad* and Virgil's *Aeneid* were the prime models for English writers of epic verse. Thus Milton, *Paradise Lost* (see vol. B, p. 1495); Wordsworth, *The Prelude* (see vol. D, p. 362); and Walcott, *Omeros* (see vol. F, p. 947). With its precise repertoire of stylistic resources, epic lent itself easily to **parodic** and **burlesque** forms, known as **mock epic;** thus Pope, *The Rape of the Lock* (see vol. C, p. 507).

epigram: a **genre.** A short, pithy poem wittily expressed, often with wounding intent. See Jonson, *Epigrams* (see vol. B, p. 1089).

epigraph (Greek "inscription"): a **genre.** Any formal statement inscribed on stone; also the brief formulation on a book's title page, or a quotation at the beginning of a poem, introducing the work's themes in the most compressed form possible.

epistle (Latin "letter"): a **genre.** The letter can be shaped as a literary form, involving an intimate address often between equals. The *Epistles* of Horace provided a model for English writers from the sixteenth century. Thus Wyatt, "Mine own John Poins" (see vol. B, p. 131), or Pope, "An Epistle to a Lady" (vol. C, p. 655). Letters can be shaped to form the matter of an extended fiction, as the eighteenth-century epistolary **novel** (e.g., Samuel Richardson's *Pamela*).

epitaph: a **genre.** A pithy formulation to be inscribed on a funeral monument. Thus Ralegh, "The Author's Epitaph, Made by Himself" (see vol. B, p. 532).

epithalamion (Greek "concerning the bridal chamber"): a **genre.** A wedding poem, celebrating the marriage and wishing the couple good fortune. Thus Spenser, *Epithalamion* (see vol. B, p. 491).

epyllion (plural "epyllia") (Greek: "little epic"): a **genre.** A relatively short poem in the meter of epic poetry. See, for example, Marlowe, *Hero and Leander* (vol. B, p 660).

essay (French "trial, attempt"): a **genre.** An informal philosophical meditation, usually in prose and sometimes in verse. The journalistic periodical essay was developed in the early eighteenth century. Thus Addison and Steele, periodical essays (see vol. C, p. 462); Pope, *An Essay on Criticism* (see vol. C, p. 490).

euphemism (Greek "sweet saying"): a **figure of thought.** The figure by which something distasteful is described in alternative, less repugnant terms (e.g., "he passed away").

exegesis (Greek "leading out"): interpretation, traditionally of the biblical text, but, by transference, of any text.

exemplum (Latin "example"): an example inserted into a usually nonfictional writing (e.g., sermon or **essay**) to give extra force to an abstract thesis. Thus Johnson's example of "Sober" in his essay "On Idleness" (see vol. C, p. 732).

fabliau (French "little story," plural *fabliaux*): a **genre.** A short, funny, often bawdy narrative in low style (see **register**) imitated and developed from French models, most subtly by Chaucer; see *The Miller's Prologue and Tale* (vol. A, p. 282).

farce (French "stuffing"): a **genre.** A play designed to provoke laughter through the often humiliating antics of stock **characters.** Congreve's *The Way of the World* (see vol. C, p. 188) draws on this tradition.

figures of speech: Literary language often employs patterns perceptible to the eye and/or to the ear. Such patterns are called "figures of speech"; in classical rhetoric they were called "schemes" (from Greek *schema*, meaning "form, figure").

figures of thought: Language can also be patterned conceptually, even outside the rules that normally govern it. Literary language in particular exploits this licensed linguistic irregularity. Synonyms for figures of thought are "trope" (Greek "twisting," referring to the irregularity of use) and "conceit" (Latin "concept," referring to the fact that these figures are perceptible only to the mind). Be careful not to confuse **trope** with **topos** (a common error).

first-person narration: relevant to **point of view,** a narrative in which the voice narrating refers to itself with forms of the first-person pronoun ("I," "me," "my," etc., or possibly "we," "us," "our"), and in which the narrative is determined by the limitations of that voice. Thus Mary Wollstonecraft Shelley, *Frankenstein.*

frame narrative: Some narratives, particularly collections of narratives, involve a frame narrative that explains the genesis of, and/or gives a perspective on, the main narrative or narratives to follow. Thus Chaucer, *Canterbury Tales*; Mary Wollstonecraft Shelley, *Frankenstein*; or Conrad, *Heart of Darkness.*

free indirect style: relevant to **point of view,** a narratorial voice that manages, without explicit reference, to imply, and often implicitly to comment on, the voice of a **character** in the narrative itself. Virginia Woolf, "A Sketch of the Past," where the voice, although strictly that of the adult narrator, manages to convey the child's manner of perception: "—I begin: the first memory. This was of red and purple flowers on a black background—my mother's dress."

genre and mode: The **style,** structure, and, often, length of a work, when coupled with a certain subject matter, raise expectations that a literary work conforms to a certain **genre** (French "kind"). Good writers might upset these expectations, but they remain aware of the expectations and thwart them purposefully. Works in different genres may nevertheless participate in the same **mode,** a broader category designating the fundamental perspectives governing various genres of writing. For mode, see **tragic, comic, satiric,** and **didactic modes.** Genres are fluid, sometimes very fluid (e.g., the **novel**); the word "usually" should be added to almost every account of the characteristics of a given genre!

georgic (Greek "farming"): a **genre**. Virgil's *Georgics* treat agricultural and occasionally scientific subjects, giving instructions on the proper management of farms. Unlike **pastoral,** which treats the countryside as a place of recreational idleness among shepherds, the georgic treats it as a place of productive labor. For an English poem that critiques both genres, see Crabbe, "The Village" (vol. C, p. 1019).

hermeneutics (from the Greek god Hermes, messenger between the gods and humankind): the science of interpretation, first formulated as such by the German philosophical theologian Friedrich Schleiermacher in the early nineteenth century.

heroic poetry: see **epic.**

hexameter (Greek "six measure"): a term of **meter.** The hexameter line (a six-stress line) is the meter of **classical** Latin **epic**; while not imitated in that form for epic verse in English, some instances of the hexameter exist. See, for example, the last line of a Spenserian stanza, *Faerie Queene* 1.1.2: "O help thou my weake wit, and sharpen my dull tong" (vol. B, p. 253), or Yeats, "The Lake Isle of Innisfree," line 1: "I will arise and go now, and go to Innisfree" (vol. F, p. 215).

homily (Greek "discourse"): a **genre**. A sermon, to be preached in church; *Book of Homilies* (see vol. B, p. 165). Writers of literary fiction sometimes exploit the homily, or sermon, as in Chaucer, *The Pardoner's Tale* (see vol. A, p. 329).

homophone (Greek "same sound"): a **figure of speech**. A word that sounds identical to another word but has a different meaning ("bear" / "bare").

hyperbaton (Greek "overstepping"): a term of **syntax**. The rearrangement, or inversion, of the expected word order in a sentence or clause. Gray, "Elegy Written in a Country Churchyard," line 38: "If Memory o'er their tomb no trophies raise" (vol. C, p. 999). Poets can suspend the expected syntax over many lines, as in the first sentences of the *Canterbury Tales* (vol. A, p. 261) and of *Paradise Lost* (vol. B, p. 1495).

hyperbole (Greek "throwing over"): a **figure of thought**. Overstatement, exaggeration; Marvell, "To His Coy Mistress," lines 11–12: "My vegetable love should grow / Vaster than empires, and more slow" (see vol. B, p. 1347); Auden, "As I Walked Out One Evening," lines 9–12: "'I'll love you, dear, I'll love you / Till China and Africa meet / And the river jumps over the mountain / And the salmon sing in the street" (see vol. F, p. 813).

hypermetrical (adj.; Greek "over measured"): a term of **meter;** the word describes a breaking of the expected metrical pattern by at least one extra syllable.

hypotaxis, or **subordination** (respectively Greek and Latin "ordering under"): a term of **syntax**. The subordination, by the use of subordinate clauses, of different elements of a sentence to a single main verb. Milton, *Paradise Lost* 9.513–15: "As when a ship by skillful steersman wrought / Nigh river's mouth or foreland, where the wind / Veers oft, as oft so steers, and shifts her sail; So varied he" (vol. B, p. 1654). The contrary principle to **parataxis.**

iamb: a term of **rhythm**. The basic foot of English verse; two syllables following the rhythmic pattern of unstressed followed by stressed and producing a rising effect. Thus, for example, "Vermont."

imitation: the practice whereby writers strive ideally to reproduce and yet renew the **conventions** of an older form, often derived from **classical** civilization. Such a practice will be praised in periods of classicism (e.g., the eighteenth century) and repudiated in periods dominated by a model of inspiration (e.g., Romanticism).

irony (Greek "dissimulation"): a **figure of thought.** In broad usage, irony designates the result of inconsistency between a statement and a context that undermines the statement. "It's a beautiful day" is unironic if it's a beautiful day; if, however, the weather is terrible, then the inconsistency between statement and context is ironic. The effect is often amusing; the need to be ironic is sometimes produced by censorship of one kind or another. Strictly, irony is a subset of allegory: whereas allegory says one thing and means another, irony says one thing and means its opposite. For an extended example of irony, see Swift's "Modest Proposal." See also **dramatic irony.**

journal (French "daily"): a **genre.** A diary, or daily record of ephemeral experience, whose perspectives are concentrated on, and limited by, the experiences of single days. Thus Pepys, *Diary* (see vol. C, p. 86).

lai: a **genre.** A short narrative, often characterized by images of great intensity; a French term, and a form practiced by Marie de France (see vol. A, p. 160).

legend (Latin "requiring to be read"): a **genre.** A narrative of a celebrated, possibly historical, but mortal **protagonist.** To be distinguished from **myth.** Thus the "Arthurian legend" but the "myth of Proserpine."

lexical set: Words that habitually recur together (e.g., January, February, March, etc.; or red, white, and blue) form a lexical set.

litotes (from Greek "smooth"): a **figure of thought.** Strictly, understatement by denying the contrary; More, *Utopia:* "differences of no slight import" (see vol. B, p. 47). More loosely, understatement; Swift, "A Tale of a Tub": "Last week I saw a woman flayed, and you will hardly believe how much it altered her person for the worse" (see vol. C, p. 274). Stevie Smith, "Sunt Leones," lines 11–12: "And if the Christians felt a little blue— / Well people being eaten often do" (see vol. F, p. 729).

lullaby: a **genre.** A bedtime, sleep-inducing song for children, in simple and regular meter. Adapted by Auden, "Lullaby" (see vol. F, p. 809).

lyric (from Greek "lyre"): Initially meaning a song, "lyric" refers to a short poetic form, without restriction of meter, in which the expression of personal emotion, often by a voice in the first person, is given primacy over narrative sequence. Thus "The Wife's Lament" (see vol. A, p. 123); Yeats, "The Wild Swans at Coole" (see vol. F, p. 223).

masque: a **genre.** Costly entertainments of the Stuart court, involving dance, song, speech, and elaborate stage effects, in which courtiers themselves participated.

metaphor (Greek "carrying across," etymologically parallel to Latin "translation"): One of the most significant **figures of thought,** metaphor designates identification or implicit identification of one thing with another with which it is not literally identifiable. Blake, "London," lines 11–12: "And the hapless Soldier's sigh / Runs in blood down Palace walls" (see vol. D, p. 141).

meter: Verse (from Latin *versus,* turned) is distinguished from prose (from Latin *prorsus,* "straightforward") as a more compressed form of expression, shaped by metrical norms. **Meter** (Greek "measure") refers to the regularly recurring sound pattern of verse lines. The means of producing sound patterns across lines differ in different poetic traditions. Verse may be **quantitative,** or determined by the quantities of syllables (set patterns of long and short syllables), as in Latin and Greek poetry. It may be **syllabic,** determined by fixed numbers of syllables in the line, as in the verse of Romance languages (e.g., French and Italian). It may be **accentual,** determined by the number of accents, or stresses in the line, with variable numbers of syllables, as in Old English and some varieties of Middle English alliterative verse. Or it may be **accentual-syllabic,** determined by the numbers of accents, but possessing a regular pattern of stressed and unstressed syllables, so as to produce regular numbers of syllables per line. Since Chaucer, English verse has worked primarily within the many possibilities of accentual-syllabic meter. The unit of meter is the **foot.** In English verse the number of feet per line corresponds to the number of accents in a line. For the types and examples of different meters, see **monometer, dimeter, trimester, tetrameter, pentameter,** and **hexameter.** In the definitions below, "u" designates one unstressed syllable, and "/" one stressed syllable.

metonymy (Greek "change of name"): one of the most significant **figures of thought.** Using a word to **denote** another concept or other concepts, by virtue of habitual association. Thus "The Press," designating printed news media. Fictional names often work by associations of this kind. Closely related to **synecdoche.**

mimesis (Greek for "imitation"): A central function of literature and drama has been to provide a plausible imitation of the reality of the world beyond the literary work; mimesis is the representation and imitation of what is taken to be reality.

mise-en-abyme (French for "cast into the abyss"): Some works of art represent themselves in themselves; if they do so effectively, the represented artifact also represents itself, and so ad infinitum. The effect achieved is called *"mise-en-abyme."* Hoccleve's *Complaint*, for example, represents a depressed man reading about a depressed man. This sequence threatens to become a *mise-en-abyme.*

monometer (Greek "one measure"): a term of **meter.** An entire line with just one stress; *Sir Gawain and the Green Knight*, line 15, "most (u) grand (/)" (see vol. A, p. 204).

myth: a genre. The narrative of **protagonists** with, or subject to, superhuman powers. A myth expresses some profound foundational truth, often by accounting for the origin of natural phenomena. To be distinguished from **legend.** Thus the "Arthurian legend" but the "myth of Proserpine."

novel: an extremely flexible **genre** in both form and subject matter. Usually in prose, giving high priority to narration of events, with a certain expectation of length, novels are preponderantly rooted in a specific, and often complex, social world; sensitive to the realities of material life; and often focused on one **character** or a small circle of central characters. By contrast with chivalric **romance** (the main European narrative genre prior to the novel), novels tend to eschew the marvelous in favor of a recognizable social world and credible action. The novel's openness allows it to participate in all modes, and to be co-opted for a huge variety of subgenres. In English literature the novel dates from the late seventeenth century and has been astonishingly successful in appealing to a huge readership, particularly in the nineteenth and twentieth centuries. The English and Irish tradition of the novel includes, for example, Fielding, Austen, the Brontë sisters, Dickens, George Eliot, Conrad, Woolf, Lawrence, and Joyce, to name but a few very great exponents of the genre.

novella: a **genre.** A short **novel,** often characterized by imagistic intensity. Conrad, *Heart of Darkness* (see vol. F, p. 73).

occupatio (Latin "taking possession"): a **figure of thought.** Denying that one will discuss a subject while actually discussing it; also known as "praeteritio" (Latin "passing by"). See Chaucer, *Nun's Priest's Tale*, lines 414–32 (see vol. A, p. 353).

ode (Greek "song"): a **genre.** A **lyric** poem in elevated, or high style (see **register**), often addressed to a natural force, a person, or an abstract quality. The Pindaric ode in English is made up of **stanzas** of unequal length, while the Horatian ode has stanzas of equal length. For examples of both types, see, respectively, Wordsworth, "Ode: Intimations of Immortality" (vol. D, p. 348); and Marvell, "An Horatian Ode" (vol. B, p. 1356), or Keats, "Ode on Melancholy" (vol. D, p. 981). For a fuller discussion, see the headnote to Jonson's "Ode on Cary and Morison" (vol. B, p. 1102).

omniscient narrator (Latin "all-knowing narrator"): relevant to **point of view.** A narrator who, in the fiction of the narrative, has complete access to both the deeds and the thoughts of all **characters** in the narrative. Thus Thomas Hardy, "On the Western Circuit" (see vol. F, p. 36).

onomatopoeia (Greek "name making"): a **figure of speech.** Verbal sounds that imitate and evoke the sounds they denote. Hopkins, "Binsey Poplars," lines 10–12 (about some felled trees): "O if we but knew what we do / When we delve [dig] or hew— / Hack and rack the growing green!" (see vol. E, p. 598).

order: A story may be told in different narrative orders. A narrator might use the sequence of events as they happened, and thereby follow what **classical** rhetoricians called the *natural order*; alternatively, the narrator might reorder the sequence of events, beginning the narration either in the middle or at the end of the sequence of events, thereby following an *artificial order*. If a narrator begins in the middle of events, he or she is said to begin *in medias res* (Latin "in the middle of the matter"). For a brief discussion of these concepts, see Spenser, *Faerie Queene*, "A Letter of the Authors" (vol. B, p. 249). Modern narratology makes a related distinction, between *histoire* (French "story") for the natural order that readers mentally reconstruct, and *discours* (French, here "narration") for the narrative as presented. See also **plot** and **story.**

ottava rima: a **verse form.** An eight-line stanza form, rhyming abababcc, using **iambic pentameter;** Yeats, "Sailing to Byzantium" (see vol. F, p. 230). Derived from the Italian poet Boccaccio, an eight-line stanza was used by fifteenth-century English poets for inset passages (e.g., Christ's speech from the Cross in Lydgate's *Testament*, lines 754–897). The form in this rhyme scheme was used in English poetry for long narrative by, for example, Byron (*Don Juan*; see vol. D, p. 669).

oxymoron (Greek "sharp blunt"): a **figure of thought.** The conjunction of normally incompatible terms; Milton, *Paradise Lost* 1.63: "darkness visible" (see vol. B, p. 1497).

panegyric: a **genre.** Demonstrative, or epideictic (Greek "showing"), rhetoric was a branch of **classical** rhetoric. Its own two main branches were the rhetoric of praise on the one hand and of vituperation on the other. Panegyric, or eulogy (Greek "sweet speaking"), or encomium (plural *encomia*), is the term used to describe the speeches or writings of praise.

parable: a **genre.** A simple story designed to provoke, and often accompanied by, **allegorical** interpretation, most famously by Christ as reported in the Gospels.

paradox (Greek "contrary to received opinion"): a **figure of thought.** An apparent contradiction that requires thought to reveal an inner consistency. Chaucer, "Troilus's Song," line 12: "O sweete harm so quainte" (see vol. A, p. 362).

parataxis, or **coordination** (respectively Greek and Latin "ordering beside"): a term of **syntax.** The coordination, by the use of coordinating conjunctions, of different main clauses in a single sentence. Malory, *Morte Darthur*: "So Sir Lancelot departed and took his sword under his arm, and so he walked in his mantel, that noble knight, and put himself in great jeopardy" (see vol. A, p. 539). The opposite principle to **hypotaxis.**

parody: a work that uses the **conventions** of a particular genre with the aim of comically mocking a **topos,** a genre, or a particular exponent of a genre. Shakespeare parodies the topos of **blazon** in Sonnet 130 (see vol. B, p. 736).

pastoral (from Latin *pastor,* "shepherd"): a **genre.** Pastoral is set among shepherds, making often refined **allusion** to other apparently unconnected subjects (sometimes politics) from the potentially idyllic world of highly literary if illiterate shepherds. Pastoral is distinguished from **georgic** by representing recreational rural idleness, whereas the georgic offers instruction on how to manage rural labor. English writers had classical models in the *Idylls* of Theocritus in Greek and Virgil's *Eclogues* in Latin. Pastoral is also called bucolic (from the Greek word for "herdsman"). Thus Spenser, *Shepheardes Calender* (see vol. B, p. 241).

pathetic fallacy: the attribution of sentiment to natural phenomena, as if they were in sympathy with human feelings. Thus Milton, *Lycidas,* lines 146–47: "With cowslips wan that hang the pensive head, / And every flower that sad embroidery wears" (see vol. B, p. 1472). For critique of the practice, see Ruskin (who coined the term), "Of the Pathetic Fallacy" (vol. E, p. 386).

pentameter (Greek "five measure"): a term of **meter.** In English verse, a five-stress line. Between the late fourteenth and the nineteenth centuries, this meter, frequently employing an iambic rhythm, was the basic line of English verse. Chaucer, Shakespeare, Milton, and Wordsworth each, for example, deployed this very flexible line as their primary resource; Milton, *Paradise Lost* 1.128: "O Prince, O Chief of many thronèd Powers" (see vol. B, p. 1499).

performative: Verbal expressions have many different functions. They can, for example, be descriptive, or constative (if they make an argument), or performative, for example. A performative utterance is one that makes something happen in the world by virtue of its utterance. "I hereby sentence you to ten years in prison," if uttered in the appropriate circumstances, itself performs an action; it makes something happen in the world. By virtue of its performing an action, it is called a "performative." See also **speech act.**

peripeteia (Greek "turning about"): the sudden reversal of fortune (in both directions) in a dramatic work.

periphrasis (Greek "declaring around"): a **figure of thought.** Circumlocution; the use of many words to express what could be expressed in few or one; Sidney, *Astrophil and Stella* 39.1–4 (vol. B, p. 593).

persona (Latin "sound through"): originally the mask worn in the Roman theater to magnify an actor's voice; in literary discourse persona (plural *personae*) refers to the narrator or speaker of a text, whose voice is coherent and whose person need have no relation to the person of the actual author of a text. Eliot, "The Love Song of J. Alfred Prufrock" (see vol. F, p. 654).

personification, or **prosopopoeia** (Greek "person making"): a **figure of thought.** The attribution of human qualities to nonhuman forces or objects; Keats, "Ode on a Grecian Urn," lines 1–2: "Thou still unvanish'd bride of quietness, / Thou fosterchild of silence and slow time" (see vol. D, p. 979).

plot: the sequence of events in a story as narrated, as distinct from **story,** which refers to the sequence of events as we reconstruct them from the plot. See also **order.**

point of view: All of the many kinds of writing involve a point of view from which a text is, or seems to be, generated. The presence of such a point of view may be powerful and explicit, as in many novels, or deliberately invisible, as in much drama. In some genres, such as the **novel,** the narrator does not necessarily tell the story from a position we can predict; that is, the needs of a particular story, not the **conventions** of the genre, determine the narrator's position. In other genres, the narrator's position is fixed by convention; in certain kinds of love poetry, for example, the narrating voice is always that of a suffering lover. Not only does the point of view significantly inform the style of a work, but it also informs the structure of that work.

protagonist (Greek "first actor"): the hero or heroine of a drama or narrative.

pun: a figure of thought. A sometimes irresolvable doubleness of meaning in a single word or expression; Shakespeare, Sonnet 135, line 1: "Whoever hath her wish, thou hast thy *Will*" (see vol. B, p. 736).

quatrain: a verse form. A stanza of four lines, usually rhyming abcb, abab, or abba. Of many possible examples, see Crashaw, "On the Wounds of Our Crucified Lord" (see vol. B, p. 1296).

refrain: usually a single line repeated as the last line of consecutive stanzas, sometimes with subtly different wording and ideally with subtly different meaning as the poem progresses. See, for example, Wyatt, "Blame not my lute" (see vol. B, p. 128).

register: The register of a word is its stylistic level, which can be distinguished by degree of technicality but also by degree of formality. We choose our words from different registers according to context, that is, audience and/or environment. Thus a chemist in a laboratory will say "sodium chloride," a cook in a kitchen "salt." A formal register designates the kind of language used in polite society (e.g., "Mr. President"), while an informal or colloquial register is used in less formal or more relaxed social situations (e.g., "the boss"). In **classical** and medieval rhetoric, these registers of formality were called *high style* and *low style*. A *middle style* was defined as the style fit for narrative, not drawing attention to itself.

rhetoric: the art of verbal persuasion. **Classical** rhetoricians distinguished three areas of rhetoric: the forensic, to be used in law courts; the deliberative, to be used in political or philosophical deliberations; and the demonstrative, or epideictic, to be used for the purposes of public praise or blame. Rhetorical manuals covered all the skills required of a speaker, from the management of style and structure to delivery. These manuals powerfully influenced the theory of poetics as a separate branch of verbal practice, particularly in the matter of style.

rhyme: a figure of speech. The repetition of identical vowel sounds in stressed syllables whose initial consonants differ ("dead" / "head"). In poetry, rhyme often links the end of one line with another. *Masculine rhyme*: full rhyme on the final syllable of the line ("decays" / "days"). *Feminine rhyme*: full rhyme on syllables that are followed by unaccented syllables ("fountains" / "mountains"). *Internal rhyme*: full rhyme within a single line; Coleridge, *The Rime of the Ancient Mariner*, line 7: "The guests are met, the feast is set" (see vol. D, p. 448). *Rhyme riche*: rhyming on **homophones**; Chaucer, *General Prologue*, lines 17–18: "seeke" / "seke." *Off rhyme* (also known as *half rhyme, near rhyme*, or *slant rhyme*): differs from perfect rhyme in changing the vowel sound and/or the concluding consonants expected of perfect rhyme; Byron, "They say that Hope is Happiness," lines 5–7: "most" / "lost." *Pararhyme*: stressed vowel sounds differ but are flanked by identical or similar consonants; Owen, "Miners," lines 9–11: "simmer" / "summer" (see vol. F, p. 163).

rhyme royal: a verse form. A stanza of seven **iambic pentameter** lines, rhyming ababbcc; first introduced by Chaucer and called "royal" because the form was used by James I of Scotland for his *Kingis Quair* in the early fifteenth century. Chaucer, "Troilus's Song" (see vol. A, p. 362).

rhythm: Rhythm is not absolutely distinguishable from **meter.** One way of making a clear distinction between these terms is to say that rhythm (from the Greek "to flow") denotes the patterns of sound within the feet of verse lines and the combination of those feet. Very often a particular meter will raise expectations that a given rhythm will be used regularly through a whole line or a whole poem. Thus in English verse the pentameter regularly uses an iambic rhythm. Rhythm, however, is much more fluid than meter, and many lines within the same poem using a single meter will frequently exploit different rhythmic possibilities. For examples of different rhythms, see **iamb, trochee, anapest, spondee,** and **dactyl.**

romance: a **genre.** From the twelfth to the sixteenth century, the main form of European narrative, in either verse or prose, was that of chivalric romance. Romance, like the later **novel,** is a very fluid genre, but romances are often characterized by (i) a tripartite structure of social integration, followed by disintegration, involving moral tests and often marvelous events, itself the prelude to reintegration in a happy ending, frequently of marriage; and (ii) aristocratic social milieux. Thus *Sir Gawain and the Green Knight* (see vol. A, p. 204); Spenser's (unfinished) *Faerie Queene* (vol. B, p. 249). The immensely popular, fertile genre was absorbed, in both domesticated and undomesticated form, by the novel. For an adaptation of romance, see Chaucer, *Wife of Bath's Tale* (vol. A, p. 300).

sarcasm (Greek "flesh tearing"): a **figure of thought.** A wounding expression, often expressed ironically; Boswell, *Life of Johnson*: Johnson [asked if any man of the modern age could have written the **epic** poem *Fingal*] replied, "Yes, Sir, many men, many women, and many children" (see vol. C, p. 844).

satire (Latin for "a bowl of mixed fruits"): a **genre.** In Roman literature (e.g., Juvenal), the communication, in the form of a letter between equals, complaining of the ills of contemporary society. The genre in this form is characterized by a first-person narrator exasperated by social ills; the letter form; a high frequency of contemporary reference; and the use of invective in **low-style** language. Pope practices the genre thus in the *Epistle to Dr. Arbuthnot* (see vol. C, p. 543). Wyatt's "Mine own John Poins" (see vol. B, p. 131) draws ultimately on a gentler, Horatian model of the genre.

satiric mode: Works in a very large variety of genres are devoted to the more or less savage attack on social ills. Thus Swift's travel narrative *Gulliver's Travels* (see vol. C, p. 279), his **essay** "A Modest Proposal" (vol. C, p. 454), Pope's mock-**epic** *The Dunciad* (vol. C, p. 555), and Gay's *Beggar's Opera* (vol. C, p. 659), to look no further than the eighteenth century, are all within a satiric mode.

scene: a subdivision of an **act,** itself a subdivision of a dramatic performance and/or text. The action of a scene usually occurs in one place.

sensibility (from Latin, "capable of being perceived by the senses"): as a literary term, an eighteenth-century concept derived from moral philosophy that stressed the social importance of fellow feeling and particularly of sympathy in social relations. The concept generated a literature of "sensibility," such as the sentimental **novel** (the most famous of which was Goethe's *Sorrows of the Young Werther* [1774]), or sentimental poetry, such as Cowper's passage on the stricken deer in *The Task* (see vol. C, p. 1024).

short story: a **genre.** Generically similar to, though shorter and more concentrated than, the **novel**; often published as part of a collection. Thus Mansfield, "The Daughters of the Late Colonel" (see vol. F, p. 698).

simile (Latin "like"): a **figure of thought.** Comparison, usually using the word "like" or "as," of one thing with another so as to produce sometimes surprising analogies. Donne, "The Storm," lines 29–30: "Sooner than you read this line did the gale, / Like shot, not feared till felt, our sails assail." Frequently used, in extended form, in **epic** poetry; Milton, *Paradise Lost* 1.338–46 (see vol. B, p. 1504).

soliloquy (Latin "single speaking"): a **topos** of drama, in which a **character,** alone or thinking to be alone on stage, speaks so as to give the audience access to his or her private thoughts. Thus Viola's soliloquy in Shakespeare, *Twelfth Night* 2.2.17–41 (vol. B, p. 758).

sonnet: a verse form. A form combining a variable number of units of rhymed lines to produce a fourteen-line poem, usually in rhyming **iambic pentameter** lines. In English there are two principal varieties: the Petrarchan sonnet, formed by an octave (an eight-line stanza, often broken into two **quatrains** having the same rhyme scheme, typically abba abba) and a sestet (a six-line stanza, typically cdecde or cdcdcd); and the Shakespearean sonnet, formed by three quatrains (abab cdcd efef) and a **couplet** (gg). The declaration of a sonnet can take a sharp turn, or "volta," often at the decisive formal shift from octave to sestet in the Petrarchan sonnet, or in the final couplet of a Shakespearean sonnet, introducing a trenchant counterstatement. Derived from Italian poetry, and especially from the poetry of Petrarch, the sonnet was first introduced to English poetry by Wyatt, and initially used principally for the expression of unrequited erotic love, though later poets used the form for many other purposes. See Wyatt, "Whoso list to hunt" (vol. B, p. 121); Sidney, *Astrophil and Stella* (vol. B, p. 586); Shakespeare, *Sonnets* (vol. B, p. 723); Wordsworth, "London, 1802" (vol. D, p. 357); McKay, "If We Must Die" (vol. F, p. 854); Heaney, "Clearances" (vol. F, p. 1104).

speech act: Words and deeds are often distinguished, but words are often (perhaps always) themselves deeds. Utterances can perform different speech acts, such as promising, declaring, casting a spell, encouraging, persuading, denying, lying, and so on. See also **performative.**

Spenserian stanza: a verse form. The stanza developed by Spenser for *The Faerie Queene*; nine **iambic** lines, the first eight of which are **pentameters,** followed by one **hexameter,** rhyming ababbcbcc. See also, for example, Shelley, *Adonais* (vol. D, p. 856), and Keats, *The Eve of St. Agnes* (vol. D, p. 961).

spondee: a term of **meter.** A two-syllable foot following the rhythmic pattern, in English verse, of two stressed syllables. Thus, for example, "Utah."

stanza (Italian "room"): groupings of two or more lines, though "stanza" is usually reserved for groupings of at least four lines. Stanzas are often joined by rhyme, often in sequence, where each group shares the same metrical pattern and, when rhymed, rhyme scheme. Stanzas can themselves be arranged into larger groupings. Poets often invent new **verse forms,** or they may work within established forms.

story: a narrative's sequence of events, which we reconstruct from those events as they have been recounted by the narrator (i.e., the **plot**). See also **order.**

stream of consciousness: usually a **first-person** narrative that seems to give the reader access to the narrator's mind as it perceives or reflects on events, prior to organizing those perceptions into a coherent narrative. Thus (though generated from a **third-person** narrative) Joyce, *Ulysses,* "Penelope" (see vol. F, p. 604).

style (from Latin for "writing instrument"): In literary works the manner in which something is expressed contributes substantially to its meaning. The expressions "sun," "mass of helium at the center of the solar system," "heaven's golden orb" all designate "sun," but do so in different manners, or styles, which produce different meanings. The manner of a literary work is its "style," the effect of which is its "tone." We often can intuit the tone of a text; from that intuition of tone we can analyze the stylistic resources by which it was produced. We can analyze the style of literary works through consideration of different elements of style; for example, **diction, figures of thought, figures of speech, meter and rhythm, verse form, syntax, point of view.**

sublime: As a concept generating a literary movement, the sublime refers to the realm of experience beyond the measurable, and so beyond the rational, produced especially by the terrors and grandeur of natural phenomena. Derived especially from the first-century Greek treatise *On the Sublime*, sometimes attributed to Longinus, the notion of the sublime was in the later eighteenth century a spur to Romanticism.

syllable: the smallest unit of sound in a pronounced word. The syllable that receives the greatest stress is called the *tonic* syllable.

symbol (Greek "token"): a **figure of thought.** Something that stands for something else, and yet seems necessarily to evoke that other thing. In Neoplatonic, and there-fore Romantic, theory, to be distinguished from **allegory** thus: whereas allegory involves connections between vehicle and tenor agreed by convention or made explicit, the meanings of a symbol are supposedly inherent to it. For discussion, see Coleridge, "On Symbol and Allegory" (vol. D, p. 507).

synecdoche (Greek "to take with something else"): a **figure of thought.** Using a part to express the whole, or vice versa; e.g., "all hands on deck." Closely related to **metonymy.**

syntax (Greek "ordering with"): Syntax designates the rules by which sentences are constructed in a given language. Discussion of meter is impossible without some reference to syntax, since the overall effect of a poem is, in part, always the product of a subtle balance of meter and sentence construction. Syntax is also essential to the understanding of prose style, since prose writers, deprived of the full shaping possibilities of meter, rely all the more heavily on syntactic resources. A working command of syntactical practice requires an understanding of the parts of speech (nouns, verbs, adjectives, adverbs, conjunctions, pronouns, prepositions, and inter-jections), since writers exploit syntactic possibilities by using particular combina-tions and concentrations of the parts of speech.

taste (from Italian "touch"): Although medieval monastic traditions used eating and tasting as a metaphor for reading, the concept of taste as a personal ideal to be cultivated by, and applied to, the appreciation and judgment of works of art in gen-eral was developed in the eighteenth century.

tercet: a **verse form.** A stanza or group of three lines, used in larger forms such as **terza rima,** the **Petrarchan sonnet,** and the **villanelle.**

terza rima: a **verse form.** A sequence of rhymed **tercets** linked by rhyme thus: aba bcb cdc, etc. first used extensively by Dante in *The Divine Comedy,* the form was adapted in English **iambic pentameters** by Wyatt and revived in the nineteenth century. See Wyatt, "Mine own John Poins" (vol. B, p. 131); Shelley, "Ode to the West Wind" (vol. D, p. 806); and Morris, "The Defence of Guinevere" (vol. E, p. 560). For modern adap-tations see Eliot, lines 78–149 (though unrhymed) of "Little Gidding" (vol. F, pp. 679–81); Heaney, "Station Island" (vol. F, p. 1102); Walcott, *Omeros* (vol. F, p. 947).

tetrameter (Greek "four measure"): a term of **meter.** A line with four stresses. Coleridge, *Christabel*, line 31: "She stole along, she nothing spoke" (see vol. D, p. 468).

theme (Greek "proposition"): In literary criticism the term designates what the work is about; the theme is the concept that unifies a given work of literature.

third-person narration: relevant to **point of view.** A narration in which the narrator recounts a narrative of **characters** referred to explicitly or implicitly by third-person pronouns ("he," she," etc.), without the limitation of a **first-person narration.** Thus Johnson, *The History of Rasselas.*

topographical poem (Greek "place writing"): a **genre.** A poem devoted to the meditative description of particular places. Thus Gray, "Ode on a Distant Prospect of Eton College" (see vol. C, p. 994).

topos (Greek "place," plural *topoi*): a commonplace in the content of a given kind of literature. Originally, in **classical** rhetoric, the topoi were tried-and-tested stimuli to literary invention: lists of standard headings under which a subject might be investigated. In medieval narrative poems, for example, it was commonplace to begin with a description of spring. Writers did, of course, render the commonplace uncommon, as in Chaucer's spring scene at the opening of *The Canterbury Tales* (see vol. A, p. 261).

tradition (from Latin "passing on"): A literary tradition is whatever is passed on or revived from the past in a single literary culture, or drawn from others to enrich a writer's culture. "Tradition" is fluid in reference, ranging from small to large referents: thus it may refer to a relatively small aspect of texts (e.g., the tradition of **iambic pentameter**), or it may, at the other extreme, refer to the body of texts that constitute a **canon.**

tragedy: a **genre.** A dramatic representation of the fall of kings or nobles, beginning in happiness and ending in catastrophe. Later transferred to other social milieux. The opposite of **comedy;** thus Shakespeare, *Othello* (see vol. B, p. 806).

tragic mode: Many genres (**epic** poetry, **legend**ary chronicles, **tragedy,** the **novel**) either do or can participate in a tragic mode, by representing the fall of noble **protagonists** and the irreparable ravages of human society and history.

tragicomedy: a **genre.** A play in which potentially tragic events turn out to have a happy, or **comic,** ending. Thus Shakespeare, *Measure for Measure.*

translation (Latin "carrying across"): the rendering of a text written in one language into another.

trimeter (Greek "three measure"): a term of **meter.** A line with three stresses. Herbert, "Discipline," line 1: "Throw away thy rod" (see vol. B, p. 1274).

triplet: a **verse form.** A **tercet** rhyming on the same sound. Pope inserts triplets among heroic **couplets** to emphasize a particular thought; see *Essay on Criticism,* 315–17 (vol. C, p. 497).

trochee: a term of **rhythm.** A two-syllable foot following the pattern, in English verse, of stressed followed by unstressed syllable, producing a falling effect. Thus, for example, "Texas."

type (Greek "impression, figure"): a **figure of thought.** In Christian allegorical interpretation of the Old Testament, pre-Christian figures were regarded as "types," or foreshadowings, of Christ or the Christian dispensation. *Typology* has been the source of much visual and literary art in which the parallelisms between old and new are extended to nonbiblical figures; thus the virtuous plowman in *Piers Plowman* becomes a type of Christ.

unities: According to a theory supposedly derived from Aristotle's *Poetics,* the events represented in a play should have unity of time, place, and action: that the play take up no more time than the time of the play, or at most a day; that the space of action should be within a single city; and that there should be no subplot. See Johnson, *The Preface to Shakespeare* (vol. C, p. 807).

vernacular (from Latin *verna*, "servant"): the language of the people, as distinguished from learned and arcane languages. From the later Middle Ages especially, the "vernacular" languages and literatures of Europe distinguished themselves from the learned languages and literatures of Latin, Greek, and Hebrew.

verse form: The terms related to **meter** and **rhythm** describe the shape of individual lines. Lines of verse are combined to produce larger groupings, called verse forms. These larger groupings are in the first instance **stanzas.** The combination of a certain meter and stanza shape constitutes the verse form, of which there are many standard kinds.

villanelle: a **verse form.** A fixed form of usually five **tercets** and a **quatrain** employing only two rhyme sounds altogether, rhyming aba for the tercets and abaa for the quatrain, with a complex pattern of two **refrains.** Derived from a French fixed form. Thomas, "Do Not Go Gentle into That Good Night" (see vol. F, p. 833).

wit: Originally a synonym for "reason" in Old and Middle English, "wit" became a literary ideal in the Renaissance as brilliant play of the full range of mental resources. For eighteenth-century writers, the notion necessarily involved pleasing expression, as in Pope's definition of true wit as "Nature to advantage dressed, / What oft was thought, but ne'er so well expressed" (*Essay on Criticism*, lines 297–98; see vol. C, p. 496–97). See also Johnson, *Lives of the Poets*, "Cowley," on "metaphysical wit" (see vol. C, p. 817). Romantic theory of the imagination deprived wit of its full range of apprehension, whence the word came to be restricted to its modern sense, as the clever play of mind that produces laughter.

zeugma (Greek "a yoking"): a **figure of thought.** A figure whereby one word applies to two or more words in a sentence, and in which the applications are surprising, either because one is unusual, or because the applications are made in very different ways; Pope, *Rape of the Lock* 3.7–8, in which the word "take" is used in two senses: "Here thou, great Anna! whom three realms obey, / Dost sometimes counsel take— and sometimes tea" (see vol. C, p. 515).

B: Publishing History, Censorship

By the time we read texts in published books, they have already been treated—that is, changed by authors, editors, and printers—in many ways. Although there are differences across history, in each period literary works are subject to pressures of many kinds, which apply before, while, and after an author writes. The pressures might be financial, as in the relations of author and patron; commercial, as in the marketing of books; and legal, as in, during some periods, the negotiation through official and unofficial censorship. In addition, texts in all periods undergo technological processes, as they move from the material forms in which an author produced them to the forms in which they are presented to readers. Some of the terms below designate important material forms in which books were produced, disseminated, and surveyed across the historical span of this anthology. Others designate the skills developed to understand these processes. The anthology's introductions to individual periods discuss the particular forms these phenomena took in different eras.

bookseller: In England, and particularly in London, commercial bookmaking and -selling enterprises came into being in the early fourteenth century. These were loose organizations of artisans who usually lived in the same neighborhoods (around St. Paul's Cathedral in London). A bookseller or dealer would coordinate the production of hand-copied books for wealthy patrons (see **patronage**), who would order books to be custom-made. After the introduction of **printing** in the late fifteenth century, authors generally sold the rights to their work to booksellers, without any further **royalties**. Booksellers, who often had their own shops, belonged to the **Stationers' Company**. This system lasted into the eighteenth century. In 1710, however, authors were for the first time granted **copyright,** which tipped the commercial balance in their favor, against booksellers.

censorship: The term applies to any mechanism for restricting what can be published. Historically, the reasons for imposing censorship are heresy, sedition, blasphemy, libel, or obscenity. External censorship is imposed by institutions having legislative sanctions at their disposal. Thus the pre-Reformation Church imposed the Constitutions of Archbishop Arundel of 1409, aimed at repressing the Lollard "heresy." After the Reformation, some key events in the history of censorship are as follows: 1547, when anti-Lollard legislation and legislation made by Henry VIII concerning treason by writing (1534) were abolished; the Licensing Order of 1643, which legislated that works be licensed, through the Stationers' Company, prior to publication; and 1695, when the last such Act stipulating prepublication licensing lapsed. Postpublication censorship continued in different periods for different reasons. Thus, for example, British publication of D. H. Lawrence's *Lady Chatterley's Lover* (1928) was obstructed (though unsuccessfully) in 1960, under the Obscene Publications Act of 1959. Censorship can also be international: although not published in Iran, Salman Rushdie's *Satanic Verses* (1988) was censored in that country, where the leader, Ayatollah Ruhollah Khomeini, proclaimed a fatwa (religious decree) promising the author's execution. Very often censorship is not imposed externally, however: authors or publishers can censor work in anticipation of what will incur the wrath of readers or the penalties of the law. Victorian and Edwardian publishers of **novels,** for example, urged authors to remove potentially offensive material, especially for serial publication in popular magazines.

codex: the physical format of most modern books and medieval manuscripts, consisting of a series of separate leaves gathered into quires and bound together, often with a cover. In late antiquity, the codex largely replaced the scroll, the standard form of written documents in Roman culture.

copy text: the particular text of a work used by a textual editor as the basis of an edition of that work.

copyright: the legal protection afforded to authors for control of their work's publication, in an attempt to ensure due financial reward. Some key dates in the history of copyright in the United Kingdom are as follows: 1710, when a statute gave authors the exclusive right to publish their work for fourteen years, and fourteen years more if the author were still alive when the first term had expired; 1842, when the period of authorial control was extended to forty-two years; and 1911, when the term was extended yet further, to fifty years after the author's death. In 1995 the period of protection was harmonized with the laws in other European countries to be the life of the author plus seventy years. In the United States no works first published before 1923 are in copyright. Works published since 1978 are, as in the United Kingdom, protected for the life of the author plus seventy years.

folio: the leaf formed by both sides of a single page. Each folio has two sides: a *recto* (the front side of the leaf, on the right side of a double-page spread in an open codex), and a *verso* (the back side of the leaf, on the left side of a double-page spread). Modern book pagination follows the pattern 1, 2, 3, 4, while medieval manuscript pagination follows the pattern 1r, 1v, 2r, 2v. "Folio" can also designate the size of a printed book. Books come in different shapes, depending originally on the number of times a standard sheet of paper is folded. One fold produces a large volume, a *folio* book; two folds produce a *quarto*, four an *octavo*, and six a very small *duodecimo*. Generally speaking, the larger the book, the grander and more expensive. Shakespeare's plays were, for example, first printed in quartos, but were gathered into a folio edition in 1623.

foul papers: versions of a work before an author has produced, if she or he has, a final copy (a "fair copy") with all corrections removed.

incunabulum (plural "incunabula"): any printed book produced in Europe before 1501. Famous incunabula include the Gutenberg Bible, printed in 1455.

manuscript (Latin, "written by hand"): Any text written physically by hand is a manuscript. Before the introduction of **printing** with moveable type in 1476, all texts in England were produced and reproduced by hand, in manuscript. This is an extremely labor-intensive task, using expensive materials (e.g., **vellum,** or **parchment**); the cost of books produced thereby was, accordingly, very high. Even after the introduction of printing, many texts continued to be produced in manuscript. This is obviously true of letters, for example, but until the eighteenth century, poetry written within aristocratic circles was often transmitted in manuscript copies.

paleography (Greek "ancient writing"): the art of deciphering, describing, and dating forms of handwriting.

parchment: animal skin, used as the material for handwritten books before the introduction of paper. See also **vellum.**

patronage, patron (Latin "protector"): Many technological, legal, and commercial supports were necessary before professional authorship became possible. Although some playwrights (e.g., Shakespeare) made a living by writing for the theater, other authors needed, principally, the large-scale reproductive capacities of **printing** and the security of **copyright** to make a living from writing. Before these conditions obtained, many authors had another main occupation, and most authors had to rely on patronage. In different periods, institutions or individuals offered material support, or patronage, to authors. Thus in Anglo-Saxon England, monasteries afforded the conditions of writing to monastic authors. Between the twelfth and the seventeenth centuries, the main source of patronage was the royal court. Authors offered patrons prestige and ideological support in return for financial support. Even as the conditions of professional authorship came into being at the beginning of the eighteenth century, older forms of direct patronage were not altogether displaced until the middle of the century.

periodical: Whereas journalism, strictly, applies to daily writing (from French *jour*, "day"), periodical writing appears at larger, but still frequent, intervals, characteristically in the form of the **essay.** Periodicals were developed especially in the eighteenth century.

printing: Printing, or the mechanical reproduction of books using moveable type, was invented in Germany in the mid-fifteenth century by Johannes Gutenberg; it quickly spread throughout Europe. William Caxton brought printing into England from the Low Countries in 1476. Much greater powers of reproduction at much lower prices transformed every aspect of literary culture.

publisher: the person or company responsible for the commissioning and publicizing of printed matter. In the early period of **printing,** publisher, printer, and bookseller were often the same person. This trend continued in the ascendancy of the **Stationers' Company,** between the middle of the sixteenth and the end of the seventeenth centuries. Toward the end of the seventeenth century, these three functions began to separate, leading to their modern distinctions.

quire: When medieval manuscripts were assembled, a few loose sheets of parchment or paper would first be folded together and sewn along the fold. This formed a quire (also known as a "gathering" or "signature"). Folded in this way, four large sheets of parchment would produce eight smaller manuscript leaves. Multiple quires could then be bound together to form a codex.

royalties: an agreed-upon proportion of the price of each copy of a work sold, paid by the publisher to the author, or an agreed-upon fee paid to the playwright for each performance of a play.

scribe: In **manuscript** culture, the scribe is the copyist who reproduces a text by hand.

scriptorium (plural "scriptoria"): a place for producing written documents and manuscripts.

serial publication: generally referring to the practice, especially common in the nineteenth century, of publishing novels a few chapters at a time, in periodicals.

Stationers' Company: The Stationers' Company was an English guild incorporating various tradesmen, including printers, publishers, and booksellers, skilled in the production and selling of books. It was formed in 1403, received its royal charter in 1557, and served as a means both of producing and of regulating books. Authors would sell the manuscripts of their books to individual stationers, who incurred the risks and took the profits of producing and selling the books. The stationers entered their rights over given books in the Stationers' Register. They also regulated the book trade and held their monopoly by licensing books and by being empowered to seize unauthorized books and imprison resisters. This system of licensing broke down in the social unrest of the Civil War and Interregnum (1640–60), and it ended in 1695. Even after the end of licensing, the Stationers' Company continued to be an intrinsic part of the **copyright** process, since the 1710 copyright statute directed that copyright had to be registered at Stationers' Hall.

subscription: An eighteenth-century system of bookselling somewhere between direct **patronage** and impersonal sales. A subscriber paid half the cost of a book before publication and half on delivery. The author received these payments directly. The subscriber's name appeared in the prefatory pages.

textual criticism: Works in all periods often exist in many subtly or not so subtly different forms. This is especially true with regard to manuscript textual reproduction, but it also applies to printed texts. Textual criticism is the art, developed from the fifteenth century in Italy but raised to new levels of sophistication from the eighteenth century, of deciphering different historical states of texts. This art involves the analysis of textual **variants,** often with the aim of distinguishing authorial from scribal forms.

variants: differences that appear among different manuscripts or printed editions of the same text.

vellum: animal skin, used as the material for handwritten books before the introduction of paper. See also **parchment.**

watermark: the trademark of a paper manufacturer, impressed into the paper but largely invisible unless held up to light.

Geographic Nomenclature

The British Isles refers to the prominent group of islands off the northwest coast of Europe, especially to the two largest, **Great Britain** and **Ireland**. At present these comprise two sovereign states: **the Republic of Ireland**, and **the United Kingdom of Great Britain and Northern Ireland**—known for short as the **United Kingdom** or the **U.K.** Most of the smaller islands are part of the **U.K.** but a few, like the **Isle of Man** and the tiny **Channel Islands,** are largely independent. The **U.K.** is often loosely referred to as "Britain" or "Great Britain" and is sometimes called simply, if inaccurately, "England." For obvious reasons, the latter usage is rarely heard among the inhabitants of the other countries of the U.K.—**Scotland, Wales,** and **Northern Ireland** (sometimes called **Ulster**). England is by far the most populous part of the kingdom, as well as the seat of its capital, London.

From the first to the fifth century C.E. most of what is now **England** and **Wales** was a province of the Roman Empire called **Britain** (in Latin, **Britannia**). After the fall of Rome, much of the island was invaded and settled by peoples from northern Germany and Denmark speaking what we now call Old English. These peoples are collectively known as the Anglo-Saxons, and the word **England** is related to the first element of their name. By the time of the Norman Conquest (1066) most of the kingdoms founded by the Anglo-Saxons and subsequent Viking invaders had coalesced into the kingdom of **England,** which, in the latter Middle Ages, conquered and largely absorbed the neighboring Celtic kingdom of **Wales.** In 1603 James VI of **Scotland** inherited the island's other throne as James I of **England,** and for the next hundred years—except for the two decades of Puritan rule—**Scotland** (both its English-speaking **Lowlands** and its Gaelic-speaking **Highlands**) and **England** (with **Wales**) were two kingdoms under a single king. In 1707 the Act of Union welded them together as **the United Kingdom of Great Britain. Ireland,** where English rule had begun in the twelfth century and been tightened in the sixteenth, was incorporated by the 1800–1801 Act of Union into **the United Kingdom of Great Britain and Ireland.** With the division of Ireland and the establishment of **the Irish Free State** after World War I, this name was modified to its present form, and in 1949 **the Irish Free State** became **the Republic of Ireland,** or **Éire.** In 1999 **Scotland** elected a separate parliament it had relinquished in 1707, and **Wales** elected an assembly it lost in 1409; neither Scotland nor Wales ceased to be part of the **United Kingdom.**

The British Isles are further divided into counties, which in **Great Britain** are also known as shires. This word, with its vowel shortened in pronunciation, forms the suffix in the names of many counties, such as **Yorkshire, Wiltshire, Somersetshire.**

The Latin names **Britannia (Britain), Caledonia (Scotland),** and **Hibernia (Ireland)** are sometimes used in poetic diction; so too is **Britain's** ancient Celtic name, **Albion.** Because of its accidental resemblance to *albus* (Latin for "white"), **Albion** is especially associated with the chalk cliffs that seem to gird much of the English coast like defensive walls.

The British Empire took its name from **the British Isles** because it was created not only by the **English** but also by the **Irish, Scots,** and **Welsh,** as well as by civilians and servicemen from other constituent countries of the empire. Some of the empire's **overseas colonies,** or **crown colonies,** were populated largely by settlers of European origin and their descendants. These predominantly white **settler colonies,** such as **Canada, Australia,** and **New Zealand,** were allowed significant self-government in the nineteenth century and recognized as **dominions** in the early twentieth century. The **white dominions** became members of **the Commonwealth of Nations**, also called **the Commonwealth, the British Commonwealth**, and **"the Old Commonwealth"** at different times, an association of sovereign states under the symbolic leadership of the British monarch.

Other **overseas colonies** of the empire had mostly indigenous populations (or, in the Caribbean, the descendants of imported slaves, indentured servants, and others). These **colonies** were granted political independence after World War II, later than the **dominions**, and have often been referred to since as **postcolonial** nations. In South and Southeast Asia, **India** and **Pakistan** gained independence in 1947, followed by other countries including **Sri Lanka** (formerly **Ceylon**), **Burma** (now **Myanmar**), **Malaya** (now **Malaysia**), and **Singapore**. In West and East Africa, the **Gold Coast** was decolonized as **Ghana** in 1957, **Nigeria** in 1960, **Sierra Leone** in 1961, **Uganda** in 1962, **Kenya** in 1963, and so forth, while in southern Africa, the white minority government of **South Africa** was already independent in 1931, though majority rule did not come until 1994. In the Caribbean, **Jamaica** and **Trinidad and Tobago** won independence in 1962, followed by **Barbados** in 1966, and other islands of the British West Indies in the 1970s and '80s. Other regions with nations emerging out of British colonial rule included Central America (**British Honduras**, now **Belize**), South America (**British Guiana**, now **Guyana**), the Pacific islands (**Fiji**), and Europe (**Cyprus, Malta**). After decolonization, many of these nations chose to remain within a newly conceived **Commonwealth** and are sometimes referred to as "**New Commonwealth**" countries. Some nations, such as **Ireland, Pakistan**, and **South Africa**, withdrew from the **Commonwealth**, though **South Africa** and **Pakistan** eventually rejoined, and others, such as **Burma** (now **Myanmar**), gained independence outside the **Commonwealth**. Britain's last major overseas colony, **Hong Kong**, was returned to Chinese sovereignty in 1997, but while Britain retains only a handful of dependent territories, such as **Bermuda** and **Montserrat**, the scope of the **Commonwealth** remains vast, with 30 percent of the world's population.

British Money

One of the most dramatic changes to the system of British money came in 1971. In the system previously in place, the pound consisted of 20 shillings, each containing 12 pence, making 240 pence to the pound. Since 1971, British money has been calculated on the decimal system, with 100 pence to the pound. Britons' experience of paper money did not change very drastically: as before, 5- and 10-pound notes constitute the majority of bills passing through their hands (in addition, 20- and 50- pound notes have been added). But the shift necessitated a whole new way of thinking about and exchanging coins and marked the demise of the shilling, one of the fundamental units of British monetary history. Many other coins, still frequently encountered in literature, had already passed. These include the groat, worth 4 pence (the word "groat" is often used to signify a trifling sum); the angel (which depicted the archangel Michael triumphing over a dragon), valued at 10 shillings; the mark, worth in its day two-thirds of a pound or 13 shillings 4 pence; and the sovereign, a gold coin initially worth 22 shillings 6 pence, later valued at 1 pound, last circulated in 1932. One prominent older coin, the guinea, was worth a pound and a shilling; though it has not been minted since 1813, a very few quality items or prestige awards (like the purse in a horse race) may still be quoted in guineas. (The table below includes some other well-known, obsolete coins.) Colloquially, a pound was (and is) called a quid; a shilling a bob; sixpence, a tanner; a copper could refer to a penny, a half-penny, or a farthing (¼ penny).

Old Currency	New Currency
1 pound note	1 pound coin (or note in Scotland)
10 shilling (half-pound note)	50 pence
5 shilling (crown)	
2½ shilling (half crown)	20 pence
2 shilling (florin)	10 pence
1 shilling	5 pence
6 pence	
2½ pence	1 penny
2 pence	
1 penny	
½ penny	
¼ penny (farthing)	

Throughout its tenure as a member of the European Union, Britain contemplated but did not make the change to the EU's common currency, the Euro. Many Britons strongly identify their country with its rich commercial history and tend to view their currency patriotically as a national symbol. Now, with the planned withdrawal of the United Kingdom from the EU, the pound seems here to stay.

Even more challenging than sorting out the values of obsolete coins is calculating for any given period the purchasing power of money, which fluctuates over time by its very nature. At the beginning of the twentieth century, 1 pound was worth about 5 American dollars, though those bought three to four times what they now do. Now, the pound buys anywhere from $1.20 to $1.50. As difficult as it is to generalize, it is clear that money used to be worth much more than it is currently. In Anglo-Saxon times, the most valuable circulating coin was the silver penny: four would buy a sheep. Beyond long-term inflationary trends, prices varied from times of plenty to those marked by poor harvests; from peacetime to wartime; from the country to the metropolis (life in London has always been very expensive); and wages varied according to the availability of labor (wages would sharply rise, for instance, during the devastating Black Death in the fourteenth century). The following chart provides a glimpse of some actual prices of given periods and their changes across time, though all the variables mentioned above prevent them from being definitive. Even from one year to the next, an added tax on gin or tea could drastically raise prices, and a lottery ticket could cost much more the night before the drawing than just a month earlier. Still, the prices quoted below do indicate important trends, such as the disparity of incomes in British society and the costs of basic commodities. In the chart on the following page, the symbol £ is used for pound, s. for shilling, d. for a penny (from Latin *denarius*); a sum would normally be written £2.19.3, i.e., 2 pounds, 19 shillings, 3 pence. (This is Leopold Bloom's budget for the day depicted in Joyce's novel *Ulysses* [1922]; in the new currency, it would be about £2.96.)

circa	1390	1590	1650	1750	1815	1875	1950
food and drink	gallon (8 pints) of ale, 1.5d.	tankard of beer, .5d.	coffee, 1d. a dish	"drunk for a penny, dead drunk for two-pence" (gin shop sign in Hogarth print)	ounce of laudanum, 3d.	pint of beer, 3d.	pint of Guinness stout, 11d.
	gallon (8 pints) of wine, 3 to 4d.	pound of beef, 2s. 5d.	chicken, 1s. 4d.	dinner at a steakhouse, 1s.	ham and potato dinner for two, 7s.	dinner in a good hotel, 5s.	pound of beef, 2s. 2d.
	pound of cinnamon, 1 to 3s.	pound of cinnamon, 10s. 6d.	pound of tea, £3 10s.	pound of tea, 16s.	bottle of French claret, 12s.	pound of tea, 2s.	dinner on railway car, 7s. 6d.
entertainment	no cost to watch a cycle play	admission to public theater, 1 to 3d.	falcon, £11 5s.	theater tickets, 1 to 5s.	admission to Covent Garden theater, 1 to 7s.	theater tickets, 6d. to 7s.	admission to Old Vic theater, 1s. 6d. to 10s. 6d.
	contributory admission to professional troupe theater	cheap seat in private theater, 6d.	billiard table, £25	admission to Vauxhall Gardens, 1s.	annual subscription to Almack's (exclusive club), 10 guineas	admission to Madam Tussaud's waxworks, 1s.	admission to Odeon cinema, Manchester, 1s 3d.
	maintenance for royal hounds at Windsor, .75d. a day	"to see a dead Indian" (quoted in *The Tempest*), 1.25d. (ten "doits")	three-quarter length portrait painting, £31	lottery ticket, £20 (shares were sold)	Jane Austen's piano, 30 guineas	annual fees at a gentleman's club, 7 to 10 guineas	tropical fish tank, £4 4s.

circa	1390	1590	1650	1750	1815	1875	1950
reading	cheap romance, 1s.	play quarto, 6d.	pamphlet, 1 to 6d.	issue of The Gentleman's Magazine, 6d.	issue of Edinburgh Review, 6s.	copy of the Times, 3d.	copy of the Times, 3d.
	a Latin Bible, 2 to £4	Shakespeare's First Folio (1623), £1	student Bible, 6s.	cheap edition of Milton, 2s.	membership in circulating library (3rd class), £1 4s. a year	illustrated edition of Through the Looking-glass, 6s.	issue of Eagle comics, 4.5d.
	payment for illuminating a liturgical book, £22 9s.	Foxe's Acts and Monuments, 24s.	Hobbes's Leviathan, 8s.	Johnson's Dictionary, folio, 2 vols., £4 10s.	1st edition of Austen's Pride and Prejudice, 18s.	1st edition of Trollope's The Way We Live Now, 2 vols., £1 1s.	Orwell's Nineteen Eighty-Four, paperback, 3s. 6d.
transportation	night's supply of hay for horse, 2d.	wherry (whole boat) across Thames, 1d.	day's journey, coach, 10s.	boat across Thames, 4d.	coach ride, outside, 2 to 3d. a mile; inside, 4 to 5d. a mile	15-minute journey in a London cab, 1s. 6d.	London tube fare, about 2d. a mile
	coach, £8	hiring a horse for a day, 12d.	coach horse, £30	coach fare, London to Edinburgh, £4 10s.	palanquin transport in Madras, 5s. a day	railway, 3rd class, London to Plymouth, 18s. 8d. (about 1d. a mile)	petrol, 3s. a gallon
	quality horse, £10	hiring a coach for a day, 10s.	fancy carriage, £170	transport to America, £5	passage, Liverpool to New York, £10	passage to India, 1st class, £50	midsize Austin sedan, £449 plus £188 4s. 2d. tax
clothes	clothing allowance for peasant, 3s. a year	shoes with buckles, 8d.	footman's frieze coat, 15s.	working woman's gown, 6s. 6d.	checked muslin, 7s. per yard	flannel for a cheap petticoat, 1s. 3d. a yard	woman's sun frock, £3 13s. 10d.

labor/incomes						
shoes for gentry wearer, 4d.	woman's gloves, £1 5s.	falconer's hat, 10s.	gentleman's suit, £8	hiring a dressmaker for a pelisse, 8s.	overcoat for an Eton schoolboy, £1 1s.	tweed sports jacket, £3 16s. 6d.
hat for gentry wearer, 10d.	fine cloak, £16	black cloth for mourning household of an earl, £100	very fine wig, £30	ladies silk stockings, 12s.	set of false teeth, £2 10s.	"Teddy boy" drape suit, £20
hiring a skilled building worker, 4d. a day	actor's daily wage during playing season, 1s.	agricultural laborer, 6s. 5d. a week	price of boy slave, £32	lowest-paid sailor on Royal Navy ship, 10s. 9d. a month	seasonal agricultural laborer, 14s. a week	minimum wage, agricultural laborer, £4 14s. per 47-hour week
wage for professional scribe, £2 3s. 4d. a year + cloak	household servant 2 to £5 a year + food, clothing	tutor to nobleman's children, £30 a year	housemaid's wage, £6 to £8 a year	contributor to *Quarterly Review*, 10 guineas per sheet	housemaid's wage, £10 to £25 a year	shorthand typist, £367 a year
minimum income to be called gentleman, £10 a year; for knighthood, 40 to £400	minimum income for eligibility for knighthood, £30 a year	Milton's salary as Secretary of Foreign Tongues, £288 a year	Boswell's allowance, £200 a year	minimum income for a "genteel" family, £100 a year	income of the "comfortable" classes, £800 and up a year	middle manager's salary, £1,480 a year
income from land of richest magnates, £3,500 a year	income from land of average earl, £4,000 a year	Earl of Bedford's income, £8,000 a year	Duke of Newcastle's income, £40,000 a year	Mr. Darcy's income, *Pride and Prejudice*, £10,000	Trollope's income, £4,000 a year	barrister's salary, £2,032 a year

The British Baronage

The English monarchy is in principle hereditary, though at times during the Middle Ages the rules were subject to dispute. In general, authority passes from father to eldest surviving son, to daughters in order of seniority if there is no son, to a brother if there are no children, and in default of direct descendants to collateral lines (cousins, nephews, nieces) in order of closeness. There have been breaks in the order of succession (1066, 1399, 1688), but so far as possible the usurpers have always sought to paper over the break with a legitimate, i.e., hereditary, claim. When a queen succeeds to the throne and takes a husband, he does not become king unless he is in the line of blood succession; rather, he is named prince consort, as Albert was to Victoria. He may father kings, but is not one himself.

The original Saxon nobles were the king's thanes, ealdormen, or earls, who provided the king with military service and counsel in return for booty, gifts, or landed estates. William the Conqueror, arriving from France, where feudalism was fully developed, considerably expanded this group. In addition, as the king distributed the lands of his new kingdom, he also distributed dignities to men who became known collectively as "the baronage." "Baron" in its root meaning signifies simply "man," and barons were the king's men. As the title was common, a distinction was early made between greater and lesser barons, the former gradually assuming loftier and more impressive titles. The first English "duke" was created in 1337; the title of "marquess," or "marquis" (pronounced "markwis"), followed in 1385, and "viscount" ("vyekount") in 1440. Though "earl" is the oldest title of all, an earl now comes between a marquess and a viscount in order of dignity and precedence, and the old term "baron" now designates a rank just below viscount. "Baronets" were created in 1611 as a means of raising revenue for the crown (the title could be purchased for about £1,000); they are marginal nobility and have never sat in the House of Lords.

Kings and queens are addressed as "Your Majesty," princes and princesses as "Your Highness," the other hereditary nobility as "My Lord" or "Your Lordship." Peers receive their titles either by inheritance (like Lord Byron, the sixth baron of that line) or from the monarch (like Alfred, Lord Tennyson, created 1st Baron Tennyson by Victoria). The children, even of a duke, are commoners unless they are specifically granted some other title or inherit their father's title from him. A peerage can be forfeited by act of attainder, as for example when a lord is convicted of treason; and, when forfeited, or lapsed for lack of a successor, can be bestowed on another family. Thus in 1605 Robert Cecil was made first earl of Salisbury in the third creation, the first creation dating from 1149, the second from 1337, the title having been in abeyance since 1539. Titles descend by right of succession and do not depend on tenure of land; thus, a title does not always indicate where a lord dwells or holds power. Indeed, noble titles do not always refer to a real place at all. At Prince Edward's marriage in 1999, the queen created him earl of Wessex, although the old kingdom of Wessex has had no political existence since the Anglo-Saxon period, and the name was all but forgotten until it was resurrected by Thomas Hardy as the setting of his novels. (This is perhaps but one of many ways in which the world of the aristocracy increasingly resembles the realm of literature.)

The king and queen	(These are all of the royal line.)
Prince and princess	
Duke and duchess	(These may or may not be of the royal
Marquess and marchioness	line, but are ordinarily remote from the
Earl and countess	succession.)
Viscount and viscountess	
Baron and baroness	
Baronet and lady	

Scottish peers sat in the parliament of Scotland, as English peers did in the parliament of England, till at the Act of Union (1707) Scottish peers were granted sixteen seats in the English House of Lords, to be filled by election. (In 1963, all Scottish lords were allowed to sit.) Similarly, Irish peers, when the Irish parliament was abolished in 1801, were granted the right to elect twenty-eight of their number to the House of Lords in Westminster. (Now that the Republic of Ireland is a separate nation, this no longer applies.) Women members (peeresses) were first allowed to sit in the House as nonhereditary Life Peers in 1958 (when that status was created for members of both genders); women first sat by their own hereditary right in 1963. Today the House of Lords still retains some power to influence or delay legislation, but its future is uncertain. In 1999, the hereditary peers (then amounting to 750) were reduced to 92 temporary members elected by their fellow peers. Holders of Life Peerages remain, as do senior bishops of the Church of England and high-court judges (the "Law Lords").

Below the peerage the chief title of honor is "knight." Knighthood, which is not hereditary, is generally a reward for services rendered. A knight (Sir John Black) is addressed, using his first name, as "Sir John"; his wife, using the last name, is "Lady Black"—unless she is the daughter of an earl or nobleman of higher rank, in which case she will be "Lady Arabella." The female equivalent of a knight bears the title of "Dame." Though the word *knight* itself comes from the Anglo-Saxon *cniht*, there is some doubt as to whether knighthood amounted to much before the arrival of the Normans. The feudal system required military service as a condition of land tenure, and a man who came to serve his king at the head of an army of tenants required a title of authority and badges of identity—hence the title of knighthood and the coat of arms. During the Crusades, when men were far removed from their land (or even sold it in order to go on crusade), more elaborate forms of fealty sprang up that soon expanded into orders of knighthood. The Templars, Hospitallers, Knights of the Teutonic Order, Knights of Malta, and Knights of the Golden Fleece were but a few of these companionships; not all of them were available at all times in England.

Gradually, with the rise of centralized government and the decline of feudal tenures, military knighthood became obsolete, and the rank largely honorific; sometimes, as under James I, it degenerated into a scheme of the royal government for making money. For hundreds of years after its establishment in the fourteenth century, the Order of the Garter was the only English order of knighthood, an exclusive courtly companionship. Then, during the late seventeenth, the eighteenth, and the nineteenth centuries, a number of additional orders were created, with names such as the Thistle, Saint Patrick, the Bath, Saint Michael, and Saint George, plus a number of special Victorian and Indian orders. They retain the terminology, ceremony, and dignity of knighthood, but the military implications are vestigial.

Although the British Empire now belongs to history, appointments to the Order of the British Empire continue to be conferred for services to that empire at home or abroad. Such honors (commonly referred to as "gongs") are granted by the monarch in her New Year's and Birthday lists, but the decisions are now made by the government in power. In recent years there have been efforts to popularize and democratize the dispensation of honors, with recipients including rock stars and actors. But this does not prevent large sectors of British society from regarding both knighthood and the peerage as largely irrelevant to modern life.

The Royal Lines of England and Great Britain

England

SAXONS AND DANES

Egbert, king of Wessex	802–839
Ethelwulf, son of Egbert	839–858
Ethelbald, second son of Ethelwulf	858–860
Ethelbert, third son of Ethelwulf	860–866
Ethelred I, fourth son of Ethelwulf	866–871
Alfred the Great, fifth son of Ethelwulf	871–899
Edward the Elder, son of Alfred	899–924
Athelstan the Glorious, son of Edward	924–940
Edmund I, third son of Edward	940–946
Edred, fourth son of Edward	946–955
Edwy the Fair, son of Edmund	955–959
Edgar the Peaceful, second son of Edmund	959–975
Edward the Martyr, son of Edgar	975–978 (murdered)
Ethelred II, the Unready, second son of Edgar	978–1016
Edmund II, Ironside, son of Ethelred II	1016–1016
Canute the Dane	1016–1035
Harold I, Harefoot, natural son of Canute	1035–1040
Hardecanute, son of Canute	1040–1042
Edward the Confessor, son of Ethelred II	1042–1066
Harold II, brother-in-law of Edward	1066–1066 (died in battle)

HOUSE OF NORMANDY

William I, the Conqueror	1066–1087
William II, Rufus, third son of William I	1087–1100 (shot from ambush)
Henry I, Beauclerc, youngest son of William I	1100–1135

HOUSE OF BLOIS

Stephen, son of Adela, daughter of William I	1135–1154

HOUSE OF PLANTAGENET

Henry II, son of Geoffrey Plantagenet by Matilda, daughter of Henry I	1154–1189
Richard I, Coeur de Lion, son of Henry II	1189–1199
John Lackland, son of Henry II	1199–1216
Henry III, son of John	1216–1272
Edward I, Longshanks, son of Henry III	1272–1307
Edward II, son of Edward I	1307–1327 (deposed)
Edward III of Windsor, son of Edward II	1327–1377
Richard II, grandson of Edward III	1377–1399 (deposed)

HOUSE OF LANCASTER

Henry IV, son of John of Gaunt, son of Edward III	1399–1413
Henry V, Prince Hal, son of Henry IV	1413–1422
Henry VI, son of Henry V	1422–1461 (deposed), 1470–1471 (deposed)

HOUSE OF YORK

Edward IV, great-great-grandson of Edward III	1461–1470 (deposed), 1471–1483
Edward V, son of Edward IV	1483–1483 (murdered)
Richard III, Crookback	1483–1485 (died in battle)

HOUSE OF TUDOR

Henry VII, married daughter of Edward IV	1485–1509
Henry VIII, son of Henry VII	1509–1547
Edward VI, son of Henry VIII	1547–1553
Mary I, "Bloody," daughter of Henry VIII	1553–1558
Elizabeth I, daughter of Henry VIII	1558–1603

HOUSE OF STUART

James I (James VI of Scotland)	1603–1625
Charles I, son of James I	1625–1649 (executed)

COMMONWEALTH & PROTECTORATE

Council of State	1649–1653
Oliver Cromwell, Lord Protector	1653–1658
Richard Cromwell, son of Oliver	1658–1660 (resigned)

HOUSE OF STUART (RESTORED)

Charles II, son of Charles I	1660–1685
James II, second son of Charles I	1685–1688

(INTERREGNUM, 11 DECEMBER 1688 TO 13 FEBRUARY 1689)

HOUSE OF ORANGE-NASSAU

William III of Orange, by	
Mary, daughter of Charles I	1689–1701
and Mary II, daughter of James II	–1694
Anne, second daughter of James II	1702–1714

Great Britain

HOUSE OF HANOVER

George I, son of Elector of Hanover and	
Sophia, granddaughter of James I	1714–1727
George II, son of George I	1727–1760
George III, grandson of George II	1760–1820
George IV, son of George III	1820–1830
William IV, third son of George III	1830–1837
Victoria, daughter of Edward, fourth son	
of George III	1837–1901

HOUSE OF SAXE-COBURG AND GOTHA

Edward VII, son of Victoria	1901–1910

HOUSE OF WINDSOR (NAME ADOPTED 17 JULY 1917)

George V, second son of Edward VII	1910–1936
Edward VIII, eldest son of George V	1936–1936 (abdicated)
George VI, second son of George V	1936–1952
Elizabeth II, daughter of George VI	1952–

Religions in Great Britain

In the late sixth century C.E., missionaries from Rome introduced Christianity to the Anglo-Saxons—actually, reintroduced it, since it had briefly flourished in the southern parts of the British Isles during the Roman occupation, and even after the Roman withdrawal had persisted in the Celtic regions of Scotland and Wales. By the time the earliest poems included in *The Norton Anthology of English Literature* were composed (i.e., the seventh century), therefore, there had been a Christian presence in the British Isles for hundreds of years. The conversion of the Germanic occupiers of England can, however, be dated only from 597. Our knowledge of the religion of pre-Christian Britain is sketchy, but it is likely that vestiges of Germanic polytheism assimilated into, or coexisted with, the practice of Christianity: fertility rites were incorporated into the celebration of Easter resurrection, rituals commemorating the dead into All-Hallows Eve and All Saints Day, and elements of winter solstice festivals into the celebration of Christmas. The most durable polytheistic remains are our days of the week, each of which except "Saturday" derives from the name of a Germanic pagan god, and the word "Easter," deriving, according to the Anglo-Saxon scholar Bede (d. 735), from the name of a Germanic pagan goddess, Eostre. In English literature such "folkloric" elements sometimes elicit romantic nostalgia. Geoffrey Chaucer's "Wife of Bath" looks back to a magical time before the arrival of Christianity in which the land was "fulfilled of fairye." Hundreds of years later, the seventeenth-century writer Robert Herrick honors the amalgamation of Christian and pagan elements in agrarian British culture in such poems as "Corinna's Gone A-Maying" and "The Hock Cart."

Medieval Christianity was fairly uniform, if complex, across Western Europe—hence called "catholic," or universally shared. The Church was composed of the so-called "regular" and "secular" orders, the regular orders being those who followed a rule in a community under an abbot or an abbess (i.e., monks, nuns, friars and canons), while the secular clergy of priests served parish communities under the governance of a bishop. In the unstable period from the sixth until the twelfth century, monasteries were the intellectual powerhouse of the Church. From the beginning of the thirteenth century, with the development of an urban Christian spirituality in Europe, friars dominated the recently invented institution of universities, as well as devoting themselves, in theory at least, to the urban poor.

The Catholic Church was also an international power structure. With its hierarchy of pope, cardinals, archbishops, and bishops, it offered a model of the centralized, bureaucratic state from the late eleventh century. That ecclesiastical power structure coexisted alongside a separate, often less centralized and feudal structure of lay authorities, with theoretically different and often competing spheres of social responsibilities. The sharing of lay and ecclesiastical authority in medieval England was sometimes a source of conflict. Chaucer's pilgrims are on their way to visit the memorial shrine to one victim of such exemplary struggle: Thomas à Becket, Archbishop of Canterbury, who opposed the policies of King Henry II, was assassinated by indirect suggestion of the king in 1170, and later made a saint. The Church, in turn, produced its own victims: Jews were subject to persecution in the late twelfth century in England, before being expelled in 1290. From the beginning of the fifteenth century, the English Church targeted Lollard heretics (see below) with capital punishment, for the first time.

As an international organization, the Church conducted its business in the universal language of Latin. Thus although in the period the largest segment of literate persons was made up of clerics, the clerical contribution to great literary writing in vernacular languages (e.g., French and English) was, so far as we know, relatively modest, with some great exceptions in the later Middle Ages (e.g., William Langland). Lay, vernacular writers of the period certainly reflect the importance of the Church as an institution and the pervasiveness of religion in the rituals that marked everyday life, as well as contesting institutional authority. From the late fourteenth century, indeed, England witnessed an active and articulate, proto-Protestant movement known as Lollardy, which attacked clerical hierarchy and promoted vernacular scriptures.

Beginning in 1517 the German monk Martin Luther, in Wittenberg, Germany, openly challenged many aspects of Catholic practice and by 1520 had completely repudiated the authority of the pope, setting in train the Protestant Reformation. Luther argued that the Roman Catholic Church had strayed far from the pattern of Christianity laid out in scripture. He rejected Catholic doctrines for which no biblical authority was to be found, such as the belief in Purgatory, and translated the Bible into German, on the grounds that the importance of scripture for all Christians made its translation into the vernacular tongue essential. Luther was not the first to advance such views— Lollard followers of the Englishman John Wycliffe had translated the Bible in the late fourteenth century. But Luther, protected by powerful German rulers, was able to speak out with impunity and convert others to his views, rather than suffer the persecution usually meted out to heretics. Soon other reformers were following in Luther's footsteps: of these, the Swiss Ulrich Zwingli and the French Jean Calvin would be especially influential for English religious thought.

At first England remained staunchly Catholic. Its king, Henry VIII, was so severe to heretics that the pope awarded him the title "Defender of the Faith," which British monarchs have retained to this day. In 1534, however, Henry rejected the authority of the pope to prevent his divorce from his queen, Catherine of Aragon, and his marriage to his mistress, Ann Boleyn. In doing so, Henry appropriated to himself ecclesiastical as well as secular authority. Thomas More, author of *Utopia*, was executed in 1535 for refusing to endorse Henry's right to govern the English church. Over the following six years, Henry consolidated his grip on the ecclesiastical establishment by dissolving the powerful, populous Catholic monasteries and redistributing their massive landholdings to his own lay followers. Yet Henry's church largely retained Catholic doctrine and liturgy. When Henry died and his young son, Edward, came to the throne in 1547, the English church embarked on a more Protestant path, a direction abruptly reversed when Edward died and his older sister Mary, the daughter of Catherine of Aragon, took the throne in 1553 and attempted to reintroduce Roman Catholicism. Mary's reign was also short, however, and her successor, Elizabeth I, the daughter of Ann Boleyn, was a Protestant. Elizabeth attempted to establish a "middle way" Christianity, compromising between Roman Catholic practices and beliefs and reformed ones.

The Church of England, though it laid claim to a national rather than pan-European authority, aspired like its predecessor to be the universal church of all English subjects. It retained the Catholic structure of parishes and dioceses and the Catholic hierarchy of bishops, though the ecclesiastical authority was now the Archbishop of Canterbury and the Church's "Supreme Governor" was the monarch. Yet disagreement and controversy persisted. Some members of the Church of England wanted to retain many of the ritual and liturgical elements of Catholicism. Others, the Puritans, advocated a more thoroughgoing reformation. Most Puritans remained within the Church of England, but a minority, the "Separatists" or "Congregationalists," split from the established church altogether. These dissenters no longer thought of the ideal church as an organization to which everybody belonged; instead, they conceived it as a more exclusive group of likeminded people, one not necessarily attached to a larger body of believers.

In the seventeenth century, the succession of the Scottish king James to the English throne produced another problem. England and Scotland were separate nations, and in the sixteenth century Scotland had developed its own national Presbyterian church, or "kirk," under the leadership of the reformer John Knox. The kirk retained fewer Catholic liturgical elements than did the Church of England, and its authorities, or "presbyters," were elected by assemblies of their fellow clerics, rather than appointed by the king. James I and his son Charles I, especially the latter, wanted to bring the Scottish kirk into conformity with Church of England practices. The Scots violently resisted these efforts, with the collaboration of many English Puritans, in a conflict that eventually developed into the English Civil War in the mid-seventeenth century. The effect of these disputes is visible in the poetry of such writers as John Milton, Robert Herrick, Henry Vaughan, and Thomas Traherne, and in the prose of Thomas Browne, Lucy Hutchinson, and Dorothy Waugh. Just as in the mid-sixteenth century, when a succession of monarchs with different religious commitments destabilized the church, so the seventeenth century endured spiritual whiplash. King Charles I's highly ritualistic Church of England was violently overturned by the Puritan victors in the Civil War—until 1660, after the death of the Puritan leader, Oliver Cromwell, when the Church of England was restored along with the monarchy.

The religious and political upheavals of the seventeenth century produced Christian sects that de-emphasized the ceremony of the established church and rejected as well its top-down authority structure. Some of these groups were ephemeral, but the Baptists (founded in 1608 in Amsterdam by the English expatriate John Smyth) and Quakers, or Society of Friends (founded by George Fox in the 1640s), flourished outside the established church, sometimes despite cruel persecution. John Bunyan, a Baptist, wrote the Christian allegory *Pilgrim's Progress* while in prison. Some dissenters, like the Baptists, shared the reformed reverence for the absolute authority of scripture but interpreted the scriptural texts differently from their fellow Protestants. Others, like the Quakers, favored, even over the authority of the Bible, the "inner light" or voice of individual conscience, which they took to be the working of the Holy Spirit in the lives of individuals.

The Protestant dissenters were not England's only religious minorities. Despite crushing fines and the threat of imprisonment, a minority of Catholics under Elizabeth and James openly refused to give their allegiance to the new church, and others remained secret adherents to the old ways. John Donne was brought up in an ardently Catholic family, and several other writers converted to Catholicism as adults—Ben Jonson for a considerable part of his career, Elizabeth Carey and Richard Crashaw permanently, and at profound personal cost. In the eighteenth century, Catholics remained objects of suspicion as possible agents of sedition, especially after the "Glorious Revolution" in 1688 deposed the Catholic James II in favor of the Protestant William and Mary. Anti-Catholic prejudice affected John Dryden, a Catholic convert, as well as the lifelong Catholic Alexander Pope. By contrast, the English colony of Ireland remained overwhelmingly Roman Catholic, the fervor of its religious commitment at least partly inspired by resistance to English occupation. Starting in the reign of Elizabeth, England shored up its own authority in Ireland by encouraging Protestant immigrants from Scotland to settle in the north of Ireland, producing a virulent religious divide the effects of which are still playing out today.

A small community of Jews had moved from France to London after 1066, when the Norman William the Conqueror came to the English throne. Although despised and persecuted by many Christians, they were allowed to remain as moneylenders to the Crown, until the thirteenth century, when the king developed alternative sources of credit. At this point, in 1290, the Jews were expelled from England. In 1655 Oliver Cromwell permitted a few to return, and in the late seventeenth and early eighteenth centuries the Jewish population slowly increased, mainly by immigration from Germany. In the mid-eighteenth century some prominent Jews had their children brought up as Christians so as to facilitate their full integration into English society: thus the nineteenth-century writer and politician Benjamin Disraeli, although he and his father were members of the Church of England, was widely considered a Jew insofar as his ancestry was Jewish.

In the late seventeenth century, as the Church of England reasserted itself, Catholics, Jews, and dissenting Protestants found themselves subject to significant legal restrictions. The Corporation Act, passed in 1661, and the Test Act, passed in 1673, excluded all who refused to take communion in the Church of England from voting, attending university, or working in government or in the professions. Members of religious minorities, as well as Church of England communicants, paid mandatory taxes in support of Church of England ministers and buildings. In 1689 the dissenters gained the right to worship in public, but Jews and Catholics were not permitted to do so.

During the eighteenth century, political, intellectual, and religious history remained closely intertwined. The Church of England came to accommodate a good deal of variety. "Low church" services resembled those of the dissenting Protestant churches, minimizing ritual and emphasizing the sermon; the "high church" retained more elaborate ritual elements, yet its prestige was under attack on several fronts. Many Enlightenment thinkers subjected the Bible to rational critique and found it wanting: the philosopher David Hume, for instance, argued that the "miracles" described therein were more probably lies or errors than real breaches of the laws of nature. Within the Church of England, the "broad church" Latitudinarians welcomed this rationalism, advocating theological openness and an emphasis on ethics rather than dogma. More radically, the Unitarian movement rejected the divinity of Christ while professing to accept his ethical teachings. Taking a different tack, the preacher John Wesley, founder of Methodism, responded to the rationalists' challenge with a newly fervent call to evangelism and personal discipline; his movement was particularly successful in Wales. Revolutions in America and France at the end of the century generated considerable millenarian excitement and fostered more new religious ideas, often in conjunction with a radical social agenda. Many important writers of the Romantic period were indebted to traditions of protestant dissent: Unitarian and rationalist protestant ideas influenced William Hazlitt, Anna Barbauld, Mary Wollstonecraft, and the young Samuel Taylor Coleridge. William Blake created a highly idiosyncratic poetic mythology loosely indebted to radical strains of Christian mysticism. Others were even more heterodox: Lord Byron and Robert Burns, brought up as Scots Presbyterians, rebelled fiercely, and Percy Shelley's writing of an atheistic pamphlet resulted in his expulsion from Oxford.

Great Britain never erected an American-style "wall of separation" between church and state, but in practice religion and secular affairs grew more and more distinct during the nineteenth century. In consequence, members of religious minorities no longer seemed to pose a threat to the commonweal. A movement to repeal the Test Act failed in the 1790s, but a renewed effort resulted in the extension of the franchise to dissenting Protestants in 1828 and to Catholics in 1829. The numbers of Roman Catholics in England were swelled by immigration from Ireland, but there were also some prominent English adherents. Among writers, the converts John Newman and Gerard Manley Hopkins are especially important. The political participation and social integration of Jews presented a thornier challenge. Lionel de Rothschild, repeatedly elected to represent London in Parliament during the 1840s and 1850s, was not permitted to take his seat there because he refused to take his oath of office "on the true faith of a Christian"; finally, in 1858, the Jewish Disabilities Act allowed him to omit these words. Only in 1871, however, were Oxford and Cambridge opened to non-Anglicans.

Meanwhile geological discoveries and Charles Darwin's evolutionary theories increasingly cast doubt on the literal truth of the Creation story, and close philological analysis of the biblical text suggested that its origins were human rather than divine. By the end of the nineteenth century, many writers were bearing witness to a world in which Christianity no longer seemed fundamentally plausible. In his poetry and prose, Thomas Hardy depicts a world devoid of benevolent providence. Matthew Arnold's poem "Dover Beach" is in part an elegy to lost spiritual assurance, as the "Sea of Faith" goes out like the tide: "But now I only hear / Its melancholy, long, withdrawing roar / Retreating." For Arnold, literature must replace religion as a source of spiritual truth, and intimacy between individuals substitute for the lost communal solidarity of the universal church.

The work of many twentieth-century writers shows the influence of a religious upbringing or a religious conversion in adulthood. T. S. Eliot and W. H. Auden embrace Anglicanism, William Butler Yeats spiritualism. James Joyce repudiates Irish Catholicism but remains obsessed with it. Yet religion, or lack of it, is a matter of individual choice and conscience, not social or legal mandate. In the past fifty years, church attendance has plummeted in Great Britain. Although 71 percent of the population still identified itself as "Christian" on the 2000 census, only about 7 percent of these regularly attend religious services of any denomination. Meanwhile, immigration from former British colonies has swelled the ranks of religions once uncommon in the British Isles—Muslim, Sikh, Hindu, Buddhist—though the numbers of adherents remain small relative to the total population.

The Universe According to Ptolemy

Ptolemy was a Roman astronomer of Greek descent, born in Egypt during the second century C.E.; for nearly fifteen hundred years after his death his account of the design of the universe was accepted as standard. During that time, the basic pattern underwent many detailed modifications and was fitted out with many astrological and pseudoscientific trappings. But in essence Ptolemy's followers portrayed the earth as the center of the universe, with the sun, planets, and fixed stars set in transparent spheres orbiting around it. In this scheme of things, as modified for Christian usage, Hell was usually placed under the earth's surface at the center of the cosmic globe, while Heaven, the abode of the blessed spirits, was in the outermost, uppermost circle, the empyrean. But in 1543 the Polish astronomer Copernicus proposed an alternative hypothesis—that the earth rotates around the sun, not vice versa; and despite theological opposition, observations with the new telescope and careful mathematical calculations insured ultimate acceptance of the new view.

The map of the Ptolemaic universe below is a simplified version of a diagram in Peter Apian's *Cosmography* (1584). In such a diagram, the Firmament is the sphere that contained the fixed stars; the Crystalline Sphere, which contained no heavenly bodies, is a late innovation, included to explain certain anomalies in the observed movement of the heavenly bodies; and the Prime Mover is the sphere that, itself put into motion by God, imparts rotation around the earth to all the other spheres.

Milton, writing in the mid-seventeenth century, used two universes. The Copernican universe, though he alludes to it, was too large, formless, and unfamiliar to be the setting for the war between Heaven and Hell in *Paradise Lost*. He therefore used the Ptolemaic cosmos, but placed Heaven well outside this smaller earth-centered universe, Hell far beneath it, and assigned the vast middle space to Chaos.

PERMISSIONS ACKNOWLEDGMENTS

TEXT CREDITS

Ancrene Riwle: "The Sweetness and Pains of Enclosure" from THE ANCRENE RIWLE, translated by M. B. Salu, 1990. ISBN 978 0 85989 341 1. Reprinted by permission of the Liverpool University Press.

Beowulf: from BEOWULF, translated by Seamus Heaney. Copyright © 2000 by Seamus Heaney. Used with permission of W. W. Norton & Company, Inc.

Geoffrey Chaucer: All excerpts are from CHAUCER'S POETRY: AN ANTHOLOGY FOR THE MODERN READER, 2nd ed., edited by E. T. Donaldson. Copyright © 1958, 1975 by Judith Anderson and Deirdre Donaldson. Used by permission of W. W. Norton & Company, Inc. *The Parliament Birds* translated by James Simpson. Copyright © 2016 by James Simpson. Reprinted by permission of the translator.

Dream of the Rood: trans. by Alfred David. Copyright © 2012 by Alfred David. Rptd. by permission of the translator.

Early Irish Lyrics: From EARLY IRISH LYRICS, edited and translated by Gerard Murphy, Four Courts Press, 1998. Reproduced with permission from Gerard Murphy and Four Courts Press.

Richard Hamer: "The Ruin," "Wulf and Eadwacer," "Riddle #21," "Riddle #26," and "Riddle #47" from A CHOICE OF ANGLO-SAXON VERSE: SELECTED WITH AN INTRODUCTION AND A PARALLEL VERSE TRANSLATION by Richard Hamer. Copyright © 1970 by Richard Hamer. Reprinted with permission of Faber and Faber Limited.

Robert Henryson: *The Cock and the Jasper* and *The Preaching of the Swallow* from THE TESTAMENT OF CRESSEID AND SEVEN FABLES by Robert Henryson, translated by Seamus Heaney. Copyright © 2009 by Seamus Heaney. Reprinted by permission of Farrar, Straus and Giroux, and Faber and Faber Limited.

Thomas Hoccleve: "My Complaint" from 'MY COMPLEINTE' AND OTHER POEMS by Thomas Hoccleve, edited by Roger Ellis, 2001. ISBN 978 0 85989 701 3. Reprinted by permission of the Liverpool University Press.

Judith: From OLD & MIDDLE ENGLISH trans. by Elaine Treharne. Rptd. with the permission of the translator.

Julian of Norwich: Excerpts reprinted from Julian of Norwich, A BOOK OF SHOWINGS, ed. by Edmund Colledge and James Walsh, by permission of the publisher. Copyright © 1978 by the Pontifical Institute of Mediaeval Studies, Toronto.

Margery Kempe: All excerpts including bibliographical citation excerpts from THE BOOK OF MARGERY KEMPE, edited by Lynn Staley (Kalamazoo, MI: Medieval Institute Publications). Copyright © 1996 by the Board of The Medieval Institute. Reprinted by permission of the publisher.

William Langland: Excerpts from PIERS PLOWMAN: AN ALLITERATIVE VERSE TRANSLATION by William Langland, translated by E. Talbot Donaldson. Translation copyright © 1990 by W. W. Norton & Company, Inc. Reprinted by permission of W. W. Norton & Company, Inc.

La Folie Tristan: from THE BIRTH OF ROMANCE: AN ANTHOLOGY, edited and translated by Judith Weiss. Copyright © 1992 by Judith Weiss.

Layamon: Excerpts from Layamon's BRUT, translated by Rosamund Allen. Reprinted by permission of The Orion Publishing Group Ltd. on behalf of the publisher, Everyman.

Marie de France: Translation of LANVAL by Alfred David. Copyright © 2000 by Alfred David. Reprinted with the permission of the translator. "Bisclavret," "Milun," and "Chevrefoil" from MARIE DE FRANCE: POETRY (NORTON CRITICAL EDITION), edited by Dorothy Gilbert. Copyright © 2015 by W. W. Norton & Company, Inc. Translation copyright © 2015 by Dorothy Gilbert. Used by permission of W. W. Norton & Company, Inc.

Medieval English Lyrics: "Foweles in the Firth" from MEDIEVAL ENGLISH LYRICS edited by Theodore Silverstein (London: Arnold, 1971), copyright © 1971. Reproduced by permission of Hodder Education.

Mystery Plays: *The Wakefield Second Shepherds' Play* translated by James Simpson. Copyright © 2016 by James Simpson. Reprinted by permission of the translator.

Sir Gawain and the Green Knight: From SIR GAWAIN AND THE GREEN KNIGHT: A NEW VERSE TRANSLATION translated by Simon Armitage. Copyright © 2007 by Simon Armitage. Used by permission of W. W. Norton & Company, Inc. and Faber and Faber Limited.

Tain Epic: *Cuchulainn's Boyhood Deeds* from THE TAIN translated by Thomas Kinsella. Copyright © 1969 by Thomas Kinsella. Used by permission of the translator.

The Wanderer: trans. by Alfred David. Copyright © 2012 by Alfred David. Rptd. by permission of the translator.

The Wife's Lament: trans. by Alfred David. Copyright © 2012 by Alfred David. Rptd. by permission of the translator.

IMAGE CREDITS

Pp. 2–3: © British Library Board. All Rights Reserved; p. 8: Cotton Nero D. IV, f.25v St. Matthew, writing, with his symbol, from the Lindisfarne Gospels, 710–721 (vellum), English School (8th century) / British Library, London, UK / © British Library Board / Bridgeman Images; p. 12: English King Harold lies dead at the Battle of Hastings during the Norman Invasion of 1066. Depicted in the Bayeux Tapestry / Universal History Archive / UIG / Bridgeman Images; p. 16: ARTstor, SCALA, Florence / ART RESOURCE, NY; p. 19: Réunion des Musées Nationaux / Art Resource, NY; p. 33: Hugh McKean / Alamy Stock Photo; p. 38: British Library, London, Great Britain / HIP / Art Resource, NY; p. 39: © The Trustees of the British Museum / Art Resource, NY; p. 139: Art Resource, NY; p. 158: The British Library, London, UK / © British Library Board. All Rights Reserved; p. 202: Musée Conde, Chantilly, France / Giraudon / The Bridgeman Art Library International; p. 229: British Library, London, UK / The Bridgeman Art Library International; p. 257: National Gallery, London, UK / The Bridgeman Art Library International; p. 300: Ellesmere Manuscript, facsimile edition, 1911, English School (15th cent.) / Private Collection / The Bridgeman Art Library International; p. 377: British Library, London, UK / © The British Library Board. All Rights Reserved / The Bridgeman Art Library International; p. 389: Prado, Madrid, Spain / The Bridgeman Art Library International; p. 390: Prado, Madrid, Spain / Giraudon / The Bridgeman Art Library International; p. 431: Österreichische Nationalbibliothek (Vienna, Austria), Codex Vindobonensis 1857, fols. 14v-15r.

COLOR INSERT CREDITS

C1: The British Museum, London / Bridgeman Art Library; C2: © British Library Board / Robana / Art Resource, NY; C3: The Pierpont Morgan Library / Art Resource, NY; C4: The British Library, Folio 170r from the Luttrell Psalter, MS additional 42130; C5: National Gallery, London, Great Britain / Art Resource, NY; C6: Corpus Christi College, University of Oxford, MS 394; C7 (top): The British Library, MS Harley 4866, Folio 88; C7 (bottom): The British Library, MS Royal 18 D II, Folio 148; C8 (top): Ms 65/1284 f.2v February: farmyard scene with peasants, from the *Tres Riches Heures du Duc de Berry* (vellum) (for facsimile copy see 65824), Limbourg Brothers (fl.1400–1416) / Musée Conde, Chantilly, France / Bridgeman Images; C8 (bottom): Louvre, Paris, France / Giraudon / The Bridgeman Art Library International.

Index